WATCH OUT FOR AQUATIC INVADERS

INVASIVE NON-NATIVE SPECIES CAN DAMAGE OUR NATIVE SPECIES AND HABITATS

DON'T LET THEM HITCH A RIDE ON YOUR BOAT

CARPET SEA SQUIRT

WIREWEED

Check and clean the prop and shaft, keel, water inlets and outlets as often as you can

Remove visible fouling and put in the bin, not back in the water

Wash off your anchor and chain before stowing and leaving an anchorage

CHINESE MITTEN CRAB

JAPANESE SKELETON SHRIMP

Lift, scrub and anti foul annually

ZEBRA MUSSEL

British Marine Federation

RYA

A joint BMF and RYA initiative

Supported by

THE CROWN ESTATE

www.thegreenblue.org.uk

Haven
Knox-Johnston
An Amlin Group Company
ACADEMY
2012 Winner for Boating Environment

Yacht Havens

Marina
Dry Stack Marina

Yacht Havens
WE LOVE BOATING

the most helpful staff

1
2
3
4
9
6 5
8 7

Prime Marina Locations... *the perfect home for your boat*

Whether you're looking for an overnight visit, an annual berth or a safe winter haven, you'll find first-rate facilities and a warm welcome from our friendly, experienced team at whichever Yacht Havens location you choose.

Attractive berthing rates and flexible contracts to save you money, superb modern facilities for your enjoyment, free Wi-Fi at every berth for your convenience, and the freedom to exchange berths with other Yacht Havens.

We can provide you with the best boating experience across the UK, and now the Netherlands. Just ask us what we can do for you.

1 Largs Yacht Haven
Largs, Ayrshire
Tel: 01475 675333

2 Troon Yacht Haven
Troon, Ayrshire
Tel: 01292 315553

3 Neyland Yacht Haven
Neyland, Pembrokeshire
Tel: 01646 601601

4 Fambridge Yacht Haven
River Crouch, Essex
Tel: 01621 740370

5 Lymington Yacht Haven
Lymington, Hampshire
Tel: 01590 677071

6 Haven Quay
Lymington, Hampshire
Tel: 01590 677072

7 Plymouth Yacht Haven
Plymouth, Devon
Tel: 01752 404231

8 Yacht Haven Quay
Plymouth, Devon
Tel: 01752 481190

NEW!
9 Jachthaven Biesbosch
Drimmelen, Netherlands
Tel: +31(0)162 68 22 49

REEDS
Aberdeen
Asset management

EASTERN
ALMANAC
2015

ADLARD COLES NAUTICAL

EDITORS **Perrin Towler and Mark Fishwick**

Free updates are available at www.reedsalmanacs.co.uk

Published by Adlard Coles Nautical 2014

Copyright © Nautical Data Ltd 2001–2003

Copyright © Adlard Coles Nautical 2004–2014

IMPORTANT SAFETY NOTE AND LEGAL DISCLAIMER

This Almanac is intended as a navigational aid only and to assist with basic planning for your passage. The information, charts, maps and diagrams in this Almanac should not be relied on for navigational purposes and should always be used in conjunction with current official hydrographic data. Whilst every care has been taken in its compilation, this Almanac may contain inaccuracies and is no substitute for the relevant official hydrographic charts and data, which should always be consulted in advance of, and whilst, navigating in the relevant area. Before setting out you should also check local conditions with the harbourmaster or other appropriate office responsible for your intended area of navigation.

Before using any waypoint or coordinate listed in this Almanac it must first be plotted on an appropriate official hydrographic chart to check its usefulness, accuracy and appropriateness for the prevailing weather and tidal conditions.

To the extent that the editors or publishers become aware that corrections are required, these will be published on the website www.reedsalmanacs.co.uk (requires registration). Readers should therefore regularly check the website for any such corrections. Data in this Almanac is corrected up to Weekly Edition 25/2014 of Admiralty Notices to Mariners.

The publishers, editors and their agents accept no responsibility for any errors or omissions, or for any accident, loss or damage (including without limitation any indirect, consequential, special or exemplary damages) arising from the use or misuse of, or reliance upon, the information contained in this Almanac.

The decision to use and rely on any of the data in this Almanac is entirely at the discretion of, and is the sole responsibility of, the Skipper or other individual in control of the vessel in connection with which it is being used or relied upon.

Adlard Coles Nautical
50 Bedford Square
London, WC1B 3DP
Tel: +44 (0)207 631 5600
Fax: +44 (0)207 631 5800
info@reedsalmanacs.co.uk
editor.britishisles@reedsalmanacs.co.uk
editor.continental@reedsalmanacs.co.uk
www.reedsalmanacs.co.uk

Aberdeen Asset Management PLC
Bow Bells House
1 Bread Street
London, EC4M 9HH
Tel: +44 (0)207 463 6000

Almanac manager
Chris Stevens

Cartography
Chris Stevens

Cover photograph
Getty Images

ISBN 978 1 4729 0702 8 – Reeds Eastern Almanac 2015

A CIP catalogue record for this book is available from the British Library.

Printed in the UK.

ADVERTISEMENT SALES

Reference Contents

REFERENCE CONTENTS vii

NAVIGATIONAL CONTENTS ix

0.1	The Almanac	2
0.2	Abbreviations and symbols	2
0.3–4	Passage planning form and notes	5
0.5	Positions from GPS	6
0.6	VHF Communications	6
0.7–8	Distress calls, Urgency and Safety calls	7
0.9	GMDSS	8
0.10–12	HM, Dutch and Belgian Coast Guard details	9
0.13–17	Weather	11

NAVTEX • MSI Broadcasts by HM CG • Broadcasts in the UK •
Dutch weather broadcasts • Belgian weather broadcasts

0.18	Automatic Identification System (AIS)	15
0.19	Overhead clearances	15
0.20	IALA buoyage	16
0.21	Flags and ensigns	17
0.22	Lights and shapes	18
0.23	Navigational lights	19
0.24	Tidal coefficients	20
0.25–26	Sun and moon: rising and setting times	21
0.27	International Code flags, IPTS	22
0.28–29	Area and harbour information	23
0.30	Environmental guidance	24
0.31	Distances across the North Sea	24

| EASTERN ENGLAND | 27 |

Ramsgate to Berwick-upon-Tweed, see page ix for detail

| NETHERLANDS AND BELGIUM | 87 |

Delfzijl to Nieuwpoort, see page ix for detail

| EASTERN SCOTLAND | 171 |

Eyemouth to Shetland Islands, see page ix for detail

| INDEX | 233 |

Navigational Contents

EAST ENGLAND	27
Area 1 Ramsgate to Great Yarmouth	28
Area Map	28
Tidal streams	30
Lights, buoys and waypoints	32
Passage information	35
Port information	36–86

NETHERLANDS AND BELGIUM	87
Area 2 Delfzijl to Nieuwpoort	87
Area Map	88
Tidal streams	90
Lights, buoys and waypoints	92
Passage information	96
Special notes for Netherlands	96
Port information	97–137
Special notes for Belgium	129

NORTH EAST ENGLAND	138
Area 3 Winterton to Berwick-upon-Tweed	138
Area Map	138
Tidal streams	140
Lights, buoys and waypoints	142
Passage information	144
Port information	144–170

EASTERN SCOTLAND	171
Area 4 SE Scotland, Eyemouth to Rattray Head	172
Area Map	172
Tidal streams	174
Lights, buoys and waypoints	176
Passage information	178
Port information	178–195
Area 5 NE Scotland, Rattray Head to Cape Wrath, including Orkney and Shetland Islands	196
Area Map	196
Tidal streams	198
Lights, buoys and waypoints	200
Passage information	202
Port information	203–231

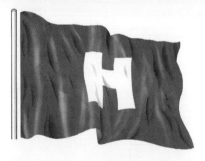

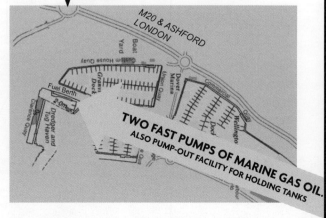

WATCH OUT FOR AQUATIC INVADERS

INVASIVE NON-NATIVE SPECIES CAN DAMAGE OUR NATIVE SPECIES AND HABITATS

DON'T LET THEM HITCH A RIDE ON YOUR BOAT

CARPET SEA SQUIRT

WIREWEED

Check and clean the prop and shaft, keel, water inlets and outlets as often as you can

Remove visible fouling and put in the bin, not back in the water

Wash off your anchor and chain before stowing and leaving an anchorage

CHINESE MITTEN CRAB

JAPANESE SKELETON SHRIMP

Lift, scrub and anti foul annually

ZEBRA MUSSEL

British Marine Federation

RYA

A joint BMF and RYA initiative

Supported by
THE CROWN ESTATE

www.thegreenblue.org.uk

Haven
Knox-Johnston
An Amlin Group Company
ACADEMY
2012 Winner for Boating Environment

On an island paradise ...

... one gem shines above all else

Accessible 3 hours either side of high water at St Peter Port, Beaucette Marina, situated on the North East of Guernsey, is the perfect base to discover the island.

All the services you would expect from a modern facility are on-hand to make your stay easy and enjoyable. Our staff are highly experienced and ready to help, so you can feel safe in the knowledge that your boat and your crew are in good hands.

Contact us by using the details below or call us on VHF 80 – call sign "Beaucette Marina',. If you are unsure of the buoyed channel or the entrance to Beaucette, please call on VHF 80 and we will send a boat out to assist you.

For more information, please visit our website at: www.beaucettemarina.com

We look forward to welcoming you.

BEAUCETTE MARINA LTD,
VALE, GUERNSEY, CHANNEL ISLANDS GY3 5BQ
T: +44 (0)1481 245000
F: +44 (0)1481 247071
E: INFO@BEAUCETTEMARINA.COM
M: +44 (0)7781 102302
W: WWW.BEAUCETTEMARINA.COM
VHF CHANNEL 80

VISITING & ANNUAL BERTHS | WATER & ELECTRICITY ON ALL BERTHS | FUEL & GAS | LAUNDRETTE | RESTAURANT | SHOWER & TOILETS | WEATHER FORECAST | FREE WIFI ACCESS | CAR HIRE | BIKE HIRE

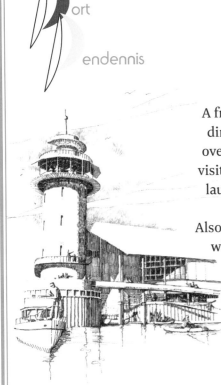
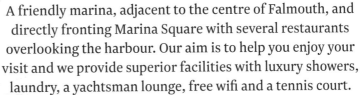

EVEN SUMMER'S BETTER WITH PREMIER!

FIRST-CLASS FACILITIES

SUPERB CUSTOMER SERVICE

SUMMER MONTHLY BERTHING

SUMMER VISITOR BERTHING

7 NIGHTS FOR 5 WITH GREAT ESCAPES

Join us overnight, tour our marinas for a week with Great Escapes or go for monthly berthing for a lazy summer break in one of our first-class marinas.
Call now or visit premiermarinas.com

GREAT ESCAPES
BUY 5 NIGHTS AND STAY 7
PREMIERMARINAS.COM

TYHA
Gold Anchor
Award Scheme

PREMIER MARINAS

Yacht Havens

Marina
Dry Stack Marina

the most helpful staff

Yacht Havens
WE
LOVE
BOATING

9 Prime Marina Locations... *the perfect home for your boat*

Whether you're looking for an overnight visit, an annual berth or a safe winter haven, you'll find first-rate facilities and a warm welcome from our friendly, experienced team at whichever Yacht Havens location you choose.

Attractive berthing rates and flexible contracts to save you money, superb modern facilities for your enjoyment, free Wi-Fi at every berth for your convenience, and the freedom to exchange berths with other Yacht Havens.

We can provide you with the best boating experience across the UK, and now the Netherlands. Just ask us what we can do for you.

1 Largs Yacht Haven
Largs, Ayrshire
Tel: 01475 675333

2 Troon Yacht Haven
Troon, Ayrshire
Tel: 01292 315553

3 Neyland Yacht Haven
Neyland, Pembrokeshire
Tel: 01646 601601

4 Fambridge Yacht Haven
River Crouch, Essex
Tel: 01621 740370

5 Lymington Yacht Haven
Lymington, Hampshire
Tel: 01590 677071

6 Haven Quay
Lymington, Hampshire
Tel: 01590 677072

7 Plymouth Yacht Haven
Plymouth, Devon
Tel: 01752 404231

8 Yacht Haven Quay
Plymouth, Devon
Tel: 01752 481190

NEW!
9 Jachthaven Biesbosch
Drimmelen, Netherlands
Tel: +31(0)162 68 22 49

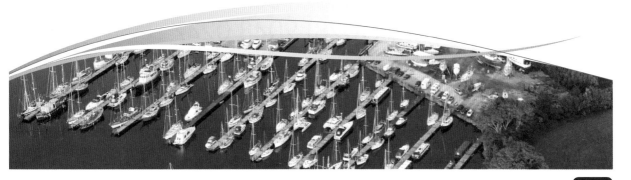

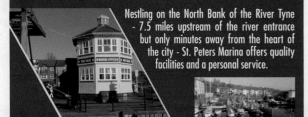

Reference data

0.1	The Almanac	2
0.2	Abbreviations and symbols	2
0.3–4	Passage planning form and notes	5
0.5	Positions from GPS	6
0.6	VHF communications	6
0.7	Distress calls	7
0.8	Urgency and Safety calls	8
0.9	GMDSS	8
0.10	HM Coastguard contact details	9
0.11	Netherlands Coast Guard	9
0.12	Belgian Coast Guard	9
–	Distress and Life Saving Signals	10
0.13	NAVTEX	11
0.14	MSI broadcasts by HM Coastguard	12
0.15	Other UK weather forecasts	12
0.16	Dutch weather forecasts	14
0.17	Belgian weather forecasts	14
0.18	Automatic Identification System (AIS)	15
0.19	Overhead clearances	15
0.20	IALA buoyage	16
0.21	Flags and ensigns	17
0.22–23	Lights and shapes/Navigation lights	18
0.24	Tidal coefficients	20
0.25–26	Sun and moon: rising and setting times	21
0.27	International Code flags, IPTS	22
0.28–29	Area and Harbour information	23
0.30–31	Environmental guidance, Distance table	24

0.1 THE ALMANAC

• Acknowledgements

The Editors thank the many official bodies and individuals for information and advice given in the compilation of this Almanac. These include: UKHO, Trinity House, Northern Lighthouse Board, HM Nautical Almanac Office, HMSO, HM Revenue & Customs, Meteorological Office, BBC, IBA, MCA, RNLI, PLA, ABP, Koninklijke Nederlandse Redding Maatschappij (KNRM), countless Harbourmasters and our many individual Harbour Agents.

• Permissions

Chartlets, tidal stream diagrams and curves are reproduced from Admiralty charts and publications (ALL, ASD, ATT and ALRS) by permission of the UKHO (Licence No GB DQ – 001 – Adlard Coles) and the Controller of HMSO.

UK and foreign tidal predictions are supplied by and with the permission of UKHO and by the German and Dutch HOs with permission to use the tidal predictions stated:

BSH (German HO): Helgoland. (Authorisation 11123/2008-07).

Rijkswaterstaat, Netherlands: Vlissingen, Hoek van Holland.

Vlaamse Hydrografie, Belgium: Zeebrugge.

Extracts from the *International Code of Signals 1969* and *Meteorological Office Weather Services for Shipping* are published by permission of the Controller of HMSO.

Ephemerides are derived from HM Nautical Almanac by permission of HM Nautical Almanac Office and the Council for the Central Laboratory of the Research Councils.

• Disclaimer

No National HO has verified the information in this product and none accepts liability for the accuracy of reproduction or any modifications made thereafter. No National HO warrants that this product satisfies national or international regulations regarding the use of the appropriate products for navigation.

Chartlets in this Almanac are not intended to be used for navigation. Always consult fully corrected official charts. See 0.29, Harbour Information, for more details.

• Improvements

Suggestions, however minor, for improving or correcting this Almanac are always welcome, especially if based on personal experience. All will be carefully considered. Please send your comments by email, if possible, direct to the relevant Editor (see below) or to info@reedsalmanacs.co.uk. Otherwise, a note to Adlard Coles Nautical (see page v) will be forwarded as necessary.

Perrin Towler (editor.britishisles@reedsalmanacs.co.uk) is responsible for Areas 1, 3, 4 and 5 (the east coasts of the UK); Mark Fishwick (editor.continental@reedsalmanacs.co.uk) is responsible for Area 2 (Netherlands and Belgium). We share the compilation of the Reference Data chapter.

• Notifying errors

Although every care has been taken in compiling this Almanac, errors may still occur. Please let us know if you spot any.

• Harbour Agents

Our harbour agents provide invaluable local information which may not appear in official sources. Vacancies are advertised on our website www.reedsalmanacs.co.uk. If you would like to earn a free copy of Reeds Nautical Almanac every year, please apply to the relevant editor, giving brief details of your experience and the area you could cover.

• Sources of corrections

This Almanac is corrected to Weekly edition No. 25/2014 of Admiralty Notices to Mariners.

Corrections to Admiralty charts and publications can be downloaded from the UKHO website or obtained from Admiralty Chart Agents (ACA) and certain Port Authorities.

• Updates

Free monthly updates, from January to June, can be downloaded at www.reedsalmanacs.co.uk. Please register online.

0.2 ABBREVIATIONS AND SYMBOLS

The following more common abbreviations and symbols feature in Reeds Almanacs. Other Admiralty chart symbols are on the flap of the inside back cover. Chart 5011 (a booklet) is the complete reference for Symbols and Abbreviations on charts.

@	Internet café/access
⌓	Alongside berth
ABP	Associated British Ports
⯇Ⅾ⯈	Shore power (electrical)
AC, ACA	Admiralty Chart, AC Agent
ACN	Adlard Coles Nautical (Publisher)
Aff Mar	Affaires Maritimes
AIS	Automatic Identification System
aka	Also known as
ALL	Admiralty List of Lights
ALRS	Admiralty List of Radio Signals
Al	Alternating light
ANWB	Association of road & waterway users (Dutch)
ATT	Admiralty Tide Tables
ATT	Atterisage (landfall/SWM) buoy
Auto	Météo Répondeur Automatique
B.	Bay, Black
Ⓑ	Bank. See also ATM
⌂	Licensed bar, Public house, Inn
BE	Belgian chart
BH	Boat Hoist (+ tons)
Bk	Broken (nature of seabed)
Bkwtr	Breakwater
BMS	Bulletin Météorologique Spécial (Strong wind/Gale warning)
Bn, bcn(s)	Beacon, beacon(s)
BSH	German Hydrographic Office/chart(s)
BST	British Summer Time (= DST)
Bu	Blue
By(s)	Buoy, buoys
BY, ⌖	Boatyard
©	Cashpoint, ATM
C.	Cape, Cabo, Cap
C	Crane (+ tons)
c	Coarse (sand; nature of seabed)
ca	Cable (approx 185m long)
Cas	Castle
CD	Chart datum (tidal)
CEVNI	Code Européen de Voies de la Navigation Intérieure (inland waterway signs etc)
cf	Compare, cross-refer to
CG	Coast Guard, HM Coastguard in UK
⌂	Chandlery
chan	Channel (navigational)
Ch	Channel (VHF)
Ch	Channel (VHF)

Ch, ✠	Church
Chy	Chimney
COG	Course Over the Ground
Col	Column, pillar, obelisk
CPA	Closest Point of Approach
CROSS	Centre Régional Opérationnel de Surveillance et Sauvetage (= MRCC)
CRS	Coast Radio Station
CRT	Canal and River Trust
⊖	Customs
D	Diesel (supply by hose)
	Diesel (by can)
Dec	Declination (of the Sun)
dest	Destroyed
DG	De-gaussing (range)
DGPS	Differential GPS
Dia	Diaphone (fog signal)
discont	Discontinued
Dn(s)	Dolphin(s)
DR	Dead Reckoning
DSC	Digital Selective Calling
DST	Daylight Saving Time
DW	Deep Water (route)
DYC	Dutch Yacht Chart(s)
DZ	Danger Zone (buoy)
E	East
ECM	East Cardinal Mark (buoy/beacon)
ED	Existence doubtful, European Datum
EEA	European Economic Area
	Electrical repairs
Ⓔ	Electronic repairs
Elev	Elevation
Ent	Entrance, entry, enter
EP, △	Estimated position
ETA	Estimated Time of Arrival
ETD	Estimated Time of Departure
F	Fixed light
f	Fine (eg sand)
F&A	Fore and aft (berth/mooring)
Fcst	Forecast
FFL	Fixed and Flashing light
Fl	Flashing light
FM	Frequency Modulation
Foc	Free of charge
Fog Det lt	Fog Detector light
Freq, Fx	Frequency
FS	Flagstaff, Flagpole
ft	Foot, feet
Ft	Fort
FV	Fishing vessel
	Fresh water supply
G	Gravel, Green
Gas	Calor Gas
Gaz	Camping Gaz
GC	Great Circle
GDOP	Geometrical Dilution of Precision (GPS)
GHA	Greenwich Hour Angle
GLA	General Lighthouse Authority
GMDSS	Global Maritime Distress & Safety System
grt	Gross Registered Tonnage
Gy	Grey
[H]	Hospital
H, h, Hrs	Hour(s)

H–, H+	Minutes before/after the whole hour
H24	Continuous
HAT	Highest Astronomical Tide
HF	High Frequency
HFP	High Focal Plane (buoy)
HIE	Highlands & Islands Enterprise
HJ	Day service only, sunrise to sunset
HM	Harbour Master
HMRC	HM Revenue & Customs
HMSO	Her Majesty's Stationery Office
HN	Night service only, sunset to sunrise
HO	Office hours, Hydrographic Office
(hor)	Horizontally disposed (lights)
hPa	Hectopascal (= 1millibar)
HT	High Tension (overhead electricity line)
HW	High Water
HX	No fixed hours
IALA	International Association of Lighthouse Authorities
iaw	In accordance with
ICAO	International Civil Aviation Organisation
IDM	Isolated Danger Mark (buoy/beacon)
IHO	International Hydrographic Organisation
IMO	International Maritime Organisation
INMARSAT	International Maritime Satellite Organisation
intens	Intensified (light sector)
IPTS	International Port Traffic Signals
IQ	Interrupted quick flashing light
IRPCS	International Regulations for the Prevention of Collisions at Sea
Is, I	Island, Islet
ISAF	International Sailing Federation
Iso	Isophase light
ITU	International Telecommunications Union
ITZ	Inshore Traffic Zone (TSS)
IUQ	Interrupted ultra quick flashing light
IVQ	Interrupted very quick flashing light
JRCC	Joint Rescue Co-ordination Centre
kn	knot(s)
Kos	Kosangas
kW	Kilowatts
L	Lake, Loch, Lough, Landing place
Lat	Latitude
LAT	Lowest Astronomical Tide
Lanby,	Large automatic navigational buoy
[LB], ♦	Lifeboat, inshore lifeboat
Ldg	Leading (light)
LF	Low frequency
L Fl	Long flash
LH	Left hand
L/L	Latitude/Longitude
LNG	Liquefied Natural Gas
LNTM	Local Notice To Mariners
LOA	Length overall
Long	Longitude
LPG	Liquefied Petroleum Gas
LT	Local time
Lt(s), ★ ☆	Light(s)
	Light float, minor
Lt V,	Light vessel; Lt float, major; Lanby
M	Moorings, nautical (sea) mile(s), Mud
m	Metre(s)
Mag	Magnetic, magnitude (of Star)

mb	Millibar (= 1 hectopascal, hPa)
MCA	Maritime and Coastguard Agency
⚒	Marine engineering repairs
MHWN	Mean High Water Neaps
MHWS	Mean High Water Springs
MHz	Megahertz
ML	Mean Level (tidal)
MLWN	Mean Low Water Neaps
MLWS	Mean Low Water Springs
MMSI	Maritime Mobile Service Identity
Mo	Morse
Mon	Monument, Monday
MRCC	Maritime Rescue Co-ordination Centre
MSI	Maritime Safety Information
N	North
Navi	Navicarte (French charts)
NB	Nota Bene, Notice Board
NCI, ©	National Coastwatch Institution
NCM	North Cardinal Mark (buoy/beacon)
NGS	Naval Gunfire Support (buoy)
NM	Notice(s) to Mariners
nps	Neap tides
NP	Naval Publication (plus number)
NT	National Trust (land/property)
Obscd	Obscured
Obstn	Obstruction
Oc	Occulting light
ODAS	Ocean Data Acquisition System (buoy)
Or	Orange
OT	Other times
OWF	Offshore wind farm
P	Petrol (supply by hose), Pebbles
⛽	Petrol (by can)
(P)	Preliminary (NM)
PA	Position approximate
Pax	Passenger(s)
PC	Portuguese chart
PD	Position doubtful
PHM	Port-hand Mark (buoy/beacon)
PLA	Port of London Authority
PO, ✉	Post Office
prom	Prominent
PSSA	Particularly Sensitive Sea Area
Pt(e), Pta	Point(e), Punta
⚓	Pump-out facility
Q	Quick flashing light
QHM	Queen's Harbour Master
R	Red, Restaurant ✗, River, Rock
Racon	Radar transponder beacon
Ramark	Radar beacon
RCD	Recreational Craft Directive
RDF	Radio Direction Finding
RG	Emergency RDF station
RH	Right hand
Rk, Rky	Rock, Rocky
RMG	Reeds Marina Guide
RNLI	Royal National Lifeboat Institution
ROI	Republic of Ireland
R/T	Radiotelephony
Ru	Ruins
RYA	Royal Yachting Association
S	South, Sand
S, St, Ste	Saint(s)
SAMU	Service d'Aide Médicale Urgente (ambulance)
SAR	Search and Rescue
SC	Sailing Club, Spanish chart
SCM	South Cardinal Mark (buoy/beacon)
SD	Sailing Directions, Semi-diameter (of sun)
SD	Sounding of doubtful depth
sf	Stiff
Sh	Shells, Shoal
SHM	Simplified Harmonic Method (tides),
SHM	Starboard-hand Mark (buoy/beacon)
SHOM	French Hydrographic Office/Chart
Si	Silt
SIGNI	Signalisation de la Navigation Intérieure
⚖	Sailmaker
⚒	Shipwright (esp wooden hulls)
SMS	Short Message Service (mobile texting)
so	Soft (eg mud)
SOG	Speed Over the Ground
SOLAS	Safety of Life at Sea (IMO Convention)
sp	Spring tides
SPM	Special Mark (buoy/beacon)
SR	Sunrise
SRR	Search and Rescue Region
SS	Sunset, Signal Station
SSB	Single Sideband (Radio)
Stbd	Starboard
subm	Submerged
SWM	Safe Water Mark (buoy/beacon)
(T), (Temp)	Temporary
tbc	To be confirmed
tbn	To be notified
TD	Temporarily discontinued (fog signal)
TE	Temporarily extinguished (light)
tfn	Till further notice
Tr, twr	Tower
T/R	Traffic Report (tells the CG your route etc)
TSS	Traffic Separation Scheme
≠	In transit with, ie ldg marks/lts
u/mkd	Unmarked (feature/hazard)
UQ	Ultra Quick flashing light
UT	Universal Time (= approx GMT)
Var	Variation (magnetic)
Vel	Velocity
(vert)	Vertically disposed (lights)
Vi	Violet
VLCC	Very large crude carrier (Oil tanker)
VNF	Voie Navigable de France (canals)
VQ	Very Quick flashing light
VTS	Vessel Traffic Service
W	West, White
WCM	West Cardinal Mark (buoy/beacon)
⚘	Wind turbine
wef	With effect from
WGS	World Geodetic System (GPS datum)
wi-fi	Wireless Fidelity (internet access)
WIP	Work in progress
Wk, ⚓ ⊕	Wreck
WPT, ⊕	Waypoint
⛅	Weather
WZ	Code for UK coastal navigation warning
Y	Yellow, Amber, Orange
YC, ⚑	Yacht Club

0.3 PASSAGE PLANNING FORM

DATE:........................... FROM: .... TO: .... DIST: ....nm

ALTERNATIVE DESTINATION(S): ....

WEATHER FORECAST: ....

....

FORECASTS AVAILABLE DURING PASSAGE: ....

....

TIDES

DATE:..	DATE:..	DATE:..
PLACE:.......................................	PLACE:.......................................	PLACE:.......................................
HW	HW	HW ....
LW	LW	LW ....
HW	HW	HW ....
LW	LW	LW ....
COEFFICIENT:	....	....
HEIGHT OF TIDE AT:	....	....
..................hrs ....m	..................hrs ....m	..................hrs ....m

DEPTH CONSTRAINTS: ....

TIDAL STREAMS AT: ....

TURNS .... AT .... TOTAL SET (FM .... TO ....): ....° .... M

TURNS .... AT .... TOTAL SET (FM .... TO ....): ....° .... M

NET TIDAL STREAM FOR PASSAGE: ....° .... M

ESTIMATED TIME: ....hrs ETD: .... ETA: ....

SUN/MOON	SUNRISE:	SUNSET: ....
	MOONRISE:	MOONSET: .... PHASE: ....

WAYPOINTS	NO	NAME	TRACK/DISTANCE (TO NEXT WAYPOINT)
	....	....	.... / ....
	....	....	.... / ....
	....	....	.... / ....
	....	....	.... / ....
	....	....	.... / ....

DANGERS   CLEARING BEARINGS/RANGES/DEPTHS

....

....

LIGHTS/MARKS EXPECTED ....

....

....

COMMUNICATIONS	PORT/MARINA	VHF	☎ ....
	PORT/MARINA	VHF	☎ ....

NOTES (CHARTS PREPARED & PAGE NUMBERS OF RELEVANT PILOTS / ALMANACS / ETC): ....

....

....

0.4 PASSAGE PLANNING

All passages by any vessel that goes to sea *must* be planned. 'Going to sea' is defined as proceeding beyond sheltered waters. Full passage planning requirements may be found in Chapter V of the International Convention for Safety of Life at Sea (SOLAS), but more digestible guidance for small craft is in the MCA's Pleasure Craft Information Pack at: **www.dft. gov.uk/mca/pleasure_craft_information_packdec07-2.pdf**.

Although the passage plan does not have to be recorded on paper, in the event of legal action a written plan is clear proof that the required planning has been completed. A suggested passage planning form is on the previous page. When completed this would constitute a reasonable passage plan. The blank form may be photocopied and/or modified.

Although spot checks on small craft are unlikely, the MCA could, following an accident or incident, take action under the Merchant Shipping Act if it could be proved that the skipper did not have a reasonable passage plan.

All passage plans should at least consider the following:

- **Weather.** Check the weather forecast and know how to get regular updates during the passage.
- **Tides.** Check tidal predictions and determine if there are any limiting depths at your port of departure, during the passage and at the port of arrival (and at alternative ports, if applicable). Tidal streams will almost certainly affect the plan.
- **Vessel.** Confirm she is suitable for the intended trip, is properly equipped, and has sufficient fuel, water and food on board.
- **Crew.** Take into account your crew's experience, expertise and stamina. Cold, tiredness and seasickness can be debilitating – and skippers are not immune.
- **Navigation.** Make sure you are aware of all navigational dangers by consulting up to date charts, pilot books and this Almanac. Never *rely* on GPS for fixing your position.
- **Contingency plan.** Consider bolt holes which can be entered *safely* in an emergency.
- **Information ashore.** Make sure someone ashore knows your plans, when they should become concerned and what action to take if necessary. Be sure to join the Coastguard Voluntary Identification Scheme.

0.5 POSITIONS FROM GPS

GPS uses the World Geodetic System 84 datum (WGS84). With the exception of much of the coast of Ireland and the west coast of Scotland, Admiralty charts of UK waters have now been converted to WGS84. Harbour chartlets in this Almanac are referenced to WGS84.

If the chart in use is not referenced to WGS84, positions read from the GPS receiver must be converted to the datum of the chart in use. This is printed on the chart and gives the Lat/Long corrections to be applied. They can be significant. There are two options:

- Set the receiver to WGS84. Before plotting positions, manually apply the corrections given on the chart. This option is advised by UKHO.
- Set the receiver to the datum of the chart in use; the datum corrections will be applied by the receiver's software. This method is not the most accurate due to the random nature of the differences.

0.6 VHF COMMUNICATIONS

Radio Telephony (R/T)

VHF radio (Marine band 156·00–174·00 MHz) is used by most vessels. Range is slightly better than the line of sight between aerials, typically about 20M between yachts and up to 65M to a shore station depending on aerial heights. It always pays to fit a good aerial, as high as possible.

VHF sets may be **Simplex**, ie transmit and receive on the same frequency, so only one person can talk at a time. **Semi-Duplex** (most modern sets), transmit and receive on different frequencies, or **full Duplex**, ie simultaneous Semi-Duplex, so conversation is normal, but two aerials are needed.

Marine VHF frequencies are known by their international channel number (Ch), as shown below.

Channels are grouped according to three main purposes, but some have more than one purpose.

> **Public correspondence:** (via Coast radio stations)
> Ch 26, 27, 25, 24, 23, 28, 04, 01, 03, 02, 07, 05, 84, 87, 86, 83, 85, 88, 61, 64, 65, 62, 66, 63, 60, 82, 78, 81.
> All channels can be used for Duplex.
>
> **Inter-ship:**
> Ch 06*, 08*, 10, 13, 09, 72*, 73, 69, 77*, 15, 17.
> These are all Simplex channels. * for use in UK.
>
> **Port Operations:**
> Simplex: Ch 12, 14, 11, 13, 09, 68, 71, 74, 69, 73, 17, 15.
> Duplex: Ch 20, 22, 18, 19, 21, 05, 07, 02, 03, 01, 04, 78, 82, 79, 81, 80, 60, 63, 66, 62, 65, 64, 61, 84.

The following channels have one specific purpose:

> **Ch 0** (156·00 MHz): SAR ops, not available to yachts.
>
> **Ch 10** (156·50 MHz), **23** (161·750 MHz), **84** (161·825 MHz) and **86** (161·925 MHz): MSI broadcasts. The optimum channel number is stated on Ch 16 in the announcement prior to the broadcast itself.
>
> **Ch 13** (156·650 MHz): Inter-ship communications relating to safety of navigation; a possible channel for calling a merchant ship if no contact on Ch 16.
>
> **Ch 16** (156·80 MHz): Distress, Safety and calling. Ch 16, in parallel with DSC Ch 70, will be monitored by ships, CG rescue centres (and, in some areas, any remaining Coast Radio Stations) for Distress and Safety until further notice. Yachts should monitor Ch 16. After an initial call, stations concerned **must** switch to a working channel, except for Distress and Safety matters.
>
> **Ch 67** (156·375 MHz): Small craft safety channel used by all UK CG centres, accessed via Ch 16.
>
> **Ch 70** (156·525 MHz): Digital Selective Calling for Distress and Safety purposes under GMDSS.
>
> **Ch 80** (157·025 MHz): Primary working channel between yachts and UK marinas.
>
> **Ch M** (157·85 MHz): Secondary working channel, formerly known as Ch 37, but no longer.
>
> **Ch M2** (161·425 MHz): for race control, with Ch M as stand-by. YCs may apply to use Ch M2.

Your position should be given as Lat/Long or the vessel's bearing and distance *from* a charted object, eg 'My position 225° Isle of May 4M' means you are 4M SW of the Isle of May (*not* 4M NE). Use the 360° True bearing notation and the 24-hour clock (0001–2359), specifying UT or LT.

0.7 DISTRESS CALLS

Distress signal - MAYDAY

Distress only applies to a situation where a *vessel or person is in grave and imminent danger and requires immediate assistance*. A MAYDAY call should usually be sent on VHF Ch 16 or MF 2182 kHz, but any frequency may be used if help would thus be obtained more quickly.

Distress, Urgency and Safety messages from vessels at sea are free of charge. A Distress call has priority over all other transmissions. If heard, cease all transmissions that may interfere with the Distress call or messages, and listen on the frequency concerned.

Brief your crew so they are all able to send a Distress message. The MAYDAY message format (below) should be displayed near the radio. Before making the call:

- Switch on radio (check main battery switch is ON)
- Select HIGH power (25 watts)
- Select VHF Ch 16 (or 2182 kHz for MF)
- Press and hold down the transmit button, and say slowly and distinctly:

- **MAYDAY MAYDAY MAYDAY**
- **THIS IS** ....
(name of boat, spoken three times)
- **MAYDAY** ....
(name of boat spoken once)
- **CALLSIGN / MMSI Number** ....
(Following a DSC alert)
- **MY POSITION IS** ....
(latitude and longitude, true bearing and
   distance *from* a known point, or general location)
- **Nature of distress** ....
(sinking, on fire etc)
- **Help required** ....
(immediate assistance)
- **Number of persons on board** ....
- **Any other important, helpful information** ....
(you are taking to the liferaft; distress rockets are
   being fired etc)
- **OVER**

On completion of the Distress message, release the transmit button and listen. The boat's position is of vital importance and should be repeated if time allows. If an acknowledgement is not received, check the set and repeat the Distress call.

Vessels with GMDSS equipment should make a MAYDAY call on Ch 16, including their MMSI and callsign, *after* sending a DSC Distress alert on VHF Ch 70 or MF 2187·5 kHz.

0.7.1 MAYDAY acknowledgement

In coastal waters an immediate acknowledgement should be expected, as follows:

> **MAYDAY** ....
> (name of station sending the Distress message, spoken three times)
>
> **THIS IS** ....
> (name of station acknowledging, spoken three times)
>
> **RECEIVED MAYDAY**

If you hear a Distress message, write down the details and, if you can help, acknowledge accordingly - but only after giving an opportunity for the nearest Coastguard station or some larger vessel to do so.

0.7.2 MAYDAY relay

If you hear a Distress message from a vessel, and it is not acknowledged, you should pass on the message as follows:

> **MAYDAY RELAY** ....
> (spoken three times)
>
> **THIS IS** ....
> (name of vessel re-transmitting the Distress message, spoken three times), followed by the intercepted message.

0.7.3 Control of MAYDAY traffic

A MAYDAY call imposes general radio silence until the vessel concerned or some other authority (eg the nearest Coastguard) cancels the Distress. If necessary the station controlling Distress traffic may impose radio silence as follows:

> **SEELONCE MAYDAY**, followed by its name or other identification, on the Distress frequency.
>
> If some other station nearby believes it necessary to do likewise, it may transmit:
>
> **SEELONCE DISTRESS**, followed by its name or other identification.

0.7.4 Relaxing radio silence

When complete radio silence is no longer necessary, the controlling station may relax radio silence as follows, indicating that restricted working may be resumed:

> **MAYDAY**
>
> **ALL STATIONS, ALL STATIONS, ALL STATIONS**
>
> **THIS IS** ....
> (name or callsign)
>
> The time ....
>
> The name of the vessel in distress ....
>
> **PRUDONCE**

Normal working on the Distress frequency may then be resumed, having listened carefully before transmitting. Subsequent calls from the casualty should be prefixed by the Urgency signal (0.8).

If Distress working continues on other frequencies these will be identified. For example, PRUDONCE on 2182 kHz, but SEELONCE on VHF Ch 16.

0.7.5 Cancelling radio silence

When the problem is resolved, the Distress call must be cancelled by the co-ordinating station using the prowords SEELONCE FEENEE as follows:

> **MAYDAY**
>
> **ALL STATIONS, ALL STATIONS, ALL STATIONS**
>
> **THIS IS** ....(name or callsign)
>
> The time ....
>
> The name of the vessel in distress ....
>
> **SEELONCE FEENEE**

0.8   URGENCY AND SAFETY CALLS

Urgency signal - PAN PAN

The radio Urgency prefix, consisting of the words PAN PAN spoken three times, indicates that a vessel, or station, has *a very urgent message concerning the safety of a ship or person*. It may be used when urgent medical advice is needed.

This is an example of an Urgency call:

> PAN PAN, PAN PAN, PAN PAN
>
> ALL STATIONS, ALL STATIONS, ALL STATIONS
>
> THIS IS YACHT SEABIRD, SEABIRD, SEABIRD
>
> Two five zero degrees Roughs Tower one point five miles
>
> Dismasted and propeller fouled
>
> Drifting west towards Cork Sands
>
> Require urgent tow
>
> **OVER**

PAN PAN messages take priority over all traffic except Distress, and are sent on Ch 16 or 2182 kHz. They should be cancelled when the urgency is over.

If the message is long (eg a medical call) or communications traffic is heavy, it may be passed on a working frequency after an initial call on Ch 16 or 2182 kHz. At the end of the initial call you should indicate that you are switching to a working frequency.

If you hear an Urgency call react in the same way as for a Distress call.

0.8.1   Safety signal - SÉCURITÉ

The word SÉCURITÉ (pronounced SAY-CURE-E-TAY) spoken three times, indicates that the station is about to transmit an important navigational or meteorological warning. Such messages usually originate from a CG Centre or a Coast Radio Station, and are transmitted on a working channel after an announcement on the distress/calling channel (Ch 16 or 2182 kHz).

Safety messages are usually addressed to 'All stations', and are often transmitted at the end of the first available silence period. An example of a Sécurité message is:

> SÉCURITÉ, SÉCURITÉ, SÉCURITÉ ....
>
> THIS IS ....
>
> (CG Centre or Coast Radio Station callsign, spoken three times)
>
> **ALL STATIONS** ....
>
> (spoken three times) followed by instructions to change channel, then the message.

0.9   GMDSS

The Global Maritime Distress and Safety System (GMDSS) came into force in 1999. Most seagoing vessels over 300 tons are required by SOLAS to comply with GMDSS, but it is not compulsory for yachts. However, it is important that the principles of the system are understood, and you should at least consider fitting compliant equipment depending on your cruising area. Full details may be found in ALRS Vol 5 (NP 285).

0.9.1   Purpose

GMDSS enables a coordinated SAR operation to be mounted rapidly and reliably anywhere at sea. To this end, terrestrial and satellite communications and navigation equipment is used to alert SAR authorities ashore and ships in the vicinity to a Distress incident or Urgency situation. GMDSS also promulgates MSI (Maritime Safety Information).

0.9.2   Sea areas

The type of equipment carried by a vessel depends of her operating area. The four GMDSS Areas are:

> **A1**   An area within R/T coverage of at least one VHF Coastguard or Coast radio station in which continuous VHF alerting is available via DSC. Range: 20–50M from the CG/CRS.
>
> **A2**   An area, excluding sea area A1, within R/T coverage of at least one MF CG/CRS in which continuous DSC alerting is available. Range: approx 50–250M from the CG/CRS.
>
> **A3**   An area between 76°N and 76°S, excluding sea areas A1 and A2, within coverage of HF or an Inmarsat satellite in which continuous alerting is available.
>
> **A4**   An area outside sea areas A1, A2 and A3, ie the polar regions, within coverage of HF.

In each Area, in addition to a Navtex receiver, certain types of radio equipment must be carried by GMDSS vessels: In A1, VHF DSC; A2, VHF and MF DSC; A3, VHF, MF and HF or SatCom; A4, VHF, MF and HF.

0.9.3   Digital Selective Calling

GMDSS comprises 'sub-systems' which are coordinated through Maritime Rescue Coordination Centres (MRCC) to ensure safety at sea. DSC is one of the 'sub-systems' of GMDSS. It uses terrestrial communications for making initial contact and, in a distress situation, provides the vessel's identity, nature of distress and position (entered manually or automatically if linked with the GPS). In all DSC messages every vessel and relevant shore station has a 9-digit Maritime Mobile Service Identity (MMSI) which is in effect an automatic electronic callsign. Dedicated frequencies are: VHF Ch 70, MF 2187·5 kHz. A thorough working knowledge of the following procedure is needed.

A typical VHF/DSC Distress alert might be sent as follows:

> • Briefly press the (red, guarded) Distress button. The set automatically switches to Ch 70 (DSC Distress channel). Press again for 5 seconds to transmit a basic Distress alert with position and time. The radio then reverts to Ch 16.
>
> • If time permits, select the nature of the distress from the menu, eg Collision, then press the Distress button for 5 seconds to send a full Distress alert.

A CG/CRS should automatically send an acknowledgement on Ch 70 before replying on Ch 16. Ships in range should reply directly on Ch 16. When a DSC Distress acknowledgement has been received, or after about 15 seconds, the vessel in distress should transmit a MAYDAY message by voice on Ch 16, including its MMSI.

0.10 HM COASTGUARD - CONTACT DETAILS OF CG CENTRES

EASTERN REGION

DOVER COASTGUARD
50°08′N 01°20′E. DSC MMSI 002320010
Langdon Battery, Swingate, Dover CT15 5NA.
☎ 01304 210008. 🖷 01304 202137.
Area: Beachy Head to Reculver Towers (51°23′N 01°12′E). Operates Channel Navigation Information Service (CNIS).

THAMES COASTGUARD
51°51′N 01°17′E. MMSI 002320009
East Terrace, Walton-on-the-Naze CO14 8PY.
☎ 01255 675518. 🖷 01255 675249.
Area: Reculver Towers to Southwold (52°19′N 01°40′E).

LONDON COASTGUARD
51°30′N 00°03′E. MMSI 002320063
Thames Barrier Navigation Centre, Unit 28,
34 Bowater Road, Woolwich, London SE18 5TF.
☎ 02083 127380. 🖷 02083 127679.
Area: River Thames from Shell Haven Pt (N bank) & Egypt Bay (S bank) up-river to Teddington Lock.

†HUMBER COASTGUARD
54°06′N 00°11′W. MMSI 002320007
Lime Kiln Lane, Bridlington, E Yorkshire YO15 2LX.
☎ 01262 672317. 🖷 01262 606915.
Area: Southwold to the Scottish border.

SCOTLAND (& NORTHERN IRELAND) REGION

†ABERDEEN COASTGUARD
57°08′N 02°05′W. MMSI 002320004
Marine House, Blaikies Quay, Aberdeen AB11 5PB.
☎ 01224 592334. 🖷 01224 212862.
Area: English border to Cape Wrath, incl Pentland Firth.

†SHETLAND COASTGUARD
60°09′N 01°08′W. MMSI 002320001
Knab Road, Lerwick ZE1 0AX.
☎ 01595 692976. 🖷 01595 694810.
Area: Orkney, Fair Isle and Shetland.

NOTE: †Monitors DSC MF 2187.5 kHz.

0.11 NETHERLANDS COAST GUARD

The national SAR agency is: SAR Commission, Directorate Transport Safety (DGG), PO Box 20904, 2500 EX The Hague, Netherlands.

The Netherlands CG at Den Helder, co-located with the Navy HQ, coordinates SAR operations as the Dutch JRCC for A1 and A2 Sea Areas. (JRCC = Joint Rescue Coordination Centre – marine & aeronautical.) Callsign is *Netherlands Coast Guard*, but *Den Helder Rescue* is used during SAR operations.

The JRCC keeps a listening watch H24 on DSC Ch 70, and MF DSC 2187·5 kHz (but not on 2182 kHz); MMSI 002442000.

Coast Guard Operations can be contacted H24 via:

In emergency:
☎ + 31 9000 111 or dial 112.

Operational telephone number:
☎ + 31 223 542300. 🖷 + 31 223 658358; ccc@kustwacht. nl If using a mobile phone, call 9000 111, especially if the International emergency number 112 is subject to delays.

Admin/info (HO):
☎+ 31 223 658300. 🖷+31 223 658303. info@kustwacht.nl
PO Box 10.000/MPC 10A, 1780 CA Den Helder.

Remote Coast Guard stations are shown on Fig 0(6). Working channels are VHF 23 and 83.

0.11.1 Medical advice
Call initially on Ch 16, DSC Ch 70 or 2187·5 kHz (MMSI 002442000). Working chans are VHF Ch 23 & 83 or MF 2824 kHz (transmit), 2520 kHz (receive).

0.11.2 Resources
The Dutch Lifeboat Ass'n (KNRM) manages 26 lifeboat stations and 13 inshore lifeboat stations along the coast. The 60 lifeboats include 13m LOA water-jet, rigid inflatables capable of 36 kn. Helicopters, fixed wing aircraft and ships of the RNLN can be called upon; also Air Force helos at Leeuwarden. The area of activity extends across the Dutch Continental Shelf and into the Waddenzee, IJsselmeer and estuaries of Zuid Holland and Zeeland.

0.12 BELGIAN COAST GUARD

The Belgian Coast Guard coordinates SAR operations from Oostende MRCC, callsign *Coast Guard Oostende*. The MRCC and *Oostende Radio* (Coast Radio Station) both keep listening watch H24 on Ch 16, 67, 2182 kHz and DSC Ch 70 and 2187·5 kHz.

Coast Guard stations
MRCC OOSTENDE
☎ +32 59 701000; 🖷 +32 59 703605
MMSI 002059981
mrcc@mrcc.be

RCC Brussels (Point of contact for COSPAS/SARSAT)
☎ +32 2 751 4615; 🖷 +32 2 7524201
rcc@mil.be

Coast radio stations
OOSTENDE Radio
☎ +32 50 558241; 🖷 +32 50 558748
rmd@mil.be
Ch 16, DSC Ch 70 and MF DSC 2187·5 kHz.
MMSI 002050480

Antwerpen Radio (remotely controlled by Oostende CRS) MMSI 002050485. Ch 16, DSC Ch 70. Working channels: Ch 07, 27

0.12.1 Resources
Offshore and inshore lifeboats are based at Nieuwpoort, Oostende and Zeebrugge.

The Belgian Air Force provides helicopters from Koksijde near the French border. The Belgian Navy also participates in SAR operations as required.

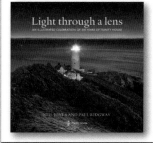

Fig 0(1)   Distress and life saving signals

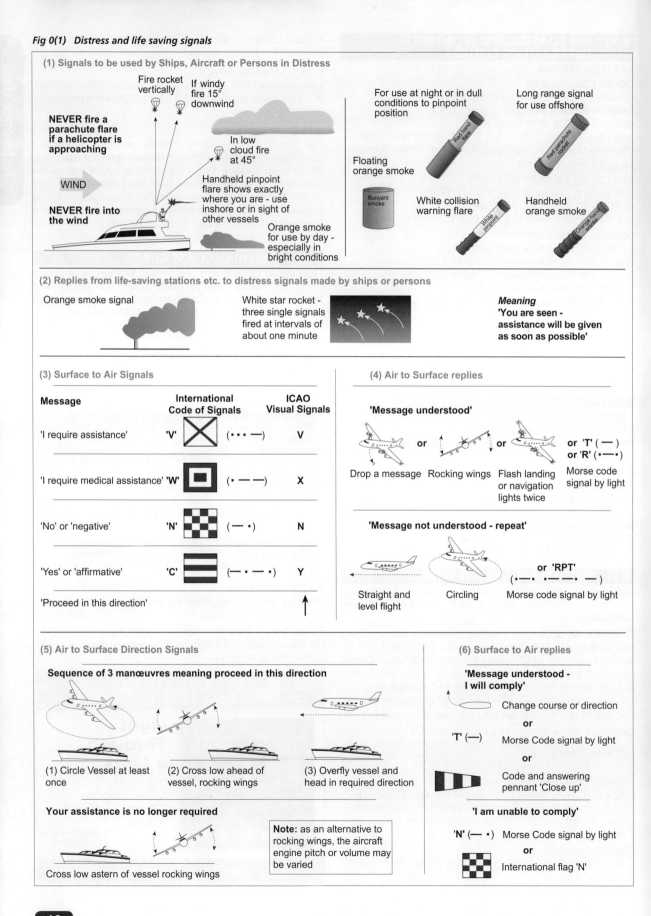

(1) Signals to be used by Ships, Aircraft or Persons in Distress

Fire rocket vertically

If windy fire 15° downwind

NEVER fire a parachute flare if a helicopter is approaching

In low cloud fire at 45°

WIND

NEVER fire into the wind

Handheld pinpoint flare shows exactly where you are - use inshore or in sight of other vessels

Orange smoke for use by day - especially in bright conditions

For use at night or in dull conditions to pinpoint position

Red hand flare

Long range signal for use offshore

Red parachute rocket

Floating orange smoke

Buoyant smoke

White collision warning flare

White pinpoint

Handheld orange smoke

Orange hand smoke

(2) Replies from life-saving stations etc. to distress signals made by ships or persons

Orange smoke signal

White star rocket - three single signals fired at intervals of about one minute

Meaning
'You are seen - assistance will be given as soon as possible'

(3) Surface to Air Signals

Message	International Code of Signals		ICAO Visual Signals
'I require assistance'	'V'	(· · · —)	V
'I require medical assistance'	'W'	(· — — —)	X
'No' or 'negative'	'N'	(— ·)	N
'Yes' or 'affirmative'	'C'	(— · — ·)	Y
'Proceed in this direction'	↑		

(4) Air to Surface replies

'Message understood'

Drop a message   **or**   Rocking wings   **or**   Flash landing or navigation lights twice   **or 'T' (—)** **or 'R' (· — ·)** Morse code signal by light

'Message not understood - repeat'

Straight and level flight   Circling   **or 'RPT'** **(· — · · — · — · —)** Morse code signal by light

(5) Air to Surface Direction Signals

Sequence of 3 manœuvres meaning proceed in this direction

(1) Circle Vessel at least once

(2) Cross low ahead of vessel, rocking wings

(3) Overfly vessel and head in required direction

Your assistance is no longer required

Cross low astern of vessel rocking wings

Note: as an alternative to rocking wings, the aircraft engine pitch or volume may be varied

(6) Surface to Air replies

'Message understood - I will comply'

Change course or direction

or

'T' (—) Morse Code signal by light

or

Code and answering pennant 'Close up'

'I am unable to comply'

'N' (— ·) Morse Code signal by light

or

International flag 'N'

0.13 NAVTEX

NAVTEX is the prime method of disseminating MSI to at least 200 miles offshore. A dedicated aerial and receiver with an LCD screen (or integrated printer) are required. The user selects which stations and message categories are recorded for automatic display or printing.

Two frequencies are used. On the international frequency, 518kHz, messages are always available in English with excellent coverage of Europe. Interference between stations is minimised by scheduling time slots and and by limiting transmission power; see Fig 6(3). NAVTEX information applies only to the geographical area for which each station is responsible.

On the national frequency 490kHz (for clarity, shown in red throughout this section) the UK issues inshore waters forecasts and coastal station actuals. Elsewhere it is used mainly for transmissions in the national language. 490khz stations have different identification letters from 518kHz stations. NAVTEX is particularly useful if preoccupied handling your vessel as you will not miss potentially important information.

0.13.1 Message categories

A*	Navigational warnings
B*	Meteorological warnings
C	Ice reports
D*	SAR info and Piracy attack warnings
E	Weather forecasts
F	Pilot service
G	AIS
H	LORAN
I	Spare
J	SATNAV
K	Other electronic Navaids
L	Navwarnings additional to A
M-U	Spare
V-Y	Special services – as allocated
Z	No messages on hand

* These categories cannot be rejected by the receiver.

0.13.2 UK 518 kHz stations

The times (UT) of weather messages are in bold; the times of an extended outlook (a further 2 or 3 days beyond the shipping forecast period) are in italics.

E – Niton	*0040*	0440	**0840**	1240	1640	**2040**
Thames clockwise to Fastnet, excluding Trafalgar.						

G – Cullercoats	*0100*	0500	**0900**	1300	1700	**2100**
Fair Isle clockwise to Thames, excluding N and S Utsire, Fisher and German Bight.						

0.13.3 UK 490 kHz stations

These provide forecasts for UK inshore waters (to 12M offshore), a national 3 day outlook for inshore waters and, at times in bold, reports of actual weather at the places listed below. To receive these reports select message category 'V' (0.13.1) on your NAVTEX receiver. Times (UT) of transmissions are listed in chronological order.

Actual Met data includes: Sea level pressure (mb), wind direction and speed (kn), weather, visibility (M), air and sea temperatures (°C), dewpoint temperature (°C) and mean wave height (m).

I – Niton	The Wash to St David's Head	0120	0520	**0920**	1320	1720	**2120**
Sandettie Lt V and other places westwards along the English Channel.							

U – Cullercoats	C. Wrath & Shetland to N Foreland	0320	0720	**1120**	**1520**	1920	**2320**
Sandettie Lt V, Manston, Shoeburyness, Weybourne, Donna Nook or Bridlington, Boulmer, Leuchars, Aberdeen, Lossiemouth, Wick, Kirkwall, Lerwick, Foula, K7 Met buoy, Sule Skerry.							

Fig 0(2) NAVTEX stations/areas – North Sea

0.13.4 Message numbering

Each message is prefixed by a group of four characters:

The 1st character is the ident of the station (eg **E** for Niton). The 2nd is the message category, see 0.13.1. The 3rd and 4th are message serial numbers from 01 to 99, then re-starting at 01. The serial number 00 is used for urgent messages which are always printed.

Messages which are corrupt or have already been printed are rejected. Weather messages, and certain other message types, are dated and timed. All NAVTEX messages end with NNNN.

0.13.5 NAVTEX coverage abroad

Selected NAVTEX stations in Metarea I, with their identity codes and transmission times are listed below. Times of weather messages are shown in **bold**. Gale warnings are usually transmitted 4 hourly.

METAREA I (Co-ordinator – UK)		Transmission times (UT)					
B –	**Oostende**, Belgium (Mostly Dutch)	**0010**	0410	0810	**1210**	1610	2010
P –	**Netherlands CG**, Den Helder	**0230**	0630	1030	**1430**	1830	2230
T –	**Oostende**, Belgium (Note 1)	0310	**0710**	1110	1510	**1910**	2310
L –	**Pinneberg**, Hamburg (In German)	0150	0550	0950	1350	**1750**	**2150**
S –	**Pinneberg**, Hamburg	**0300**	**0700**	**1100**	**1500**	**1900**	**2300**
V –	**Oostende**, Belgium (Note 2)	0330	0730	1130	1530	1930	2330
L –	**Rogaland**, Norway	**0150**	0550	0950	**1350**	1750	2150

Note 1 Forecasts and strong wind warnings for Thames and Dover, plus nav info for the Belgian coast.
2 No weather information, only Nav warnings.

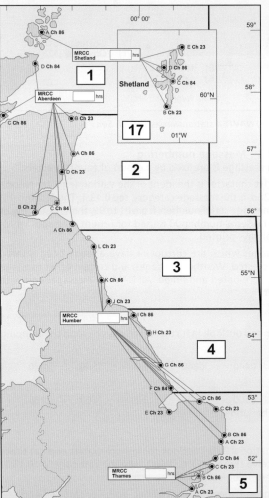

Fig 0(3) Boundaries of the areas used by the CG for forecasts covering inshore waters.

0.14 MSI BROADCASTS BY HM COASTGUARD

HM CG Centres routinely broadcast MSI (Maritime Safety Information) every 3 hours at the times in the Table below. The broadcast channel is pre-stated on Ch 16.

Each broadcast contains one of 3 different Groups of MSI:

Group A, the full broadcast, contains the Shipping forecast, a new Inshore waters forecast and 24 hrs outlook, Gale warnings, a Fisherman's 3 day forecast (1 Oct-31 Mar*), Navigational (WZ) warnings and Subfacts & Gunfacts where appropriate ‡. Times of 'A' broadcasts are in bold.

Group B contains a new Inshore waters forecast, plus the previous outlook, and Gale warnings. 'B' broadcast times are in plain type.

Group C is a repeat of the Inshore forecast and Gale warnings (as per the previous Group A or B) plus new Strong wind warnings. 'C' broadcast times are italicised.

‡ Subfacts and Gunfacts are broadcast (occas) by Aberdeen Coastguard.

0.15 OTHER UK WEATHER BROADCASTS

BBC Radio 4 Shipping forecast
BBC Radio 4 broadcasts shipping forecasts at:

0048, 0520 LT[1]	LW, MW, FM
1201 LT	LW only
1754 LT	LW, FM (Sat/Sun)

[1] Includes weather reports from coastal stations

Frequencies

LW		198 kHz
MW	Tyneside:	603 kHz
	London:	720 kHz
	Aberdeen:	1449 kHz
FM	England:	92·4–94·6 MHz
	Scotland:	91·3–96·1 MHz
		103·5–104·9 MHz

Broadcasts of shipping and inshore waters forecasts by HM Coastguard

Coastguard	Shipping forecast areas	Inshore areas	B	C	A	C	B	C	A	C
					Broadcast times LT					
Thames	Dover, Wight, Thames, Humber	5, 6	0110	*0410*	**0710**	*1010*	1310	*1610*	**1910**	*2210*
Humber*	Humber, German Bight, Dogger, Tyne	3–5	0150	*0450*	**0750**	*1050*	1350	*1650*	**1950**	*2250*
Aberdeen‡*	Tyne, Forth, Cromarty, Forties, Fair Is	1, 2	0130	*0430*	**0730**	*1030*	1330	*1630*	**1930**	*2230*
Shetland*	Cromarty, Viking, Fair Isle, Faeroes	1, 16	0110	*0410*	**0710**	*1010*	1310	*1610*	**1910**	*2210*

The Shipping Forecast contains:

Time of issue; summary of gale warnings in force at that time; a general synopsis of weather systems and their expected development and movement over the next 24 hours; sea area forecasts for the same 24 hours, including wind direction/ force, weather and visibility in each; and an outlook for the following 24 hours.

Gale warnings for all affected areas are broadcast at the earliest break in Radio 4 programmes after receipt, as well as after the next news bulletin.

Weather reports from coastal stations follow the 0048 and 0520 shipping forecasts. They include wind direction and force, present weather, visibility, and sealevel pressure and tendency, if available. The stations are shown in Fig 0(4).

0.15.1 BBC Radio 4 Inshore waters forecast

A forecast for UK inshore waters (up to 12M offshore), valid for 24 hrs, is broadcast after the 0048 and 0520 coastal station reports. It includes forecasts of wind direction and force, weather, visibility and sea state.

Reports of actual weather are broadcast from all the stations below after the 0048 inshore waters forecast and also after the 0520 forecast, except those in italics: Lerwick. *Wick**; *Aberdeen*, Leuchars, *Boulmer*; Bridlington; Sandettie LV*, Greenwich LV*.

These stations are shown in Fig 0(5). An asterisk* denotes an automatic station.

0.15.2 Terms used in weather bulletins

Speed of movement of pressure systems	
Slowly	< 15 knots
Steadily	15–25 knots
Rather quickly	25–35 knots
Rapidly	35–45 knots
Very rapidly	> 45 knots

Visibility	
Good	> 5 miles
Moderate	2–5 miles
Poor	1000 metres–2 miles
Fog	Less than 1000 metres

Timing of gale warnings	
Imminent:	Within 6 hrs from time of issue
Soon:	6–12 hrs from time of issue
Later:	>12 hrs from time of issue

Barometric pressure changes (tendency)

Rising or falling slowly: Pressure change of 0·1 to 1·5 hPa/mb in the preceding 3 hours.

Rising or falling: Pressure change of 1·6 to 3·5 hPa/ mb in the preceding 3 hours.

Rising or falling quickly: Pressure change of 3·6 to 6 hPa/mb in the preceding 3 hours.

Rising or falling very rapidly: Pressure change of more than 6 hPa/mb in the preceding 3 hours.

Now rising (or falling): Pressure has been falling (rising) or steady in the preceding 3 hours, but at the observation time was definitely rising (falling).

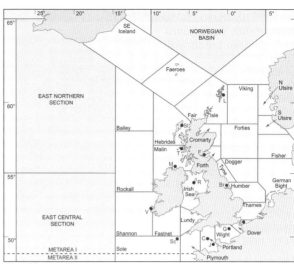

Fig 0(4) UK - Forecast areas

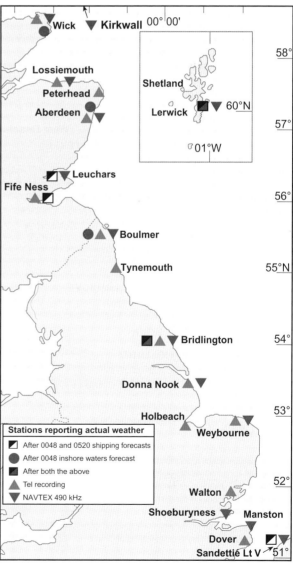

Fig 0(5) Stations reporting actual weather via BBC Radio 4, NAVTEX, telephone recordings or SMS

0.16   DUTCH WEATHER FORECASTS

Netherlands Coastguard
VHF weather broadcasts Fig 0(6)

Forecasts for Dutch coastal waters (7 areas up to 30M offshore) and inland waters (IJsselmeer, Markermeer and Oosterschelde) are transmitted in **English** and Dutch at 0805, 1305, 1905, 2305 LT on the VHF channels shown below, **without** prior announcement on Ch 16 or DSC 70.

Westkapelle	Ch 23	Hoorn	Ch 83
Woensdrecht	Ch 83	Wezep	Ch 23
Renesse	Ch 83	Kornwerderzand	Ch 23
Scheveningen	Ch 23	West Terschelling	Ch 83
Schoorl	Ch 83	Schiermonnikoog	Ch 23
Den Helder	Ch 23	Appingedam	Ch 83

Gale warnings are broadcast on receipt and at 0333, 0733, 1133, 1533, 1933 and 2333 UT.

MF weather broadcasts

Forecasts for areas Dover, Thames, Humber, German Bight, Dogger, Fisher, Forties and Viking are broadcast in **English** by Scheveningen at 0940 and 2140 UT on 3673 kHz. Gale warnings for these areas are broadcast in **English** on receipt and at 0333, 0733, 1133, 1533, 1933 and 2333 UT.

0.16.1   Radio Noord-Holland (FM)

Coastal forecasts for northern areas, gale warnings and wind strength are broadcast in Dutch, Mon-Fri at 0730, 0838, 1005, 1230 and 1705LT; Sat/Sun 1005, by:

Wieringermeer 93.9 MHz and **Haarlem** 97.6 MHz.

0.16.2   Omroep Zeeland (FM)

Coastal forecasts for southern areas, synopsis, gale warnings and wind strength are broadcast in Dutch, Mon-Fri at 0715, 0915, 1215 and 1715LT; Sat/Sun 1015, by:

Philippine 97.8 MHz and **Goes** 101.9 MHz.

0.17   BELGIAN WEATHER FORECASTS

Coast Radio Stations

Oostende Radio broadcasts in **English** and Dutch on VHF Ch 27 and 2761 kHz: Strong wind warnings on receipt and at 0820 and 1720 UT, together with a forecast for sea areas Thames and Dover.

Antwerpen Radio broadcasts in **English** and Dutch on VHF Ch 24 for the Schelde estuary: Gale warnings on receipt and at every odd H+05. Also strong wind warnings (F6+) on receipt and at every H+03 and H+48.

Fig 0(6) Netherlands CRS broadcasts, showing the boundaries and names of coastal areas referred to above

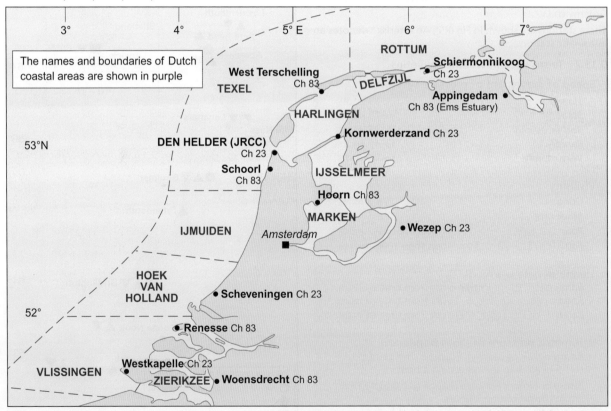

0.18 AUTOMATIC IDENTIFICATION SYSTEM (AIS)

Automatic Identification System (AIS) allows information to be provided to other ships and shore authorities; it is required by SOLAS to be fitted to most vessels over 300 GRT. AIS is also widely used to assist in collision avoidance by automatically and continuously identifying, tracking and displaying other vessels' movements.

Each ship's course and speed vector is shown by a symbol on an AIS screen or overlaid on radar, chart plotter or PC. This data may also appear in a text box as heading, COG & SOG, range, CPA, position, ship's name, and her status – under power or sail, anchored, constrained by draught, restricted in her ability to manoeuvre, not under command, fishing etc.

Many lights, buoys and other aids to navigation (AtoN) are now fitted with AIS, and the number is growing rapidly. On Admiralty charts, these are shown by a magenta circle and the notation 'AIS'. Not all transmitted information is available to all users; it depends on the display system fitted.

Caveats: Many vessels are not fitted with AIS, and some may not have it switched on; some only display 3 lines of text, not a plot; in busy areas only the strongest signals may be shown; AIS may distract a bridge watchkeeper from his visual and radar watch; unlike eyes and radar, AIS does not yet feature in the Colregs; GPS/electronic failures invalidate AIS.

AIS is not mandatory for leisure craft, but it is worth considering. Accurate and continuous display of other ships' courses and speeds removes any doubts when these parameters are derived solely from basic radar information.

AIS sets suitable for small craft are available. Later sets can receive aids to navigation (A2N) data, showing virtual marks and MMSI numbers from buoys and lighthouses. *It is not a radar* despite what some advertisements may imply.

0.19 CALCULATING CLEARANCES BELOW OVERHEAD OBJECTS

A diagram often helps when calculating vertical clearance below bridges, power cables etc. Fig 0(7) shows the relationship to CD. The height of such objects as shown on the chart is usually measured above HAT, so the actual clearance will almost always be more. The height of HAT above CD is given at the foot of each page of the tide tables. Most Admiralty charts now show clearances above HAT, but check the **Heights** block below the chart title.

To calculate clearances, insert the dimensions into the following formula, carefully observing the conventions for brackets:

Masthead clearance = (Height of object above HAT + height of HAT above CD) minus (height of tide at the time + height of the masthead above waterline)

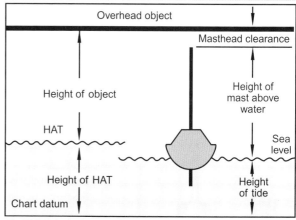

Fig 0(7) Calculating masthead clearance

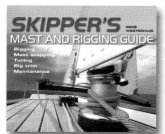

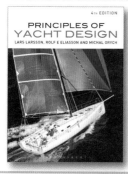

0.20   IALA BUOYAGE

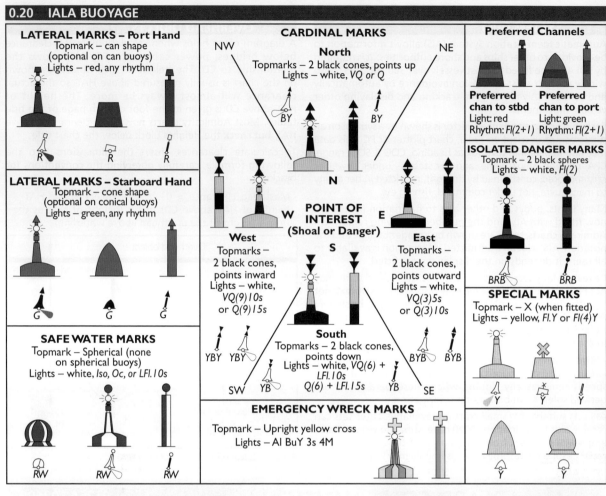

LATERAL MARKS – Port Hand
Topmark – can shape
(optional on can buoys)
Lights – red, any rhythm

LATERAL MARKS – Starboard Hand
Topmark – cone shape
(optional on conical buoys)
Lights – green, any rhythm

SAFE WATER MARKS
Topmark – Spherical (none on spherical buoys)
Lights – white, Iso, Oc, or LFl.10s

CARDINAL MARKS

North
Topmarks – 2 black cones, points up
Lights – white, VQ or Q

West
Topmarks – 2 black cones, points inward
Lights – white, VQ(9)10s or Q(9)15s

POINT OF INTEREST
(Shoal or Danger)

East
Topmarks – 2 black cones, points outward
Lights – white, VQ(3)5s or Q(3)10s

South
Topmarks – 2 black cones, points down
Lights – white, VQ(6) + LFl.10s Q(6) + LFl.15s

EMERGENCY WRECK MARKS
Topmark – Upright yellow cross
Lights – Al BuY 3s 4M

Preferred Channels
Preferred chan to stbd
Light: red
Rhythm: Fl(2+1)

Preferred chan to port
Light: green
Rhythm: Fl(2+1)

ISOLATED DANGER MARKS
Topmark – 2 black spheres
Lights – white, Fl(2)

SPECIAL MARKS
Topmark – X (when fitted)
Lights – yellow, Fl.Y or Fl(4)Y

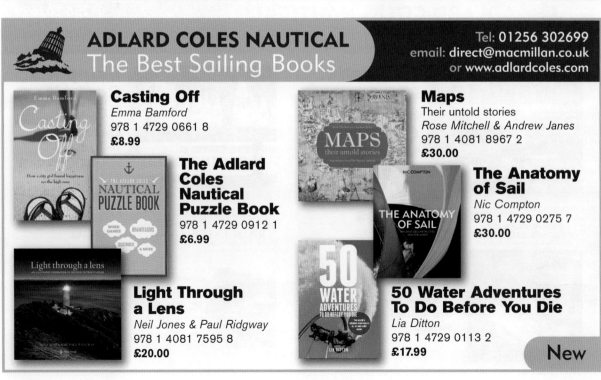

0.21 FLAGS AND ENSIGNS

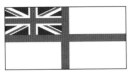
UK WHITE ENSIGN

UK BLUE ENSIGN

UK RED ENSIGN

AUSTRALIA

AUSTRIA

BASQUE FLAG

BELGIUM

CANADA

CYPRUS

DENMARK

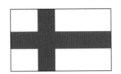
FINLAND

FRANCE

GERMANY

GREECE

GUERNSEY

JERSEY

IRELAND

ISRAEL

ITALY

LIBERIA

MALTA

MONACO

MOROCCO

NETHERLANDS

NEW ZEALAND

NORWAY

PANAMA

POLAND

PORTUGAL

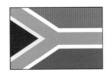
SOUTH AFRICA

SPAIN

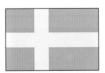
SWEDEN

SWITZERLAND

TUNISIA

TURKEY

USA

0.22 LIGHTS AND SHAPES

Vessels being towed and towing

Vessel towed shows sidelights (forward) and sternlight

Tug shows two masthead lights, sidelights, sternlight, yellow towing light

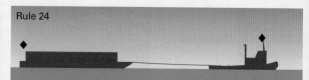

Towing by day — Length of tow more than 200m

Towing vessel and tow display diamond shapes. By night, the towing vessel shows three masthead lights instead of two as for shorter tows

Motor sailing

Cone point down, forward. At night the lights of a power-driven vessel underway

Vessel fishing

All-round red light over all-round white, plus sidelights and sternlight when making way

Fishing/Trawling

A shape consisting of two cones point to point in a vertical line one above the other

Vessel trawling

All-round green light over all-round white, plus sidelights and sternlight when making way

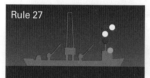

Vessel restricted in her ability to manoeuvre

All-round red, white, red lights vertically, plus normal steaming lights when making way

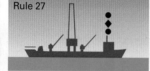

Three shapes in a vertical line: ball, diamond, ball

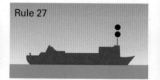

Not under command

Two all-round red lights, plus sidelights and sternlight when making way

Two balls vertically

Dredger

All round red, white, red lights vertically, plus two all-round red lights (or two balls) on foul side, and two all-round green (or two diamonds) on clear side

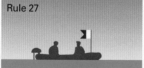

Divers down

Letter 'A' International Code

Constrained by draught

Three all-round red lights in a vertical line, plus normal steaming lights. By day — a cylinder

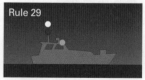

Pilot boat

All-round white light over all-round red, plus sidelights and sternlight when underway, or anchor light

Vessel at anchor

All-round white light; if over 50m, a second light aft and lower

Ball forward

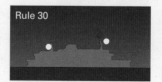

Vessel aground

Anchor light(s), plus two all-round red lights in a vertical line

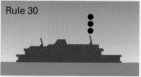

Three balls in a vertical line

0.23 NAVIGATION LIGHTS

LIGHTS FOR TYPICAL YACHT WITH 3 OPTIONAL VARIANTS

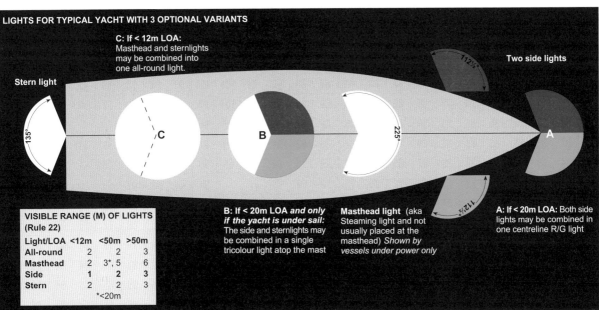

Stern light

C: If < 12m LOA: Masthead and sternlights may be combined into one all-round light.

Two side lights

135° / 225° / 112½°

B: If < 20m LOA and only if the yacht is under sail: The side and sternlights may be combined in a single tricolour light atop the mast

Masthead light (aka Steaming light and not usually placed at the masthead) *Shown by vessels under power only*

A: If < 20m LOA: Both side lights may be combined in one centreline R/G light

VISIBLE RANGE (M) OF LIGHTS (Rule 22)			
Light/LOA	<12m	<50m	>50m
All-round	2	2	3
Masthead	2	3*, 5	6
Side	1	2	3
Stern	2	2	3
		*<20m	

PLAN VIEWS OF LIGHTS FOR SAILING VESSELS UNDERWAY AND UNDER SAIL ONLY
Note: If motor-sailing, the lights appropriate for a power-driven vessel must be shown, as below

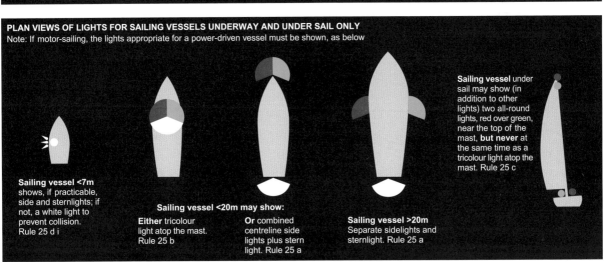

Sailing vessel <7m shows, if practicable, side and sternlights; if not, a white light to prevent collision. Rule 25 d i

Sailing vessel <20m may show:

Either tricolour light atop the mast. Rule 25 b

Or combined centreline side lights plus stern light. Rule 25 a

Sailing vessel >20m Separate sidelights and sternlight. Rule 25 a

Sailing vessel under sail may show (in addition to other lights) two all-round lights, red over green, near the top of the mast, **but never** at the same time as a tricolour light atop the mast. Rule 25 c

PLAN VIEWS OF LIGHTS FOR POWER-DRIVEN VESSELS UNDERWAY AND SAILING CRAFT UNDER POWER

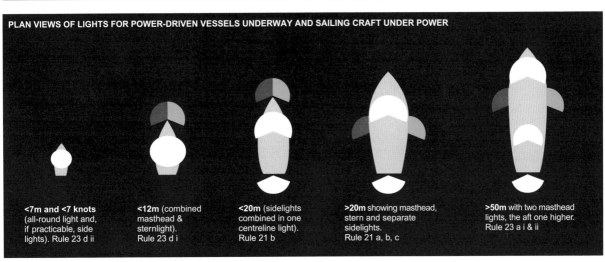

<7m and <7 knots (all-round light and, if practicable, side lights). Rule 23 d ii

<12m (combined masthead & sternlight). Rule 23 d i

<20m (sidelights combined in one centreline light). Rule 21 b

>20m showing masthead, stern and separate sidelights. Rule 21 a, b, c

>50m with two masthead lights, the aft one higher. Rule 23 a i & ii

0.24 TIDAL COEFFICIENTS 2015

Date	Jan am	Jan pm	Feb am	Feb pm	Mar am	Mar pm	Apr am	Apr pm	May am	May pm	June am	June pm	July am	July pm	Aug am	Aug pm	Sept am	Sept pm	Oct am	Oct pm	Nov am	Nov pm	Dec am	Dec pm
1	59	62	63	68	46	51	62	67	65	69	75	78	79	83	99	103	114	111	108	102	76	68	65	59
2	65	69	72	76	57	62	72	76	74	77	81	84	87	90	105	106	107	102	95	86	61	53	53	48
3	73	76	79	82	67	72	79	82	80	83	86	88	93	94	106	104	95	88	78	68	47	42	44	41
4	79	81	84	85	76	79	85	86	85	87	89	89	95	96	101	97	79	71	60	52	39	38	39	39
5	83	84	86	86	82	85	88	89	88	88	88	87	95	93	92	86	62	55	45			40		40
6	85	85	85	85	86	88	89	88	87	86	85	82	91	87	79	72	48		41	39	42	46	42	46
7	84	83	83	81	88	88	87	85	84	82	79	76	84	79	65	59	44	43	40	43	51	56	50	54
8	81	79	78	75	87	86	82	79	79	75	72	69	75	70		54	44	47	47	53	60	65	58	63
9	76	73	72	67	84	81	75	70	71	66	66	63	66		51	50	52	57	58	63	69	72	67	71
10	70	66	63	58	78	74	65	60	62	58		62	62	60	51	54	62	68	68	72	75	78	75	78
11	62	57	54	49	70	65	55	51	56	54	61	62	58	59	57	62	72	76	76	79	80	82	81	83
12	53	49	44	41	60	55	47			54	63	66	60	63	66	71	79	82	81	83	84	84	85	86
13	45	42	39		50	45	46	47	56	60	70	74	66	70	75	78	84	85	85	85	85	84	86	86
14	40	39	39	42	42	41	50	56	65	71	77	81	73	77	81	83	86	86	86	85	63	81	85	84
15		40	47	54		42	63	72	77	83	84	87	80	82	85	86	86	85	84	83	79	76	82	79
16	42	47	62	71	46	53	80	88	88	93	89	90	84	85	86	85	83	81	81	78	72	69	76	73
17	52	59	79	88	61	71	95	101	97	100	91	90	86	86	84	83	78	75	75	71	64	60	69	66
18	66	73	96	103	80	89	106	110	101	102	89	88	85	83	80	78	71	67	66	62	56	53	62	60
19	80	87	109	113	97	105	112	113	101	99	85	82	81	79	74	71	62	57	57	52	50	50	58	58
20	93	98	116	118	110	115	112	109	97	93	79	75	76	73	67	62	52	47	47	44	51			59
21	103	106	117	115	118	119	105	100	89	84	71	67	69	65	57	53	42	39	41		54	58	61	65
22	109	109	111	106	118	115	94	87	78	72	62	58	61	56	48	43	37		41	44	64	71	69	74
23	109	107	99	91	111	105	79	72	67	61	53	49	52	48	39	37	37	41	50	56	77	84	79	83
24	104	99	82	74	98	90	64	57	55	50	46	43	44	41		36	47	55	65	73	90	95	87	91
25	93	87	65	56	82	73	50	44	48	42		41		39	38	42	64	72	82	89	99	102	93	95
26	79	72	49	43	64	55	40			40	40	40	38	40	48	55	82	90	97	103	104	104	96	95
27	65	58		40	48	42	37	37	39	40	42	45	42	47	63	71	98	105	108	111	104	102	94	92
28	52	49	40	42	38		39	42	42	45	49	54	52	58	79	87	110	114	113	113	99	95	90	86
29		47			36	38	46	51	49	53	59	64	65	71	95	101	117	117	112	109	90	84	82	78
30	48	50			41	46	56	60	57	62	69	74	78	84	107	111	116	113	104	98	78	72	73	68
31	54	58			52	57			66	70			90	95	113	114			92	84			63	57

Tidal coefficients indicate the magnitude of the tide on any particular day without having to look up and calculate the range, and thus determine whether it is springs, neaps or somewhere in between. This table is valid for all areas covered by this Almanac. Typical values are:

120	Very big spring tide
95	**Mean spring tide**
70	Average tide
45	**Mean neap tide**
20	Very small neap tide

Times are in UT - add 1 hour in non-shaded areas to convert to BST

0.25 SUNRISE/SET TIMES 2015

The table shows times of Sunrise (SR) and Sunset (SS) for every 3rd day as the times of Sunrise and Sunset never change by more than 8 minutes (and often by only 1–3 minutes) between the given dates.

The table is based on Longitude 0°, so longitude corrections are required. To calculate this add 4 minutes of time for every degree West of Greenwich; subtract if East.

LATITUDE 56°N

	Rise JANUARY	Set	Rise FEBRUARY	Set	Rise MARCH	Set	Rise APRIL	Set	Rise MAY	Set	Rise JUNE	Set
1	08 31	15 36	07 55	16 32	06 52	17 33	05 32	18 37	04 17	19 39	03 22	20 34
4	08 30	15 40	07 50	16 39	06 45	17 40	05 24	18 44	04 10	19 45	03 19	20 38
7	08 29	15 44	07 44	16 45	06 37	17 46	05 16	18 50	04 04	19 51	03 17	20 41
10	08 26	15 49	07 37	16 52	06 29	17 52	05 08	18 56	03 58	19 56	03 15	20 44
13	08 24	15 54	07 31	16 59	06 22	17 59	05 01	19 02	03 52	20 02	03 14	20 47
16	08 20	15 59	07 24	17 05	06 14	18 05	04 53	19 08	03 46	20 08	03 13	20 49
19	08 17	16 05	07 17	17 12	06 06	18 11	04 46	19 14	03 41	20 13	03 13	20 50
22	08 12	16 11	07 10	17 18	05 58	18 17	04 38	19 20	03 36	20 19	03 14	20 51
25	08 08	16 17	07 02	17 25	05 50	18 23	04 31	19 26	03 31	20 24	03 14	20 51
28	08 03	16 24	06 55	17 31	05 42	18 29	04 24	19 33	03 27	20 28	03 16	20 50
31	07 57	16 30			05 34	18 35			03 24	20 33		

	Rise JULY	Set	Rise AUGUST	Set	Rise SEPTEMBER	Set	Rise OCTOBER	Set	Rise NOVEMBER	Set	Rise DECEMBER	Set
1	03 18	20 49	04 03	20 08	05 03	18 55	06 02	17 36	07 06	16 20	08 06	15 31
4	03 21	20 47	04 09	20 02	05 09	18 48	06 08	17 28	07 13	16 14	08 11	15 29
7	03 24	20 45	04 15	19 56	05 15	18 40	06 14	17 21	07 19	16 08	08 15	15 27
10	03 27	20 42	04 20	19 49	05 21	18 32	06 20	17 13	07 25	16 02	08 19	15 26
13	03 31	20 39	04 26	19 42	05 27	18 24	06 26	17 05	07 32	15 56	08 23	15 25
16	03 36	20 35	04 32	19 35	05 33	18 16	06 32	16 58	07 38	15 51	08 26	15 25
19	03 40	20 31	04 38	19 28	05 39	18 08	06 39	16 50	07 44	15 46	08 28	15 26
22	03 45	20 26	04 44	19 21	05 44	18 00	06 45	16 43	07 50	15 42	08 30	15 27
25	03 51	20 21	04 50	19 13	05 50	17 52	06 51	16 36	07 56	15 38	08 31	15 29
28	03 56	20 16	04 56	19 06	05 56	17 44	06 58	16 29	08 01	15 34	08 32	15 31
31	04 01	20 10	05 01	18 58			07 04	16 22			08 31	15 34

0.26 MOONRISE/SET TIMES 2015

The table gives the times of Moonrise (MR) and Moonset (MS) for every 3rd day; interpolation is necessary for other days. The aim is simply to indicate whether the night in question will be brightly moonlit, partially moonlit or pitch black – depending, of course, on the level of cloud cover. The table is based on Longitude 0°. To correct for longitude, add 4 minutes of time for every degree West; subtract if East. ** Indicates that the phenomenon does not occur.

LATITUDE 56°N

	Rise JANUARY	Set	Rise FEBRUARY	Set	Rise MARCH	Set	Rise APRIL	Set	Rise MAY	Set	Rise JUNE	Set
1	13 20	04 20	14 32	05 58	13 26	04 36	15 35	04 26	16 42	03 31	18 59	03 11
4	15 40	07 17	17 42	07 32	16 39	06 00	18 54	05 26	20 06	04 40	21 54	05 22
7	18 48	09 03	21 00	08 34	19 57	07 00	22 15	06 38	23 08	06 35	23 42	08 52
10	22 06	10 08	** **	09 36	23 17	08 06	00 17	08 39	00 34	09 47	00 32	12 53
13	00 20	11 07	02 35	11 10	01 25	09 52	02 32	12 00	02 01	13 45	01 48	16 51
16	03 47	12 34	05 23	14 09	03 57	13 01	03 58	16 07	03 17	17 52	03 43	20 12
19	06 50	15 22	07 09	18 22	05 33	17 13	05 19	20 19	05 05	21 28	06 39	22 13
22	08 44	19 29	08 27	22 36	06 53	21 29	07 16	23 43	07 52	23 43	09 59	23 24
25	10 00	23 38	10 02	01 07	08 40	** **	10 09	01 10	11 09	00 36	13 18	00 02
28	11 24	02 10	12 27	03 57	11 19	02 35	13 23	02 31	14 28	01 37	16 41	01 11
31	13 35	05 13			14 30	04 04			17 52	02 42		

	Rise JULY	Set	Rise AUGUST	Set	Rise SEPTEMBER	Set	Rise OCTOBER	Set	Rise NOVEMBER	Set	Rise DECEMBER	Set
1	19 46	03 10	20 16	05 32	20 02	08 44	19 36	10 23	20 52	12 13	21 53	11 54
4	21 46	06 36	21 34	09 45	21 40	12 42	22 04	13 33	** **	13 50	00 07	12 59
7	23 03	10 40	23 01	13 43	** **	15 36	00 09	15 21	02 21	14 53	03 25	13 59
10	** **	14 39	00 25	16 51	02 17	17 16	03 26	16 27	05 39	15 55	06 43	15 26
13	01 39	18 03	03 20	18 46	05 35	18 21	06 43	17 27	08 54	17 29	09 30	18 01
16	04 25	20 14	06 38	19 55	08 52	19 22	09 58	18 51	11 30	20 10	11 16	21 39
19	07 44	21 29	09 56	20 55	12 05	20 50	12 45	21 14	13 09	23 52	12 29	00 18
22	11 03	22 28	13 13	22 14	14 49	23 26	14 37	** **	14 24	02 35	13 54	04 20
25	14 23	23 41	16 10	** **	16 39	01 54	15 58	03 36	15 58	06 43	16 14	07 49
28	17 32	00 59	18 12	03 03	18 00	06 11	17 28	07 53	18 33	10 03	19 33	09 54
31	19 45	04 12	19 35	07 18			19 51	11 23			22 57	11 05

0.27 INTERNATIONAL CODE OF SIGNALS

Code flags, phonetic alphabet (NATO/ITU), Morse code, single-letter signals. INTERNATIONAL PORT TRAFFIC SIGNALS.

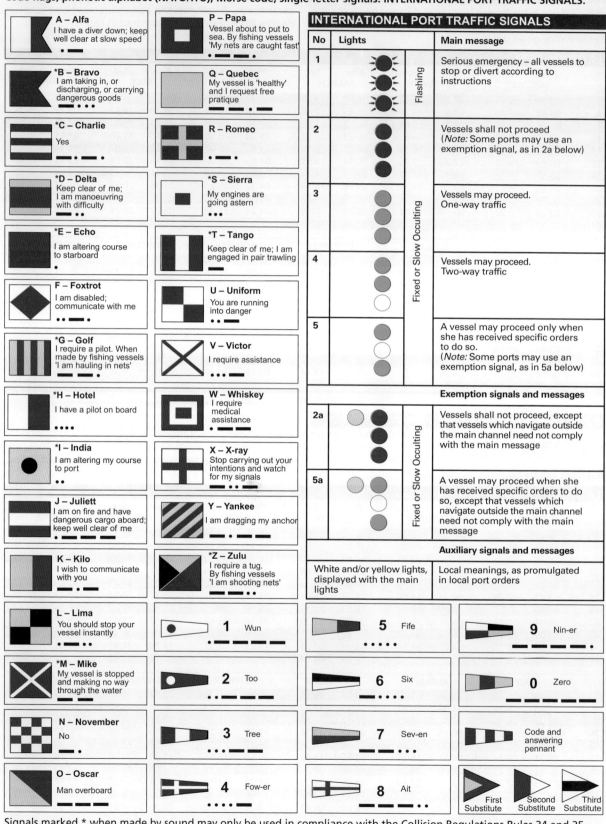

A – Alfa
I have a diver down; keep well clear at slow speed

*B – Bravo
I am taking in, or discharging, or carrying dangerous goods

*C – Charlie
Yes

*D – Delta
Keep clear of me; I am manoeuvring with difficulty

*E – Echo
I am altering course to starboard

F – Foxtrot
I am disabled; communicate with me

*G – Golf
I require a pilot. When made by fishing vessels 'I am hauling in nets'

*H – Hotel
I have a pilot on board

*I – India
I am altering my course to port

J – Juliett
I am on fire and have dangerous cargo aboard; keep well clear of me

K – Kilo
I wish to communicate with you

L – Lima
You should stop your vessel instantly

*M – Mike
My vessel is stopped and making no way through the water

N – November
No

O – Oscar
Man overboard

P – Papa
Vessel about to put to sea. By fishing vessels 'My nets are caught fast'

Q – Quebec
My vessel is 'healthy' and I request free pratique

R – Romeo

*S – Sierra
My engines are going astern

*T – Tango
Keep clear of me; I am engaged in pair trawling

U – Uniform
You are running into danger

V – Victor
I require assistance

W – Whiskey
I require medical assistance

X – X-ray
Stop carrying out your intentions and watch for my signals

Y – Yankee
I am dragging my anchor

*Z – Zulu
I require a tug. By fishing vessels 'I am shooting nets'

1 Wun

2 Too

3 Tree

4 Fow-er

INTERNATIONAL PORT TRAFFIC SIGNALS

No	Lights		Main message
1		Flashing	Serious emergency – all vessels to stop or divert according to instructions
2		Fixed or Slow Occulting	Vessels shall not proceed (*Note:* Some ports may use an exemption signal, as in 2a below)
3			Vessels may proceed. One-way traffic
4			Vessels may proceed. Two-way traffic
5			A vessel may proceed only when she has received specific orders to do so. (*Note:* Some ports may use an exemption signal, as in 5a below)

Exemption signals and messages

2a		Fixed or Slow Occulting	Vessels shall not proceed, except that vessels which navigate outside the main channel need not comply with the main message
5a			A vessel may proceed when she has received specific orders to do so, except that vessels which navigate outside the main channel need not comply with the main message

Auxiliary signals and messages

White and/or yellow lights, displayed with the main lights	Local meanings, as promulgated in local port orders

5 Fife

9 Nin-er

6 Six

0 Zero

7 Sev-en

Code and answering pennant

8 Ait

First Substitute   Second Substitute   Third Substitute

Signals marked * when made by sound may only be used in compliance with the Collision Regulations Rules 34 and 35.

0.28 AREA INFORMATION

The 5 geographic Areas are arranged as follows:

An Area map which includes harbours, principal lights, TSS, MRCCs, NCI stations, airports, main ferry routes, magnetic variation and a distance table. Wind farms and other offshore energy installations are not routinely shown.

Tidal stream chartlets showing hourly rates and set.

Lights, buoys and waypoints (LBW) listing positions and characteristics of selected lights and other marks, their daytime appearance, fog signals and Racons. Arcs of visibility and alignment of sector/leading lights are true bearings as seen from seaward. Lights are white unless otherwise stated; any colours are shown between the bearings of the relevant arcs. AIS is widely fitted to navigational marks, but not normally shown in LBW. See the relevant official charts/publications for details.

Passage Information (PI) is at Section 4 in each Area. Further information is geographically arranged between the harbour entries.

Special notes giving data specific to a country or area.

Harbour information (see below).

0.29 HARBOUR INFORMATION

Each harbour entry is arranged as follows:

HARBOUR NAME followed by the County or Unitary Council (or foreign equivalent) and the lat/long of the harbour entrance, or equivalent, for use as the final waypoint.

Harbour ratings (❀ ☙ ✿), inevitably subjective, which grade a port based on the following criteria:

Ease of access:

❀❀❀ *Can be entered in almost any weather from most directions and at all states of tide, by day or night.*

❀❀ *Accessible in strong winds from most directions; possible tidal or pilotage constraints.*

❀ *Only accessible in calm, settled conditions by day with little or no swell; possible bar and difficult pilotage.*

Facilities available:

☙☙☙ *Good facilities for vessel and crew.*

☙☙ *Most domestic needs catered for, but limited boatyard facilities.*

☙ *Possibly some domestic facilities, but little else.*

Ambience:

✿✿✿ *An attractive place; well worth visiting.*

✿✿ *Average for this part of the coast.*

✿ *Holds no particular attraction.*

CHARTS show Admiralty (AC), Imray, and foreign charts, all smallest scale first. Admiralty Leisure Folios (56XX), which cover most of the UK, Channel Islands and Ireland, and Imray 2000 series folios (2X00) are also shown.

TIDES include a time difference (usually on Dover in the UK), ML, Duration and the harbour's Standard Port. Time and height differences for nearby Secondary Ports are also shown. Tidal coefficients are tabled at 0.24.

SHELTER assesses how protected a harbour is from wind, sea, surge and swell. It warns of any access difficulties and advises on safe berths and anchorages.

NAVIGATION gives guidance on the approach and entry, and shows the position of the approach waypoint with its bearing and distance to the harbour entrance or next significant feature. Some waypoints may not be shown on the chartlet. Access times are only stated where a lock, gate, sill or other obstruction restricts entry. Otherwise the minimum charted depth of water in the approaches, where it is less than 2m, is usually shown, but always consult up to date official charts.

Chartlets are based on official charts augmented with local information. Due to their scale, they may not cover the whole area referred to in the text nor do they show every depth, mark, light or feature.

The chartlets are not intended to be used for navigation; positions taken from them should not be used as waypoints in chart plotters. The publisher and editors disclaim any responsibility for resultant accidents or damage if they are so used. The largest scale official chart, properly corrected, should always be used.

Drying areas and an indicative 5m depth contour are shown as: Dries   <5m   >5m

Wrecks around the UK which are of archaeological or historic interest are protected by law. Sites are listed under harbour entries or in Passage Information. Unauthorised interference, including anchoring and diving on these sites, may lead to a substantial fine.

LIGHTS AND MARKS describes, in more detail than is shown on the chartlets, any unusual characteristics of marks, their appearance by day and features not listed elsewhere.

COMMUNICATIONS shows the telephone area code followed by local telephone and VHF contact details for: MRCC/CG, weather, police, doctor/medical, harbourmaster/office, other. Marina contact details are not usually duplicated if they are shown under the marina entry. International telephone calls from/to the UK are described in Special Notes, as are national numbers for emergency services: normally 112 in the EU; 999 in the UK. Radio callsigns, if not obvious, are in *italics*.

FACILITIES describes berthing options and facilities in harbours, marinas and yacht clubs (see the free **Reeds Marina Guide** for detailed marina plans in the UK, Channel Islands and Ireland). Water, electricity, showers and toilets are available in marinas unless otherwise stated. Most yacht clubs welcome visiting crews who belong to a recognised club and arrive by sea. Any rail and air links are also shown.

The overnight cost of a visitor's alongside berth (AB), *correct with regard to information supplied at the time of going to press (Summer 2014)*, is the average charge per metre LOA (unless otherwise stated) during high season, usually June to Sept. It includes VAT, harbour dues and, where possible, any tourist taxes (per head). The cost of pile moorings, ⚓s or ⚓s, where these are the norm, may also be given. Shore electricity is usually free abroad but extra in the UK.

The number of ❶ berths is a marina's estimate of how many visitors may be accommodated at any one time. It is always advisable to call the marina beforehand.

TransEurope Marinas (www.transeuropemarinas.com) is an expanding grouping of independent marinas in the UK and abroad. Many hold Blue Flags and 4 or 5 Gold Anchor Awards; it is a condition of membership that they are well-equipped and maintain high standards. They operate a discounted reciprocal berthing scheme and are shown by the symbol ⓐ.

Rover Tickets, offering good discounts, are available for many berthing facilities in Scotland and the offlying islands.

0.30 ENVIRONMENTAL GUIDANCE

- Comply with regulations for navigation and conduct within Marine Nature Reserves, Particularly Sensitive Sea Areas (PSSA) and National Water Parks.
- In principle never ditch rubbish at sea, keep it on board and dispose of it in harbour refuse bins.
- Readily degradable foodstuffs may be ditched at sea when >3M offshore (>12M in the English Channel).
- Foodstuffs and other materials which are not readily degradable should never be ditched at sea.
- Sewage. If you do not have a holding tank, only use the onboard heads when well offshore. A holding tank should be fitted as soon as possible as many countries require them. Pump-out facilities (⊅) are shown in the text. Do not pump out holding tanks until more than 3M offshore.
- Do not discharge foul water into a marina, anchorage or moorings area and minimise on washing-up water.
- Deposit used engine oil and oily waste ashore at a recognised facility. Do not allow an automatic bilge pump to discharge oily bilge water overboard.
- Dispose of toxic waste, (eg some antifoulings, cleaning chemicals, old batteries) at an approved disposal facility.
- Row ashore whenever possible – to minimise noise, wash and disturbance. Land at recognised places.
- Respect wild birds, plants, fish and marine animals. Avoid protected nesting sites and breeding colonies.
- Do not anchor or dry out on vulnerable seabed species, eg soft corals, eel grass.

0.31 DISTANCES (M) ACROSS THE NORTH SEA

Approximate distances in nautical miles are by the most direct route, avoiding dangers and allowing for TSS.

Norway to France / UK	Bergen	Stavanger	Lindesnes	Skagen	Esjberg	Sylt (List)	Brunsbüttel	Helgoland	Bremerhaven	Willhelmshaven	Delfzijl	Den Helder	IJmuiden	Scheveningen	Roompotsluis	Vlissingen	Zeebrugge	Oostende	Nieuwpoort	Dunkerque
Lerwick	210	226	288	403	428	442	517	470	510	500	493	486	497	505	551	550	552	555	562	588
Kirkwall	278	275	323	438	439	452	516	467	507	497	481	460	473	481	515	514	516	519	526	545
Wick	292	283	323	437	428	440	498	449	489	479	458	433	444	451	485	484	486	489	496	514
Inverness	356	339	381	485	461	462	529	479	519	509	487	460	471	478	513	512	514	517	524	542
Fraserburgh	288	266	296	410	383	384	451	404	444	434	412	385	396	403	430	429	431	434	441	456
Aberdeen	308	279	298	411	371	378	433	382	432	412	386	353	363	369	401	400	402	405	412	426
Dundee	362	329	339	451	394	401	448	396	436	426	395	352	359	364	390	389	385	388	395	412
Port Edgar	391	355	362	472	409	413	457	405	445	435	401	355	361	366	391	390	386	389	396	413
Berwick	374	325	320	431	356	361	408	355	395	385	355	310	315	320	342	341	337	340	347	364
Hartlepool	409	353	340	440	340	331	367	312	352	342	302	241	243	247	266	265	261	264	271	288
Grimsby	463	395	362	452	324	318	342	291	332	325	288	187	182	185	199	198	190	191	201	198
Kings Lynn	485	416	379	466	330	333	343	292	344	336	283	184	183	183	197	195	187	188	198	195
Lowestoft	508	431	380	453	308	300	295	262	284	271	218	118	104	98	95	99	87	87	89	106
Harwich	540	461	410	483	330	331	320	287	309	296	243	147	126	114	94	100	84	77	80	80
Brightlingsea	558	479	428	501	348	349	338	305	327	314	261	165	144	105	108	106	92	88	86	87
Burnham/Crouch	567	488	437	510	357	358	347	314	336	323	270	174	151	112	109	115	99	92	93	95
London Bridge	620	543	490	560	400	408	395	361	382	374	320	222	199	149	153	149	134	125	126	114
Sheerness	580	503	450	520	360	367	353	319	340	334	280	180	157	109	113	109	94	85	86	74
Ramsgate	575	498	446	516	368	346	339	305	323	315	262	161	144	121	89	85	77	65	58	42
Dover	588	511	459	529	378	359	352	328	336	328	275	174	155	132	101	92	79	65	58	44

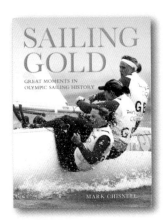
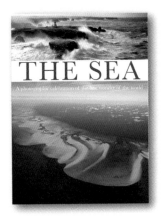
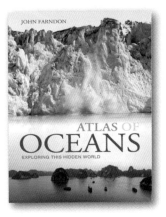

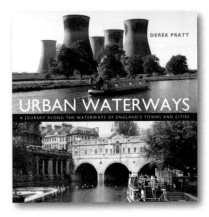
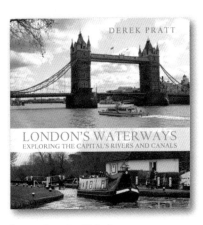

Eastern England

Ramsgate to Berwick-upon-Tweed

AREA 1 – EAST ENGLAND

1.1	Area map and Distance table – Ramsgate to Great Yarmouth	28
1.2	Tidal stream charts	30
1.3	Lights, buoys and waypoints	32
1.4	Passage information	35
1.5	Ramsgate	36
1.6	Thames Estuary	37
1.7	Thames Estuary tidal stream charts	38
	Margate tide tables/curves	40
1.8	Whitstable	44
	Margate • Herne Bay	
1.9	The Swale	45
1.10	Queenborough	46
	Sheerness tide tables and curves	47
1.11	River Medway	50
1.12	River Thames, London Bridge, Tide tables and curves	52
	Holehaven • Gravesend • Thames Barrier • Gallions Point Marina • South Dock Marina • Poplar Dock Marina • Limehouse Basin • St Katharine Haven • Chelsea Harbour • Brentford Dock	
1.13	Southend-on-Sea and Leigh-on-Sea	60
1.14	River Roach/Havengore	61
1.15	Burnham-on-Crouch Tide tables and curves	62
1.16	River Blackwater	66
1.17	River Colne	67
1.18	Walton Backwaters Tide tables and curves	69
1.19	River Stour	74
1.20	River Orwell/Harwich Tide tables and curves	75
1.21	River Deben	79
1.22	River Ore/Alde	80
1.23	Southwold	81
1.24	Lowestoft, tide tables and curves	82
1.25	Great Yarmouth	86
	Norfolk Broads	

AREA 2 – NETHERLANDS AND BELGIUM
See page 87

AREA 3 – NORTH EAST ENGLAND

3.1	Area map and Distance table – Blakeney to Berwick-upon-Tweed	138
3.2	Tidal stream charts	140
3.3	Lights, buoys and waypoints	142
3.4	Passage information	144
3.5	Blakeney	144
3.6	Wells-next-the-Sea	145
	Burnham Overy Staithe • Brancaster Staithe	
3.7	King's Lynn	146
3.8	Wisbech	146
3.9	Boston	147
	River Welland • Wainfleet	
3.10	River Humber/Immingham Tide tables and curves	148
	Grimsby • Hull • South Ferriby • Brough • Goole • Naburn	
3.11	Bridlington	155
	Filey	
3.12	Scarborough	155
3.13	Whitby	156
	Runswick Bay • River Tees • Middlesbrough	
3.14	Hartlepool/River Tees Tide tables/curves	157
3.15	Seaham	162
3.16	Sunderland	162
3.17	River Tyne/North Shields Tide tables and curves	157
	Cullercoats	
3.18	Blyth	167
	Newbiggin	
3.19	Amble	168
	Boulmer • Craster • Newton Haven and Beadnell Bay • Seahouses (N Sunderland) • Farne Islands	
3.20	Holy Island	169
3.21	Berwick-upon-Tweed	170

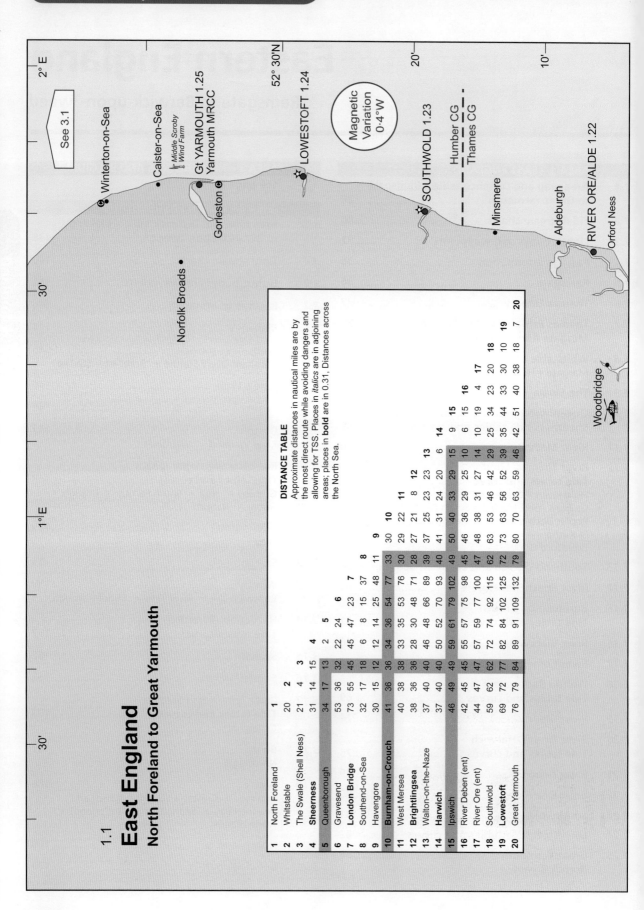

1.1 East England
North Foreland to Great Yarmouth

Map labels: See 3.1 · Winterton-on-Sea · Caister-on-Sea · Middle Scroby Wind Farm · Gt YARMOUTH 1.25 / Yarmouth MRCC · Gorleston · LOWESTOFT 1.24 · Magnetic Variation 0·4°W · SOUTHWOLD 1.23 · Humber CG / Thames CG · Minsmere · Aldeburgh · RIVER ORE/ALDE 1.22 · Orford Ness · Woodbridge · Norfolk Broads · 2°E · 1°E · 52°30'N · 30' · 20' · 10'

DISTANCE TABLE

Approximate distances in nautical miles are by the most direct route while avoiding dangers and allowing for TSS. Places in *italics* are in adjoining areas; places in **bold** are in 0.31. Distances across the North Sea.

		1	2	3	4	5	6	7	8	9	10	11	12	13	14	15	16	17	18	19	20
1	North Foreland	1																			
2	Whitstable	20	2																		
3	The Swale (Shell Ness)	21	4	3																	
4	**Sheerness**	31	14	15	4																
5	Queenborough	34	17	13	2	5															
6	Gravesend	53	36	32	22	24	6														
7	**London Bridge**	73	55	45	45	47	23	7													
8	Southend-on-Sea	32	17	18	6	8	15	37	8												
9	Havengore	30	15	12	12	14	25	48	11	9											
10	**Burnham-on-Crouch**	41	36	34	36	36	54	77	33	30	10										
11	West Mersea	40	38	33	35	35	53	76	30	29	22	11									
12	**Brightlingsea**	38	36	36	28	30	48	71	28	27	21	8	12								
13	Walton-on-the-Naze	37	40	40	46	48	66	89	39	37	25	23	23	13							
14	**Harwich**	37	40	40	50	52	70	93	40	41	31	24	20	6	14						
15	Ipswich	46	49	49	59	61	79	102	49	50	40	33	29	15	9	15					
16	River Deben (ent)	42	45	45	55	57	75	98	45	46	36	29	25	10	6	15	16				
17	River Ore (ent)	44	47	47	57	59	77	100	47	48	38	31	27	14	10	19	4	17			
18	Southwold	59	62	62	74	74	102	115	72	63	53	46	42	29	25	34	23	20	18		
19	**Lowestoft**	69	72	77	82	84	102	125	72	73	63	56	52	44	35	44	33	30	10	19	
20	Great Yarmouth	76	79	84	89	91	109	132	79	80	70	63	59	59	42	51	40	38	18	7	20

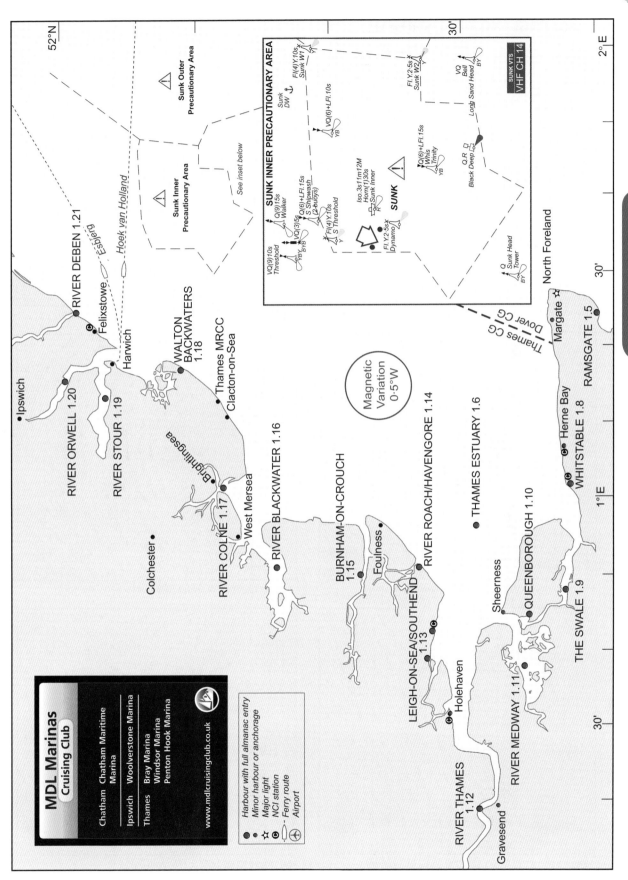

E England

EAST ENGLAND TIDAL STREAMS

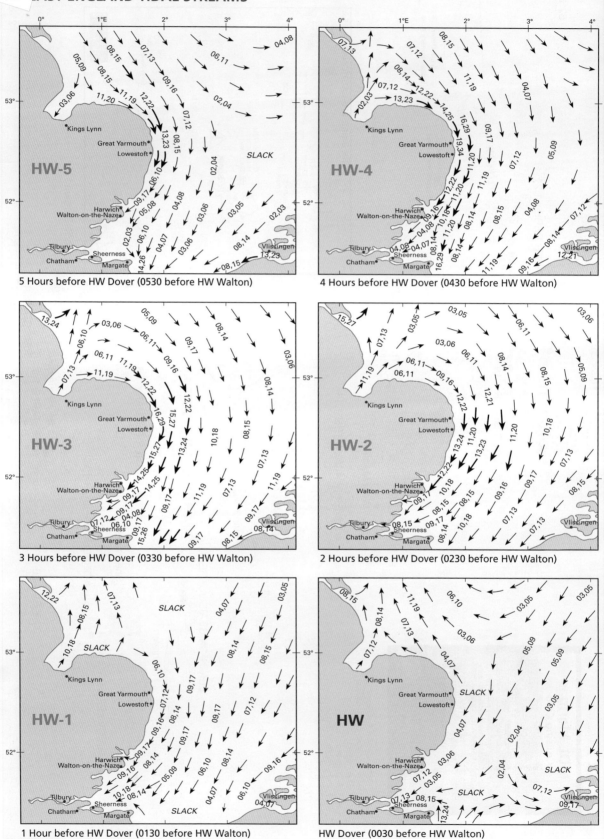

5 Hours before HW Dover (0530 before HW Walton)

4 Hours before HW Dover (0430 before HW Walton)

3 Hours before HW Dover (0330 before HW Walton)

2 Hours before HW Dover (0230 before HW Walton)

1 Hour before HW Dover (0130 before HW Walton)

HW Dover (0030 before HW Walton)

Thames Estuary 1.7   Northward 3.2   Eastward 2.3

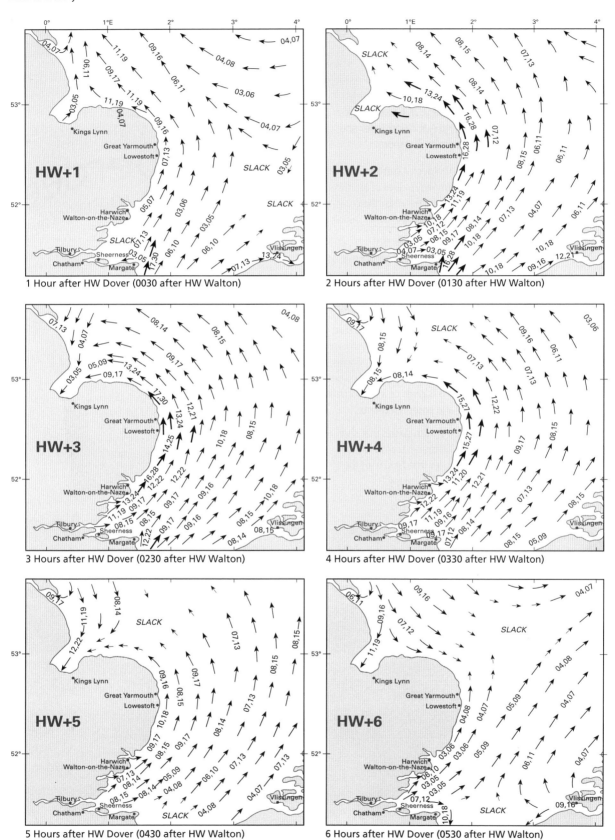

HW+1

1 Hour after HW Dover (0030 after HW Walton)

HW+2

2 Hours after HW Dover (0130 after HW Walton)

HW+3

3 Hours after HW Dover (0230 after HW Walton)

HW+4

4 Hours after HW Dover (0330 after HW Walton)

HW+5

5 Hours after HW Dover (0430 after HW Walton)

HW+6

6 Hours after HW Dover (0530 after HW Walton)

E England

Aberdeen Asset Management and sailing

Aberdeen Asset Management's association with sailing stretches around the world - from title sponsorship of the legendary UK Cowes Week since 2011, to the Farr 40 Australian Series and the Extreme Sailing Series in Singapore.

Clients now associate Aberdeen Asset Management with sailing and their company values of teamwork, diligence and dedication are shared by the crews who participate in Cowes Week and other sailing events around the globe.

Aberdeen Asset Management sees sponsorship as an opportunity to stand out from the competition in an environment that Sponsorship Manager, Jill Maxwell, describes as a 'somewhat cluttered'.

Jill says: "When sponsoring sailing, we make sure we are strategic and clever - investing only in events that hit our target audience. For example, Cowes Week is an event that is very well attended by one of our target audiences. This gives us a platform to speak to both existing and potential clients."

"We like to align ourselves with sports that share our own ethos. Sailing illustrates team work and dedication - both attributes that fit in with the nature of our work and our company."

Shirley Robertson OBE

14 Extremes Sailing Series, Singapore

Aberdeen Asset Management Farr 40 Queensland Championship

Aberdeen Asset Management Dad Vail Regatta, Philadelphia

Shirley Robertson OBE Q&A

What does the role of Global Sailing Ambassador at Aberdeen Asset Management Cowes Week mean to you personally?
It is an honour to be able to represent the event each year as it holds many special memories for me. The Isle of Wight has a huge history and legacy of sailing so it felt natural for me to set up home in Cowes. Each Cowes Week is unique with so many stories to be told and to be an official part of it is wonderful.

How important is it that sailing is promoted as an accessible sport?
Very. The good thing about sailing is that there is a role for everyone, even if you are not the strongest person on board. London 2012 was a really good thing for Aberdeen Asset Management Cowes Week in that it put a focus on sailing as well as sport everywhere. We hope that continues.

You entered the history books as the first British woman to win two Olympic gold medals at consecutive games, what did that mean to you?
Everything. As an Olympic athlete you never really know if you are going to walk away with anything, so winning that first gold in Sydney was pretty special. It was definitely my proudest career moment to date.

What is it like being a female in a mostly male dominated sport?
When I first started sailing there were few women sailing at all – that came later. You do get used to being a female in a male dominated sport and sailing is still predominately male, however we are seeing signs of change. My Olympic career really started when the lottery funding came in because I had always had to raise my own money. Now that lots more women are involved in sailing the demographic is changing and the mind-set of females is changing. Participation from women in Aberdeen Asset Management Cowes Week is up 150% over the last 15 years and this is something we celebrate with 'Ladies Day' on Thursday 7th August.

Was being an athlete your only career option?
It has been such a long time I couldn't imagine not sailing. I have always loved sport and the outdoors and I am now working with the media so I am still very close to it. The hardest and best part of my journalism career has been the Olympics, it is my world. I had to try not to cry before the athletes did. I could empathise as I know that it means the world to them.

Are the Solent waters your favourite place to sail?
I have sailed all over the world but yes, I really enjoy sailing on the Solent. The Solent is a tricky, busy place with so many boats but it's also a very unique place. It's definitely a challenge.

At the Aberdeen Asset Management Cowes Week you have amateur sailors competing against Olympic and world champions, do you think this is what differentiates Cowes Week from other regattas?
Definitely. The great thing about Aberdeen Asset Management Cowes Week is that everybody can be a part of it regardless of age and experience. And yet its success is not just because of the sailing but also down to the appeal of the entire event. To be a spectator, sitting on the green and enjoying the hospitality, is to have a really great day out.

1.3 LIGHTS, BUOYS AND WAYPOINTS

Bold print = light with a nominal range of 15M or more. CAPITALS = place or feature. *CAPITAL ITALICS* = light-vessel, light float or Lanby. *Italics* = Fog signal. ***Bold italics*** = Racon. Some marks/buoys are fitted with AIS (<u>MMSI No</u>); see relevant charts.

IMPORTANT NOTE. Regular changes are made to Thames Estuary buoyage. Check Notices to Mariners for the latest information.

BROADSTAIRS AND NORTH FORELAND

Broadstairs Knoll ⬙ Fl R 2·5s; 51°20'·88N 01°29'·48E.
Pier SE End ⚓ 2 FR (vert) 7m 4M; 51°21'·50N 01°26'·74E.
Elbow ⬙ Q; 51°23'·23N 01°31'·59E.

North Foreland ☆ 51°22'·49N 01°26'·70E; Fl (5) WR 20s 57m **W19M, R16M, R15M**; W 8-sided twr; vis: shore-W-150°-R(**16M**)-181°-R(**15M**)-200°-W-011°; H24; <u>992351020</u>.

THAMES ESTUARY – SOUTHERN

(Direction of buoyage generally East to West)

APPROACHES to THAMES ESTUARY
Foxtrot 3 ⬳ 51°24'·15N 02°00'·38E; Fl 10s 12m **15M**; *Racon (T) 10M*; *Horn 10s*; <u>992351033</u>.
Falls Hd ⬙ Q; 51°28'·23N 01°49'·89E.
Drill Stone ⬙ Q (3) 10s; 51°25'·88N 01°42'·89E.
Thanet N ⬙ VQ 15s; 51°28'·28N 01°38'·06E.
NE Spit ⬙ VQ (3); *Racon (T) 10M*; 5s; 51°27'·93N 01°29'·89E; <u>992351037</u>.
East Margate ⬳ Fl R 2·5s; 51°27'·03N 01°26'·40E.
Elbow ⬙ Q; 51°23'·23N 01°31'·59E.
Foreness Pt Outfall ⬳ Fl R 5s; 51°24'·61N 01°26'·02E.
Longnose ⬳ 51°24'·15N 01°26'·08E.
Longnose Spit ⬙ Fl R 2·5s 5m 2M; 51°23'·93N 01°25'·68E.

MARGATE and GORE CHANNEL
SE Margate ⬙ Q (3) 10s; 51°24'·05N 01°20'·40E.
S Margate ⬥ Fl G 2·5s; 51°23'·83N 01°16'·65E.
Copperas ⬥ QG; 51°23'·81N 01°11'·18E.
Reculver ⬳ QR; 51°23'·63N 01°12'·56E.

HERNE BAY
Beltinge Bay Bn ⬙ Fl Y 5s; 51°22'·73N 01°08'·63E.
Landing Stage ⚓ Q 18m 4M, (isolated); 51°22'·91N 01°06'·89E.
N Pier Hd ⚓ 2 FR (vert); 51°22'·43N 01°07'·27E.

WHITSTABLE
Whitstable Street ⬳ ; 51°24'·00N 01°01'·54E. (See The Swale.)
Oyster ⬳ Fl (2) R 10s; 51°22'·14N 01°01'·16E.
W Quay Dn ⚓ Fl G 5s 2m.

THE SWALE
Whitstable Street ⬳ Fl R 2s; 51°24'·00N 01°01'·54E.
Columbine ⬥ Fl G 2s; 51°24'·26N 01°01'·34E.
Columbine Spit ⬥ Fl (3) G 10s; 51°23'·86N 01°00'·03E.
Ham Gat ⬥ Q G; 51°23'·08N 00°58'·32E.
Pollard Spit ⬳ Q R; 51°22'·98N 00°58'·57E.
Sand End ⬥ Fl G 5s; 51°21'·43N 00°55'·90E.
Receptive Point ⬥ Fl G 10s; 51°20'·86N 00°54'·41E.
Queenborough Spit ⬙ Q (3) 10s; 51°25'·81N 00°43'·93E.
South Oaze ⬳ Fl R 2s; 51°21'·34N 00°56'·01E.

QUEENS CHANNEL and FOUR FATHOMS CHANNEL
E Margate ⬳ Fl R 2·5s; 51°27'·03N 01°26'·40E.
Spaniard ⬙ Q (3) 10s; 51°26'·23N 01°04'·00E.
Spile ⬥ Fl G 2·5s; 51°26'·43N 00°55'·70E.

PRINCES CHANNEL
Tongue Sand E ⬙ VQ (3) 5s; 51°29'·48N 01°22'·21E.
Tongue Sand N ⬙ Q; 51°29'·68N 01°22'·03E.
Princes Outer ⬙ VQ (6) + L Fl 10s; 51°28'·89N 01°20'·43E.
Princes North ⬥ Q G; 51°29'·25N 01°18'·35E.
Princes South ⬳ Q R; 51°28'·74N 01°18'·26E.

Princes No.1 ⬥ Fl (4) G 15s; 51°29'·23N 01°16'·02E.
Princes No.2 ⬳ Fl (2) R 5s; 51°28'·81N 01°13'·08E.
Princes No.3 ⬥ Fl (2) G 5s; 51°29'·33N 01°13'·10E.
Princes No.4 ⬳ Fl R 10s; 51°28'·83N 01°09'·90E.
Princes No.5 ⬥ Fl (3) G 10s; 51°29'·39N 01°10'·00E.
Princes Mid ⬙ Fl Y 5s; 51°29'·19N 01°09'·00E.
Shivering Sand Twr N ⬙ Q; 51°30'·01N 01°04'·76E.
Shivering Sand Twr S ⬙ Q (6) + L Fl 15s; *Bell*; 51°29'·75N 01°04'·83E.
Princes No.8 ⬳ Fl (2) R 5s; 51°29'·14N 01°03'·00E.
Princes Inner ⬙ Fl Y 2·5s; 51°29'·59N 01°03'·47E.

FOULGER'S GAT and KNOB CHANNEL
N Edinburgh Channel is not buoyed. Foulger's Gat, lies within the boundary of the London Array Wind Farm.
Long Sand Outer ⬳ L Fl 10s; 51°34'·61N 01°28'·34E.
Long Sand Middle ⬳ Iso 5s; 51°35'·60N 01°26'·45E.
Long Sand Inner ⬳ Mo 'A' 15s; 51°38'·78N 01°25'·44E.
SE Knob ⬥ Fl G 5s; 51°30'·89N 01°06'·41E.
Knob ⬙ Iso 5s; *Whis*; 51°30'·69N 01°04'·28E.

OAZE DEEP
Oaze Deep ⬥ Fl (2) G 5s; 51°30'·03N 01°00'·70E.
Red Sand Trs N ⬳ Fl (3) R 10s; *Bell*; 51°28'·73N 00°59'·32E.
N Oaze ⬳ QR; 51°30'·03N 00°57'·65E.
Oaze ⬙ Fl (4) Y 10s; 51°29'·06N 00°56'·93E.
W Oaze ⬙ Iso 5s; 51°29'·06N 00°55'·43E.
Oaze Bank ⬥ Q G 5s; 51°29'·36N 00°56'·95E.
Cant ⬙ (unlit); 51°27'·77N 00°53'·36E.
East Cant ⬳ QR; 51°28'·53N 00°55'·60E.

MEDWAY, SHEERNESS
Medway ⬙ Mo (A) 6s; 51°28'·83N 00°52'·81E.
No. 1 ⬥ Fl G 2·5s; 51°28'·55N 00°50'·50E.
No. 2 ⬙ Q; 51°28'·33N 00°50'·52E.
No. 7 ⬥ Fl G 10s; 51°27'·91N 00°47'·52E.
No. 9 ⬥ Fl G 5s; 51°27'·74N 00°46'·61E.
No. 11 ⬥ Fl (3) G 10s; 51°27'·51N 00°45'·80E.
Grain Hard ⬥ Fl G 5s; 51°26'·98N 00°44'·17E.
Isle of Grain ☆ Q 20m 13M; RW ◇ on R twr; 51°26'·70N 00°43'·38E.
Queenborough Spit ⬙ Q (3) 10s; 51°25'·81N 00°43'·93E.

RIVER THAMES

SEA REACH, NORE and YANTLET
Sea Reach 1 (N) ⬙ Fl Y 2·5s; *Racon (T) 10M*; 51°29'·59N 00°52'·71E.
Sea Reach 1 (S) ⬳ Fl R 2·5s; 51°29'·39N 00°52'·45E.
Sea Reach 2 (N) ⬥ Fl R 2·5s; 51°29'·49N 00°49'·73E.
Sea Reach 2 (S) ⬳ Fl R 2·5s; 51°29'·30N 00°49'·75E.
South East Leigh ⬙ Q(6) + L Fl 15s; 51°29'·41N 00°47'·06E.
Sea Reach 3 (S) ⬳ Q R; 51°29'·22N 00°46'·71E.
Sea Reach 4 (N) ⬥ Fl G (2) 5s; 51°29'·69N 00°44'·19E.
Sea Reach 4 (S) ⬳ Fl R (2) 5s; 51°29'·50N 00°44'·12E.
Sea Reach 5 (N) ⬥ VQ G; 51°30'·04N 00°41'·47E.
Sea Reach 5 (S) ⬳ VQ R; 51°29'·85N 00°41'·43E.
Sea Reach 6 (N) ⬥ Fl G 5s; 51°30'·13N 00°39'·87E.
Sea Reach 6 (S) ⬳ Fl R 5s; 51°29'·93N 00°39'·84E.
Sea Reach 7 (N) ⬙ Fl Y 2·5s; 51°30'·21N 00°36'·94E.
Sea Reach 7 (S) ⬳ Fl R 2·5s; *Racon (T) 10M*; 51°30'·01N 00°36'·91E.
Nore Swatch ⬳ Fl (4) R 15s; 51°28'·28N 00°45'·55E.
Mid Swatch ⬥ Fl G 5s; 51°28'·68N 00°44'·16E.
W Nore Sand ⬳ Fl (3) R 10s; 51°29'·41N 00°40'·85E.
East Blyth ⬳ Fl (2) R 10s; 51°29'·72N 00°37'·80E.
Mid Blyth ⬙ Q; 51°30'·08N 00°32'·38E.

LEIGH-ON-SEA and SOUTHEND-ON-SEA
Leigh ⬥; 51°31'·07N 00°42'·56E.
Southend Pier E End ⚓ 2 FG (vert) 7m; *Horn Mo (N) 30s, Bell (1)*
SE Leigh ⬙ Q (6) + L Fl 15s; 51°29'·42N 00°47'·07E.

LOWER HOPE REACH
West Blyth ⬳ Q R; 51°29'·57N 00°28'·39E.
Mucking 1 ⬥ Q G; 51°29'·70N 00°37'·28E.
Lower Hope ⬳ Fl R 5s; 51°29'·32N 00°28'·02E.
Mucking 3 ⬥ Fl G 2·5s; 51°29'·33N 00°27'·68E.

Mucking 5 ⚲ Fl (3) G 10s; 51°28'·76N 00°27'·19E.
Mucking 7 ⚲ Fl G 5s; 51°28'·03N 00°26'·77E.
Bell Ovens ⚲ Q G; 51°27'·50N 00°26'·35E.
Higham ⚲ Fl (2) R 5s; 51°27'·40N 00°26'·85E.
Tilbury ⚲ Q(6) + L Fl 15s; 51°27'·16N 00°25'·50E.

GRAVESEND
Shornmead ⚡ Fl (2) WR 10s 12m, W11/7M, R11M; vis 070°-W-084°-R(Intens)-089°-W(Intens)-094°-W-250°; 51°26'·92N 00°26'·24E.
Northfleet Upper ☆ Oc WRG 10s 30m **W16M**, R12M, G12M; vis:126°-R-149°-W-159°-G-268°-W-279°; 51°26'·93N 00°20'·06E.

THAMES TIDAL BARRIER
Spans B, C, D, E, F, G are navigable. Spans C – F are for large ships.
Eastbound small craft/yachts use Span B (51°29'·73N 00°02'·23E)
Westbound small craft/yachts use Span G (51°29'·91N 00°02'·21E).
Red X indicates span closed Green → indicates span open.
W lights show either side of open spans in poor visibility.

KENTISH KNOCK
Kentish Knock ⚲ Q (3) 10s; 51°38'·08N 01°40·43E.
S Knock ⚲ Q (6) + L Fl 15s; *Bell*; 51°34'·13N 01°34'·29E.

KNOCK JOHN CHANNEL
No. 7 ⚲ Fl (4) G 15s; 51°32'·03N 01°06'·40E.
No. 5 ⚲ Fl (3) G 10s; 51°32'·49N 01°07'·75E.
No. 4 ⚲ QR 10s; 51°32'·40 N 01°08'·08E.
No. 2 ⚲ Fl (3) R 10s; 51°33'·03N 01°09'·63E.
No. 3 ⚲ Q (6) + L Fl 15s; 51°33'·29N 01°09'·83E.
No. 1 ⚲ Fl G 5s; 51°33'·75N 01°10'·72E.
Knock John ⚲ Fl (2) R 5s; 51°33'·61N 01°11'·37E.

BLACK DEEP
No. 12 ⚲ Fl (4) R 15s; 51°33'·83N 01°13'·50E.
No. 11 ⚲ Fl (3) G 10s; 51°34'·33N 01°13'·40E.
No. 10 ⚲ Fl (3) R 10s; 51°34'·74N 01°15'·60E.
No. 9 ⚲ Q (6) + L Fl 15s; 51°35'·13N 01°15'·09E.
No. 8 ⚲ Q (9) 15s; 51°36'·36N 01°20'·43E.
No. 7 ⚲ QG. 51°37'·08N 01°17'·69E.
No. 6 ⚲ Fl R 2·5s; 51°38'·53N 01°24'·41E.
No. 5 ⚲ VQ (3) 5s; 51°39'·53N 01°23'·00E.
No. 4 ⚲ Fl (2) R 5s; 51°41'·42N 01°28'·49E.
Long Sand Bcn ⚲ ; 51°41'·48N 01°29'·49E.
No. 3 ⚲ Fl (3) G 15s; 51°42'·39N 01°26'·66E.
No. 1 ⚲ Fl G 5s; 51°44'·03N 01°28'·09E.
No. 2 ⚲ Fl (4) R 15s; 51°45'·63N 01°32'·20E.
SHM ⚲ Fl Y 2·5s; *Racon (T) 10M*; 51°29'·59N 00°52'·71E.

SUNK
Sunk Head Tower ⚲ Q; *Whis*; 51°46'·63N 01°30'·51E.
Black Deep ⚲ QR; 51°48'·10N 01°36'·60E.
Long Sand Head ⚲ VQ; *Whis*; 51°47'·90N 01°39'·42E.
SUNK CENTRE ⬚ 51°50'·11N 01°46'·02E; Fl (2) 20s 12m **16M**;
Racon (C) 10M; Horn (2) 60s; 992351094.
Dynamo ⚲ Fl Y 2·5s; 51°29'·59N 00°52'·71E.
Trinity ⚲ Q (6) + L Fl 15s; 51°49'·03N 01°36'·39E.
SUNK INNER ⬚ 51°51'·17N 01°34'·40E; Iso 3s 11m 12M; *Racon (C) 10M*; Horn 30s; 992351027.

FISHERMANS GAT
Outer Fisherman ⚲ Q (3) 10s; 51°34'·02N 01°25'·10E.
Fisherman No. 1 ⚲ Fl G 2·5s (sync); 51°34'·50N 01°23'·52E.
Fisherman No. 2 ⚲ Fl R 2·5s (sync); 51°34'·30N 01°23'·50E.
Fisherman No. 3 ⚲ Fl G 5s; 51°34'·78N 01°22'·65E.
Fisherman No. 4 ⚲ Fl (2) R 5s; 51°34'·77N 01°22'·08E.
Fisherman No. 5 ⚲ Fl (2) G 5s; 51°35'·25N 01°21'·84E.
Fisherman No. 6 ⚲ Fl (3) R 10s; 51°35'·08N 01°21'·56E.
Inner Fisherman ⚲ Q R; 51°36'·10N 01°19'·97E.

BARROW DEEP
SW Barrow ⚲ Q(6) + L Fl 15s; *Bell*; 51°32'·29N 01°00'·31E.
Barrow No. 14 ⚲ Fl R 2·5s; 51°31'·83N 01°00'·43E.
Barrow No. 13 ⚲ Fl (2) G 5s; 51°32'·82N 01°03'·07E.
Barrow No. 12 ⚲ Fl (2) G 5s; 51°32'·77N 01°04'·13E.
Barrow No.11 ⚲ Fl (3) G 10s; 51°34'·08N 01°06'·70E.

Barrow No. 9 ⚲ VQ (3) 5s; 51°35'·34N 01°10'·30E.
Barrow No. 8 ⚲ Fl (2) R 5s; 51°35'·03N 01°11'·40E.
Barrow No. 6 ⚲ Fl (4) R 15s; 51°37'·30N 01°14'·69E.
Barrow No. 5 ⚲ Fl G 10s; 51°40'·03N 01°16'·20E.
Barrow No. 4 ⚲ VQ (9) 10s; 51°39'·88N 01°17'·48E.
Barrow No. 3 ⚲ Q (3) 10s; *Racon (M)10M*; 51°42'·02N 01°20'·24E.
Barrow No. 2 ⚲ Fl (2) R 5s; 51°41'·98N 01°22'·89E.

WEST SWIN and MIDDLE DEEP
Blacktail (W) ⚲ ; 51°31'·46N 00°55'·19E.
Maplin ⚲ Q G (sync with W Swin); *Bell*; 51°33'·66N 01°01'·40E.
W Swin ⚲ Q R (sync with Maplin); 51°33'·40N 01°01'·97E.
Maplin Edge ⚲ Fl G 2.5s; 51°35'·33N 01°03'·64E.
Maplin Bank ⚲ Fl (3) R 10s; 51°35'·50N 01°04'·70E.

EAST SWIN and KING'S CHANNEL
NE Maplin ⚲ Fl G 5s; *Bell*; 51°37'·43N 01°04'·90E.
W Hook Middle ⚲ 51°39'·18N 01°07'·97E.
S Whitaker ⚲ Fl (2) G 10s; 51°40'·17N 01°09'·11E.
N Middle ⚲ Q; 51°41'·35N 01°12'·61E.
W Sunk ⚲ Q (9) 15s; 51°44'·33N 01°25'·80E.
Gunfleet Spit ⚲ Q (6) + L Fl 15s; *Bell*; 51°45'·33N 01°21'·70E.

WHITAKER CHANNEL and RIVER CROUCH
Whitaker ⚲ Q (3) 10s; *Bell*; 51°41'·43N 01°10'·51E.
Inner Whitaker ⚲ VQ (6) + L Fl 10s; 51°40'·76N 01°08'·40E.
Swin Spitway ⚲ Iso 10s; *Bell*; 51°41'·95N 01°08'·35E.
Whitaker 1 ⚲ Fl G 5s (sync Whit 2), 51° 40'.69N 01° 06'.67E.
Whitaker 2 ⚲ Fl R 5s (sync Whit 1), 51° 40'.41N 01° 06'.78E.
Whitaker 3 ⚲ Fl(2) G 5s (sync Whit 4) 51° 40'.41N 01° 04'.74E.
Whitaker 4 ⚲ Fl(2) R 5s (sync Whit 4) 51° 40'.16N 01° 04'.91E.
Whitaker 5 ⚲ Fl(3) G 10s (sync Whit 6) 51° 40'.03N 01° 03'.22E.
Whitaker 6 ⚲ Fl(3) R 10s(sync Whit 5) 51° 39'.77N 01° 03'.43E.
Whitaker 7 ⚲ Fl(4) G 10s(sync Whit 8) 51° 39'.54N 01° 02'.00E.
Whitaker 8 ⚲ Fl(4) R 10s(sync Whit 7), 51° 39'.35N 01° 02'.00E.
Swallowtail 1 ⚲ Fl Y 5s, 51° 41'.38N 01° 08'.20E.
Swallowtail 2 ⚲ Fl Y 10s, 51° 41'.19N 01° 06'.28E.
Swallowtail 3 ⚲ Fl Y 15s, 51° 40.84N 01° 04.39E.
Swallowtail 4 ⚲ (2) Y 10s, 51° 40'.52N 01° 03'.47E.
Buxey Edge ⚲ Fl G 10s, 51° 40'.65N 01° 03'.48E.
Swallowtail ⚲ VQ (9) 10s, 51° 40'.04N 01° 02'.65E.
Sunken Buxey ⚲ VQ; 51°39'·59N 01°00'·77E.
Buxey No. 1 ⚲ VQ (6) + L Fl 10s; 51°39'·18N 01°01'·13E.
Buxey No. 2 ⚲ Q; 51°39'·08N 01°00'·23E.
Outer Crouch 1 ⚲ Fl G 5s (sync Cro 2) 51° 38'.71N 00° 59'.00E.
Outer Crouch 2 ⚲ Fl R 5s (sync Cro 1) 51° 38'.62N 00° 59'.20E.
Outer Crouch 3 ⚲ Fl G 10s (sync Cro 4) 51° 38'.10N 00° 57'.83E.
Outer Crouch 4 ⚲ Fl R 10s (sync Cro 3) 51° 37'.95N 00° 58'.00E.
Crouch ⚲ Q.Fl, 51° 37.650N 00° 56.582E.
Inner Crouch ⚲ L Fl 10s, 51° 37'.19N 00° 55'.09E.
Branklet (RGR) **Pref Chan to Stbd,** Comp grp Fl (R) 2+1 10s, 51° 36'.99N 00° 52'.10E.

GOLDMER GAT and WALLET
NE Gunfleet ⚲ Q (3) 10s; 51°49'·93N 01°27'·79E.
Wallet No. 2 ⚲ Fl R 5s; 51°48'·88N 01°22'·99E.
Wallet No. 4 ⚲ Fl (4) R 10s; 51°46'·53N 01°17'·23E.
Wallet Spitway ⚲ L Fl 10s; *Bell*; 51°42'·86N 01°07'·30E.
Knoll ⚲ Q; 51°43'·88N 01°05'·07E.
Eagle ⚲ QG; 51°44'·13N 01°03'·82E.
N Eagle ⚲ Q; 51°44'·71N 01°04'·32E.
NW Knoll ⚲ Fl (2) R 5s; 51°44'·35N 01°02'·17E.
Colne Bar ⚲ Fl (2) G 5s; 51°44'·61N 01°02'·57E.
Bench Head ⚲ Fl (3) G 10s; 51°44'·69N 01°01'·10E.

RIVER BLACKWATER
The Nass ⚲ VQ (3) 5s 6m 2M; 51°45'·83N 00°54'·83E.
Thirslet ⚲ Fl (3) G 10s; 51°43'·73N 00°50'·39E.
No. 1 ⚲ ; 51°43'·44N 00°48'·02E.

RIVER COLNE and BRIGHTLINGSEA
Inner Bench Head No. 2 ⚲ Fl (2) R 5s; 51°45'·96N 01°01'·74E.
Colne Pt No. 1 ⚲ Fl G 3s; 51°46'·01N 01°01'·92E.
No. 8 ⚲ Fl R 3s; 51°46'·90N 01°01'·30E.

E England

No. 9 ⚓ Fl G 3s; 51°47'·36N 01°01'·07E.
Ldg lts 041°. Front, FR 7m 4M; W □, R stripe on post; vis: 020°-080°; 51°48'·39N 01°01'·20E. Rear, 50m from front, FR 10m 4M; W □, R stripe on post. FR lts are shown on 7 masts between 1·5M and 3M NW when firing occurs.

WALTON BACKWATERS
Pye End ⚓ L Fl 10s; 51°55'·03N 01°17'·90E.
No. 2 ⚓ Fl (2) 5s; 51°54'·62N 01°16'·80E.
Crab Knoll No. 3 ⚓ Fl G 5s; 51°54'·41N 01°16'·41E.

HARWICH APPROACHES

(Direction of buoyage is North to South)

MEDUSA CHANNEL
Medusa ⚓ Fl G 5s; 51°51'·23N 01°20'·35E.
Stone Banks ⚓ FlR 5s; 51°53'·19N 01°19'·23E.
Pennyhole ⚓ ; 51°53'·55N 01°18'·00E (Mar–Sep).

CORK SAND and ROUGH SHOALS
S Cork ⚓ Q (6) + L Fl 15s; 51°51'·33N 01°24'·09E.
SE Roughs Tower ⚓ Q (3) 10s; 51°53'·64N 01°28'·94E.
NW Roughs Tower ⚓ VQ (9) 10s; 51°53'·81N 01°28'·77E.
Cork Sand ⚓ Fl (3) R 10s; 51°55'·51N 01°25'·42E.

HARWICH CHANNEL
S Threshold ⚓ Fl (4) Y 10s; 51°52'·20N 01°33'·14E.
S Shipwash ⚓⚓ 2 By(s) Q (6) + L Fl 15s; 51°52'·71N 01°33'·97E.
Outer Tidal Bn ⚓ Mo (U) 15s 2m 3M; 51°52'·85N 01°32'·34E.
E Fort Massac ⚓ VQ (3) 5s; 51°53'·36N 01°32'·79E.
W Fort Massac ⚓ VQ (9) 10s; 51°53'·36N 01°32'·49E.
Walker ⚓ Q (9)15s; 51°53'·79N 01°33'·90E.
N Threshold ⚓ Fl Y 5s; 51°54'·49N 01°33'·47E.
SW Shipwash ⚓ Fl Y 2·5s; 51°54'·75N 01°34'·21E.
Haven ⚓ Mo (A) 5s; 51°55'·76N 01°32'·56E.
W Shipwash ⚓ Fl (2) R 10s; 51°57'·13N 01°35'·89E.
NW Shipwash ⚓ Fl R 5s; 51°58'·98N 01°37'·01E.
Harwich App (HA) ⚓ Iso 5s; 51°56'·75N 01°30'·66E.
Cross ⚓ Fl (3) Y 10s; 51°56'·23N 01°30'·48E.
Harwich Chan No. 1 ⚓ Fl Y 2·5s; *Racon (T) 10M*; 51°56'·13N 01°27'·06E.
Harwich Chan No. 3 ⚓ Fl (3) Y 10s; 51°56'·04N 01°25'·54E.
Harwich Chan No. 5 ⚓ Fl (5) Y 10s; 51°55'·96N 01°24'·01E.
Harwich Chan No. 7 ⚓ Fl (3) Y 10s; 51°55'·87N 01°22'·49E.
S Bawdsey ⚓ Q (6) + L Fl 15s; *Whis*; 51°57'·23N 01°30'·19E.
Washington ⚓ QG; 51°56'·52N 01°26'·59E.
Felixstowe Ledge ⚓ Fl (3) G 10s; 51°56'·30N 01°23'·72E.
Wadgate Ledge ⚓ Fl (4) G 15s; 51°56'·16N 01°21'·99E.
Platters ⚓ Q (6) + L Fl 15s; 51°55'·64N 01°20'·97E.
Rolling Ground ⚓ QG; 51°55'·55N 01°19'·75E.
Beach End ⚓ Fl (2) G 5s; 51°55'·62N 01°19'·21E.
Cork Sand Yacht Bn ⚓ VQ 2M; 51°55'·21N 01°25'·20E.
Rough ⚓ VQ; 51°55'·19N 01°31'·00E.
Pitching Ground ⚓ Fl (4) R 15s; 51°55'·43N 01°21'·05E.
Inner Ridge ⚓ QR; 51°55'·38N 01°20'·20E.
Deane ⚓ L Fl R 6s; 51°55'·36N 01°19'·28E.
Landguard ⚓ Q; 51°55'·45N 01°18'·84E.

RIVERS STOUR AND ORWELL

RIVER STOUR and HARWICH
Shotley Spit ⚓ Q (6) + L Fl 15s; 51°57'·21N 01°17'·69E.
Shotley Marina Lock E side Dir lt 339·5° 3m 1M (uses Moiré pattern); Or structure; 51°57'·46N 01°16'·60E.
Guard ⚓ Fl R 5s; *Bell*; 51°57'·07N 01°17'·86E.

RIVER ORWELL and IPSWICH
Suffolk Yacht Harbour. Ldg lts Front Iso Y 1M; 51°59'·73N 01°16'·09E. Rear Oc Y 4s 1M.

HARWICH TO ORFORD NESS

FELIXSTOWE, R DEBEN and WOODBRIDGE HAVEN
Woodbridge Haven ⚓ Mo(A)15s; 51°58'·20N 01°23'·85E.
Deben ⚓ ; 51°59'·30N 01°23'·53E.

RIVERS ORE and ALDE
Orford Haven ⚓ L Fl 10s; *Bell*. 52°02'·04N 01°28'·38E.

OFFSHORE MARKS
S Galloper ⚓ Q (6) L Fl 15s; *Racon (T) 10M*; 51°43'·98N 01°56'·43E.
N Galloper ⚓ Q; 51°49'·84N 01°59'·99E.
S Inner Gabbard ⚓ Q (6) + L Fl 15s. 51°49'·92N 01°51'·89E.
N Inner Gabbard ⚓ Q; 51°59'·20N 01°56'·00E.
Outer Gabbard ⚓ Q (3) 10s; *Racon (O) 10M*; 51°57'·83N 02°04'·19E.
NHR-SE ⚓ Fl G 5s; 51°45'·39N 02°39'·89E.

SHIPWASH and BAWDSEY BANK
E Shipwash ⚓ VQ (3) 5s; 51°57'·08N 01°37'·89E.
NW Shipwash ⚓ Fl R 5s; 51°58'·98N 01°37'·01E.
N Shipwash ⚓ Q 7M; *Racon (M) 10M*; *Whis*; 52°01'·73N 01°38'·27E; 992351069.
S Bawdsey ⚓ Q (6) + L Fl 15s; *Whis*; 51°57'·23N 01°30'·22E.
Mid Bawdsey ⚓ Fl (3) G 10s; 51°58'·88N 01°33'·59E.
NE Bawdsey ⚓ Fl G 10s; 52°01'·73N 01°36'·09E.

CUTLER and WHITING BANKS
Cutler ⚓ QG; 51°58'·51N 01°27'·48E.
SW Whiting ⚓ Q (6) + L Fl 10s; 52°00'·96N 01°30'·69E.
Whiting Hook ⚓ Fl R 10s; 52°02'·98N 01°31'·82E.
NE Whiting ⚓ Q (3) 10s; 52°03'·61N 01°33'·32E.

ORFORD NESS TO WINTERTON

(Direction of buoyage is South to North)
Orford Ness Lt Ho (dis) 52°05'·04N 01°34'·45E; W ○ twr, R bands.
Aldeburgh Ridge ⚓ QR; 52°06'·49N 01°36'·95E.

SOUTHWOLD
Southwold ☆ 52°19'·63N 01°40'·89E; Fl 10s 37m **W24M**; vis 204°-W-032·5°, 992351019.

LOWESTOFT and APPR VIA STANFORD CHANNEL
E Barnard ⚓ Q (3) 10s; 52°25'·14N 01°46'·38E.
Newcome Sand ⚓ QR; 52°26'·28N 01°46'·97E.
S Holm ⚓ VQ (6) + L Fl 10s; 52°26'·85N 01°47'·15E.
Stanford ⚓ Fl R 2·5s; 52°27'·35N 01°46'·67E.
SW Holm ⚓ Fl (2) G 5s; 52°27'·87N 01°46'·99E.
Kirkley ⚓ Oc WRG 10s 17m, W8M, R6M, G6M, vis: 210°-G-224°-W-229°-R-313°; 52°27'·71N 01°44'·54E.
Outer Hbr S Pier Hd ⚓ Oc R 5s 12m 6M; *Horn (4) 60s*; Tfc sigs; 52°28'·29N 01°45'·36E.
N Newcome ⚓ Fl (4) R 15s; 52°28'·39N 01°46'·37E.
Lowestoft ☆ 52°29'·22N 01°45'·35; Fl 15s 37m **23M**; W twr; part obscd 347°- shore.

LOWESTOFT NORTH ROAD and CORTON ROAD
Lowestoft Ness SE ⚓ Q (6) + L Fl 15s; 52°28'·84N 01°46'·25E.
Lowestoft Ness N ⚓ VQ (3) 5s; *Bell*; 52°28'·89N 01°46'·23E.
W Holm ⚓ Fl (3) G 10s; 52°29'·80N 01°47'·09E.
NW Holm ⚓ Fl (4) G 15s; 52°31'·93N 01°46'·70E.

GREAT YARMOUTH APPROACH via HOLM CHANNEL
E Newcome ⚓ Fl (2) R 5s; 52°28'·51N 01°49'·21E.
Holm Approach ⚓ Q (3) 10s; 52°30'·88N 01°50'·22E.
Holm Sand ⚓ Q (9) 15s; 52°33'·18N 01°46'·54E.
S Corton ⚓ Q (6) + L Fl 15s; *Bell*; 52°32'·94N 01°49'·12E.
NE Holm ⚓ Fl R 2·5s; 52°32'·69N 01°48'·48E.
Mid Corton ⚓ Fl G 2·5s; 52°33'·62N 01°48'·01E.
N Holm ⚓ Q. 52°33'·93N 01°47'·23E.

GREAT YARMOUTH and GORLESTON
W Corton ⚓ Fl (3) G 10s; 52°34'·12N 01°47'·50E.
Gorleston South Pier Hd ⚓ Fl R 3s 11m 11M; vis: 235°-340°; 52°34'·33N 01°44'·28E.
N Pier Hd ⚓ QG 8m 6M; vis: 176°-078°; *Horn(3) 60s*; 52°34'·38N 01°44'·38E.

1.4 PASSAGE INFORMATION

Reference books include: *East Coast Rivers* (NDL/Harber, latest edition 2008), *East Coast Pilot* (Imray), Admiralty NP 28 *Dover Strait Pilot* and NP54 *North Sea (West) Pilot*. See also www.eastcoastsailing.co.uk. The area is well covered by Admiralty Leisure Folios: 5606 covers the Thames Estuary from Ramsgate to Tower Bridge, 5607 the northern Thames Estuary to Orford Ness, and 5614 from Orford Ness northwards. More Passage Information is threaded between the harbours of this Area.

THE THAMES ESTUARY

(AC 1183, 1975, 1607, 1606, 1609) The sandbanks shift constantly in the Thames Estuary; charted depths cannot be relied upon, and an accurate echo sounder is vital. Up to date charts showing the latest buoyage changes and a detailed tidal stream atlas are essential. The commercial deep water route from the Sunk Inner precautionary area to the Yantlet runs through Black Deep and Knock John Channel. It is well marked, as are Barrow Deep, Princes Channel and Fisherman's Gat. The lesser channels and swatchways, which are convenient for yachtsmen, particularly when crossing the estuary, are mainly unmarked and unlit. They should be used with great caution. Good visibility is needed to pick out buoys and marks, and to avoid shipping. Care should be exercised when plotting electronic waypoints. Many former navigation marks and towers have been removed or allowed to disintegrate. Those that are still standing may be in very shallow water.

Newcomers to the estuary are advised to choose a period of neap tides when minimum depths are greater and tidal streams weaker. If a crossing at springs is unavoidable, keep in deep water even if that involves a longer passage.

Careful consideration needs to be given to wind strength and direction for each of the several course changes during a typical crossing. It is easy to find yourself trapped between shoals, down-wind and down-stream.

▶ *Study the tides carefully so as to work the streams to best advantage and to ensure sufficient depth at the times and places where you expect to be, or might be later. In principle it is best to make most of the crossing on a rising tide. However, a typical passage from N Foreland to the Blackwater will take 7-9 hours, so some adverse stream is almost inevitable. The stream at springs runs at 3kn in places, mostly along the channels but sometimes across the intervening banks. A short, steep sea may be raised with the wind against tide.* ◀

CROSSING THE THAMES ESTUARY

(AC 1183, 1975, 1607, 1606, 1609) *Crossing the Thames Estuary* (Imray) gives 32 suggested routes. Making N from N Foreland to Orford Ness or beyond it may be better to keep to seaward of the main banks, via Kentish Knock and Long Sand Head buoys, thence to N Shipwash lt buoy, 14M further N.

Bound NW from North Foreland it is approximately 35M to the mouths of the Rivers Crouch, Blackwater or Colne. One route is through the Princes Channel, thence N of the Oaze Deep precautionary area and S of the Knob and West Barrow banks to the West Swin, before turning NE into Middle Deep and the East Swin. The Wallet Spitway then leads NW to the Colne and Blackwater. Many routes may be followed, depending on wind direction, tidal conditions and confidence in electronic aids in the absence of marks. Passage over Sunk Sand and Knock John bank is best avoided, particularly in winds >F5.

Southbound from the Colne or Blackwater, leave 1-2 hours before HW and make best speed to skirt or cross the shoals while there is sufficient depth of water. The latter part of the passage will then be in generally deeper water of Edinburgh Channel, Fisherman's or Foulger's Gat or (keeping appropriately clear of the turbines in the London Array), with a favourable S-going stream just starting off North Foreland.

From the NE follow Goldmer Gat and the Wallet (for Rivers Colne/Blackwater) or King's Channel and Whittaker Channel for the River Crouch.

London VTS has radar coverage from Greenwich to a line between the Naze and Margate. Keep a listening watch on VHF Ch 69 to monitor shipping activity. If really necessary, *London VTS* may be able to give navigational help to yachts; Thames CG at Walton-on-the-Naze may also assist.

NORTH FORELAND TO LONDON BRIDGE

North Foreland has a conspic lt ho (AC 1828), with buoys offshore.
▶ *From HW Dover –0120 to +0045 the stream runs N from The Downs and W into Thames Estuary. From HWD +0045 to +0440 the N-going stream from The Downs meets the E-going stream from Thames Estuary, which in strong winds causes a bad sea. From HWD –0450 to –0120 the streams turn W into Thames Estuary and S towards The Downs. If bound for London, round N Foreland against the late ebb in order to carry a fair tide from Sheerness onward.* ◀

The most direct route from North Foreland to the Thames and Medway is via South, Gore and Copperas Channels, then Overland Passage, Four Fathoms Channel and The Cant. Minimum depth is about 2m but may be significantly less off Reculver and leaving Copperas Channel. It is not well marked. Beware of Kentish Flats wind farm (30 turbines) with submarine cables to Herne Bay. An alternative, deeper route is east of Margate Sand and the Tongue, via the Princes Channel to the Oaze Deep. The N & S Edinburgh Channels are unmarked but navigable with caution.
▶ *W-going streams begin at approx HW Sheerness –0600 and E-going at HW Sheerness +0030.* ◀

Margate or Whitstable afford little shelter for yachts. The Swale provides an interesting inside route S of the Isle of Sheppey with access to Sheerness and the R Medway. If sailing from N Foreland to the Thames, Queenborough offers the first easily accessible, all-tide, deep-water shelter. In the east part of The Swale, Harty Ferry provides a sheltered anchorage, but not in strong winds from N or E. The Medway Channel is the main approach to Sheerness from The Warp.

CROSSING FROM THAMES/ORWELL TO BELGIUM OR THE NETHERLANDS

(ACs 1408, 1406, 1610, 1630, 1872, 1183) Up to date charts are *essential*. Thanet Wind Farm is now established 6Nm ENE of N Foreland and bounded by cardinal buoys. The southern North Sea is an extremely busy area with several large and complex Traffic Separation Schemes and associated Precautionary Areas which should be avoided if at all possible. Where practicable, navigate outside the schemes using any available ITZs, and always cross a TSS on a heading at 90° to the traffic flow in accordance with the Collision Regulations. From the Thames to Zeebrugge, the most direct route crosses the Nord Hinder South TSS in the vicinity of F3 light float. This is a focal point for dense crossing traffic. The very busy area around West Hinder must then be negotiated. A longer but much safer route (or if bound for Dunkerque, Nieuwpoort or Oostende) via S Falls, Sandettié and Dyck minimises time spent in the TSS and provides the option of breaking the passage in Ramsgate.

From the Orwell (or adjacent rivers) to the Netherlands, it may be best to pass north of the Sunk Inner and Sunk Outer TSS/Precautionary Areas before setting course for Hoek van Holland. From S Shipwash make for N Inner Gabbard before setting course for NHR-S to cross the North Hinder TSS to NHR-SE, then pass S of the Maas-West TSS leaving MW1, MW3 and MW5 buoys to port before shaping up for MV-N buoy.

▶ *Care must be taken throughout with the tidal streams, which may be setting across the yacht's track.* ◀ The whole area is relatively shallow, and in bad weather seas are steep and short. *(See also Area 2.)*

1.5 RAMSGATE

Kent 51°19'·51N 01°25'·50E ⊕⊕⊕♦♦♦✿✿

CHARTS AC 323, 1828, 1827, 5605/6; Imray C30, C8, C1, 2100

TIDES +0030 Dover; ML 2·7; Duration 0530

Standard Port DOVER (←—)

Times				Height (metres)			
High Water		Low Water		MHWS	MHWN	MLWN	MLWS
0000	0600	0100	0700	6·8	5·3	2·1	0·8
1200	1800	1300	1900				
Differences RAMSGATE							
+0030	+0030	+0017	+0007	−1·6	−1·3	−0·7	−0·2
RICHBOROUGH							
+0015	+0015	+0030	+0030	−3·4	−2·6	−1·7	−0·7

NOTE: HW Broadstairs is approx HW Dover +0037.

SHELTER Options: (a) Inner Marina, min depth 2m. Access approx HW ±2 via flap gate and lifting bridge; (b) W Marina, min 2m, access H24; (c) E Marina, min 2m, access H24. Larger vessels can berth on outer wavebreak pontoons of both W and E marinas.

NAVIGATION WPT 51°19'·43N 01°27'·70E, 270°/1·45M to S bkwtr. Commercial shipping uses the well-marked main E-W chan dredged 7·5m. *Due to silting, depths may be significantly less than shown; parts of Eastern Marina, particularly, almost dry at LWS.* Latest information may be obtained from Port Control.

For ent/dep yachts must use the Recommended Yacht Track on the S side of the main buoyed chan. Ent/dep under power, or advise Port Control if unable to motor. Ent/dep Royal Hbr directly; cross the turning basin without delay keeping close to the W Pier to avoid shoal patch alongside E Pier. Holding area to the S of the S bkwtr must be used by yachts to keep the hbr ent clear for freight vessels. Beware Dike Bank to the N and Quern Bank close S of the chan. Cross Ledge and Brake shoals are further S. Speed limit 5kn. See www.rma.eu.com.

LIGHTS AND MARKS Ldg lts 270°: front Dir Oc WRG 10s 10m 5M; rear, Oc 5s 17m 5M. N bkwtr hd = QG 10m 5M; S bkwtr hd = VQ R 10m 5M. At E Pier, **IPTS** (Sigs 2 and 3) visible from seaward and from within Royal Hbr, control appr into hbr limits (abeam Nos 1 & 2 buoys) and ent/exit to/from Royal Hbr. In addition a Fl Orange lt = ferry is under way; no other vessel may enter Hbr limits from seaward or leave Royal Hbr. Ent to inner marina controlled by separate IPTS to stbd of ent. Siren sounded approx 10 mins before gate closes; non-opening indicated by red ball or light.

COMMUNICATIONS (Code 01843) MRCC (01304) 210008; Police 101; Dr 852853; Ⓗ 225544. Marina Office 572110, Hbr Office 572100; Broadstairs HM 861879.

Listen and contact *Ramsgate Port Control* on Ch 14 when intending to enter or leave Royal Hbr. Only when in Royal Hbr call *Ramsgate Marina* Ch 80 for a berth. Ramsgate Dock Office must be called on Ch 14 for information on Inner Marina Lock.

FACILITIES Note: No animals are allowed in Ramsgate Harbour, including the marinas.

Marina www.portoframsgate.co.uk ☎ 572100; 510+300 Ⓥ £2.96, ⚓, ⬢, ▣, ✕, ✎, ▣, Ⓔ, ⚠, ◰, ACA, Gaz, BH (40 ton), ⚓ £32/craft <5tons.

Royal Hbr P & D (0600-2200).

Royal Temple YC ☎ 591766, ▭.

Town: Gas, Gaz, ☷, ✕, ▭, ✉, Ⓑ, ⇌.

ADJACENT HARBOUR

SANDWICH, Kent, 51°16'·83N 01°21'·20E. AC 1827 1828. Richborough differences above; ML 1·4m; Duration 0520. HW Sandwich Town quay is HW Richborough +1. Access via narrow drying channel to Sandwich; arrive off ent at HW Dover. Visitors should seek local know-ledge before arriving by day; night ent definitely not advised. The chan is marked by small lateral buoys and beacons. Visitors' berths on S bank of the River Stour at Town Quay ☎ (01304) 612162. Limited turning room before the swing bridge (opens 1H notice ☎ 01304 620644 or Mobile 0860 378792), 1·7m clearance when closed. Facilities: ⚓ HW±2; ✉, Ⓑ, ☷, ✕, ▭, ⇌, ✈ (Manston).

Marina ☎ 613783 50 ⚓ + some Ⓥ, £2.20, (max LOA 18m, 2·1m draft), ⚓, ▣ & ▣, ✕, ✎, ⚠, ◰, ⚓, BH (15 ton), Gas.

Sandwich Sailing and Motorboat Club ☎ 617650 and **Sandwich Bay Sailing and Water Ski Clubs** offer some facilities. The port is administered by Sandwich Port & Haven Commissioners.

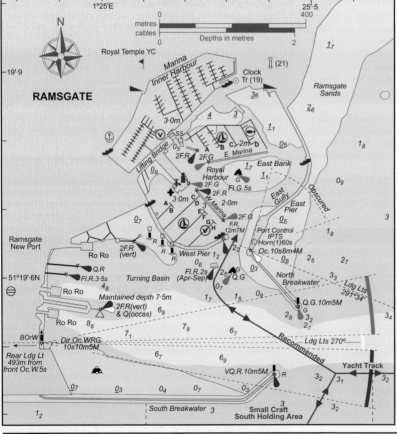

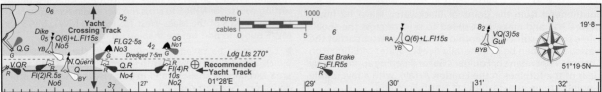

1.6 THAMES ESTUARY

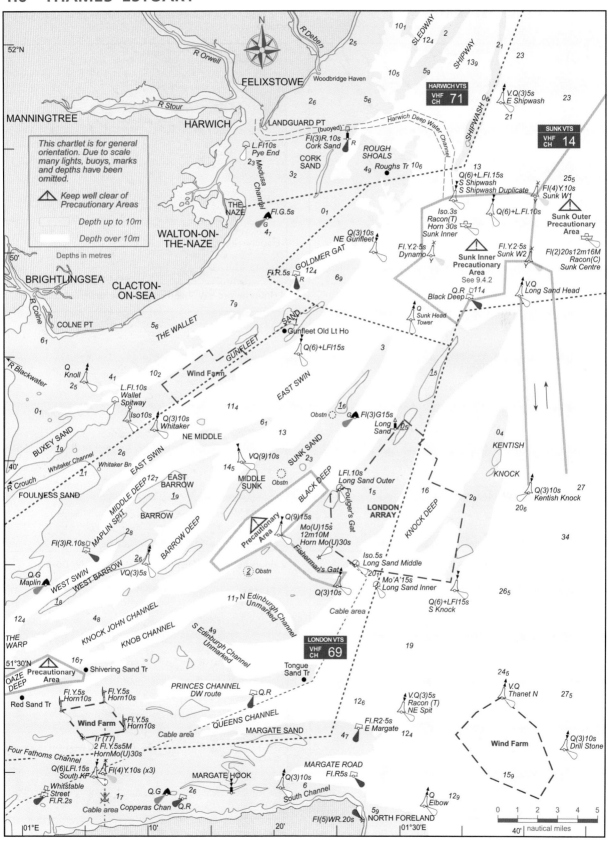

1.7 THAMES ESTUARY TIDAL STREAMS

Due to very strong rates of tidal streams in some areas, eddies may occur. Where possible, some indication of these is shown, but in many areas there is insufficient information or eddies are unstable.

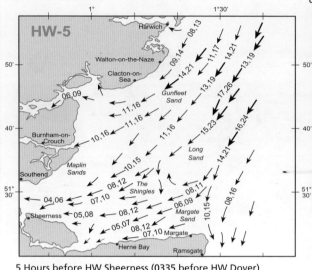

5 Hours before HW Sheerness (0335 before HW Dover)

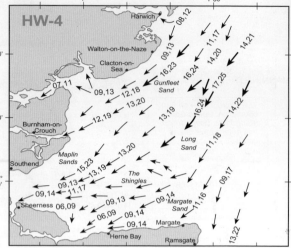

4 Hours before HW Sheerness (0235 before HW Dover)

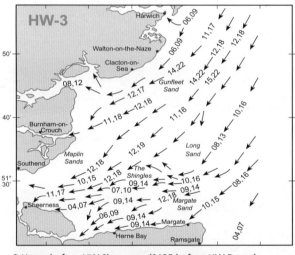

3 Hours before HW Sheerness (0135 before HW Dover)

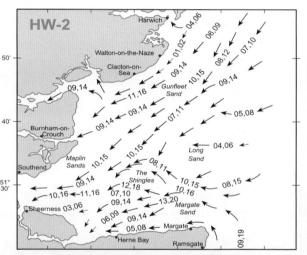

2 Hours before HW Sheerness (0035 before HW Dover)

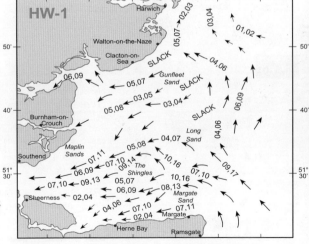

1 Hour before HW Sheerness (0025 after HW Dover)

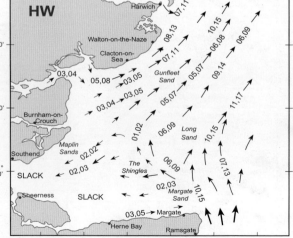

HW Sheerness (0125 after HW Dover)

Due to very strong rates of tidal streams in some areas, eddies may occur. Where possible, some indication of these is shown, but in many areas there is insufficient information or eddies are unstable.

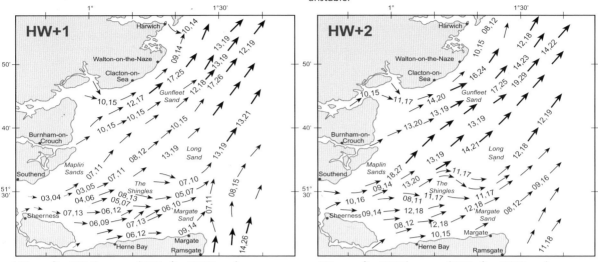

1 Hour after HW Sheerness (0225 after HW Dover)

2 Hours after HW Sheerness (0325 after HW Dover)

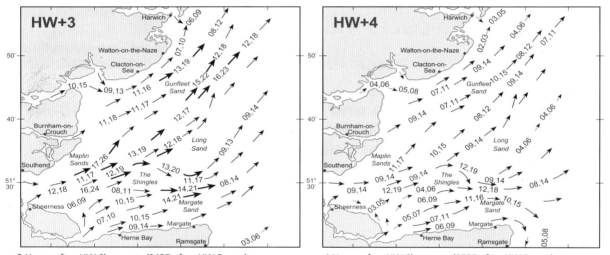

3 Hours after HW Sheerness (0425 after HW Dover)

4 Hours after HW Sheerness (0525 after HW Dover)

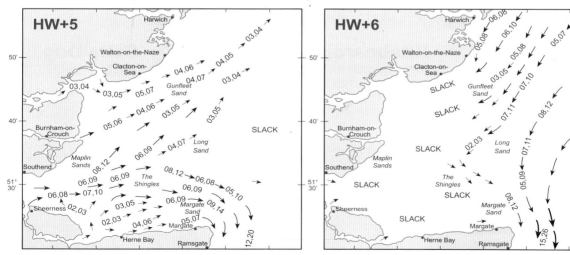

5 Hours after HW Sheerness (0600 before HW Dover)

6 Hours after HW Sheerness (0500 before HW Dover)

E England

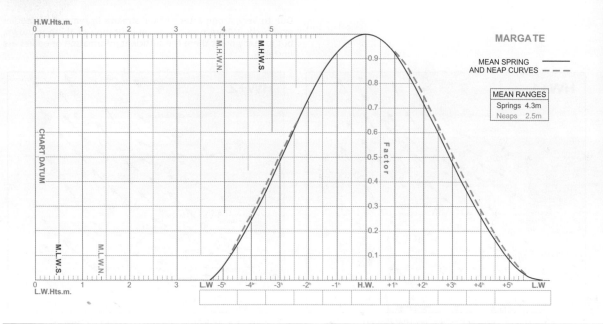

MARGATE

MEAN SPRING
AND NEAP CURVES

MEAN RANGES
Springs 4.3m
Neaps 2.5m

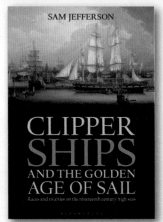

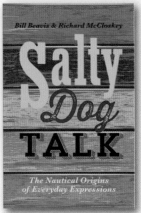

MARGATE LAT 51°23'N LONG 1°23'E

TIMES AND HEIGHTS OF HIGH AND LOW WATERS

STANDARD TIME (UT)
For Summer Time add ONE hour in **non-shaded areas**

Dates in red are **SPRINGS**
Dates in blue are **NEAPS**

YEAR 2015

E England

JANUARY

Day	Time	m	Time	m		Day	Time	m	Time	m
1 TH	0225	1.2	1504	0.9		**16** F	0135	1.5	1416	1.2
	0833	4.3	2123	4.3			0741	4.0	2029	4.1
2 F	0332	1.1	1602	1.0		**17** SA	0257	1.3	1523	1.1
	0941	4.4	2221	4.4			0856	4.1	2133	4.3
3 SA	0433	0.9	1652	0.9		**18** SU	0400	1.0	1618	0.9
	1040	4.5	2310	4.5			0959	4.3	2227	4.5
4 SU	0525	0.8	1734	0.9		**19** M	0454	0.8	1708	0.8
	1128	4.5	2349	4.6			1054	4.5	2315	4.6
5 M	0609	0.7	1812	0.9		**20** TU	0545	0.6	1754	0.7
○	1208	4.6				●	1145	4.7		
6 TU	0022	4.7	1245	4.6		**21** W	0001	4.8	1234	4.9
	0649	0.6	1848	0.9			0633	0.5	1839	0.6
7 W	0055	4.7	1320	4.6		**22** TH	0046	4.9	1323	5.0
	0725	0.6	1922	0.9			0719	0.3	1923	0.6
8 TH	0129	4.7	1356	4.6		**23** F	0133	5.0	1412	5.0
	0758	0.6	1954	0.9			0805	0.3	2008	0.6
9 F	0205	4.7	1431	4.5		**24** SA	0219	5.0	1459	4.9
	0829	0.6	2025	1.0			0850	0.3	2052	0.7
10 SA	0241	4.6	1507	4.4		**25** SU	0304	4.9	1545	4.7
	0900	0.7	2058	1.1			0934	0.3	2137	0.8
11 SU	0316	4.5	1543	4.3		**26** M	0350	4.8	1632	4.5
	0933	0.8	2135	1.2			1019	0.5	2225	0.9
12 M	0352	4.3	1620	4.2		**27** TU	0440	4.6	1726	4.3
	1011	0.9	2218	1.3			1110	0.7	◑ 2323	1.1
13 TU	0431	4.2	1704	4.0		**28** W	0540	4.4	1832	4.2
	1055	1.0	◑ 2309	1.4			1212	0.9		
14 W	0519	4.0	1757	3.9		**29** TH	0036	1.2	1324	1.1
	1150	1.2					0652	4.2	1944	4.1
15 TH	0012	1.5	1259	1.2		**30** F	0156	1.3	1436	1.2
	0619	3.9	1909	3.9			0808	4.2	2056	4.1
						31 SA	0313	1.2	1543	1.2
							0925	4.2	2202	4.3

FEBRUARY

Day	Time	m	Time	m		Day	Time	m	Time	m
1 SU	0424	1.0	1640	1.1		**16** M	0332	1.0	1555	1.0
	1030	4.3	2255	4.4			0936	4.3	2205	4.4
2 M	0518	0.8	1724	1.0		**17** TU	0434	0.8	1649	0.8
	1119	4.4	2337	4.5			1039	4.5	2259	4.6
3 TU	0559	0.7	1759	1.0		**18** W	0528	0.5	1738	0.7
	1158	4.5	○				1132	4.8	● 2347	4.8
4 W	0010	4.6	1231	4.5		**19** TH	0618	0.4	1825	0.6
	0633	0.6	1831	0.9			1222	4.9		
5 TH	0039	4.7	1301	4.6		**20** F	0033	5.0	1310	5.0
	0704	0.6	1903	0.9			0704	0.2	1909	0.5
6 F	0110	4.7	1332	4.6		**21** SA	0119	5.1	1357	5.0
	0734	0.5	1933	0.8			0748	0.2	1953	0.5
7 SA	0144	4.7	1406	4.6		**22** SU	0205	5.1	1442	4.9
	0803	0.6	2004	0.9			0830	0.2	2035	0.6
8 SU	0219	4.7	1440	4.6		**23** M	0249	5.0	1524	4.8
	0832	0.6	2035	0.9			0909	0.3	2117	0.7
9 M	0252	4.6	1513	4.4		**24** TU	0331	4.9	1604	4.5
	0902	0.7	2109	1.0			0948	0.5	2201	0.8
10 TU	0323	4.4	1546	4.3		**25** W	0416	4.7	1650	4.3
	0935	0.8	2144	1.1			1031	0.8	◑ 2252	1.0
11 W	0356	4.3	1622	4.1		**26** TH	0510	4.4	1751	4.1
	1012	0.9	2227	1.2			1127	1.1		
12 TH	0439	4.2	1710	4.0		**27** F	0001	1.2	1244	1.3
	1059	1.1	◑ 2323	1.3			0621	4.1	1908	4.0
13 F	0534	4.0	1812	3.9		**28** SA	0126	1.3	1406	1.4
	1203	1.2					0743	4.0	2024	4.0
14 SA	0042	1.4	1329	1.3						
	0649	3.9	1941	3.9						
15 SU	0217	1.3	1451	1.1						
	0821	4.0	2101	4.1						

MARCH

Day	Time	m	Time	m		Day	Time	m	Time	m
1 SU	0251	1.2	1522	1.3		**16** M	0147	1.2	1423	1.2
	0905	4.1	2136	4.1			0754	4.0	2032	4.1
2 M	0408	1.0	1623	1.2		**17** TU	0307	0.9	1532	1.0
	1012	4.2	2233	4.3			0916	4.3	2141	4.4
3 TU	0501	0.8	1707	1.1		**18** W	0412	0.7	1629	0.8
	1102	4.4	2316	4.5			1022	4.6	2238	4.6
4 W	0539	0.7	1741	1.0		**19** TH	0508	0.4	1719	0.7
	1141	4.4	2350	4.5			1116	4.8	2328	4.8
5 TH	0609	0.6	1812	0.9		**20** F	0557	0.3	1805	0.6
○	1211	4.5				●	1204	4.9		
6 F	0018	4.6	1238	4.5		**21** SA	0014	5.0	1251	4.9
	0637	0.6	1841	0.8			0642	0.2	1850	0.5
7 SA	0049	4.7	1307	4.6		**22** SU	0100	5.1	1336	4.9
	0706	0.5	1912	0.8			0725	0.2	1935	0.5
8 SU	0121	4.7	1340	4.6		**23** M	0146	5.1	1418	4.9
	0734	0.5	1942	0.8			0805	0.2	2018	0.5
9 M	0155	4.7	1414	4.6		**24** TU	0229	5.0	1458	4.7
	0803	0.5	2014	0.8			0841	0.4	2059	0.6
10 TU	0228	4.6	1446	4.4		**25** W	0311	4.9	1535	4.5
	0832	0.6	2046	0.8			0917	0.6	2140	0.7
11 W	0257	4.5	1514	4.3		**26** TH	0354	4.6	1616	4.3
	0904	0.7	2119	0.9			0956	0.9	2227	0.9
12 TH	0327	4.4	1548	4.2		**27** F	0444	4.3	1711	4.1
	0938	0.9	2158	1.0			1046	1.1	◑ 2329	1.1
13 F	0408	4.3	1635	4.1		**28** SA	0549	4.1	1829	3.9
	1022	1.0	◑ 2251	1.2			1158	1.4		
14 SA	0504	4.1	1738	4.0		**29** SU	0050	1.3	1329	1.5
	1125	1.2					0712	3.9	1947	3.9
15 SU	0008	1.3	1254	1.3		**30** M	0216	1.2	1449	1.4
	0619	4.0	1903	3.9			0832	4.0	2056	4.0
						31 TU	0331	1.0	1551	1.3
							0939	4.1	2156	4.2

APRIL

Day	Time	m	Time	m		Day	Time	m	Time	m
1 W	0425	0.9	1637	1.1		**16** TH	0348	0.6	1605	0.8
	1031	4.3	2243	4.4			1000	4.5	2213	4.6
2 TH	0503	0.7	1713	1.0		**17** F	0444	0.4	1656	0.7
	1110	4.4	2319	4.5			1055	4.7	2305	4.8
3 F	0536	0.6	1746	0.9		**18** SA	0532	0.3	1744	0.6
	1141	4.5	2351	4.6			1143	4.8	● 2352	4.9
4 SA	0606	0.6	1818	0.8		**19** SU	0617	0.3	1831	0.5
	1209	4.5	○				1227	4.8		
5 SU	0022	4.6	1239	4.6		**20** M	0038	5.0	1311	4.9
	0636	0.5	1849	0.7			0658	0.3	1916	0.4
6 M	0056	4.7	1313	4.6		**21** TU	0124	5.0	1352	4.8
	0705	0.5	1921	0.7			0737	0.4	2001	0.4
7 TU	0131	4.7	1348	4.6		**22** W	0209	5.0	1431	4.7
	0735	0.5	1954	0.7			0814	0.5	2042	0.5
8 W	0205	4.6	1421	4.5		**23** TH	0251	4.8	1509	4.5
	0806	0.6	2027	0.7			0850	0.7	2123	0.7
9 TH	0237	4.5	1451	4.4		**24** F	0333	4.6	1548	4.3
	0839	0.7	2103	0.8			0928	0.9	2206	0.8
10 F	0310	4.4	1527	4.3		**25** SA	0419	4.3	1635	4.1
	0916	0.8	2144	0.9			1013	1.2	◑ 2300	1.0
11 SA	0353	4.3	1616	4.2		**26** SU	0515	4.0	1741	3.9
	1002	1.0	2237	1.0			1112	1.4		
12 SU	0450	4.2	1718	4.0		**27** M	0010	1.2	1236	1.6
	1105	1.2	◑ 2353	1.1			0633	3.9	1903	3.9
13 M	0604	4.0	1838	4.0		**28** TU	0130	1.2	1404	1.5
	1230	1.2					0748	3.9	2011	3.9
14 TU	0124	1.0	1357	1.2		**29** W	0239	1.1	1508	1.3
	0734	4.1	2005	4.1			0852	4.0	2109	4.1
15 W	0243	0.8	1508	1.0		**30** TH	0334	0.9	1558	1.1
	0855	4.3	2115	4.4			0945	4.2	2159	4.3

Chart Datum: 2·5 metres below Ordnance Datum (Newlyn). HAT is 5·2 metres above Chart Datum.

STANDARD TIME (UT)
For Summer Time add ONE hour in **non-shaded areas**

MARGATE LAT 51°23′N LONG 1°23′E
TIMES AND HEIGHTS OF HIGH AND LOW WATERS

Dates in red are SPRINGS
Dates in blue are NEAPS

YEAR 2015

MAY

Day	Time	m	Day	Time	m
1 F	0419 / 1029 / 1639 / 2242	0.8 / 4.3 / 1.0 / 4.4	16 SA	0417 / 1032 / 1634 / 2241	0.5 / 4.6 / 0.7 / 4.7
2 SA	0458 / 1105 / 1717 / 2319	0.7 / 4.4 / 0.9 / 4.5	17 SU	0506 / 1120 / 1724 / 2331	0.4 / 4.7 / 0.6 / 4.8
3 SU	0533 / 1137 / 1753 / 2354	0.6 / 4.5 / 0.9 / 4.6	18 M ●	0551 / 1205 / 1812	0.4 / 4.7 / 0.5
4 M ○	0606 / 1210 / 1827	0.6 / 4.6 / 0.7	19 TU	0018 / 0632 / 1247 / 1900	4.9 / 0.5 / 4.7 / 0.4
5 TU	0029 / 0637 / 1246 / 1902	4.6 / 0.6 / 4.6 / 0.6	20 W	0105 / 0713 / 1328 / 1945	4.9 / 0.5 / 4.7 / 0.4
6 W	0107 / 0710 / 1323 / 1937	4.7 / 0.6 / 4.6 / 0.6	21 TH	0149 / 0752 / 1407 / 2028	4.8 / 0.6 / 4.7 / 0.5
7 TH	0145 / 0744 / 1400 / 2014	4.6 / 0.6 / 4.6 / 0.6	22 F	0232 / 0828 / 1445 / 2107	4.7 / 0.8 / 4.5 / 0.6
8 F	0224 / 0821 / 1437 / 2053	4.6 / 0.7 / 4.5 / 0.7	23 SA	0312 / 0905 / 1523 / 2146	4.5 / 1.0 / 4.4 / 0.8
9 SA	0304 / 0903 / 1518 / 2138	4.5 / 0.8 / 4.4 / 0.7	24 SU	0354 / 0945 / 1605 / 2230	4.3 / 1.1 / 4.2 / 0.9
10 SU	0350 / 0952 / 1607 / 2234	4.4 / 0.9 / 4.3 / 0.8	25 M ☽	0440 / 1033 / 1655 / 2325	4.1 / 1.3 / 4.1 / 1.0
11 M ☽	0445 / 1054 / 1705 / 2345	4.3 / 1.1 / 4.2 / 0.8	26 TU	0540 / 1133 / 1803	3.9 / 1.5 / 3.9
12 TU	0554 / 1210 / 1818	4.2 / 1.1 / 4.1	27 W	0033 / 0655 / 1255 / 1919	1.1 / 3.9 / 1.5 / 3.9
13 W	0104 / 0715 / 1331 / 1938	0.8 / 4.2 / 1.1 / 4.2	28 TH	0145 / 0800 / 1416 / 2020	1.1 / 3.9 / 1.4 / 4.0
14 TH	0218 / 0831 / 1441 / 2047	0.7 / 4.3 / 1.0 / 4.4	29 F	0245 / 0856 / 1514 / 2114	1.0 / 4.1 / 1.3 / 4.1
15 F	0322 / 0936 / 1540 / 2147	0.6 / 4.5 / 0.8 / 4.6	30 SA	0335 / 0944 / 1602 / 2202	0.9 / 4.2 / 1.1 / 4.3
			31 SU	0420 / 1027 / 1646 / 2245	0.8 / 4.3 / 0.9 / 4.4

JUNE

Day	Time	m	Day	Time	m
1 M	0501 / 1106 / 1727 / 2325	0.7 / 4.4 / 0.8 / 4.5	16 TU ●	0530 / 1147 / 1800	0.7 / 4.6 / 0.6
2 TU ○	0539 / 1144 / 1806	0.7 / 4.5 / 0.7	17 W	0003 / 0613 / 1228 / 1847	4.7 / 0.6 / 4.7 / 0.5
3 W	0005 / 0614 / 1223 / 1845	4.6 / 0.7 / 4.6 / 0.6	18 TH	0048 / 0654 / 1307 / 1931	4.8 / 0.7 / 4.7 / 0.5
4 TH	0046 / 0650 / 1303 / 1924	4.6 / 0.7 / 4.7 / 0.6	19 F	0131 / 0732 / 1344 / 2011	4.7 / 0.8 / 4.7 / 0.5
5 F	0129 / 0729 / 1344 / 2005	4.7 / 0.6 / 4.7 / 0.5	20 SA	0211 / 0808 / 1422 / 2048	4.6 / 0.8 / 4.6 / 0.6
6 SA	0214 / 0810 / 1426 / 2049	4.7 / 0.6 / 4.6 / 0.5	21 SU	0249 / 0843 / 1459 / 2123	4.5 / 0.9 / 4.5 / 0.7
7 SU	0259 / 0855 / 1510 / 2136	4.6 / 0.7 / 4.6 / 0.6	22 M	0327 / 0919 / 1537 / 2200	4.4 / 1.1 / 4.4 / 0.8
8 M	0347 / 0945 / 1558 / 2231	4.5 / 0.9 / 4.5 / 0.6	23 TU	0406 / 0959 / 1618 / 2242	4.2 / 1.2 / 4.3 / 0.9
9 TU ☽	0439 / 1042 / 1652 / 2333	4.4 / 1.1 / 4.4 / 0.7	24 W ☽	0450 / 1046 / 1704 / 2333	4.1 / 1.3 / 4.1 / 1.0
10 W	0541 / 1148 / 1757	4.3 / 1.1 / 4.3	25 TH	0542 / 1142 / 1801	3.9 / 1.4 / 4.0
11 TH	0042 / 0654 / 1302 / 1910	0.7 / 4.3 / 1.1 / 4.3	26 F	0035 / 0651 / 1255 / 1916	1.1 / 3.9 / 1.5 / 3.9
12 F	0151 / 0806 / 1414 / 2019	0.7 / 4.3 / 1.1 / 4.4	27 SA	0148 / 0801 / 1421 / 2022	1.1 / 4.0 / 1.4 / 4.0
13 SA	0255 / 0911 / 1517 / 2123	0.7 / 4.4 / 0.9 / 4.5	28 SU	0251 / 0859 / 1522 / 2119	1.0 / 4.1 / 1.2 / 4.2
14 SU	0353 / 1010 / 1615 / 2223	0.6 / 4.5 / 0.8 / 4.6	29 M	0343 / 0951 / 1614 / 2211	0.9 / 4.3 / 1.0 / 4.3
15 M	0444 / 1102 / 1709 / 2316	0.6 / 4.6 / 0.7 / 4.7	30 TU	0431 / 1037 / 1702 / 2259	0.8 / 4.4 / 0.9 / 4.5

JULY

Day	Time	m	Day	Time	m
1 W	0514 / 1121 / 1747 / 2344	0.8 / 4.5 / 0.7 / 4.6	16 TH ●	0559 / 1214 / 1836	0.8 / 4.6 / 0.6
2 TH ○	0555 / 1202 / 1830	0.7 / 4.6 / 0.6	17 F	0035 / 0636 / 1249 / 1914	4.7 / 0.8 / 4.7 / 0.5
3 F	0029 / 0635 / 1245 / 1913	4.7 / 0.7 / 4.7 / 0.5	18 SA	0112 / 0713 / 1323 / 1950	4.6 / 0.8 / 4.7 / 0.5
4 SA	0116 / 0717 / 1329 / 1957	4.7 / 0.6 / 4.8 / 0.4	19 SU	0148 / 0747 / 1358 / 2023	4.6 / 0.9 / 4.7 / 0.6
5 SU	0203 / 0801 / 1415 / 2042	4.8 / 0.6 / 4.8 / 0.4	20 M	0223 / 0820 / 1434 / 2055	4.5 / 0.9 / 4.6 / 0.7
6 M	0251 / 0846 / 1500 / 2129	4.8 / 0.7 / 4.8 / 0.4	21 TU	0258 / 0853 / 1510 / 2127	4.5 / 1.0 / 4.6 / 0.7
7 TU	0338 / 0933 / 1546 / 2218	4.7 / 0.8 / 4.7 / 0.5	22 W	0334 / 0928 / 1545 / 2202	4.3 / 1.1 / 4.4 / 0.9
8 W ☽	0427 / 1024 / 1636 / 2313	4.5 / 0.9 / 4.6 / 0.6	23 TH	0411 / 1007 / 1624 / 2243	4.2 / 1.2 / 4.3 / 1.0
9 TH	0523 / 1123 / 1734	4.4 / 1.0 / 4.5	24 F ☽	0452 / 1054 / 1708 / 2333	4.1 / 1.3 / 4.1 / 1.1
10 F	0015 / 0628 / 1233 / 1843	0.7 / 4.3 / 1.1 / 4.4	25 SA	0542 / 1152 / 1804	4.0 / 1.5 / 4.0
11 SA	0123 / 0738 / 1347 / 1954	0.8 / 4.2 / 1.1 / 4.4	26 SU	0038 / 0648 / 1311 / 1919	1.3 / 3.9 / 1.5 / 4.0
12 SU	0230 / 0847 / 1457 / 2105	0.9 / 4.3 / 1.0 / 4.4	27 M	0158 / 0809 / 1438 / 2035	1.2 / 4.0 / 1.3 / 4.1
13 M	0332 / 0952 / 1602 / 2212	0.9 / 4.4 / 0.9 / 4.5	28 TU	0307 / 0914 / 1542 / 2140	1.1 / 4.2 / 1.1 / 4.3
14 TU	0429 / 1048 / 1702 / 2308	0.9 / 4.5 / 0.8 / 4.6	29 W	0403 / 1010 / 1637 / 2236	1.0 / 4.4 / 0.9 / 4.5
15 W	0517 / 1135 / 1752 / 2354	0.9 / 4.6 / 0.6 / 4.6	30 TH	0452 / 1059 / 1727 / 2326	0.9 / 4.6 / 0.7 / 4.7
			31 F ○	0538 / 1144 / 1814	0.8 / 4.7 / 0.5

AUGUST

Day	Time	m	Day	Time	m
1 SA	0014 / 0621 / 1229 / 1859	4.8 / 0.7 / 4.8 / 0.4	16 SU	0051 / 0651 / 1300 / 1924	4.6 / 0.9 / 4.7 / 0.6
2 SU	0102 / 0704 / 1314 / 1944	4.8 / 0.6 / 4.9 / 0.3	17 M	0121 / 0724 / 1333 / 1954	4.6 / 0.9 / 4.8 / 0.6
3 M	0150 / 0748 / 1400 / 2028	4.9 / 0.6 / 5.0 / 0.3	18 TU	0154 / 0756 / 1408 / 2023	4.6 / 0.9 / 4.7 / 0.6
4 TU	0237 / 0832 / 1445 / 2112	4.9 / 0.6 / 5.0 / 0.3	19 W	0228 / 0827 / 1442 / 2053	4.6 / 0.9 / 4.7 / 0.7
5 W	0323 / 0916 / 1529 / 2156	4.8 / 0.7 / 4.9 / 0.5	20 TH	0302 / 0900 / 1515 / 2124	4.4 / 1.0 / 4.5 / 0.8
6 TH	0408 / 1003 / 1616 / 2244	4.6 / 0.9 / 4.8 / 0.6	21 F	0335 / 0934 / 1549 / 2200	4.3 / 1.1 / 4.4 / 1.0
7 F ☽	0457 / 1056 / 1710 / 2341	4.4 / 1.0 / 4.6 / 0.9	22 SA ☽	0411 / 1014 / 1628 / 2243	4.2 / 1.2 / 4.2 / 1.3
8 SA	0558 / 1202 / 1817	4.3 / 1.1 / 4.4	23 SU	0455 / 1106 / 1719 / 2343	4.1 / 1.4 / 4.1 / 1.3
9 SU	0051 / 0710 / 1321 / 1932	1.0 / 4.1 / 1.2 / 4.3	24 M	0553 / 1218 / 1827	3.9 / 1.5 / 4.0
10 M	0205 / 0823 / 1440 / 2051	1.1 / 4.2 / 1.2 / 4.3	25 TU	0104 / 0714 / 1353 / 1954	1.4 / 3.9 / 1.4 / 4.0
11 TU	0316 / 0934 / 1555 / 2204	1.2 / 4.3 / 1.0 / 4.4	26 W	0230 / 0838 / 1510 / 2111	1.3 / 4.1 / 1.2 / 4.3
12 W	0419 / 1034 / 1656 / 2300	1.1 / 4.4 / 0.8 / 4.5	27 TH	0336 / 0943 / 1612 / 2215	1.1 / 4.3 / 0.9 / 4.5
13 TH	0507 / 1122 / 1743 / 2345	1.0 / 4.6 / 0.7 / 4.6	28 F	0430 / 1037 / 1706 / 2308	0.9 / 4.6 / 0.7 / 4.7
14 F ●	0545 / 1200 / 1820	1.0 / 4.6 / 0.6	29 SA ○	0518 / 1124 / 1754 / 2357	0.8 / 4.8 / 0.5 / 4.9
15 SA	0020 / 0619 / 1231 / 1853	4.7 / 0.8 / 4.7 / 0.6	30 SU	0603 / 1209 / 1840	0.7 / 4.9 / 0.4
			31 M	0044 / 0647 / 1254 / 1924	5.0 / 0.6 / 5.0 / 0.4

Chart Datum: 2·5 metres below Ordnance Datum (Newlyn). HAT is 5·2 metres above Chart Datum.

》 FREE monthly updates from 《
www.reedsalmanac.co.uk

STANDARD TIME (UT)
For Summer Time add ONE hour in **non-shaded areas**

MARGATE   LAT 51°23'N   LONG 1°23'E
TIMES AND HEIGHTS OF HIGH AND LOW WATERS

Dates in red are **SPRINGS**
Dates in blue are NEAPS

YEAR 2015

E England

SEPTEMBER

Time	m		Time	m
1 TU	0131 5.0 / 0731 0.6 / 1340 5.1 / 2006 0.3	**16** W	0123 4.7 / 0732 0.8 / 1341 4.8 / 1951 0.7	
2 W	0217 5.0 / 0814 0.6 / 1426 5.1 / 2047 0.4	**17** TH	0157 4.6 / 0803 0.9 / 1415 4.7 / 2020 0.7	
3 TH	0301 4.8 / 0857 0.7 / 1509 5.0 / 2127 0.6	**18** F	0230 4.5 / 0834 0.9 / 1447 4.6 / 2050 0.9	
4 F	0342 4.6 / 0941 0.8 / 1554 4.8 / 2210 0.8	**19** SA	0301 4.4 / 0907 1.0 / 1518 4.4 / 2123 1.0	
5 SA	0427 4.4 / 1030 1.0 / 1646 4.6 / 2303 1.1	**20** SU	0332 4.3 / 0944 1.1 / 1554 4.3 / 2203 1.2	
6 SU	0524 4.2 / 1134 1.2 / 1751 4.3	**21** M	0415 4.1 / 1032 1.3 / 1645 4.1 / 2300 1.4	
7 M	0016 1.3 / 0639 4.1 / 1256 1.3 / 1912 4.2	**22** TU	0513 4.0 / 1140 1.4 / 1753 4.0	
8 TU	0140 1.4 / 0757 4.1 / 1421 1.2 / 2036 4.2	**23** W	0022 1.5 / 0629 3.9 / 1316 1.3 / 1920 4.1	
9 W	0259 1.4 / 0911 4.2 / 1541 1.0 / 2150 4.4	**24** TH	0156 1.4 / 0802 4.1 / 1440 1.1 / 2045 4.3	
10 TH	0404 1.2 / 1013 4.4 / 1640 0.9 / 2244 4.5	**25** F	0309 1.1 / 0914 4.3 / 1546 0.8 / 2153 4.6	
11 F	0451 1.1 / 1101 4.5 / 1723 0.7 / 2327 4.6	**26** SA	0406 0.9 / 1011 4.6 / 1641 0.6 / 2248 4.8	
12 SA	0527 1.0 / 1138 4.6 / 1756 0.7 / 2359 4.6	**27** SU	0455 0.8 / 1100 4.8 / 1730 0.4 / 2336 5.0	
13 SU	0558 0.9 / 1206 4.7 / 1825 0.6 ●	**28**	0541 0.7 / 1146 5.0 / 1816 0.3 ○	
14 M	0024 4.6 / 0629 0.9 / 1235 4.7 / 1853 0.6	**29** TU	0021 5.0 / 0626 0.6 / 1231 5.1 / 1858 0.3	
15 TU	0052 4.7 / 0701 0.8 / 1306 4.8 / 1923 0.6	**30** W	0107 5.0 / 0711 0.5 / 1318 5.2 / 1940 0.4	

OCTOBER

Time	m		Time	m
1 TH	0151 5.0 / 0755 0.6 / 1404 5.1 / 2019 0.5	**16** F	0127 4.7 / 0741 0.8 / 1348 4.7 / 1950 0.8	
2 F	0233 4.8 / 0838 0.6 / 1449 5.0 / 2057 0.7	**17** SA	0201 4.6 / 0813 0.8 / 1422 4.6 / 2022 0.9	
3 SA	0314 4.7 / 0922 0.8 / 1534 4.8 / 2138 0.9	**18** SU	0231 4.5 / 0847 0.9 / 1454 4.5 / 2056 1.0	
4 SU	0356 4.4 / 1009 0.9 / 1623 4.5 / 2227 1.2 ◑	**19** M	0303 4.4 / 0925 1.0 / 1533 4.3 / 2138 1.2	
5 M	0448 4.2 / 1109 1.1 / 1726 4.2 / 2335 1.5	**20** TU	0347 4.2 / 1012 1.1 / 1624 4.2 / 2234 1.3 ◑	
6 TU	0603 4.0 / 1226 1.3 / 1847 4.1	**21** W	0446 4.1 / 1118 1.2 / 1730 4.1 / 2351 1.4	
7 W	0105 1.6 / 0724 4.0 / 1352 1.2 / 2009 4.1	**22** TH	0558 4.0 / 1246 1.2 / 1854 4.1	
8 TH	0230 1.5 / 0836 4.1 / 1509 1.1 / 2120 4.3	**23** F	0122 1.4 / 0726 4.1 / 1409 1.0 / 2019 4.3	
9 F	0335 1.4 / 0938 4.3 / 1607 0.9 / 2215 4.5	**24** SA	0238 1.2 / 0842 4.3 / 1517 0.7 / 2127 4.6	
10 SA	0423 1.2 / 1027 4.4 / 1649 0.8 / 2256 4.5	**25** SU	0339 0.9 / 0942 4.6 / 1613 0.6 / 2223 4.8	
11 SU	0500 1.0 / 1106 4.6 / 1722 0.7 / 2328 4.6	**26** M	0430 0.8 / 1034 4.8 / 1703 0.4 / 2312 4.9	
12 M	0533 0.9 / 1137 4.6 / 1752 0.7 / 2354 4.6	**27** TU	0518 0.7 / 1122 5.0 / 1749 0.4 / 2357 5.0 ○	
13 TU	0605 0.9 / 1207 4.7 / 1823 0.7 ●	**28** W	0605 0.6 / 1208 5.1 / 1832 0.4	
14 W	0021 4.7 / 0637 0.8 / 1239 4.8 / 1852 0.7	**29** TH	0041 4.9 / 0651 0.5 / 1256 5.1 / 1913 0.5	
15 TH	0053 4.7 / 0709 0.8 / 1313 4.7 / 1921 0.7	**30** F	0124 4.9 / 0738 0.6 / 1344 5.1 / 1954 0.6	
		31 SA	0206 4.8 / 0823 0.6 / 1429 4.9 / 2032 0.8	

NOVEMBER

Time	m		Time	m
1 SU	0247 4.7 / 0906 0.7 / 1514 4.7 / 2111 1.0	**16** M	0212 4.6 / 0833 0.8 / 1442 4.5 / 2039 0.9	
2 M	0328 4.5 / 0951 0.8 / 1601 4.5 / 2156 1.3	**17** TU	0249 4.5 / 0914 0.8 / 1523 4.4 / 2124 1.1	
3 TU	0415 4.3 / 1044 1.0 / 1657 4.2 / 2253 1.5 ◑	**18** W	0334 4.3 / 1003 0.9 / 1613 4.3 / 2218 1.2	
4 W	0518 4.0 / 1150 1.2 / 1811 4.0	**19** TH	0428 4.2 / 1105 1.0 / 1714 4.2 / 2326 1.3 ◑	
5 TH	0013 1.7 / 0641 3.9 / 1308 1.2 / 1928 4.0	**20** F	0533 4.2 / 1221 1.0 / 1829 4.2	
6 F	0144 1.7 / 0751 4.0 / 1420 1.2 / 2034 4.1	**21** SA	0048 1.3 / 0652 4.2 / 1338 0.9 / 1950 4.3	
7 SA	0252 1.5 / 0852 4.1 / 1518 1.0 / 2130 4.3	**22** SU	0205 1.2 / 0809 4.3 / 1446 0.7 / 2059 4.5	
8 SU	0344 1.3 / 0944 4.3 / 1604 0.9 / 2215 4.4	**23** M	0310 1.0 / 0913 4.5 / 1545 0.6 / 2158 4.7	
9 M	0427 1.1 / 1027 4.4 / 1643 0.8 / 2251 4.5	**24** TU	0406 0.8 / 1010 4.7 / 1637 0.5 / 2250 4.8	
10 TU	0505 1.0 / 1105 4.5 / 1719 0.8 / 2322 4.6	**25** W	0457 0.7 / 1101 4.8 / 1724 0.5 / 2336 4.8 ○	
11 W	0541 0.9 / 1138 4.6 / 1753 0.7 / 2353 4.7 ●	**26** TH	0547 0.6 / 1151 4.9 / 1809 0.5	
12 TH	0615 0.8 / 1212 4.7 / 1824 0.7	**27** F	0019 4.9 / 0636 0.5 / 1239 5.0 / 1852 0.6	
13 F	0026 4.7 / 0648 0.7 / 1248 4.7 / 1854 0.7	**28** SA	0102 4.9 / 0724 0.5 / 1326 5.0 / 1933 0.7	
14 SA	0101 4.7 / 0721 0.7 / 1326 4.7 / 1926 0.8	**29** SU	0144 4.8 / 0809 0.5 / 1412 4.8 / 2012 0.9	
15 SU	0137 4.7 / 0756 0.7 / 1403 4.6 / 2000 0.8	**30** M	0224 4.7 / 0852 0.6 / 1455 4.7 / 2050 1.0	

DECEMBER

Time	m		Time	m
1 TU	0304 4.5 / 0933 0.8 / 1538 4.4 / 2129 1.2	**16** W	0239 4.6 / 0907 0.6 / 1516 4.5 / 2114 0.9	
2 W	0346 4.4 / 1016 0.9 / 1624 4.2 / 2215 1.4	**17** TH	0323 4.5 / 0955 0.7 / 1604 4.4 / 2204 1.1	
3 TH	0434 4.2 / 1108 1.1 / 1721 4.0 / 2311 1.6 ◑	**18** F	0413 4.4 / 1050 0.8 / 1657 4.3 / 2303 1.2 ◑	
4 F	0539 4.0 / 1212 1.2 / 1834 3.9	**19** SA	0510 4.3 / 1155 0.8 / 1803 4.3	
5 SA	0029 1.7 / 0658 3.9 / 1324 1.2 / 1941 4.0	**20** SU	0013 1.2 / 0619 4.3 / 1306 0.8 / 1920 4.3	
6 SU	0158 1.6 / 0802 4.0 / 1426 1.1 / 2038 4.1	**21** M	0131 1.2 / 0737 4.3 / 1416 0.8 / 2031 4.4	
7 M	0259 1.4 / 0858 4.1 / 1519 1.0 / 2129 4.2	**22** TU	0242 1.1 / 0846 4.4 / 1519 0.8 / 2135 4.5	
8 TU	0350 1.2 / 0948 4.2 / 1605 0.9 / 2213 4.4	**23** W	0345 0.9 / 0951 4.5 / 1615 0.7 / 2232 4.6	
9 W	0434 1.1 / 1032 4.4 / 1647 0.9 / 2252 4.5	**24** TH	0442 0.8 / 1049 4.7 / 1706 0.7 / 2322 4.7	
10 TH	0515 0.9 / 1111 4.5 / 1726 0.8 / 2328 4.6	**25** F	0537 0.6 / 1140 4.8 / 1753 0.7 ○	
11 F	0553 0.8 / 1149 4.6 / 1800 0.7 ●	**26** SA	0005 4.8 / 0626 0.5 / 1228 4.8 / 1836 0.7	
12 SA	0003 4.7 / 0630 0.7 / 1227 4.6 / 1833 0.8	**27** SU	0047 4.8 / 0713 0.5 / 1312 4.8 / 1917 0.8	
13 SU	0041 4.7 / 0706 0.7 / 1307 4.7 / 1908 0.8	**28** M	0126 4.8 / 0756 0.5 / 1354 4.7 / 1954 0.9	
14 M	0119 4.7 / 0743 0.6 / 1349 4.7 / 1946 0.8	**29** TU	0204 4.7 / 0834 0.6 / 1434 4.6 / 2030 1.0	
15 TU	0159 4.7 / 0823 0.6 / 1432 4.6 / 2028 0.8	**30** W	0242 4.6 / 0910 0.7 / 1512 4.5 / 2104 1.1	
		31 TH	0319 4.5 / 0945 0.8 / 1550 4.3 / 2142 1.2	

Chart Datum: 2·5 metres below Ordnance Datum (Newlyn). HAT is 5·2 metres above Chart Datum.

1.8 WHITSTABLE

Kent **51°21'·86N 01°01'·46E** ✳☸◊◊✿✿

CHARTS AC 5606, 1607, 2571; Imray C1, 2100

TIDES +0135 Dover; ML 3·0; Duration 0605

Standard Port MARGATE (←)

Times				Height (metres)			
High Water		Low Water		MHWS	MHWN	MLWN	MLWS
0100	0700	0100	0700	4·8	3·9	1·4	0·5
1300	1900	1300	1900				
Differences HERNE BAY							
+0022	+0020	+0019	+0017	+0·6	+0·3	+0·2	+0·1
WHITSTABLE APPROACHES							
+0042	+0029	+0025	+0050	+0·6	+0·6	+0·1	0·0

SHELTER Good, except in strong winds from NNW to NE. Harbour dries up to 0·4m. Yacht berths are limited since priority is given to commercial shipping. Fender board needed against piled quays or seek a mooring to NW of harbour (controlled by YC).

NAVIGATION WPT 51°22'·65N 01°01'·10E, 345°/0·83M to W Quay dolphin. From E keep well seaward of Whitstable Street, a hard drying sandspit, which extends 1M N from the coast; shoals a further 1M to seaward are marked by Whitstable Street NCM lt buoy. From W avoid Columbine and Pollard Spits.

Approach, not before half flood, via Oyster PHM lt buoy to harbour entrance. Entry best at HW±1.

LIGHTS AND MARKS Off head of W Quay on a dolphin, ⚡ Fl G 5s, covers the approaches.

COMMUNICATIONS (Code 01227) MRCC (01255) 675518; Police 101; Dr 594400. HM 274086.

Whitstable Harbour Radio VHF Ch **09** 12 16 (Mon–Fri: 0830–1700 LT. Other times: HW –3 to HW+1). Tidal info on request.

FACILITIES www.canterbury.gov.uk HM ☎ 274086, ⌷ £10, ⬇, D.
Whitstable YC ☎ 272942, M, ✕, ▬ HW ±3, L, ⬇, ⬜.
Services: ✎, C,⬛, ACA, △, Gas, Ⓔ.
Town: ▣, ⒑, ☷, ✕, ⬜, ✉, Ⓑ, ⇌, ✈ Lydd/Manston.

MINOR HARBOURS WEST OF NORTH FORELAND
MARGATE, Kent, **51°23'·43N 01°22'·65E**. AC 5606,1 827, 1828, 323; Imray Y7, C1; Stanfords 5, 8. HW+0045 on Dover; ML 2·6; Duration 0610; Standard Port (←). Small hbr drying 3m, inside bkwtr (Stone Pier) FR 17m 4M; exposed to NW'lies. Appr's: from E, via Longnose NCM buoy, keeping about 5ca offshore; from N, via Margate PHM lt buoy; from W via Gore Chan and S Chan to SE Margate ECM lt buoy. Facilities: Margate YC ☎ (01843) 292602, ⬜.

Town, 10 Slips all HW±2, check suitability with Foreshore Office ☎ (01843) 577529, ⒑ & ⒓, ✕, ☷, ⬜, ✉, Ⓑ, ⇌, ✈ Manston.

HERNE BAY, Kent, **51°22'·40N 01°07'·22E**. AC 5606, 1607. Close E of Pavillion (old pier), 400m long bkwtr 'Neptunes Arm' gives well sheltered drying ⚓ for craft <8m. Exposed to strong NE'lies at HW springs when Thames Barrier closed as seas may then top the bkwtr. 3 Slips (HW±2½ to HW±3). Foreshore Manager ☎ (01227) 266719. Herne Bay SC ☎ (01227) 375650. Lts: QW 8m 4M is 6ca offshore (former pier hd); bkwtr hd 2FR (vert); pier hd 2FG (vert); R bn on B dolphin, Fl Y 5s, is approx 1M ENE of bkwtr hd. Reculvers twrs are conspic 3M to the E.

Town, ⒑ & ⒓, Ⓔ, ✕, ☷, ⬜, ✉, Ⓑ, ▣, ⇌, ✈ Lydd/Manston.

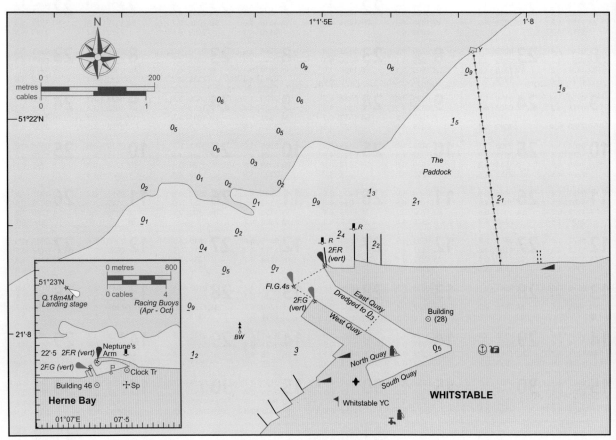

1.9 THE SWALE

Kent ✿✿❋◊◊◊✿✿

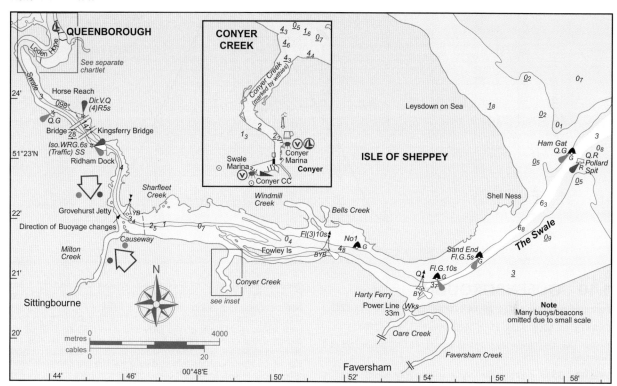

CHARTS

AC 5606, 2482, 2571, 2572, 1834, 3683; Imray Y18, C1, 2100

TIDES

Queenborough +0130 Dover; Harty Ferry +0120 Dover; ML (Harty Ferry) 3·0; Duration 0610. Faversham HW differences are –0·2m on Sheerness; no other data.

Standard Port SHEERNESS (⟶)

Times				Height (metres)			
High Water		Low Water		MHWS	MHWN	MLWN	MLWS
0200	0800	0200	0700	5·8	4·7	1·5	0·6
1400	2000	1400	1900				
Differences R. SWALE (Grovehurst Jetty)							
–0007	0000	0000	+0016	0·0	0·0	0·0	–0·1

Grovehurst Jetty is close N of the ent to Milton Creek.

SHELTER

Excellent in the Swale, the 14M chan between the Isle of Sheppey and the N Kent coast, from Shell Ness in the E to Queenborough in the W. Yachts can enter the drying creeks of Faversham, Oare, Conyer, and Milton. Beware wrecks at ent to Faversham Creek. Many moorings line the chan from Faversham to Conyer Creeks. See Queenborough for all-tide access.

NAVIGATION

E ent WPT: Whitstable Street lit PHM, 51°24′·00N 01°01′·54E, at ent to well marked buoyed chan. Speed limit 8kn. The middle section from 1·5M E of Conyer Creek to 0·5M E of Milton Creek is narrowed by drying mudbanks and carries least depths of 0·4m. At Milton Creek direction of buoyage changes. There are numerous oyster beds in the area. Kingsferry Bridge opens for masted craft on request, but subject to railway trains; temp anchs off SW bank. The power lines crossing SE of the br have a clearance of 30m. **W ent** is marked by Queenborough Spit ECM buoy, Q (3) 10s, 1M S of Garrison Pt, at 51°25′·81N 00°43′·93E.

LIGHTS AND MARKS

See chartlet and 1.3. In W Swale lights intended for large coasters using the narrow chan are:

No 5 Bn Oc WRG 6s; vis: 161°-G-166°-W-167°-R-172°. Round Loden Hope bend: two Q WG and one Q WRG on bns; keep in G sectors. See Queenborough chartlet. Horse Reach ldg lts 113°: front QG 7m 5M; rear Fl G 3s 10m 6M. Dir lt 098°, VQ (4) R 5s 6m 5M. Kingsferry Bridge: Dir WRG, 142°-G-147°-W-148°-R-153° 9m. Lts on bridge: two x 2 FG (vert) on SW buttresses; two x 2 FR (vert) on NE. Road bridge has a vertical clearance of 28m.

Kingsferry Bridge traffic sigs:

No lts	= Bridge down (3·35m MHWS).
Al Q ●/◐	= Centre span lifting.
F ●	= Bridge open (29m MHWS).
Q ●	= Centre span lowering. Keep clear.
Q ◉	= Bridge out of action.

Request bridge opening on VHF Ch 10 (or Ch 74 if no response).

COMMUNICATIONS

(Code 01795) MRCC (01255) 675518; Police 101; Dr or Ⓗ via Medway Navigation Service 663025. HM (Medway Ports Ltd) 596593;

Medway VTS VHF Ch **74** 16 22 (H24); Kingsferry Bridge Ch 10 (H24).

FACILITIES

FAVERSHAM: Town 🛒, ✕, 🍴, Gas, ✉, Ⓑ, ⇌, ✈ Gatwick.

OARE CREEK: Services: ⌂, M, C (8 ton), ⚒, 🔧, ✕,🛠; **Hollow Shore Cruising Club,** 🍴.

CONYER CREEK: Swale Marina ☎ 521562; ⌂(dredged 2m) £14/craft, ⚓, 🔧, D, P, Gas, BH (30 ton), ⚒, ✕, C (30ton), ▬, ⛽, ▣; **Conyer CC. Conyer Marina ☎** 521711 ⌂ £10,🛠, △, Rigging, BY, ⚒, ✕, 🔧, Ⓔ, ▬, D.

MILTON CREEK (Sittingbourne): Crown Quay M, ⚓.

Town 🛒, ✕, 🍴, ✉, Ⓑ, ⇌, ✈ (Gatwick); also the Dolphin Yard Sailing Barge Museum.

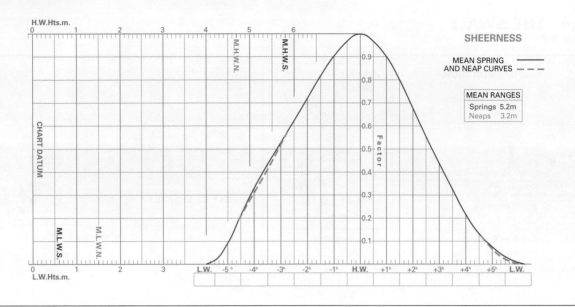

SHEERNESS

MEAN SPRING ——————
AND NEAP CURVES ‑ ‑ ‑ ‑ ‑

MEAN RANGES
Springs 5.2m
Neaps 3.2m

1.10 QUEENBOROUGH

Kent (Isle of Sheppey) **51°25'·04N 00°44'·19E** ⚓️⚓️⚓️💧💧💧🌸🌸

CHARTS AC 5606, 1834, 2572, 3683; Imray C1, Y18, 2100

TIDES Use 1.11 Sheerness, 2M to the N. +0130 Dover; ML 3·0; Duration 0610

SHELTER Good, except near HW in strong N'ly winds. The first deep-water refuge W of N Foreland, accessible at all tides from Garrison Pt (1.11); or from the Swale (1.9) on the tide. An all-tide pontoon/jetty (5m depth at end) on E bank is for landing/short stay only; both sides of the jetty are foul. 2 Y ⚓️s (raft up to 4 craft <10m each) lie N of the jetty and a pair Gy ⚓️s (raft up to 6 craft <10m each) lie to the S; also single visitors Y ⚓️s Nos 14-26 for craft <10m, with HM's permission craft >10m berth on W side of Concrete Lighter. When ⚓️s are full the hbr controller will offer spare buoys. Smaller R buoys (numbered) are for locals. ⚓ is discouraged due to commercial traffic. Speed limit 8kn.

NAVIGATION WPT: see R Medway for appr via Garrison Pt. Enter the river at Queenborough Spit ECM buoy, Q (3) 10s, 51°25'·75N 00°43'·93E. The chan narrows between drying banks and moorings. See The Swale if approaching from the E.

LIGHTS AND MARKS Lights as chartlet. Note: No 5 Bn Dir Oc WRG 6s, vis 161°-G-166°-W-167°-R-172°, on river bend covers the appr chan. All-tide landing 2 FR (vert). Concrete lighter Fl G 3s.

COMMUNICATIONS (Code 01795) MRCC (01255) 675518; Police 101; Dr 583828; Ⓗ (01634) 830000 (Gillingham). HM 662051.

Monitor *Medway VTS* VHF Ch **74** for tfc info. Call Ch 08 *Sheppey One* (Q'boro HM) for berths, also water taxi at weekends only (£1.20 to landing).

FACILITIES HM/Hbr Controller, ⚓️ and ◯ on concrete lighter 9/day or £48/week. Tokens for all-tide-landing gate may be purchased at the YC, local grocery or pubs. ⚓ on all-tide landing jetty.

Queenborough YC Wed, Fri, Sat evenings, Sat, Sun lunchtimes, M, 🚿, 🚻, 🅿, ✕, 🍺.

The Creek ☎ 07974 349018, (HW±1½) ⚓, Scrubbing berth (⚓, ⬦, 🛠).

Services: ✎, ✕, 🛒, ⚓, BY, C (10 ton), Gas.

Town 🅿 & 🏧, 🛒, ✕, 🍺, ✉, ⇄, ✈ (Gatwick).

STANDARD TIME (UT)
For Summer Time add ONE hour in **non-shaded areas**

SHEERNESS LAT 51°27′N LONG 0°45′E
TIMES AND HEIGHTS OF HIGH AND LOW WATERS

Dates in red are **SPRINGS**
Dates in blue are NEAPS

YEAR 2015

E England

JANUARY

Time	m	Time	m
1 0237 0900 TH 1528 2143	1.3 5.2 1.1 5.3	**16** 0139 0813 F 1436 2054	1.6 4.8 1.4 5.0
2 0348 1007 F 1632 2243	1.2 5.3 1.1 5.4	**17** 0306 0926 SA 1546 2200	1.5 5.0 1.2 5.2
3 0455 1106 SA 1725 2334	1.1 5.4 1.0 5.5	**18** 0413 1030 SU 1645 2258	1.2 5.3 1.0 5.5
4 0551 1156 SU 1809	0.9 5.5 1.0	**19** 0513 1126 M 1739 2350	0.9 5.6 0.8 5.7
5 0019 0636 M 1241 ○ 1846	5.6 0.8 5.6 1.0	**20** 0610 1216 TU 1830 ●	0.7 5.8 0.7
6 0059 0717 TU 1321 1920	5.6 0.7 5.7 0.9	**21** 0037 0704 W 1304 1918	5.9 0.5 6.0 0.6
7 0135 0754 W 1357 1952	5.6 0.7 5.7 0.9	**22** 0122 0754 TH 1350 2005	6.0 0.3 6.1 0.5
8 0209 0827 TH 1432 2022	5.6 0.7 5.6 1.0	**23** 0205 0842 F 1435 2049	6.1 0.2 6.2 0.5
9 0241 0857 F 1505 2052	5.6 0.8 5.5 1.0	**24** 0249 0927 SA 1521 2131	6.1 0.2 6.1 0.6
10 0312 0925 SA 1538 2122	5.5 0.8 5.4 1.1	**25** 0333 1009 SU 1608 2211	6.0 0.3 5.9 0.8
11 0345 0955 SU 1613 2155	5.4 0.9 5.3 1.2	**26** 0419 1049 M 1657 2252	5.8 0.5 5.6 0.9
12 0420 1028 M 1652 2233	5.2 1.1 5.1 1.4	**27** 0510 1132 TU 1751 ◑ 2341	5.6 0.8 5.4 1.1
13 0501 1108 TU 1737 ◑ 2318	5.0 1.2 4.9 1.5	**28** 0608 1225 W 1853	5.3 1.0 5.1
14 0551 1158 W 1833	4.9 1.3 4.8	**29** 0044 0717 TH 1336 2003	1.3 5.1 1.3 5.0
15 0017 0655 TH 1308 1942	1.6 4.7 1.4 4.8	**30** 0204 0834 F 1453 2116	1.4 5.0 1.3 5.0
		31 0325 0949 SA 1605 2223	1.3 5.1 1.3 5.2

FEBRUARY

Time	m	Time	m
1 0441 1053 SU 1706 2318	1.1 5.3 1.2 5.3	**16** 0345 1004 M 1619 2234	1.2 5.2 1.1 5.4
2 0539 1145 M 1752	0.9 5.4 1.1	**17** 0453 1107 TU 1719 2330	0.9 5.6 0.8 5.6
3 0004 0624 TU 1228 ○ 1829	5.5 0.8 5.6 1.0	**18** 0556 1200 W 1814 ●	0.6 5.9 0.7
4 0043 0701 W 1305 1901	5.6 0.7 5.6 0.9	**19** 0019 0652 TH 1248 1904	5.9 0.4 6.1 0.5
5 0118 0735 TH 1338 1932	5.6 0.7 5.6 0.9	**20** 0104 0741 F 1334 1951	6.1 0.2 6.2 0.4
6 0149 0806 F 1409 2003	5.6 0.6 5.7 0.9	**21** 0148 0827 SA 1418 2034	6.2 0.1 6.3 0.4
7 0219 0835 SA 1439 2033	5.7 0.6 5.6 0.9	**22** 0231 0909 SU 1502 2114	6.2 0.1 6.2 0.5
8 0249 0904 SU 1510 2102	5.6 0.7 5.6 0.9	**23** 0314 0948 M 1545 2152	6.1 0.3 6.0 0.6
9 0319 0933 M 1542 2131	5.5 0.8 5.4 1.0	**24** 0358 1023 TU 1630 2229	5.9 0.5 5.7 0.8
10 0351 1001 TU 1617 2200	5.4 0.9 5.3 1.2	**25** 0445 1059 W 1719 ◑ 2311	5.7 0.8 5.4 1.0
11 0427 1031 W 1656 2235	5.2 1.1 5.1 1.3	**26** 0539 1144 TH 1816	5.3 1.1 5.0
12 0510 1110 TH 1745 ◑ 2326	5.1 1.2 5.0 1.4	**27** 0008 0646 F 1250 1926	1.3 5.0 1.4 4.8
13 0607 1209 F 1850	4.9 1.4 4.8	**28** 0131 0806 SA 1417 2046	1.5 4.8 1.6 4.8
14 0038 0724 SA 1342 2010	1.5 4.8 1.5 4.8		
15 0223 0850 SU 1513 2128	1.5 4.9 1.3 5.0		

MARCH

Time	m	Time	m
1 0303 0928 SU 1536 2159	1.4 4.9 1.5 5.0	**16** 0150 0820 M 1443 2057	1.4 4.9 1.4 5.0
2 0422 1035 M 1642 2257	1.2 5.2 1.3 5.2	**17** 0321 0941 TU 1555 2209	1.1 5.3 1.1 5.3
3 0520 1126 TU 1730 2343	1.0 5.4 1.1 5.4	**18** 0433 1046 W 1658 2307	0.8 5.6 0.9 5.6
4 0603 1207 W 1808	0.8 5.5 1.0	**19** 0539 1140 TH 1755 2357	0.5 5.9 0.7 5.9
5 0021 0638 TH 1243 ○ 1840	5.5 0.7 5.6 0.9	**20** 0635 1229 F 1846 ●	0.3 6.1 0.5
6 0055 0710 F 1314 1911	5.6 0.7 5.6 0.9	**21** 0043 0722 SA 1314 1932	6.1 0.1 6.2 0.4
7 0125 0740 SA 1343 1941	5.7 0.6 5.7 0.8	**22** 0127 0806 SU 1357 2015	6.2 0.1 6.2 0.3
8 0154 0810 SU 1412 2013	5.7 0.6 5.7 0.7	**23** 0210 0846 M 1439 2055	6.3 0.1 6.1 0.4
9 0223 0841 M 1442 2043	5.7 0.6 5.7 0.8	**24** 0253 0923 TU 1521 2132	6.2 0.3 5.9 0.5
10 0254 0910 TU 1513 2111	5.6 0.7 5.6 0.9	**25** 0336 0956 W 1603 2208	6.0 0.6 5.7 0.7
11 0326 0936 W 1547 2136	5.5 0.9 5.5 1.0	**26** 0422 1029 TH 1648 2246	5.7 0.9 5.3 1.0
12 0401 1002 TH 1625 2207	5.4 1.0 5.3 1.1	**27** 0513 1109 F 1740 ◑ 2337	5.3 1.2 5.0 1.2
13 0444 1037 F 1711 ◑ 2254	5.2 1.2 5.1 1.2	**28** 0616 1207 SA 1848	1.5 5.0 1.5 4.7
14 0538 1134 SA 1812	5.0 1.4 4.9	**29** 0056 0734 SU 1336 2008	1.4 4.8 1.7 4.6
15 0004 0651 SU 1304 1932	1.4 4.9 1.5 4.8	**30** 0232 0856 M 1500 2125	1.4 4.8 1.6 4.8
		31 0348 1005 TU 1607 2226	1.2 5.1 1.4 5.1

APRIL

Time	m	Time	m
1 0446 1057 W 1658 2313	1.0 5.3 1.2 5.3	**16** 0411 1023 TH 1633 2242	0.7 5.7 0.9 5.6
2 0531 1139 TH 1739 2352	0.8 5.5 1.0 5.5	**17** 0517 1118 F 1732 2334	0.5 5.9 0.7 5.9
3 0607 1213 F 1813	0.8 5.6 0.9	**18** 0612 1207 SA 1824 ●	0.4 6.1 0.5
4 0025 0639 SA 1245 ○ 1845	5.6 0.7 5.6 0.8	**19** 0020 0659 SU 1252 1911	6.0 0.3 6.1 0.4
5 0057 0711 SU 1314 1918	5.6 0.6 5.7 0.7	**20** 0106 0741 M 1335 1955	6.2 0.2 6.1 0.4
6 0127 0743 M 1344 1952	5.7 0.6 5.8 0.7	**21** 0150 0821 TU 1416 2036	6.2 0.3 6.1 0.4
7 0159 0816 TU 1416 2024	5.7 0.6 5.8 0.7	**22** 0233 0857 W 1457 2114	6.1 0.5 5.9 0.5
8 0231 0847 W 1448 2055	5.7 0.7 5.7 0.8	**23** 0317 0930 TH 1538 2150	5.9 0.7 5.6 0.7
9 0305 0916 TH 1523 2123	5.6 0.9 5.6 0.9	**24** 0401 1002 F 1620 2226	5.6 1.0 5.3 1.0
10 0343 0945 F 1602 2156	5.5 1.0 5.4 1.0	**25** 0450 1039 SA 1708 ◑ 2310	5.3 1.3 5.0 1.2
11 0427 1023 SA 1648 2243	5.3 1.2 5.2 1.1	**26** 0546 1129 SU 1807	5.0 1.6 4.8
12 0522 1120 SU 1748 2351	5.2 1.3 5.0 1.2	**27** 0015 0654 M 1244 1920	1.4 4.8 1.7 4.6
13 0633 1243 M 1905	5.0 1.5 4.9	**28** 0149 0810 TU 1413 2037	1.4 4.7 1.7 4.7
14 0129 0758 TU 1416 2029	1.2 5.1 1.3 5.0	**29** 0302 0920 W 1521 2142	1.3 4.9 1.5 4.9
15 0258 0918 W 1528 2142	1.0 5.3 1.1 5.3	**30** 0400 1016 TH 1616 2233	1.1 5.2 1.3 5.2

Chart Datum: 2·90 metres below Ordnance Datum (Newlyn). HAT is 6·3 metres above Chart Datum.

SHEERNESS LAT 51°27'N LONG 0°45'E
TIMES AND HEIGHTS OF HIGH AND LOW WATERS

STANDARD TIME (UT)
For Summer Time add ONE hour in **non-shaded areas**

Dates in red are SPRINGS
Dates in blue are NEAPS

YEAR **2015**

MAY

Day	Time	m	Time	m	Time	m	Time	m
1 F	0448	0.9	1100	5.4	1701	1.1	2315	5.4
16 SA	0451	0.6	1055	5.8	1706	0.8	2311	5.7
2 SA	0528	0.8	1138	5.5	1741	1.0	2352	5.5
17 SU	0547	0.5	1145	5.9	1802	0.6		
3 SU	0605	0.8	1212	5.6	1817	0.9		
18 M ●	0000	5.9	0634	0.5	1231	6.0	1850	0.5
4 M ○	0027	5.6	0640	0.7	1245	5.7	1853	0.8
19 TU	0047	6.0	0717	0.5	1314	6.0	1936	0.4
5 TU	0102	5.7	0715	0.7	1319	5.8	1931	0.7
20 W	0132	6.0	0756	0.6	1356	5.9	2019	0.5
6 W	0136	5.7	0752	0.7	1353	5.8	2008	0.7
21 TH	0217	5.9	0833	0.7	1437	5.8	2058	0.6
7 TH	0212	5.7	0828	0.7	1428	5.7	2045	0.7
22 F	0300	5.8	0906	0.9	1516	5.6	2134	0.7
8 F	0250	5.7	0903	0.8	1505	5.6	2120	0.8
23 SA	0343	5.6	0938	1.1	1556	5.4	2208	0.9
9 SA	0331	5.6	0938	1.0	1547	5.5	2159	0.9
24 SU	0427	5.3	1012	1.3	1638	5.1	2246	1.1
10 SU	0418	5.5	1020	1.1	1635	5.3	2247	1.0
25 M ☽	0514	5.1	1054	1.5	1727	4.9	2334	1.2
11 M ☽	0514	5.3	1115	1.3	1733	5.1	2351	1.0
26 TU	0610	4.9	1149	1.7	1828	4.7		
12 TU	0621	5.2	1227	1.4	1845	5.0		
27 W	0043	1.4	0712	4.7	1305	1.7	1936	4.7
13 W	0115	1.0	0738	5.2	1348	1.3	2003	5.1
28 TH	0203	1.3	0819	4.8	1424	1.6	2043	4.8
14 TH	0236	0.9	0853	5.4	1500	1.1	2114	5.3
29 F	0307	1.2	0920	5.0	1526	1.5	2142	5.0
15 F	0346	0.7	0958	5.6	1605	1.0	2216	5.5
30 SA	0359	1.1	1013	5.2	1618	1.2	2233	5.2
31 SU	0446	0.9	1058	5.4	1705	1.1	2317	5.4

JUNE

Day	Time	m	Time	m	Time	m	Time	m
1 M	0529	0.9	1139	5.6	1748	0.9	2358	5.5
16 TU ●	0612	0.7	1214	5.8	1835	0.6		
2 TU ○	0610	0.8	1218	5.7	1831	0.8		
17 W	0034	5.8	0655	0.7	1259	5.8	1921	0.6
3 W	0038	5.6	0650	0.8	1257	5.8	1913	0.7
18 TH	0120	5.8	0734	0.8	1340	5.8	2004	0.5
4 TH	0118	5.7	0731	0.7	1335	5.8	1956	0.6
19 F	0203	5.8	0811	0.8	1419	5.7	2043	0.6
5 F	0158	5.8	0812	0.7	1414	5.8	2039	0.6
20 SA	0244	5.7	0844	1.0	1457	5.6	2119	0.7
6 SA	0239	5.8	0853	0.8	1454	5.7	2122	0.6
21 SU	0323	5.6	0915	1.1	1533	5.5	2150	0.8
7 SU	0324	5.8	0934	0.9	1538	5.6	2206	0.7
22 M	0401	5.4	0946	1.2	1610	5.3	2221	1.0
8 M	0412	5.6	1018	1.0	1626	5.5	2253	0.8
23 TU	0441	5.2	1021	1.4	1650	5.1	2257	1.1
9 TU ☽	0506	5.5	1108	1.1	1721	5.3	2349	0.8
24 W ☽	0525	5.0	1104	1.5	1736	4.9	2344	1.2
10 W	0608	5.4	1209	1.2	1825	5.2		
25 TH	0615	4.9	1158	1.6	1833	4.8		
11 TH	0057	0.9	0717	5.3	1319	1.3	1937	5.2
26 F	0044	1.3	0714	4.8	1307	1.7	1939	4.7
12 F	0210	0.9	0827	5.4	1430	1.2	2048	5.3
27 SA	0201	1.4	0818	4.8	1427	1.6	2046	4.8
13 SA	0319	0.8	0933	5.5	1538	1.1	2153	5.4
28 SU	0309	1.2	0921	5.0	1533	1.4	2148	5.0
14 SU	0425	0.8	1033	5.6	1644	0.9	2252	5.6
29 M	0405	1.1	1018	5.3	1629	1.2	2243	5.3
15 M	0523	0.8	1126	5.7	1743	0.8	2345	5.7
30 TU	0456	1.1	1109	5.5	1720	1.0	2332	5.5

JULY

Day	Time	m	Time	m	Time	m	Time	m
1 W	0544	0.9	1155	5.7	1810	0.8		
16 TH ●	0024	5.7	0637	1.0	1245	5.7	1909	0.7
2 TH ○	0018	5.7	0629	0.8	1238	5.8	1858	0.7
17 F	0108	5.7	0715	0.9	1325	5.7	1949	0.6
3 F	0102	5.8	0714	0.7	1320	5.9	1946	0.6
18 SA	0148	5.7	0750	0.9	1402	5.7	2025	0.6
4 SA	0146	5.9	0800	0.7	1402	5.9	2034	0.4
19 SU	0225	5.7	0822	1.0	1436	5.7	2058	0.7
5 SU	0230	6.0	0844	0.7	1444	5.9	2120	0.4
20 M	0259	5.6	0852	1.0	1508	5.6	2127	0.8
6 M	0315	6.0	0928	0.7	1528	5.8	2205	0.4
21 TU	0333	5.5	0921	1.1	1541	5.5	2155	0.9
7 TU	0402	5.9	1010	0.9	1614	5.7	2249	0.6
22 W	0407	5.4	0952	1.2	1615	5.3	2225	1.0
8 W ☽	0452	5.7	1055	1.0	1705	5.6	2336	0.7
23 TH	0443	5.2	1027	1.4	1652	5.1	2301	1.2
9 TH	0548	5.5	1146	1.1	1803	5.4		
24 F ☽	0525	5.0	1109	1.5	1738	4.9	2347	1.3
10 F	0032	0.9	0651	5.3	1249	1.2	1910	5.3
25 SA	0615	4.9	1202	1.6	1837	4.8		
11 SA	0140	1.0	0759	5.3	1401	1.3	2023	5.2
26 SU	0049	1.4	0719	4.8	1317	1.7	1950	4.7
12 SU	0251	1.0	0908	5.3	1515	1.2	2134	5.3
27 M	0214	1.4	0831	4.9	1446	1.6	2105	4.9
13 M	0400	1.1	1014	5.4	1627	1.1	2239	5.4
28 TU	0326	1.3	0940	5.2	1555	1.3	2211	5.2
14 TU	0503	1.0	1111	5.5	1732	0.9	2336	5.6
29 W	0426	1.1	1040	5.4	1655	1.2	2309	5.5
15 W	0555	1.0	1201	5.6	1824	0.8		
30 TH	0520	0.9	1132	5.7	1751	0.8	2359	5.7
31 F ○	0611	0.8	1219	5.8	1845	0.6		

AUGUST

Day	Time	m	Time	m	Time	m	Time	m
1 SA	0046	5.9	0659	0.7	1304	6.0	1935	0.4
16 SU	0128	5.7	0727	1.0	1340	5.8	2000	0.7
2 SU	0131	6.1	0746	0.6	1347	6.1	2023	0.3
17 M	0201	5.7	0758	0.9	1411	5.7	2031	0.7
3 M	0216	6.2	0832	0.6	1429	6.1	2108	0.2
18 TU	0232	5.7	0828	1.0	1441	5.7	2059	0.7
4 TU	0300	6.1	0915	0.6	1512	6.1	2151	0.3
19 W	0302	5.6	0857	1.0	1511	5.6	2127	0.8
5 W	0345	6.0	0955	0.8	1556	6.0	2232	0.5
20 TH	0333	5.5	0925	1.1	1542	5.5	2155	1.0
6 TH	0432	5.8	1036	0.9	1644	5.8	2313	0.7
21 F	0406	5.4	0954	1.3	1616	5.3	2225	1.1
7 F ☽	0523	5.6	1121	1.1	1738	5.5		
22 SA ☽	0443	5.2	1028	1.4	1657	5.1	2301	1.3
8 SA	0001	1.0	0622	5.3	1218	1.3	1844	5.3
23 SU	0527	5.0	1113	1.5	1748	4.9	2354	1.5
9 SU	0105	1.2	0730	5.1	1334	1.4	1959	5.1
24 M	0626	4.9	1219	1.7	1859	4.8		
10 M	0222	1.3	0844	5.1	1456	1.3	2118	5.2
25 TU	0117	1.6	0742	4.8	1359	1.6	2024	4.9
11 TU	0338	1.3	0955	5.2	1616	1.2	2228	5.3
26 W	0250	1.5	0903	5.0	1524	1.4	2141	5.2
12 W	0446	1.2	1057	5.4	1722	1.0	2325	5.5
27 TH	0357	1.2	1011	5.4	1631	1.0	2245	5.5
13 TH	0539	1.1	1147	5.6	1812	0.8		
28 F	0456	1.0	1109	5.7	1732	0.7	2339	5.9
14 F ●	0012	5.7	0619	1.1	1230	5.7	1852	0.7
29 SA ○	0551	0.8	1158	5.9	1828	0.7		
15 SA	0053	5.7	0654	1.0	1307	5.7	1928	0.7
30 SU	0027	6.1	0641	0.6	1243	6.1	1918	0.3
31 M	0112	6.2	0729	0.6	1326	6.1	2005	0.2

Chart Datum: 2·90 metres below Ordnance Datum (Newlyn). HAT is 6·3 metres above Chart Datum.

》》 FREE monthly updates from 《《
www.reedsalmanac.co.uk

STANDARD TIME (UT)
For Summer Time add ONE hour in **non-shaded areas**

SHEERNESS   LAT 51°27′N   LONG 0°45′E
TIMES AND HEIGHTS OF HIGH AND LOW WATERS

Dates in red are **SPRINGS**
Dates in blue are **NEAPS**

YEAR **2015**

E England

SEPTEMBER

Date	Time m	Time m	Time m	Time m
1 TU	0156 6.3	0814 0.5	1409 6.3	2049 0.2
16 W	0201 5.8	0802 0.9	1412 5.8	2029 0.7
2 W	0239 6.2	0856 0.6	1451 6.2	2130 0.3
17 TH	0231 5.7	0832 1.0	1442 5.7	2058 0.8
3 TH	0323 6.1	0936 0.7	1535 6.1	2208 0.5
18 F	0301 5.7	0900 1.1	1514 5.6	2126 1.0
4 F	0408 5.8	1014 0.9	1622 5.8	2244 0.8
19 SA	0333 5.5	0927 1.2	1547 5.4	2153 1.2
5 SA	0456 5.5	1056 1.1	1714 5.5	◖2327 1.1
20 SU	0408 5.4	0956 1.3	1627 5.3	2224 1.3
6 SU	0551 5.2	1149 1.3	1819 5.2	
21 M	0451 5.2	1037 1.4	1716 5.1	◖2314 1.5
7 M	0027 1.4	0659 5.0	1307 1.5	1936 5.0
22 TU	0546 5.0	1140 1.6	1823 4.9	
8 TU	0151 1.6	0816 4.9	1438 1.4	2059 5.1
23 W	0032 1.7	0700 4.8	1317 1.6	1948 4.9
9 W	0313 1.5	0933 5.1	1600 1.2	2211 5.3
24 TH	0214 1.6	0826 5.0	1454 1.3	2112 5.2
10 TH	0424 1.4	1036 5.4	1704 1.0	2307 5.5
25 F	0328 1.3	0941 5.3	1605 1.0	2220 5.6
11 F	0517 1.2	1126 5.6	1751 0.8	2352 5.7
26 SA	0430 1.0	1041 5.7	1710 0.7	2315 5.9
12 SA	0556 1.1	1207 5.7	1828 0.8	
27 SU	0527 0.8	1133 5.9	1807 0.5	
13 SU ●	0030 5.7	0629 1.0	1242 5.7	1859 0.7
28 M ○	0004 6.2	0619 0.7	1219 6.1	1857 0.3
14 M	0103 5.8	0701 1.0	1314 5.8	1930 0.7
29 TU	0050 6.3	0707 0.6	1303 6.3	1942 0.2
15 TU	0133 5.8	0731 0.9	1343 5.8	1959 0.7
30 W	0134 6.3	0753 0.5	1346 6.3	2025 0.3

OCTOBER

Date	Time m	Time m	Time m	Time m
1 TH	0216 6.3	0835 0.5	1430 6.3	2104 0.4
16 F	0201 5.8	0808 0.9	1417 5.7	2030 0.9
2 F	0259 6.2	0915 0.7	1514 6.1	2140 0.7
17 SA	0233 5.7	0839 1.0	1450 5.7	2100 1.0
3 SA	0342 5.8	0953 0.8	1600 5.8	2215 1.0
18 SU	0306 5.6	0908 1.1	1525 5.5	2128 1.2
4 SU ◖	0428 5.5	1033 1.1	1652 5.5	2254 1.3
19 M	0342 5.5	0938 1.2	1606 5.4	2202 1.3
5 M	0520 5.2	1122 1.3	1754 5.2	2349 1.6
20 TU	0425 5.3	1019 1.3	1656 5.2	◖2251 1.5
6 TU	0625 4.9	1237 1.5	1909 5.0	
21 W	0518 5.1	1119 1.4	1800 5.0	
7 W	0111 1.8	0742 4.8	1412 1.5	2030 5.0
22 TH	0004 1.6	0628 4.9	1248 1.5	1920 5.0
8 TH	0239 1.7	0901 5.0	1530 1.3	2143 5.2
23 F	0138 1.6	0752 5.0	1424 1.3	2043 5.3
9 F	0349 1.5	1006 5.2	1631 1.1	2240 5.5
24 SA	0256 1.4	0909 5.3	1537 1.0	2152 5.6
10 SA	0443 1.3	1056 5.5	1717 0.9	2324 5.6
25 SU	0400 1.1	1012 5.6	1643 0.7	2250 5.9
11 SU	0525 1.2	1138 5.6	1754 0.8	
26 M	0459 0.9	1105 5.9	1741 0.5	2340 6.1
12 M	0001 5.7	0559 1.1	1213 5.7	1826 0.8
27 TU ○	0554 0.7	1154 6.1	1832 0.4	
13 TU ●	0033 5.7	0631 1.0	1244 5.7	1856 0.8
28 W	0026 6.2	0644 0.6	1240 6.2	1917 0.4
14 W	0102 5.8	0703 0.9	1314 5.8	1927 0.7
29 TH	0111 6.2	0731 0.5	1325 6.3	1959 0.4
15 TH	0131 5.8	0736 0.9	1345 5.8	1959 0.8
30 F	0154 6.2	0815 0.5	1410 6.2	2038 0.6
31 SA	0236 6.0	0856 0.6	1455 6.0	2114 0.8

NOVEMBER

Date	Time m	Time m	Time m	Time m
1 SU	0319 5.8	0935 0.8	1542 5.8	2148 1.1
16 M	0246 5.7	0858 0.9	1510 5.6	2114 1.1
2 M	0403 5.5	1014 1.0	1631 5.5	2224 1.4
17 TU	0324 5.5	0934 1.0	1553 5.5	2151 1.2
3 TU ◖	0451 5.2	1058 1.2	1727 5.2	2311 1.6
18 W	0408 5.4	1016 1.1	1644 5.3	2239 1.4
4 W	0549 4.9	1159 1.4	1833 4.9	
19 TH	0500 5.2	1111 1.2	1744 5.2	◖2343 1.5
5 TH	0019 1.8	0659 4.8	1329 1.5	1947 4.9
20 F	0604 5.1	1226 1.2	1857 5.1	
6 F	0149 1.8	0814 4.8	1444 1.4	2059 5.0
21 SA	0102 1.5	0720 5.1	1353 1.1	2013 5.3
7 SA	0301 1.7	0923 5.0	1544 1.2	2159 5.2
22 SU	0221 1.4	0836 5.3	1507 1.0	2123 5.5
8 SU	0359 1.5	1017 5.2	1633 1.0	2246 5.4
23 M	0328 1.2	0942 5.5	1614 0.8	2223 5.7
9 M	0445 1.3	1101 5.4	1714 0.9	2325 5.6
24 TU	0430 1.0	1040 5.7	1714 0.7	2316 5.9
10 TU	0525 1.1	1139 5.6	1749 0.9	2359 5.7
25 W ○	0530 0.8	1132 5.9	1807 0.6	
11 W ●	0602 1.0	1214 5.6	1823 0.8	
26 TH	0005 6.0	0623 0.7	1222 6.0	1853 0.6
12 TH	0031 5.7	0636 0.9	1247 5.7	1856 0.8
27 F	0051 6.0	0712 0.5	1309 6.1	1935 0.6
13 F	0104 5.8	0712 0.8	1321 5.7	1931 0.8
28 SA	0135 6.0	0758 0.5	1355 6.1	2014 0.7
14 SA	0137 5.8	0748 0.8	1356 5.7	2006 0.8
29 SU	0217 5.9	0841 0.6	1440 5.9	2050 0.9
15 SU	0210 5.8	0823 0.9	1432 5.7	2040 0.9
30 M	0259 5.7	0920 0.7	1525 5.7	2123 1.1

DECEMBER

Date	Time m	Time m	Time m	Time m
1 TU	0340 5.5	0956 0.9	1610 5.5	2157 1.3
16 W	0312 5.6	0936 0.8	1544 5.7	2145 1.0
2 W	0423 5.3	1033 1.1	1658 5.2	2235 1.5
17 TH	0356 5.5	1018 0.9	1633 5.5	2229 1.2
3 TH ◖	0511 5.0	1118 1.3	1751 5.0	2326 1.7
18 F	0445 5.4	1058 0.9	1728 5.4	◖2323 1.3
4 F	0608 4.8	1220 1.4	1852 4.8	
19 SA	0542 5.3	1205 1.0	1833 5.2	
5 SA	0034 1.8	0714 4.7	1340 1.5	1957 4.8
20 SU	0028 1.4	0650 5.2	1319 1.1	1944 5.2
6 SU	0158 1.8	0823 4.8	1448 1.4	2102 4.9
21 M	0144 1.3	0804 5.2	1435 1.0	2054 5.3
7 M	0306 1.6	0925 4.9	1543 1.2	2157 5.1
22 TU	0257 1.2	0915 5.3	1545 0.9	2159 5.5
8 TU	0401 1.4	1018 5.1	1630 1.1	2244 5.3
23 W	0405 1.1	1019 5.5	1650 0.9	2257 5.6
9 W	0448 1.2	1103 5.3	1713 1.0	2325 5.5
24 TH	0511 0.9	1117 5.7	1745 0.8	2349 5.7
10 TH	0531 1.0	1144 5.5	1752 0.9	
25 F ○	0609 0.7	1209 5.8	1833 0.8	
11 F ●	0003 5.6	0611 0.9	1224 5.6	1830 0.8
26 SA	0036 5.8	0659 0.6	1258 5.9	1915 0.8
12 SA	0041 5.7	0651 0.9	1301 5.7	1908 0.8
27 SU	0120 5.8	0745 0.5	1343 5.9	1954 0.8
13 SU	0117 5.8	0732 0.8	1339 5.8	1947 0.8
28 M	0202 5.8	0827 0.6	1426 5.8	2029 0.9
14 M	0154 5.8	0814 0.8	1419 5.8	2026 0.8
29 TU	0241 5.7	0904 0.7	1507 5.7	2101 1.0
15 TU	0232 5.7	0855 0.7	1500 5.7	2105 0.9
30 W	0319 5.6	0938 0.7	1546 5.5	2131 1.2
31 TH	0356 5.4	1007 0.9	1625 5.3	2203 1.3

Chart Datum: 2·90 metres below Ordnance Datum (Newlyn). HAT is 6·3 metres above Chart Datum.

1.11 RIVER MEDWAY (SHEERNESS TO ROCHESTER)

Kent **51°27'·03N 00°44'·50E** (Off Garrison Pt) ❄❄❄◊◊◊✿✿✿

CHARTS AC 5606, 1835, 1834, 1185, 2482, 3683; IMRAY C1, Y18, 2100

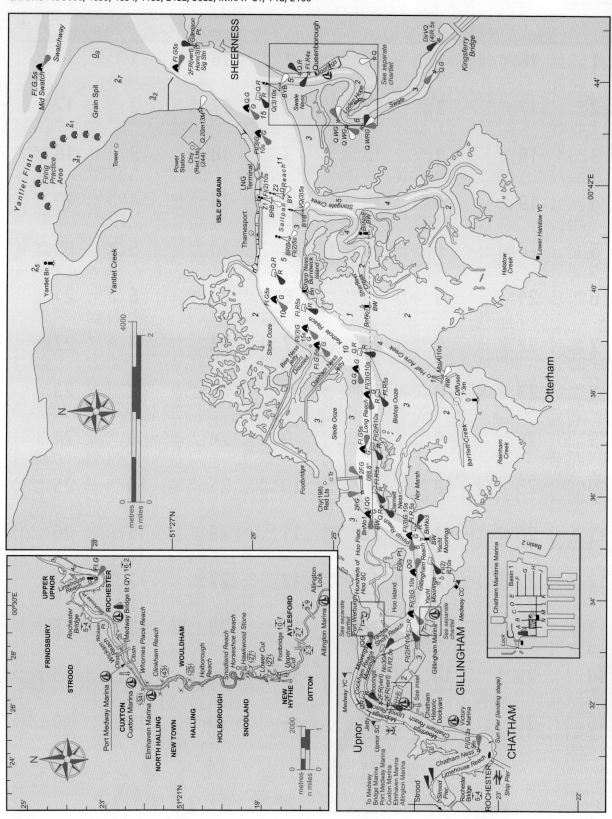

TIDES +0130 Dover; ML 3·1; Duration 0610
Standard Port SHEERNESS (→)

Times				Height (metres)			
High Water		Low Water		MHWS	MHWN	MLWN	MLWS
0200	0800	0200	0700	5·8	4·7	1·5	0·6
1400	2000	1400	1900				
Differences BEE NESS							
+0002	+0002	0000	+0005	+0·2	+0·1	0·0	0·0
BARTLETT CREEK							
+0016	+0008	ND	ND	+0·1	0·0	ND	ND
DARNETT NESS							
+0004	+0004	0000	+0010	+0·2	+0·1	0·0	–0·1
CHATHAM (Lock Approaches)							
+0010	+0012	+0012	+0018	+0·3	+0·1	–0·1	–0·2
UPNOR							
+0015	+0015	+0015	+0025	+0·2	+0·2	–0·1	–0·1
ROCHESTER (STROOD PIER)							
+0018	+0018	+0018	+0028	+0·2	+0·2	–0·2	–0·3
WOULDHAM							
+0030	+0025	+0035	+0120	–0·2	–0·3	–1·0	–0·3
NEW HYTHE							
+0035	+0035	+0220	+0240	–1·6	–1·7	–1·2	–0·3
ALLINGTON LOCK							
+0050	+0035	ND	ND	–2·1	–2·2	–1·3	–0·4

SHELTER There are 4 marinas down-river of Rochester Bridge and 5 above. Sheerness is solely a commercial hbr. See Queenborough for access to/from The Swale. Lower reaches of the Medway are exposed to strong NE winds, but Stangate and Half Acre Creeks are secure in all winds and give access to lesser creeks. There are good ⚓s in Sharfleet Creek; with sufficient rise of the tide it is possible to go via the 'back-door' into Half Acre Creek. Speed limit is 6kn W of Folly Pt (Hoo Island).

NAVIGATION WPT 51°28'·84N 00°52'·78E, Medway SWM buoy, 253°/4·5M to No 11 SHM buoy, then follow recommended route 240°/1M to Grain Hard SHM buoy. The wreck of the *Richard Montgomery* is visible 2M NE of estuary ent and a Military Wreck depth 22 in Kethole Reach. There is a huge area to explore, although much of it dries to mud. Some minor creeks are buoyed. The river is well buoyed/marked up to Rochester and tidal up to Allington Lock (21·6M). Above Rochester bridge the river shoals appreciably and in the upper reaches there is only about 1m at LW.

Bridge Clearances (HAT), going up-river:

Rochester	5·4m
Medway (M2)	16·2m
New Hythe (footbridge)	10·7m
Aylesford (pedestrian)	2·3m
Aylesford (road)	2·7m
Maidstone bypass (M20)	8·9m

LIGHTS AND MARKS See 1.3 and chartlet for details of most lts. NB: not all buoys are shown due to small scale. Isle of Grain lt Q 20m 13M. Power stn chy (242m) Oc and FR lts. Tfc Sigs: Powerful lt, Fl 7s, at Garrison Pt means large vessel under way: if shown up river = inbound; if to seaward = outbound.

COMMUNICATIONS (Codes 01634 Medway) MRCC (01255) 675518; Police 101; Dr via Medway Navigation Service (01795) 663025; Sheerness HM (01795) 596593.

Medway VTS VHF Ch **74** 16 (H24). Monitor Ch 74 underway and Ch 16 at ⚓. Radar assistance is available on request Ch 22. Ch **80** M for marinas: Gillingham, Hoo (H24), Chatham Maritime (H24), Medway Bridge (0900-1700LT) and Port Medway (0800-2000LT).

YACHT CLUBS Sheppey YC (01795) ☎ 663052;
Lower Halstow YC ☎ (01227) 458554;
Medway Cruising Club (Gillingham) ☎ 856489, ▱, M, L, ⚓;
Hoo Ness YC ☎ 250052, ▱, ✕, M, L, ⚓;
Hundred of Hoo SC ☎ 250102;
Medway Motor Cruising Club ☎ 827194;
Medway Motor YC ☎ (01622) 737647;
Medway YC (Upnor) ☎ 718399; **Upnor SC** ☎ 718043;
Royal Engineers YC ☎ 844555; **RNSA Medway** ☎ 200970;
Rochester CC ☎ 841350, ▱, ✕, M, ⚓, L, ▣;
Strood YC ☎ 718261, ▱, M, C (1·5 ton), ⚓, L, ◣.

FACILITIES (☎ code 01634 unless otherwise stated) All moorings run by YCs or marinas. Slips at Commodores Hard, and Gillingham.

Marinas (From seaward to Rochester Bridge)

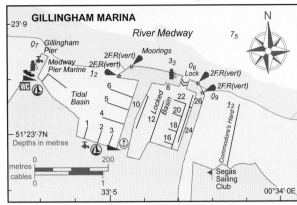

Gillingham Marina cross-tide, esp. the ebb, off the lock ent are reduced by a timber baffle at 90° to the stream (close W of lock). An angled pontoon deflects the stream and is also the fuel berth; the outboard end is lit by 2FR (vert).⚓ (252+12🅥s) ☎ 280022, prebook. £2·90 locked basin (access via lock (width 6m) HW±4½), £2·00 tidal basin HW±2, P, ✎, ⬚, Ⓔ, ✗, Gas, Gaz, ⬚, BH (65 ton), ⇕, C (1 ton), ꕥ, ▱.

Medway Pier Marine ☎ 851113, D, ⚓, ◣, C (6 ton), BY, Ⓔ.

Port Werburgh (120+ residential ⬭ only), ☎ 252107, ▣, BY, BH; access to W basin HW±2½; HW±3 to E basin (via sill 1m above CD); an unlit WCM buoy marks chan ent; 4 waiting buoys in river.

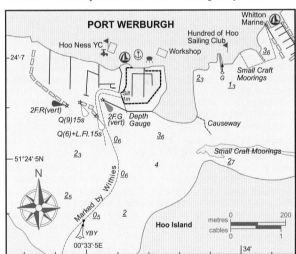

Chatham Maritime Marina – see inset on previous page (←) ☎ 899200, (300 ⬭), access via lock H24 and sill 1.3m below CD (1.5m at MLWS), £3.20. C(15T), ⚓, ⬚▷, P, D, ✎, ⬥, ⬚, BY, BH.
Victory Marina ☎ 07785 971797, 🅥, ⚓, ⬚▷.

Marinas (Up-river from Rochester Bridge)

Medway Bridge Marina (160+4 visitors) ☎ 843576, £1.20, ◣, D, P, ✎, ⬚, Ⓔ, ✗, C (3 ton), BH (10 ton), Gas, Gaz, ⬥, ⬚, ꕥ, ✕, ▱;

Port Medway Marina (50) ☎ 720033, BH (16 ton), C, ⇕;

Cuxton Marina (150+some 🅥) ☎ 721941, ✎, ⬚, Ⓔ, ✗, ⬚, BH (12 ton), ◣;

Elmhaven Marina (60) ☎ 240489, ✎, ⬚, ✗, C;

Allington Lock operates HW–3 to +2, ☎ (01622) 752864.

Allington Marina (120) ☎ (01622) 752057, above the lock; ⬚, ✎, ⬚, ✗, P, D, ◣, C (10 ton), ⚓, Gas, Gaz.

Towns: All facilities ✕, ꕥ, ▣, ✉, ⇌, ✈ (Gatwick).

1.12 RIVER THAMES

CHARTS AC 5606, 1185,1186, 2151, 3337, 2484, 3319. Imray C1, C2, Y18, 2100

TIDES The river is tidal up to Teddington. +0252 Dover; ML 3·6; Duration 0555.

Standard Port LONDON BRIDGE (→)

Times				Height (metres)			
High Water		Low Water		MHWS	MHWN	MLWN	MLWS
0300	0900	0400	1100	7·1	5·9	1·3	0·5
1500	2100	1600	2300				
Differences TILBURY							
−0055	−0040	−0050	−0115	−0·7	−0·5	+0·1	0·0
WOOLWICH (GALLIONS POINT)							
−0020	−0020	−0035	−0045	−0·1	0·0	+0·2	0·0
ALBERT BRIDGE							
+0025	+0020	+0105	+0110	−0·9	−0·8	−0·7	−0·4
HAMMERSMITH BRIDGE							
+0040	+0035	+0205	+0155	−1·4	−1·3	−1·0	−0·5
KEW BRIDGE							
+0055	+0050	+0255	+0235	−1·8	−1·8	−1·2	−0·5
TEDDINGTON (RICHMOND) LOCK							
+0105	+0055	+0325	+0305	−2·2	−2·7	−0·9	−0·5

Tide Boards, showing height of tide above CD, are at Lower Pool (Met Police Boatyard), King's Reach (Temple Stairs), Nine Elms Reach (Cringle Wharf) and Battersea Reach (Plantation Wharf). Above Putney the **height** of LW may be below CD if the water flow over Teddington Weir is low; warnings are broadcast by London VTS. Thames Barrier closure will alter predicted water levels greatly.

SHELTER Very good in marinas. PLA Drawdocks, arrowed, are drying inlets offering emergency refuge, but subject to wash.

NAVIGATION WPT 51°29'·62N 00°44'·17E, Sea Reach No 4 buoy, 276°/6·8M to abm Holehaven Creek and 37·8M to Tower Bridge. Pleasure craft should always keep clear of commercial vessels. To clear tanker berths off Holehaven, Coryton and Thames Haven yachts should navigate following small craft crossing routes:-

Inward from north: Keep close to SHM buoys & bcns. At W Leigh Middle ensure the fairway is clear, then cross to the S side of Yantlet Channel. Make for E Blyth buoy before turning onto the inward track, so as to clear outward vessels passing close to the PHM buoys. It is safe to pass S of Tanker, Cliffe Fleet, West Blyth and Lower Hope buoys. When safe, cross to the N side in Lower Hope Reach as quickly as possible.

Outward to north: as above in reverse, but cross to the N side between Sea Reach Nos 4 & 5 buoys.

Inward from the south: Keep well south of Yantlet Channel, crossing to the N side in Lower Hope Reach as described above.

Sea Reach, keep well S of the main chan to clear tankers turning off Canvey Is and Coryton. Keep at least 60m clear of oil/gas jetties and give a wide berth to London Gateway container terminal. Warning lights are displayed at Cliffe and Canvey Is when large ships are manoeuvring.

Lower Hope Reach, hold the NW bank until Ovens SHM; long groynes extend from the N bank for the next 2M. Tilbury Landing Stage is used by the Gravesend ferry and cruise liners.

Gravesend Reach, beware 6 groynes off the N bank, WSW of Coalhouse Pt, which project almost into the fairway. Outer ends marked by SHM beacons, Fl G 2·5s. *No inside passage exists.*

Above **Gravesend** keep to stbd side of channel – do not cut corners.

Northfleet Hope, beware ships/tugs turning into Tilbury Docks; container berths and a grain terminal are close up-river. A light, Iso 6s, on Tilbury Cargo Jetty (51°27'·06N 00°20'·95E) is shown when vessels are manoeuvring off Tilbury Dock locks or for a berth in Northfleet Hope. *Proceed with caution.*

Above **Cherry Garden Pier** vessels > 40m LOA and tugs/tows always have priority. Very heavy traffic/frequent River Ferries from/to Greenwich, Tower of London and Westminster. Police and PLA launches are always willing to assist.

Speed limits. Minimise wash. 8kn speed limit applies at Canvey Is, Coryton and Thurrock when gas tankers are berthed, in all creeks and above Wandsworth Bridge. Voluntary 12kn speed limit to Wandsworth Bridge.

Exclusion Zones. These are in place off the Houses of Parliament on the North Embankment and government offices below Vauxhall Br on the S side of the river.

The Port of London Authority (PLA), London River House, Royal Pier Road, Gravesend, Kent DA12 2BG, ☎ 01474 562200, publish (download free from www.pla.co.uk) *Recreational Users' Guide; General Directions; Permanent Notices to Mariners; Port of London River Byelaws; Tide Tables* and a *Port Handbook.*

LIGHTS AND MARKS See 1.3 and chartlets. Glare from shore lts can make navigation by night difficult or even hazardous. Some ⚓s show F.Bu lights; High Speed Craft show Fl.Y lights.

COMMUNICATIONS Port of London Authority: www.pla.co.uk HM: lower district ☎ 01474 562200, upper district ☎ 020 7743 7912 Thames CG ☎ 01255 675518; London CG ☎ 020 8312 7380 Port Controller Gravesend ☎ 01474 560311, Police Marine Support Unit ☎ 020 7275 4421; Thames Barrier Navigation Centre ☎ 020 8855 0315; Tower Bridge ☎ 020 7940 3984; Richmond lock 020 8940 0634; Teddington lock 020 8940 8723.

London VTS works from centres at Gravesend and the Thames Barrier, dividing the estuary/river into three sectors. Routine MSI broadcasts are made at the times shown (in brackets) below.

Sector 1: Outer limits – Sea Reach No 4 buoy. Ch **69** (H +15, H +45)

Sector 2: Sea Reach 4 – Crayfordness. Ch **68** (H and H +30)

Sector 3: Crayfordness – Teddington. Ch **14** (H +15 and H +45)

PLA launches *Thames Patrol* Ch 69, 68, 14. Police launches *Thames Police* Ch 14. **Do not** use tug Channels 8, 10, 13, 36, 72, 77. **In emergency** call *London Coastguard* Ch 16, 67, co-located with London VTS at the Thames Barrier Navigation Control and covering from Canvey Island to Teddington. *Thames Coastguard* covers the area to seaward of Canvey Island. The RNLI operates four LB stations at Gravesend, Victoria Embankment (Waterloo Br), Chiswick and Teddington.

HARBOURS IN SEA REACH and GRAVESEND REACH

HOLEHAVEN CREEK, Essex, 51°30'·57N 00°33'·16E. AC 2484, 1186. HW +0140 on Dover; use differences for Coryton (at 1.13); ML 3·0m; Duration 0610. Shelter is good, but beware swell from passing traffic. Keep to Canvey Is side on ent. Temp ⚓ in lee of Chainrock jetty or call PLA ☎ 01474 562462 for possible mooring. 5ca N of ent an overhead oil pipe (2 FY horiz) crosses chan with 11m clearance, plus. 2 FG (vert) on all jetty heads, plus Chainrock SHM buoy Fl G 5s. ⚓ from Lobster Smack pub, 🛒 & 🍴 from Canvey Village (1M); all other facilities on Canvey Is.

GRAVESEND, Kent, 51°26'·61N 00°22'·92E. AC 1186, 2151. HW +0150 on Dover; ML 3·3m; Duration 0610. Use Tilbury diffs. ⚓ E of Club's Jetty close to S shore, but remote from town.

Gravesend SC www.gravesendsailingclub.co.uk ☎ 07538 326623.

PLA 🅰s are upriver, £25/night. **London River Moorings** ☎ 01474 535700 All tide 🅰s £25/night, half tide ⌓. New all tide landing stage available.

Embankment Marina www.theembankmentmarina.co.uk ☎ 01474 535700; £25/night. Lock into Canal Basin HW −1 to HW Tilbury by arrangement: 1 Apr-31 Oct, 0800-2000; Winter 1000-1600. Lock closes at local HW. Out of hours openings up to HW by arrangement with lock keeper. D, Gas, ⌓, M, Ⓔ, ⚒, 🍴, ⚓, slip.

Town Tourist info ☎ (01474) 337600, Ⓔ, ⚒, 🍴, ✕, 🛒 & 🍴, BH (70 ton) at Denton Wharf, ✕, 🚆.

Thurrock YC 51°28'·28N 00°19'·47E at Grays, ☎ 01375 373720. 1 🅰, 🛒 & 🍴 (2M), ⌓, ✕ (occas). M-F 1000-1500; Thu 2000-2300.

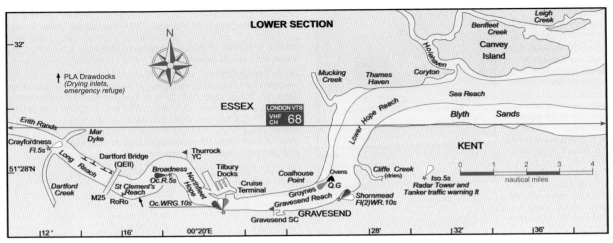

CANVEY ISLAND TO CRAYFORDNESS (AC 1185, 1186, 2484, 2151)

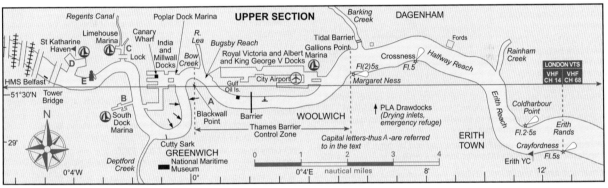

CRAYFORDNESS TO TOWER BRIDGE (AC 2484, 2151, 3337)

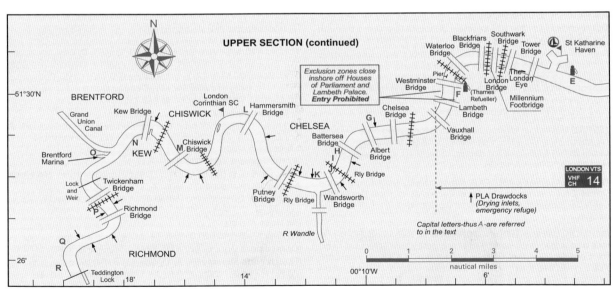

TOWER BRIDGE TO TEDDINGTON (AC 3319)

OBSTRUCTIONS

THAMES TIDAL BARRIER **51°29´·91N 00°02´·21E** (Span G), AC 5606, 2484, 3337. At Woolwich Reach are 9 piers between which gates can be rotated upwards from the river bed to form a barrier. Piers are numbered 1-9 from N to S; Spans are lettered A-K from S to N (see diagram). A, H, J & K are not navigable. C-F, with depth 5·8m and 61m wide, are for larger ships. Spans B and G, with 1·25m, are for small craft: W-bound via G and E-bound via B (51°29´·73N 00°02´·24E). On N side of river (Spans E and F) a cross-tide component is reported.

Small craft should not navigate between Thames Refinery Jetty and Gulf Oil Island, unless intending to transit the Barrier. Yachts must transit the barrier under power, not sail. When all spans are closed, keep 200m clear to avoid turbulence. It is dangerous to transit a span closed to navigation as the gate may be semi-raised.

In reduced visibility, open spans are marked by high intensity lts. *London VTS* broadcasts information on Ch **14** at H + 15 / H + 45.

CONTROL AND COMMUNICATIONS The Thames Barrier Navigation Centre controls all traffic in a Zone from Margaret Ness (51°30´·5N 00°05´·56E) to Blackwall Point (51°30´·3N 00°00´·2E), using the callsign *London VTS* on VHF Ch **14**, 22, 16.

Inbound call *London VTS* to obtain clearance to proceed through the Barrier when passing Margaret Ness (51°30´·54N 00°05´·50E).

Outbound call *London VTS* to obtain clearance to proceed through the Barrier when passing Blackwall Point (51°30´·30N 00°00´·18E).

Non-VHF craft should, if possible, pre-notify the Thames Barrier Control ☎ 020 8855 0315; then observe all visual signals, proceed with caution keeping clear of larger vessels and use spans B or G as appropriate. Call before and after transiting the barrier.

There are fixed warning noticeboards (CEVNI) at: Barking Creek (N bank) Blackwall Stairs (N bank) Blackwall Point (S bank).

TESTING The Barrier is completely closed for testing once a month for about 3hrs, LW ±1½. Visit www.pla.co.uk (navigation safety) or call ☎ 020 8305 4188 for details. In Sept/Oct an annual closure lasts about 10 hrs, LW to LW.

THAMES GATEWAY CABLE CAR Joining the O2 Millennium Dome site at Greenwich with the Excel Centre at Victoria Docks, the Cable Car crosses the river between 2 pylons giving an air draught of 60m.

RICHMOND WEIR & TEDDINGTON LOCK At **Richmond** a half-tide lock and a weir with overhead sluice gates give access up-river; fee payable. 3 R discs (3 ● lts at night) in a ▽ show when the sluice gates are down (closed) and maintaining at least 1·72m between Richmond and Teddington bridges. The half-tide lock, on the Surrey bank, must then be used. At other times (approx HW ±2) two ◐ lights at each arch = weir open to navigation. Pass freely below the 3 central arches.

Teddington lock marks the end of the tidal Thames (semi-tidal above Richmond). Red/green lights indicate which of the launch or barge locks is in operation.

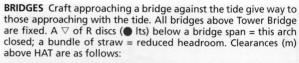

North Bank / South Bank diagram showing Thames Tidal Barrier spans and piers, LONDON VTS VHF CH 14, small craft channels, F.W (in fog) markings, 3F.R lights, compass rose, cables scale 0 to 1.

BRIDGES

BRIDGES Craft approaching a bridge against the tide give way to those approaching with the tide. All bridges above Tower Bridge are fixed. A ▽ of R discs (● lts) below a bridge span = this arch closed; a bundle of straw = reduced headroom. Clearances (m) above HAT are as follows:

Tower Bridge fog horn sounds a 10s blast every 20s when bascules are open for shipping; standby signal is a bell 30s. On bridge arches between Tower and Wandsworth bridges high intensity white signal lts are electronically triggered by one or more large vessels approaching a bridge. Iso W 4s means a single large vessel, VQ a second large vessel, nearing the same bridge. Other vessels keep clear of that arch. NB air-draught boards at Harrods Depository and Chiswick Eyot for Hammersmith Bridge.

Dartford (QEII)	53	Albert	4.5
Tower (closed)	8·0	Battersea road	5·0
Tower (open)	42	Battersea rail	5·5
London	8·2	Wandsworth	5·3
Cannon St	6·7	Fulham	6·3
Southwark	6·8	Putney	4·8
Millennium	8·4	Hammersmith	3·1
Blackfriars rail	6·8	Barnes	4·9
Blackfriars road	6·5	Chiswick	6·1
Waterloo	8·1	Kew rail	5·0
Charing Cross	6·5	Kew road	4·7
Westminster	4·8	Richmond foot	5·0
Lambeth	5·9	Twickenham	8·5*
Vauxhall	5·2	Richmond rail	8·0*
Victoria Railway	5·5	Richmond road	7·9*
Chelsea	6·1	* Above maintained water level

FACILITIES

Marinas See overleaf for Gallions Point and Poplar Dock. Other marinas and YCs (Bold red letters in brackets appear on River Thames chartlets):

(A) Greenwich YC ☎ 0844 736 5846; VHF Ch M. ⚓, ⛽, ⚒.

(B) South Dock Marina ☎ 020 7252 2244, (details overleaf).

(C) Limehouse Marina ☎ 020 7308 9930, (details overleaf).

(D) St Katharine Haven ☎ 020 7264 5312, (details overleaf).

West India Dock ☎ 020 7517 5500; group bookings (min 6) only.

Hermitage Moorings (3·5ca downstream of Tower bridge) ☎ 020 7481 2122; VHF Ch M/80. 2 ♥ on pontoons (max 40m LOA); £30/£40 per night; ⚓, ⌖, 🚾/shower, ⛽.

(E) Fuel Barge ☎ 020 7481 1774; VHF Ch 14 *Heiko*. D & Gas, M-F 0630-1430. W/ends Apr-Oct, HW±2, between 0600 & 1800.

(F) Westminster Petroleum Ltd Fuel barge moored off Houses of Parliament. Open Mon-Fri (and Sat from Easter to mid-Oct). Call *Thames Refueller* VHF Ch 14, ☎ 07831 110681, D, Gas, dry stores.

(G) Cadogan 020 8748 2715, give 24 hrs notice. Chiswick 020 8742 2713. Dove 020 8748 2715. St Katharine 020 7488 0555. Putney 020 7378 1211. 020 7930 2062 for Kew Pier and Richmond Lndg Stage.

(H) Chelsea Yacht & Boat Co ☎ 020 7352 1427, M, Gas.

(I) Chelsea Harbour ☎ 020 7225 9100, (details overleaf).

(J) Imperial Wharf Marina, pier@imperialwharfmarina.co.uk. ☎ 07932 603284, 270m pontoon, 2m at MLWS, £4/m/night, ⚓, ⌖, visitors welcome.

(K) Hurlingham YC ☎ 020 8788 5547, M.

Chiswick Pier, ☎ 020 8742 2713, £0.95m, long pontoon, 2FG (vert). All tide access, max draft 1·4m. ⚓, ⌖, ⛽. Visitors welcome.

(L) Chiswick Quay Marina (50) ☎ 020 8994 8743, Access HW±2 via lock, M, ⚓, BY, M, ⚒, 🛒, ⚒.

(M) Dove Marina.

(N) Kew Marina ☎ 020 8940 8364, M, ⌖, D, P, Gas, △.

(O) Brentford Dock ☎ 020 8232 8941, (details overleaf).

(P) Richmond Slipway BY, ⌖, D, Gas, M, ⚓, ⚒, 🛒, ⚒.

(Q) Eel Pie Island BY ⌖, ⌖, ⚒, M, Gas, C (6 ton), ⚒, 🛒, ⚓.

(R) Swan Island Hbr D, M, ⚒, 🛒, ⚒, ⚓, Gas, ⚓, ⌂, C (30t), ⌖.

Piers where landing may be possible, by prior arrangement:- Call London River Services ☎ 020 7941 2400 for: Greenwich, Tower, Millennium, Embankment, Bankside, Festival, Westminster, Millbank, Blackfriars and Waterloo.

MARINAS ON THE TIDAL THAMES, from seaward to Bentford
AC 2484, 3337, 3319

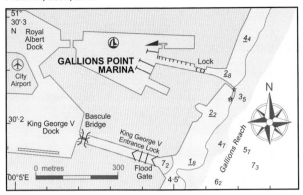

GALLIONS POINT MARINA, 51°30'·30N 00°04'·66E sited in the entry
basin for Royal Albert Dock. www.gallionspoint marina.co.uk ☎
020 7476 7054. Ch M/80, when vessel expected. 2 x ☆s 2FG (vert)
on river pier. 8m depth in basin. Access via lock (width 7·6m)
HW±5; Locking £5 each way; H24 security, ⌂ from £12/yacht, WC,
Showers, ♂, P & D, ⚒, Gas, P & D, ⚒, slip. DLR from N Woolwich
to central London, until 0030. Woolwich ferry & foot tunnel 15
mins walk. ✈ (City) is adjacent.

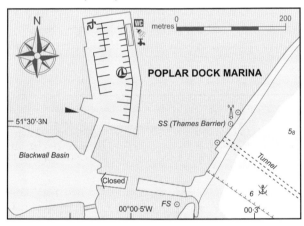

POPLAR DOCK MARINA, 51°30'·07N 00°00'·50W (lock entrance).
☎ 020 7308 9930, *but no visitors berths*. Tides: India & Millwall
Docks ent. 4·5M below Tower Bridge. Canary Wharf twrs (244m)
are conspic 4ca W of marina. Enter via West India Entrance Lock
(spanned by Docklands 'Blue Bridge'). Lock (300m x 24m) opens
0700-1700LT at HW for outbound and HW-1 to HW+1 for arrivals,
foc, but OT £20. Least width 12·1m into marina. VHF Ch 13 (H24).
Facilities: ▬, ▢, ✗, ▦, ♂, ▢, &; Dr ☎ 020 7237 1078; Ⓗ ☎ 020
7955 5000; Police ☎ 101. ⇌, Blackwall DLR, Canary Wharf Tube,
✈ City.

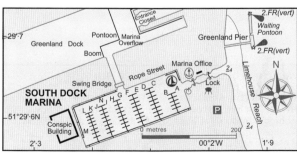

SOUTH DOCK MARINA (B), 51°29'·65N 00°01'·97W. ☎ 020 7252
2244 Mob 0795 662 10710 (OH 0700-1900 Mon-Fri / 0800-1700 w/e)
Tides as for Surrey Dock Greenland Ent. 1·1M above Greenwich,

2·5M below Tower Bridge. Baltic Quay building at SW end of marina
is conspic with five arched rooftops. Waiting pontoon at Greenland
Pier. Approx access via lock (width 6·4m) HW-2 to HW+1½ for 2m
draft. (250 + Ⓥ, £22·62< 9·5m, £24·89 <15m, £33·89 < 20m, £39·60 >
20·5m).VHF Ch **M** 80; Dr ☎ 237 1078; Ⓗ; ♂ ☎ 020 7955 5000; Police
☎ 101. **Facilities:** ⚒, ✗, ▣, ▢, C (20 ton), ▢, ✗, ▦, ▢, &, ⇌, Surrey
Quays and Canada Water tube, ✈ City Airport.

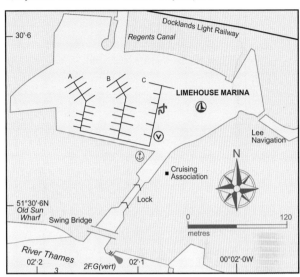

LIMEHOUSE MARINA (C), 51°30'·57N 00°02'·27W www.bwml.co.uk
☎ 020 7308 9930. Entry HW±3 via swing bridge/lock (width 8m)
0800-1800LT daily Apr-Sep; 0800-1600 Oct-Mar; other times by
prior arrangement (24hrs notice) to BWML Lock control ☎ 020
7308 9930, beware cross-tide at lock cut, mid flood/ebb. Waiting
pontoon in lock entrance is accessible outside LW±2. Call VHF Ch
80 *Limehouse Marina*.
Facilities: (90 berths, from £28·00/craft Ⓥ) H24 security, &, ⚓, ♂,
▢, ▢, ⇌, DLR; also entry to Regents Canal and Lee Navigation.
Visitors welcome at CA clubhouse.

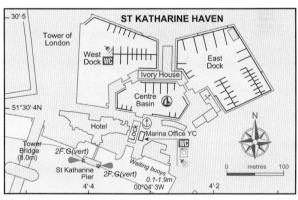

ST KATHARINE HAVEN (D), 51°30´·36N 00°04´·35W www.skdocks.
co.uk ☎ 020 77264 5312 HW +0245 on Dover. Tides as London
Bridge. Beware of cross tide at mid-flood/ebb. Good shelter under
all conditions. Tower Bridge and the Tower of London are uniquely
conspic, close up-river. Six Y waiting buoys are close downstream of
entrance. Berthing on St Katharine Pier, 30m upriver, is strictly by
prior arrangement and only for shoal draft vessels with permission.
Pleasure launches berth on S side of pier.

St Katharine Haven Ch **80** M. Lock (41m x 12·5m with 2 small lifting
bridges), access HW −2 to HW +1½, season 0600-2030, winter 0800-
1800LT; other times by prior arrangement. R/G traffic lights at entr.

Facilities: (160 inc Ⓥ in 3 basins) usually Centre Basin or East Dock;
typically £4·50 (+electricity) ♂, @, ▢, ✗, ▦, ▢.

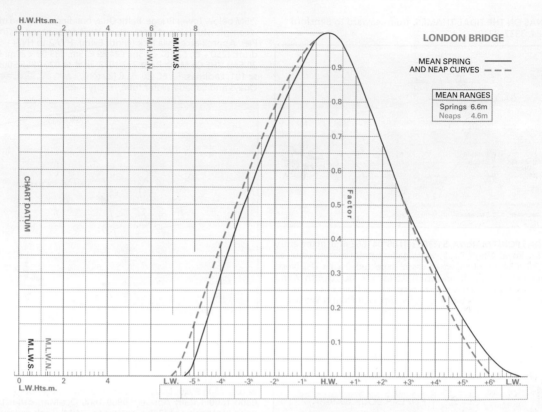

LONDON BRIDGE

MEAN SPRING ——————
AND NEAP CURVES – – – – –

MEAN RANGES	
Springs	6.6m
Neaps	4.6m

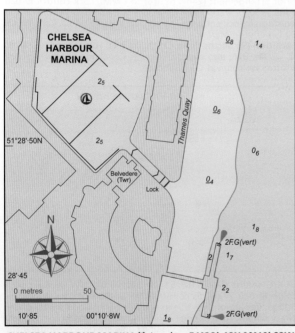

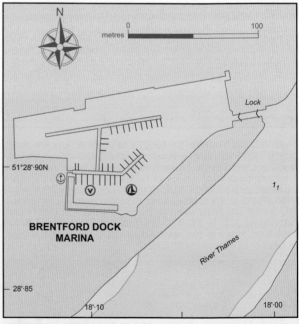

CHELSEA HARBOUR MARINA (I), London, **51°28′·48N 00°10′·82W**. Tides: see Albert Bridge. Good shelter in all conditions, 5M above Tower Bridge, reached via 14 fixed bridges. Battersea railway bridge is 120m upstream. Belvedere Tower (80m high with tide ball) is conspic, next to the lock and bascule bridge. Max sizes for lock: LOA 24m, beam 5·5m, draft 1·8m. Lock opens when there is 2·5m water above sill; tide gauge outside; R/G traffic lights. Limited waiting berths and shore access on Chelsea Hbr Pier (1·7m) close upriver. **Marina**, 50+10 Ⓥ £25 < 12m, £30 > 12m. Mobile ☎ 07770 542783. VHF Ch 80. ⌂, ✕, Ⓑ, ▣, showers, ⌷, ⌸, ⚓, 🛒.

BRENTFORD DOCK MARINA (O), 51°28′·92N 00°18′·05W, 1100m beyond Kew bridge. AC 3319. Tides, see Kew Bridge. 60 ⬭ inc Ⓥ, £20 for all LOA. Mobile ☎ 07970 143 987. No VHF. Access approx HW±2½ via lock 4·8m x 9·8m (longer LOA during freeflow); 15m waiting pontoon. **Facilities:** ⬭, ▣, ✕, ⬭, ⚒, ⚓, Gas, ⌂, ✕, ▤; Gunnersbury & Ealing tubes. Ent to Grand Union Canal via lock is nearby: M, ⬭.

STANDARD TIME (UT)
For Summer Time add ONE hour in **non-shaded areas**

LONDON BRIDGE   LAT 51°30'N   LONG 0°05'W
TIMES AND HEIGHTS OF HIGH AND LOW WATERS

Dates in red are **SPRINGS**
Dates in blue are NEAPS

YEAR 2015

E England

JANUARY

Time	m		Time	m
1 0412	1.3	**16**	0240	1.7
1021	6.4		0929	5.8
TH 1646	1.1	F	1534	1.4
2302	6.4		2210	6.0
2 0527	1.2	**17**	0427	1.6
1128	6.5		1045	6.2
F 1802	1.1	SA	1703	1.2
			2318	6.3
3 0006	6.5	**18**	0547	1.2
0636	1.0		1147	6.6
SA 1227	6.6	SU	1809	1.0
1902	1.0			
4 0059	6.6	**19**	0018	6.7
0732	0.7		0656	0.9
SU 1317	6.8	M	1244	6.9
1950	1.0		1914	0.9
5 0144	6.7	**20**	0113	6.9
0820	0.5		0801	0.6
M 1400	6.9	TU	1336	7.2
○ 2032	1.0	●	2018	0.8
6 0223	6.8	**21**	0203	7.1
0903	0.6		0858	0.4
TU 1440	7.0	W	1425	7.4
2108	1.0		2112	0.7
7 0259	6.8	**22**	0250	7.2
0940	0.6		0949	0.2
W 1516	7.0	TH	1513	7.5
2138	1.1		2200	0.6
8 0331	6.8	**23**	0335	7.3
1010	0.7		1034	0.0
TH 1549	6.9	F	1559	7.5
2203	1.1		2243	0.5
9 0401	6.7	**24**	0418	7.3
1035	0.7		1115	0.0
F 1621	6.8	SA	1644	7.4
2232	1.1		2322	0.6
10 0432	6.7	**25**	0501	7.2
1102	0.7		1152	0.1
SA 1652	6.7	SU	1730	7.2
2303	1.1			
11 0503	6.5	**26**	0000	0.7
1131	0.8		0545	7.0
SU 1725	6.5	M	1227	0.4
2335	1.2		1818	6.9
12 0536	6.4	**27**	0040	0.9
1159	0.9		0634	6.8
M 1801	6.3	TU	1305	0.6
		◑	1911	6.6
13 0006	1.4	**28**	0125	1.1
0614	6.2		0730	6.5
TU 1230	1.1	W	1353	0.9
◑ 1843	6.1		2011	6.3
14 0043	1.5	**29**	0222	1.3
0700	6.0		0837	6.3
W 1310	1.2	TH	1454	1.2
1935	5.9		2116	6.1
15 0133	1.6	**30**	0332	1.4
0758	5.8		0948	6.2
TH 1406	1.4	F	1604	1.4
2050	5.8		2231	6.1
		31	0449	1.4
			1103	6.2
		SA	1723	1.3
			2345	6.2

FEBRUARY

Time	m		Time	m
1 0610	1.1	**16**	0512	1.2
1210	6.4		1120	6.5
SU 1836	1.2	M	1742	1.1
			2354	6.6
2 0042	6.5	**17**	0632	0.9
0711	0.8		1223	6.9
M 1303	6.7	TU	1857	0.9
1928	1.1			
3 0128	6.7	**18**	0053	6.9
0800	0.7		0746	0.5
TU 1347	6.8	W	1319	7.2
○ 2011	1.0	●	2005	0.7
4 0208	6.8	**19**	0145	7.1
0841	0.6		0845	0.2
W 1425	6.9	TH	1409	7.4
2049	1.0		2100	0.5
5 0242	6.8	**20**	0232	7.3
0917	0.6		0935	0.0
TH 1459	6.9	F	1456	7.6
2122	1.0		2148	0.4
6 0313	6.9	**21**	0317	7.5
0948	0.6		1019	-0.1
F 1528	6.9	SA	1541	7.6
2151	1.0		2231	0.3
7 0341	6.9	**22**	0359	7.6
1016	0.5		1058	-0.1
SA 1556	6.9	SU	1625	7.5
2219	0.9		2309	0.4
8 0409	6.9	**23**	0441	7.5
1042	0.5		1131	0.1
SU 1625	6.8	M	1708	7.2
2248	0.9		2343	0.5
9 0439	6.8	**24**	0523	7.2
1109	0.6		1200	0.4
M 1657	6.7	TU	1751	6.9
2316	1.0			
10 0511	6.6	**25**	0016	0.7
1133	0.8		0607	6.9
TU 1731	6.5	W	1231	0.7
2342	1.1	◐	1837	6.5
11 0546	6.4	**26**	0054	1.0
1158	0.9		0658	6.6
W 1809	6.3	TH	1310	1.1
			1930	6.1
12 0012	1.2	**27**	0142	1.3
0627	6.2		0759	6.2
TH 1232	1.0	F	1408	1.4
◑ 1854	6.1		2035	5.9
13 0055	1.3	**28**	0251	1.5
0719	6.1		0913	6.0
F 1320	1.2	SA	1525	1.6
1954	5.9		2155	5.8
14 0154	1.5			
0831	5.9			
SA 1431	1.4			
2124	5.9			
15 0327	1.6			
1006	6.1			
SU 1626	1.3			
2245	6.2			

MARCH

Time	m		Time	m
1 0411	1.4	**16**	0250	1.4
1035	6.0		0936	6.1
SU 1646	1.5	M	1558	1.4
2317	6.0		2215	6.1
2 0536	1.2	**17**	0444	1.2
1148	6.3		1054	6.5
M 1805	1.3	TU	1718	1.1
			2329	6.5
3 0018	6.4	**18**	0609	0.8
0644	0.9		1202	6.9
TU 1242	6.6	W	1839	0.8
1901	1.1			
4 0105	6.6	**19**	0031	6.9
0732	0.7		0728	0.4
W 1325	6.8	TH	1259	7.2
1946	1.0		1947	0.6
5 0144	6.8	**20**	0124	7.2
0813	0.6		0825	0.1
TH 1403	6.8	F	1349	7.4
○ 2025	0.9	●	2042	0.4
6 0219	6.9	**21**	0210	7.4
0849	0.6		0914	0.0
F 1435	6.9	SA	1436	7.5
2101	0.9		2129	0.3
7 0249	6.9	**22**	0254	7.6
0921	0.5		0957	-0.1
SA 1503	6.9	SU	1519	7.5
2132	0.9		2212	0.2
8 0317	7.0	**23**	0336	7.7
0950	0.5		1035	0.0
SU 1529	7.0	M	1602	7.4
2202	0.8		2249	0.3
9 0345	7.0	**24**	0418	7.6
1018	0.5		1106	0.3
M 1559	6.9	TU	1643	7.2
2231	0.8		2322	0.4
10 0415	6.9	**25**	0459	7.3
1045	0.6		1131	0.5
TU 1631	6.8	W	1724	6.8
2258	0.9		2352	0.7
11 0448	6.8	**26**	0542	7.0
1108	0.7		1157	0.8
W 1704	6.6	TH	1806	6.4
2322	1.0			
12 0523	6.6	**27**	0023	0.9
1133	0.8		0629	6.6
TH 1741	6.4	F	1232	1.1
2350	1.0	◑	1852	6.1
13 0603	6.5	**28**	0105	1.2
1205	0.9		0726	6.2
F 1825	6.2	SA	1323	1.5
◑			1953	5.8
14 0029	1.1	**29**	0208	1.4
0653	6.2		0837	5.9
SA 1251	1.1	SU	1443	1.7
1922	6.0		2112	5.7
15 0125	1.3	**30**	0332	1.4
0801	6.0		0957	5.9
SU 1358	1.4	M	1608	1.6
2046	5.9		2236	5.8
		31	0449	1.2
			1113	6.2
		TU	1724	1.4
			2343	6.2

APRIL

Time	m		Time	m
1 0559	0.9	**16**	0543	0.7
1211	6.5		1139	6.9
W 1825	1.1	TH	1815	0.8
2 0032	6.5	**17**	0007	6.9
0652	0.7		0703	0.4
TH 1256	6.7	F	1238	7.2
1913	1.0		1923	0.6
3 0114	6.7	**18**	0100	7.2
0736	0.6		0800	0.2
F 1333	6.8	SA	1328	7.3
1956	0.9	●	2018	0.4
4 0149	6.9	**19**	0147	7.4
0815	0.6		0848	0.1
SA 1406	6.8	SU	1414	7.4
○ 2034	0.8		2107	0.3
5 0221	7.0	**20**	0231	7.5
0850	0.5		0931	0.2
SU 1434	6.9	M	1457	7.4
2109	0.8		2150	0.2
6 0250	7.0	**21**	0313	7.6
0922	0.5		1008	0.3
M 1503	7.0	TU	1538	7.3
2142	0.7		2228	0.3
7 0320	7.1	**22**	0356	7.5
0953	0.5		1038	0.5
TU 1534	6.9	W	1619	7.1
2214	0.7		2301	0.4
8 0352	7.1	**23**	0437	7.3
1021	0.6		1101	0.7
W 1608	6.8	TH	1658	6.7
2242	0.8		2329	0.6
9 0427	6.9	**24**	0520	6.9
1046	0.7		1127	0.9
TH 1643	6.6	F	1738	6.4
2307	0.8		2358	0.8
10 0504	6.8	**25**	0604	6.5
1114	0.8		1202	1.2
F 1721	6.4	SA	1821	6.1
2336	0.9	◐		
11 0547	6.6	**26**	0035	1.1
1149	0.9		0655	6.1
SA 1806	6.2	SU	1248	1.5
			1914	5.8
12 0015	1.0	**27**	0129	1.3
0638	6.4		0800	5.9
SU 1236	1.2	M	1354	1.7
◑ 1903	6.0		2027	5.6
13 0109	1.1	**28**	0248	1.4
0746	6.2		0913	5.8
M 1346	1.4	TU	1521	1.7
2022	5.9		2145	5.7
14 0236	1.3	**29**	0404	1.2
0914	6.3		1023	6.0
TU 1537	1.4	W	1638	1.5
2150	6.1		2254	6.0
15 0421	1.0	**30**	0507	1.0
1031	6.6		1126	6.3
W 1656	1.1	TH	1740	1.2
2304	6.5		2351	6.4

Chart Datum: 3·20 metres below Ordnance Datum (Newlyn). HAT is 7·7 metres above Chart Datum.

STANDARD TIME (UT)
For Summer Time add ONE hour in **non-shaded areas**

LONDON BRIDGE LAT 51°30'N LONG 0°05'W
TIMES AND HEIGHTS OF HIGH AND LOW WATERS

Dates in **red** are **SPRINGS**
Dates in blue are **NEAPS**

YEAR 2015

MAY

Time	m	Time	m
1 0603	0.8	**16** 0632	0.5
1216	6.5	1215	7.0
F 1834	1.0	SA 1857	0.7
2 0036	6.6	**17** 0037	7.0
0653	0.7	0732	0.4
SA 1257	6.7	SU 1307	7.1
1921	0.9	1954	0.5
3 0116	6.8	**18** 0126	7.2
0737	0.6	0821	0.4
SU 1333	6.8	M 1353	7.1
2004	0.8	● 2043	0.3
4 0150	6.9	**19** 0210	7.4
0817	0.6	0905	0.5
M 1406	6.9	TU 1437	7.1
○ 2044	0.7	2128	0.3
5 0223	7.0	**20** 0254	7.4
0854	0.6	0943	0.6
TU 1439	6.9	W 1518	7.1
2122	0.7	2208	0.3
6 0257	7.1	**21** 0336	7.4
0929	0.6	1014	0.7
W 1514	6.9	TH 1558	6.9
2158	0.6	2242	0.4
7 0333	7.1	**22** 0418	7.2
1001	0.6	1037	0.9
TH 1551	6.8	F 1637	6.7
2230	0.6	2310	0.6
8 0411	7.0	**23** 0459	6.9
1031	0.7	1104	1.0
F 1628	6.7	SA 1714	6.4
2259	0.7	2337	0.8
9 0452	6.9	**24** 0541	6.5
1105	0.8	1138	1.2
SA 1709	6.5	SU 1753	6.2
2331	0.7		
10 0537	6.7	**25** 0011	1.0
1144	1.0	0625	6.2
SU 1755	6.3	M 1219	1.4
		◑ 1837	5.9
11 0011	0.8	**26** 0056	1.1
0630	6.5	0718	6.0
M 1234	1.2	TU 1310	1.6
◐ 1852	6.2	1937	5.7
12 0107	1.0	**27** 0155	1.3
0738	6.4	0824	5.8
TU 1348	1.4	W 1416	1.7
2007	6.1	2053	5.7
13 0234	1.0	**28** 0311	1.3
0856	6.4	0930	5.9
W 1516	1.3	TH 1539	1.7
2127	6.3	2202	5.9
14 0358	0.9	**29** 0418	1.1
1008	6.6	1032	6.1
TH 1632	1.1	F 1650	1.4
2238	6.5	2302	6.2
15 0514	0.7	**30** 0515	0.9
1115	6.8	1128	6.3
F 1747	0.9	SA 1749	1.2
2342	6.8	2354	6.5
		31 0609	0.8
		1217	6.5
		SU 1843	1.0

JUNE

Time	m	Time	m
1 0039	6.7	**16** 0109	7.0
0659	0.7	0755	0.7
M 1300	6.7	TU 1338	6.9
1933	0.8	● 2022	0.4
2 0120	6.9	**17** 0155	7.1
0746	0.7	0840	0.7
TU 1340	6.8	W 1422	6.9
○ 2020	0.7	2108	0.3
3 0200	7.0	**18** 0239	7.2
0829	0.7	0920	0.8
W 1420	6.9	TH 1503	6.9
2104	0.6	2150	0.4
4 0239	7.1	**19** 0321	7.2
0910	0.7	0954	0.9
TH 1500	6.9	F 1541	6.9
2146	0.5	2226	0.5
5 0320	7.2	**20** 0401	7.1
0950	0.7	1021	1.0
F 1540	6.9	SA 1618	6.7
2226	0.4	2255	0.6
6 0401	7.1	**21** 0440	6.8
1028	0.7	1047	1.0
SA 1621	6.8	SU 1652	6.5
2303	0.5	2320	0.7
7 0445	7.0	**22** 0516	6.6
1106	0.9	1118	1.1
SU 1703	6.6	M 1727	6.4
2338	0.5	2350	0.8
8 0531	6.9	**23** 0554	6.4
1149	0.9	1154	1.2
M 1750	6.5	TU 1804	6.2
9 0019	0.6	**24** 0025	0.9
0624	6.7	0634	6.1
TU 1240	1.0	W 1234	1.4
◑ 1844	6.4	◐ 1846	6.0
10 0113	0.7	**25** 0107	1.1
0727	6.6	0725	5.9
W 1343	1.2	TH 1320	1.6
1951	6.3	1944	5.8
11 0222	0.8	**26** 0159	1.2
0836	6.5	0831	5.8
TH 1453	1.2	F 1418	1.7
2104	6.4	2104	5.7
12 0332	0.8	**27** 0311	1.3
0944	6.6	0937	5.9
F 1605	1.1	SA 1542	1.7
2212	6.5	2211	5.9
13 0442	0.8	**28** 0424	1.2
1050	6.6	1039	6.1
SA 1718	1.0	SU 1702	1.4
2317	6.7	2310	6.2
14 0558	0.7	**29** 0525	1.0
1154	6.7	1137	6.4
SU 1830	0.8	M 1804	1.1
15 0016	6.8	**30** 0004	6.6
0703	0.7	0621	0.9
M 1250	6.8	TU 1230	6.6
1930	0.6	1902	0.9

JULY

Time	m	Time	m
1 0053	6.8	**16** 0145	7.0
0716	0.8	0820	0.9
W 1318	6.8	TH 1410	6.8
1957	0.7	● 2050	0.4
2 0139	7.0	**17** 0228	7.1
0809	0.8	0901	0.9
TH 1403	6.9	F 1449	6.9
○ 2049	0.5	2132	0.4
3 0224	7.2	**18** 0307	7.1
0859	0.7	0937	0.9
F 1448	7.0	SA 1525	6.9
2138	0.4	2208	0.5
4 0308	7.3	**19** 0344	7.0
0946	0.6	1007	1.0
SA 1531	7.0	SU 1558	6.8
2224	0.2	2236	0.5
5 0352	7.3	**20** 0417	6.9
1030	0.6	1032	1.0
SU 1613	7.0	M 1629	6.7
2306	0.2	2301	0.6
6 0437	7.3	**21** 0449	6.7
1111	0.6	1100	1.0
M 1656	6.9	TU 1700	6.6
2345	0.2	2327	0.7
7 0523	7.1	**22** 0521	6.5
1152	0.7	1131	1.1
TU 1740	6.8	W 1732	6.4
		2356	0.8
8 0023	0.4	**23** 0554	6.3
0613	6.9	1203	1.2
W 1237	0.9	TH 1807	6.2
◑ 1830	6.7		
9 0107	0.5	**24** 0026	1.0
0709	6.7	0632	6.1
TH 1327	1.0	F 1237	1.4
1929	6.6	◐ 1848	6.0
10 0200	0.7	**25** 0101	1.2
0812	6.5	0720	5.9
F 1427	1.1	SA 1320	1.6
2037	6.5	1943	5.8
11 0302	0.9	**26** 0149	1.3
0917	6.4	0831	5.7
SA 1535	1.2	SU 1420	1.7
2145	6.5	2110	5.8
12 0408	1.0	**27** 0308	1.4
1025	6.4	0951	5.9
SU 1648	1.1	M 1603	1.6
2254	6.5	2226	6.0
13 0523	1.0	**28** 0441	1.3
1134	6.5	1059	6.2
M 1804	0.9	TU 1725	1.2
2359	6.6	2329	6.4
14 0637	0.9	**29** 0547	1.0
1235	6.6	1200	6.5
TU 1910	0.7	W 1831	0.9
15 0056	6.8	**30** 0026	6.8
0733	0.9	0649	0.9
W 1326	6.7	TH 1256	6.8
2003	0.5	1936	0.6
		31 0119	7.1
		0753	0.8
		F 1345	7.0
		○ 2035	0.4

AUGUST

Time	m	Time	m
1 0207	7.3	**16** 0249	7.0
0850	0.7	0916	0.9
SA 1431	7.2	SU 1504	7.0
2127	0.2	2142	0.5
2 0253	7.5	**17** 0321	7.0
0940	0.6	0947	0.9
SU 1516	7.3	M 1534	7.0
2214	0.0	2211	0.5
3 0338	7.5	**18** 0350	7.0
1025	0.5	1014	0.9
M 1558	7.3	TU 1602	7.0
2257	-0.1	2235	0.5
4 0423	7.4	**19** 0418	6.9
1106	0.4	1041	0.9
TU 1640	7.3	W 1631	6.8
2335	0.0	2300	0.6
5 0507	7.2	**20** 0448	6.7
1144	0.5	1109	1.0
W 1723	7.1	TH 1701	6.6
		2326	0.8
6 0010	0.2	**21** 0519	6.5
0553	6.9	1136	1.2
TH 1223	0.7	F 1734	6.4
1809	6.9	2350	0.9
7 0046	0.5	**22** 0554	6.3
0644	6.6	1202	1.3
F 1305	0.9	SA 1812	6.2
◑ 1902	6.7	◐	
8 0129	0.8	**23** 0017	1.1
0742	6.4	0635	6.0
SA 1357	1.1	SU 1237	1.4
2006	6.5	1859	6.0
9 0227	1.1	**24** 0059	1.3
0847	6.2	0730	5.8
SU 1503	1.3	M 1330	1.5
2117	6.3	2004	5.8
10 0335	1.3	**25** 0201	1.5
0958	6.1	0856	5.7
M 1617	1.2	TU 1450	1.6
2231	6.3	2141	5.9
11 0451	1.3	**26** 0357	1.5
1114	6.2	1021	6.0
TU 1739	1.0	W 1647	1.3
2343	6.5	2256	6.4
12 0613	1.1	**27** 0516	1.2
1219	6.5	1131	6.4
W 1851	0.7	TH 1801	0.9
13 0042	6.8	**28** 0000	6.8
0711	1.0	0625	0.9
TH 1310	6.7	F 1231	6.8
1944	0.5	1916	0.6
14 0131	7.0	**29** 0057	7.2
0759	0.9	0736	0.8
F 1353	6.9	SA 1323	7.1
● 2029	0.4	○ 2018	0.3
15 0212	7.0	**30** 0147	7.4
0840	0.9	0835	0.6
SA 1431	6.9	SU 1410	7.3
2109	0.5	2111	0.1
		31 0234	7.6
		0926	0.5
		M 1454	7.5
		2157	-0.1

Chart Datum: 3·20 metres below Ordnance Datum (Newlyn). HAT is 7·7 metres above Chart Datum.

》 FREE monthly updates from 《
www.reedsalmanac.co.uk

STANDARD TIME (UT)
For Summer Time add ONE hour in **non-shaded areas**

LONDON BRIDGE LAT 51°30'N LONG 0°05'W

TIMES AND HEIGHTS OF HIGH AND LOW WATERS

Dates in red are SPRINGS
Dates in blue are NEAPS

YEAR 2015

E England

SEPTEMBER

Time	m	Time	m
1 TU 0319 1010 1537 2239	7.6 0.4 7.6 -0.1	**16** W 0320 0952 1534 2206	7.0 0.8 7.0 0.5
2 W 0402 1051 1619 2315	7.5 0.4 7.5 0.1	**17** TH 0347 1020 1603 2232	6.9 0.8 7.0 0.6
3 TH 0445 1128 1701 2347	7.3 0.5 7.3 0.3	**18** F 0417 1047 1634 2256	6.8 0.9 6.8 0.8
4 F 0529 1202 1745	6.9 0.7 7.1	**19** SA 0449 1111 1707 2319	6.6 1.1 6.6 1.0
5 SA 0017 0614 1240 1834 ◑	0.7 6.6 0.9 6.7	**20** SU 0523 1135 1745 2346	6.4 1.2 6.4 1.1
6 SU 0054 0708 1325 1934	1.0 6.2 1.1 6.4	**21** M 0602 1208 1830 ◑	6.1 1.2 6.2
7 M 0147 0812 1429 2047	1.4 6.0 1.3 6.2	**22** TU 0025 0653 1256 1930	1.2 5.9 1.3 6.0
8 TU 0301 0928 1546 2205	1.6 5.9 1.3 6.2	**23** W 0123 0807 1407 2100	1.5 5.7 1.5 6.0
9 W 0422 1049 1710 2322	1.5 6.1 1.1 6.4	**24** TH 0316 0944 1614 2225	1.7 5.9 1.3 6.4
10 TH 0545 1156 1827	1.3 6.4 0.8	**25** F 0448 1100 1732 2333	1.3 6.4 0.9 6.9
11 F 0022 0646 1248 1919	6.8 1.0 6.7 0.6	**26** SA 0600 1203 1852	1.0 6.8 0.5
12 SA 0110 0733 1330 2001	6.9 0.9 6.9 0.5	**27** SU 0032 0714 1257 1956	7.2 0.7 7.2 0.3
13 SU 0149 0814 1406 ● 2038	7.0 0.9 6.9 0.5	**28** M 0123 0814 1345 ○ 2048	7.5 0.6 7.4 0.1
14 M 0224 0850 1438 2111	7.0 0.9 7.0 0.5	**29** TU 0211 0905 1430 2134	7.6 0.4 7.6 0.0
15 TU 0254 0923 1506 2139	7.0 0.9 7.0 0.5	**30** W 0255 0951 1513 2215	7.6 0.3 7.7 0.1

OCTOBER

Time	m	Time	m
1 TH 0338 1031 1555 2250	7.5 0.3 7.6 0.3	**16** F 0319 0959 1536 2203	7.0 0.8 7.1 0.7
2 F 0421 1108 1637 2319	7.3 0.4 7.4 0.6	**17** SA 0350 1027 1610 2229	6.9 0.9 7.0 0.8
3 SA 0503 1140 1721 2345	6.9 0.6 7.1 0.9	**18** SU 0424 1052 1645 2255	6.7 1.0 6.8 1.0
4 SU 0546 1213 1809 ◑	6.5 0.9 6.7	**19** M 0459 1117 1724 2326	6.5 1.0 6.6 1.1
5 M 0019 0633 1254 1904	1.2 6.1 1.1 6.3	**20** TU 0539 1150 1811 ◑	6.2 1.1 6.4
6 TU 0107 0733 1353 2015	1.5 5.9 1.4 6.1	**21** W 0006 0629 1237 1909	1.3 6.0 1.2 6.2
7 W 0222 0851 1513 2132	1.8 5.7 1.4 6.0	**22** TH 0102 0737 1344 2032	1.5 5.9 1.4 6.1
8 TH 0348 1013 1631 2249	1.7 5.9 1.2 6.3	**23** F 0246 0910 1543 2156	1.7 6.0 1.2 6.4
9 F 0506 1123 1744 2352	1.4 6.2 0.9 6.6	**24** SA 0420 1029 1702 2305	1.4 6.4 0.9 6.6
10 SA 0610 1216 1840	1.2 6.6 0.7	**25** SU 0534 1134 1821	1.0 6.8 0.6
11 SU 0040 0659 1259 1923	6.8 1.0 6.8 0.6	**26** M 0006 0648 1230 1928	7.2 0.8 7.1 0.3
12 M 0120 0742 1336 2001	6.9 0.9 6.9 0.6	**27** TU 0059 0749 1320 ○ 2022	7.3 0.6 7.4 0.2
13 TU 0154 0820 1408 ● 2035	6.9 0.9 7.0 0.6	**28** W 0147 0842 1405 2108	7.4 0.4 7.5 0.3
14 W 0223 0855 1437 2107	7.0 0.8 7.1 0.6	**29** TH 0232 0928 1449 2149	7.4 0.3 7.6 0.4
15 TH 0250 0928 1505 2136	7.0 0.8 7.1 0.6	**30** F 0316 1010 1533 2225	7.4 0.3 7.6 0.6
		31 SA 0358 1048 1616 2252	7.2 0.4 7.4 0.8

NOVEMBER

Time	m	Time	m
1 SU 0439 1120 1700 2317	6.9 0.6 7.1 1.1	**16** M 0406 1040 1629 2241	6.7 0.8 6.9 0.9
2 M 0520 1149 1746 2349	6.5 0.9 6.7 1.3	**17** TU 0443 1108 1711 2316	6.6 0.9 6.8 1.1
3 TU 0603 1225 1837 ◐	6.1 1.1 6.3	**18** W 0525 1143 1758 2359	6.4 0.9 6.6 1.3
4 W 0031 0655 1315 1939	1.6 5.8 1.3 6.0	**19** TH 0615 1229 1856 ◐	6.2 1.0 6.4
5 TH 0133 0806 1431 2051	1.9 5.7 1.4 5.9	**20** F 0055 0717 1334 2010	1.5 6.1 1.2 6.3
6 F 0300 0924 1546 2202	1.9 5.7 1.3 6.0	**21** SA 0224 0840 1515 2128	1.6 6.1 1.1 6.5
7 SA 0419 1035 1650 2308	1.7 6.0 1.1 6.3	**22** SU 0351 0958 1632 2237	1.4 6.4 0.9 6.7
8 SU 0523 1134 1747	1.4 6.3 0.9	**23** M 0505 1105 1747 2340	1.2 6.7 0.7 6.9
9 M 0001 0617 1222 1836	6.6 1.2 6.6 0.8	**24** TU 0620 1204 1858	0.9 7.0 0.6
10 TU 0044 0705 1302 1921	6.7 1.0 6.8 0.7	**25** W 0036 0724 1257 ○ 1954	7.1 0.7 7.2 0.5
11 W 0120 0748 1337 ● 2000	6.8 0.9 6.9 0.7	**26** TH 0127 0818 1345 2042	7.2 0.5 7.3 0.5
12 TH 0152 0827 1409 2036	6.9 0.8 7.0 0.7	**27** F 0213 0907 1431 2125	7.2 0.4 7.5 0.6
13 F 0223 0904 1441 2109	6.9 0.8 7.1 0.8	**28** SA 0257 0951 1515 2202	7.2 0.3 7.5 0.8
14 SA 0256 0939 1515 2140	6.9 0.8 7.1 0.8	**29** SU 0339 1030 1559 2231	7.1 0.4 7.2 1.0
15 SU 0330 1012 1551 2209	6.9 0.8 7.0 0.8	**30** M 0420 1103 1642 2255	6.8 0.6 7.0 1.1

DECEMBER

Time	m	Time	m
1 TU 0459 1131 1724 2325	6.5 0.8 6.7 1.3	**16** W 0435 1112 1702 2318	6.7 0.7 7.0 1.0
2 W 0537 1201 1808	6.3 1.0 6.3	**17** TH 0517 1147 1749	6.6 0.7 6.8
3 TH 0003 0619 1241 1858 ◐	1.5 6.0 1.2 6.1	**18** F 0002 0604 1231 ◐ 1842	1.1 6.5 0.8 6.6
4 F 0050 0712 1335 2000	1.7 5.8 1.3 5.9	**19** SA 0055 0700 1328 1949	1.3 6.3 1.0 6.4
5 SA 0150 0827 1449 2106	1.9 5.6 1.4 5.9	**20** SU 0203 0811 1445 2101	1.4 6.3 1.0 6.4
6 SU 0313 0939 1558 2210	1.9 5.7 1.3 6.0	**21** M 0320 0929 1600 2210	1.4 6.3 1.0 6.5
7 M 0430 1042 1657 2309	1.7 6.0 1.1 6.2	**22** TU 0436 1038 1713 2316	1.3 6.5 0.9 6.6
8 TU 0531 1138 1752	1.4 6.3 1.0	**23** W 0553 1142 1829	1.1 6.7 0.8
9 W 0001 0625 1225 1841	6.5 1.2 6.6 0.9	**24** TH 0018 0701 1240 1929	6.8 0.8 6.9 0.8
10 TH 0046 0715 1306 1928	6.7 1.0 6.8 0.9	**25** F 0112 0758 1331 ○ 2020	6.9 0.6 7.1 0.8
11 F 0125 0801 1344 ● 2010	6.8 0.9 6.9 0.9	**26** SA 0200 0849 1418 2105	7.0 0.4 7.2 0.8
12 SA 0202 0844 1421 2049	6.9 0.8 7.0 0.9	**27** SU 0244 0934 1502 2144	7.0 0.4 7.2 0.9
13 SU 0240 0925 1459 2126	6.9 0.7 7.1 0.9	**28** M 0325 1015 1545 2216	7.0 0.6 7.2 1.0
14 M 0318 1004 1538 2202	6.9 0.6 7.1 0.8	**29** TU 0403 1049 1624 2240	6.9 0.6 7.0 1.1
15 TU 0356 1040 1619 2238	6.8 0.6 7.1 0.9	**30** W 0439 1114 1702 2306	6.7 0.7 6.7 1.2
		31 TH 0513 1139 1738 2339	6.5 0.8 6.5 1.3

Chart Datum: 3·20 metres below Ordnance Datum (Newlyn). HAT is 7·7 metres above Chart Datum.

1.13 SOUTHEND-ON-SEA/LEIGH-ON-SEA

Essex 51°31'·07N 00°42'·57E ❀❀❀❀❀

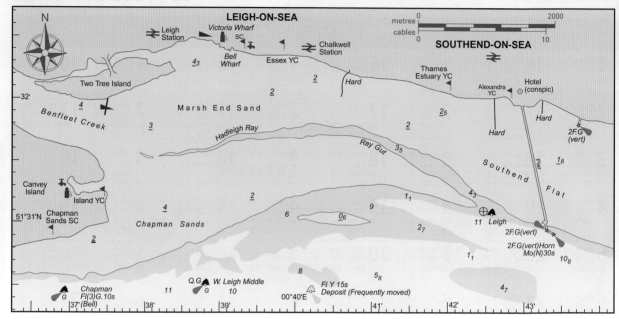

CHARTS AC 5606, 1183, 1185; Imray C1, C2, Y18, 2100

TIDES +0125 Dover; ML 3·0; Duration 0610

Standard Port SHEERNESS (←—)

Times				Height (metres)			
High Water		Low Water		MHWS	MHWN	MLWN	MLWS
0200	0800	0200	0700	5·8	4·7	1·5	0·6
1400	2000	1400	1900				
Differences SOUTHEND-ON-SEA							
–0005	–0005	–0005	–0005	+0·1	0·0	–0·1	–0·1
CORYTON							
+0005	+0010	+0010	+0010	+0·4	+0·3	0·0	0·0

SHELTER The whole area dries soon after half ebb, except Ray Gut (0·4–4·8m) which leads to Leigh Creek and Hadleigh Ray, either side of Two Tree Island, thence to Benfleet Creek where the limit of W navigation is the Tidal Barrier just above Benfleet YC; all are buoyed, but echo-sounder is essential. Craft can take the ground alongside Bell Wharf or Victoria Wharf. It is also possible to secure at the end of Southend Pier to collect stores, ⚓. NOTE: Southend-on-Sea and Leigh-on-Sea are both part of the lower PLA Area and an 8kn speed limit is enforced in inshore areas.

NAVIGATION WPT 51°31'·07N 00°42'·57E, Leigh SHM buoy, at ent to Ray Gut; this SHM buoy can be left close to port on entering Ray Gut, since there is now more water NE of it than to the SW. Appr from Shoeburyness, keep outside the W Shoebury SHM buoy, Fl G 2·5s.

Beware some 3000 small boat moorings 1M either side of Southend Pier. Speed limit in Canvey Island/Hadleigh Ray areas is 8kn.

LIGHTS AND MARKS See chartlet.

COMMUNICATIONS (Code 01702) MRCC (01255) 675518; Essex Police Marine Section (01268) 775533; Police 101; Dr 225500; Ⓗ 348911. HM ☎ 215620; HM Leigh-on-Sea 710561.

Port Control London: *London VTS* VHF Ch 68 inward from Sea Reach No4, *London VTS* VHF Ch 69 seaward from Sea Reach No 4.

FACILITIES
SOUTHEND-ON-SEA: Southend Pier ☎ 215620, ▭ (craft not to be unattended), £17/night <40' LOA, £37/night 40'-50', £76/night > 50' (short stay free), M, L. **Alexandra YC** ☎ 340363, ▭, ⚓; **Thorpe Bay YC** ☎ 587563, ▭, L, ▬, ✕, ⚓; **Thames Estuary YC** ☎ 345967; **Halfway YC** ☎ 582025, pre-book 1 🅟, ⚓. **Town** ◨, ACA, Ⓔ, ☍, ✕, ▭, ✉, Ⓑ, ≈, ✈.

LEIGH-ON-SEA: Essex YC ☎ 478404, ⚓, ▭; **Leigh on Sea SC** ☎ 476788, ⚓, ▭; **Bell Wharf**, ▭ 24hrs free then £11/night; **Victoria Wharf** ▭ 24hrs free then £11/night, D, ⚓, ▬ (Two Tree Is HW±2½); **Town**: ⚒, ▣, ✕, C, ◨, ⚓.

CANVEY ISLAND: (Code 01268) Access via drying channels. **Services:** ▬, M, D, ⚓, ⚒, ▣, ✕, C, Gas, ◨. **Island YC** ☎ 510360, ▭ (max 9m LOA), dries; **Benfleet YC** (on S side of Benfleet Creek on Canvey Island) ☎ 792278, M, ▬, ⚓, D (by day), ◨, ⚒, ▣, ✕, C, ▭, ☍, 🖰.

SHOEBURYNESS TO RIVER COLNE

(Charts 1185, 1975) Maplin and Foulness Sands extend nearly 6M NE from Foulness Pt, the extremity being marked by Whitaker bn. On N side of Whitaker chan leading to R. Crouch and R Roach lies Buxey Sand, inshore of which is the Ray Sand chan (dries), a convenient short cut between R. Crouch and R. Blackwater with sufficient rise of tide.

To seaward of Buxey Sand and the Spitway, Gunfleet Sand extends 10M NE, marked by buoys and dries in places. ▶ *A conspic disused lt tr stands on SE side of Gunfleet Sand, about 6M SSE of the Naze tr, and here the SW-going (flood) stream begins about*

HW Sheerness +0600, and the NE-going stream at about HW Sheerness –0030, sp rates 2kn. ◀

The Rivers Blackwater and Colne share a common estuary which is approached from the NE via NE Gunfleet lt buoy; thence along Goldmer Gat and the Wallet towards Knoll and Eagle lt buoys. For the Colne turn NNW via Colne Bar buoy towards Inner Bench Hd buoy keeping in mid-chan. For R Blackwater, head WNW for NW Knoll and Bench Hd buoys. From the S or SE, make for the Whitaker ECM buoy, thence through the Spitway, via Swin Spitway and Wallet Spitway buoys to reach Knoll buoy and deeper water.

1.14 RIVER ROACH/HAVENGORE

Essex **51°36'·98N 00°52'·14E** (Branklet SPM buoy), R Roach ✿✿✿✿✿✿✿✿. **51°33'·62N 00°50'·52E**, Havengore Bridge ✿✿✿

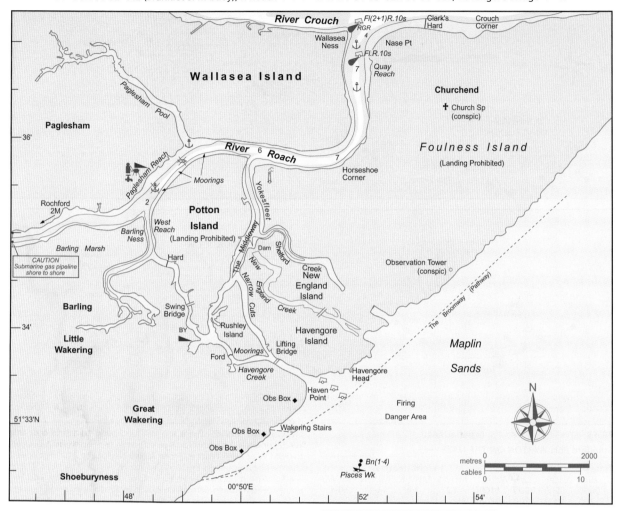

E England

CHARTS AC 5607, 1185, 3750; Imray C1, Y17, 2100, 2000

TIDES +0110 Dover; ML 2·7; Duration 0615

Standard Port WALTON-ON-THE-NAZE (→)

Times				Height (metres)			
High Water		Low Water		MHWS	MHWN	MLWN	MLWS
0000	0600	0500	1100	4·2	3·4	1·1	0·4
1200	1800	1700	2300				
Differences ROCHFORD							
+0050	+0040	DR	DR	–0·8	–1·1	DR	DR

SHELTER Good. The Roach gives sheltered sailing and access to a network of secluded creeks, including Havengore (the 'backdoor' from the Crouch to the Thames Estuary). No ⌒ available in the area. ⚓s behind sea-walls can be found for all winds at: Quay Reach (often more protected than the Crouch), Paglesham Reach, West Reach, Barling Reach and Yokes Fleet. An ⚓ light is essential due to freighters H24. Speed limit 8kn. Crouch Hbr Authority controls R Roach and Crouch, out to Foulness Pt.

NAVIGATION Normal access H24 to the Roach is from R Crouch; the ent between Branklet buoy and Nase Pt is narrowed by mudbanks. Unlit buoys up-river to Barling Ness, above which few boats go. To exit at Havengore Creek, appr via Middleway and Narrow Cuts to reach the bridge before HW.

Entry via **Havengore Creek** is possible in good weather, with great care and adequate rise of tide (max draft 1·5m at HW sp). Shoeburyness Range is usually active Mon-Fri 0600-1700LT; give 24hrs notice to Range Officer by ☎. Subsequent clearance on VHF by Havengore lifting bridge (☎ HW±2, HJ); no passage unless bridge raised. Least water is over the shifting bar, just inside creek ent. From the S, cross Maplin Sands at HW –1 from S Shoebury SHM buoy, leaving Pisces wreck (conspic, 1M from ent) to port.

LIGHTS AND MARKS Unlit, but night entry to R Roach may be possible.

COMMUNICATIONS (Code 01702 Southend MRCC (01255) 675518; Dr 218678. Crouch HM (01621) 783602; Range Officer 383211; Havengore Br 383436; Swing Br to Potton Island 219491.

VHF Ch 72 16 is worked by Range Officer (*Shoe Base*) (HO); Radar Control (*Shoe Radar*) (HO); & Bridge keeper (*Shoe Bridge*) (HW±2 by day). Radar guidance may be available.

FACILITIES Paglesham (East End) ⚓, D, slip, ⛽, ↘ (from BY), ✕, ⌂; **Gt Wakering:** ⎘, P, D, ⚓, ↘, ⛽, ✕, C, ⚓ (from BY); at Rochford **Wakering YC** ☎ 530926, M, L, ⌂. **Towns** Gt Wakering & Rochford; ⎙, ✕, ⌂, ✉ (Great Wakering and Barling); most facilities, Ⓑ and ⇌ in Rochford and Shoeburyness, ✈ (Southend).

1.15 BURNHAM-ON-CROUCH

Essex 51°37'·50N 00°48'·23E (Yacht Hbr) ✺✺✺🌢🌢🌢❀❀✿

CHARTS AC 5607, 1183, 1975, 3750; Imray C1, Y17, 2100, 2000

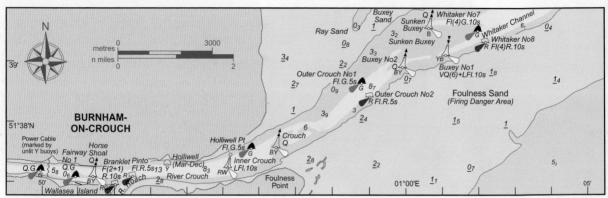

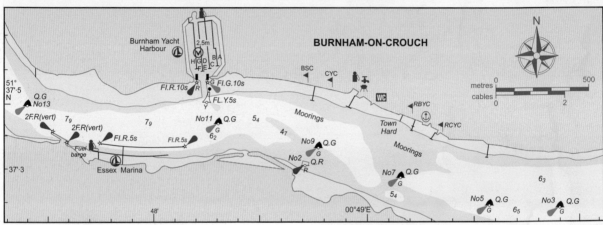

TIDES +0115 Dover; ML 2·5; Duration 0610

Standard Port WALTON-ON-THE-NAZE (→)

Times				Height (metres)			
High Water		Low Water		MHWS	MHWN	MLWN	MLWS
0000	0600	0500	1100	4·2	3·4	1·1	0·4
1200	1800	1700	2300				
Differences WHITAKER BEACON							
+0022	+0024	+0033	+0027	+0·6	+0·5	+0·2	+0·1
HOLLIWELL POINT							
+0034	+0037	+0100	+0037	+1·1	+0·9	+0·3	+0·1
NORTH FAMBRIDGE							
+0115	+0050	+0130	+0100	+1·1	+0·8	0·0	−0·1
HULLBRIDGE							
+0115	+0050	+0135	+0105	+1·1	+0·8	0·0	−0·1
BATTLESBRIDGE							
+0120	+0110	DR	DR	−1·8	−2·0	DR	DR

SHELTER River is exposed to most winds. Cliff Reach (off W edge of lower chartlet) is sheltered from SW'lies. ⚓ prohib in fairway but possible just E or W of the moorings.

NAVIGATION Appr from East Swin or the Wallet via Swin Spitway SWM / Whitaker ECM, into the well marked Whitaker Channel.

Near Sunken Buxey seas can be hazardous with strong wind over tide. Ray Sand Chan (dries 1·7m), usable on the tide by shoal draft boats as a short cut from/to the Blackwater. Shoeburyness Artillery ranges lie E and S of Foulness Pt, clear of fairway. The buoyed chan leads either side of shoal patch 0·7 marked by Sunken Buxey NCM and Buxey No1 SCM. R Crouch is navigable to Battlesbridge, 10M beyond Burnham. No landing on Foulness or Bridgemarsh Is. Wallasea Wetlands are being developed; keep well clear of ships using unloading pontoon at Ringwood Pt. Anchoring is prohibited in swinging area between Horse Shoal and No 3 SHM buoy. Work is expected to be complete by 2019.

LIGHTS AND MARKS There are few landmarks to assist entry, but Whitaker Chan, Swallow Tail Bank and the river are well lit/buoyed to 0·5M W of Essex Marina. From Buxey No2 steer 240° in buoyed channel past Foulness Pt, N of Crouch NCM into the river. There is a 1·3M unlit gap between Inner Crouch SWM lit buoy, and the entrance to R Roach, which is marked by Pinto PHM and Branklet PCM en-route Horse Shoal NCM.

COMMUNICATIONS (Code Maldon 01621) MRCC (01255) 675518; Police 101; Dr 782054. HM 783602.

VHF Ch 80 for: Crouch HM Launch (0900-1700LT, w/e); Essex Marina; Burnham Yacht Harbour; W Wick Marina (1000-1700), also Ch M.

FACILITIES There are five marinas or yacht hbrs. Speed limit in moorings is 8kn.

BURNHAM, Burnham Yacht Hbr ☎ 782150, access H24, some ⚓s, (350) £2·50, 🔌 +£2, ⚒, ☐, D, ⚓, ✗, 🛒, 🅿, BY, BH (30 ton), ✗, ☐, 🛢. **Royal Corinthian YC** ☎ 782105, 🍽, ⚓, M, L, ✗, ☐.
Royal Burnham YC ☎ 782044, ⚓, L, ✗, ☐. **Crouch YC** ☎ 782252, L, ✗, ☐. **Services:** 🍽, BY, C (15 ton), D, P, ⚓, ✗, 🛒, ✗, M, ⚒, 🅿, ACA, Gas, 🛢, Gaz. **Town** 🍴, ✗, ☐, ✉, Ⓑ, ⇌, ✈ (Southend).

ALTHORNE, Bridgemarsh Marina £20 /craft/night.

WALLASEA ISLAND, Essex Marina (400) ☎ (01702) 258531, £2·13, BY, Gas, ☐, C (13 ton), BH (40 ton), 🅿, D, P, LPG, 🛒, M, ⚓, ✗, ✗, ⚒. Ferry to Burnham Town Hard at w/ends in season, ☎ 07704060482. **Essex YC.** ACA.

FAMBRIDGE, Fambridge Yacht Haven ⚓ www.yachthavens.com ☎ 740370; 170 + 🍽 ❼ £2·50, short stay <3 hrs < 15m £5, ⚓s £1·50. Min 1m depth in approach. M, ✗, ⚓, BY, BH (25ton), C (5 ton), 🛒, ⚒ (£6-£15), Gas, Gaz, 🅿, showers, YC, ☐, 🍴. ❼ pontoon (with electricity and water) at Fambridge Yacht Station, £5/night.

Brandy Hole Yacht Stn (120) ☎ (01702) 230248, L, M, ⚓, ✗, ⚒, Gas, Gaz, ☐, BY, D, Access via drying channel.

STANDARD TIME (UT)
For Summer Time add ONE hour in **non-shaded areas**

BURNHAM-ON-CROUCH   LAT 51°37′N   LONG 0°48′E
TIMES AND HEIGHTS OF HIGH AND LOW WATERS

Dates in red are **SPRINGS**
Dates in blue are **NEAPS**

YEAR 2015

E England

JANUARY

Time	m	Time	m
1 0249 0.8 / 0854 4.6 / TH 1533 0.5 / 2134 4.8		**16** 0147 1.2 / 0806 4.2 / F 1439 0.9 / 2050 4.5	
2 0359 0.6 / 0958 4.8 / F 1632 0.4 / 2231 5.0		**17** 0308 1.1 / 0925 4.3 / SA 1550 0.8 / 2158 4.7	
3 0458 0.3 / 1055 5.0 / SA 1724 0.4 / 2323 5.1		**18** 0423 0.9 / 1032 4.6 / SU 1653 0.6 / 2257 4.9	
4 0551 0.2 / 1147 5.1 / SU 1811 0.4		**19** 0526 0.6 / 1128 5.0 / M 1748 0.5 / 2350 5.2	
5 0011 5.1 / 0639 0.1 / M 1235 5.1 / ○ 1853 0.5		**20** 0620 0.3 / 1219 5.2 / TU 1837 0.3 ●	
6 0054 5.1 / 0722 0.1 / TU 1317 5.0 / 1930 0.6		**21** 0038 5.3 / 0709 0.0 / W 1308 5.5 / 1923 0.2	
7 0131 4.9 / 0801 0.2 / W 1354 4.9 / 1958 0.7		**22** 0123 5.5 / 0755 -0.1 / TH 1354 5.6 / 2006 0.2	
8 0200 4.8 / 0832 0.4 / TH 1424 4.7 / 2018 0.8		**23** 0207 5.5 / 0840 -0.2 / F 1439 5.6 / 2049 0.2	
9 0223 4.7 / 0857 0.5 / F 1451 4.6 / 2043 0.8		**24** 0249 5.5 / 0924 -0.2 / SA 1524 5.5 / 2132 0.3	
10 0250 4.7 / 0924 0.6 / SA 1523 4.6 / 2117 0.8		**25** 0333 5.4 / 1009 -0.1 / SU 1610 5.3 / 2216 0.4	
11 0326 4.7 / 0959 0.6 / SU 1601 4.7 / 2158 0.9		**26** 0418 5.2 / 1055 0.1 / M 1659 5.1 / 2304 0.5	
12 0408 4.7 / 1041 0.7 / M 1646 4.6 / 2243 1.0		**27** 0507 4.9 / 1145 0.3 / TU 1752 4.8 / ☽ 2357 0.7	
13 0455 4.6 / 1130 0.7 / TU 1736 4.6 / ☽ 2334 1.1		**28** 0604 4.7 / 1242 0.5 / W 1853 4.6	
14 0548 4.4 / 1225 0.8 / W 1833 4.5		**29** 0058 0.8 / 0712 4.4 / TH 1349 0.7 / 2001 4.4	
15 0034 1.2 / 0649 4.3 / TH 1329 0.9 / 1938 4.4		**30** 0214 0.8 / 0829 4.4 / F 1504 0.7 / 2110 4.5	
		31 0335 0.7 / 0940 4.5 / SA 1611 0.6 / 2212 4.7	

FEBRUARY

Time	m	Time	m
1 0441 0.5 / 1040 4.7 / SU 1707 0.5 / 2306 4.8		**16** 0359 1.0 / 1005 4.4 / M 1634 0.7 / 2233 4.6	
2 0535 0.3 / 1133 4.8 / M 1754 0.5 / 2355 4.9		**17** 0509 0.6 / 1107 4.8 / TU 1732 0.5 / 2329 5.0	
3 0623 0.1 / 1220 4.9 / TU 1837 0.5 ○		**18** 0604 0.2 / 1200 5.2 / W 1821 0.2 ●	
4 0038 5.0 / 0704 0.1 / W 1302 4.9 / 1912 0.5		**19** 0018 5.3 / 0652 -0.1 / TH 1249 5.5 / 1906 0.0	
5 0115 4.9 / 0740 0.2 / TH 1336 4.8 / 1938 0.6		**20** 0105 5.5 / 0737 -0.4 / F 1335 5.6 / 1949 -0.1	
6 0143 4.8 / 0808 0.3 / F 1402 4.7 / 1957 0.6		**21** 0148 5.6 / 0821 -0.4 / SA 1419 5.7 / 2031 -0.1	
7 0203 4.8 / 0830 0.4 / SA 1426 4.7 / 2020 0.6		**22** 0230 5.7 / 0903 -0.4 / SU 1503 5.6 / 2112 0.0	
8 0228 4.9 / 0855 0.4 / SU 1455 4.8 / 2052 0.6		**23** 0313 5.6 / 0945 -0.3 / M 1547 5.4 / 2154 0.1	
9 0302 4.9 / 0928 0.4 / M 1533 4.9 / 2128 0.6		**24** 0357 5.4 / 1028 0.0 / TU 1633 5.1 / 2238 0.2	
10 0342 4.9 / 1006 0.5 / TU 1615 4.9 / 2208 0.6		**25** 0444 5.1 / 1114 0.3 / W 1723 4.7 / ☽ 2327 0.5	
11 0426 4.8 / 1048 0.6 / W 1702 4.8 / 2252 0.8		**26** 0538 4.7 / 1205 0.6 / TH 1819 4.4	
12 0515 4.6 / 1136 0.7 / TH 1754 4.6 / ☽ 2342 1.0		**27** 0023 0.7 / 0642 4.4 / F 1307 0.8 / 1928 4.2	
13 0611 4.4 / 1235 0.9 / F 1853 4.4		**28** 0134 0.8 / 0803 4.2 / SA 1428 0.9 / 2044 4.2	
14 0045 1.1 / 0718 4.2 / SA 1342 1.0 / 2006 4.3			
15 0220 1.2 / 0846 4.2 / SU 1520 1.0 / 2126 4.4			

MARCH

Time	m	Time	m
1 0303 0.8 / 0920 4.3 / SU 1545 0.9 / 2150 4.4		**16** 0129 1.1 / 0810 4.1 / M 1447 1.1 / 2050 4.1	
2 0415 0.6 / 1022 4.5 / M 1643 0.7 / 2246 4.6		**17** 0332 1.0 / 0939 4.4 / TU 1612 0.8 / 2206 4.4	
3 0511 0.4 / 1114 4.7 / TU 1731 0.6 / 2334 4.8		**18** 0447 0.5 / 1044 4.8 / W 1711 0.5 / 2305 4.8	
4 0557 0.1 / 1200 4.8 / W 1812 0.5		**19** 0541 0.1 / 1138 5.2 / TH 1800 0.2 / 2355 5.2	
5 0017 4.9 / 0636 0.2 / TH 1240 4.8 / ○ 1846 0.5		**20** 0629 -0.2 / 1226 5.5 / F 1845 -0.1 ●	
6 0054 4.9 / 0710 0.2 / F 1313 4.8 / 1913 0.5		**21** 0041 5.5 / 0713 -0.4 / SA 1312 5.6 / 1928 -0.2	
7 0122 4.9 / 0737 0.3 / SA 1338 4.8 / 1935 0.5		**22** 0126 5.7 / 0756 -0.5 / SU 1356 5.7 / 2010 -0.2	
8 0145 4.9 / 0800 0.3 / SU 1402 4.8 / 1959 0.4		**23** 0209 5.7 / 0837 -0.4 / M 1439 5.5 / 2051 -0.2	
9 0210 4.9 / 0827 0.3 / M 1431 4.9 / 2030 0.4		**24** 0252 5.6 / 0918 -0.2 / TU 1522 5.3 / 2132 -0.1	
10 0242 5.0 / 0859 0.3 / TU 1507 5.0 / 2104 0.4		**25** 0336 5.4 / 0959 0.1 / W 1606 5.0 / 2215 0.1	
11 0321 5.0 / 0935 0.4 / W 1548 5.0 / 2142 0.4		**26** 0422 5.1 / 1042 0.4 / TH 1652 4.7 / 2301 0.3	
12 0404 5.0 / 1015 0.5 / TH 1633 4.8 / 2224 0.6		**27** 0513 4.7 / 1129 0.7 / F 1744 4.3 / ☽ 2353 0.6	
13 0451 4.8 / 1100 0.7 / F 1722 4.6 / ☽ 2312 0.8		**28** 0614 4.3 / 1235 1.1 / SA 1850 4.0	
14 0544 4.5 / 1153 0.9 / SA 1817 4.3		**29** 0057 0.8 / 0733 4.1 / SU 1338 1.1 / 2009 4.0	
15 0009 1.0 / 0645 4.3 / SU 1303 1.1 / 1923 4.1		**30** 0220 0.8 / 0852 4.1 / M 1503 1.1 / 2119 4.1	
		31 0337 0.7 / 0954 4.3 / TU 1607 0.9 / 2216 4.4	

APRIL

Time	m	Time	m
1 0434 0.5 / 1046 4.5 / W 1656 0.8 / 2305 4.6		**16** 0418 0.5 / 1018 4.8 / TH 1644 0.5 / 2237 4.8	
2 0520 0.4 / 1130 4.7 / TH 1738 0.6 / 2347 4.7		**17** 0514 0.1 / 1112 5.1 / F 1735 0.2 / 2329 5.1	
3 0559 0.3 / 1209 4.8 / F 1814 0.5		**18** 0603 -0.2 / 1202 5.4 / SA 1822 0.0 ●	
4 0024 4.8 / 0632 0.3 / SA 1243 4.8 / ○ 1844 0.5		**19** 0017 5.4 / 0647 -0.3 / SU 1248 5.6 / 1906 -0.2	
5 0056 4.9 / 0702 0.3 / SU 1311 4.9 / 1911 0.4		**20** 0103 5.6 / 0730 -0.3 / M 1332 5.6 / 1949 -0.2	
6 0124 4.9 / 0731 0.3 / M 1339 5.0 / 1940 0.3		**21** 0148 5.6 / 0812 -0.2 / TU 1415 5.4 / 2031 -0.2	
7 0153 5.0 / 0801 0.3 / TU 1410 5.1 / 2011 0.3		**22** 0231 5.5 / 0852 0.0 / W 1457 5.2 / 2113 -0.1	
8 0226 5.0 / 0834 0.3 / W 1445 5.1 / 2046 0.3		**23** 0315 5.3 / 0932 0.3 / TH 1538 4.9 / 2156 0.1	
9 0304 5.0 / 0910 0.4 / TH 1525 5.0 / 2125 0.4		**24** 0400 5.0 / 1012 0.5 / F 1621 4.6 / 2241 0.3	
10 0347 5.0 / 0950 0.5 / F 1609 4.9 / 2208 0.5		**25** 0448 4.6 / 1056 0.8 / SA 1707 4.3 / ☽ 2330 0.5	
11 0434 4.8 / 1036 0.7 / SA 1657 4.6 / 2256 0.6		**26** 0543 4.3 / 1147 1.0 / SU 1803 4.0	
12 0526 4.6 / 1129 0.9 / SU 1750 4.4 / ☽ 2353 0.8		**27** 0026 0.7 / 0651 4.0 / M 1248 1.2 / 1916 3.9	
13 0627 4.3 / 1235 1.1 / M 1852 4.2		**28** 0132 0.8 / 0808 4.0 / TU 1359 1.3 / 2034 3.9	
14 0111 0.9 / 0745 4.2 / TU 1411 1.1 / 2014 4.1		**29** 0242 0.8 / 0913 4.1 / W 1510 1.2 / 2135 4.1	
15 0303 0.8 / 0911 4.4 / W 1542 0.9 / 2135 4.4		**30** 0342 0.7 / 1006 4.3 / TH 1608 1.0 / 2226 4.4	

Chart Datum: 2·35 metres below Ordnance Datum (Newlyn). HAT is 5·8 metres above Chart Datum.

〉〉 FREE monthly updates from 〈〈
www.reedsalmanac.co.uk

STANDARD TIME (UT)
For Summer Time add ONE hour in **non-shaded areas**

BURNHAM-ON-CROUCH   LAT 51°37'N   LONG 0°48'E
TIMES AND HEIGHTS OF HIGH AND LOW WATERS

Dates in red are **SPRINGS**
Dates in blue are **NEAPS**

YEAR 2015

MAY

	Time	m		Time	m
1 F	0432 1051 1655 2310	0.5 4.6 0.8 4.6	**16** SA	0447 1046 1709 2304	0.2 5.1 0.3 5.1
2 SA	0515 1132 1736 2350	0.4 4.8 0.6 4.7	**17** SU	0537 1137 1800 2354	0.0 5.3 0.1 5.3
3 SU	0553 1209 1813	0.4 4.9 0.5	**18** M ●	0624 1225 1847	-0.1 5.4 -0.1
4 M ○	0027 0629 1244 1849	4.8 0.3 5.0 0.4	**19** TU	0042 0708 1310 1932	5.5 -0.1 5.4 -0.1
5 TU	0102 0704 1317 1923	4.9 0.3 5.1 0.4	**20** W	0128 0750 1353 2016	5.4 0.0 5.3 -0.1
6 W	0137 0739 1352 1959	5.0 0.4 5.1 0.3	**21** TH	0213 0830 1434 2059	5.3 0.2 5.1 0.4
7 TH	0213 0815 1428 2035	5.0 0.4 5.1 0.4	**22** F	0256 0908 1513 2140	5.1 0.5 4.8 0.2
8 F	0253 0852 1508 2116	5.0 0.5 5.0 0.4	**23** SA	0338 0945 1550 2221	4.8 0.7 4.6 0.4
9 SA	0336 0934 1551 2200	4.9 0.6 4.9 0.5	**24** SU	0421 1024 1629 2305	4.5 0.9 4.4 0.5
10 SU	0423 1021 1638 2251	4.8 0.8 4.7 0.6	**25** M ◐	0507 1108 1713 2353	4.3 1.1 4.2 0.7
11 M ◐	0515 1115 1730 2350	4.6 0.9 4.5 0.7	**26** TU	0559 1159 1807	4.0 1.2 4.0
12 TU	0615 1220 1830	4.5 1.0 4.3	**27** W	0046 0700 1258 1916	0.8 3.9 1.3 3.9
13 W	0107 0726 1342 1944	0.7 4.4 1.1 4.3	**28** TH	0145 0808 1402 2032	0.8 4.0 1.2 4.0
14 TH	0236 0843 1506 2103	0.6 4.5 0.9 4.4	**29** F	0244 0910 1506 2134	0.7 4.2 1.1 4.2
15 F	0349 0950 1614 2208	0.4 4.8 0.6 4.7	**30** SA	0340 1003 1605 2227	0.6 4.4 1.0 4.4
			31 SU	0432 1051 1657 2314	0.5 4.7 0.8 4.6

JUNE

	Time	m		Time	m
1 M	0519 1135 1745 2358	0.4 4.9 0.6 4.8	**16** TU ●	0607 1206 1833	0.1 5.2 0.0
2 TU ○	0603 1217 1829	0.4 5.1 0.5	**17** W	0026 0652 1252 1920	5.3 0.3 5.2 0.0
3 W	0040 0645 1257 1911	5.0 0.4 5.1 0.4	**18** TH	0113 0735 1335 2004	5.2 0.2 5.1 0.3
4 TH	0121 0725 1336 1953	5.1 0.4 5.2 0.3	**19** F	0157 0813 1414 2045	5.2 0.4 4.9 0.3
5 F	0202 0804 1416 2034	5.1 0.4 5.1 0.3	**20** SA	0237 0847 1448 2123	4.9 0.6 4.7 0.3
6 SA	0244 0844 1456 2117	5.1 0.5 5.1 0.3	**21** SU	0314 0916 1518 2157	4.7 0.7 4.6 0.5
7 SU	0328 0927 1539 2203	5.0 0.6 4.9 0.4	**22** M	0349 0949 1551 2232	4.5 0.8 4.5 0.6
8 M	0414 1013 1625 2253	4.9 0.7 4.8 0.5	**23** TU	0427 1027 1630 2313	4.4 0.9 4.4 0.6
9 TU	0505 1106 1715 2351	4.8 0.8 4.6 0.5	**24** W ●	0509 1112 1716	4.2 1.0 4.3
10 W	0602 1206 1812	4.6 0.9 4.5	**25** TH	0000 0558 1204 1809	0.7 4.2 1.1 4.1
11 TH	0057 0706 1316 1920	0.6 4.5 0.9 4.4	**26** F	0053 0656 1303 1915	0.8 4.1 1.2 4.0
12 F	0210 0816 1433 2035	0.5 4.5 0.8 4.5	**27** SA	0152 0803 1408 2032	0.8 4.2 1.1 4.1
13 SA	0321 0923 1545 2143	0.4 4.7 0.6 4.7	**28** SU	0253 0910 1516 2141	0.8 4.3 1.1 4.3
14 SU	0423 1022 1648 2243	0.3 4.9 0.4 5.0	**29** M	0354 1010 1622 2239	0.7 4.6 0.9 4.5
15 M	0517 1116 1742 2336	0.1 5.1 0.2 5.2	**30** TU	0451 1103 1720 2331	0.5 4.8 0.7 4.8

JULY

	Time	m		Time	m
1 W	0543 1152 1813	0.4 5.0 0.5	**16** TH ●	0014 0639 1238 1907	5.1 0.2 5.0 0.0
2 TH ○	0019 0631 1238 1901	5.0 0.4 5.1 0.3	**17** F	0101 0721 1320 1950	5.1 0.3 5.0 0.0
3 F	0105 0716 1322 1947	5.2 0.3 5.2 0.0	**18** SA	0142 0757 1356 2027	5.0 0.4 4.8 0.1
4 SA	0149 0758 1403 2031	5.3 0.3 5.2 0.1	**19** SU	0218 0825 1424 2058	4.8 0.6 4.7 0.3
5 SU	0233 0840 1444 2115	5.3 0.4 5.2 0.1	**20** M	0247 0847 1448 2124	4.7 0.7 4.7 0.5
6 M	0317 0922 1526 2200	5.2 0.4 5.1 0.1	**21** TU	0316 0914 1518 2153	4.6 0.7 4.6 0.5
7 TU	0403 1006 1611 2247	5.1 0.5 5.0 0.2	**22** W	0349 0949 1555 2229	4.6 0.7 4.6 0.6
8 W	0451 1054 1659 2338	5.0 0.6 4.8 0.3	**23** TH	0429 1029 1638 2312	4.5 0.8 4.5 0.6
9 TH	0544 1147 1753	4.8 0.7 4.7	**24** F ◐	0515 1114 1727	4.5 0.9 4.4
10 F	0035 0642 1249 1857	0.5 4.6 0.8 4.5	**25** SA	0002 0606 1207 1823	0.7 4.4 1.0 4.2
11 SA	0142 0749 1402 2011	0.6 4.5 0.8 4.4	**26** SU	0100 0707 1311 1932	0.8 4.3 1.1 4.1
12 SU	0256 0858 1521 2124	0.6 4.5 0.7 4.6	**27** M	0207 0818 1429 2056	0.9 4.2 1.1 4.1
13 M	0404 1002 1630 2228	0.5 4.7 0.4 4.8	**28** TU	0319 0931 1550 2208	0.9 4.4 1.0 4.4
14 TU	0502 1059 1728 2324	0.3 4.9 0.2 5.0	**29** W	0428 1035 1700 2308	0.7 4.6 0.7 4.7
15 W	0553 1150 1820	0.3 5.0 0.0	**30** TH	0526 1129 1757	0.5 4.9 0.4
			31 F ○	0000 0617 1219 1847	5.0 0.3 5.1 0.1

AUGUST

	Time	m		Time	m
1 SA	0048 0703 1304 1934	5.3 0.2 5.3 -0.1	**16** SU	0125 0735 1336 2000	4.9 0.4 4.8 0.1
2 SU	0133 0746 1347 2018	5.5 0.1 5.4 -0.2	**17** M	0156 0758 1400 2025	4.8 0.5 4.7 0.3
3 M	0217 0828 1429 2101	5.5 0.1 5.4 -0.2	**18** TU	0220 0817 1421 2046	4.7 0.5 4.7 0.4
4 TU	0301 0909 1510 2144	5.5 0.2 5.3 -0.1	**19** W	0244 0843 1449 2114	4.7 0.5 4.8 0.4
5 W	0345 0951 1554 2227	5.3 0.2 5.2 0.0	**20** TH	0316 0915 1525 2148	4.8 0.5 4.8 0.4
6 TH	0431 1036 1640 2314	5.1 0.3 5.0 0.2	**21** F	0356 0953 1607 2228	4.8 0.6 4.8 0.5
7 F ◐	0521 1125 1732	4.8 0.5 4.8	**22** SA ◐	0440 1034 1654 2313	4.7 0.7 4.6 0.7
8 SA	0007 0616 1222 1834	0.5 4.6 0.6 4.5	**23** SU	0529 1122 1746	4.6 0.8 4.4
9 SU	0110 0722 1332 1950	0.7 4.4 0.7 4.3	**24** M	0007 0624 1220 1848	0.9 4.4 1.0 4.2
10 M	0229 0835 1458 2109	0.7 4.3 0.7 4.4	**25** TU	0117 0731 1339 2011	1.0 4.2 1.1 4.1
11 TU	0345 0944 1614 2215	0.7 4.5 0.5 4.6	**26** W	0244 0853 1520 2138	1.0 4.2 1.0 4.3
12 W	0446 1043 1713 2311	0.5 4.7 0.2 4.8	**27** TH	0405 1007 1640 2244	0.9 4.5 0.7 4.7
13 TH	0537 1135 1804	0.4 4.9 0.0	**28** F	0507 1106 1738 2338	0.6 4.8 0.3 5.1
14 F ●	0001 0622 1222 1848	5.0 0.3 5.0 -0.1	**29** SA ○	0559 1156 1828	0.3 5.1 -0.1
15 SA	0046 0701 1302 1928	5.0 0.3 4.9 0.0	**30** SU	0027 0644 1243 1913	5.4 0.1 5.4 -0.3
			31 M	0113 0727 1326 1956	5.6 0.0 5.5 -0.4

Chart Datum: 2·35 metres below Ordnance Datum (Newlyn). HAT is 5·8 metres above Chart Datum.

〉〉 FREE monthly updates from 〈〈
www.reedsalmanac.co.uk

STANDARD TIME (UT)
For Summer Time add ONE hour in **non-shaded areas**

BURNHAM-ON-CROUCH LAT 51°37'N LONG 0°48'E
TIMES AND HEIGHTS OF HIGH AND LOW WATERS

Dates in red are **SPRINGS**
Dates in blue are **NEAPS**

YEAR 2015

E England

SEPTEMBER

Time	m	Time	m
1 0157 0809 TU 1408 2038	5.7 -0.1 5.6 -0.4	**16** 0152 0748 W 1357 2011	4.8 0.5 4.9 0.3
2 0240 0849 W 1450 2119	5.6 0.0 5.5 -0.2	**17** 0216 0815 TH 1425 2040	4.9 0.4 4.9 0.3
3 0323 0931 TH 1534 2201	5.4 0.0 5.4 0.0	**18** 0248 0847 F 1501 2114	5.0 0.4 5.0 0.4
4 0408 1014 F 1620 2246	5.2 0.2 5.1 0.2	**19** 0327 0924 SA 1542 2152	5.0 0.5 4.9 0.5
5 0456 1101 SA 1711 ☽ 2335	4.9 0.6 4.8 0.5	**20** 0410 1005 SU 1628 2236	4.9 0.6 4.7 0.7
6 0550 1156 SU 1812	4.5 0.6 4.5	**21** 0458 1052 M 1719 ☽ 2328	4.7 0.7 4.5 0.9
7 0035 0655 M 1305 1930	0.8 4.3 0.7 4.2	**22** 0551 1148 TU 1818	4.5 0.9 4.3
8 0156 0812 TU 1434 2052	0.9 4.2 0.7 4.3	**23** 0032 0652 W 1301 1934	1.1 4.2 1.1 4.1
9 0320 0924 W 1552 2159	0.9 4.3 0.5 4.5	**24** 0204 0812 TH 1451 2107	1.2 4.2 1.0 4.2
10 0423 1023 TH 1651 2254	0.7 4.6 0.3 4.8	**25** 0338 0935 F 1616 2218	1.0 4.4 0.7 4.6
11 0513 1114 F 1739 2342	0.5 4.8 0.1 4.9	**26** 0443 1038 SA 1714 2313	0.7 4.8 0.2 5.1
12 0557 1159 SA 1821	0.4 5.0 0.0	**27** 0534 1130 SU 1803	0.3 5.1 -0.1
13 0024 0634 SU 1239 ● 1857	5.0 0.4 5.0 0.1	**28** 0002 0620 M 1218 ○ 1848	5.4 0.1 5.5 -0.3
14 0101 0705 M 1312 1926	4.9 0.4 4.9 0.2	**29** 0049 0704 TU 1302 1931	5.6 -0.1 5.7 -0.4
15 0129 0728 TU 1336 1948	4.8 0.5 4.8 0.3	**30** 0133 0746 W 1346 2012	5.7 -0.1 5.7 -0.4

OCTOBER

Time	m	Time	m
1 0216 0828 TH 1429 2053	5.6 -0.1 5.7 -0.2	**16** 0151 0751 F 1407 2011	5.0 0.4 5.0 0.4
2 0259 0910 F 1513 2135	5.5 0.0 5.5 0.0	**17** 0224 0824 SA 1442 2046	5.1 0.4 5.0 0.5
3 0343 0954 SA 1600 2218	5.2 0.1 5.3 -0.3	**18** 0302 0902 SU 1524 2126	5.0 0.5 5.0 0.6
4 0430 1041 SU 1651 ☽ 2307	4.8 0.3 4.8 0.6	**19** 0345 0944 M 1610 2211	4.9 0.6 4.8 0.7
5 0522 1135 M 1751	4.5 0.6 4.5	**20** 0433 1033 TU 1701 ☽ 2303	4.7 0.8 4.6 0.9
6 0004 0625 TU 1241 1906	0.9 4.2 0.7 4.2	**21** 0524 1130 W 1759	4.5 0.9 4.4
7 0117 0744 W 1403 2028	1.1 4.1 0.8 4.2	**22** 0006 0623 TH 1242 1909	1.1 4.3 1.0 4.3
8 0242 0857 TH 1520 2133	1.1 4.2 0.6 4.4	**23** 0130 0737 F 1423 2034	1.2 4.2 1.0 4.4
9 0349 0957 F 1618 2227	0.9 4.5 0.4 4.7	**24** 0303 0900 SA 1546 2147	1.1 4.4 0.7 4.7
10 0440 1047 SA 1705 2313	0.7 4.8 0.3 4.8	**25** 0412 1007 SU 1646 2245	0.7 4.8 0.3 5.1
11 0523 1131 SU 1745 2354	0.6 4.9 0.2 4.9	**26** 0507 1102 M 1736 2335	0.4 5.2 0.0 5.4
12 0601 1210 M 1820	0.5 5.0 0.2	**27** 0555 1151 TU 1822 ○	0.5 5.5 -0.2
13 0029 0631 TU 1243 ● 1848	4.9 0.5 5.0 0.3	**28** 0023 0640 W 1239 1905	5.6 -0.2 5.7 -0.2
14 0059 0657 W 1311 1914	4.9 0.5 5.0 0.3	**29** 0108 0725 TH 1324 1948	5.7 -0.1 5.8 -0.2
15 0124 0723 TH 1337 1941	4.9 0.5 5.0 0.4	**30** 0152 0808 F 1409 2029	5.6 -0.1 5.7 0.2
		31 0235 0852 SA 1454 2111	5.4 0.0 5.5 0.2

NOVEMBER

Time	m	Time	m
1 0319 0937 SU 1541 2154	5.1 0.2 5.2 0.5	**16** 0244 0849 M 1512 2109	5.1 0.5 5.0 0.7
2 0404 1024 M 1630 2241	4.8 0.4 4.8 0.8	**17** 0327 0933 TU 1558 2155	4.9 0.6 4.9 0.8
3 0453 1117 TU 1727 ☽ 2334	4.5 0.6 4.5 1.1	**18** 0413 1023 W 1648 2247	4.8 0.7 4.8 1.0
4 0550 1216 W 1834	4.2 0.7 4.2	**19** 0504 1121 TH 1745 ☽ 2349	4.6 0.9 4.6 1.1
5 0037 0701 TH 1324 1949	1.2 4.0 0.8 4.1	**20** 0601 1232 F 1850	4.4 0.9 4.5
6 0149 0817 F 1434 2055	1.3 4.1 0.8 4.3	**21** 0104 0708 SA 1357 2005	1.2 4.3 0.9 4.5
7 0259 0919 SA 1533 2149	1.1 4.3 0.6 4.5	**22** 0228 0826 SU 1515 2116	1.1 4.4 0.7 4.8
8 0355 1010 SU 1621 2236	1.0 4.5 0.5 4.7	**23** 0341 0936 M 1617 2216	0.8 4.7 0.5 5.1
9 0441 1056 M 1702 2317	0.8 4.8 0.5 4.8	**24** 0440 1036 TU 1710 2310	0.5 5.1 0.2 5.3
10 0522 1136 TU 1740 2354	0.7 4.9 0.4 5.0	**25** 0533 1128 W 1759 ○ 2359	0.2 5.4 0.2 5.5
11 0558 1213 W 1814 ●	0.6 5.0 0.4	**26** 0622 1218 TH 1845	0.0 5.6 0.4
12 0028 0630 TH 1247 1845	5.0 0.5 5.0 0.4	**27** 0046 0708 F 1306 1928	5.5 -0.1 5.7 0.1
13 0100 0703 F 1319 1917	5.1 0.5 5.1 0.5	**28** 0131 0754 SA 1352 2011	5.5 -0.1 5.6 0.2
14 0131 0735 SA 1353 1951	5.1 0.5 5.1 0.5	**29** 0214 0839 SU 1437 2052	5.3 0.0 5.4 0.4
15 0206 0810 SU 1430 2028	5.1 0.5 5.1 0.6	**30** 0256 0924 M 1522 2133	5.1 0.2 5.1 0.7

DECEMBER

Time	m	Time	m
1 0337 1009 TU 1608 2215	4.8 0.4 4.8 0.9	**16** 0313 0934 W 1549 2145	5.0 0.5 5.0 0.8
2 0419 1055 W 1656 2301	4.5 0.6 4.5 1.1	**17** 0358 1022 TH 1638 2236	4.9 0.6 4.9 0.9
3 0506 1145 TH 1750 ☽ 2352	4.3 0.7 4.2 1.3	**18** 0446 1116 F 1731 ☽ 2333	4.7 0.7 4.7 1.0
4 0601 1239 F 1851	4.1 0.8 4.1	**19** 0540 1219 SA 1831	4.6 0.8 4.6
5 0050 0709 SA 1336 1956	1.3 4.0 0.9 4.1	**20** 0039 0642 SU 1330 1938	1.1 4.5 0.9 4.6
6 0152 0821 SU 1433 2056	1.3 4.0 0.8 4.3	**21** 0154 0755 M 1445 2047	1.0 4.5 0.7 4.7
7 0254 0922 M 1527 2148	1.2 4.2 0.8 4.5	**22** 0311 0909 TU 1553 2151	0.9 4.6 0.5 4.9
8 0351 1013 TU 1617 2235	1.0 4.5 0.6 4.7	**23** 0418 1014 W 1651 2248	0.6 4.9 0.3 5.1
9 0441 1100 W 1702 2318	0.8 4.7 0.6 4.9	**24** 0516 1110 TH 1743 2340	0.3 5.2 0.2 5.3
10 0527 1143 TH 1745 2359	0.7 4.9 0.5 5.1	**25** 0609 1203 F 1831 ○	0.1 5.4 0.2
11 0610 1224 F 1825 ●	0.5 5.0 0.5	**26** 0029 0658 SA 1252 1915	5.4 -0.1 5.5 0.2
12 0038 0650 SA 1303 1903	5.2 0.4 5.1 0.5	**27** 0115 0744 SU 1338 1957	5.3 -0.1 5.4 0.3
13 0116 0730 SU 1342 1941	5.2 0.4 5.2 0.5	**28** 0157 0829 M 1422 2036	5.2 0.3 5.2 0.5
14 0153 0809 M 1422 2019	5.2 0.4 5.2 0.6	**29** 0235 0910 TU 1503 2111	5.0 0.1 5.0 0.7
15 0232 0850 TU 1504 2100	5.1 0.4 5.1 0.7	**30** 0310 0948 W 1541 2144	4.8 0.3 4.7 0.9
		31 0344 1026 TH 1619 2221	4.6 0.5 4.5 1.0

Chart Datum: 2·35 metres below Ordnance Datum (Newlyn). HAT is 5·8 metres above Chart Datum.

1.16 RIVER BLACKWATER

Essex 51°45′·33N 00°54′·90E ✹✹✹☼☾☾☾☾⚓⚓⚓

CHARTS AC 5607, 1183, 1975, 3741; Imray C1, Y17, 2000

TIDES Maldon +0130 Dover; ML 2·8; Duration 0620)

Standard Port WALTON-ON-THE-NAZE (→)

Times				Height (metres)			
High Water		Low Water		MHWS	MHWN	MLWN	MLWS
0000	0600	0500	1100	4·2	3·4	1·1	0·4
1200	1800	1700	2300				
Differences SUNK HEAD							
0000	+0002	−0002	+0002	−0·3	−0·3	−0·1	−0·1
WEST MERSEA							
+0035	+0015	+0055	+0010	+0·9	+0·4	+0·1	+0·1
BRADWELL							
+0035	+0023	+0047	+0004	+1·0	+0·8	+0·2	0·0
OSEA ISLAND							
+0057	+0045	+0050	+0007	+1·1	+0·9	+0·1	0·0
MALDON							
+0107	+0055	ND	ND	−1·3	−1·1	ND	ND

SHELTER Good, as appropriate to wind. ⚓ in creeks restricted by oyster beds and many moorings.

NAVIGATION WPT Knoll NCM, Q, 51°43′·88N 01°05′·07E, 287°/6·7M to Nass bn, ECM VQ (3) 5s. Speed limit 8kn W of Osea Is.

WEST MERSEA Min depth 0·6m in approach to Nass Bn. Avoid oyster beds between Cobmarsh and Packing Marsh Is and in Salcott Chan. ⚓ in Mersea Quarters in 5-6m (exposed). There is a pontoon for landing (limited waiting); also pile moorings in Ray Channel.

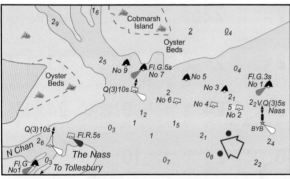

TOLLESBURY FLEET Proceed via S Chan up Woodrolfe Creek. A tide gauge shows depth over marina ent sill (approx 2·4m at MHWS and 1·4m at MHWN). Speed limits: Tollesbury Fleet S Chan 8kn; Woodrolfe Creek upper reaches 4kn.

BRADWELL No dangers, power station is conspic 7ca NNE. Creek only suitable for small craft and gets very crowded. Ent has SCM bn Q with tide gauge in creek; leave to **STBD** on entry. 4 PHM buoys, 3 SHM withies and 2 B/W △ ldg bns mark the channel which doglegs past a SHM buoy to marina entrance. Min depth 0·2m in approach channel.

MALDON From S of Osea Is, 'The Doctor', No 3 SHM buoy on with Blackwater SC lt, Iso G 5s, lead 300° approx up the chan; or No 3 and No 8 buoys in line at 305°.

LIGHTS AND MARKS See chartlets and 1.3.

COMMUNICATIONS Codes (01621 Maldon; 01206 Colchester/W Mersea) MRCC (01255) 675518; Police 101; Dr 854118.

Bradwell and Tollesbury Marinas Ch **80** M (HO); Blackwater Marina Ch M, 0900-2300; Heybridge Lock Ch 80 HW −2+1; Clark and Carter launch: call CC1.

FACILITIES

WEST MERSEA (01206). **W Mersea YC** 382947, ✗, ⌹, showers; launch service call YC 1 on Ch M or ☎ 07752 309435. **Town** ⓘ & ⌂, ⚓, ✎, ⊞, ⌹, ☒, ✗, ⌹, ✉, Ⓑ, ⇌ (bus to Colchester, Ⓗ ☎ 01206-853535), ✈ (Southend/Stansted).

TOLLESBURY (01621). **Tollesbury Marina** ④ (220+20 Ⓥ) ☎ 869202, £2·00, marina@woodrolfe.com. Sill to marina dries 1·9m; ⚓, D, BH (20t), Gas, Gaz, LPG, ⊞, ✎, ✗, C (5 ton), ⌹, ✗, ⌹, ⓔ. **Tollesbury Cruising Club** ☎ 869561, ⌹, ✗, M. **Village** ⓘ, ⌸, ✗, ⌹, ✉, Ⓑ (Tues, Thurs 1000-1430), ⇌ (bus to Witham), ✈ (Southend or Cambridge).

BRADWELL (01621). **Bradwell Marina** (300, some Ⓥ) ☎ 776235. Min depth 0·2m in approach channel. £2·00, short stay £3/hr. ⚓, D, P, ✎, ⊞, ✗, BH (45t), ⌹, ✗, ⌹. **Bradwell Quay YC** ☎ 890173, M, ⚓, ⌹, L, ⚓. **Town** ✉, ⇌ (bus/taxi to Southminster), ✈ (Southend).

MAYLANDSEA (01621). **Blackwater Marina** (230, all dry) ☎ 740264, £10/craft, ⚓, D, ✗, ⌹, ✗, ⌹; 150 moorings (£5/craft) in chan. Taxi to Southminster ⇌.

MALDON (01621). **Maldon Quay** Beyond No 8 buoy, the chan which shifts and carries 0·2m, is lit and buoyed. Access near HW; pontoons dry to soft mud. HM/River bailiff ☎ 856487, Mob 07818 013723; ⌯ £15, ⚓, M, P, D, ⚓. **Maldon Little Ship Club** ☎ 854139, ⌹. **Services:** ✗, ⌹, M, ACA, ⌂, ✎, ⊞, Ⓔ. **Town** ✉, Ⓑ, ⇌ (bus to Chelmsford, Ⓗ ☎ (01245) 440761), ✈ (Southend, Cambridge or Stansted).

HEYBRIDGE BASIN (01621). **Lock** ☎ 853506, opens HW −1 to HW approx. A SHM buoy opposite the lock marks the deep water ent. Access to Chelmer & Blackwater Canal (not navigable). **Blackwater SC** ☎ 853923, L, ⚓. **Services:** at CRS Marine ☎ 854684, Mobile 07850 543873 (pontoon outside lock), ⚓, L, M, ⚓, ✎, ⊞, ✗, C. Bus to Heybridge/Maldon.

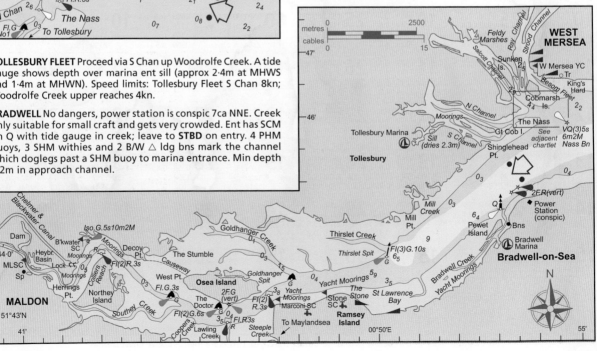

1.17 RIVER COLNE

Essex **51°47'·98N 01°00'·60E** (Brightlingsea)

CHARTS AC 5607, 1183, 1975, 3741; Imray C1, Y17, 2000

TIDES +0050 Dover; ML 2·5; Duration 0615

Standard Port WALTON-ON-THE-NAZE (→)

Times				Height (metres)			
High Water		Low Water		MHWS	MHWN	MLWN	MLWS
0000	0600	0500	1100	4·2	3·4	1·1	0·4
1200	1800	1700	2300				
Differences BRIGHTLINGSEA							
+0025	+0021	+0046	+0004	+0·8	+0·4	+0·1	0·0
COLCHESTER							
+0035	+0025	DR	DR	0·0	−0·3	DR	DR
CLACTON-ON-SEA							
+0012	+0010	+0025	+0008	+0·3	+0·1	+0·1	+0·1

SHELTER Suitable shelter can be found from most winds. Brightlingsea outer hbr is exposed to W'lies. In the creek S of Cindery Island are moorings (as shown) and long pontoons in about 1·5m, with possible ⌒ for **Ⓥ**s. ⚓ prohib in Brightlingsea Hbr, but there are ⚓s to the NW of Mersea Stone Pt and in Pyefleet

Chan, E of Pewit Island. R Colne is navigable for 4·5m draft to Wivenhoe and Rowhedge, where the river dries; and to The Hythe, Colchester (3m draft).

NAVIGATION WPT Colne Bar By, SHM Fl (2) G 5s, 51°44'·61N 01°02'·57E, 340°/3·6M to Mersea Stone. Extensive mud and sand banks flank the entrance channel. Large coasters use the Brightlingsea Reach; at HW sand barges regularly visit Ballast Quay below the tidal barrier at Wivenhoe. The ent to Brightlingsea Creek is narrow at LW and carries about 1m.

Tidal barrier 2ca below Wivenhoe church is usually open (30m wide) allowing unrestricted passage; keep to stbd, max speed 5kn. 3 F R (vert), shown on N Pier, visible up/downstream indicate barrier gates are shut; see also LIGHTS AND MARKS.

Speed limits in approaches and up-river (by buoy no): No13–15 = 8kn; No15–18 = no spd limit; No18–34 = 8kn; No 34 – Colchester = 5kn; Brightlingsea Harbour = 4kn.

LIGHTS AND MARKS Bateman's Tr (conspic) by Westmarsh Pt Fl(3) 20s. Brightlingsea ldg lts/marks 041°; FR 7/10m 4M, W□ on R striped posts; adjusted to suit channel. Pass Spit SCM, and follow lateral marks to NCM (Q) where chan is divided by Cindery Is. Pyefleet Chan and other creeks are unlit.

Lit lateral buoys up to Wivenhoe. Passage through flood barrier marked by 2FR/FG (vert) each side and there are bns, QR/QG, up/downstream on the banks.

COMMUNICATIONS (Brightlingsea 01206) MRCC (01255) 675518; Police 101; Dr 302522; HM (Brightlingsea) 302200, mob 07952 734814.

Brightlingsea Harbour Radio VHF Ch 68. *Waterside Marina* Ch 80.

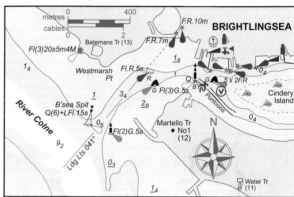

FACILITIES

BRIGHTLINGSEA:

Town Hard ☎ (01206) 302200, D, L, ⚓. Pontoon berths £10 < 26ft, £11 < 36ft, £12 > 36ft, ⚓ at fuel jetty, ⎯ £8.

Waterside Marina ☎ (01206) 308709, sill 1m above CD; £10-£14 (inc ⚡).

Colne YC ☎ 302594, L, ⚓, wi-fi, ✕, 🗑.

Brightlingsea SC ⎯, 🗑.

Services: ⚒, ✎, 🅿, Ⓔ, ⚠, BY, C (mobile), 🗑 supply 🕐 & 🕐 (HO), ACA, Gas.

Town 🍴, ✕, 🗑, ✉, Ⓑ, Bus (Wivenhoe or Colchester for ⟲), ✈ (Southend or Stansted).

WIVENHOE: Wivenhoe SC ☎ 822132. ⌒ (drying **Ⓥ** berths may be available on the inside pontoons – first come first served, no charge).

Village 🕐, 🛒, 🗑, ✉, ⟲.

ROWHEDGE: Quay ⌒(drying) some **Ⓥ**.

RIVER COLNE TO HARWICH

(Chart AC 1975, 1593) 4M SW of the Naze tr at Hollands Haven a conspic radar twr (67m, unlit) is an excellent daymark. From the S, approach Walton and Harwich via the Medusa chan about 1M E of Naze tr. At N end of this chan, 1M off Dovercourt, Pye End buoy marks chan SSW to Walton Backwaters. Harwich and Landguard Pt are close to the N. Making Harwich from the SE beware the drying Cork Sand, which lies N/S.

Sunk Inner SWM buoy, 11M E of The Naze, marks the outer apprs to Harwich, an extensive and well sheltered hbr accessible at all times (chart AC 2693).

- Harwich, Felixstowe Docks and Ipswich are referred to collectively as the Haven Ports.
- Small craft should give plenty of sea room to shipping manoeuvring to board/disembark Pilots in the Sunk Inner Precautionary Area, see Thames Estuary chartlet.
- The Harwich DW channel begins 1·5M NNW of Sunk Inner buoy and runs N between Rough and Shipwash shoals, then W past the Cork Sand PHM lt buoy. Constantly used by commercial shipping, approach should be via the recommended track for yachts.

Approaching from NE and 2M off the ent to R. Deben, beware Cutler shoal, with least depth of 1·2m, marked by SHM buoy on E side; Wadgate Ledge and the Platters are about 1·5M ENE of Landguard Point. ▶ *S of Landguard Point the W-going (flood) stream begins at HW Harwich +0600, and the E-going stream at HW Harwich, sp rates about 1·5kn. Note: HW Harwich is never more than 7 mins after HW Walton; LW times are about 10 mins earlier.* ◀

HARWICH TO ORFORD NESS

(Chart AC 2052) Shipwash shoal, buoyed and with a drying patch, runs NNE from 9M E of Felixstowe to 4M SSE of Orford Ness. Inshore of this is Shipway Chan, then Bawdsey Bank, buoyed with depths of 2m, on which the sea breaks in E'ly swell.

The Sledway Chan lies between Bawdsey Bank and Whiting Bank (buoyed) which is close SW of Orford Ness, and has depths less than 1m. Hollesley Chan, about 1M wide, runs inshore W and N of this bank. In the SW part of Hollesley B is the ent to Orford Haven and the R Ore/Alde. ▶ *There are overfalls S of Orford Ness on both the ebb and flood streams. 2M E of Orford Ness the SW-going stream begins at HW Harwich +0605, sp rate 2·5kn; the NE-going stream begins at HW Harwich –0010, sp rate 3kn.* ◀

Note: The direction of local buoyage becomes S to N off Orford Ness (52°05'N).

ORFORD NESS TO GREAT YARMOUTH

(Chart AC 1543) N of Orford Ness seas break on Aldeburgh Ridge (1·3m), but the coast is clear of offlying dangers past Aldeburgh and Southwold, as far as Benacre Ness, 5M S of Lowestoft. Sizewell power stn is a conspic 3 bldg 1·5M N of Thorpe Ness. Keep 1·5M offshore to avoid fishing floats.

▶ *Lowestoft is best approached from both S and E by the buoyed/lit Stanford chan, passing E of Newcome Sand and SW of Holm Sand; beware possible strong set across hbr ent.* ◀ From the N, approach through Cockle Gatway, Caister Road, Yarmouth Road, passing Great Yarmouth (beware of prohibited area N of harbour entrance); then proceed S through Gorleston, Corton and Lowestoft North Roads (buoyed). ▶ *1M E of hbr ent, the S-going stream begins at HW Dover –0600, and the N-going at HW Dover, sp rates 2·6kn.* ◀

Scroby Sands Wind Farm consists of 30 turbines centred on 52°39'·00N 01°47'·00E. Each turbine is 61m high, with 80m diameter blades and clearance height of 18m and six of the perimeter ones are lit. Vessels to keep well clear and not enter the area.

In the approaches to Great Yarmouth from seaward the banks are continually changing; use the buoyed chans which, from N and S, are those described in the preceding paragraph. But from the E the shortest approach is via Corton ECM lt buoy and the Holm Channel leading into Gorleston Road. ▶ *The sea often breaks on North Scroby, Middle Scroby and Caister Shoal (all of which dry), and there are heavy tide rips over parts of Corton and South Scroby Sands, Middle and South Cross Sands, and Winterton Overfalls.* ◀

▶ *1M NE of ent to Gt Yarmouth the S-going stream begins at HW Dover –0600, and the N-going at HW Dover –0015, sp rates 2·3kn. Breydon Water (tidal) affects streams in the Haven; after heavy rain the out-going stream at Brush Quay may exceed 5kn.* ◀ About 12M NE of Great Yarmouth lie Newarp Banks, on which the sea breaks in bad weather.

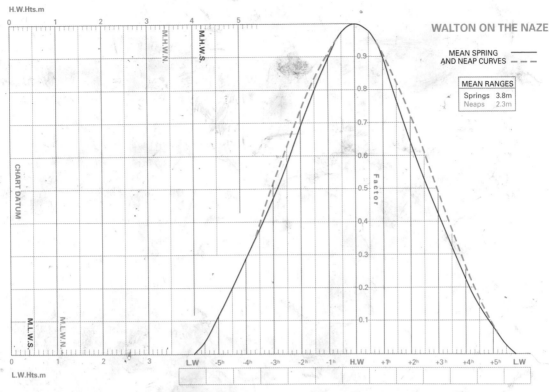

WALTON ON THE NAZE

MEAN SPRING
AND NEAP CURVES

MEAN RANGES
Springs 3.8m
Neaps 2.3m

1.18 WALTON BACKWATERS

Essex **51°54'·57N 01°16'·79E** (No 2 PHM buoy) ❀❀♓♓♓♻♻

CHARTS AC 5607, 2052, 2695; Imray C1, Y16, 2000

TIDES +0030 Dover; ML 2·2; Duration 0615. Walton is a Standard Port. Predictions are for Walton Pier, ie to seaward. Time differences for Bramble Creek (N of Hamford Water) are +10, –7, –5, +10 mins; height differences are all +0·3m.

SHELTER Good in all weather, but ent not advised if a big sea is running from the NE. Good ⚓s in Hamford Water (clear of Oakley Creek) and in N end of Walton Chan, 2ca S of Stone Pt on E side.

NAVIGATION From S, appr via Medusa Chan; from N and E via the Harwich recomended yacht track (1.19). WPT Pye End SWM buoy, L Fl 10s, 51°55'·05N 01°17'·89E, 234°/1·1M to Crab Knoll SHM at chan ent. NB this stretch carries only 0·9m. Beware lobster pots off the Naze and Pye Sands and oyster beds in the Backwaters. Buoys may be moved to suit channel changes.

At narrow ent to Walton Chan leave NCM buoy to stbd, and 3 PHM buoys close to port. Fm No.9 SHM expect significant shoaling, ebb>4kn and strong back eddies ivo Stone Pt. Best water to E side, but beware tidal sheer and vessels with strong tide under them.

LIGHTS AND MARKS Naze Tr (49m) is conspic 3M S of Pye End buoy. 2M NNE at Felixstowe, cranes and Y flood lts are conspic D/N. No.9 SHM Fl G 5s.

COMMUNICATIONS (Code 01255)   MRCC 675518; Police 101; Ⓗ 421145; HM 851899.

Titchmarsh Marina Ch 80, 0800-2000 in season.

FACILITIES
Titchmarsh Marina 420 inc Ⓥ, <8m £17, <10m £19, <12m £20; short stay (max 3 hrs) £5/hr. ☎ 672185. Access over sill 1·3m (tide gauge at entrance) berths dredged to approx 2m; pontoons on R Twizzle. D, Gas, Gaz, LPG, ⚒, ⚓, ▣, C (10 ton), BH (35 ton), ▬, ✕, ▣. **Walton & Frinton YC,** ☎ 678161, ✕, ▣. **Yacht Basin** (60) run by YC; appr dries. ◎ (long stay), ⚡, ▣, ▬, M, D, C (½ ton), ▣.

Town P, ⚓, ☷, ✕, ▣, ✉, ⇌, ✈ (Southend/Cambridge/Stansted).

WALTON-ON-THE-NAZE LAT 51°51'N LONG 1°17'E
TIMES AND HEIGHTS OF HIGH AND LOW WATERS

STANDARD TIME (UT)
For Summer Time add ONE hour in **non-shaded areas**

Dates in red are **SPRINGS**
Dates in blue are **NEAPS**

YEAR 2015

JANUARY

Time	m		Time	m
1 0152	1.0	**16** 0116	1.3
0816	3.8	0721	3.5
TH 1435	0.7	F 1352	1.0
2056	3.8	2000	3.6
2 0302	0.9	**17** 0230	1.1
0919	3.9	0832	3.6
F 1538	0.8	SA 1453	0.8
2153	4.0	2107	3.8
3 0405	0.8	**18** 0329	0.8
1012	4.0	0934	3.9
SA 1630	0.8	SU 1547	0.7
2242	4.1	2205	4.0
4 0457	0.6	**19** 0423	0.6
1058	4.1	1028	4.1
SU 1713	0.8	M 1637	0.7
2325	4.1	2257	4.1
5 0541	0.5	**20** 0513	0.4
1140	4.1	1117	4.3
M 1751	0.8	TU 1724	0.6
○		● 2345	4.3
6 0005	4.2	**21** 0602	0.3
0621	0.4	1205	4.5
TU 1219	4.2	W 1809	0.5
1826	0.8		
7 0042	4.2	**22** 0649	0.1
0657	0.4	1253	4.6
W 1256	4.1	TH 1854	0.5
1859	0.8		
8 0116	4.2	**23** 0118	4.5
0731	0.4	0735	0.1
TH 1332	4.1	F 1340	4.6
1929	0.8	1940	0.5
9 0149	4.1	**24** 0203	4.5
0802	0.4	0821	0.1
F 1407	4.0	SA 1427	4.5
1957	0.8	2025	0.6
10 0222	4.1	**25** 0248	4.4
0832	0.5	0907	0.2
SA 1442	3.9	SU 1515	4.3
2028	0.9	2112	0.7
11 0256	4.0	**26** 0334	4.3
0904	0.6	0954	0.3
SU 1518	3.8	M 1605	4.1
2103	1.0	2202	0.8
12 0332	3.8	**27** 0423	4.1
0939	0.7	1045	0.5
M 1556	3.7	TU 1700	3.9
2144	1.1	☽ 2259	0.9
13 0413	3.7	**28** 0521	3.9
1022	0.8	1145	0.7
TU 1642	3.6	W 1803	3.7
☽ 2233	1.2		
14 0503	3.6	**29** 0006	1.0
1116	0.9	0631	3.7
W 1740	3.5	TH 1252	0.8
2340	1.3	1916	3.6
15 0608	3.5	**30** 0122	1.0
1234	1.0	0749	3.6
TH 1850	3.5	F 1407	1.0
		2032	3.6
		31 0245	1.0
		0900	3.7
		SA 1522	1.0
		2136	3.8

FEBRUARY

Time	m		Time	m
1 0358	0.8	**16** 0302	0.8
0959	3.8	0910	3.8
SU 1618	0.9	M 1524	0.8
2228	3.9	2144	3.8
2 0450	0.6	**17** 0402	0.6
1046	3.9	1010	4.0
M 1701	0.9	TU 1619	0.7
2311	4.0	2239	4.1
3 0530	0.5	**18** 0456	0.3
1127	4.0	1102	4.3
TU 1736	0.8	W 1708	0.6
○ 2349	4.1	● 2328	4.3
4 0605	0.4	**19** 0546	0.2
1203	4.1	1150	4.5
W 1808	0.8	TH 1755	0.5
5 0023	4.2	**20** 0014	4.5
0636	0.4	0633	0.0
TH 1238	4.1	F 1237	4.6
1839	0.7	1841	0.4
6 0056	4.2	**21** 0100	4.6
0706	0.4	0719	0.0
F 1312	4.1	SA 1323	4.6
1908	0.7	1925	0.4
7 0127	4.2	**22** 0144	4.6
0736	0.4	0802	0.0
SA 1344	4.1	SU 1408	4.5
1935	0.7	2008	0.5
8 0158	4.1	**23** 0227	4.6
0804	0.4	0843	0.1
SU 1415	4.0	M 1453	4.3
2004	0.7	2052	0.5
9 0229	4.1	**24** 0310	4.4
0832	0.5	0924	0.3
M 1447	3.9	TU 1540	4.1
2036	0.8	2137	0.6
10 0301	4.0	**25** 0356	4.2
0902	0.6	1009	0.6
TU 1521	3.8	W 1630	3.8
2112	0.9	☽ 2228	0.8
11 0337	3.8	**26** 0449	3.9
0937	0.7	1103	0.8
W 1601	3.7	TH 1728	3.6
2153	1.0	2330	0.9
12 0420	3.7	**27** 0557	3.6
1023	0.8	1210	0.9
TH 1651	3.6	F 1840	3.4
☽ 2249	1.1		
13 0516	3.6	**28** 0048	1.0
1130	1.0	0720	3.5
F 1758	3.5	SA 1334	1.1
		2003	3.4
14 0014	1.2		
0630	3.5		
SA 1307	1.0		
1916	3.4		
15 0153	1.0		
0755	3.6		
SU 1423	0.9		
2036	3.6		

MARCH

Time	m		Time	m
1 0225	1.0	**16** 0121	0.9
0839	3.6	0725	3.6
SU 1501	1.1	M 1356	1.0
2114	3.6	2008	3.5
2 0343	0.8	**17** 0237	0.7
0941	3.7	0849	3.8
M 1600	1.0	TU 1501	0.8
2207	3.8	2122	3.8
3 0433	0.6	**18** 0340	0.5
1029	3.9	0952	4.1
TU 1641	0.9	W 1558	0.7
2250	3.9	2219	4.1
4 0510	0.5	**19** 0436	0.3
1108	4.0	1044	4.3
W 1715	0.8	TH 1649	0.5
2327	4.0	2308	4.3
5 0541	0.4	**20** 0526	0.1
1143	4.0	1131	4.4
TH 1746	0.7	F 1737	0.4
○		● 2353	4.5
6 0000	4.1	**21** 0612	0.0
0609	0.4	1216	4.5
F 1216	4.1	SA 1823	0.4
1815	0.7		
7 0031	4.2	**22** 0037	4.6
0637	0.3	0656	0.0
SA 1247	4.1	SU 1302	4.5
1844	0.6	1907	0.4
8 0102	4.2	**23** 0120	4.7
0706	0.3	0738	0.1
SU 1318	4.1	M 1346	4.5
1913	0.6	1950	0.4
9 0133	4.2	**24** 0203	4.6
0734	0.4	0816	0.2
M 1349	4.0	TU 1430	4.3
1942	0.6	2032	0.4
10 0204	4.1	**25** 0246	4.4
0801	0.4	0854	0.4
TU 1420	4.0	W 1513	4.1
2013	0.7	2115	0.5
11 0235	4.0	**26** 0330	4.2
0830	0.5	0935	0.7
W 1453	3.9	TH 1600	3.8
2046	0.7	2201	0.7
12 0310	4.0	**27** 0421	3.9
0904	0.6	1025	0.9
TH 1532	3.8	F 1654	3.6
2125	0.8	☽ 2257	0.8
13 0352	3.8	**28** 0525	3.6
0948	0.8	1129	1.1
F 1619	3.7	SA 1801	3.4
☽ 2217	0.9		
14 0445	3.7	**29** 0011	1.0
1052	1.0	0645	3.4
SA 1721	3.5	SU 1252	1.3
2336	1.0	1922	3.3
15 0556	3.5	**30** 0147	1.0
1230	1.1	0807	3.5
SU 1840	3.4	M 1424	1.2
		2039	3.5
		31 0311	0.8
		0913	3.6
		TU 1529	1.1
		2136	3.7

APRIL

Time	m		Time	m
1 0402	0.7	**16** 0316	0.4
1002	3.8	0930	4.1
W 1612	0.9	TH 1534	0.7
2220	3.8	2155	4.1
2 0438	0.6	**17** 0412	0.2
1041	3.9	1023	4.2
TH 1647	0.8	F 1626	0.5
2257	4.0	2245	4.3
3 0509	0.5	**18** 0502	0.2
1115	4.0	1111	4.4
F 1720	0.7	SA 1716	0.4
2330	4.1	● 2330	4.5
4 0538	0.4	**19** 0549	0.1
1148	4.0	1155	4.4
SA 1750	0.6	SU 1803	0.4
○			
5 0002	4.2	**20** 0014	4.6
0607	0.4	0632	0.1
SU 1220	4.1	M 1240	4.4
1820	0.6	1849	0.3
6 0035	4.2	**21** 0057	4.6
0636	0.4	0713	0.2
M 1252	4.1	TU 1323	4.4
1850	0.5	1933	0.3
7 0107	4.2	**22** 0140	4.5
0704	0.4	0751	0.2
TU 1324	4.1	W 1406	4.2
1922	0.5	2015	0.4
8 0140	4.2	**23** 0223	4.3
0733	0.5	0828	0.6
W 1357	4.0	TH 1449	4.1
1954	0.6	2056	0.5
9 0213	4.1	**24** 0306	4.1
0804	0.5	0906	0.6
TH 1432	3.9	F 1533	3.8
2028	0.6	2138	0.6
10 0250	4.0	**25** 0355	3.8
0841	0.7	0950	1.0
F 1511	3.8	SA 1622	3.6
2109	0.7	☽ 2228	0.8
11 0334	3.9	**26** 0454	3.6
0927	0.9	1047	1.2
SA 1559	3.7	SU 1723	3.5
2202	0.8	2332	0.9
12 0428	3.8	**27** 0605	3.4
1034	1.0	1203	1.3
SU 1659	3.6	M 1832	3.4
☽ 2320	0.8		
13 0536	3.6	**28** 0053	0.9
1207	1.1	0719	3.4
M 1816	3.5	TU 1330	1.1
		1945	3.4
14 0057	0.8	**29** 0212	0.9
0703	3.6	0827	3.5
TU 1329	1.0	W 1441	1.2
1942	3.6	2049	3.6
15 0212	0.6	**30** 0312	0.8
0826	3.8	0922	3.7
W 1436	0.8	TH 1533	1.0
2057	3.8	2139	3.7

Chart Datum: 2·16 metres below Ordnance Datum (Newlyn). HAT is 4·7 metres above Chart Datum.

WALTON-ON-THE-NAZE   LAT 51°51'N   LONG 1°17'E

TIMES AND HEIGHTS OF HIGH AND LOW WATERS

STANDARD TIME (UT)
For Summer Time add ONE hour in **non-shaded areas**

Dates in red are SPRINGS
Dates in blue are NEAPS

YEAR **2015**

E England

MAY

Time	m	Time	m
1 0355	0.6	**16** 0348	0.3
1005	3.8	1002	4.2
F 1614	0.8	SA 1605	0.6
2219	3.9	2222	4.2
2 0432	0.6	**17** 0439	0.3
1042	3.9	1051	4.3
SA 1650	0.7	SU 1656	0.5
2256	4.0	2308	4.4
3 0505	0.5	**18** 0526	0.3
1117	4.0	1136	4.3
SU 1724	0.6	M 1746	0.4
2331	4.1	● 2353	4.5
4 0537	0.5	**19** 0610	0.4
1151	4.1	1220	4.3
M 1757	0.6	TU 1833	0.3
○			
5 0007	4.2	**20** 0036	4.5
0607	0.5	0651	0.4
TU 1227	4.1	W 1304	4.3
1830	0.5	1917	0.3
6 0043	4.2	**21** 0120	4.4
0638	0.5	0730	0.6
W 1303	4.1	TH 1346	4.2
1905	0.5	2000	0.4
7 0119	4.2	**22** 0202	4.3
0711	0.5	0806	0.7
TH 1340	4.1	F 1427	4.1
1941	0.5	2039	0.5
8 0157	4.2	**23** 0245	4.1
0747	0.6	0841	0.8
F 1418	4.0	SA 1508	3.9
2019	0.5	2117	0.6
9 0238	4.1	**24** 0331	3.9
0829	0.7	0920	1.0
SA 1500	3.9	SU 1553	3.7
2104	0.6	2200	0.7
10 0324	4.0	**25** 0423	3.7
0920	0.8	1007	1.1
SU 1548	3.8	M 1645	3.6
2201	0.6	◗ 2252	0.8
11 0418	3.9	**26** 0523	3.5
1027	1.0	1108	1.3
M 1647	3.7	TU 1744	3.5
◗ 2315	0.7		
12 0525	3.8	**27** 0000	0.9
1146	1.0	0625	3.5
TU 1759	3.6	W 1231	1.3
		1846	3.5
13 0036	0.6	**28** 0112	0.9
0645	3.8	0728	3.5
W 1302	1.0	TH 1347	1.2
1917	3.7	1949	3.5
14 0147	0.5	**29** 0215	0.8
0801	3.9	0828	3.6
TH 1409	0.8	F 1447	1.1
2030	3.9	2047	3.7
15 0250	0.4	**30** 0307	0.7
0907	4.0	0920	3.7
F 1509	0.7	SA 1536	0.9
2130	4.1	2137	3.8
		31 0353	0.7
		1005	3.9
		SU 1618	0.8
		2220	4.0

JUNE

Time	m	Time	m
1 0432	0.6	**16** 0508	0.6
1045	4.0	1121	4.2
M 1657	0.7	TU 1733	0.4
2301	4.1	● 2337	4.3
2 0509	0.6	**17** 0552	0.6
1125	4.1	1205	4.2
TU 1735	0.6	W 1820	0.4
○ 2342	4.2		
3 0544	0.6	**18** 0020	4.3
1205	4.2	0633	0.6
W 1813	0.5	TH 1247	4.2
		1904	0.3
4 0022	4.3	**19** 0103	4.3
0619	0.5	0711	0.7
TH 1246	4.2	F 1328	4.2
1852	0.4	1944	0.4
5 0104	4.3	**20** 0144	4.2
0657	0.5	0747	0.8
F 1328	4.2	SA 1407	4.1
1934	0.4	2021	0.4
6 0146	4.3	**21** 0225	4.1
0738	0.6	0819	0.9
SA 1410	4.1	SU 1445	4.0
2017	0.4	2056	0.5
7 0230	4.2	**22** 0306	3.9
0824	0.7	0852	0.9
SU 1454	4.1	M 1524	3.9
2105	0.4	2131	0.6
8 0317	4.1	**23** 0349	3.8
0917	0.8	0930	1.0
M 1542	4.0	TU 1607	3.8
2201	0.5	2212	0.7
9 0411	4.0	**24** 0438	3.6
1016	0.9	1016	1.2
TU 1637	3.9	W 1657	3.6
◗ 2305	0.5	◗ 2304	0.8
10 0514	3.9	**25** 0533	3.5
1124	1.0	1116	1.3
W 1741	3.8	TH 1754	3.5
11 0014	0.5	**26** 0012	0.9
0624	3.8	0631	3.5
TH 1234	1.0	F 1241	1.3
1852	3.8	1854	3.5
12 0121	0.5	**27** 0122	0.9
0735	3.9	0731	3.5
F 1342	1.0	SA 1356	1.2
2003	3.9	1956	3.6
13 0224	0.5	**28** 0222	0.9
0843	3.9	0830	3.6
SA 1446	0.8	SU 1454	1.0
2107	4.0	2054	3.7
14 0324	0.5	**29** 0315	0.8
0943	4.0	0926	3.8
SU 1546	0.7	M 1546	0.9
2202	4.1	2147	3.9
15 0419	0.5	**30** 0402	0.7
1034	4.1	1016	3.9
M 1642	0.6	TU 1632	0.7
2251	4.3	2235	4.0

JULY

Time	m	Time	m
1 0445	0.7	**16** 0539	0.7
1102	4.1	1152	4.2
W 1716	0.6	TH 1810	0.4
2320	4.2	●	
2 0525	0.6	**17** 0006	4.2
1146	4.2	0616	0.7
TH 1759	0.5	F 1232	4.2
○		1849	0.4
3 0004	4.3	**18** 0047	4.2
0605	0.6	0652	0.7
F 1232	4.3	SA 1310	4.2
1842	0.4	1925	0.4
4 0050	4.4	**19** 0125	4.2
0647	0.6	0726	0.8
SA 1316	4.3	SU 1345	4.2
1927	0.3	1958	0.4
5 0135	4.4	**20** 0202	4.1
0731	0.6	0756	0.9
SU 1400	4.3	M 1419	4.1
2012	0.3	2029	0.5
6 0221	4.4	**21** 0238	4.0
0817	0.6	0825	0.9
M 1445	4.3	TU 1453	4.1
2100	0.3	2059	0.6
7 0308	4.3	**22** 0314	3.9
0906	0.7	0858	0.9
TU 1531	4.2	W 1529	3.9
2150	0.3	2132	0.7
8 0359	4.1	**23** 0352	3.7
0959	0.8	0936	1.0
W 1621	4.1	TH 1609	3.8
◗ 2246	0.4	2211	0.8
9 0456	4.0	**24** 0435	3.6
1059	0.9	1022	1.2
TH 1719	4.0	F 1657	3.6
2348	0.5	◗ 2302	0.9
10 0600	3.9	**25** 0530	3.5
1205	1.0	1123	1.3
F 1825	3.9	SA 1757	3.5
11 0053	0.6	**26** 0016	1.1
0709	3.8	0634	3.5
SA 1315	1.0	SU 1255	1.3
1937	3.9	1905	3.5
12 0159	0.7	**27** 0136	1.1
0821	3.8	0742	3.5
SU 1425	0.9	M 1412	1.1
2046	3.9	2014	3.6
13 0306	0.8	**28** 0239	1.0
0926	3.9	0843	3.7
M 1534	0.8	TU 1513	0.9
2147	4.0	2117	3.8
14 0406	0.8	**29** 0334	0.8
1021	4.0	0949	3.9
TU 1635	0.6	W 1607	0.7
2239	4.1	2211	4.0
15 0456	0.8	**30** 0423	0.8
1109	4.1	1040	4.1
W 1726	0.5	TH 1656	0.6
2324	4.2	2300	4.2
		31 0508	0.7
		1128	4.2
		F 1743	0.4
		○ 2347	4.4

AUGUST

Time	m	Time	m
1 0552	0.6	**16** 0027	4.2
1214	4.4	0631	0.8
SA 1829	0.3	SU 1247	4.3
		1859	0.4
2 0033	4.5	**17** 0102	4.2
0635	0.6	0702	0.8
SU 1259	4.5	M 1319	4.3
1915	0.2	1929	0.4
3 0120	4.6	**18** 0135	4.2
0719	0.6	0732	0.8
M 1344	4.5	TU 1351	4.2
1959	0.2	1958	0.5
4 0205	4.6	**19** 0208	4.1
0804	0.6	0759	0.9
TU 1428	4.5	W 1422	4.1
2044	0.2	2025	0.6
5 0252	4.4	**20** 0239	4.0
0850	0.7	0829	0.9
W 1512	4.4	TH 1454	4.0
2130	0.3	2053	0.7
6 0340	4.2	**21** 0311	3.9
0938	0.8	0903	0.9
TH 1559	4.3	F 1528	3.9
2219	0.5	2126	0.8
7 0432	4.0	**22** 0348	3.7
1033	0.9	0942	1.0
F 1653	4.1	SA 1607	3.8
◗ 2316	0.7	◗ 2207	1.0
8 0532	3.8	**23** 0434	3.6
1136	0.9	1032	1.2
SA 1758	3.9	SU 1659	3.6
		2306	1.1
9 0022	0.8	**24** 0536	3.5
0642	3.7	1149	1.3
SU 1248	1.0	M 1809	3.5
1914	3.8		
10 0135	1.0	**25** 0044	1.2
0759	3.7	0653	3.5
M 1408	1.0	TU 1331	1.2
2029	3.8	1933	3.6
11 0251	1.0	**26** 0206	1.1
0910	3.8	0813	3.6
TU 1529	0.8	W 1442	1.0
2134	3.9	2048	3.8
12 0357	1.0	**27** 0307	0.9
1008	4.0	0922	3.8
W 1630	0.7	TH 1541	0.7
2227	4.1	2149	4.0
13 0445	0.9	**28** 0400	0.8
1055	4.1	1018	4.1
TH 1716	0.5	F 1634	0.5
2312	4.1	2240	4.3
14 0524	0.8	**29** 0449	0.7
1136	4.2	1107	4.3
F 1755	0.5	SA 1723	0.3
● 2351	4.2	○ 2328	4.5
15 0558	0.8	**30** 0534	0.6
1212	4.2	1152	4.5
SA 1828	0.4	SU 1810	0.2
		31 0014	4.6
		0618	0.5
		M 1237	4.6
		1855	0.1

Chart Datum: 2·16 metres below Ordnance Datum (Newlyn). HAT is 4·7 metres above Chart Datum.

STANDARD TIME (UT)
For Summer Time add ONE hour in **non-shaded areas**

WALTON-ON-THE-NAZE   LAT 51°51'N   LONG 1°17'E
TIMES AND HEIGHTS OF HIGH AND LOW WATERS

Dates in red are **SPRINGS**
Dates in blue are **NEAPS**

YEAR **2015**

SEPTEMBER

Day	Time	m	Time	m	Time	m	Time	m
1	0059	4.7	0703	0.5	TU 1321	4.7	1939	0.1
16	0106	4.2	0706	0.7	W 1320	4.3	1924	0.5
2	0145	4.6	0747	0.5	W 1404	4.7	2021	0.2
17	0136	4.2	0734	0.7	TH 1351	4.2	1950	0.6
3	0230	4.5	0831	0.6	TH 1448	4.5	2103	0.4
18	0206	4.1	0804	0.8	F 1422	4.1	2017	0.7
4	0316	4.2	0917	0.7	F 1533	4.3	2148	0.6
19	0238	4.0	0835	0.8	SA 1455	4.0	2048	0.8
5	0405	4.0	1008	0.8	SA 1625	4.1	2242	0.9
20	0313	3.8	0911	0.9	SU 1534	3.9	2127	1.0
6	0503	3.8	1108	0.9	SU 1730	3.8	2348	1.1
21	0356	3.7	0957	1.0	M 1622	3.7	2221	1.2
7	0613	3.6	1221	1.0	M 1850	3.7		
22	0453	3.6	1106	1.1	TU 1727	3.6	2353	1.3
8	0107	1.2	0733	3.6	TU 1350	1.0	2011	3.7
23	0609	3.5	1252	1.1	W 1853	3.6		
9	0233	1.2	0849	3.7	W 1516	0.9	2118	3.9
24	0131	1.2	0736	3.6	TH 1411	0.9	2019	3.8
10	0340	1.1	0948	3.9	TH 1614	0.7	2211	4.0
25	0238	1.0	0853	3.8	F 1513	0.6	2125	4.1
11	0427	1.0	1034	4.1	F 1657	0.6	2253	4.1
26	0335	0.8	0952	4.1	SA 1609	0.4	2218	4.3
12	0503	0.9	1113	4.2	SA 1730	0.5	2329	4.2
27	0425	0.7	1042	4.3	SU 1659	0.3	2306	4.5
13	0535	0.8	1147	4.2	SU 1800	0.5		
28	0512	0.6	1128	4.5	M 1746	0.2	2351	4.6
14	0002	4.2	0606	0.8	M 1219	4.3	1828	0.5
29	0558	0.5	1212	4.7	TU 1831	0.1		
15	0035	4.2	0637	0.7	TU 1250	4.3	1857	0.5
30	0036	4.7	0644	0.5	W 1256	4.7	1914	0.2

OCTOBER

Day	Time	m	Time	m	Time	m	Time	m
1	0121	4.6	0728	0.5	TH 1340	4.7	1955	0.3
16	0107	4.2	0711	0.7	F 1323	4.2	1918	0.6
2	0206	4.4	0812	0.5	F 1423	4.6	2035	0.5
17	0139	4.1	0742	0.7	SA 1356	4.2	1946	0.7
3	0251	4.2	0857	0.6	SA 1508	4.3	2117	0.8
18	0212	4.0	0814	0.7	SU 1431	4.1	2020	0.8
4	0338	4.0	0945	0.7	SU 1559	4.1	2207	1.0
19	0248	3.9	0850	0.8	M 1511	4.0	2101	1.0
5	0432	3.7	1041	0.8	M 1702	3.8	2310	1.2
20	0331	3.8	0937	0.9	TU 1600	3.8	2157	1.1
6	0539	3.5	1151	1.0	TU 1822	3.6		
21	0425	3.6	1043	1.0	W 1702	3.7	2322	1.3
7	0031	1.4	0659	3.5	W 1320	1.0	1942	3.7
22	0537	3.5	1220	0.9	TH 1823	3.7		
8	0200	1.3	0817	3.6	TH 1445	0.9	2052	3.8
23	0056	1.2	0702	3.6	F 1340	0.8	1949	3.8
9	0311	1.2	0918	3.8	F 1545	0.7	2144	4.0
24	0207	1.0	0821	3.8	SA 1444	0.6	2058	4.1
10	0359	1.0	1005	4.0	SA 1626	0.6	2226	4.1
25	0306	0.8	0924	4.1	SU 1541	0.4	2154	4.3
11	0436	0.9	1043	4.1	SU 1658	0.6	2301	4.1
26	0400	0.7	1016	4.3	M 1633	0.3	2243	4.5
12	0509	0.8	1117	4.2	M 1727	0.5	2334	4.2
27	0449	0.6	1103	4.5	TU 1721	0.2	2329	4.6
13	0540	0.7	1148	4.2	TU 1756	0.5		
28	0538	0.5	1148	4.6	W 1806	0.2		
14	0005	4.2	0611	0.7	W 1219	4.3	1824	0.5
29	0014	4.6	0625	0.4	TH 1232	4.7	1849	0.3
15	0036	4.2	0641	0.7	TH 1251	4.3	1852	0.6
30	0059	4.5	0711	0.4	F 1317	4.6	1931	0.5
31	0143	4.4	0756	0.4	SA 1401	4.5	2011	0.7

NOVEMBER

Day	Time	m	Time	m	Time	m	Time	m
1	0227	4.2	0840	0.5	SU 1446	4.3	2051	0.9
16	0154	4.1	0801	0.6	M 1415	4.1	2003	0.8
2	0312	4.0	0925	0.6	M 1535	4.0	2135	1.1
17	0233	4.0	0841	0.7	TU 1457	4.0	2048	0.9
3	0402	3.8	1015	0.8	TU 1633	3.8	2230	1.3
18	0316	3.9	0929	0.7	W 1546	3.9	2146	1.1
4	0502	3.6	1116	0.9	W 1744	3.6	2342	1.4
19	0409	3.8	1034	0.8	TH 1646	3.8	2300	1.2
5	0613	3.5	1233	1.0	TH 1859	3.6		
20	0514	3.7	1154	0.8	F 1759	3.8		
6	0108	1.4	0728	3.5	F 1351	0.9	2010	3.7
21	0022	1.2	0630	3.7	SA 1310	0.7	1919	3.9
7	0223	1.3	0834	3.6	SA 1455	0.8	2107	3.8
22	0135	1.0	0749	3.8	SU 1414	0.5	2030	4.0
8	0320	1.1	0926	3.8	SU 1542	0.7	2151	3.9
23	0238	0.9	0856	4.0	M 1513	0.4	2130	4.2
9	0402	1.0	1006	3.9	M 1619	0.7	2229	4.0
24	0335	0.7	0952	4.2	TU 1607	0.4	2222	4.3
10	0439	0.8	1042	4.0	TU 1653	0.6	2303	4.1
25	0429	0.6	1041	4.4	W 1658	0.4	2310	4.4
11	0513	0.7	1116	4.1	W 1725	0.6	2336	4.2
26	0520	0.5	1127	4.5	TH 1745	0.4	2355	4.5
12	0546	0.7	1150	4.2	TH 1755	0.6		
27	0610	0.4	1213	4.6	F 1830	0.5		
13	0009	4.2	0618	0.6	F 1225	4.3	1823	0.6
28	0040	4.4	0657	0.3	SA 1258	4.5	1912	0.6
14	0043	4.2	0651	0.6	SA 1300	4.2	1853	0.7
29	0124	4.4	0742	0.4	SU 1342	4.4	1951	0.6
15	0118	4.2	0725	0.6	SU 1336	4.2	1926	0.7
30	0207	4.2	0825	0.4	M 1426	4.2	2028	0.9

DECEMBER

Day	Time	m	Time	m	Time	m	Time	m
1	0249	4.0	0906	0.5	TU 1512	4.0	2106	1.1
16	0225	4.1	0836	0.5	W 1448	4.2	2042	0.8
2	0333	3.9	0948	0.7	W 1603	3.8	2150	1.2
17	0308	4.0	0925	0.5	TH 1536	4.1	2136	0.9
3	0423	3.7	1037	0.8	TH 1701	3.6	2245	1.4
18	0357	3.9	1022	0.6	F 1631	3.9	2239	1.0
4	0522	3.5	1138	0.9	F 1805	3.5		
19	0454	3.8	1129	0.6	SA 1737	3.8	2349	1.1
5	0002	1.4	0625	3.5	SA 1249	0.9	1909	3.5
20	0602	3.8	1239	0.6	SU 1850	3.8		
6	0124	1.4	0731	3.5	SU 1353	0.9	2011	3.6
21	0102	1.0	0718	3.5	M 1345	0.6	2003	3.9
7	0230	1.3	0832	3.6	M 1450	0.9	2106	3.7
22	0210	0.9	0830	3.9	TU 1447	0.6	2109	4.0
8	0323	1.1	0923	3.7	TU 1538	0.8	2151	3.9
23	0314	0.8	0932	4.1	W 1546	0.6	2206	4.1
9	0407	0.9	1006	3.9	W 1619	0.7	2231	4.0
24	0413	0.6	1025	4.2	TH 1641	0.6	2256	4.2
10	0446	0.8	1046	4.0	TH 1656	0.7	2309	4.1
25	0508	0.5	1113	4.3	F 1730	0.6	2342	4.3
11	0523	0.7	1125	4.1	F 1730	0.7	2346	4.2
26	0559	0.4	1159	4.4	SA 1814	0.6		
12	0559	0.6	1203	4.2	SA 1803	0.7		
27	0026	4.3	0645	0.3	SU 1243	4.4	1855	0.7
13	0025	4.2	0635	0.5	SU 1243	4.3	1837	0.6
28	0109	4.3	0728	0.3	M 1326	4.3	1933	0.6
14	0105	4.2	0713	0.4	M 1323	4.3	1914	0.7
29	0149	4.2	0807	0.4	TU 1408	4.2	2008	0.9
15	0144	4.2	0753	0.4	TU 1404	4.2	1956	0.7
30	0227	4.1	0843	0.5	W 1449	4.0	2039	1.0
31	0305	4.0	0918	0.5	TH 1531	3.8	2113	1.0

Chart Datum: 2·16 metres below Ordnance Datum (Newlyn). HAT is 4·7 metres above Chart Datum.

1.19 & 20   RIVERS STOUR AND ORWELL

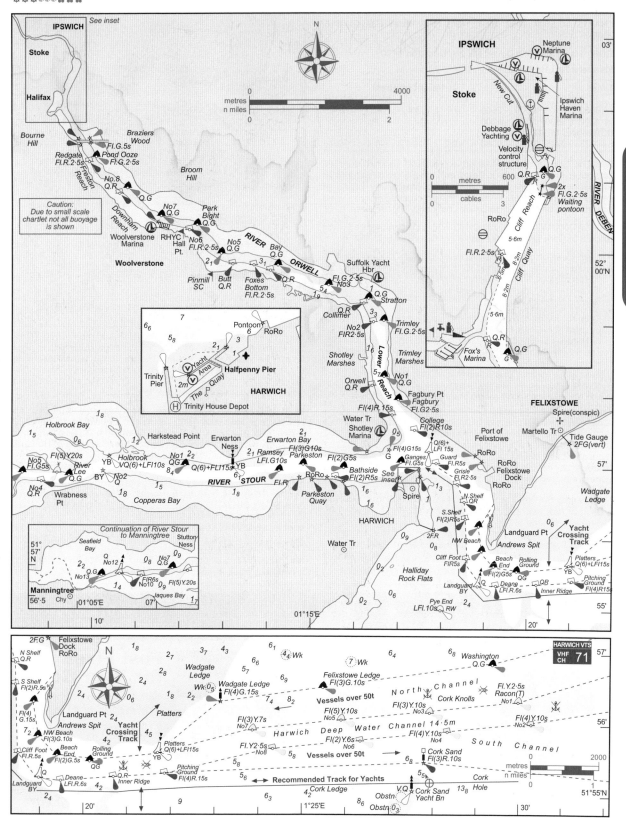

E England

1.19 RIVER STOUR

Essex/Suffolk **51°57'·06N 01°17'·77E** (Guard PHM buoy)
✦✦✦✦✦✦✦✦✦

CHARTS AC 5607, 2052, 2693, 1491, 1594; Imray C29, C1, Y16, 2000

TIDES Harwich +0050 Dover; ML 2·1; Duration 0630
Standard Port HARWICH (→)

Times				Height (metres)			
High Water		Low Water		MHWS	MHWN	MLWN	MLWS
0000	0600	0000	0600	4·0	3·4	1·1	0·4
1200	1800	1200	1800				
Differences MISTLEY							
+0025	+0015	+0005	0000	+0·2	+0·1	−0·1	−0·1

SHELTER Good at Shotley Marina; access (H24) via chan dredged 2m, outer limits lit, to lock. Enter only on F.G tfc lt. ⌒ also at Halfpenny Pier (H24) and Manningtree (dries). No yachts at Parkeston Quay. ⚓s off Wrabness Pt (untenable in some wind against tide conditions), Holbrook Creek and Stutton Ness.

NAVIGATION WPT 51°55'·33N 01°25'·50E, on recommended yacht track, S of Cork Sand Bn (see also River Orwell page).

- Keep clear of commercial shipping. Outside the hbr, yachts should cross the DW chan at 90° between Rolling Ground and Platters buoys. Stay clear of the DW chan (Y lit SPMs) using Recommended Yacht Track, running S and W of DW chan to beyond Harwich.

- Caution: Bkwtr, ESE of Blackman's Hd, covers at HW; marked by PHM lit Bn, only 5ca W of main chan. Beware of passing W of Harwich Shelf ECM buoy without sufficient height of tide. The Guard Shoal (0·8m), about 2ca S of Guard PHM, lies close to the Recommended Yacht Track. R Stour is well marked; sp limit 8kn. Beware 'The Horse' 4ca NE and drying bank 1½ca NW of Wrabness Pt. Mistley Quay local knowledge advised for the narrow, tortuous chan to Manningtree.

Special local sound signals
Commercial vessels may use these additional signals:

Four short and rapid blasts followed by one short blast	} =	I am turning short around to stbd.
Four short and rapid blasts followed by two short blasts	} =	I am turning short around to port.
One prolonged blast	=	I am leaving dock, quay or ⚓.

LIGHTS AND MARKS The R Stour to Mistley is lit. Shotley Marina: a Dir lt at lock indicates the dredged chan (2·0m) by Inogen (or Moiré) visual marker lt which is a square, ambered display; a vert B line indicates on the appr centre line 339°. If off the centre line, arrows indicate the direction to steer to regain it.

COMMUNICATIONS (Code 01255) MRCC 675518; Police 101; Dr 201299; Ⓗ 201200. Harwich HM 243030; Hbr Ops 243000.

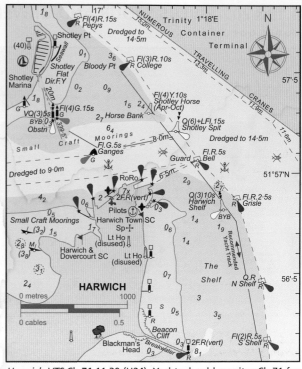

HARWICH

Harwich VTS Ch **71** 11 20 (H24). Yachts should monitor Ch 71 for traffic info, but not transmit. ⚓, tidal and (possibly) help in poor vis may be available on request. The Hbr Patrol launch listens on Ch 11 (summer weekends, 0800–1800). Hbr Radar Ch 20. Shotley Marina Ch **80** (lock master). Monitor Ch 14 for an information service by Dover CG for the Sunk TSS.

FACILITIES HARWICH Halfpenny Pier Available Apr–Oct, no reservations. Free 0900-1600; overnight: £1·00/m up to 20m, £30 > 20m, max stay 72hrs, ⚓, showers. **Town** 🅿 & 🅿, Gas, 🔧⚓🏪, ✕, ✉, Ⓑ, 🍴, 🖴, ✕, ⚡, ➤ (Cambridge). **Ferries:** Hook of Holland: 2/day; 6¼ Hrs; Stena (www.stenaline.co.uk) Esbjerg: 3/week; 18 Hrs; DFDS Seaways (dfdsseaways.com).

SHOTLEY (01473) **Shotley Marina** sales@shotleymarina.co.uk ☎ 788982 (H24), 350 (visitors welcome), £2·50, access H24 via lock (width 7m); D(H24), 🖴, 🛢, 🔧, 🏪, Ⓔ, ✕, BH (40 ton), BY, C, 🍴, 🖴, ⚓, 🖴, ✕, Gas, Gaz, Ferries to Harwich.
Shotley SC ☎ 787500, ➤, ⚓, 🖴.

WRABNESS: M, ⚓, 🍴.

MANNINGTREE, ⌒ (drying), ⚓. Stour SC ☎ (01206) 393924, M (drying but free), ⚓, 🖴, showers. **Town** 🍴, Gas.

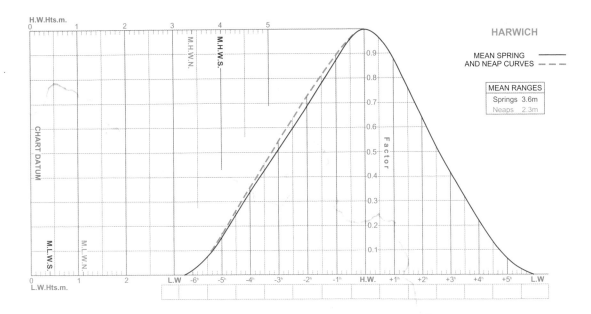

HARWICH

MEAN SPRING
AND NEAP CURVES – – –

MEAN RANGES
Springs 3.6m
Neaps 2.3m

1.20 RIVER ORWELL

Suffolk **51°57'·06N 01°17'·77E** (Guard PHM by)

CHARTS AC 5607, 2052, 2693, 1491; Imray C29, C1, Y16, 2000

TIDES Pin Mill +0100 Dover; Ipswich +0115 Dover; ML 2·4; Duration 0555

Standard Port HARWICH (➝)

Times				Height (metres)			
High Water		Low Water		MHWS	MHWN	MLWN	MLWS
0000	0600	0000	0600	4·0	3·4	1·1	0·4
1200	1800	1200	1800				
Differences IPSWICH							
+0015	+0025	0000	+0010	+0·2	0·0	–0·1	–0·1

SHELTER Good. Ent and river well marked, but many unlit moorings line both banks. ⚓s above Shotley Pt on W side, or off Pinmill. No yacht facilities at Felixstowe. Ⓥ's (pre-book) at Suffolk Yacht Hbr, Woolverstone Marina, Fox's Marina (Ipswich), Neptune Marina, Ipswich Haven Marina, the latter two accessed via Prince Philip Lock; *call Ch 68 at Orwell Bridge.*

NAVIGATION Approach/entry from seaward as for R Stour. WPT Shotley Spit SCM buoy, Q (6)+L Fl 15s, 51°57'·21N 01°17'·68E, at river ent. A *Yachting Guide to Harwich Harbour and its Rivers* has much useful info; it can be obtained free from Harwich Haven Authority, The Quay, Harwich CO12 3HH; ☎ (01255) 243030.

- Keep clear of the many large ships, ferries from/to Harwich, Felixstowe and Ipswich, especially container ships turning between Trinity container terminal, Shotley Spit and Guard buoys.
- Major harbour works planned for 2015 to cater for larger container ships. Advise referral to NM. Ch 71 should be monitored whilst in Harwich Harbour but only used in emergency. Call sign Harwich VTS. Harwich HM 01255 243030. Refer also to 1.19 River Stour.
- 6kn speed limit in R Orwell. Ipswich Dock ent closed when tide >4.6m above CD. Ipswich New Cut entrance, *Velocity Control Structure is raised from seabed when required with the top of it just below sea level*; 3 FR (vert) = no passage.

LIGHTS AND MARKS Suffolk Yacht Hbr appr marked by SWM then four bns and ldg lts: front Iso Y; rear Oc Y 4s.

A14 bridge lts: Centre FY (clearance 38m)
No 9 Pier 2 FR (vert) } shown up and
No 10 Pier 2 FG (vert) } down stream.
● and ● tfc lts control ent to Ipswich Dock (H24).
Ipswich New Cut: 3 FR (vert) when closed to navigation.

COMMUNICATIONS (Code 01473) MRCC (01255) 675518; Police 101; Ⓗ 712233; Orwell Navigation Service 211066, Ipswich HM 211771, Ipswich Lock Control 213526.

Ipswich Port Radio and *Ipswich Lock Control* VHF Ch 68 (H24). Once above Shotley Pt or anywhere in the area, monitor Ch 68 continuously in fog. Suffolk Yacht Hbr, Woolverstone Marina, Fox's Marina: Ch 80 M. Neptune Marina: Ch M, 80 (0800-1730LT). Ipswich Haven Marina Ch M 80.

FACILITIES

LEVINGTON Suffolk Yacht Hbr (SYH) info@syharbour.co.uk ☎ 659240, Ch 80. Access H24; 550 ⌒ + Ⓥ, £2·64; ⚓ (launching £25·00), ⛽, ⊕, ⊙ P & D (0815-1750); ✕, ⚒, ☎, Ⓔ, △, BH (10/60t), C (15t), ⚓, ⬚, Gas, Gaz, LPG.

Haven Ports YC ☎ 659658, ✕, ⬚.

Town ✉, Ⓑ (Felixstowe), ⇌ (bus to Ipswich), ✈ (Cambridge).

PIN MILL King's Boatyard ☎ 780258; M (£10 proceeds to RNLI, 07714 260568), L, ⚓, ⚓, ⊙, ✕, ⚒, ☎, △, C (6t), ⬚ (1M), Gas, Gaz, LPG.

Haven Ports YC ☎ 659658, ✕, ⬚.

Pin Mill SC ☎ 780271.

WOOLVERSTONE Marina ☎ 780206 (H24), Mob 07803 968209. 235 ⌒ inc Ⓥ £2·88 inc electricity, ⚓, D (HO), Gas, Gaz, ⊙, ⛽, ⚒, ☎, △, ⚓, BY, C (20t), ⬚, ✕.

Royal Harwich YC www.royalharwichyachtclub.co.uk ☎ 780319. ⌒, £2·11, ✕, ⬚.

Town Chelmondiston: ✉, ⬚.

IPSWICH, Fox's Marina ④ ☎ 689111. 75 + ⌒ Ⓥ £2·59. Ch 80, ⛽, P, D (0800-1730), Gas, Gaz, ⚒, ☎, Ⓔ, ✕, △, Rigger, ⚓, ACA, BH (44/70 t), BY, C (7t), ⬚, wi-fi. **Marina YC** ☎ 684111, ⬚ ✕.

Orwell YC ☎ 602288, ⚓, ⚓, ⬚, ⬚,

Prince Philip Lock near city centre gives H24 access to:

Neptune Marina 150+ ⌒ Ⓥ, £2·64, ☎ 215204; D (0800-1700).

Ipswich Haven Marina 320+ ⌒ Ⓥ, £2·47 ☎ 236644; D (0800-1900), ⊙, ✕, ⚒, ☎, Ⓔ, BH (70t), BY, C, Gas, Gaz, ✕, ⬚.

Town ✉, Ⓑ, ⛾ & ⛾, ⇌, ✈ (Cambridge/Norwich).

Harwich tides

HARWICH   LAT 51°57′N   LONG 1°17′E

TIMES AND HEIGHTS OF HIGH AND LOW WATERS

STANDARD TIME (UT)
For Summer Time add ONE hour in **non-shaded areas**

Dates in red are **SPRINGS**
Dates in blue are **NEAPS**

YEAR **2015**

JANUARY

Time	m	Time	m
1 0141 1.0 / 0808 3.5 / TH 1419 0.8 / 2047 3.6		**16** 0057 1.2 / 0725 3.3 / F 1340 0.9 / 1957 3.4	
2 0244 0.9 / 0911 3.6 / F 1514 0.7 / 2145 3.7		**17** 0205 1.1 / 0830 3.4 / SA 1440 0.8 / 2101 3.6	
3 0341 0.8 / 1007 3.8 / SA 1604 0.7 / 2237 3.9		**18** 0307 0.9 / 0933 3.6 / SU 1535 0.7 / 2202 3.8	
4 0432 0.6 / 1058 3.9 / SU 1649 0.7 / 2323 3.9		**19** 0403 0.7 / 1030 3.8 / M 1625 0.6 / 2255 3.9	
5 0518 0.5 / 1144 3.9 / M 1729 0.7 / ○		**20** 0453 0.5 / 1122 4.0 / TU 1712 0.5 / ● 2344 4.1	
6 0006 4.0 / 0600 0.5 / TU 1227 3.9 / 1806 0.8		**21** 0540 0.3 / 1211 4.2 / W 1755 0.4	
7 0045 3.9 / 0638 0.5 / W 1305 3.9 / 1839 0.8		**22** 0031 4.2 / 0625 0.2 / TH 1258 4.3 / 1838 0.4	
8 0118 3.9 / 0711 0.5 / TH 1338 3.8 / 1909 0.8		**23** 0117 4.2 / 0709 0.1 / F 1344 4.3 / 1920 0.4	
9 0149 3.8 / 0741 0.5 / F 1409 3.8 / 1940 0.8		**24** 0201 4.2 / 0754 0.1 / SA 1431 4.2 / 2004 0.5	
10 0220 3.8 / 0813 0.6 / SA 1443 3.7 / 2016 0.9		**25** 0246 4.1 / 0839 0.2 / SU 1518 4.0 / 2049 0.6	
11 0256 3.8 / 0851 0.6 / SU 1522 3.7 / 2055 0.9		**26** 0331 4.0 / 0926 0.3 / M 1607 3.8 / 2138 0.7	
12 0337 3.7 / 0934 0.7 / M 1606 3.6 / 2139 1.0		**27** 0421 3.8 / 1020 0.5 / TU 1701 3.6 / ◑ 2234 0.9	
13 0424 3.5 / 1023 0.8 / TU 1656 3.5 / ◑ 2231 1.1		**28** 0520 3.6 / 1129 0.7 / W 1803 3.4 / 2351 1.0	
14 0519 3.4 / 1125 0.9 / W 1753 3.4 / 2340 1.2		**29** 0630 3.4 / 1245 0.9 / TH 1913 3.3	
15 0621 3.3 / 1234 1.0 / TH 1854 3.4		**30** 0113 1.1 / 0744 3.4 / F 1353 0.9 / 2022 3.4	
		31 0223 0.9 / 0852 3.5 / SA 1452 0.9 / 2124 3.5	

FEBRUARY

Time	m	Time	m
1 0325 0.8 / 0952 3.6 / SU 1545 0.9 / 2218 3.7		**16** 0242 0.9 / 0909 3.5 / M 1515 0.8 / 2138 3.6	
2 0418 0.6 / 1044 3.8 / M 1631 0.8 / 2306 3.9		**17** 0346 0.6 / 1013 3.8 / TU 1608 0.6 / 2236 3.9	
3 0504 0.5 / 1130 3.9 / TU 1712 0.7 / ○ 2349 3.9		**18** 0439 0.4 / 1106 4.1 / W 1655 0.4 / ● 2327 4.1	
4 0545 0.5 / 1211 3.9 / W 1748 0.7		**19** 0526 0.2 / 1155 4.2 / TH 1739 0.3	
5 0027 3.9 / 0619 0.5 / TH 1248 3.8 / 1819 0.7		**20** 0014 4.2 / 0610 0.2 / F 1242 4.3 / 1821 0.3	
6 0101 3.9 / 0648 0.5 / F 1319 3.8 / 1848 0.7		**21** 0059 4.3 / 0652 0.0 / SA 1327 4.3 / 1903 0.3	
7 0130 3.8 / 0716 0.5 / SA 1346 3.8 / 1918 0.7		**22** 0142 4.3 / 0734 0.0 / SU 1411 4.2 / 1946 0.3	
8 0158 3.8 / 0747 0.5 / SU 1416 3.8 / 1951 0.7		**23** 0225 4.2 / 0817 0.1 / M 1454 4.1 / 2029 0.4	
9 0229 3.8 / 0821 0.5 / M 1451 3.8 / 2026 0.7		**24** 0308 4.1 / 0901 0.3 / TU 1539 3.9 / 2114 0.6	
10 0305 3.8 / 0857 0.6 / TU 1531 3.7 / 2105 0.8		**25** 0354 3.9 / 0949 0.5 / W 1626 3.6 / ◑ 2206 0.8	
11 0346 3.7 / 0937 0.7 / W 1618 3.6 / 2149 0.8		**26** 0447 3.6 / 1051 0.8 / TH 1722 3.3 / 2317 1.0	
12 0434 3.5 / 1025 0.8 / TH 1712 3.4 / ◑ 2242 1.1		**27** 0555 3.4 / 1213 1.0 / F 1835 3.2	
13 0536 3.3 / 1130 1.0 / F 1814 3.4 / 2355 1.2		**28** 0048 1.0 / 0720 3.3 / SA 1326 1.1 / 1954 3.2	
14 0645 3.3 / 1300 1.0 / SA 1921 3.3			
15 0126 1.1 / 0757 3.3 / SU 1414 0.9 / 2030 3.4			

MARCH

Time	m	Time	m
1 0202 0.9 / 0832 3.4 / SU 1428 1.0 / 2059 3.4		**16** 0050 1.0 / 0730 3.3 / M 1350 1.0 / 2002 3.3	
2 0306 0.8 / 0932 3.6 / M 1523 0.9 / 2154 3.6		**17** 0222 0.8 / 0848 3.5 / TU 1456 0.7 / 2114 3.5	
3 0400 0.6 / 1023 3.8 / TU 1610 0.8 / 2243 3.8		**18** 0329 0.6 / 0954 3.8 / W 1549 0.6 / 2214 3.8	
4 0444 0.5 / 1109 3.9 / W 1651 0.7 / 2326 3.9		**19** 0422 0.3 / 1048 4.1 / TH 1636 0.4 / 2306 4.1	
5 0522 0.4 / 1150 3.9 / TH 1725 0.7 / ○		**20** 0508 0.1 / 1136 4.3 / F 1720 0.3 / ● 2353 4.2	
6 0005 3.9 / 0552 0.4 / F 1226 3.9 / 1755 0.7		**21** 0550 0.0 / 1221 4.3 / SA 1802 0.2	
7 0039 3.9 / 0619 0.4 / SA 1256 3.8 / 1825 0.6		**22** 0037 4.3 / 0631 0.0 / SU 1305 4.3 / 1844 0.2	
8 0107 3.8 / 0648 0.5 / SU 1321 3.8 / 1855 0.6		**23** 0121 4.3 / 0712 0.0 / M 1348 4.2 / 1926 0.2	
9 0134 3.8 / 0719 0.5 / M 1348 3.8 / 1927 0.6		**24** 0203 4.3 / 0753 0.2 / TU 1429 4.1 / 2009 0.3	
10 0203 3.8 / 0751 0.5 / TU 1421 3.8 / 2001 0.6		**25** 0245 4.1 / 0834 0.4 / W 1511 3.9 / 2053 0.5	
11 0236 3.8 / 0825 0.5 / W 1500 3.8 / 2038 0.7		**26** 0330 3.9 / 0919 0.7 / TH 1554 3.6 / 2142 0.7	
12 0315 3.7 / 0903 0.6 / TH 1543 3.6 / 2120 0.8		**27** 0419 3.6 / 1014 0.9 / F 1643 3.4 / ◑ 2249 0.9	
13 0401 3.6 / 0947 0.8 / F 1635 3.4 / ◑ 2211 0.9		**28** 0522 3.4 / 1137 1.2 / SA 1750 3.2	
14 0500 3.4 / 1044 1.0 / SA 1738 3.3 / 2315 1.0		**29** 0021 1.0 / 0649 3.2 / SU 1256 1.2 / 1918 3.1	
15 0613 3.3 / 1210 1.1 / SU 1848 3.2		**30** 0135 0.9 / 0805 3.3 / M 1400 1.1 / 2027 3.3	
		31 0237 0.8 / 0905 3.5 / TU 1456 1.0 / 2124 3.5	

APRIL

Time	m	Time	m
1 0331 0.6 / 0957 3.7 / W 1544 0.9 / 2213 3.7		**16** 0306 0.5 / 0931 3.8 / TH 1527 0.6 / 2149 3.8	
2 0414 0.5 / 1042 3.9 / TH 1624 0.7 / 2257 3.8		**17** 0400 0.3 / 1025 4.1 / F 1615 0.4 / 2242 4.0	
3 0449 0.5 / 1123 3.9 / F 1658 0.7 / 2336 3.9		**18** 0446 0.1 / 1114 4.2 / SA 1700 0.3 / ● 2330 4.2	
4 0519 0.5 / 1158 3.9 / SA 1729 0.6 / ○		**19** 0528 0.1 / 1159 4.3 / SU 1744 0.2	
5 0011 3.8 / 0548 0.5 / SU 1228 3.8 / 1800 0.6		**20** 0015 4.3 / 0609 0.1 / M 1243 4.3 / 1826 0.2	
6 0041 3.8 / 0620 0.5 / M 1254 3.8 / 1833 0.6		**21** 0059 4.3 / 0650 0.0 / TU 1325 4.2 / 1909 0.2	
7 0109 3.8 / 0652 0.5 / TU 1322 3.9 / 1906 0.5		**22** 0142 4.3 / 0730 0.3 / W 1405 4.0 / 1951 0.3	
8 0139 3.8 / 0725 0.5 / W 1355 3.9 / 1940 0.5		**23** 0225 4.1 / 0810 0.5 / TH 1445 3.9 / 2035 0.5	
9 0214 3.9 / 0759 0.5 / TH 1433 3.8 / 2018 0.5		**24** 0309 4.0 / 0851 0.5 / F 1527 3.7 / 2122 0.6	
10 0254 3.8 / 0838 0.6 / F 1516 3.7 / 2101 0.6		**25** 0356 3.7 / 0939 1.0 / SA 1613 3.4 / ◑ 2222 0.8	
11 0342 3.6 / 0924 0.8 / SA 1606 3.5 / 2152 0.7		**26** 0452 3.4 / 1050 1.2 / SU 1709 3.3 / 2345 0.9	
12 0440 3.5 / 1019 1.0 / SU 1708 3.3 / ◑ 2255 0.9		**27** 0605 3.2 / 1216 1.3 / M 1826 3.2	
13 0552 3.3 / 1136 1.1 / M 1822 3.2		**28** 0057 0.9 / 0725 3.3 / TU 1324 1.2 / 1944 3.2	
14 0027 0.9 / 0711 3.4 / TU 1324 1.0 / 1938 3.3		**29** 0158 0.8 / 0829 3.4 / W 1421 1.1 / 2045 3.4	
15 0201 0.7 / 0827 3.6 / W 1431 0.9 / 2049 3.5		**30** 0249 0.7 / 0922 3.6 / TH 1509 0.9 / 2137 3.6	

Chart Datum: 2·02 metres below Ordnance Datum (Newlyn). HAT is 4·4 metres above Chart Datum.

》》 **FREE** monthly updates from 《《
www.reedsalmanac.co.uk

STANDARD TIME (UT)
For Summer Time add ONE
hour in **non-shaded areas**

HARWICH   LAT 51°57'N   LONG 1°17'E
TIMES AND HEIGHTS OF HIGH AND LOW WATERS

Dates in red are **SPRINGS**
Dates in blue are **NEAPS**

YEAR 2015

E England

	MAY				JUNE				JULY				AUGUST		
	Time	m	Time	m	Time	m	Time	m	Time	m	Time	m	Time	m	Time	m

MAY

1 0332 0.6 / 1009 3.7 / F 1550 0.8 / 2222 3.7
16 0334 0.3 / 1001 4.0 / SA 1553 0.5 / 2218 4.0

2 0408 0.6 / 1050 3.9 / SA 1625 0.7 / 2303 3.8
17 0423 0.3 / 1052 4.1 / SU 1641 0.4 / 2308 4.1

3 0443 0.5 / 1126 3.9 / SU 1700 0.6 / 2339 3.8
18 0507 0.2 / 1138 4.2 / M 1726 0.3 / ● 2355 4.2

4 0518 0.5 / 1157 3.9 / M 1736 0.6 / ○
19 0549 0.3 / 1223 4.2 / TU 1811 0.3

5 0013 3.8 / 0554 0.5 / TU 1228 3.9 / 1812 0.5
20 0040 4.2 / 0629 0.4 / W 1305 4.1 / 1854 0.3

6 0046 3.8 / 0630 0.5 / W 1300 3.9 / 1848 0.5
21 0124 4.1 / 0709 0.5 / TH 1345 4.0 / 1937 0.3

7 0120 3.9 / 0705 0.5 / TH 1336 3.9 / 1925 0.5
22 0207 4.0 / 0748 0.7 / F 1424 3.9 / 2020 0.4

8 0159 3.9 / 0741 0.6 / F 1415 3.8 / 2005 0.5
23 0249 3.9 / 0826 0.8 / SA 1503 3.7 / 2103 0.6

9 0242 3.8 / 0822 0.6 / SA 1459 3.7 / 2050 0.6
24 0333 3.7 / 0907 1.0 / SU 1546 3.6 / 2152 0.7

10 0332 3.7 / 0909 0.8 / SU 1549 3.6 / 2142 0.6
25 0421 3.5 / 0959 1.2 / M 1636 3.4 / ◗ 2253 0.8

11 0430 3.6 / 1004 0.9 / M 1650 3.4 / ◗ 2244 0.7
26 0515 3.3 / 1110 1.3 / TU 1734 3.3

12 0539 3.5 / 1117 1.1 / TU 1803 3.4
27 0000 0.9 / 0618 3.3 / W 1226 1.3 / 1840 3.2

13 0012 0.7 / 0653 3.5 / W 1253 1.0 / 1916 3.4
28 0100 0.8 / 0729 3.3 / TH 1328 1.2 / 1948 3.3

14 0135 0.6 / 0803 3.6 / TH 1403 0.9 / 2023 3.6
29 0153 0.8 / 0832 3.4 / F 1421 1.0 / 2048 3.4

15 0240 0.5 / 0906 3.8 / F 1501 0.7 / 2123 3.8
30 0241 0.7 / 0924 3.6 / SA 1507 0.9 / 2140 3.5

31 0326 0.6 / 1009 3.7 / SU 1551 0.8 / 2226 3.7

JUNE

1 0410 0.6 / 1049 3.8 / M 1633 0.7 / 2307 3.8
16 0447 0.5 / 1121 4.0 / TU 1712 0.4 / ● 2340 4.1

2 0451 0.5 / 1127 3.9 / TU 1714 0.6 / ○ 2347 3.8
17 0531 0.5 / 1206 4.1 / W 1758 0.3

3 0532 0.5 / 1204 3.9 / W 1755 0.5
18 0026 4.1 / 0612 0.6 / TH 1249 4.0 / 1842 0.4

4 0026 3.9 / 0611 0.5 / TH 1243 3.9 / 1835 0.4
19 0110 4.0 / 0651 0.7 / F 1328 4.0 / 1924 0.4

5 0107 4.0 / 0650 0.5 / F 1322 3.9 / 1916 0.4
20 0151 3.9 / 0728 0.7 / SA 1405 3.9 / 2003 0.4

6 0149 4.0 / 0729 0.6 / SA 1404 3.9 / 1959 0.4
21 0230 3.8 / 0802 0.8 / SU 1441 3.8 / 2040 0.5

7 0235 3.9 / 0812 0.6 / SU 1449 3.8 / 2044 0.4
22 0308 3.7 / 0838 0.9 / M 1519 3.7 / 2118 0.6

8 0325 3.8 / 0859 0.7 / M 1539 3.7 / 2135 0.4
23 0349 3.6 / 0920 1.0 / TU 1603 3.6 / 2204 0.7

9 0421 3.7 / 0952 0.8 / TU 1637 3.6 / ◗ 2235 0.5
24 0434 3.5 / 1011 1.1 / W 1653 3.5 / ◖ 2300 0.8

10 0524 3.6 / 1057 1.0 / W 1744 3.5 / 2351 0.6
25 0524 3.4 / 1116 1.2 / TH 1749 3.3

11 0631 3.6 / 1219 1.0 / TH 1852 3.5
26 0001 0.9 / 0620 3.3 / F 1225 1.2 / 1848 3.3

12 0107 0.6 / 0737 3.6 / F 1333 0.9 / 1958 3.6
27 0101 0.9 / 0720 3.4 / SA 1328 1.1 / 1950 3.3

13 0212 0.5 / 0840 3.7 / SA 1436 0.8 / 2100 3.7
28 0157 0.8 / 0822 3.5 / SU 1424 1.0 / 2051 3.4

14 0310 0.5 / 0939 3.9 / SU 1532 0.6 / 2158 3.9
29 0250 0.7 / 0921 3.6 / M 1518 0.9 / 2148 3.6

15 0401 0.5 / 1032 4.0 / M 1624 0.5 / 2251 4.0
30 0341 0.7 / 1014 3.8 / TU 1607 0.7 / 2238 3.8

JULY

1 0428 0.6 / 1101 3.9 / W 1654 0.6 / 2325 3.9
16 0515 0.7 / 1151 4.0 / TH 1747 0.4 / ●

2 0513 0.5 / 1145 4.0 / TH 1739 0.4 / ○
17 0013 4.0 / 0555 0.7 / F 1234 4.0 / 1829 0.4

3 0010 4.0 / 0555 0.5 / F 1229 4.0 / 1823 0.3
18 0056 4.0 / 0633 0.7 / SA 1312 4.0 / 1907 0.4

4 0055 4.1 / 0636 0.5 / SA 1312 4.0 / 1906 0.3
19 0134 3.9 / 0706 0.8 / SU 1346 3.9 / 1941 0.5

5 0140 4.1 / 0718 0.5 / SU 1355 4.0 / 1950 0.2
20 0208 3.8 / 0737 0.8 / M 1417 3.9 / 2011 0.5

6 0226 4.1 / 0801 0.6 / M 1440 4.0 / 2036 0.2
21 0240 3.8 / 0810 0.9 / TU 1451 3.8 / 2044 0.6

7 0315 4.0 / 0847 0.6 / TU 1528 3.9 / 2124 0.3
22 0315 3.7 / 0847 0.9 / W 1529 3.7 / 2123 0.6

8 0407 3.9 / 0936 0.7 / W 1620 3.8 / 2218 0.4
23 0355 3.6 / 0930 1.0 / TH 1613 3.6 / 2210 0.8

9 0503 3.7 / 1034 0.9 / TH 1721 3.7 / 2325 0.6
24 0442 3.5 / 1020 1.1 / F 1705 3.5 / ◖ 2308 0.9

10 0606 3.6 / 1146 1.0 / F 1827 3.6
25 0535 3.4 / 1125 1.2 / SA 1803 3.3

11 0039 0.7 / 0711 3.6 / SA 1304 1.0 / 1934 3.5
26 0015 1.0 / 0633 3.4 / SU 1239 1.2 / 1904 3.3

12 0147 0.7 / 0816 3.6 / SU 1413 0.9 / 2041 3.6
27 0120 1.0 / 0735 3.4 / M 1346 1.1 / 2009 3.4

13 0247 0.7 / 0919 3.7 / M 1515 0.7 / 2142 3.7
28 0220 0.9 / 0839 3.5 / TU 1448 1.0 / 2114 3.5

14 0342 0.7 / 1015 3.8 / TU 1611 0.6 / 2238 3.9
29 0316 0.8 / 0942 3.7 / W 1545 0.8 / 2213 3.8

15 0430 0.7 / 1105 4.0 / W 1701 0.5 / 2328 4.0
30 0408 0.7 / 1037 3.9 / TH 1637 0.6 / 2305 4.0

31 0455 0.6 / 1126 4.0 / F 1724 0.4 / ○ 2353 4.1

AUGUST

1 0539 0.5 / 1212 4.1 / SA 1809 0.2
16 0037 4.0 / 0611 0.8 / SU 1251 4.0 / 1843 0.5

2 0040 4.2 / 0620 0.5 / SU 1257 4.2 / 1852 0.1
17 0112 3.9 / 0641 0.8 / M 1323 3.9 / 1911 0.5

3 0126 4.3 / 0702 0.4 / M 1341 4.2 / 1935 0.1
18 0142 3.8 / 0710 0.8 / TU 1351 3.9 / 1938 0.5

4 0211 4.2 / 0745 0.5 / TU 1425 4.2 / 2018 0.1
19 0209 3.8 / 0741 0.8 / W 1420 3.9 / 2010 0.6

5 0257 4.1 / 0829 0.5 / W 1509 4.1 / 2104 0.2
20 0240 3.8 / 0816 0.8 / TH 1454 3.8 / 2045 0.6

6 0345 4.0 / 0916 0.6 / TH 1557 3.9 / 2154 0.4
21 0318 3.8 / 0854 0.9 / F 1533 3.7 / 2125 0.8

7 0437 3.8 / 1009 0.8 / F 1653 3.7 / ◗ 2255 0.7
22 0402 3.6 / 0937 1.0 / SA 1620 3.6 / ◖ 2211 0.9

8 0536 3.6 / 1117 1.0 / SA 1759 3.6
23 0454 3.5 / 1029 1.2 / SU 1718 3.4 / 2315 1.1

9 0011 0.8 / 0643 3.4 / SU 1239 1.0 / 1913 3.5
24 0553 3.4 / 1142 1.3 / M 1824 3.3

10 0123 0.9 / 0754 3.4 / M 1354 1.0 / 2025 3.5
25 0041 1.1 / 0657 3.3 / TU 1309 1.2 / 1933 3.3

11 0226 0.9 / 0859 3.6 / TU 1500 0.8 / 2128 3.7
26 0152 1.1 / 0805 3.4 / W 1422 1.0 / 2045 3.5

12 0323 0.9 / 0956 3.8 / W 1558 0.7 / 2223 3.9
27 0254 0.9 / 0913 3.6 / TH 1525 0.8 / 2151 3.8

13 0413 0.8 / 1047 3.9 / TH 1647 0.5 / 2312 4.0
28 0348 0.8 / 1013 3.9 / F 1619 0.5 / 2246 4.0

14 0457 0.8 / 1132 4.0 / F 1731 0.4 / ● 2356 4.0
29 0436 0.6 / 1105 4.1 / SA 1707 0.3 / ○ 2334 4.2

15 0536 0.8 / 1214 4.1 / SA 1810 0.4
30 0519 0.5 / 1152 4.2 / SU 1750 0.1

31 0020 4.4 / 0601 0.4 / M 1237 4.3 / 1832 0.1

Chart Datum: 2·02 metres below Ordnance Datum (Newlyn). HAT is 4·4 metres above Chart Datum.

》》 FREE monthly updates from 《《
www.reedsalmanac.co.uk

Harwich tides – River Deben

HARWICH LAT 51°57'N LONG 1°17'E
TIMES AND HEIGHTS OF HIGH AND LOW WATERS

Dates in red are **SPRINGS**
Dates in blue are **NEAPS**

YEAR 2015

SEPTEMBER

Time	m		Time	m
1 0106	4.4	**16** 0113	3.9	
0643	0.4	0643	0.8	
TU 1320	4.4	W 1322	3.9	
1913	0.1	1906	0.6	
2 0149	4.3	**17** 0137	3.9	
0725	0.4	0715	0.8	
W 1402	4.3	TH 1349	3.9	
1955	0.1	1937	0.6	
3 0233	4.2	**18** 0206	3.9	
0809	0.5	0748	0.8	
TH 1446	4.2	F 1420	3.9	
2039	0.3	2010	0.7	
4 0318	4.0	**19** 0242	3.8	
0855	0.6	0824	0.8	
F 1531	4.0	SA 1457	3.8	
2126	0.5	2047	0.8	
5 0406	3.8	**20** 0323	3.7	
0946	0.8	0904	0.9	
SA 1624	3.8	SU 1540	3.7	
☽ 2223	0.8	2128	0.9	
6 0502	3.5	**21** 0412	3.6	
1051	1.0	0952	1.0	
SU 1731	3.5	M 1636	3.5	
2342	1.1	☾ 2220	1.1	
7 0614	3.3	**22** 0513	3.4	
1218	1.1	1054	1.2	
M 1853	3.4	TU 1747	3.3	
		2340	1.3	
8 0058	1.2	**23** 0623	3.3	
0730	3.3	1229	1.2	
TU 1335	1.0	W 1903	3.3	
2007	3.5			
9 0204	1.1	**24** 0124	1.2	
0836	3.5	0734	3.4	
W 1441	0.9	TH 1356	1.0	
2109	3.7	2019	3.5	
10 0301	1.0	**25** 0230	1.0	
0933	3.7	0845	3.6	
TH 1538	0.7	F 1502	0.7	
2203	3.9	2127	3.8	
11 0351	0.9	**26** 0325	0.8	
1023	3.9	0947	3.9	
F 1627	0.5	SA 1557	0.5	
2251	4.0	2223	4.1	
12 0435	0.8	**27** 0413	0.6	
1108	4.0	1039	4.1	
SA 1708	0.5	SU 1644	0.2	
2334	4.1	2312	4.3	
13 0513	0.8	**28** 0458	0.5	
1149	4.1	1127	4.3	
SU 1743	0.5	M 1728	0.1	
●		○ 2358	4.4	
14 0012	4.0	**29** 0540	0.4	
0545	0.8	1212	4.4	
M 1226	4.0	TU 1809	0.1	
1811	0.5			
15 0046	3.9	**30** 0042	4.4	
0614	0.8	0622	0.3	
TU 1256	3.9	W 1256	4.4	
1838	0.6	1849	0.1	

OCTOBER

Time	m		Time	m
1 0125	4.4	**16** 0106	3.9	
0705	0.3	0651	0.7	
TH 1339	4.4	F 1321	3.9	
1931	0.2	1909	0.6	
2 0208	4.2	**17** 0136	3.9	
0749	0.4	0727	0.7	
F 1422	4.3	SA 1354	3.9	
2013	0.4	1942	0.7	
3 0251	4.0	**18** 0212	3.9	
0834	0.6	0801	0.7	
SA 1508	4.1	SU 1432	3.9	
2058	0.7	2018	0.8	
4 0336	3.8	**19** 0252	3.8	
0924	0.7	0841	0.8	
SU 1558	3.8	M 1516	3.8	
☽ 2151	1.0	2101	0.9	
5 0427	3.5	**20** 0338	3.6	
1028	0.9	0929	0.9	
M 1702	3.5	TU 1609	3.6	
2308	1.2	☾ 2151	1.1	
6 0536	3.3	**21** 0436	3.4	
1155	1.0	1027	1.0	
TU 1827	3.4	W 1718	3.4	
		2256	1.3	
7 0030	1.2	**22** 0549	3.3	
0658	3.3	1149	1.0	
W 1311	1.0	TH 1837	3.4	
1942	3.4			
8 0136	1.3	**23** 0048	1.3	
0806	3.4	0705	3.4	
TH 1414	0.9	F 1328	0.9	
2043	3.6	1953	3.6	
9 0234	1.2	**24** 0201	1.1	
0903	3.6	0816	3.6	
F 1509	0.7	SA 1436	0.7	
2136	3.8	2100	3.8	
10 0325	1.0	**25** 0259	0.9	
0953	3.8	0918	3.8	
SA 1557	0.6	SU 1531	0.5	
2223	4.0	2157	4.1	
11 0408	0.9	**26** 0349	0.7	
1039	4.0	1013	4.1	
SU 1636	0.6	M 1620	0.3	
2306	4.1	2247	4.3	
12 0445	0.8	**27** 0435	0.5	
1120	4.0	1102	4.3	
M 1708	0.6	TU 1704	0.2	
2344	4.0	○ 2334	4.4	
13 0517	0.8	**28** 0520	0.4	
1156	4.0	1156	4.4	
TU 1737	0.6	W 1746	0.1	
●				
14 0016	4.0	**29** 0018	4.4	
0547	0.7	0603	0.3	
W 1227	3.9	TH 1237	4.4	
1805	0.6	1826	0.3	
15 0042	3.9	**30** 0102	4.3	
0618	0.7	0647	0.3	
TH 1253	3.9	F 1318	4.4	
1837	0.6	1908	0.4	
		31 0144	4.2	
		0731	0.4	
		SA 1402	4.2	
		1950	0.6	

NOVEMBER

Time	m		Time	m
1 0226	4.0	**16** 0151	3.9	
0816	0.5	0745	0.6	
SU 1447	4.0	M 1416	3.9	
2032	0.8	1959	0.8	
2 0309	3.8	**17** 0231	3.8	
0905	0.7	0827	0.7	
M 1536	3.8	TU 1501	3.8	
2119	1.1	2042	0.9	
3 0355	3.6	**18** 0316	3.7	
1004	0.9	0914	0.7	
TU 1632	3.5	W 1554	3.7	
☽ 2223	1.3	2132	1.0	
4 0453	3.4	**19** 0410	3.5	
1122	1.0	1010	0.8	
W 1746	3.4	TH 1659	3.5	
2350	1.4	☾ 2232	1.2	
5 0611	3.3	**20** 0520	3.4	
1236	1.0	1121	0.9	
TH 1904	3.4	F 1813	3.5	
		2359	1.2	
6 0101	1.4	**21** 0637	3.4	
0725	3.3	1254	0.8	
F 1338	0.9	SA 1926	3.6	
2007	3.5			
7 0200	1.2	**22** 0125	1.1	
0825	3.5	0747	3.6	
SA 1432	0.8	SU 1405	0.7	
2102	3.7	2031	3.8	
8 0252	1.1	**23** 0229	0.9	
0917	3.7	0850	3.8	
SU 1518	0.7	M 1504	0.5	
2150	3.8	2130	4.0	
9 0336	1.0	**24** 0324	0.7	
1004	3.8	0948	4.0	
M 1557	0.7	TU 1555	0.4	
2233	3.9	2223	4.2	
10 0413	0.8	**25** 0414	0.6	
1046	3.9	1040	4.1	
TU 1630	0.6	W 1641	0.3	
2311	4.0	○ 2312	4.2	
11 0447	0.8	**26** 0501	0.4	
1124	3.9	1129	4.2	
W 1703	0.6	TH 1725	0.4	
● 2343	4.0	2358	4.3	
12 0521	0.7	**27** 0547	0.4	
1157	3.9	1215	4.3	
TH 1738	0.6	F 1807	0.4	
13 0012	4.0	**28** 0042	4.2	
0556	0.7	0632	0.3	
F 1228	3.9	SA 1301	4.2	
1812	0.6	1848	0.5	
14 0041	4.0	**29** 0125	4.1	
0632	0.6	0716	0.4	
SA 1300	3.9	SU 1345	4.2	
1846	0.7	1929	0.7	
15 0114	4.0	**30** 0206	4.0	
0708	0.6	0801	0.5	
SU 1336	3.9	M 1429	4.0	
1921	0.7	2009	0.9	

DECEMBER

Time	m		Time	m
1 0246	3.8	**16** 0219	3.9	
0846	0.6	0817	0.5	
TU 1514	3.8	W 1452	3.9	
2049	1.0	2029	0.8	
2 0328	3.7	**17** 0304	3.8	
0934	0.7	0903	0.5	
W 1601	3.6	TH 1543	3.8	
2135	1.2	2117	0.9	
3 0415	3.5	**18** 0354	3.7	
1033	0.9	0955	0.6	
TH 1654	3.4	F 1641	3.7	
☽ 2238	1.4	☾ 2212	1.0	
4 0512	3.4	**19** 0455	3.6	
1142	0.9	1057	0.7	
F 1757	3.3	SA 1748	3.6	
		2320	1.1	
5 0000	1.4	**20** 0608	3.5	
0619	3.3	1218	0.7	
SA 1246	0.9	SU 1857	3.6	
1908	3.3			
6 0110	1.3	**21** 0046	1.1	
0729	3.3	0718	3.5	
SU 1340	0.9	M 1334	0.7	
2013	3.4	2003	3.6	
7 0206	1.2	**22** 0159	1.0	
0830	3.4	0825	3.6	
M 1428	0.8	TU 1438	0.6	
2107	3.6	2106	3.8	
8 0254	1.1	**23** 0301	0.8	
0923	3.6	0927	3.8	
TU 1512	0.8	W 1533	0.6	
2154	3.7	2203	3.9	
9 0336	0.9	**24** 0357	0.6	
1010	3.7	1023	3.9	
W 1554	0.7	TH 1623	0.5	
2235	3.8	2255	4.0	
10 0417	0.8	**25** 0447	0.5	
1052	3.8	1115	4.1	
TH 1634	0.7	F 1708	0.5	
2312	3.9	○ 2342	4.1	
11 0457	0.7	**26** 0535	0.4	
1130	3.9	1203	4.1	
F 1714	0.6	SA 1751	0.6	
● 2347	4.0			
12 0537	0.6	**27** 0027	4.1	
1207	3.9	0620	0.4	
SA 1753	0.6	SU 1248	4.1	
		1832	0.6	
13 0023	4.0	**28** 0109	4.1	
0616	0.6	0704	0.4	
SU 1245	4.0	M 1331	4.1	
1830	0.6	1910	0.7	
14 0100	3.9	**29** 0148	4.0	
0656	0.5	0745	0.4	
M 1324	4.0	TU 1411	3.9	
1907	0.7	1946	0.8	
15 0138	3.9	**30** 0225	3.9	
0735	0.5	0824	0.5	
TU 1406	4.0	W 1450	3.8	
1946	0.7	2020	0.9	
		31 0302	3.8	
		0900	0.6	
		TH 1529	3.7	
		2058	1.0	

Chart Datum: 2·02 metres below Ordnance Datum (Newlyn). HAT is 4·4 metres above Chart Datum.

1.21 RIVER DEBEN

Suffolk **51°59'·38N 01°23'·58E** (Felixstowe Ferry) ❄△△△✿✿✿

CHARTS AC 5607, 2052, 2693; Imray C29, C1, C28, Y16, 2000

TIDES Woodbridge Haven +0025 Dover; Woodbridge +0105 Dover; ML 1·9; Duration 0635

Standard Port WALTON-ON-THE-NAZE (←)

Times				Height (metres)			
High Water		Low Water		MHWS	MHWN	MLWN	MLWS
0100	0700	0100	0700	4·2	3·4	1·1	0·4
1300	1900	1300	1900				
Differences FELIXSTOWE PIER (51° 57'N 1° 21'E)							
−0005	−0007	−0018	−0020	−0·5	−0·4	0·0	0·0
BAWDSEY							
−0016	−0020	−0030	−0032	−0·8	−0·6	−0·1	−0·1
WOODBRIDGE HAVEN (Entrance)							
0000	−0005	−0020	−0025	−0·5	−0·5	−0·1	+0·1
WOODBRIDGE (Town)							
+0045	+0025	+0025	−0020	−0·2	−0·3	−0·2	0·0

SHELTER Good in Tide Mill Yacht Hbr (TMYH) Woodbridge. ⚓s upriver, clear of moorings: N of Horse Sand; off Ramsholt, The Rocks, Waldringfield, The Tips, Methersgate, Kyson Pt and Woodbridge.

NAVIGATION WPT 51°58'·20N 01°23'·85E Woodbridge Haven SWM buoy, thence NNW'ly past W Knoll PHM to Mid Knoll SHM and then head north up-river to the entrance hugging the sea wall/W bank until close to Deben PHM. Chartlet shows the ent at latest survey (2013), showing west'ly movement of the Knolls. Depths can change significantly and buoyage is often adjusted Visitors may obtain updates at www.debenestuarypilot.co.uk.

Cross the shifting shingle bar HW−3 to HW+2 depending on draft. When Horse Sand is covered there is approx 2m at the bar. Best to enter after half-flood, and leave on the flood. The ent is only 1ca wide and in strong on-shore winds gets dangerously choppy; channel is well buoyed/marked. Keep to the W shore until PHM opposite the SC, then move E of Horse Sand. No commercial traffic. 8kn max speed N of Green Reach.

LIGHTS AND MARKS See 1.3 and chartlets.

COMMUNICATIONS (Code 01473) MRCC (01255) 675518; Police 101.

HM mob 07803 476621, Asst HM mob 07860 191768.
Pilotage for river entr, call *Odd Times* Ch 08 or HM on mobile.

FACILITIES
FELIXSTOWE FERRY (01394), M, L, ⚓, ⚒, ⊞, ✗, 🛢, 🛒, ✕, ⊡;
Felixstowe Ferry SC ☎ 283785; BY ☎ 282173, M (200), ⚓(£10), Gas.
RAMSHOLT HM ☎ 07930 304061. M, ⚓, ✗, ⊡.

WALDRINGFIELD AC 2693. Craft >11m should anchor at the Rocks (NW of Prettyman's Pt) or upriver at The Tips. Possibly ⚓ for <11m by arrangement with HM waldringfieldhm @ btinternet.com ☎ 736291 mob 07925 081062; BY may have ⚓, ☎ 736260 VHF 80; C, ⚓. Sailing Club www.waldringfieldsc.com ⊡ (Wed and Sat evenings only).

WOODBRIDGE (01394) **Tide Mill Yacht Hbr**, 200+🅥 (max 24m) £2. info@tidemillyachtharbour.co.uk; ☎ 385745. Ent by No 26 PHM. Depth over sill, dries 1·5m, is 1·6m at MHWN and 2·5m MHWS, with very accurate tide gauge and 6 waiting buoys. M, L, D, ⚓, ⋺▷, 🔧, ✕, ⚒, ⊞, Ⓔ, △, 🛢, 🛒, Gas/Gaz, 🅁, C (18 ton), ACA.
Woodbridge Cruising Club, ☎ 386737.
Deben YC. www.debenyachtclub.co.uk .
Town 🏧, D, 🛒, ✕, ⊡, ⊠, Ⓑ, ⇌, ✈ (Cambridge, Norwich).

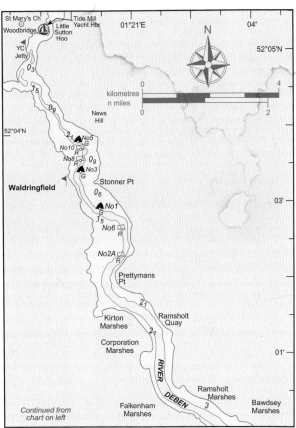

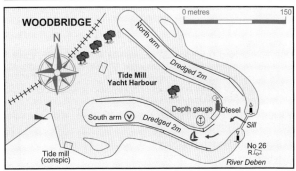

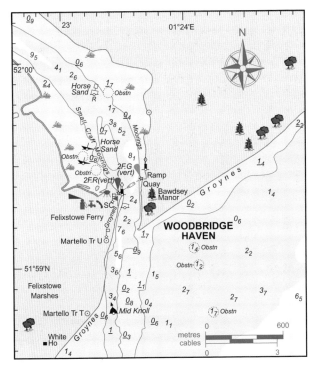

1.22 RIVER ORE/ALDE

Suffolk **52°02′·13N 01°27′·49E** (Ent) ⊛🌢🌢🌢✿✿✿

CHARTS AC 5607, 1543, 2052, 2693, 2695; Imray C29, C28, 2000

TIDES Ent. +0015 Dover Slaughden Quay +0155 Dover; ML1·6; Duration 0620

Standard Port WALTON-ON-THE-NAZE (←)

Times				Height (metres)			
High Water		Low Water		MHWS	MHWN	MLWN	MLWS
0100	0700	0100	0700	4·2	3·4	1·1	0·4
1300	1900	1300	1900				
Differences ORFORD HAVEN BAR							
−0026	−0030	−0036	−0038	−1·0	−0·8	−0·1	0·0
ORFORD QUAY							
+0040	+0040	+0055	+0055	−1·4	−1·1	0·0	+0·2
SLAUGHDEN QUAY							
+0105	+0105	+0125	+0125	−1·3	−0·8	−0·1	+0·2
IKEN CLIFF							
+0130	+0130	+0155	+0155	−1·3	−1·0	0·0	+0·2

SHELTER Good shelter within the river, but the entrance should not be attempted in strong E/ESE onshore winds and rough seas or at night. The only safe anchorage is in Short Gull; no anchoring in mooring areas. Landing on Havergate Island bird sanctuary is prohibited. ⚓ at Orford have small pick-up buoys marked V. Possible use of private mooring via Upson's BY at Slaughden.

NAVIGATION WPT Orford Haven SWM buoy, 52°01′·85N 01°28′·21E, is moved as required. For latest position call Thames CG ☎ (01255) 675518. Proceed NW'ly to Oxley PHM shaping a more NNW'ly course to leave Weir SHM and North Shoal to starboard.

Chartlet is based on surveys carried out in 2013, but depths can change significantly. North Shoal has fragmented and the entr moved to the N. For regularly updated local information see *eastcoastsailing.co.uk*, call Small Craft Deliveries: ☎ (01394) 387672, sales@scd-charts.co.uk; or local marinas or chandlers.

- The bar (approx 0·5m) shifts after onshore gales and is dangerous in rough or confused seas. These result from tidal streams offshore running against those within the shingle banks. Sp ebb reaches 6kn.
- Without local info do not enter before half flood or at night. For a first visit, appr at about LW+2½ in settled conditions and at nps.
- Beware Horse Shoal close WNW of N Weir Pt and shoals S & SW of Dove Pt (SW tip of Havergate Island).

R Ore (re-named R Alde between Orford and Slaughden Quay) is navigable up to Snape. The upper reaches are shallow and winding, and marked by withies with red and green topmarks. Shellfish beds on the E bank centred on 52°08′·0N 01°35′·6E.

LIGHTS AND MARKS As chartlet. Ent and river are unlit. Oxley and Weir buoys are seasonal Apr-Oct and the Or bn on the shore of Oxley Marshes is not maintained. Shingle Street, about 2ca S of ent, is identified by Martello tr 'AA', CG Stn, terrace houses and DF aerial. Up-river, Orford Ch and Castle are conspic; also Martello Tr 'CC', 3ca S of Slaughden Quay.

COMMUNICATIONS (Codes 01394 Orford; 01728 Aldeburgh) MRCC (01255) 675518; Police 101; Orford Dr 450315 (HO); Aldeburgh Dr 452027 (HO). Harbourmaster 07528 092635; Small Craft Deliveries (pilotage info) 382655.

Chantry on Ch 08.

FACILITIES

ORFORD: Orford Quay for ⚓ phone HM for availability (max 1 hour with competent crew); M (marked 'V'; call HM. No rafting) £8/night collected by launch 'Chantry'; L, ⚓, D(cans), Orford SC (OSC) visitors may use showers (£6 deposit, key held in Quay Office), ✕, 🛏, Internet (White Lion Hotel Aldeburgh).

Village (¼M) 🏧 & 🏧 (HO), Gas, Gaz, ✉, 🛒, ✕, 🛏, ⇌ (twice daily bus to Woodbridge).

ALDEBURGH: Slaughden Quay L, ⚓, ⚓, BH (20 ton).

Aldeburgh YC (AYC) ☎ 452562, 🛏.

Slaughden SC (SSC). **Services:** M (via Upson's BY if any vacant) £5, ✕, ⚓, D, ⚒, BY, Gas, Gaz, P.

Town (¾M) 🏧, 🛒, ✕, 🛏, ✉, Ⓑ, ⇌ (bus to Wickham Market), ✈ (Norwich).

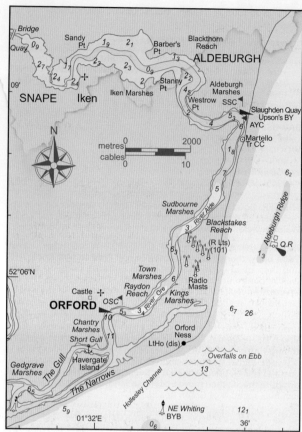

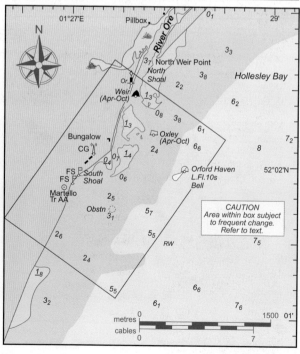

1.23 SOUTHWOLD

Suffolk 52°18'·78N 01°40'·54E ❋❋⚓⚓⚓⚓✿✿✿

CHARTS AC 5614, 1543, 2695; Imray C29, C28

TIDES –0105 Dover; ML 1·5; Duration 0620

Standard Port LOWESTOFT (→)

Times				Height (metres)			
High Water		Low Water		MHWS	MHWN	MLWN	MLWS
0300	0900	0200	0800	2·4	2·1	1·0	0·5
1500	2100	1400	2000				
Differences SOUTHWOLD							
+0105	+0105	+0055	+0055	0·0	0·0	–0·1	0·0
MINSMERE SLUICE							
+0110	+0110	+0110	+0110	0·0	–0·1	–0·2	–0·2
ALDEBURGH (seaward)							
+0130	+0130	+0115	+0120	+0·3	+0·2	–0·1	–0·2
ORFORD NESS							
+0135	+0135	+0135	+0125	+0·4	+0·6	–0·1	0·0

NOTE: HW time differences (above) for Southwold apply up the hbr. At the ent mean HW is HW Lowestoft +0035.

SHELTER Good, but the ent is dangerous in strong winds from N through E to S. Visitors berth (must book ahead) on a staging 6ca from the ent, on N bank near to the Harbour Inn. If rafted, shore lines are essential due to current.

NAVIGATION WPT 52°18'·09N 01°41'·69E, 315°/1M to N Pier lt.

- Enter on the flood as the ebb runs up to 6kn. Shoals are unpredictable up to ¼M offshore; a sand and shingle bar, extent/depth variable, lies off the ent and a shoal builds inside N Pier. Obtain details of appr chans from HM before entering.
- Enter between piers in midstream. When chan widens keep close to The Knuckle (2 FG vert), turn stbd towards LB House; keep within 3m of quay wall until it ends, then resume midstream.
- **Caution** Rowing ferry (which has right of way at all times) 3ca and unlit low footbridge 7.5ca upstream of ent.

LIGHTS AND MARKS See 1.3 and chartlet. Walberswick ✠ in line with N Pier lt = 268°. Hbr ent opens on 300°. 3 FR (vert) at N pier = port closed. Lt ho, W ○ tr, Fl 10s 24M, in Southwold town, 0·86M NNE of hbr ent.

COMMUNICATIONS (Code 01502) MRCC (01262) 672317; Police 101; Dr 722326; Ⓗ 723333. HM 724712.
Southwold Port Radio Ch **12** 16 (as reqd).

FACILITIES Hbr southwoldharbour@waveney.gov.uk ⌣<20' £11·60 20-30' £15.10, 30-40' £18.60, ⚓, 🛢 also by bowser 100 litres min, BY, 🪣, ⚒, ✖, ▬ HW±3 (Hbr dues £5.95), BH (20 ton). **Southwold SC; Town** (¾M), Gas, Gaz, Kos, ✖, 🛒, ✉, Ⓑ, ⇌ (bus to Brampton/Darsham), ✈ (Norwich).

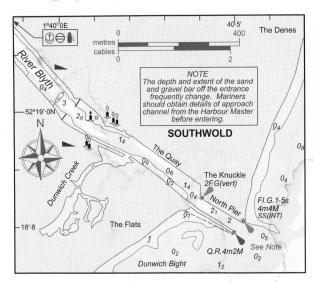

SOUTHWOLD

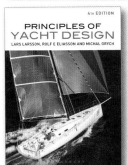
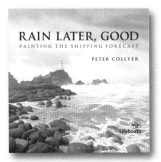
E England

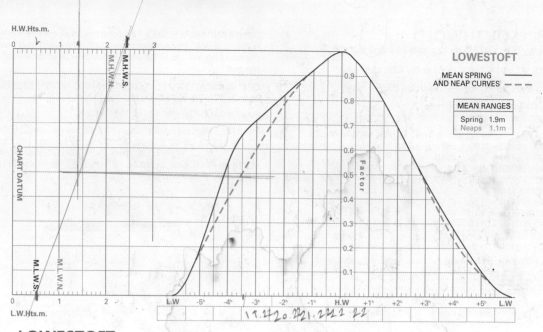

1.24 LOWESTOFT

Suffolk 52°28'·31N 01°45'·39E ✿✿✿♨♨♨✿✿✿

CHARTS AC 1543, 1535, 5614; Imray C29, C28

TIDES −0133 Dover; ML 1·6; Duration 0620

SHELTER Good; accessible H24. Wind over tide, especially on the ebb, can make the entrance lively. Fairway is dredged to 4·7m. RN&S YC yacht basin in the SW corner of Outer Hbr with 2m to 2·5m; no berthing on N side of S Pier. Lowestoft Haven Marina has facilities 1.5M upriver with additional berths in Hamilton Dock.

NAVIGATION Keep watch on Ch 14; req permission from *Harbour Control* to enter/leave harbour and pass (either way) between Outer Harbour and Waveney/Hamilton Docks to deconflict with helicopter movements. Sands continually shift and buoys are moved to suit. Beware shoals and drying areas esp S of hbr ent; do not cross banks in bad weather, nor at mid flood/ebb. Speed limit in harbour is 4 kn.

From S, WPT is E Barnard ECM buoy, Q (3) 10s, 52°25'·15N 01°46'·36E; thence via Stanford Chan E of Newcome Sand QR, Stanford Fl R 2.5s and N Newcome Fl (4) R 15s, all PHM buoys. S Holm SCM, VQ (6)+L Fl 10s, and SW Holm SHM, Fl (2) G 5s, buoys mark the seaward side of this channel.

From E, WPT is Holm Approach ECM buoy, Q (3) 10s, 52°30'·88N 01°50'·22E, then via Holm Chan (buoyed) into Corton Road. Or approach direct to S Holm SCM buoy for Stanford Channel.

From N, appr via Yarmouth, Gorleston and Corton Roads.

Bridge to Inner Hbr (Lake Lothing and Lowestoft CC) lifts at the following times (20 mins notice required): daily 0300, 0500, 0700, 0945, 1115, 1430, 1600, 1800; W/Es + BHs only 1900, 2100 and 2400. Small craft may pass under the bridge (clearance 2·2m) at any time but call on Ch 14. Craft are to await bridge opening on pontoon at E end of Trawl Dock. **Vessels may only transit bridge chan when G lights shown on N side of appr** (showing Br locked in position).

LIGHTS AND MARKS Lowestoft lt ho, W twr, is 1M N of entrance.

Traffic Signals shown on E arm of RN&SYC Yacht Basin to exit, and tip of S Pier for entry/exit:

3 FR (vert) = Do not proceed
GWG (vert) = proceed only as/when instructed

Bridge Sigs (on N bank each side of bridge):
● = bridge operating, keep 150m clear.
● = vessels may pass through bridge channel.

COMMUNICATIONS (Code 01502) MRCC (01262) 672317; Police 101; H 01493 452452. HM & Bridge Control 572286; Mutford Bridge and Lock 531778 (+Ansafone, checked daily at 0830, 1300 & 1730); Oulton Broad Yacht Stn 574946; Pilot 572286 ext 243.

Lowestoft Hbr Control (ABP) VHF Ch **14** 16 11 (H24). *Lowestoft Haven Marina* Ch **80**, 37. *Oulton Broad YS and Mutford Lock Control* Ch 73. Pilot Ch 14. RN & SYC Ch 14, 80.

FACILITIES

Royal Norfolk & Suffolk YC (www.rnsyc.net) admin@rnsyc.org.uk, ☎ 566726, £2·30 inc YC facilities, ✕, 🛎.

Lowestoft Cruising Club www.lowestoftcruisingclub.co.uk, ☎ 07913 391950, ⚓(max 13m) £2·00, 🔌, ⚓, ⚓(emergency).

Lowestoft Haven Marina ⚓ www. lowestofthavenmarina.com ☎ 580300, 140 ⚓, £2·21 (+ 47 ⚓ in Hamilton Dock, £2·37).

Services: @, BH (70 tons), 🔧, ⛽, ✂, D, Gas, Gaz, 🛢, ♿, Ⓔ, ACA.

Town 🏨, ✕, 🏪, ✉, 🚇, Ⓑ, ⇌, ✈ (Norwich).

Entry to the Broads: See Gt Yarmouth & www.norfolkbroads.com. Passage to Oulton Broad from Lake Lothing is via two bridges and Mutford Lock (width 5·9m). The lock is available 0800-1200 and 1300-1730 daily; 0800-1200 and 1300-1930 at weekends/Bank Holidays; 0900-1200 only 1 Nov to 31 Mar. Charge is £11/day. Booking 24 hours in advance is recommended, ☎ 01502 531778 or Ch 73. Oulton Broad Yacht Station ☎ (01502) 574946. From Oulton Broad, access into the R Waveney is via Oulton Dyke.

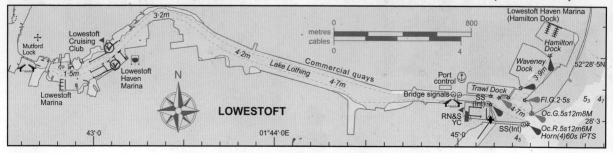

STANDARD TIME (UT)
For Summer Time add ONE hour in **non-shaded areas**

LOWESTOFT LAT 52°28'N LONG 1°45'E
TIMES AND HEIGHTS OF HIGH AND LOW WATERS

Dates in red are **SPRINGS**
Dates in blue are **NEAPS**

YEAR **2015**

E England

JANUARY

Day	Time m	Time m	Time m	Time m
1 TH	0548 2.4	1222 0.8	1850 2.3	
2 F	0047 1.0	0653 2.4	1320 0.9	1939 2.4
3 SA	0149 0.9	0756 2.4	1413 1.0	2023 2.5
4 SU	0241 0.8	0849 2.4	1458 0.9	2104 2.5
5 M ○	0327 0.7	0936 2.4	1538 0.9	2142 2.6
6 TU	0409 0.6	1018 2.4	1613 0.9	2219 2.6
7 W	0447 0.6	1057 2.4	1645 0.9	2254 2.6
8 TH	0523 0.6	1133 2.3	1714 0.9	2328 2.6
9 F	0557 0.7	1206 2.3	1743 1.0	
10 SA	0003 2.5	0630 0.7	1240 2.2	1814 1.0
11 SU	0041 2.5	0704 0.8	1316 2.2	1852 1.1
12 M	0121 2.4	0741 0.9	1358 2.1	1935 1.2
13 TU ☽	0205 2.3	0825 0.9	1449 2.1	2026 1.2
14 W	0257 2.3	0921 1.0	1612 2.1	2128 1.3
15 TH	0406 2.2	1038 1.0	1722 2.2	2259 1.3
16 F	0525 2.2	1146 1.0	1816 2.2	
17 SA	0013 1.1	0626 2.2	1241 0.9	1904 2.3
18 SU	0110 1.0	0721 2.3	1331 0.8	1950 2.4
19 M	0202 0.8	0814 2.4	1420 0.8	2034 2.5
20 TU ●	0255 0.6	0905 2.5	1510 0.7	2117 2.6
21 W	0347 0.5	0952 2.5	1558 0.6	2201 2.7
22 TH	0437 0.3	1038 2.6	1645 0.6	2245 2.7
23 F	0524 0.3	1124 2.5	1729 0.7	2330 2.8
24 SA	0610 0.3	1210 2.5	1811 0.7	
25 SU	0015 2.7	0655 0.4	1257 2.4	1854 0.8
26 M	0102 2.7	0742 0.6	1349 2.3	1940 0.9
27 TU ☽	0153 2.6	0835 0.7	1457 2.2	2034 1.0
28 W	0256 2.4	0940 0.8	1619 2.2	2149 1.1
29 TH	0423 2.3	1055 0.9	1724 2.2	2318 1.1
30 F	0540 2.3	1203 1.0	1825 2.2	
31 SA	0032 1.0	0655 2.3	1307 1.0	1923 2.3

FEBRUARY

Day	Time m	Time m	Time m	Time m
1 SU	0138 0.9	0800 2.3	1402 1.0	2010 2.4
2 M	0230 0.8	0847 2.3	1446 1.0	2049 2.4
3 TU ○	0313 0.7	0927 2.3	1523 0.9	2125 2.5
4 W	0352 0.6	1003 2.4	1556 0.9	2159 2.5
5 TH	0427 0.6	1035 2.3	1625 0.8	2232 2.6
6 F	0500 0.6	1106 2.3	1652 0.8	2304 2.6
7 SA	0531 0.6	1135 2.3	1720 0.8	2338 2.6
8 SU	0601 0.6	1206 2.3	1751 0.9	
9 M	0013 2.5	0631 0.7	1242 2.2	1825 0.9
10 TU	0051 2.4	0704 0.8	1317 2.2	1905 1.0
11 W	0131 2.3	0743 0.9	1401 2.2	1952 1.1
12 TH ☽	0218 2.3	0831 1.0	1455 2.1	2048 1.1
13 F	0318 2.2	0936 1.0	1617 2.1	2208 1.2
14 SA	0449 2.2	1116 1.1	1734 2.2	2342 1.1
15 SU	0604 2.2	1214 1.0	1831 2.2	
16 M	0046 0.9	0706 2.3	1310 0.9	1922 2.4
17 TU	0143 0.7	0802 2.4	1403 0.8	2010 2.5
18 W ●	0239 0.5	0851 2.5	1454 0.7	2056 2.6
19 TH	0332 0.4	0937 2.5	1543 0.6	2141 2.7
20 F	0420 0.2	1021 2.6	1629 0.5	2226 2.8
21 SA	0506 0.2	1104 2.6	1712 0.5	2311 2.8
22 SU	0550 0.2	1148 2.5	1754 0.6	2356 2.8
23 M	0632 0.3	2.5	1835 0.7	
24 TU	0043 2.7	0715 0.5	1320 2.3	1919 0.8
25 W ☽	0135 2.5	0802 0.7	1414 2.2	2011 0.9
26 TH	0240 2.3	0901 0.9	1530 2.1	2121 1.0
27 F	0411 2.2	1025 1.1	1646 2.1	2258 1.0
28 SA	0532 2.2	1144 1.1	1753 2.2	

MARCH

Day	Time m	Time m	Time m	Time m
1 SU	0014 0.9	0651 2.2	1252 1.1	1858 2.2
2 M	0119 0.8	0752 2.3	1347 1.1	1950 2.3
3 TU	0210 0.7	0835 2.3	1430 1.0	2029 2.4
4 W	0251 0.7	0910 2.3	1504 0.9	2103 2.4
5 TH ○	0327 0.6	0941 2.4	1534 0.8	2134 2.5
6 F	0400 0.6	1009 2.3	1602 0.8	2206 2.5
7 SA	0431 0.5	1036 2.4	1629 0.7	2239 2.5
8 SU	0501 0.6	1104 2.3	1658 0.7	2313 2.5
9 M	0530 0.6	1135 2.3	1730 0.8	2348 2.5
10 TU	0601 0.7	1208 2.3	1804 0.8	
11 W	0024 2.4	0633 0.7	1245 2.3	1841 0.9
12 TH	0103 2.3	0710 0.8	1327 2.2	1925 0.9
13 F ☽	0150 2.3	0756 0.9	1417 2.2	2020 1.0
14 SA	0248 2.2	0854 1.1	1521 2.1	2134 1.0
15 SU	0420 2.1	1025 1.1	1646 2.1	2316 1.0
16 M	0547 2.2	1149 1.1	1756 2.2	
17 TU	0023 0.8	0651 2.3	1249 1.0	1853 2.3
18 W	0122 0.6	0747 2.4	1344 0.8	1944 2.4
19 TH	0219 0.5	0834 2.5	1436 0.7	2033 2.6
20 F ●	0312 0.3	0917 2.5	1525 0.6	2120 2.7
21 SA	0359 0.2	1000 2.6	1610 0.5	2206 2.8
22 SU	0444 0.2	1042 2.6	1653 0.5	2252 2.8
23 M	0526 0.2	1124 2.5	1735 0.5	2338 2.7
24 TU	0607 0.4	1207 2.4	1817 0.5	
25 W	0026 2.6	0647 0.6	1252 2.3	1901 0.6
26 TH	0120 2.4	0733 0.8	1341 2.3	1951 0.8
27 F ☽	0228 2.3	0822 1.0	1441 2.2	2057 0.9
28 SA	0357 2.2	0943 1.2	1558 2.1	2233 0.9
29 SU	0514 2.2	1118 1.3	1709 2.1	2346 0.9
30 M	0631 2.2	1225 1.2	1817 2.1	
31 TU	0046 0.8	0730 2.2	1321 1.1	1916 2.2

APRIL

Day	Time m	Time m	Time m	Time m
1 W	0138 0.7	0812 2.3	1403 1.0	1959 2.3
2 TH	0219 0.7	0846 2.3	1437 0.9	2033 2.3
3 F	0255 0.6	0914 2.3	1507 0.9	2105 2.4
4 SA ○	0328 0.6	0939 2.4	1535 0.8	2138 2.5
5 SU	0358 0.6	1006 2.4	1605 0.7	2213 2.5
6 M	0429 0.6	1035 2.4	1637 0.7	2248 2.5
7 TU	0501 0.6	1108 2.4	1711 0.7	2324 2.4
8 W	0533 0.7	1142 2.4	1747 0.7	
9 TH	0002 2.4	0607 0.7	1220 2.3	1825 0.8
10 F	0043 2.3	0645 0.8	1301 2.3	1909 0.8
11 SA	0131 2.2	0731 1.0	1351 2.2	2003 0.9
12 SU ☽	0231 2.2	0828 1.1	1449 2.2	2117 0.9
13 M	0404 2.2	0949 1.2	1603 2.2	2252 0.8
14 TU	0531 2.2	1121 1.1	1720 2.2	
15 W	0000 0.7	0633 2.3	1225 1.0	1822 2.3
16 TH	0059 0.5	0727 2.4	1321 0.9	1917 2.4
17 F	0156 0.4	0813 2.5	1415 0.7	2008 2.5
18 SA ●	0248 0.3	0856 2.5	1505 0.6	2058 2.6
19 SU	0336 0.3	0938 2.5	1551 0.5	2146 2.7
20 M	0420 0.3	1020 2.6	1635 0.4	2235 2.7
21 TU	0502 0.4	1102 2.5	1718 0.4	2323 2.6
22 W	0542 0.5	1144 2.5	1801 0.5	
23 TH	0013 2.5	0621 0.7	1228 2.4	1845 0.6
24 F	0107 2.3	0701 0.9	1313 2.3	1933 0.7
25 SA ☽	0212 2.2	0746 1.1	1404 2.2	2033 0.8
26 SU	0332 2.2	0823 1.3	1505 2.2	2157 0.9
27 M	0444 2.1	1033 1.3	1617 2.1	2310 0.8
28 TU	0553 2.1	1146 1.3	1723 2.1	
29 W	0007 0.8	0654 2.2	1241 1.2	1821 2.1
30 TH	0057 0.8	0740 2.2	1326 1.1	1912 2.2

Chart Datum: 1·50 metres below Ordnance Datum (Newlyn). HAT is 2·9 metres above Chart Datum.

LOWESTOFT LAT 52°28'N LONG 1°45'E
TIMES AND HEIGHTS OF HIGH AND LOW WATERS

STANDARD TIME (UT)
For Summer Time add ONE hour in **non-shaded** areas

Dates in red are **SPRINGS**
Dates in blue are **NEAPS**

YEAR 2015

MAY

Day	Time m	Time m	Time m	Time m
1 F	0139 0.7	0815 2.3	1402 1.0	1954 2.3
2 SA	0216 0.7	0842 2.3	1434 0.9	2032 2.3
3 SU	0250 0.6	0908 2.4	1506 0.8	2109 2.4
4 M	0324 0.6	0936 2.4	1540 0.7	2147 2.4
5 TU	0358 0.6	1008 2.4	1617 0.6	2225 2.4
6 W	0434 0.6	1043 2.5	1655 0.6	2304 2.4
7 TH	0510 0.7	1120 2.4	1735 0.6	2345 2.4
8 F	0548 0.7	1159 2.4	1816 0.7	
9 SA	0029 2.3	0628 0.9	1243 2.4	1902 0.7
10 SU	0120 2.3	0715 1.0	1331 2.3	1957 0.7
11 M	0221 2.2	0810 1.1	1427 2.3	2108 0.7
12 TU	0348 2.2	0920 1.2	1531 2.3	2229 0.7
13 W	0512 2.2	1048 1.1	1647 2.3	2335 0.6
14 TH	0612 2.3	1156 1.1	1754 2.3	
15 F	0034 0.5	0704 2.4	1256 0.9	1851 2.4
16 SA	0131 0.5	0751 2.4	1353 0.8	1946 2.5
17 SU	0224 0.4	0835 2.5	1445 0.6	2039 2.6
18 M	0313 0.4	0917 2.5	1534 0.5	2131 2.6
19 TU	0358 0.5	1000 2.6	1620 0.4	2222 2.6
20 W	0439 0.5	1042 2.5	1704 0.4	2311 2.5
21 TH	0519 0.7	1124 2.5	1747 0.5	
22 F	0001 2.4	0556 0.8	1206 2.5	1829 0.5
23 SA	0051 2.3	0634 1.0	1248 2.4	1914 0.6
24 SU	0147 2.2	0712 1.1	1332 2.3	2005 0.7
25 M	0253 2.1	0755 1.2	1421 2.3	2108 0.8
26 TU	0403 2.1	0850 1.3	1518 2.2	2222 0.9
27 W	0505 2.1	1040 1.4	1626 2.2	2322 0.9
28 TH	0603 2.1	1149 1.3	1729 2.2	
29 F	0012 0.8	0653 2.2	1238 1.2	1824 2.2
30 SA	0056 0.8	0732 2.2	1319 1.1	1913 2.2
31 SU	0135 0.8	0804 2.3	1358 1.0	1959 2.3

JUNE

Day	Time m	Time m	Time m	Time m
1 M	0213 0.7	0835 2.4	1436 0.8	2042 2.3
2 TU	0251 0.6	0909 2.4	1517 0.7	2124 2.4
3 W	0331 0.6	0944 2.5	1559 0.6	2206 2.4
4 TH	0412 0.6	1022 2.5	1643 0.6	2249 2.4
5 F	0453 0.7	1102 2.5	1727 0.5	2333 2.4
6 SA	0534 0.7	1143 2.5	1812 0.6	
7 SU	0019 2.4	0617 0.8	1228 2.5	1859 0.6
8 M	0110 2.3	0702 0.9	1315 2.5	1952 0.6
9 TU	0207 2.3	0754 1.0	1407 2.4	2053 0.6
10 W	0324 2.2	0854 1.1	1506 2.4	2203 0.6
11 TH	0447 2.2	1011 1.1	1618 2.4	2310 0.6
12 F	0547 2.3	1127 1.1	1730 2.4	
13 SA	0011 0.6	0641 2.4	1233 1.0	1831 2.4
14 SU	0109 0.6	0730 2.4	1334 0.9	1931 2.4
15 M	0204 0.6	0816 2.5	1431 0.7	2029 2.4
16 TU	0254 0.6	0900 2.5	1521 0.6	2123 2.5
17 W	0339 0.7	0942 2.6	1607 0.5	2213 2.5
18 TH	0420 0.7	1024 2.6	1651 0.5	2300 2.4
19 F	0459 0.8	1105 2.6	1732 0.5	2345 2.4
20 SA	0534 0.9	1144 2.5	1812 0.5	
21 SU	0029 2.3	0607 1.0	1222 2.5	1851 0.6
22 M	0112 2.2	0640 1.1	1301 2.4	1932 0.7
23 TU	0159 2.1	0716 1.1	1343 2.4	2016 0.8
24 W	0256 2.1	0759 1.2	1430 2.3	2110 0.9
25 TH	0406 2.1	0851 1.3	1527 2.2	2219 0.9
26 F	0504 2.1	1007 1.3	1639 2.2	2321 0.9
27 SA	0555 2.2	1140 1.3	1743 2.2	
28 SU	0011 0.9	0642 2.2	1236 1.2	1838 2.2
29 M	0057 0.9	0725 2.3	1323 1.0	1930 2.3
30 TU	0140 0.8	0804 2.4	1409 0.9	2019 2.3

JULY

Day	Time m	Time m	Time m	Time m
1 W	0224 0.8	0843 2.4	1456 0.7	2106 2.4
2 TH	0308 0.7	0923 2.5	1543 0.6	2151 2.4
3 F	0353 0.7	1003 2.6	1631 0.5	2236 2.5
4 SA	0438 0.7	1045 2.6	1718 0.4	2321 2.5
5 SU	0522 0.7	1128 2.7	1804 0.4	
6 M	0006 2.4	0605 0.8	1212 2.6	1850 0.4
7 TU	0054 2.4	0649 0.9	1258 2.6	1938 0.5
8 W	0146 2.3	0736 1.0	1347 2.6	2032 0.6
9 TH	0251 2.3	0830 1.0	1443 2.5	2135 0.6
10 F	0416 2.2	0937 1.1	1555 2.4	2244 0.7
11 SA	0521 2.3	1101 1.1	1713 2.4	2349 0.8
12 SU	0618 2.3	1214 1.0	1821 2.3	
13 M	0050 0.8	0712 2.4	1321 0.9	1928 2.4
14 TU	0149 0.8	0801 2.4	1420 0.8	2029 2.4
15 W	0240 0.7	0846 2.5	1511 0.6	2119 2.4
16 TH	0324 0.8	0927 2.6	1555 0.5	2204 2.4
17 F	0404 0.8	1007 2.6	1636 0.5	2245 2.4
18 SA	0439 0.9	1044 2.6	1714 0.5	2324 2.4
19 SU	0511 0.9	1120 2.6	1750 0.6	
20 M	0000 2.3	0540 0.9	1156 2.6	1823 0.6
21 TU	0035 2.3	0610 1.0	1231 2.5	1857 0.7
22 W	0109 2.2	0643 1.1	1310 2.5	1932 0.8
23 TH	0148 2.2	0723 1.1	1352 2.4	2012 0.9
24 F	0236 2.1	0809 1.2	1441 2.3	2101 1.0
25 SA	0346 2.1	0906 1.3	1544 2.2	2209 1.1
26 SU	0501 2.2	1031 1.3	1704 2.2	2325 1.0
27 M	0557 2.2	1155 1.2	1809 2.2	
28 TU	0022 1.0	0647 2.3	1253 1.1	1906 2.3
29 W	0112 0.9	0734 2.4	1345 0.9	2000 2.3
30 TH	0200 0.8	0818 2.5	1436 0.7	2050 2.4
31 F	0249 0.8	0901 2.6	1527 0.6	2136 2.5

AUGUST

Day	Time m	Time m	Time m	Time m
1 SA	0337 0.7	0943 2.7	1616 0.4	2220 2.6
2 SU	0423 0.7	1026 2.8	1703 0.3	2303 2.6
3 M	0508 0.7	1109 2.8	1748 0.3	2347 2.5
4 TU	0551 0.7	1153 2.8	1833 0.3	
5 W	0032 2.5	0633 0.8	1239 2.8	1917 0.4
6 TH	0121 2.4	0717 0.9	1327 2.7	2006 0.6
7 F	0217 2.3	0807 1.0	1423 2.5	2103 0.8
8 SA	0336 2.3	0911 1.1	1541 2.4	2217 0.9
9 SU	0450 2.3	1040 1.1	1706 2.3	2330 1.0
10 M	0552 2.3	1200 1.0	1821 2.3	
11 TU	0037 1.0	0652 2.4	1310 0.9	1933 2.3
12 W	0138 1.0	0746 2.4	1409 0.8	2028 2.4
13 TH	0229 1.0	0830 2.5	1457 0.7	2111 2.4
14 F	0310 1.0	0909 2.6	1538 0.6	2149 2.4
15 SA	0345 0.9	0945 2.6	1615 0.5	2224 2.4
16 SU	0417 0.9	1020 2.6	1650 0.5	2257 2.4
17 M	0446 0.9	1054 2.6	1722 0.6	2327 2.4
18 TU	0514 0.9	1127 2.6	1752 0.6	2357 2.3
19 W	0543 0.9	1202 2.6	1822 0.7	
20 TH	0029 2.3	0615 0.9	1239 2.5	1853 0.8
21 F	0106 2.3	0652 1.0	1318 2.4	1929 0.9
22 SA	0148 2.3	0736 1.1	1403 2.3	2012 1.0
23 SU	0238 2.2	0829 1.2	1500 2.2	2108 1.1
24 M	0349 2.2	0940 1.3	1624 2.2	2232 1.2
25 TU	0511 2.2	1119 1.2	1745 2.2	2350 1.1
26 W	0610 2.3	1225 1.0	1848 2.3	
27 TH	0047 1.0	0702 2.4	1321 0.9	1943 2.4
28 F	0139 0.9	0750 2.5	1415 0.7	2032 2.5
29 SA	0229 0.8	0835 2.6	1507 0.5	2117 2.6
30 SU	0319 0.7	0919 2.8	1557 0.3	2159 2.6
31 M	0405 0.7	1003 2.9	1643 0.2	2242 2.6

Chart Datum: 1·50 metres below Ordnance Datum (Newlyn). HAT is 2·9 metres above Chart Datum.

》》 **FREE** monthly updates from 《《
www.reedsalmanac.co.uk

STANDARD TIME (UT)
For Summer Time add ONE hour in **non-shaded areas**

LOWESTOFT   LAT 52°28'N   LONG 1°45'E
TIMES AND HEIGHTS OF HIGH AND LOW WATERS

Dates in red are **SPRINGS**
Dates in blue are NEAPS

YEAR 2015

E England

SEPTEMBER

Time	m	Time	m
1 0450	0.6	**16** 0448	0.9
1048	2.9	1059	2.6
TU 1727	0.2	W 1718	0.7
2325	2.6	2323	2.4
2 0532	0.6	**17** 0518	0.9
1133	2.9	1134	2.6
W 1810	0.3	TH 1747	0.7
		2356	2.4
3 0008	2.5	**18** 0551	0.9
0614	0.7	1210	2.5
TH 1219	2.8	F 1818	0.8
1852	0.5		
4 0055	2.5	**19** 0031	2.4
0658	0.8	0627	1.0
F 1309	2.7	SA 1249	2.4
1937	0.7	1853	0.9
5 0146	2.4	**20** 0112	2.4
0748	0.9	0709	1.0
SA 1408	2.5	SU 1333	2.3
2030	0.9	1935	1.0
6 0252	2.3	**21** 0159	2.3
0851	1.0	0800	1.1
SU 1534	2.4	M 1427	2.3
2145	1.1	2028	1.2
7 0413	2.3	**22** 0257	2.3
1023	1.1	1017	1.0
M 1700	2.3	TU 1547	2.2
2311	1.2	2142	1.2
8 0521	2.3	**23** 0415	2.3
1144	1.0	1046	1.1
TU 1818	2.3	W 1724	2.3
		2317	1.2
9 0021	1.2	**24** 0531	2.3
0626	2.4	1159	1.0
W 1252	0.9	TH 1829	2.4
1928	2.4		
10 0123	1.2	**25** 0021	1.1
0724	2.4	0628	2.4
TH 1349	0.8	F 1256	0.8
2016	2.4	1923	2.5
11 0211	1.1	**26** 0116	1.0
0809	2.5	0719	2.5
F 1434	0.7	SA 1351	0.6
2054	2.4	2011	2.5
12 0249	1.0	**27** 0207	0.9
0845	2.5	0807	2.7
SA 1513	0.6	SU 1444	0.4
2127	2.4	2054	2.6
13 0322	1.0	**28** 0257	0.8
0919	2.6	0854	2.8
SU 1547	0.5	M 1533	0.3
● 2158	2.4	○ 2136	2.7
14 0352	0.9	**29** 0344	0.7
0952	2.6	0940	2.9
M 1620	0.6	TU 1619	0.3
2226	2.5	2218	2.7
15 0420	0.9	**30** 0430	0.6
1025	2.6	1026	2.9
TU 1649	0.6	W 1703	0.3
2254	2.5	2301	2.7

OCTOBER

Time	m	Time	m
1 0513	0.6	**16** 0456	0.8
1113	2.9	1108	2.5
TH 1745	0.4	F 1716	0.8
2344	2.6	2327	2.5
2 0557	0.6	**17** 0531	0.9
1202	2.8	1145	2.5
F 1827	0.6	SA 1749	0.8
3 0029	2.5	**18** 0003	2.5
0641	0.7	0608	0.9
SA 1254	2.6	SU 1225	2.4
1909	0.8	1825	0.9
4 0118	2.4	**19** 0043	2.4
0731	0.8	0650	1.0
SU 1357	2.4	M 1310	2.3
◑ 1958	1.1	1908	1.1
5 0216	2.4	**20** 0130	2.4
0833	0.9	0740	1.0
M 1524	2.3	TU 1405	2.3
2105	1.3	◑ 2000	1.2
6 0329	2.3	**21** 0224	2.3
1001	1.0	0845	1.0
TU 1645	2.3	W 1519	2.2
2243	1.3	2106	1.3
7 0442	2.3	**22** 0330	2.3
1119	0.9	1017	1.0
W 1800	2.3	TH 1702	2.3
2355	1.3	2240	1.3
8 0548	2.3	**23** 0448	2.4
1222	0.9	1131	0.8
TH 1907	2.4	F 1806	2.4
		2352	1.2
9 0055	1.3	**24** 0554	2.4
0649	2.4	1229	0.7
F 1317	0.8	SA 1900	2.5
1954	2.4		
10 0143	1.2	**25** 0048	1.1
0737	2.4	0648	2.6
SA 1402	0.8	SU 1325	0.6
2030	2.4	1947	2.6
11 0221	1.1	**26** 0142	0.9
0815	2.5	0739	2.7
SU 1440	0.7	M 1418	0.5
2101	2.4	2030	2.6
12 0253	1.0	**27** 0234	0.8
0848	2.5	0829	2.8
M 1514	0.7	TU 1508	0.4
2128	2.5	○ 2113	2.7
13 0323	0.9	**28** 0324	0.7
0922	2.6	0918	2.8
TU 1545	0.7	W 1554	0.4
● 2154	2.5	2155	2.7
14 0352	0.9	**29** 0411	0.6
0957	2.6	1008	2.8
W 1615	0.7	TH 1638	0.4
2222	2.5	2238	2.7
15 0423	0.8	**30** 0456	0.5
1032	2.6	1057	2.8
TH 1645	0.7	F 1721	0.6
2253	2.5	2322	2.6
		31 0541	0.6
		1148	2.7
		SA 1802	0.7

NOVEMBER

Time	m	Time	m
1 0006	2.6	**16** 0556	0.8
0626	0.6	1207	2.4
SU 1242	2.5	M 1805	0.9
1843	0.9		
2 0053	2.5	**17** 0021	2.5
0715	0.7	0639	0.8
M 1344	2.4	TU 1254	2.3
1928	1.1	1848	1.0
3 0144	2.4	**18** 0107	2.5
0813	0.8	0729	0.9
TU 1502	2.3	W 1348	2.3
◑ 2021	1.3	1939	1.1
4 0244	2.4	**19** 0159	2.4
0929	0.9	0831	0.9
W 1619	2.3	TH 1456	2.3
2151	1.4	◑ 2039	1.2
5 0354	2.3	**20** 0257	2.4
1045	0.9	0949	0.9
TH 1727	2.3	F 1634	2.3
2316	1.4	2158	1.3
6 0501	2.3	**21** 0407	2.4
1145	0.9	1102	0.8
F 1832	2.3	SA 1740	2.4
		2318	1.2
7 0016	1.3	**22** 0520	2.5
0600	2.3	1202	0.7
SA 1238	0.9	SU 1834	2.4
1922	2.4		
8 0106	1.3	**23** 0020	1.1
0652	2.3	0620	2.5
SU 1323	0.8	M 1259	0.6
2000	2.4	1922	2.5
9 0146	1.2	**24** 0118	1.0
0736	2.4	0715	2.6
M 1402	0.8	TU 1353	0.5
2030	2.4	2007	2.6
10 0220	1.0	**25** 0213	0.8
0815	2.5	0809	2.7
TU 1436	0.8	W 1444	0.5
2056	2.5	○ 2051	2.6
11 0252	0.9	**26** 0306	0.7
0852	2.5	0902	2.7
W 1508	0.7	TH 1532	0.5
● 2122	2.5	2135	2.7
12 0325	0.9	**27** 0355	0.6
0930	2.5	0954	2.7
TH 1541	0.7	F 1617	0.6
2153	2.6	2218	2.7
13 0400	0.8	**28** 0442	0.5
1008	2.5	1046	2.6
F 1615	0.7	SA 1659	0.7
2226	2.6	2302	2.7
14 0437	0.8	**29** 0527	0.5
1046	2.5	1136	2.5
SA 1650	0.8	SU 1739	0.8
2302	2.6	2346	2.6
15 0516	0.8	**30** 0612	0.6
1125	2.4	1227	2.4
SU 1726	0.9	M 1818	1.0
2340	2.5		

DECEMBER

Time	m	Time	m
1 0029	2.5	**16** 0004	2.6
0658	0.7	0633	0.7
TU 1322	2.3	W 1241	2.4
1857	1.1	1834	1.0
2 0114	2.5	**17** 0049	2.5
0747	0.8	0721	0.7
W 1425	2.2	TH 1331	2.3
1940	1.3	1921	1.1
3 0203	2.4	**18** 0137	2.5
0846	0.9	0816	0.7
TH 1538	2.2	F 1430	2.3
◑ 2030	1.4	● 2015	1.1
4 0257	2.3	**19** 0231	2.5
0957	1.0	0921	0.7
F 1643	2.2	SA 1556	2.2
2155	1.5	2120	1.2
5 0404	2.3	**20** 0334	2.4
1101	1.0	1032	0.7
SA 1743	2.2	SU 1712	2.3
2324	1.4	2241	1.2
6 0509	2.3	**21** 0451	2.4
1155	0.9	1137	0.7
SU 1837	2.3	M 1808	2.4
		2354	1.1
7 0020	1.3	**22** 0559	2.5
0605	2.3	1236	0.7
M 1241	0.9	TU 1900	2.4
1920	2.4		
8 0105	1.2	**23** 0057	1.0
0656	2.3	0658	2.5
TU 1322	0.9	W 1333	0.7
1953	2.4	1948	2.5
9 0144	1.1	**24** 0158	0.8
0743	2.3	0757	2.5
W 1359	0.8	TH 1426	0.7
2023	2.4	2033	2.5
10 0222	1.0	**25** 0254	0.7
0826	2.4	0854	2.5
TH 1435	0.8	F 1516	0.7
2054	2.5	○ 2118	2.6
11 0300	0.9	**26** 0344	0.6
0907	2.4	0947	2.6
F 1512	0.8	SA 1600	0.7
● 2128	2.5	2202	2.6
12 0340	0.8	**27** 0431	0.5
0948	2.4	1036	2.5
SA 1550	0.8	SU 1641	0.8
2204	2.6	2245	2.6
13 0422	0.7	**28** 0514	0.5
1029	2.5	1123	2.5
SU 1630	0.8	M 1719	0.9
2242	2.6	2326	2.6
14 0505	0.7	**29** 0556	0.5
1111	2.4	1208	2.4
M 1710	0.8	TU 1754	1.0
2322	2.6		
15 0548	0.7	**30** 0005	2.6
1154	2.4	0636	0.6
TU 1751	0.9	W 1252	2.3
		1827	1.0
		31 0045	2.5
		0717	0.7
		TH 1337	2.2
		1902	1.1

Chart Datum: 1·50 metres below Ordnance Datum (Newlyn). HAT is 2·9 metres above Chart Datum.

1.25 GREAT YARMOUTH

Norfolk 52°34'·36N 01°44'·39E ✲✲⬨⬨

CHARTS AC 5614, 1543, 1535, 1534; Imray C29, C28

TIDES −0210 Dover; ML 1·5; Duration 0620

Standard Port LOWESTOFT (←)

Times				Height (metres)			
High Water		Low Water		MHWS	MHWN	MLWN	MLWS
0300	0900	0200	0800	2·4	2·1	1·0	0·5
1500	2100	1400	2000				

Differences GORLESTON (To be used for Great Yarmouth)

−0035	−0035	−0030	−0030	0·0	0·0	0·0	0·0

CAISTER-ON-SEA

−0120	−0120	−0100	−0100	0·0	−0·1	0·0	0·0

WINTERTON-ON-SEA

−0225	−0215	−0135	−0135	+0·8	+0·5	+0·2	+0·1

• Rise of tide occurs mainly during 3.5 hours after LW. From HW Lowestoft −3 until HW the level is usually within 0·3m of predicted HW. Flood tide runs until about HW +15 and ebb until about LW +25.

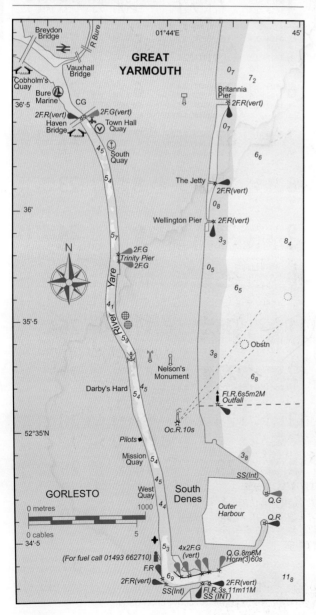

SHELTER Excellent on Town Hall Quay, close S of Haven Bridge; Yachts and small craft are not allowed in the outer harbour and ⚓ prohibited in the commercial hbrs, R Yar and its approaches.

NAVIGATION WPT 52°34'·43N 01°45'·56E, 264°/1M to front ldg lt.

- Access is H24, subject to clearance, but small craft must not attempt ent in strong SE winds which cause dangerous seas, especially on the ebb. Except at local slack water, which occurs at HW+1½ and LW+1¾, tidal streams at the ent are strong.
- On the flood, the stream eddies NW past S pier, thence up-river; a QY tidal lt on S pier warns of this D/N. Beware being set onto the N pier.
- Temporary shoaling may occur in the ent during strong E'lies, with depths 1m less than those charted.
- Beware strong tidal streams that sweep through the Haven Bridge. Proceed slowly past Bure Marine.
- Outer Harbour is for commercial vessels only.

LIGHTS AND MARKS See 1.3 and Chartlet. Gorleston Pier lt, Fl R 3s, is on R brick building (W lower half floodlit). Entrance and bend marked by five 2FG(vert) and seven 2FR(vert).

TRAFFIC SIGNALS Port operations advise on Ch 12, this should always be heeded. **Inbound:** now IALA sigs on S pier: 3 Fl ● = hbr closed; 3F ● = do not proceed; 3 F ● = vessels may proceed, oneway; ●○○ = proceed only when told to; **Outbound:** 3 ● (vert) = no vessel to go down river south of LB shed. Haven and Breydon bridges: 3 ● (vert) = passage prohib.

COMMUNICATIONS (Code 01493) MRCC (01262) 672317; Police 101; HM 335511; Breydon Bridge 651275.

Yarmouth Radio Ch **12** (H24). *Breydon Bridge* Ch 12 (OH).

FACILITIES Town Hall Quay (50m stretch) ⌓ £15/yacht, then £7 for successive days. **Burgh Castle Marina** (top of Breydon Water 5M) (90+10 visitors) ☎ 780331, £16, ⚓, D, ⚓, ⚒, ▣, ⚒, ▢, ⛽, ▢, 🛒, ✗, ▢, Access HW ±4 for 1m draft; diving ACA; **Goodchild Marine Services** (top of Breydon Water 5M) (27+6✓ £12.50) ☎ 782301, D, ⚓, ⚒, ▣, C (32 tons, including mast stepping), ⚓, Access 6ft at LW; **Services:** ⌓, L, M, ✗, ⚓, ACA. **Town** ▣ & ▣, ▢, 🛒, ✗, ▢, ✉, Ⓑ, ⚒, ✈ (Norwich).

NORFOLK BROADS: The Broads comprise about 120 miles of navigable rivers and lakes in Norfolk and Suffolk. The main rivers (Bure, Yare and Waveney) are tidal, flowing into the sea at Great Yarmouth. The N Broads have a 2·3m headroom limit. Br clearances restrict cruising to R Yare (Great Yarmouth to Norwich, but note that 3M E of Norwich, Postwick viaduct on S bypass has 10.7m HW clearance) and River Waveney (Lowestoft to Beccles). The Broads may be entered also at Lowestoft (1.24). Broads Navigation Authority ☎ (01603) 610734.

Entry to the Broads: Pass up R Yare at slack LW, under Haven Bridge (1·8m HAT) thence to Breydon Water via Breydon Bridge (4·0m) or to R Bure. Both bridges lift in co-ordination to pass small craft in groups. All br lifts on request to Hbr Office (01493) 335503 during office hrs. Weekend and bank holiday lifts to be requested working afternoon before. Call the Bridge Officer on VHF Ch 12. R Bure has two fixed bridges (2·3m MHWS).

Tidal data on the rivers and Broads is based on the time of LW at Yarmouth Yacht Stn (mouth of R Bure), which is LW Gorleston +0100 (see TIDES). Add the differences below to time of LW Yarmouth Yacht Stn to get local LW times:

R Bure		R Waveney		R Yare	
Acle Bridge	+0230	Berney Arms	+0100	Reedham	+0130
Horning	+0300	St Olaves	+0130	Cantley	+0200
Potter Heigham	+0300	Oulton Broad	+0300	Norwich	+0300

LW at Breydon (mouth of R Yare) is LW Yarmouth Yacht Stn +0100. Tide starts to flood on Breydon Water whilst still ebbing from R Bure. Max draft is 1·8m; 2m with care. Tidal range 0·6m to 1·8m.

Licences (compulsory) are obtainable from: The Broads Authority, 18 Colegate, Norwich NR3 1BQ, ☎ 01603-610734; the Info Centre, Yarmouth Yacht Stn or the River Inspectors. *Hamilton's Guide to the Broads* is recommended. www.hamilton publications.com.

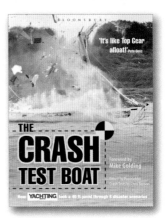
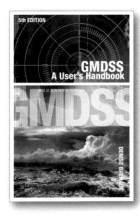
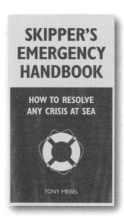

Netherlands & Belgium

Delfzijl to Nieuwpoort

2.1	Area map. *2.1A* The Staande Mastroute	88
2.2	Tidal stream charts	90
2.3	Lights, buoys and waypoints	92
2.4	Passage information	96
2.5	Special notes for the Netherlands	96
2.6	TSS off the Northern Netherlands	97
	Helgoland tide tables	98

NETHERLANDS

2.7	Delfzijl Termunterzijl • Eemshaven • Schiermonnikoog	101
2.8	Lauwersoog Zoutkamp • Oostmahorn • Nes (Ameland)	101
2.9	Het Vlie (Zeegat van Terschelling)	103
2.10	West Terschelling	104
2.11	Vlieland	104
2.12	Harlingen	105
2.13	Oudeschild	105
2.14	Den Helder	106
2.15	IJsselmeer	107
2.16	IJmuiden	109
2.17	Noordzeekanaal	110
2.18	Amsterdam	110
2.19	Scheveningen	112
2.20	TSS and VTS off Southern Netherlands and Belgium	113
	Hoek van Holland tides	114
2.21/A	Maas TSS/Precautionary Area and Maasgeul	117
2.22	Hoek van Holland and Nieuwe Waterweg VTS	118
2.23	Rotterdam	119
2.24	Haringvliet (Stellendam and Hellevoetsluis)	120
2.25	Roompotsluis (Oosterschelde)	121
2.26	Westerschelde	122
	Ellewoutsdijk • Hoedekenskerke • Hansweert • Walsoorden • Paal, Doel, Lillo	
2.27	Vlissingen, Tide tables/curves	124
2.28	Breskens	128
2.29	Terneuzen	128

BELGIUM

2.30	Special notes for Belgium	129
2.31	Antwerpen	129
2.32	Zeebrugge, Tide tables/curves	131
	Area 2 Distance table	131
2.33	Blankenberge	135
2.34	Oostende	135
2.35	Nieuwpoort	137

Netherlands

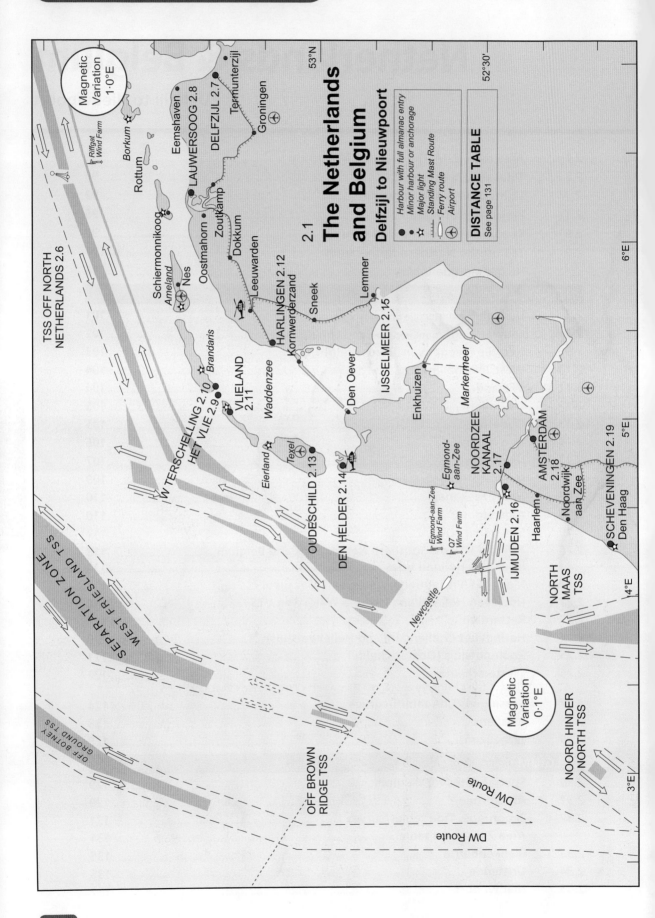

2.1

The Netherlands and Belgium
Delfzijl to Nieuwpoort

- ● Harbour with full almanac entry
- ● Minor harbour or anchorage
- ☆ Major light
- ⟋ Standing Mast Route
- --- Ferry route
- ⊕ Airport

DISTANCE TABLE
See page 131

Magnetic Variation 1·0°E

Magnetic Variation 0·1°E

53°N

52°30'

6°E

5°E

4°E

3°E

Riffgat Wind Farm
Borkum
Rottum
Eemshaven
LAUWERSOOG 2.8
DELFZIJL 2.7
Termunterzijl
Groningen
Zoutkamp
Oostmahorn
Dokkum
Schiermonnikoog
Ameland
Nes
Leeuwarden
HARLINGEN 2.12
Kornwerderzand
Sneek
Lemmer
Brandaris
VLIELAND 2.11
HET VLIE 2.9
W TERSCHELLING 2.10
Waddenzee
Den Oever
IJSSELMEER 2.15
Enkhuizen
Markermeer
Eierland
Texel
OUDESCHILD 2.13
DEN HELDER 2.14
Egmond-aan-Zee
Egmond-aan-Zee Wind Farm
Q7 Wind Farm
NOORDZEE KANAAL 2.17
AMSTERDAM
Haarlem
Noordwijk aan Zee
IJMUIDEN 2.16
SCHEVENINGEN 2.19
Den Haag

TSS OFF NORTH NETHERLANDS 2.6

SEPARATION ZONE
WEST FRIESLAND TSS

OFF BOTNEY GROUND TSS

OFF BROWN RIDGE TSS

DW Route

DW Route

Newcastle

NORTH MAAS TSS

NOORD HINDER NORTH TSS

88

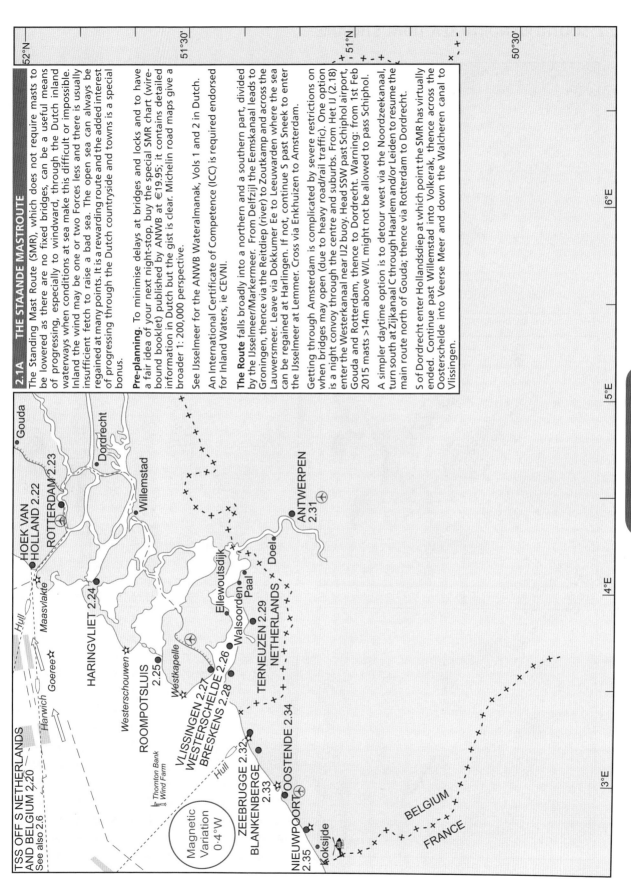

2.1A   THE STAANDE MASTROUTE

The Standing Mast Route (SMR), which does not require masts to be lowered as there are no fixed bridges, can be a useful means of progressing, especially to windward, through the Dutch inland waterways when conditions at sea make this difficult or impossible. Inland the wind may be one or two Forces less and there is usually insufficient fetch to raise a bad sea. The open sea can always be regained at many points. It is a rewarding route and the added interest of progressing through the Dutch countryside and towns is a special bonus.

Pre-planning. To minimise delays at bridges and locks and to have a fair idea of your next night-stop, buy the special SMR chart (wire-bound booklet) published by ANWB at €19.95; it contains detailed information in Dutch but the gist is clear. Michelin road maps give a broader 1: 200,000 perspective.

See IJsselmeer for the ANWB Wateralmanak, Vols 1 and 2 in Dutch.

An International Certificate of Competence (ICC) is required endorsed for Inland Waters, ie CEVNI.

The Route falls broadly into a northern and a southern part, divided by the IJsselmeer/Markermeer. From Delfzijl the Eemskanaal leads to Groningen, thence via the Reitdiep (river) to Zoutkamp and across the Lauwersmeer. Leave via Dokkumer Ee to Leeuwarden where the sea can be regained at Harlingen. If not, continue S past Sneek to enter the IJsselmeer at Lemmer. Cross via Enkhuizen to Amsterdam.

Getting through Amsterdam is complicated by severe restrictions on when bridges may open (due to heavy road/rail traffic). One option is a night convoy through the centre and suburbs. From Het IJ (2.18) enter the Westerkanaal near IJ2 buoy. Head SSW past Schiphol airport, Gouda and Rotterdam, thence to Dordrecht. Warning: from 1st Feb 2015 masts >14m above W/L might not be allowed to pass Schiphol.

A simpler daytime option is to detour west via the Noordzeekanaal, turn south at Zijkanaal C through Haarlem and/or Leiden to resume the main route north of Gouda; thence via Rotterdam to Dordrecht.

S of Dordrecht enter Hollandsdiep at which point the SMR has virtually ended. Continue past Willemstad into Volkerak, thence across the Oosterschelde into Veerse Meer and down the Walcheren canal to Vlissingen.

2.2 SOUTHERN NORTH SEA TIDAL STREAMS

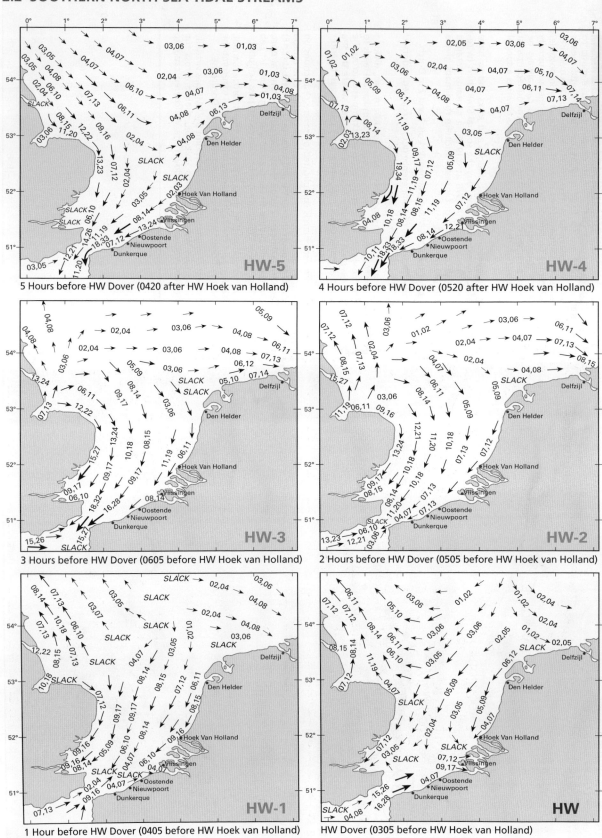

5 Hours before HW Dover (0420 after HW Hoek van Holland)

4 Hours before HW Dover (0520 after HW Hoek van Holland)

3 Hours before HW Dover (0605 before HW Hoek van Holland)

2 Hours before HW Dover (0505 before HW Hoek van Holland)

1 Hour before HW Dover (0405 before HW Hoek van Holland)

HW Dover (0305 before HW Hoek van Holland)

South-westward 1.2   North-westward 3.2

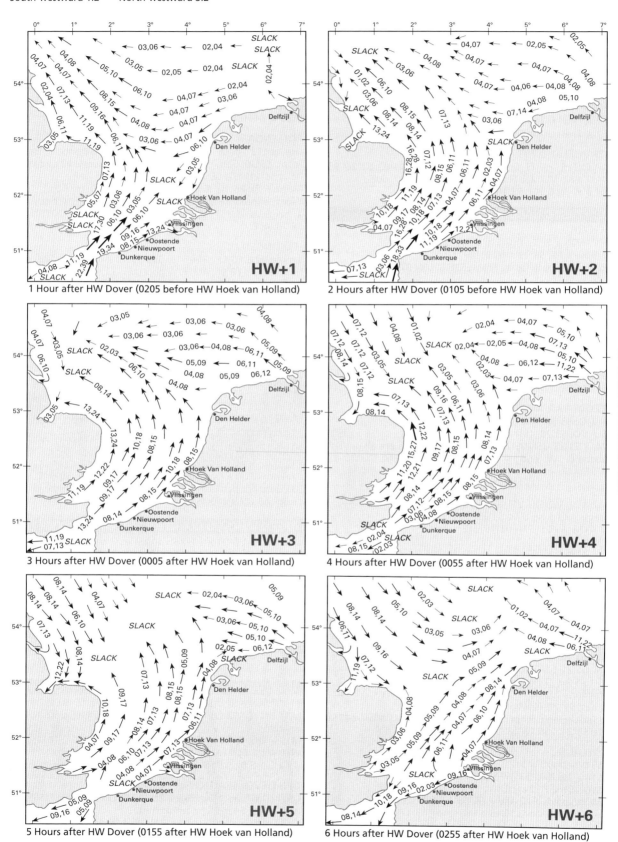

1 Hour after HW Dover (0205 before HW Hoek van Holland)

2 Hours after HW Dover (0105 before HW Hoek van Holland)

3 Hours after HW Dover (0005 after HW Hoek van Holland)

4 Hours after HW Dover (0055 after HW Hoek van Holland)

5 Hours after HW Dover (0155 after HW Hoek van Holland)

6 Hours after HW Dover (0255 after HW Hoek van Holland)

Netherlands

2.3 LIGHTS, BUOYS AND WAYPOINTS

Bold print = light with a nominal range of 15M or more. CAPITALS = place or feature. *CAPITAL ITALICS* = light-vessel, light float or Lanby. *Italics* = Fog signal. ***Bold italics*** = Racon. Many marks/buoys are fitted with AIS (<u>MMSI No</u>); see relevant charts.

TSS OFF NORTHERN NETHERLANDS

TERSCHELLING-GERMAN BIGHT TSS
TG1/Ems ⚓ IQ G 13s; 53°43'·33N 06°22'·24E.
TE5 ⚓ Fl (3) G 10s; 53°37'·79N 05°53'·69E.
TE1 ⚓ Fl (3) G 10s; 53°29'·58N 05°11'·31E.

OFF VLIELAND TSS
VL-CENTER 🔶 Fl 5s 12M; ***Racon C, 12–15M***; 53°26'·93N 04°39'·88E. VL7 ⚓ L Fl G 10s; 53°26'·40N 04°57'·60E.
VL1 ⚓ Fl (2) G 10s; 53°10'·96N 04°35'·31E.

DELFZIJL TO HARLINGEN

DELFZIJL
PS3/BW26 ⚓ Fl (2+1) G 12s; 53°19'·25N 07°00'·32E.
W mole ⚡ FG; 53°19'·01N 07°00'·27E.
Ldg lts 203° both Iso 4s. Front, 53°18'·63N 07°00'·17E.

SCHIERMONNIKOOG AND LAUWERSOOG
WG (Westgat) ⚓ Iso 8s; ***Racon N***; 53°32'·55N 06°00'·70E.
WRG ⚓ Q; 53°32'·87N 06°03'·24E.
AM ⚓ VQ; 53°30'·95N 05°44'·72E.
Schiermonnikoog ☆ Fl (4) 20s 43m **28M**; dark R ○ twr. Same twr: F WR 29m **W15M**, R12M; 210°-W-221°-R-230°. 53°29'·20N 06°08'·79E.
Lauwersoog W mole ⚡ FG; *Horn (2) 30s*; 53°24'·68N 06°12'·00E.

ZEEGAT VAN AMELAND
BR ⚓ Q; 53°30'·66N 05°33'·52E.
TS ⚓ VQ; 53°28'·15N 05°21'·53E.
WA ⚓ 53°28'·35N 05°28'·64E. (Westgat buoys are all unlit)
Ameland, W end ☆ Fl (3) 15s 57m **30M**; 53°26'·89N 05°37'·42E.

NES
VA2-R1 ⚓ VQ(6) + L Fl 10s; 53°25'·71N 05°45'·88E.
Reegeul R3 ⚡ Iso G 4s; 53°25'·80N 05°45'·93E.
R7 ⚡ QG; 53°25'·91N 05°46'·21E.

HET VLIE (ZEEGAT VAN TERSCHELLING)
ZS (Zuider Stortemelk) ⚓ Iso 4s; ***Racon T***; 53°19'·56N 04°55'·80E.
ZS1 ⚓ VQ G; 53°19'·29N 04°57'·19E.
ZS3 ⚓ Fl G 5s; 53° 19'·38N 04° 57'·19E
ZS5 ⚓ L Fl G 8s; 53°18'·55N 05°00'·86E.
ZS11-VS2 ⚓ Q (9) 15s; 53°18'·66N 05°05'·95E.

NOORD MEEP/SLENK TO WEST TERSCHELLING
WM3 ⚓ Iso G 2s; 53°17'·45N 05°12'·28E.
NM 4-S 21 ⚓ VQ (3) 5s; 53°19'·02N 05°15'·47E.
SG 15-S 2 ⚓ Q (9) 15s; 53°20'·44N 05°11'·70E.
Brandaris Twr ☆ Fl 5s 54m **29M**; Y □ twr partly obscured by dunes; 53°21'·62N 05°12'·86E.
W Terschelling W hbr mole ⚡ FR 5m 5M; R post, W bands; *Horn 15s*; 53°21'·26N 05°13'·09E. E pier hd ⚡ FG 4m 4M.

VLIELAND
VS3 (Vliesloot) ⚓ VQ G; 53°18'·27N 05°06'·25E.
VS14 ⚓ Iso R 4s; 53°17'·58N 05°05'62E.
VS16-VB1 ⚓ Fl (2+1) R 10s; 53°17'·62N 05°05'·19E.
E/W mole hds ⚡ FG and ⚡ FR; 53°17'·68N 05°05'·51E.
Ldg lts 282° ⚡ Iso 4s 10/16m 1M, synch; 53°17'·75N 05°04'·47W (100m apart); mainly for the ferry terminal at E Vlieland.
E Vlieland (Vuurduin) ☆ Iso 4s 54m **20M**; 53°17'·75N 05°03'·49E.

APPROACHES TO HARLINGEN (selected marks):
VLIESTROOM buoys are frequently moved.
VL1 ⚓ QG; 53°18'·99N 05°08'·82E. VL 2 ⚓ QR; 53°19'·40N 05°09'·19E.
VL 11 ⚓ Iso G 8s; 53°16'·42N 05°09'·70E.

BLAUWE SLENK
BS1-IN2 ⚓ VQ (3) 5s; 53°15'·41N 05°09'·41E.
BS13 ⚓ QG; 53°13'·31N 05°17'·13E. BS19 ⚓ VQ G; 53°11'·90N 05°18'·28E.
BS23 ⚓ L Fl G 8s; 53°11'·42N 05°19'·60E.

POLLENDAM
Ldg lts 112°, both Iso 6s 8/19m 13M (H24); B masts, W bands. Front, 53°10'·52N 05°24'·19E. Use only between P2 and P6.
P2 ⚓ 53°11'·47N 05°20'·38E on the training wall.
P4, Iso R 8s; P6, Iso R 4s; P8, Iso R 8s; and P10, Iso R 2s.
Yachts should keep outboard of P1 thru 7 SHM buoys. P1 ⚓ Iso G 2s; 53°11'·39N 05°20'·32E. P7 ⚓ VQ G; 53°10'·68N 05°23'·45E.

HARLINGEN
S mole hd ⚡ FG 9m; *Horn (3) 30s;* 53°10'·56N 05°24'·18E.
N mole hd ⚡ FR 9m 4M; R/W pedestal; 53°10'·59N 05°24'·32E.

TEXEL AND THE WADDENZEE

TEXEL (from NW and W)
Eierland ☆ Fl (2) 10s 52m **29M**; R ○ twr; 53°10'·93N 04°51'·31E.
TX ⚓ Q(9) 15s; 53°06'·81N 04°41'·19E

MOLENGAT (from the N)
MG-A,Y ⚓ ; 53°02'·54N 04°41'·88E.
MG-B, Y ⚓ 53°02'·00N 04°42'·11E
MG-D, Y ⚓ ; 53°00'·90N 04°42'·04E;
MG-G, Y ⚓ ; 52°59'·30N 04°42'·56E;
MG-H, Y ⚓ ; 52°58'·91N 04°43'·10E.

OUDESCHILD
T12 ⚓ Iso R 8s; 53°02'·23N 04°51'·52E.
Oudeschild Dir ⚡ Oc 6s; intens 291°; 53°02'·40N 04°50'·94E; leads 291° into hbr between N mole head FG 6m; and S mole head ⚡ FR 6m; 53°02'·33N 04°51'·17E.

APPROACHES TO KORNWERDERZAND SEALOCK
DOOVE BALG (From Texelstroom eastward)
T23 ⚓ VQ G; 53°03'·60N 04°55'·85E, 066°/3M from Oudeschild.
T29 ⚓ 53°03'·25N 05°00'·05E.
D1 ⚓ Iso G 4s; 53°02'·18N 05°03'·42E.
D21 ⚓ Iso G 8s; 53°03'·55N 05°15'·71E.
BO2-WG1 ⚓ Q (6) + L Fl 10s; 53°05'·00N 05°17'·91E.

KORNWERDERZAND SEALOCK
W mole ⚡ FG 9m 7M; *Horn Mo(N) 30s;* 53°04'·78N 05°20'·03E.
E mole ⚡ FR 9m 7M; 53°04'·70N 05°20'·08E.
W mole elbow ⚡ Iso G 6s 6m 7M; 53°04'·61N 05°19'·90E.

APPROACHES TO DEN OEVER SEALOCK
MALZWIN and VISJAGERSGAATJE CHANS TO DEN OEVER
MH4-M1 ⚓ VQ (9) 10s; 52°58'·14N 04°47'·49E, close N Den Helder.
M15 ⚓ QG; 52°59'·39N 04°55'·48E (hence use DYC 1811.3).
VG1-W2 ⚓ Fl (2+1) G 10s; 52°59'·00N 04°56'·85E.
O9 ⚓ Iso G 8s; 52°56'·63N 05°02'·38E.

DEN OEVER SEALOCK
Ldg lts 131°, both Oc 10s 6m 7M; 127°-137°. Front, 52°56'·32N 05°02'·98E. Rear, 280m from front.
E end of swing bridge, ⚡ Iso WRG 5s 14m 10/7M; 226°-G-231°-W-235°-R-290°-G-327°-W-335°-R-345°; 52°56'·12N 05°02'·52E.

ZEEGAT VAN TEXEL AND DEN HELDER

OFFSHORE MARKS W and SW OF DEN HELDER
NH (Noorderhaaks) ⚲ VQ; 53°00'·24N 04°35'·37E.
MR ⚲ Q (9) 15s; 52°56'·77N 04°33'·82E.
ZH (Zuiderhaaks) ⚲ VQ (6) + L Fl 10s; 52°54'·65N 04°34'·72E.
Vinca G wreck ⚲ Q (9) 15s; *Racon D*; 52°45'·93N 04°12'·31E.

SCHULPENGAT (from the SSW)
Schulpengat Dir ☆ 026·5°, Dir WRG, Al WR, Al WG, **W22M R/G18M**; church spire; 025.1°–FG–025.6°–AlWG–026.3°–FW–026.7°–Al WR–027.4°–F R–027.9°; shown H24.
Schilbolsnol ☆ F WRG 27m **W15M**, R12M, G11M; 338°-W-002°-G-035°-W(ldg sector for Schulpengat)-038°-R-051°-W-068°; post; 53°00'·50N 04°45'·70E (on Texel).
SG ⚲ Mo (A) 8s; *Racon Z*; 52°52'·90N 04°37'·90E.
S1 ▲ Iso G 4s; 52°53'·53N 04°38'·82E.
S7 ▲ QG; 52°56'·25N 04°40'·92E. S6A ⚲ QR; 52°56'·52N 04°40'·51E.
S10 ⚲ Iso R 8s; 52°57'·59N 04°41'·57E. S14-MG17 ⚲, see Molengat.
S11 ▲ Iso G 8s; 52°57'·55N 04°43'·25E.
Huisduinen ⚹ F WR 26m W14M, R11M; 070°-W-113°-R-158°-W-208°; □ twr; 52°57'·14N 04°43'·30E (abeam S10 PHM buoy).
Kijkduin ☆ Fl (4) 20s 56m **30M**; vis 360°, except where obsc'd by dunes on Texel; brown twr; 52°57'·33N 04°43'·58E (mainland).

MARSDIEP and DEN HELDER
T1 ▲ Fl (3) G 10s; 52°57'·99N 04°44'·62E.
T3 ▲ Iso G 8s; 52°58'·07N 04°46'·42E.
Den Helder ldg lts 191°, both Oc G 5s 16/25m 3M, synch. Front, vis 183·5°-198·5°; B ▽ on bldg; 52°57'·37N 04°47'·08E.
Marinehaven, W bkwtr head ⚹ QG 11m 8M; *Horn 20s*; 52°57'·95N 04°47'·07E (Harssens Island).
W side, ⚹ Fl G 5s 9m 4M (H24); 180°-067°; 52°57'·78N 04°47'·08E.
Yacht hbr (KMYC), ent ⚹ FR & FG; 165m SW of ⚹ Fl G 5s, above.
E side, MH6 ⚲ Iso R 4s; 52°57'·99N 04°47'·41E.
Ent E side, ⚹ QR 9m 4M (H24); 52°57'·77N 04°47'·37E.

DEN HELDER TO AMSTERDAM

Zanddijk Grote Kaap ⚹ OcWRG 10s 30m W11M, R8M, G8M; 041°-G-088°-W-094°-R-131°; brown twr; 52°52'·86N 04°42'·88E.
Petten ⚲ VQ (9) 10s; 52°47'·33N 04°36'·78E (Power stn outfall).
Egmond-aan-Zee ☆ Iso WR 10s 36m **W18M**; 010°-W-175°-R-188°; W ○ twr; 52°36'·99N 04°37'·16E.
Wind farm approx 6·4M W of Egmond-aan-Zee is marked by: a Meteomast, Mo (U) 15s 11m 10M; 52°36'·36N 04°23'·41E; and by L Fl Y 15s; Horn Mo (U) 30s on 5 of the peripheral wind turbines.

IJMUIDEN
Baloeran ⚲ Q (9) 15s; 52°29'·21N 04°32'·00E.
IJmuiden ⚲ Mo (A) 8s; *Racon Y, 10M*; 52°28'·45N 04°23'·92E.
Ldg lts 100·5° (FW 5M by day; 090·5°-110·5°). **Front** ☆ F WR 30m **W16M**, R13M; 050°-W-122°-R-145°-W-160°; (Tidal and traffic sigs); dark R ○ twrs; 52°27'·70N 04°34'·47E. **Rear** ☆ Fl 5s 52m **29M**; 019°-199° (FW 5M by day; 090·5°-110·5°); 560m from front.
S bkwtr hd ⚹ FG 14m 10M (in fog Fl 3s); W twr, G bands; 52°27'·82N 04°31'·93E.
N bkwtr hd ⚹ FR 15m 10M; 52°28'·05N 04°32'·55E.
IJM 1 ▲ Iso G 5s; 52°27'·75N 04°33'·59E.
S outer chan ⚹ Iso G 6s; 52°27'·75N 04°33'·81E. ⚹ Iso R 6s, 52°27'·84N 04°34'·39E (Forteiland). Kleine Sluis 52°27'·84N 04°35'·43E.

AMSTERDAM
IJ8 ⚲ Iso R 8s (for Sixhaven marina); 52°22'·86N 04°54'·37E.
Oranjesluizen, N lock 52°22'·93N 04°57'·60E (for IJsselmeer).

AMSTERDAM TO ROTTERDAM

Noordwijk-aan-Zee ☆ Oc (3) 20s 32m **18M**; W□twr; 52°14'·88N 04°26'·02E.

SCHEVENINGEN
Lighthouse ☆ Fl (2) 10s 48m **29M**; 014°-244°; brown twr; 52°06'·23N 04°16'·13E, 5ca E of hbr ent.

Ldg lts 156°, both Iso 4s 14M, H24; synch; Gy masts. Front 52°05'·99N 04°15'·44E; rear 250m from front. Intens at night.
SCH ⚲ Iso 4s; 52°07'·76N 04°14'·12E.
KNS ⚲ Q (9)15s; 52°06'·41N 04°15'·32E.
W mole ⚹ FG 12m 9M; G twr, W bands; 52°06'·23N 04°15'·16E.
E mole ⚹, FR 12m 9M; R twr, W bands; 52°06'·24N 04°15'·37E.
Inner ldg lts 131°: both Iso G 4s synch; Gy posts. Front 52°05'·81N 04°15'·89E. Rear, 34m from front.

NOORD HINDER N & S TSS and JUNCTION
NHR-N ⚲ L Fl 8s; *Racon K, 10M*; 52°10'·91N 03°04'·76E.
Noord Hinder ⚲ Fl (2) 10s; *Horn (2) 30s*; *Racon T, 12-15M*; 52°00'·10N 02° 51'·11E.
NHR-S ⚲ Fl Y 10s; 51°51'·37N 02°28'·72E.
NHR-SE ▲ Fl G 5s; 51°45'·42N 02°39'·96E.
Birkenfels ⚲ Q (9) 15s; 51°38'·98N 02°31'·75E.
Twin ⚲ Fl (3) Y 9s; 51°32'·00N 02°22'·59E.
Garden City ⚲ Q (9) 15s; 51°29'·20N 02°17'·54E.

APPROACHES TO HOEK VAN HOLLAND
Europlatform ⚑ Mo (U) 15s; W structure, R bands; helicopter platform; *Horn Mo(U) 30s;* 51°59'·89N 03°16'·46E.
Goeree ☆ Fl (4) 20s 32m **28M**; R/W chequered twr on platform; helicopter platform; *Horn (4) 30s*; *Racon T, 12-15M;* 51°55'·42N 03°40'·03E.
Maasvlakte ☆ Fl (5) 20s 67m **28M**, H24; 340°-267°; W twr, B bands; 51°58'·20N 04°00'·84E, 1·5M SSW of Maas ent.
Maas Center ⚲ Iso 4s; *Racon M, 10M;* 52°00'·92N 03°48'·79E.
MO ⚲ Mo (A) 8s; 52°01'·10N 03°58'·19E.
MN3 ▲ Fl (3) G 10s; 52°07'·04N 04°00'·00E.
MN1 ▲ Fl G 5s; 52°02'·23N 04°01'·91E.

HOEK VAN HOLLAND
Maasmond ldg lts 112° (for deep draught vessels): both Iso 4s 30/46m **21M**; 101°-123°, synch; W twr, B bands. **Front**, 51°58'·88N 04°04'·88E (NW end of Splitsingsdam). **Rear**, 0·6M from front.
Indusbank N ⚲ VQ; 52°02'·89N 04°03'·57E.
MVN ⚲ VQ; 51°59'·61N 04°00'·23E.
MV ⚲ Q (9) 15s; 51°58'·40N 03°56'·58E.
Maas 1 ▲ L Fl G 5s; 51°59'·35N 04°01'·68E.
Nieuwe Waterweg ldg lts 107°: both Iso R 6s 29/43m **18M**; 099.5°-114.5°; R twr, W bands. Front, 51°58'·55N 04°07'·52E. Rear, 450m from front.
Noorderdam Head ⚹ FR 25m 10M (In fog Al Fl WR 6s; 278°-255°); R twr, W bands; 51°59'·67N 04°02'·80E.
Nieuwe Zuiderdam ⚹ FG 25m 10M, 330°-307°; (In fog Al Fl WG 6s); G twr, W bands; 51°59'·14N 04°02'·49E.

ROTTERDAM
Maassluis ⚹ FG 6m; 51°54'·94N 04°14'·81E; and FR.
Vlaardingen ⚹ FG; 51°53'·99N 04°20'·95E; and FR.
Spuihaven, W ent ⚹ FR; 51°53'·98N 04°23'·97E.
Veerhaven, E ent ⚹ FG; 51°54'·42N 04°28'·75E; and FR.
City marina ent, 51°54'·64N 04°29'·76E.

APPROACHES TO HARINGVLIET

Buitenbank , Iso 4s; 51°51'·16N 03°25'·71E.
Hinder ⚲ Q (9) 15s; 51°54'·55N 03°55'·42E.
SH ⚲ VQ (9) 10s; 51°49'·49N 03°45'·79E.
Westhoofd ☆ Fl (3) 15s 55m **30M**; R □ tr; 51°48'·79N 03°51'·85E.
Ooster ⚲ Q (9) 15s; 51°47'·90N 03°41'·27E.

SLIJKGAT
SG ⚲ Iso 4s; 51°51'·95N 03°51'·42E.
SG 2 ⚲ Iso R 4s; 51°51'·71N 03°53'·45E.
SG 5 ▲ Iso G 4s; 51°50'·00N 03°55'·56E.
SG 11 ▲ Iso G 4s; 51°50'·81N 03°58'·52E.
P1 ▲ Iso G 4s; 51°51'·30N 04°01'·12E.
P3 ▲ Iso G 8s; 51°51'·12N 04°01'·45E.
P9 ▲ Iso G 8s; 51°49'·98N 04°02'·15E.

Netherlands

STELLENDAM

N mole ≼ FG; *Horn (2) 15s;* 51°49'·88N 04°02'·03E.
Buitenhaven ≼ Oc 6s; 51°49'·73N 04°01'·75E.

APPROACHES TO OOSTERSCHELDE

OUTER APPROACHES

Schouwenbank ⊚ Mo (A) 8s; *Racon O, 10M;* 51°44'·94N 03°14'·32E.
Middelbank ⊚ Iso 8s; 51°40'·86N 03°18'·20E.
MW ⊰ Q (9) 15s; 51°44'·55N 03°24'·04E (Schouwendiep).
MD 3 ⚲ Fl G 5s; 51°42'·70N 03°26'·98E.
SW Thornton ⊚ Iso 8s; 51°30'·98N 02°50'·90E.
Wind farm, Thornton Bank in □ 5.5M x 2.7M centred on 51°32'·58N 2°57'·56E: 54 turbines all R lts, the 11 perimeter turbines are lit Mo U Y 15s, Horn Mo U 30s.
Rabsbank ⊚ Iso 4s; 51°38'·25N 03°09'·93E.
Westpit ⊚ Iso 8s; 51°33'·65N 03°09'·92E.
ZSB ⊰ VQ (9) 10s; 51°36'·57N 03°15'·62E.
OG1 ⚲ QG; 51°36'·14N 03°20'·08E.

WESTGAT, OUDE ROOMPOT and ROOMPOTSLUIS

West Schouwen ☆ Fl (2+1)15s 57m **30M**; Gy twr, R diagonals on upper part; 51°42'·52N 03°41'·50E, 5·8M N of Roompotsluis.
OG-WG ⊰ VQ (9) 10s; 51°37'·18N 03°23'·82E.
WG1 ⚲ Iso G 8s; 51°38'·00N 03°26'·24E.
WG4 ≼ L Fl R 8s; 51°38'·62N 03°28'·78E.
WG7 ⚲ Iso G 4s 51°39'·40N 03°32'·67E.
WG-GB (Geul van de Banjaard) ⛵ 51°39'·72N 03°32'·69E.
OR1 ⚹ 51°39'·15N 03°33'·59E.
OR5 ⚲ Iso G 8s; 51°38'·71N 03°35'·53E.
OR11 ⚲ Iso G 4s; 51°36'·98N 03°38'·40E.
OR12 ⚳ Iso R 4s; 51°37'·27N 03°39'·25E.
OR-R ⊰ VQ (3) 5s; 51°36'·41N 03°38'·96E.
Roompotsluis ldg lts 073·5°, both Oc G 5s; synch. Front, 51°37'·33N 03°40'·75E. Rear, 280m from front.
N bkwtr ≼ FR 7m; 51°37'·31N 03°40'·09E.

WESTKAPELLE TO VLISSINGEN

OOSTGAT

Ldg lts 149·5°: Front, Noorderhoofd Oc WRG 10s 20m; W13M, R/G10M; 353°-R-008°-G-029°-W-169°; R ○ twr, W band; 51°32'·40N 03°26'·21E, 0·73M from rear (Westkapelle).
Westkapelle ☆, rear, Fl 3s 50m **28M**; obsc'd by land on certain brgs; □ twr, R top; 51°31'·75N 03°26'·83E.
Kaloo ⊚ Iso 8s; 51°35'·55N 03°23'·24E. Chan is well buoyed/lit.
OG5 ⚲ Iso G 8s; 51°33'·95N 03°25'·92E.
OG-GR ⊰ VQ (3) 5s; 51°32'·74N 03°24'·71E.
Molenhoofd ≼ Oc WRG 6s 10m; 306°-R-329°-W-349°-R-008°-G-034·5°-W-036·5°-G-144°-W-169°-R-198°; W mast R bands; 51°31'·58N 03°26'·05E.
Zoutelande FR 21m 12M; 321°-352°; R □ twr; 51°30'·28N 03°28'·41E.
Kaapduinen, ldg lts 130°: both Oc 5s 25/34m 13M; synch; Y □ twrs, R bands. Front, 115°-145°; 51°28'·47N 03°30'·99E. Rear, 107·5°-152·5°; 220m from front.
Fort de Nolle ≼ Oc WRG 9s 11m W6M, R/G4M; 293°-R-309°-W-324·5°-G-336·5°-R-014°-G-064°-R-099·5°-W-110·5°-G-117°-R-130°; W col, R bands; 51°26'·94N 03°33'·12E.
Ldg lts 117°: Front, Leugenaar, Oc R 5s 6m 7M; intens 108°-126°; W&R pile; 51°26'·43N 03°34'·14E.
Rear, Sardijngeul Oc WRG 5s 8m W12M, R9M, G8M; synch; 245°-R-272°-G-281°-W-123°-R-147°; R △, W bands on R & W mast; 550m from front; 51°26'·30N 03°34'·56E.

OFFSHORE: W HINDER TSS TO SCHEUR CHANNEL

West Hinder ☆ Fl (4) 30s 23m 13M; *Horn Mo (U) 30s;* **Racon W**; 51°23'·30N 02°26'·27E.
WH Zuid ⊰ Q (6) + L Fl 15s; 51°22'·78N 02°26'·25E.

Oost-Dyck ⊰ Q; 51°21'·38N 02°31'·12E.
Bergues N ⊰ Q; 51°19'·96N 02°24'·53E.
Oost-Dyck West ⊰ Q (9) 15s; 51°17'·15N 02°26'·32E.
Oostdyck radar twr; ≼ Mo (U) 15s 15m 12M on 4 corners; *Horn Mo (U) 30s;* **Racon O**. R twr, 3 W bands, with adjacent red twr/helipad; 51°16'·49N 02°26'·85E.
AN ⚳ Fl (4) R 20s; 51°23'·45N 02°36'·92E.
AZ ⚲ Fl (3) G 10s; 51°21'·15N 02°36'·92E.
KB2 ⊰ VQ; 51°21'·04N 02°42'·22E.
KB ⊰ Q; *Racon K;* 51°21'·03N 02°42'·83E.
MBN ⊰ Q; 51°20'·82N 02°46'·29E.
Akkaert-SW ⊰ Q (9) 15s; 51°22'·28N 02°46'·34E.
VG ⊰ Q ; 51°23'·38N 02°46'·21E, Vaargeul 1.
VG1 ⚲ VQ G; 51°25'·03N 02°49'·04E.
VG2 ⚳ Q (6) + L Fl R 15s; *Racon V;* 51°25'·96N 02°48'·16E.
VG3 ⚲ QG; 51°25'·05N 02°52'·92E.
VG5 ⚲ Fl G 5s; 51°24'·63N 02°57'·92E.
VG7 ⊰ Q ; 51°24'·53N 02°59'·92E.
Goote Bank ⊰ Q (3) 10s; 51°26'·95N 02°52'·72E.
A1 ⊰ Iso 8s; 51°22'·36N 02°53'·33E.
A1bis ⊰ L Fl 10s; 51°21'·68N 02°58'·02E.

WESTERSCHELDE APPROACHES

SCHEUR CHANNEL

S1 ⚲ Fl G 5s; 51°23'·14N 03°00'·12E.
S3 ⊰ Q; 51°24'·30N 03°02'·92E.
MOW 0 ⊙ Fl (5) Y 20s; *Racon S, 10M;* 51°23'·67N 03°02'·75E.
S5 ⚲ Fl G 5s; 51°23'·70N 03°06'·30E.
S7 ⚲ Fl G 5s; 51°23'·98N 03°10'·42E.
S9 ⚲ QG; 51°24'·42N 03°14'·99E.
S12 ⚳ Fl (4) R 10s; 51°24'·67N 03°18'·22E.
S-W ⊰ Q; 51°24'·13N 03°18'·22E, here Wielingen chan merges.
S14 ⚳ Fl R 5s; 51°24'·58N 03°19'·67E.

WIELINGEN CHANNEL

BVH ⚳ Q (6) + L Fl R 15s; 51°23'·15N 03°12'·04E.
MOW3 tide gauge ≼ Fl (5) Y 20s; *Racon H, 10M;* 51°23'·38N 03°11'·92E.
W ⚲ Fl (3) G 15s; 51°23'·27N 03°14'·92E.
W1 ⚲ Fl G 5s; 51°23'·48N 03°18'·22E.
Fort Maisonneuve ⊰ VQ (9) 10s; wreck; 51°24'·20N 03°21'·50E.
W3 ⚲ Iso G 8s; 51°23'·96N 03°21'·49E.
W5 ⚲ Iso G 4s; 51°24'·31N 03°24'·50E.
W7 ⚲ Iso G 8s; 51°24'·60N 03°27'·27E.
W9 ⚲ Iso G 4s; 51°24'·96N 03°30'·43E.
Nieuwe Sluis ≼ Oc WRG 10s 26m W14M, R11M, G10M; 055°-R-089°-W-093°-G-105°-R-134°-W-136·5°-G-156·5°-W-236·5°-G-243°-W-254°-R-292°-W-055°; B 8-sided twr, W bands; 51°24'·41N 03°31'·29E.
Songa ⚲ QG; 51°25'·26N 03°33'·66E.
W10 ⚳ QR; 51°25'·85N 03°33'·28E.

VLISSINGEN

Koopmanshaven, W mole root, ≼ Iso WRG 3s 15m W12M, R10M, G9M; 253°-R-277°-W-283°-R-296°- W-306·5°-G-013°-W-024°-G-033°-W-035°-G-039°-W-055°-G-084·5°-R-092°-G-111°-W-114°; R pylon; 51°26'·37N 03°34'·52E.
Sardijngeul Oc WRG 5s; 51°26'·30N 03°34'·56E: see OOSTGAT last 3 lines. E mole head, ≼ FG 7m; W mast; 51°26'·32N 03°34'·67E.
Buitenhaven ent, W side ≼ FR 10m 5M; also Iso WRG 4s: W073°-324°, G324°-352°, W352°-017°, G017°-042°, W042°-056°, R056°-073°; W post, R bands; tfc sigs; 51°26'·38N 03°36'·06E.
Buitenhaven ent, E side ≼ FG 7m 4M; 51°26'·41N 03°36'·38E.
Schone Waardin ≼ Oc WRG 9s 10m W13M, R10M, G9M; 235°-R-271°-W-288°-G-335°-R-341°-G-026°-W-079°-R-091°; R mast, W bands; 51°26'·54N 03°37'·91E (1M E of Buitenhaven ent).

BRESKENS
ARV-VH ⚓ Q; 51°24'·71N 03°33'·89E.
VH2 (Vaarwaterlangs Hoofdplaat) ⌑ 51°24'·34N 03°33'·90E.
Yacht hbr, W mole ⚡ FG 7m; in fog FY; Gy post; 51°24'·03N 03°34'·06E. E mole ⚡ FR 6m; Gy mast; 51°23'·95N 03°34'·09E.

WESTERSCHELDE: TERNEUZEN TO PAAL

TERNEUZEN
Nieuw Neuzenpolder ldg lts 125°, both Oc 5s 6/16m 9/13M; intens 117°-133°; synch. Front, W col, B bands; 51°20'·97N 03°47'·24E. Rear, B & W twr; 365m from front.
Oost Buitenhaven E mole ⚡ FR 5M; 51°20'·56N 03°49'·19E.
Former ferry hbr (W part) & marinas (E part), W mole head ⚡ FG, Gy mast; 51°20'·57N 03°49'·64E. E mole, FR.
W mole ⚡ Oc WRG 5s 15m W9M, R7M, G6M; 090°-R-115°-W-120°-G-130°-W-245°-G-249°-W-279°-G-245°-W-279°-R-004°; B & W post; 51°20'·54N 03°49'·58E, close SW of ⚡ FG.

HANSWEERT
W mole ⚡ Oc WRG 10s 9m W9M, R7M, G6M; (in fog FY); 288°-R-311°-G-320°-W-332·5°-G-348·5°-R-042·5°-R-061·5°-W-078°-G-099°-W-114·5°-R-127·5°-W-288°; R twr, W bands; 51°26'·41N 04°00'·53E.

BELGIUM
ZANDVLIET TO ANTWERPEN

ZANDVLIET
Dir ⚡ 118·3°,WRG 20m W4M, R/ G3M; 116·63°-Oc G-117·17°- FG-117·58°-Alt GW-118·63°-F-118·63°-Alt RW-119·18°-FR-119·58°-Oc R-120·13°; 51°20'·61N 04°16'·47E, near Zandvliet locks.

ANTWERPEN
No 107 ⚓ Iso G 8s, 51°14'·12N 04°23'·80E (Kattendijksluis for Willemdok ⊕).
Royerssluis, ldg lts 091°, both FR. Ent FR/FG.
No. 109 ⚓ Iso G 8s; 51°13'·88N 04°23'·87E, (off Linkeroever ⊕).
Linkeroever marina ⚓ F WR 9m W3M, R2M; shore-W-283°- R-shore; B ⊙, R lantern; 51°13'·91N 04°23'·70E. Marina ent, FR/FG.

COASTAL MARKS
SWW ⌑ Fl (4) R 20s; 51°21'·95N 03°00'·94E; Wandelaar.
WBN ⬥ QG; 51°21'·50N 03°02'·59E; Wandelaar.
Oostende Bank N ⚓ Q; 51°21'·20N 02°52'·93E.
Wenduine Bank E ⌑ QR; 51°18'·83N 03°01'·64E.
Wenduine Bank W ⚓ Q (9) 15s; 51°17'·23N 02°52'·76E.
Nautica Ena wreck ⚓ Q; 51°18'·08N 02°52'·79E.
Oostendebank E ⌑ Fl (4) R 20s; 51°17'·35N 02°51'·91E.
Oostendebank W ⚓ Q (9)15s; 51°16'·20N 02°44'·74E.
LST 420 ⚓ Q (9)15s; 51°15'·45N 02°40'·67E.
MBN ⚓ Q; 51°20'·82N 02°46'·29E.
Middelkerke Bank ⬥ Fl G 5s; 51°18'·19N 02°42'·75E.
Middelkerke Bank S ⌑ Q (9) R 15s; 51°14'·73N 02°41'·89E.
D1 ⚓ Q (3) 10s; 51°13'·95N 02°38'·59E.
BT Ratel ⌑ Fl (4) R 15s; 51°11'·63N 02°27'·92E; Buiten Ratel.

ZEEBRUGGE TO THE FRENCH BORDER

ZEEBRUGGE
AW ⚓ Iso 8s; 51°22'·41N 03°07'·05E.
Ldg lts 136°, both Oc 5s 22/45m 8M; 131°-141°; H24, synch; W cols, R bands. Front, 51°20'·71N 03°13'·11E. Rear, 890m SE.
SZ ⚓ Q (3) 10s; 51°23'·30N 03°08'·65E (Scheur Channel).
Z ⬥ QG; 51°22'·48N 03°09'·95E.
WZ ⚓ Q (9) 15s; 51°22'·57N 03°10'·72E.
W outer mole ⚡ Oc G 7s 31m 7M; G vert strip lts visible from seaward; 057°-267°; *Horn (3) 30s;* IPTS; 51°21'·74N 03°11'·17E.

E outer mole ⚡ Oc R 7s 31m 7M; R vert strip lts visible from seaward; 087°-281°; *Bell 25s;* 51°21'·78N 03°11'·86E.
Ldg lts 154°: Front, Oc WR 6s 20m 3M, 135°-W-160°-R-169°; W pylon, R bands; 51°20'·33N 03°12'·89E. Rear, Oc 6s 38m 3M, H24, synch; 520m from front.
Leopold II mole ☆ Oc WR 15s 22m, **W20M, R18M**; 068°-W-145°-R-212°-W-296°; IPTS; *Horn (3+1) 90s;* 51°20'·85N 03°12'·17E. Entrance to Marina and FV hbr 51°19'·88N 03°11'·85E.

BLANKENBERGE
Promenade pier Fl (3) Y 20s, 8m 4M; 51°19'·28N 03°08'·18E.
Lt ho ☆ Fl (2) 8s 30m **20M**; 065°-245°; W twr, B top; 51°18'·75N 03°06'·85E.
Ldg lts 134°, both FR 5/9m 3/10M, R cross (X) topmarks on masts; front 51°18'·70N 03°08'·82E; rear 81m from front.
E pier ⚡ FR 12m 11M; R290°-245°(315°); W ○ twr; 51°18'·91N 03°06'·56E.
W pier ⚡ FG 14m 11M; intens 065°-290°, unintens 290°-335°; W ○ twr; 51°18'·89N 03°06'·42E.
OBST 4 – OBST 14 are eleven ⚓s Q approx 3ca offshore, marking Spoil Ground between Blankenberge and Oostende.

OOSTENDE
Oostendebank East ⌑ Fl (4) R 20s; 51°17'·35N 02°51'·91E.
Wenduinebank West ⚓ Q (9) 15s; 51°17'·23N 02°52'·76E.
Buitenstroombank ⚓ Q; 51°15'·17N 02°51'·71E.
Binnenstroombank ⚓ Q (3) 10s; 51°14'·47N 02°53'·65E.
Ldg lts 143°: both Iso 4s (triple vert) 36/46m 4M, 068°-218°; X on metal mast, R/W bands. Front, 51°13'·80N 02°55'·89E.
Oostende lt ho ☆ Fl (3) 10s 65m **27M**; obsc 069·5°-071°; Gy twr, 2 sinusoidal Bu bands; 51°14'·18N 02°55'·84E.
IPTS is shown from sig mast 51°14'·25N 02°55'·44E, plus QY when chan closed for ferry.
Inner W pier ⚡ FG 12m 10M; G057°-327°(270°); W ○ twr 51°14'·31N 02°55'·03E.

NIEUWPOORT
Zuidstroombank ⌑ Fl R 5s; 51°12'·28N 02°47'·37E.
Weststroombank ⌑ Fl (4) R 20s; 51°11'·34N 02°43'·03E.
Wreck 4 ⚓ Q (6) + L Fl 15s; 51°10'·90N 02°405'·03E.
Nieuwpoort Bank ⚓ Q (9) 15s; 51°10'·16N 02°36'·09E.
Oostduinkerke ⚓ Q; 51°09'·15N 02°39'·44E.
Lt ho ☆ Fl (2) R 14s 28m **16M**; R/W twr; 51°09'·27N 02°43'·79E.
E pier ⚡ FR 10m 10M; R025°-250°(225°), R307°-347°(40°); W ○ twr; 51°09'·41N 02°43'·08E.
W pier ⚡ FG 10m 9M; G025°-250°(225°), G284°-324°(40°); W ○ twr; 51°09'·35N 02°43'·00E.
⚡ QG 51°08'·65N 02°44'·31E marks the Y-junction where the channel forks stbd for KYCN and port for WSKLM and VVW-N.

WESTDIEP and PASSE DE ZUYDCOOTE
Den Oever wreck 2 ⚓ Q; 51°08'·11N 02°37'·43E.
Wreck 1 ⚓ Q; 51°08'·32N 02°35'·03E (adjacent to ⌑ next line).
Wave recorder ⌑ Fl (5) Y 20s; 51°08'·25N 02°34'·98E.
Trapegeer ⬥ Fl G 10s; 51°08'·41N 02°34'·36E.
E12 ⚓ VQ (6) + L Fl 10s; 51°07'·89N 02°30'·68E.
French waters, for continuity:
CME ⚓ Q (3) 10s; 51°07'·30N 02°30'·00E.
E11 ⚓ Fl G 4s; 51°06'·90N 02°30'·90E.
E10 ⚓ Fl (2) R 6s; 51°06'·30N 02°30'·47E.
E9 ⚓ Fl (2) G 6s; 51°05'·64N 02°29'·68E.
E8 ⚓ Fl (3) R 12s; 51°05'·16N 02°28'·67E.

Netherlands

2.4 PASSAGE INFORMATION

More Passage Information is threaded between harbours in this Area. **Bibliography:** *N Sea Passage Pilot* (Imray/Navin). *Cruising Guide to the Netherlands* (Imray/Navin). NP 55 *N Sea (East) Pilot*. NP 28 *Dover Strait Pilot*. *Hafenhandbuch Nordsee* (DSV-Verlag).

CHARTS, PSSA AND TSS

While AC 2182A, 1405/06/08, 1630/31/32/33, 1872 suffice for coastal passages and entry to the main ports, larger scale **Dutch yacht charts** (1800 series) are essential for exploring the cruising grounds along this coast or entering the smaller hbrs. Inland, the ANWB booklet-style chart (€19.95) of the *Staande-Mast Route* (Fixed Mast Route; see Stande Maastroute) is very detailed with copious, but intelligible, notes in Dutch.

From the Ems estuary west to Den Helder a **Particularly Sensitive Sea Area** (PSSA) extends 3M seaward from the West Frisian Islands. Yachts should carefully avoid damaging the maritime environment and marine organisms living in it.

The Terschelling-German Bight TSS, Off Vlieland TSS and Off Texel TSS lie between 5 and 10M to seaward of the West Frisian Islands. Cruising yachts are advised to navigate within this relatively narrow ITZ. Further offshore, and particularly in and near the Off Vlieland TSS, West Friesland TSS and Botney Ground TSS, navigation is further complicated by the many oil and gas fields. For general notes on North Sea oil & gas installations, see Area 3. Up to date charts are essential, particularly AC 1406, 1408 and 1423.

CROSSING THE NORTH SEA TO THE UK

From ports S of Hoek van Holland make for NHR-SE, to cross the TSS for destinations between Harwich and Great Yarmouth (AC 1406, 1408, 1872, 2449, 3371). From ports N of Hoek van Holland passages can be more problematic. For example, a route from IJmuiden to the Humber crosses two DW routes, N and NW of Brown Ridge, and then runs into extensive offshore Gas Fields. These might cause you to opt for two shorter legs, stopping a night at Great Yarmouth. Similar thinking might apply if coming out of Den Helder, even if a stop at Great Yarmouth might incur some southing. From east of Den Helder, make ground west via the ITZ before taking departure.

2.5 SPECIAL NOTES: NETHERLANDS

PROVINCES are given in lieu of UK 'counties'.

CHARTS The following types of chart are available from agents. The Chart catalogue (HP7) is downloadable from www.hydro.nl:

- Zeekaarten (equivalent to AC) are issued by the Royal Netherlands Navy Hydrographer and corrected by Notices to Mariners (*Berichten aan Zeevarenden* or *BaZ*).
- 1800 series *voor Kust-en Binnenwateren* (coastal and inland waters) are yacht charts (DYC) issued annually in March by the Hydrographer in 8 folios (1801-1812, excluding 1802/4/6 & 8); about 9 loose double-sided sheets (54 x 38cm) per folio.

TIME ZONE is –0100, but add 1 hr for DST in the summer months.

TIDES HP 33 *Waterstanden & Stromen* (Tide tables and tidal streams in **English** and Dutch, €22·50) is most useful especially if cruising Dutch waters for any length of time. It contains tide tables for 15 Dutch and 2 Belgian coastal ports; and 8 tidal stream atlases, including Westerschelde, Oosterschelde and the Maas.

REGULATIONS Discharge of toilet waste from recreational boats is forbidden in all Dutch waters, including inland waterways, lakes and the Waddenzee. Carry evidence (receipts) that any red diesel in your tanks is duty paid.

MARINAS Most marinas are private YCs or Watersport Associations (WSV or WV): *Gemeentelijke (Gem)* = municipal. Marinas with >50 berths must have a pump-out unit ✪. Sometimes (in Belgium also) berth-holders show a green tally if a berth is free, or a red tally if returning same day, but check with HM. Duty-free fuel (coloured red) is not available for leisure craft and may only be carried in the tank, NOT in cans. A tourist tax (Touristenbelasting) of €0.55–€1.82/head/night is often levied. VAT (BTW) is 21%. A useful website covering other marinas is www.allejachthavens.nl

CUSTOMS Ports of entry are: Delfzijl, Lauwersoog, W Terschelling, Vlieland*, Harlingen, Kornwerderzand, Den Helder, IJmuiden, Scheveningen, Hoek van Holland, Maassluis, Schiedam, Vlaardingen, Rotterdam, Roompot*, Vlissingen, Terneuzen and Breskens. *Summer only. Den Oever and Stellendam are *not* Ports of entry.

FERRIES TO THE UK IJmuiden-Newcastle; Hoek van Holland-Harwich; Rotterdam (Europoort)-Hull.

BUOYAGE Buoys are often named by the abbreviations of the banks or chans which they mark (eg VL = Vliestroom). A division buoy has the abbreviations of both chans meeting there, eg VL2-SG2 = as above, plus Schuitengat.

Some minor, tidal channels are marked by withies: SHM bound ⚲; PHM unbound ⚲. On tidal flats (eg Friesland) where the direction of main flood stream is uncertain, bound withies are on the S side of a chan and unbound on the N side; the banks thus marked are steep-to. In minor chans the buoyage may be moved without notice to accommodate changes.

The SIGNI buoyage system is used in the IJsselmeer, but not in the Eems, Waddenzee and Westerschelde.

SIGNALS When **motor-sailing** yachts must by law hoist a ▼ and when **at anchor** a black ball ●; these laws are rigidly enforced.

IPTS are widely used at coastal ports. Local signals, if any, are given where possible.

Sluicing signals may be shown by day: A blue board, with the word 'SPUIEN' on it; by night 3 ● in a △; sometimes both at once.

Storm warning signals, lts only, are shown by day & night at West Terschelling, Den Helder and IJmuiden; see Reference Data.

R/T In emergency call *Den Helder Rescue* Ch 16 for Netherlands CG (see Reference Data); or the working channel of a VTS sector or nearest lock or bridge. Monitor TSS info broadcasts and VTS sector channels. Ch 30/31 is for Dutch marinas (UK VHF sets need to be modified). Note: Do not use Ch M in Dutch waters, where it is a salvage frequency. Ch 13 is for commercial ship-ship calling. English is the second language and widely spoken.

TELEPHONE To call UK from the Netherlands, dial 00-44; then the UK area code minus the prefix 0, followed by the number required. To call the Netherlands from UK dial 00-31 then the area code minus the prefix 0 followed by two or three digits, followed by a 7 or 6 digits subscriber no. Mobile phone Nos start 06.

Emergency: Fire, Police, Ambulance, dial 112 (free); Non-emergency 0900 8844 (local tariff).

PUBLIC HOLIDAYS New Year's Day, Easter Sun and Mon, Queen's Birthday (30 April), Liberation Day (5 May), Ascension Day, Whit Mon, Christmas and Boxing Days.

BRITISH CONSULS Contact British Consulate-General, Koningslaan 44, 1075 AE Amsterdam; ☎ 020 676 4343. Or British Embassy, Lange Voorhout 10, 2514 ED The Hague; ☎ 070 4270 427.

INLAND WATERWAYS The sealocks at Kornwerderzand, Den Oever (IJsselmeer), IJmuiden, Stellendam and Roompotsluis are fully covered. The Staandemast (mast-up) route (Area map) and the IJsselmeer are outlined. Lack of space precludes detailed coverage of other harbours in the very extensive and enjoyable inland seas, waterways and canals.

Regulations. All craft must carry a copy of waterway regulations, *Binnenvaartpolitiereglement (BPR)*, as given in Dutch in the annual ANWB *Wateralmanak Vol 1* or available separately. Vol 2, also in Dutch, is essential reading; it gives pictograph details of marinas and the opening hours of bridges and locks.

Qualifications. Craft >15m LOA or capable of more than 20kph (11kn) must be skippered by the holder of an RYA Coastal Skipper's Certificate or higher qualification; *plus* an International Certificate of Competence (ICC) endorsed for Inland waterways, ie CEVNI.

Bridges and locks mostly work VHF Ch 18, 20 or 22, but CEVNI light signals (shown up/down-stream) largely negate the need for R/T. The most commonly seen signals include:

●   = Bridge closed (opens on request).

To request bridges to open, call on VHF low power (1 watt), or sound 'K' (—·—).

● over ●   = Bridge about to open.
●   = Bridge open.

2.6 TSS OFF THE NORTHERN NETHERLANDS

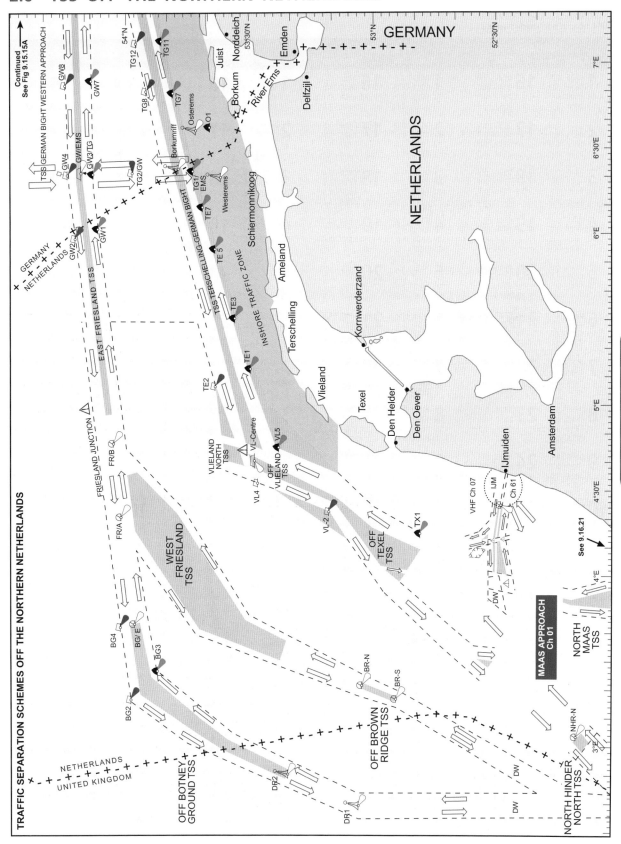

STANDARD TIME UT –01
Subtract 1 hour for UT
For German Summer Time add
ONE hour in **non-shaded areas**

HELGOLAND LAT 54°11'N LONG 7°53'E
TIMES AND HEIGHTS OF HIGH AND LOW WATERS

Dates in **red** are **SPRINGS**
Dates in **blue** are **NEAPS**

YEAR 2015

JANUARY

Time	m	Time	m
1 0226 / 0815 / TH 1505 / 2053	0.9 / 3.0 / 0.8 / 2.9	**16** 0126 / 0715 / F 1405 / 1957	1.0 / 2.8 / 0.9 / 2.8
2 0341 / 0925 / F 1612 / 2156	0.8 / 3.0 / 0.8 / 3.0	**17** 0245 / 0830 / SA 1519 / 2108	1.0 / 2.9 / 0.8 / 2.9
3 0446 / 1025 / SA 1711 / 2251	0.7 / 3.0 / 0.7 / 3.1	**18** 0357 / 0940 / SU 1626 / 2210	0.8 / 2.9 / 0.7 / 3.0
4 0541 / 1117 / SU 1801 / 2339	0.6 / 3.0 / 0.6 / 3.1	**19** 0500 / 1040 / M 1724 / 2304	0.7 / 3.0 / 0.6 / 3.1
5 0628 / 1203 / M 1842 / ○	0.6 / 3.0 / 0.6	**20** 0556 / 1133 / TU 1816 / ● 2353	0.5 / 3.1 / 0.6 / 3.2
6 0019 / 0708 / TU 1242 / 1918	3.2 / 0.5 / 3.0 / 0.6	**21** 0647 / 1223 / W 1907	0.4 / 3.1 / 0.5
7 0057 / 0744 / W 1318 / 1952	3.2 / 0.6 / 3.0 / 0.6	**22** 0040 / 0737 / TH 1312 / 1956	3.3 / 0.4 / 3.1 / 0.4
8 0133 / 0819 / TH 1354 / 2026	3.3 / 0.6 / 3.0 / 0.7	**23** 0128 / 0827 / F 1400 / 2042	3.3 / 0.4 / 3.1 / 0.4
9 0206 / 0851 / F 1427 / 2057	3.3 / 0.7 / 3.0 / 0.7	**24** 0213 / 0912 / SA 1444 / 2124	3.4 / 0.3 / 3.0 / 0.4
10 0237 / 0921 / SA 1459 / 2127	3.2 / 0.7 / 3.0 / 0.7	**25** 0257 / 0956 / SU 1527 / 2207	3.3 / 0.3 / 3.0 / 0.4
11 0308 / 0953 / SU 1533 / 2201	3.2 / 0.8 / 2.9 / 0.8	**26** 0343 / 1040 / M 1613 / 2252	3.3 / 0.5 / 3.0 / 0.5
12 0343 / 1027 / M 1610 / 2236	3.1 / 0.8 / 2.9 / 0.9	**27** 0433 / 1125 / TU 1701 / ☽ 2340	3.2 / 0.6 / 2.9 / 0.6
13 0419 / 1102 / TU 1648 / ☽ 2317	3.1 / 0.8 / 2.8 / 0.9	**28** 0526 / 1212 / W 1755	3.1 / 0.7 / 2.8
14 0503 / 1146 / W 1737	3.0 / 0.9 / 2.8	**29** 0036 / 0627 / TH 1312 / 1901	0.7 / 2.9 / 0.8 / 2.8
15 0013 / 0602 / TH 1249 / 1843	1.0 / 2.9 / 0.9 / 2.8	**30** 0150 / 0742 / F 1428 / 2019	0.8 / 2.9 / 0.9 / 2.8
		31 0315 / 0901 / SA 1548 / 2134	0.8 / 2.8 / 0.8 / 2.9

FEBRUARY

Time	m	Time	m
1 0431 / 1011 / SU 1655 / 2237	0.7 / 2.9 / 0.7 / 3.0	**16** 0325 / 0910 / M 1558 / 2143	0.7 / 2.8 / 0.7 / 2.9
2 0529 / 1106 / M 1746 / 2325	0.6 / 2.9 / 0.6 / 3.1	**17** 0439 / 1021 / TU 1705 / 2244	0.5 / 2.9 / 0.6 / 3.1
3 0614 / 1149 / TU 1827	0.5 / 2.9 / 0.6	**18** 0540 / 1118 / W 1802 / 2336	0.4 / 3.0 / 0.5 / 3.2
4 0004 / 0652 / W 1226 / ○ 1902	3.2 / 0.5 / 3.0 / 0.6	**19** 0633 / 1207 / TH 1853 / ●	0.3 / 3.1 / 0.4
5 0040 / 0727 / TH 1300 / 1936	3.2 / 0.5 / 3.0 / 0.5	**20** 0023 / 0723 / F 1255 / 1941	3.3 / 0.2 / 3.1 / 0.3
6 0113 / 0759 / F 1331 / 2007	3.2 / 0.5 / 3.0 / 0.5	**21** 0110 / 0811 / SA 1342 / 2027	3.3 / 0.2 / 3.1 / 0.3
7 0144 / 0828 / SA 1401 / 2036	3.2 / 0.6 / 3.0 / 0.5	**22** 0157 / 0857 / SU 1427 / 2110	3.3 / 0.2 / 3.1 / 0.3
8 0213 / 0857 / SU 1432 / 2106	3.2 / 0.6 / 3.0 / 0.6	**23** 0242 / 0939 / M 1509 / 2151	3.3 / 0.3 / 3.1 / 0.3
9 0244 / 0928 / M 1506 / 2139	3.1 / 0.6 / 2.9 / 0.6	**24** 0326 / 1018 / TU 1550 / 2232	3.2 / 0.4 / 3.0 / 0.4
10 0317 / 1000 / TU 1540 / 2211	3.1 / 0.6 / 2.9 / 0.6	**25** 0410 / 1055 / W 1631 / ☾ 2313	3.1 / 0.5 / 3.0 / 0.5
11 0349 / 1028 / W 1610 / 2241	3.1 / 0.7 / 2.9 / 0.7	**26** 0457 / 1136 / TH 1718	3.0 / 0.7 / 2.9
12 0421 / 1059 / TH 1646 / ☾ 2323	3.0 / 0.7 / 2.8 / 0.8	**27** 0003 / 0552 / F 1231 / 1820	0.6 / 2.8 / 0.9 / 2.8
13 0508 / 1151 / F 1743	2.8 / 0.8 / 2.7	**28** 0114 / 0706 / SA 1350 / 1942	0.7 / 2.7 / 0.9 / 2.8
14 0030 / 0619 / SA 1309 / 1903	0.8 / 2.7 / 0.8 / 2.7		
15 0157 / 0746 / SU 1438 / 2029	0.8 / 2.7 / 0.8 / 2.8		

MARCH

Time	m	Time	m
1 0244 / 0833 / SU 1519 / 2109	0.8 / 2.7 / 0.8 / 2.8	**16** 0123 / 0714 / M 1405 / 1956	0.7 / 2.6 / 0.8 / 2.8
2 0409 / 0952 / M 1636 / 2218	0.7 / 2.7 / 0.7 / 2.9	**17** 0258 / 0845 / TU 1534 / 2117	0.5 / 2.7 / 0.7 / 2.9
3 0512 / 1049 / TU 1728 / 2306	0.6 / 2.8 / 0.6 / 3.0	**18** 0417 / 1000 / W 1645 / 2221	0.5 / 2.9 / 0.5 / 3.1
4 0554 / 1130 / W 1807 / 2343	0.5 / 2.9 / 0.5 / 3.1	**19** 0520 / 1059 / TH 1743 / 2315	0.3 / 3.0 / 0.4 / 3.2
5 0629 / 1204 / TH 1841 / ○	0.4 / 2.9 / 0.5	**20** 0614 / 1148 / F 1834 / ●	0.2 / 3.0 / 0.3
6 0016 / 0702 / F 1235 / 1914	3.1 / 0.4 / 3.0 / 0.4	**21** 0003 / 0704 / SA 1234 / 1922	3.1 / 0.1 / 3.1 / 0.2
7 0048 / 0733 / SA 1305 / 1945	3.1 / 0.4 / 3.0 / 0.4	**22** 0050 / 0750 / SU 1320 / 2008	3.3 / 0.1 / 3.1 / 0.2
8 0119 / 0802 / SU 1336 / 2014	3.1 / 0.4 / 3.0 / 0.4	**23** 0136 / 0835 / M 1404 / 2051	3.3 / 0.2 / 3.1 / 0.2
9 0150 / 0832 / M 1407 / 2046	3.1 / 0.5 / 3.0 / 0.4	**24** 0222 / 0915 / TU 1445 / 2132	3.3 / 0.3 / 3.1 / 0.3
10 0221 / 0904 / TU 1441 / 2120	3.1 / 0.5 / 3.0 / 0.4	**25** 0305 / 0952 / W 1524 / 2211	3.2 / 0.4 / 3.1 / 0.3
11 0255 / 0936 / W 1514 / 2151	3.1 / 0.5 / 3.0 / 0.4	**26** 0347 / 1026 / TH 1603 / 2249	3.1 / 0.5 / 3.0 / 0.5
12 0326 / 1003 / TH 1542 / 2218	3.0 / 0.5 / 2.9 / 0.5	**27** 0430 / 1103 / F 1646 / ☾ 2334	2.9 / 0.6 / 2.9 / 0.6
13 0354 / 1028 / F 1612 / ☾ 2252	2.9 / 0.6 / 2.8 / 0.6	**28** 0522 / 1155 / SA 1745	2.7 / 0.8 / 2.8
14 0434 / 1112 / SA 1703 / 2353	2.7 / 0.7 / 2.7 / 0.8	**29** 0039 / 0632 / SU 1310 / 1904	0.7 / 2.6 / 0.8 / 2.8
15 0542 / 1229 / SU 1823	2.6 / 0.8 / 2.7	**30** 0206 / 0758 / M 1441 / 2032	0.7 / 2.5 / 0.8 / 2.8
		31 0334 / 0920 / TU 1603 / 2146	0.6 / 2.6 / 0.7 / 2.9

APRIL

Time	m	Time	m
1 0441 / 1020 / W 1658 / 2235	0.5 / 2.8 / 0.6 / 3.0	**16** 0353 / 0936 / TH 1620 / 2155	0.4 / 2.8 / 0.5 / 3.1
2 0523 / 1059 / TH 1736 / 2310	0.4 / 2.9 / 0.5 / 3.0	**17** 0455 / 1035 / F 1718 / 2250	0.3 / 2.9 / 0.4 / 3.2
3 0555 / 1132 / F 1811 / 2345	0.4 / 2.9 / 0.5 / 3.0	**18** 0550 / 1126 / SA 1812 / ● 2342	0.2 / 3.0 / 0.4 / 3.2
4 0629 / 1206 / SA 1846 / ○	0.4 / 2.9 / 0.4	**19** 0641 / 1213 / SU 1902	0.2 / 3.1 / 0.2
5 0019 / 0702 / SU 1238 / 1920	3.0 / 0.4 / 3.0 / 0.4	**20** 0030 / 0727 / M 1256 / 1947	3.2 / 0.2 / 3.1 / 0.2
6 0053 / 0734 / M 1310 / 1952	3.0 / 0.4 / 3.0 / 0.3	**21** 0115 / 0809 / TU 1338 / 2030	3.2 / 0.3 / 3.2 / 0.2
7 0125 / 0807 / TU 1343 / 2026	3.0 / 0.4 / 3.0 / 0.3	**22** 0200 / 0849 / W 1420 / 2110	3.1 / 0.3 / 3.2 / 0.3
8 0159 / 0840 / W 1417 / 2100	3.0 / 0.4 / 3.0 / 0.3	**23** 0243 / 0925 / TH 1500 / 2149	3.1 / 0.4 / 3.1 / 0.3
9 0233 / 0913 / TH 1450 / 2133	3.0 / 0.4 / 3.0 / 0.3	**24** 0325 / 1000 / F 1539 / 2227	2.9 / 0.5 / 3.0 / 0.4
10 0307 / 0942 / F 1522 / 2203	2.9 / 0.4 / 3.0 / 0.4	**25** 0408 / 1037 / SA 1622 / 2310	2.8 / 0.6 / 3.0 / 0.6
11 0340 / 1012 / SA 1556 / 2239	2.9 / 0.6 / 2.9 / 0.5	**26** 0457 / 1124 / SU 1714 / ☾	2.7 / 0.8 / 2.9
12 0422 / 1057 / SU 1646 / ☾ 2338	2.8 / 0.7 / 2.8 / 0.6	**27** 0006 / 0557 / M 1230 / 1822	0.7 / 2.6 / 0.8 / 2.8
13 0527 / 1210 / M 1800	2.7 / 0.8 / 2.8	**28** 0120 / 0712 / TU 1351 / 1941	0.7 / 2.5 / 0.8 / 2.8
14 0103 / 0653 / TU 1342 / 1929	0.6 / 2.7 / 0.8 / 2.9	**29** 0241 / 0830 / W 1511 / 2054	0.6 / 2.6 / 0.7 / 2.9
15 0235 / 0822 / W 1509 / 2050	0.6 / 2.7 / 0.7 / 3.0	**30** 0350 / 0933 / TH 1612 / 2149	0.5 / 2.7 / 0.6 / 2.9

Chart Datum: 1·68 metres below Normal Null (German reference level). HAT is 3·0 metres above Chart Datum.

STANDARD TIME UT –01
Subtract 1 hour for UT
For German Summer Time add
ONE hour in **non-shaded areas**

HELGOLAND   LAT 54°11'N LONG 7°53'E
TIMES AND HEIGHTS OF HIGH AND LOW WATERS

Dates in red are **SPRINGS**
Dates in blue are **NEAPS**

YEAR 2015

Netherlands

MAY

Time	m		Time	m
1 0437	0.4	**16** 0427	0.3	
1017	2.8	1008	2.9	
F 1655	0.5	SA 1652	0.4	
2230	3.0	2226	3.1	
2 0514	0.4	**17** 0524	0.3	
1054	2.9	1102	3.0	
SA 1734	0.5	SU 1749	0.4	
2309	3.0	2321	3.2	
3 0552	0.4	**18** 0618	0.3	
1132	3.0	1151	3.1	
SU 1815	0.5	M 1842	0.3	
2348	3.0	●		
4 0630	0.4	**19** 0012	3.1	
1210	3.0	0705	0.3	
M 1853	0.4	TU 1235	3.1	
○		1927	0.2	
5 0024	3.1	**20** 0056	3.1	
0706	0.4	0745	0.3	
TU 1244	3.1	W 1315	3.2	
1929	0.4	2008	0.3	
6 0100	3.0	**21** 0140	3.0	
0742	0.4	0823	0.4	
W 1319	3.1	TH 1357	3.2	
2005	0.4	2049	0.3	
7 0137	3.0	**22** 0223	3.0	
0818	0.4	0901	0.4	
TH 1354	3.1	F 1438	3.2	
2042	0.3	2128	0.4	
8 0215	3.0	**23** 0306	2.9	
0853	0.4	0938	0.5	
F 1431	3.1	SA 1519	3.1	
2118	0.3	2207	0.5	
9 0254	2.9	**24** 0347	2.9	
0928	0.5	1015	0.6	
SA 1508	3.1	SU 1559	3.1	
2155	0.4	2247	0.6	
10 0335	2.9	**25** 0431	2.8	
1008	0.6	1056	0.8	
SU 1550	3.1	M 1644	3.0	
2240	0.5	◑ 2333	0.7	
11 0422	2.8	**26** 0521	2.7	
1057	0.7	1148	0.8	
M 1642	3.0	TU 1737	2.9	
◑ 2338	0.5			
12 0523	2.8	**27** 0030	0.7	
1203	0.7	0620	2.6	
TU 1749	3.0	W 1253	0.8	
		1841	2.9	
13 0052	0.6	**28** 0137	0.7	
0639	2.7	0727	2.6	
W 1323	0.7	TH 1405	0.8	
1908	3.0	1950	2.8	
14 0213	0.5	**29** 0245	0.6	
0758	2.8	0832	2.7	
TH 1443	0.6	F 1512	0.7	
2024	3.1	2053	2.9	
15 0325	0.4	**30** 0342	0.5	
0909	2.8	0926	2.8	
F 1552	0.5	SA 1606	0.7	
2128	3.1	2145	3.0	
		31 0430	0.5	
		1013	2.9	
		SU 1655	0.6	
		2232	3.0	

JUNE

Time	m		Time	m
1 0515	0.5	**16** 0556	0.4	
1057	3.0	1131	3.1	
M 1741	0.6	TU 1824	0.3	
2316	3.0	● 2356	3.1	
2 0558	0.5	**17** 0644	0.4	
1139	3.1	1216	3.1	
TU 1825	0.5	W 1909	0.3	
○ 2357	3.1			
3 0639	0.4	**18** 0041	3.0	
1218	3.1	0724	0.4	
W 1905	0.4	TH 1257	3.2	
		1950	0.3	
4 0037	3.1	**19** 0123	3.0	
0720	0.4	0802	0.4	
TH 1256	3.2	F 1338	3.2	
1946	0.4	2030	0.4	
5 0119	3.1	**20** 0205	3.0	
0800	0.4	0840	0.5	
F 1337	3.2	SA 1419	3.3	
2027	0.4	2108	0.5	
6 0202	3.0	**21** 0245	3.0	
0840	0.4	0916	0.6	
SA 1417	3.2	SU 1457	3.2	
2108	0.4	2145	0.6	
7 0244	3.0	**22** 0323	2.9	
0920	0.5	0951	0.7	
SU 1459	3.2	M 1534	3.2	
2151	0.4	2221	0.7	
8 0330	2.9	**23** 0401	2.9	
1006	0.6	1027	0.8	
M 1546	3.2	TU 1612	3.1	
2241	0.5	2259	0.7	
9 0421	2.9	**24** 0442	2.8	
1057	0.6	1108	0.8	
TU 1640	3.2	W 1654	3.0	
◐ 2337	0.5	◑ 2341	0.8	
10 0519	2.8	**25** 0527	2.8	
1156	0.6	1157	0.8	
W 1740	3.1	TH 1744	2.9	
11 0040	0.5	**26** 0032	0.8	
0624	2.8	0622	2.7	
TH 1303	0.6	F 1257	0.8	
1848	3.1	1845	2.9	
12 0148	0.5	**27** 0135	0.8	
0733	2.8	0726	2.8	
F 1416	0.7	SA 1406	0.8	
1959	3.1	1952	2.9	
13 0256	0.5	**28** 0242	0.7	
0841	2.9	0830	2.8	
SA 1526	0.6	SU 1514	0.8	
2106	3.1	2056	2.9	
14 0400	0.5	**29** 0343	0.6	
0943	3.0	0929	2.9	
SU 1630	0.5	M 1614	0.7	
2207	3.1	2154	3.0	
15 0500	0.4	**30** 0438	0.6	
1039	3.0	1021	3.0	
M 1730	0.4	TU 1708	0.6	
2304	3.1	2246	3.0	

JULY

Time	m		Time	m
1 0529	0.6	**16** 0626	0.5	
1110	3.1	1202	3.2	
W 1758	0.6	TH 1853	0.4	
2333	3.1	●		
2 0616	0.5	**17** 0027	3.0	
1154	3.2	0706	0.5	
TH 1844	0.5	F 1242	3.2	
○		1933	0.4	
3 0019	3.1	**18** 0107	3.0	
0702	0.5	0744	0.5	
F 1238	3.2	SA 1321	3.3	
1930	0.4	2011	0.5	
4 0105	3.1	**19** 0144	3.0	
0747	0.5	0820	0.6	
SA 1322	3.3	SU 1358	3.3	
2016	0.4	2046	0.6	
5 0150	3.1	**20** 0220	3.1	
0831	0.5	0853	0.6	
SU 1405	3.3	M 1431	3.3	
2100	0.4	2118	0.6	
6 0234	3.0	**21** 0253	3.0	
0913	0.6	0924	0.7	
M 1449	3.3	TU 1505	3.2	
2145	0.4	2150	0.7	
7 0320	3.0	**22** 0328	3.0	
0958	0.5	0958	0.7	
TU 1537	3.3	W 1540	3.2	
2235	0.4	2225	0.7	
8 0411	3.0	**23** 0405	2.9	
1049	0.5	1033	0.8	
W 1630	3.2	TH 1617	3.1	
◐ 2327	0.5	2258	0.8	
9 0505	2.9	**24** 0442	2.9	
1142	0.6	1110	0.8	
TH 1726	3.2	F 1655	3.0	
		◑ 2336	0.8	
10 0020	0.6	**25** 0524	2.8	
0602	2.9	1157	0.9	
F 1240	0.6	SA 1745	2.9	
1827	3.1			
11 0119	0.6	**26** 0029	0.8	
0705	2.9	0621	2.8	
SA 1348	0.7	SU 1302	0.9	
1935	3.1	1851	2.8	
12 0226	0.7	**27** 0139	0.8	
0813	2.9	0732	2.8	
SU 1503	0.7	M 1419	0.9	
2047	3.0	2006	2.8	
13 0337	0.7	**28** 0255	0.8	
0921	3.0	0844	2.9	
M 1615	0.6	TU 1534	0.8	
2153	3.0	2118	2.9	
14 0443	0.6	**29** 0404	0.7	
1023	3.0	0949	3.0	
TU 1716	0.5	W 1639	0.7	
2252	3.0	2221	3.0	
15 0539	0.5	**30** 0503	0.6	
1116	3.1	1044	3.1	
W 1808	0.4	TH 1735	0.6	
2343	3.0	2315	3.1	
		31 0557	0.6	
		1134	3.2	
		F 1826	0.5	
		○		

AUGUST

Time	m		Time	m
1 0003	3.1	**16** 0046	3.1	
0646	0.5	0724	0.6	
SA 1220	3.3	SU 1300	3.3	
1915	0.4	1947	0.5	
2 0049	3.2	**17** 0120	3.1	
0734	0.5	0757	0.6	
SU 1305	3.4	M 1333	3.3	
2003	0.4	2019	0.6	
3 0135	3.1	**18** 0151	3.1	
0819	0.4	0827	0.6	
M 1350	3.4	TU 1404	3.2	
2048	0.3	2048	0.6	
4 0219	3.1	**19** 0222	3.1	
0901	0.4	0857	0.6	
TU 1435	3.4	W 1436	3.2	
2132	0.4	2118	0.7	
5 0304	3.1	**20** 0256	3.0	
0945	0.4	0929	0.7	
W 1522	3.3	TH 1510	3.2	
2218	0.5	2152	0.7	
6 0352	3.0	**21** 0331	3.0	
1032	0.5	1003	0.7	
TH 1613	3.3	F 1544	3.1	
2305	0.6	2222	0.8	
7 0442	3.0	**22** 0404	3.0	
1121	0.6	1034	0.8	
F 1705	3.2	SA 1616	3.0	
◐ 2351	0.7	◑ 2250	0.8	
8 0533	3.0	**23** 0437	2.9	
1213	0.7	1110	0.9	
SA 1801	3.1	SU 1656	2.9	
		2333	0.9	
9 0045	0.8	**24** 0525	2.8	
0633	2.9	1207	0.9	
SU 1320	0.8	M 1758	2.8	
1909	2.9			
10 0155	0.9	**25** 0043	1.0	
0746	2.9	0638	2.8	
M 1442	0.8	TU 1329	0.9	
2028	2.9	1921	2.7	
11 0316	0.9	**26** 0209	0.9	
0904	3.0	0803	2.8	
TU 1603	0.7	W 1457	0.9	
2143	2.9	2046	2.8	
12 0429	0.8	**27** 0332	0.8	
1012	3.1	0919	3.0	
W 1707	0.6	TH 1613	0.7	
2243	3.0	2158	2.9	
13 0526	0.7	**28** 0441	0.6	
1104	3.1	1021	3.1	
TH 1755	0.5	F 1714	0.6	
2330	3.0	2256	3.1	
14 0609	0.6	**29** 0538	0.6	
1147	3.2	1112	3.2	
F 1836	0.5	SA 1807	0.5	
●		○ 2345	3.1	
15 0010	3.0	**30** 0629	0.5	
0647	0.6	1159	3.3	
SA 1225	3.2	SU 1856	0.4	
1913	0.5			
		31 0031	3.2	
		0716	0.4	
		M 1244	3.4	
		1944	0.3	

Chart Datum: 1·68 metres below Normal Null (German reference level). HAT is 3·0 metres above Chart Datum.

STANDARD TIME UT –01
Subtract 1 hour for UT
For German Summer Time add
ONE hour in **non-shaded areas**

HELGOLAND   LAT 54°11'N LONG 7°53'E
TIMES AND HEIGHTS OF HIGH AND LOW WATERS

Dates in red are **SPRINGS**
Dates in blue are **NEAPS**

YEAR 2015

SEPTEMBER

Time	m		Time	m
1 0116	3.2	**16** 0123	3.1
0802	0.4	0801	0.6
TU 1331	3.4	W 1338	3.2
2030	0.3	2018	0.6
2 0200	3.2	**17** 0154	3.1
0845	0.4	0832	0.6
W 1417	3.4	TH 1408	3.2
2113	0.4	2048	0.7
3 0244	3.2	**18** 0226	3.1
0928	0.4	0904	0.6
TH 1503	3.3	F 1441	3.1
2155	0.5	2120	0.7
4 0327	3.1	**19** 0259	3.1
1011	0.5	0936	0.7
F 1550	3.2	SA 1514	3.1
2236	0.7	2149	0.7
5 0412	3.1	**20** 0330	3.0
1055	0.6	1004	0.7
SA 1638	3.1	SU 1544	3.0
☽ 2318	0.8	2215	0.8
6 0500	3.0	**21** 0400	3.0
1144	0.8	1036	0.8
SU 1733	3.0	M 1622	2.9
		☾ 2253	0.9
7 0010	1.0	**22** 0445	2.9
0600	2.9	1128	0.9
M 1250	0.9	TU 1721	2.7
1842	2.8		
8 0122	1.0	**23** 0000	1.1
0718	2.9	0556	2.8
TU 1416	0.9	W 1250	1.0
2007	2.8	1846	2.7
9 0251	1.0	**24** 0132	1.1
0844	3.0	0726	2.9
W 1546	0.9	TH 1425	0.9
2130	2.8	2017	2.9
10 0413	0.9	**25** 0303	1.0
0958	3.1	0849	3.0
TH 1654	0.7	F 1547	0.7
2232	2.9	2134	2.9
11 0510	0.8	**26** 0416	0.8
1049	3.2	0955	3.1
F 1738	0.6	SA 1651	0.6
2313	3.0	2234	3.0
12 0549	0.7	**27** 0515	0.7
1126	3.2	1047	3.3
SA 1812	0.6	SU 1744	0.4
2346	3.0	2324	3.1
13 0623	0.6	**28** 0607	0.6
1206	3.2	1135	3.3
SU 1845	0.6	M 1834	0.4
●		○	
14 0019	3.1	**29** 0010	3.2
0658	0.6	0655	0.5
M 1234	3.2	TU 1222	3.4
1918	0.6	1921	0.4
15 0052	3.1	**30** 0055	3.2
0731	0.6	0741	0.4
TU 1307	3.2	W 1309	3.4
1949	0.6	2007	0.4

OCTOBER

Time	m		Time	m
1 0138	3.2	**16** 0128	3.1
0826	0.5	0808	0.6
TH 1356	3.4	F 1343	3.1
2049	0.5	2021	0.6
2 0221	3.3	**17** 0159	3.1
0908	0.4	0840	0.6
F 1442	3.3	SA 1415	3.1
2129	0.5	2052	0.6
3 0301	3.2	**18** 0231	3.1
0949	0.5	0912	0.6
SA 1526	3.1	SU 1448	3.0
2206	0.7	2121	0.7
4 0343	3.1	**19** 0303	3.1
1030	0.6	0942	0.7
SU 1612	3.0	M 1522	3.0
☽ 2246	0.9	2151	0.9
5 0430	3.1	**20** 0337	3.1
1117	0.8	1016	0.8
M 1705	2.9	TU 1602	2.9
2336	1.0	☾ 2231	1.0
6 0528	3.0	**21** 0422	3.0
1219	0.9	1108	1.0
TU 1812	2.7	W 1700	2.8
		2335	1.1
7 0047	1.1	**22** 0529	2.9
0644	2.9	1225	1.0
W 1342	1.0	TH 1819	2.8
1936	2.7		
8 0216	1.1	**23** 0102	1.1
0812	2.9	0654	3.0
TH 1513	0.9	F 1355	0.9
2101	2.8	1948	2.8
9 0342	1.0	**24** 0232	1.0
0929	3.0	0818	3.1
F 1625	0.8	SA 1518	0.8
2205	2.9	2106	2.9
10 0442	0.9	**25** 0347	0.9
1021	3.1	0926	3.2
SA 1709	0.7	SU 1623	0.6
2245	3.0	2208	3.0
11 0520	0.7	**26** 0447	0.7
1056	3.1	1021	3.2
SU 1740	0.6	M 1718	0.5
2316	3.0	2300	3.1
12 0553	0.7	**27** 0542	0.6
1130	3.1	1113	3.3
M 1811	0.6	TU 1810	0.4
2349	3.1	○ 2348	3.2
13 0628	0.7	**28** 0634	0.6
1206	3.1	1202	3.3
TU 1846	0.6	W 1858	0.4
●			
14 0024	3.1	**29** 0033	3.2
0703	0.6	0721	0.5
W 1240	3.1	TH 1249	3.3
1919	0.6	1942	0.5
15 0056	3.1	**30** 0115	3.2
0736	0.6	0805	0.5
TH 1312	3.1	F 1335	3.3
1950	0.6	2024	0.6
		31 0157	3.3
		0848	0.5
		SA 1421	3.2
		2103	0.7

NOVEMBER

Time	m		Time	m
1 0238	3.3	**16** 0209	3.2
0928	0.6	0854	0.6
SU 1505	3.1	M 1431	3.0
2141	0.7	2103	0.7
2 0320	3.2	**17** 0244	3.2
1008	0.7	0928	0.7
M 1550	3.0	TU 1509	3.0
2219	0.9	2139	0.9
3 0404	3.1	**18** 0323	3.2
1053	0.8	1008	0.8
TU 1640	2.8	W 1553	2.9
☽ 2306	1.0	2223	1.0
4 0457	3.1	**19** 0410	3.1
1148	1.0	1100	0.9
W 1740	2.7	TH 1648	2.9
		☾ 2322	1.0
5 0009	1.1	**20** 0511	3.1
0604	3.0	1208	0.9
TH 1258	1.0	F 1758	2.8
1852	2.7		
6 0127	1.1	**21** 0037	1.0
0721	2.9	0626	3.1
F 1419	1.0	SA 1327	0.9
2010	2.7	1918	2.8
7 0249	1.1	**22** 0159	1.0
0837	3.0	0746	3.1
SA 1532	0.9	SU 1445	0.8
2118	2.8	2034	2.9
8 0355	0.9	**23** 0315	0.9
0937	3.0	0857	3.2
SU 1624	0.8	M 1552	0.7
2205	2.9	2139	3.0
9 0441	0.8	**24** 0420	0.8
1019	3.1	0957	3.2
M 1701	0.7	TU 1652	0.6
2241	3.0	2235	3.1
10 0518	0.8	**25** 0520	0.7
1057	3.1	1053	3.2
TU 1737	0.7	W 1748	0.5
2318	3.1	○ 2327	3.2
11 0557	0.7	**26** 0614	0.6
1135	3.1	1145	3.2
W 1814	0.7	TH 1837	0.5
● 2355	3.1		
12 0636	0.7	**27** 0012	3.2
1212	3.1	0702	0.5
TH 1850	0.7	F 1232	3.2
		1920	0.5
13 0030	3.2	**28** 0054	3.3
0711	0.6	0745	0.5
F 1247	3.1	SA 1316	3.2
1924	0.6	2000	0.6
14 0103	3.2	**29** 0136	3.3
0746	0.6	0828	0.6
SA 1321	3.1	SU 1403	3.1
1958	0.7	2041	0.7
15 0136	3.2	**30** 0220	3.3
0820	0.6	0910	0.6
SU 1356	3.1	M 1448	3.1
2031	0.7	2120	0.7

DECEMBER

Time	m		Time	m
1 0301	3.3	**16** 0233	3.3
0950	0.7	0921	0.6
TU 1530	3.0	W 1500	3.0
2158	0.8	2133	0.7
2 0342	3.2	**17** 0314	3.3
1030	0.8	1005	0.7
W 1614	2.9	TH 1545	3.0
2239	1.0	2220	0.8
3 0426	3.1	**18** 0403	3.2
1115	0.9	1056	0.7
TH 1703	2.8	F 1638	2.9
☽ 2328	1.1	☽ 2313	0.9
4 0518	3.0	**19** 0458	3.2
1208	1.0	1154	0.8
F 1759	2.7	SA 1738	2.9
5 0029	1.1	**20** 0015	0.9
0620	2.9	0602	3.1
SA 1312	1.0	SU 1259	0.8
1905	2.7	1847	2.8
6 0140	1.1	**21** 0127	0.9
0730	2.9	0715	3.1
SU 1422	1.0	M 1411	0.8
2013	2.8	2000	2.9
7 0251	1.0	**22** 0243	0.9
0838	3.0	0829	3.1
M 1526	0.9	TU 1523	0.8
2113	2.9	2110	3.0
8 0351	1.0	**23** 0356	0.8
0934	3.0	0937	3.1
TU 1618	0.8	W 1629	0.7
2202	3.0	2212	3.1
9 0441	0.9	**24** 0501	0.9
1022	3.1	1038	3.1
W 1702	0.8	TH 1729	0.6
2245	3.1	2308	3.1
10 0526	0.8	**25** 0558	0.6
1105	3.1	1133	3.1
TH 1744	0.8	F 1820	0.5
2327	3.1	○ 2356	3.2
11 0609	0.7	**26** 0647	0.6
1145	3.1	1220	3.1
F 1823	0.7	SA 1903	0.5
●			
12 0005	3.2	**27** 0038	3.3
0648	0.7	0730	0.6
SA 1224	3.1	SU 1303	3.1
1902	0.7	1942	0.6
13 0041	3.2	**28** 0120	3.3
0727	0.6	0812	0.6
SU 1303	3.1	M 1347	3.1
1941	0.7	2023	0.6
14 0118	3.2	**29** 0203	3.3
0806	0.6	0853	0.7
M 1343	3.1	TU 1429	3.1
2018	0.7	2102	0.7
15 0156	3.3	**30** 0242	3.3
0843	0.6	0931	0.7
TU 1421	3.1	W 1508	3.0
2054	0.7	2137	0.7
		31 0318	3.3
		1005	0.8
		TH 1545	2.9
		2211	0.8

Chart Datum: 1·68 metres below Normal Null (German reference level). HAT is 3·0 metres above Chart Datum.

》 **FREE** monthly updates from 《《
www.reedsalmanac.co.uk

2.7 DELFZIJL

Groningen **53°18'·99N 07°00'·45E** ✷✷✷✷♵♵✿✿

CHARTS AC 3631, 3632; DYC 1812.6; Zeekaart 1555; Imray C26; ANWB A

TIDES –0025 Dover; ML 2·1; Duration 0605

Standard Port HELGOLAND (←—)

Times				Height (metres)			
High Water		Low Water		MHWS	MHWN	MLWN	MLWS
0200	0700	0200	0800	3·2	2·8	0·9	0·5
1400	1900	1400	2000				
Differences DELFZIJL							
+0020	–0005	–0040	0000	+0·5	+0·6	–0·1	–0·1
EEMSHAVEN							
–0025	–0045	–0115	–0045	0·0	+0·1	–0·1	–0·1
HUIBERTGAT							
–0150	–0150	–0210	–0210	–0·5	–0·4	–0·2	–0·2
SCHIERMONNIKOOG							
–0120	–0130	–0240	–0220	–0·3	–0·2	–0·2	–0·2

SHELTER Good in Handelshaven, where at Neptunus Marina a floating jetty acts as a wavebreak.

NAVIGATION From the E or N, WPT 53°38'·96N 06°27'·06E (Riffgat SWM buoy) 121°/4·2M to Nos 11/12 buoys. See also TSS off the Northern Netherlands.

From the W, WPT 53°36'·93N 06°19'·39E (Westereems SWM buoy) 091°/8·2M to join Riffgat at Nos 11/12 buoys.

Huibertgat lies parallel to and S of Westereems. It is marked by unlit R/W buoys H1-H5, least depths about 9m but prone to silt.

From Nos 11/12 buoys follow the well marked/lit river channel for approx 25M via Randzelgat or Alte Eems, Dukegat and Ostfriesisches Gatje to enter Zeehavenkanaal abeam Knock lt ho. Beware strong cross tides at the ent (Lat/Long under title).

INLAND ROUTE TO IJSSELMEER See Area Map and IJsselmeer.

LIGHTS AND MARKS See chartlet and Lights, buoys & waypoints. From the river, appr ldg lts 203°, both Iso 4s. Hbr ent, FG on W arm and FR on E arm (in fog, FY). Zeehavenkanaal, 2·5M long, has Fl G lts to N and Fl R to S. Entry sigs on both piers: 2 ● = No entry, unless cleared by Hbr office on VHF Ch 14.

COMMUNICATIONS (Code 0596) All vessels, except leisure craft, must call *Delfzijl Radar* VHF Ch 03 (H24) for VTS, co-ordinated with Ems Traffic; Traffic, weather and tidal info is broadcast every even H+10 on VHF Ch 14 in Dutch and English on request; *Ems Traffic* VHF Ch 15, 18, 20 & 21 (H24) broadcasts every H + 50 weather and tidal info in German, and gale warnings for coastal waters between Die Ems and Die Weser, see also Emden; CG (Police) 613831; Police 112; ⊖ 0598 696560; Brit Consul (020) 6764343; 🏥 644444; Port HM 640400, VHF Ch 66; HM 't Dok 616560; Eemskanaal Sea locks 613293, VHF Ch 26.

FACILITIES Neptunus Yacht Hbr (4·4m, 53°19'·80N 06°55'·86E) ☎ 615004, €0·24 per gross ton, D (not 0900-1700), ⌂, M. **Yacht Hbr 't Dok** at N end of the Old Eemskanaal in 4m, ⌑ €0·41, D. Note: Eems (Dutch) = Ems (German). **Ems Canal** L, ⚓, ⌑. **Motor Boat Club Abel Tasman** ☎ 616560 D, ⌷, ⌇, ⌂, M. **Services:** ⌂, ACA, DYC Agent, ⚒, ⍯, Gaz. **Town** P, D, ⌇, R, ⌂, Ⓑ, ⊠, ⇌, ✈ (Groningen/ Eelde). Ferry: Hoek van Holland.

MINOR HARBOUR 1·3M ESE OF DELFZIJL ENTRANCE
TERMUNTERZIJL Groningen, **53°18'·20N 07°02'·21E**. AC 3632; Zeekaart 1555; DYC 1812.6. HW –0025 on Dover (UT); use Differences Delfzijl. Ent (1·3M ESE of Delfzijl ent) is close to BW13 SHM buoy Fl G 5s (53°18'·63N 07°02'·32E); thence chan marked by 7 R and 7 G unlit bns. Yachts berth in Vissershaven (0·9m), stbd of ent, or on pontoons (1m) to port of ent, €0·36. HM ☎ (0596) 601891 (Apr-Sept), VHF Ch 09, ⚓, ⍟, ⌂, about.

COMMERCIAL HARBOUR AT MOUTH OF THE EEMS (EMS)
EEMSHAVEN, Groningen, **53°27'·66N 06°50'·27E**. AC 3631, 3632, Zeekaart 1555, DYC 1812.5/.6. HW –0100 (approx) on Dover. Eemshaven is a modern commercial port, but may be used by yachts as a port of refuge. Outer appr via Hubertgat (see TSS N

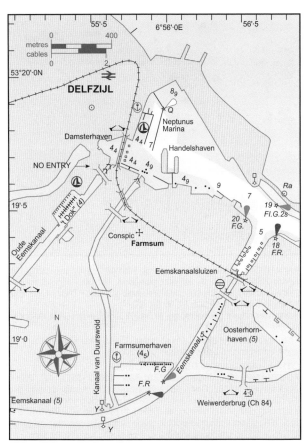

Netherlands) or Westereems; inner appr via Randzelgat or Alte Eems, passing the outer anchorage for merchant ships. From the nearest buoy, A16 PHM Fl R 4s, the hbr ent bears 137°/1·6M. Call *Eemshaven Radar* Ch 01 (H24) for VTS info; and *Eemshaven Port Control* Ch 66 for info and clearance to enter.

There are many wind turbines S, W and NW of the port. A power stn chy (128m high) is conspic 2M ESE of the port; as are white-roofed bldgs at the port. Enter on 175°, ldg lts Iso 4s, between mole hds, FG and FR. Inner ldg lts, both Iso R 4s, leads 195° to S end of port. Here yachts turn 90° stbd into Emmahaven, marked by FG and FR, and berth on floating jetty in SW corner. HM ☎ (Delfzijl Port Authority) (0596) 640400; ⊖ 0598 696560; other ☎ numbers see Delfzijl. No special facilities for yachts, but dues are €0·24 per gross ton.

2.8 LAUWERSOOG

Friesland, **53°24'·68N 06°12'·04E**

CHARTS AC 1632/3; Imray C26; Zeekaart 1458; DYC 1812.3

TIDES HW –0150 on Dover; ML 1·7m. See Harlingen.

SHELTER Outer hbr suffers swell in bad weather; complete shelter in Noordergat Marina.

NAVIGATION See Schiermonnikoog (facing page); continue to Z15 SHM buoy for hbr ent. Await lock on pontoons at W end of FV basin. Lock hrs (LT) **April-Oct**: Mon-Sat 0700-1900; Sun 0800-2000. **Nov-Mar**: Mon-Sat 0700-1200, 1300-1800; Sun shut. A firing range 1·5m ENE of hbr ent is marked by Fl Y 10s bcns, alternating W/R when the range is active; info broadcasts on Ch 71.

LIGHTS AND MARKS See chartlet and Lights, buoys & waypoints.

COMMUNICATIONS (Code 0519) ⊖ 0598 696560; Port HM 349023, VHF Ch 05, 11; Lock 349043, VHF Ch 84; Range broadcast Ch 71.

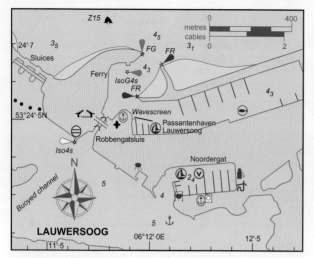

FACILITIES **Noordergat Marina**, ☎ 349040; www.noordergat.nl (2·4m-2·8m). ♥s berth on first pontoon, €1·00 + €1·15 tourist tax/head. Gaz, BY, BH (30 ton); D (E end of hbr); P (ferry terminal, W end of hbr), ⚓, ◻, ⊾, ⌂, R, ⬚, YC.

Passantenhaven Lauwersoog, ☎ 349023. 60 berths (visitors only), €1.50, D&P (can), ⬚.

The Staande Mastroute (Area map, Delfzijl-Harlingen) can be entered from the Lauwersmeer at Dokkum.

OTHER HARBOURS IN THE LAUWERSMEER

ZOUTKAMP, Groningen, **53°20'·38N 06°17'·55E**. AC 2593, Zeekaarten 1458, DYC 1812·4; non-tidal. Appr down the Zoutkamperril (2·6-4.5m); approx 2ca before lock/bridge, Hunzegat marina (1·5-2·1m) is to port. ☎ (0595) 402875, SC, ⊾. Beyond the lock (FR lts) and close to port is Oude Binnenhaven marina (2m), €1·25 + €1·15 tourist tax/head; C, ✎, ◻, ✗, C (20 ton), BH.

Town D, P, ⚓, Gaz, ✉, R, ⬚, Dr.

OOSTMAHORN, Friesland, **53°22'·94N 06°09'·63E**. AC 2593, Zeekaarten 1458, DYC 1812·4. Non-tidal hbr on W side of Lauwersmeer; lock in as for Lauwersoog. Floating bns with Y flags mark fishing areas. Main hbr with FR and FG lts at ent has marina (2·2-3·0m). VHF Ch 10. HM ☎ (0519) 321445; €0·91, D, P, ⚓, C, BY, BH (15T), ⬚, Gaz, R. Approx 450m to the SSE, next to the Voorm Veerhaven (ferry hbr), is a tiny marina with 1·5-2m.

MINOR HARBOURS IN THE WEST FRISIAN ISLANDS

SCHIERMONNIKOOG, Friesland, **53°28'·07N 06°10'·05E**. AC 3761; Zeekaart 1458; DYC 1812.3. HW –0150 on Dover. See Delfzijl. WPT 53°32'·35N 06°00'·70E, (WG SWM buoy, Iso 8s, Racon N), 149°/1·0M to WG1 SHM buoy, VQ G, at the ent to Westgat; buoyed/lit, but in bad weather dangerous due to shoals (2·6m) at seaward end, shifting chan, frequent buoy movements. Call Schiermonnikoog ☆, VHF Ch 5 for update. Follow Westgat chan into Zoutkamperlaag either to Lauwersoog or Schiermonnikoog; leave at Z4 & Z6-GVS bys to enter buoyed Gat van Schiermonnikoog (GVS).

Follow GVS bys to ent of Groote Siege (GS bys), turn to port at GS6 into Reegeul chan, marked by withies, and eastwards towards the small yacht hbr of Schiermonnikoog, (1·3-1·5m), 1·5m max depth at HW in apprs. Picturesque, but busy in season; €2·00/m. HM VHF Ch 31; ☎ (0519) 531544 (May-Sept). Facilities: ⚓, ◻, R.

Note: Lt ho Fl (4) 20s, R twr, conspic 1.35M NNW of yacht hbr. CG at lt ho, 48M radius radar surveillance of the Terschelling/German Bight TSS and coordinates local SAR operations. VHF Ch 05, 10, 16, 67 and 37 (all H24); ☎ 0519 531247.

NES, Ameland, Friesland, **53°26'·22N 05°46'·53E**. AC 2593, Zeekaart 1458, DYC 1811.10 & .2. HW –0055 on Dover; ML 1·6m; Duration 0625. See Harlingen. Shelter in all but E/S winds. Appr from WA SWM buoy via Westgat, Borndiep and Molengat to VA2-R1 SCM lt perch, VQ(6) + L Fl 10s, beware sandbanks; dangerous in >F6 from SW-N-NE. Lts: see Lights, buoys & waypoints. **Yacht hbr** ('t Leije Gat) HM ☎ (0519) 542159. 140 berths, €0·66/m² + €1·18 p/p daily tourist tax. L Fl R 8s and L Fl G 8s piles at ent. Pontoons N end hbr (0·8m) beyond ferry; W side dries . **Facilities:** Gas, YC.

This chain of islands stretches from the River Ems estuary W and SSW for some 85M along the Dutch coast to Den Helder (AC 1632, 1633). The islands have similar characteristics – being long, low and narrow, with the major axis parallel to the coast. Texel is the largest and, with Vlieland and Terschelling, lies furthest offshore.

Between the islands, narrow channels (*zeegat* in Dutch, *Seegat* in German) give access to/from the North Sea. Most of these channels are shallow for at least part of their length, and in these shoal areas a dangerous sea builds up in a strong onshore wind against the outgoing (ebb) tide. The Westerems and the Zeegaten van Terschelling and van Texel are safe for yachts in W–NE winds up to force 6. All the others are unsafe in strong onshore winds.

▶*The flood stream along this coast is E-going, so it starts to run in through the zeegaten progressively from W to E. Where the tide meets behind each island, as it flows in first at the W end and a little later at the E end, a bank is formed, called a wantij (Dutch) or Wattenhoch (German).◀*

These banks between the islands and the coast are major obstacles to E/W progress inside the islands. The chans are narrow and winding, marked by buoys and/or withies (⌇ ⌇) in the shallower parts, and they mostly dry; so that it is essential to time the tide correctly.

This is an area most suited to shallow-draft yachts that can take the ground easily. Whilst the zeegaten are described briefly below, the many channels inside the islands and across the Waddenzee are mentioned only for general orientation.

DELFZIJL TO AMELAND

The Ems estuary (AC 1633, 3631) flows seaward past the SW side of the German island of Borkum. It gives access to **Delfzijl**, **Termunterzijl** and **Emden**. Hubertgat, which runs parallel to and S of the main Westerems chan, is slightly more direct when bound to/from the W, but in both these chans there is a dangerous sea in strong NW winds over the ebb. Hubertgat is now sparsely buoyed and unlit, but is quite acceptable to yachts. ▶*The E-going (flood) stream begins at HW Helgoland +0530, and the W-going (ebb) stream begins at HW Helgoland –0030, sp rates 1·5kn.◀*

Friesche Zeegat (DYC 1812.3 & .9), between Schiermonnikoog and Ameland, contains two channels: Westgat marked by 'WG' buoys, but increasing shoaling and buoy shifting reported, and Plaatgat, a unmarked channel, which is considered to be dangerous. In strong winds the sea breaks across the whole estuary. Westgat trends SE past Wierumergronden and N7-FA-1 platform, the S past Het Rif and Engelsmanplaat (a prominent sandbank) into Zoutkamperlaag, the main channel (buoys prefixed 'Z') to **Lauwersoog**. Here locks give access to the Lauwersmeer and inland waterways.

Zeegat van Ameland (DYC 1811.6), between Ameland and Terschelling, is fronted by the sandbank of Bornrif about 3M offshore. The main entrance is also called Westgat, with buoys prefixed by letters 'WA', all unlit except WA12 QR. The channel runs ESE close N of Terschelling, and divides into Boschgat (BG) at the E end of West Terschelling and Borndiep (BB) the wider, deeper channel. This skirts the W end of Ameland and at WA22-WG1 buoy gives access via the Molengat to the small ferry port and yacht hbr at Nes.

▶*In Westgat the flood stream begins at HW Helgoland +0425, and the ebb stream at HW Helgoland –0150, sp rates 2kn.◀* A dangerous sea develops in strong onshore winds.

TERSCHELLING TO TEXEL AND DEN HELDER

Zeegat Het Vlie, aka Zeegat van Terschelling (AC 112 and DYC 1811.4, .5 and .9), between Terschelling and Vlieland, gives access to the hbrs of **Vlieland, West Terschelling and Harlingen**; it is also a northern approach to the sealock at Kornwerderzand. Shallow banks extend more than 5M seaward narrowing the ITZ to only 4M wide.

▶*The E-going (flood) stream begins at HW Helgoland +0325, while the W-going (ebb) stream begins at HW Helgoland –0230, sp rates 2·5kn.*◀

The main chan (buoyed/lit) through the banks is Zuider Stortemelk (buoys prefixed 'ZS') running ESE close N of Vlieland into Vliesloot (VS) which leads to **Oost Vlieland** hbr. The Stortemelk (SM) forks eastward at SM1-ZS10 buoy towards the deeper wider channel of Vliestroom.

Approach **West Terschelling** via West Meep and Slenk, **not** by the shorter Schuitengat Zuid which is badly silted. From Zuider Stortemelk the Vliestroom, a deep well buoyed chan (buoys prefixed 'VL'), runs S about 4M until its junction with Blauwe Slenk (BS) and Inschot (IN). Blauwe Slenk runs ESE to **Harlingen**; from Harlingen a S-going channel 'Boontjes' leads via the locks at Kornwerderzand into the IJsselmeer.

Eierlandsche Gat (DYC 1811.7), between Vlieland and Texel, consists of dangerous shoals, shallow and unmarked chans used only by fishermen, *and should not be attempted by strangers.*

Zeegat van Texel (AC 1546/DYC 1811.2) lies between Texel and Den Helder, and gives access to the **Waddenzee** and IJsselmeer via locks at Den Oever or Kornwerderzand. Haaksgronden shoals extend 5M seaward. The 2 appr channels are: Molengat from the

N along the Texel shore (see next para), and from the SSW the well marked/lit main chan Schulpengat, buoys prefixed 'S'; but strong SW winds cause rough seas against ▶*the SW-going (ebb) stream which begins at HW Helgoland – 0330, while the NE-going (flood) stream begins at HW Helgoland +0325, sp rates 1·5kn.*◀

Serious shoaling in the Molengat has reduced this to a fair weather channel for small craft in daylight only, least depth 3.5m, marked along E side by Y spar buoys and Y SPM's at N and S entrances. Do not attempt in fresh NE wind or swell.

▶*In Molengat the N-going (ebb) stream begins at HW Helgoland –0145, and the S-going (flood) stream at HW Helgoland +0425, sp rates 1·25kn.*◀

From the N the Schulpengat involves a southerly deviation of approx 15M and leads W of the very dangerous Zuider Haaks which should be avoided in bad weather.

E of **Den Helder** and the Marsdiep, the flood makes in three main directions through the SW Waddenzee:

- to E and SE through Malzwin and Visjagersgaatje (keeping to the ctr of the channel) to **Den Oever** (where the lock into IJsselmeer is only available during daylight hours); thence NE along the Afsluitdijk, and then N towards Harlingen;

- to NE and E through Texelstroom and Doove Balg towards Kornwerderzand; and

- from Texelstroom, NE and N through Scheurrak, Omdraai and Inschot, where it meets the flood stream from Zeegat van Terschelling. The ebb runs in reverse. The **Kornwerderzand** locks (available H24), near NE end of Afsluitdijk, also give access to the IJsselmeer.

2.9 HET VLIE (ZEEGAT VAN TERSCHELLING)

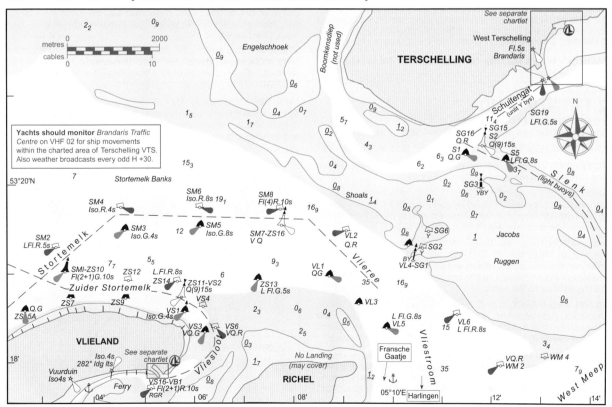

2.10 WEST TERSCHELLING

WEST FRISIAN ISLANDS 53°21'·26N 05°13'·13E ✳✳✳✤◊◊◊❀❀

CHARTS AC 1633, 112; Zeekaart 1456; DYC 1811.4/.5; Imray C25

TIDES –0300 Dover; ML 1·4; Duration No data
Standard Port HELGOLAND (←)

Times				Height (metres)			
High Water		Low Water		MHWS	MHWN	MLWN	MLWS
0200	0700	0200	0800	3·2	2·8	0·9	0·5
1400	1900	1400	2000				
Differences WEST TERSCHELLING							
–0220	–0250	–0335	–0310	–0·8	–0·6	–0·3	–0·2
VLIELAND-HAVEN							
–0250	–0320	–0355	–0330	–0·8	–0·6	–0·3	–0·1

SHELTER Good in the marina; very crowded in season.

NAVIGATION WPT 53°19'·58N 04°55'·77E (ZS buoy) 099°/6·2M to ZS11-VS2 buoy via Zuider Stortemelk which is well marked/lit. In strong W/NW'lies beware dangerous seas from ZS to ZS5/6 buoys. Stortemelk, the deeper N'ly route, is no shorter and is more exposed. From Vlieree (Vlieland Roads) make for the West Meep Channel. Call *Brandaris* Ch 02 or 04; see Communications.

> **Note**: Schuitengat-Zuid, a former approach channel, **is no longer an option for the foreseeable future.**
>
> West Meep/Slenk is long, but wide, safe and 3·2m deep; hence easier for visitors. Route: WM2, 4 & 6 buoys, NM4–S21 buoy to enter Slenk buoyed/lit chan leading NW into the inner Schuitengat (11m) at SG15/S2 WCM buoy. Expect much commercial traffic and ferries in Slenk.

Ameland can be reached if draft <1.5m by the inshore channels across the Waddenzee (Meep, Noorder Balgen and Oosterom; DYC 1811.4 & .6). Leave at HW –3 to arrive at HW.

LIGHTS AND MARKS Hbr lts as chartlet and Lights, buoys and waypoints. The square, yellow Brandaris light tower dominates the town and hbr.

COMMUNICATIONS (Code 0562) Coast Guard 442341; *Brandaris* (VTS) Ch 02, 04 broadcasts weather, visibility, traffic, tidal data at H+30 in Dutch and English. Yachts must monitor Ch 02; ⊖ 442884; Dr 442181; Port HM 443337 (H24), VHF Ch 12; Marina Ch 31 HO.

FACILITIES Marina Stichting Passantenhaven ☎ 443337 (H24 Apr-

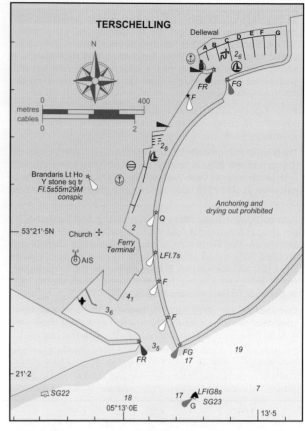

Oct). info@jachthaventerschelling.nl. www.waddenhavens.nl Notices on pontoons A-G indicate berths by LOA and type of boat (yacht, motor cruiser or traditional craft). 500 ⚓, €0·70/m² + €1·30 p/p daily tourist tax, inc ⚡, ⚓, shwrs, ▣, D at marina ent, @, ▬, C, Gaz, ✎, ⚓, Chart agent, ⚓.

Village is an easy walk: ⚓, ⛟, R, ⚓, ✉, ☏ (5km), Ⓑ. ✈ Amsterdam. Ferry to Harlingen, thence ⇌ for Hook-Harwich.

2.11 VLIELAND

WEST FRISIAN ISLANDS
Friesland 53°17'·68N 05°05'·49E ✳✳✳◊◊❀❀

CHARTS AC 1633, 112; Zeekaart 1456; DYC 1811.4/.5; Imray C26

TIDES –0300 Dover; ML 1·4; Duration 0610. See West Terschelling. The Dutch use Harlingen as a Standard Port.

SHELTER Good in yacht hbr. Two ⚓s, both affected by swell in strong SE-SW'lies near HW: (a) in up to 3m ½M S of the hbr or (b) in 4-9m 1M W of the hbr (beyond the ferry pier). Do not ⚓ in buoyed chan from hbr ent to ferry pier (no ⚓).

NAVIGATION From ZS buoy (WPT) follow W Terschelling Navigation, lines 1-3. At ZS11-VS2 and VS1 buoys turn S into Vliesloot (narrow and in places only 2·5m MLWS). Keep in mid-chan past VS3-VS7 buoys to hbr ent (strong current across); tight berths difficult in SW wind.

LIGHTS AND MARKS A dk R lt ho (W lantern, R top) stands on Vuurduin, 1·2M W of hbr. Hbr lts as chartlet. Tfc sigs: R Flag or ●● at ent = hbr closed (full). The 282° ldg lts (Lights, bys & waypoints & W Terschelling) lead toward the ferry terminal in E Vlieland.

COMMUNICATIONS (Code 0562) CG 442341; All vessels in Zeegat van Terschelling and N Waddenzee must monitor Ch 02 for *Brandaris Traffic Centre VTS;* Police 451312; ⊖ 058 2949488 (Leeuwarden); Brit Consul (020) 6764343; Dr 451307; HM 451729, mob 06 201 33086, VHF Ch 12.

FACILITIES Yacht Hbr ☎ 451729. www.waddenhavens.nl 300 inc **Ⓥ**; finger berths on all pontoons in 2m. €0·70 per m² + €1·35 p/p daily tourist tax; dinghy slip, ▣, ⚓, ☏ & ☏ (10 mins); D at Harlingen and Terschelling.

Village ☏, Gaz, ⛟, R, @, ✉, Ⓑ, ✈ (Amsterdam). Ferry as West Terschelling.

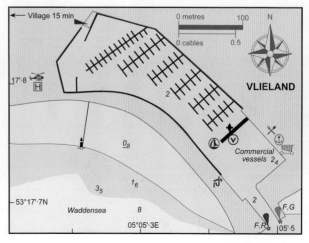

2.12 HARLINGEN

Friesland 53°10'·58N 05°24'·23E ✳ ✳ ♿ ♿ ✿ ✿

CHARTS AC 1633, 112; Zeekaart 1454, 1456; DYC 1811·5; ANWB B; Imray C26

TIDES –0210 Dover; ML 1·2; Duration 0520

Standard Port HELGOLAND (←)

Times				Height (metres)			
High Water		Low Water		MHWS	MHWN	MLWN	MLWS
0200	0700	0200	0800	3·2	2·8	0·9	0·5
1400	1900	1400	2000				
Differences LAUWERSOOG							
–0130	–0145	–0235	–0220	–0·3	–0·2	–0·2	0·0
HARLINGEN							
–0155	–0245	–0210	–0130	–0·8	–0·7	–0·4	–0·1
NES (AMELAND)							
–0135	–0150	–0245	–0225	–0·3	–0·2	–0·2	0·0

SHELTER Very good in Noorderhaven. Beware strong flood stream across outer hbr ent; it can be rough at HW in W/ NW'lies.

NAVIGATION WPT 53°11'·48N 05°19'·63E [abeam BS23 buoy] 110°/2·8M to hbr ent. See West Terschelling for appr, thence to the WPT via buoyed Vliestroom and Blauwe Slenk chans; the latter is narrow for the last 2½M. A small craft chan, at least 1·8m, lies parallel to Pollendam trng wall and outboard of the main chan SHM buoys; it is marked by SPM buoys A–N in season. Beware ferries passing very close. Caution: When Pollendam is covered, tidal streams sweep across it.

LIGHTS AND MARKS See chartlet and Lights, buoys and waypoints. Ldg lts 111°, both Iso 6s, H24; B masts, W bands. 2 ch spires are conspic almost on ldg line.

COMMUNICATIONS (Code 0517) Coast Guard 0223 542300; Brandaris Traffic Ctre (0562) 442341, VHF Ch 02; Police 0900 8844/112; ⊜ 088 151444; British Consul (020) 6764343; Ⓗ 058 2866666; Doctor 412544; Harlingen Port Control 412512, VHF Ch

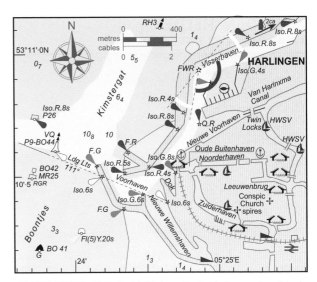

11; HM 492300, VHF Ch 11 (Not on Sun); Harinxma Canal locks VHF Ch 22.

FACILITIES Lifting bridges across the Oude Buitenhaven and Noorderhaven open in unison 2 x per hr 0600-2200 in season (on request in winter), but are shut at times of boat trains/ferries and at a tidal height exceeding LAT + 2·54m. Fuel available in the NE corner of the Nieuwe Industriehaven.

Noorderhaven Yacht Hbr ☎ 415666, ⬚, ⬚, ⚓, △, Ⓔ, Gaz, Diving/ salvage (by arrangement) ⬚, R, ⬚, ⬚.

Harlinger Watersportvereningen (HWSV) ☎ 416898 info@harlingerwatersportvereningen.nl, useful small marina just inside the locks, 100+ ⬚ inc ♥ €1·20 + €0·75 p/p daily tourist tax, inc ⬚, ⬚, shwrs; ⬚, ⬚, @. **Town** ⬚, R, ⬚, ⊠, Ⓑ, ⇌, ✈ (Amsterdam). Ferry: See Hoek van Holland.

2.13 OUDESCHILD

Texel, 53°02'·35N 04°51'·18E ✳ ✳ ✳ ♿ ♿ ✿ ✿

CHARTS AC 1631, 1546; Zeekaart 1546, 1454; DYC 1811·3

TIDES –0355 Dover; ML 1·1m; Duration 0625

Standard Port HELGOLAND (←)

Times				Height (metres)			
High Water		Low Water		MHWS	MHWN	MLWN	MLWS
0200	0700	0200	0800	3·2	2·8	0·9	0·5
1400	1900	1400	2000				
Differences OUDESCHILD							
–0310	–0420	–0445	–0400	–1·4	–1·1	–0·4	–0·2

SHELTER Very good in marina (2·4m) in far NE basin. ⚓ prohib. Visitors are always welcome.

NAVIGATION From Waddenzee appr via Doove Balg and Texelstroom. From seaward, app via Schulpengat or Molengat into Marsdiep (Den Helder). Thence NE via Texelstroom for 3·5M to WPT 53°02'·26N 04°51'·55E (abeam T12 PHM buoy), 291°/400m to hbr ent, keeping the dir lt, Oc 6s, midway between FR and FG mole hd lts. Speed limit 5kn.

LIGHTS AND MARKS See chartlet and Lights, buoys and waypoints. Dir lt Oc 6s, on G mast, is vis only on brg 291°. FR/FG lts are on R/G masts with W bands.

COMMUNICATIONS (Code 0222) Coast Guard 316270; Police/ ambulance 0900 8844 or 112; ⊜ via HM; Port HM 312710, mobile 06 1502 8380, VHF Ch 12 0800-2000LT; Marina VHF Ch 31; See Den Helder for VTS and radar assistance/info on request.

FACILITIES

Waddenhaven Texel Marina 250 berths ☎ 321227. info@waddenhaventexel.nl €0·70/m² + €1·60pp tourist tax D & P, ◄,

⬚, ♂, ♿, ⬚, R, mini ⬚ in season, bike hire, Gaz, Internet desk.

YC WSV Texel, members only. Dry dock (FVs only).

Village (walking distance), ⬚, △, Gaz, ⬚, Ⓑ, ⊠, ⬚, R. Ferry from 't Horntje to Den Helder. UK ferries from Hook/Rotterdam. ✈ Amsterdam.

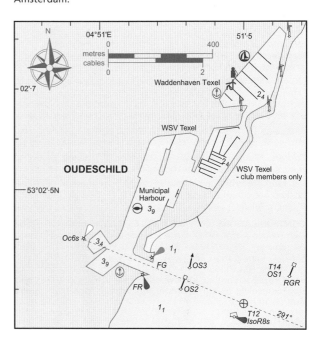

2.14 DEN HELDER
Noord Holland 52°57'·94N 04°47'·24E

CHARTS AC 1408, 1631, 1546, 126; Zeekaart 1454, 1546; DYC 1811.2, 1801.10; ANWB F; Imray C25

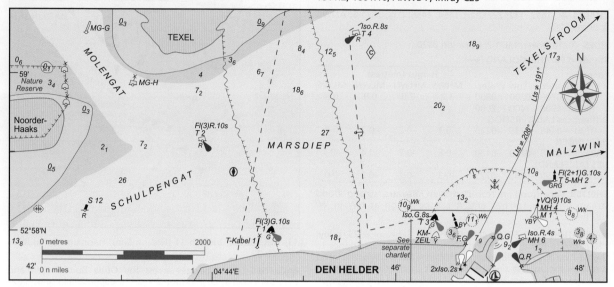

TIDES –0430 Dover; ML 1·1; Duration 0540

Standard Port HELGOLAND (←—)

Times				Height (metres)			
High Water		Low Water		MHWS	MHWN	MLWN	MLWS
0200	0700	0200	0800	3·2	2·8	0·9	0·5
1400	1900	1400	2000				
Differences DEN HELDER							
–0410	–0520	–0520	–0430	–1·3	–1·1	–0·4	–0·2
K13A PLATFORM (53°13'·0N 03°13'·1E; 58M WNW of Den Helder)							
–0420	–0430	–0520	–0530	–1·4	–1·4	–0·3	–0·3

SHELTER Good in all yacht hbrs (see Facilities). Hbr speed limit 5kn. Den Helder is the main base of the Royal Netherlands Navy which manages the Marinehaven Willemsoord and KMYC.

NAVIGATION Caution: fast ferries to/from Texel, many FVs and offshore service vessels, strong tidal streams across the hbr ent.

Schulpengate leads into Marsdiep for the hbr ent. It is well marked/lit. WPT 52°52'·90N 04°37'·90E (SG (SWM) buoy, Mo (A) 8s, Racon Z) 026·5°/6M towards S14/MG17 SCM lt buoy.

Although closed as a shipping chan in Apr 2013 due to silting, the Molengat remains a viable fair weather chan for smaller craft, least depth 3.5m, with Y ⌐ marking E side. Do not attempt at night or in fresh NE wind or swell.

LIGHTS AND MARKS See chartlet and Lights, buoys & waypoints. Schulpengat: Dir lt Al WRG and F WRG. Kijkduin lt ho, R twr, is conspic 2·3M WSW of hbr. Hbr 191° ldg lts; front B ▲ on bldg; rear B ▼ on B lattice twr. A 60m radar twr is conspic on E side of hbr.

Entry sigs, from Hbr Control twr (W side of ent): ring of R lts = No entry/exit, except for the vessel indicated by Hbr Control Ch 62.

Bridges: Moorman bridge operates H24 7/7, giving access to Nieuwe Diep, Koopvaarder Lock and N Holland Canal.

Van Kinsbergen bridge is operated by HM, on request, Mon-Fri. All bridges are closed 0705-0810, 1200-1215, 1245-1300, 1600-1700, Mon-Fri. All LT.

COMMUNICATIONS (Code 0223) VTS 657522, monitor VHF Ch 62 *Den Helder Traffic* (VTS) in the Schulpengat and Marsdiep; info on request; Police 112/09008844; Water Police 616767; ⊖ 0255 566707; Immigration 08000543; British Consul (020) 676 4343; Ⓗ 696969; HM 613955, VHF Ch 14 (H24), also remote control of van Kinsbergen bridge; *Koopvaarders Lock* VHF Ch 22 (H24), also remote control of Burgemeester Vissersbrug; Moorman bridge VHF Ch 18 (H24).

FACILITIES KMJC is hard to stbd on entering Naval Hbr. ☎ 652645,

mob 0651007528, VHF Ch 31, www.kmjc.eu €1·90 + €1·20/head draught <4m, D, ⚓, ⬚, ⬜, R.

Willemsoord Marina through Zeedoksluis (Ch 14) ☎ 616100, www.willemsoord.nl €1·65 + €1·20/head, D, R.

In or near **Binnenhaven**, YCs/marinas (MWV, HWN and Breewijd) can only be reached via the Rijkshaven, Moorman bridge, Nieuwe Diep and lock: **MWV YC** ☎ 652173, www.marinewatersport.nl €1·10 + €1·20/head. P (at garage), D, ⬚. **HWN YC** ☎ 624422, www.wsvhwn.nl €1·00 + €1·20/head. **YC WSOV Breewijd** ☎ 615500 €0·75 + €1·20/head. **Councilharbour** ☎ 613955 €1·05 + €1·20/head. **Nauticadam (Den Helder marina)** ☎ 637444, €0·75 + €1·20/head, Ch 31, ⬚, ⚓, 🔧, ⬚, 🔧, C, ⬚, ⬛, R, ⬜.

Services: ⬚, △, Gaz. **Boatyard:** Jachtwerf Den Helder ☎ 636964, BH (40 ton), 🔧.

Town P, ⬚, 🛒, R, ⬜, ✉, Ⓑ, ⇌, ✈ (Amsterdam). Ferry: Hook-Harwich; Rotterdam-Hull, IJmuiden-Newcastle.

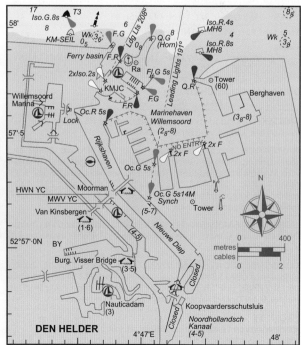

2.15 IJSSELMEER

CHARTS Zeekaart 1351, 1454; In-date DYC 1810, sheets 3-5, are essential to avoid live firing ranges, fishing areas and other hazards; 1810 also has many hbr chartlets.

TIDES The IJsselmeer is non-tidal. Tides seaward of Den Oever and Kornwerderzand locks: –0230 Dover; ML 1·2

Standard Port HELGOLAND (←)

Times				Height (metres)			
High Water		Low Water		MHWS	MHWN	MLWN	MLWS
0200	0700	0200	0800	3·2	2·8	0·9	0·5
1400	1900	1400	2000				
Differences DEN OEVER							
–0245	–0410	–0400	–0305	–1·2	–1·0	–0·5	–0·2
KORNWERDERZAND							
–0210	–0315	–0300	–0215	–1·0	–0·8	–0·4	–0·2

SHELTER Excellent in the marinas, but in the IJsselmeer strong winds can get up very quickly and often raise short, steep seas.

NAVIGATION Enter from sea by Den Oever or Kornwerderzand locks; also from IJmuiden via the Noordzeekanaal and Amsterdam.

Speed limits: 10·5kn in buoyed chans and <250m from shore. Hbr limits vary; see Special notes for the ANWB *Wateralmanak*.

A firing range, operational Tues to Thurs 1000–1900LT, extends S from Breezanddijk (53°01'·0N 05°12'·5E) to 3M NE of Medemblik then NNW to Den Oever (DYC 1811.3 & 1810.3). Call *Schietterrein Breezanddijk* (range control) Ch 71. Firing times are broadcast on VHF Ch 01 by Centrale Meldpost at H +15 on the day of firing, after weather forecasts.

R/T Nav info VHF Ch 01. Sealocks: Kornwerderzand 18; Den Oever 20. Enkhuizen naviduct 22; Lelystad 20; Oranjesluizen 18.

SEALOCKS Standard signals, see Special notes.

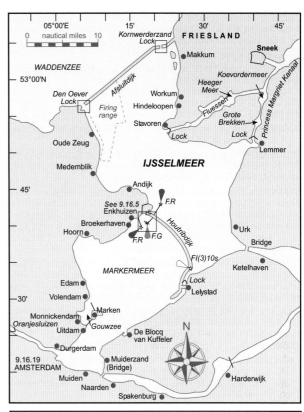

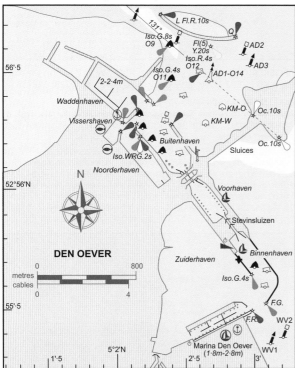

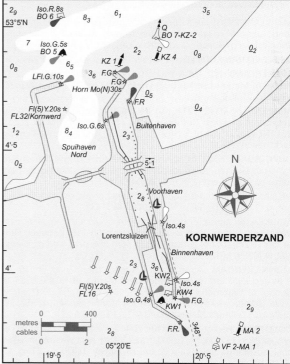

DEN OEVER SEALOCK AND MARINA Approach from seaward via the buoyed/lit Malzwin and Wierbalg channels. Enter on 131° ldg line, then 220° towards Buitenhaven. 2 swing bridges (52°56'·05N 05°02'·50E) and lock open in unison HO. If NW-bound, await lock opening in Binnenhaven. Marina (2-3m) HM ☎ (0227) 511789, D, P, C (30 ton), ▨.

KORNWERDERZAND SEALOCK From seaward approach from the W via Doove Balg; from NW via shallow Inschot chan; or from N via Boontjes. Entrance to Buitenhaven has FR/G and Iso G 6s lts. When two road bridges (53°04'·44N 05°20'·09E) have opened, yachts enter the smaller Lorentz E lock, operates H24. N-bound, follow 348° ldg lts, Iso 4s, to FR/G at ent. Await lock in Binnenhaven (3·6m). HM ☎ (0517) 578170. ⊜ 058 2949444.

FACILITIES clockwise from Kornwerderzand. Overnight fees range from approx €0·80 – €1·80/metre LOA. Most berths are bows on to a pontoon, stern lines to piles; there are few ⚓s.

IJSSELMEER EAST

MAKKUM: About 1M SE of Kornwerderzand, MA5 SHM buoy, Iso G4s, marks the buoyed chan. FR/FG lts lead 090·5° into Makkum. To stbd, **Marina Makkum** (2·5-2·8m) ☎ (0515) 232828, P, D, ⚓, Gaz, ⬛, ⬛, R, ⬛. 5 other marinas/YCs are further E; BY, ⚒, C (30 ton), BH (40 ton). **Town** ⓑ, Dr, ⬛, R.

WORKUM: 5M S of Makkum; FW ldg lts 081° along buoyed chan to **It Soal Marina** ☎ (0515) 542937, BY, ⚒, C, D, ⬛, Gaz, BH.

HINDELOOPEN: WV Hylper Haven HM ☎ (0514) 522009, P, D, ⚒, ⬛, ⚒. **Old Hbr** D, P, ⚒, ⬛, ⚒. **Jachthaven Hindeloopen** (500) HM ☎ (0514) 524554, P, D, ⬛, BH (65 ton), ⬛, R, ⬛.

STAVOREN: Ent Buitenhaven 048° on Dir lt Iso 4s between FR/G. Marina, €1·00, E of ent in Oudehaven, ☎ (0514) 681216, VHF Ch 74. Or, 1km S, ent Nieuwe Voorhaven (FR/G & Fl 5s Dir lt) then via lock to **Marina Stavoren** (3m) ☎ (0514) 684684, BY, ⚒, C, P, D, ⚓, Gaz, BH (65 ton); **Outer Marina** (3·5m) close S of Nieuwe Voorhaven. Also 3 other marinas. **Town** ⬛, Dr, ⬛, R, ⬛.

LEMMER: Appr on ldg lts 038°, Iso 8s, to KL5/VL2 By; then ldg lts 083°, Iso 8s, through Lemstergeul. Lastly FG and Iso G 4s lead 065° into town and some 14 marinas. **Jachthaven Friese Hoek** (275) HM ☎ (0514) 568135. Services: BY, ⚒, GAZ, ⚓, BH (30 ton), ⬛, ⬛.

URK: Hbr ent ½M SE of lt ho. Dir lt Iso G 4s to hbr ent, FR/G. Hbr has 4 basins; keep NNW to berth in Nieuwe Haven, Westhaven or Oosthaven (3·3m). **Westhaven** ⬛, ⬛, ⚓; **Oosthaven** ⚒, ⬛, ⚒, ⓔ, ⬛. **Town** EC Tues; ⓑ, ⬛, Dr.

LELYSTAD: Flevo is 2M NNE of lock. (550) ☎ (0320) 279800, BY, ⚒, C, P, D, Gaz, ⬛, BH (50 ton), R, ⬛, ⬛. **Deko Marina** is close N of the lock; ☎ (0320) 269000, ⚓, C, R. **WV Lelystad, Houtribhaven** (560) HM ☎ (0320) 260198, D, ⬛, ⬛, ⬛, R, ⬛, BH (20 ton). S of lock **Bataviahaven** (150), Ch 14, HM ☎ 06 511 77049. **Marina Lelystadhaven** ☎ (0320) 260326, R.

MARKERMEER is divided from the IJsselmeer by the Houtribdijk 13M long. Access from sea via IJmuiden, Noordzeekanaal, Amsterdam/Oranjesluizen. Hbrs clockwise from Lelystad to Enkhuizen:

DE BLOCQ VAN KUFFELER: (8·5M SW Lelystad), ☎ 06 2751 2497, R.

MUIDERZAND: Ent 1M N of Hollandsebrug (12·7m cl'nce at SE corner of Markermeer) at buoys IJM5 & IJM7/JH2. **Marina** ☎ (036) 5369151, D, P, C, ⚒, R, ⬛.

MUIDEN: Ldg lts Q 181° into **KNZ & RV Marina** (2·6m), W of ent; home of Royal Netherlands YC (150 berths). HM ☎ (0294) 261450, www.knzrv.nl €1·95, ⬛, ⬛, ⬛, ⬛, R. On E bank **Stichting Jachthaven** (70) ☎ (0294) 261223, €1·60, D, P.

DURGERDAM: ½M E of overhead power lines (70m); convenient for Oranjesluizen. Keep strictly in buoyed chan. **WV Durgerdam** Berth to stbd of ent (1·8m). ☎ 06-14750510.

UITDAM Appr from MIJ5 buoy Fl Y 5s via buoyed chan to FR/FG at ent. C (9 ton), P, D, Gaz, ⬛. HM ☎ (020) 4031433.

MARKEN (picturesque show piece): Ent Gouwzee from N, abeam Volendam, thence via buoyed chan; Dir FW lt 116° between FR/G at hbr (2·2m). Lt ho, conspic, Oc 8s 16m 9M, on E end of island. HM ☎ (0299) 601253, free on quay, ⬛, R, ⓑ, ⬛, ⬛.

MONNICKENDAM: Appr as for Marken, then W to MO10 Iso R 8s and 236° ldg lts FR. **Hemmeland Marina** ☎ (0299) 655555, (2·0m), C. **Waterland Marina** ☎ 652000, (2·5m), ⬛, C (15 ton) www.jachthavenwaterland.nl. **Marina Monnickendam** ☎ 652595, (2·0m), C. **Zeilhoek Marina** ☎ 651463, (2·5m), BY.

VOLENDAM: Fork stbd to old hbr (2·4m). Dir lt Fl 5s 313°. FR/FG at ent. ☎ 06 51337494, ⚒, C, P, D, Gaz, ⚓. Fork port via unlit buoyed chan to **Marina Volendam** (2·7m) HM(0299) 320262. C (16t), ⚓, ⬛, B, R.

EDAM: Appr via unlit chan keeping Iso W 8s between FG /R at narrow ent; beware commercial traffic. **Jachthaven WSV De Zeevang** (2·2m) S side of outer hbr. ☎ (0299) 350174, ⚒, ⬛, ⚒. Or lock into the Oorgat and via S canal into Nieuwe Haven. **Town** ⬛, ⬛, ⬛, Gaz, ⓑ.

HOORN: Radio twr (80m) 1·5M ENE of hbr. Iso 4s 15m 10M and FR/G at Hbr ent. Four options: To port **Grashaven** (700) HM ☎

(0229) 215208, ⬛, ⬛, ⬛, ⚒, ⬛, ⚒, C. To stbd ⚓ in **Buitenhaven** (1·6m). Ahead & to stbd **WSV Hoorn**, (100) ☎ 213540. Ahead to **Binnenhaven** (2·5m) via narrow lock (open H24) ⬛, P. **Town** ⬛, ⬛, ⬛, R, Dr, ⬛, ⬛, ⓑ, Gaz, ⬛.

ENKHUIZEN: 036° ldg lts Iso 4s; 230° ldg lts Iso 8s. Yachts transit the Houtribdijk via a 'Naviduct', ie a twin-chambered lock above the road tunnel below (see chartlet), saving long delays for boat & road traffic; call Ch 22. Krabbersgat lock & bridge, the former bottleneck for both road and sea traffic, can still be used by boats with <6m air clearance.
Compagnieshaven (500) HM ☎ (0228) 313353, P, D, ⬛, BH (12), Gaz; **Buyshaven** (195) ☎ 315660, ⬛, ⬛; **Buitenhaven** ☎ 312444.
Town EC Mon; Market Wed; C, ⬛, ⬛, ⚓, ⚒, ⬛, ⚒, ⓑ, ⬛, ⬛, ⬛, Dr, ⬛, ⬛.

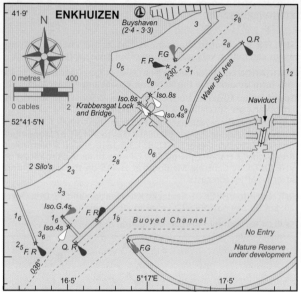

BROEKERHAVEN: Small yacht hbr 1·5M SW of Enkhuizen. Appr from KG15-BR2 buoy. WSV de Broekerhaven ☎ (0228) 518798.

IJSSELMEER WEST

ANDIJK: Visitors use **Stichting Jachthaven Andijk**, the first of 2 marinas; (600) ☎ (0228) 593075, narrow ent with tight turn between FR/G lts. ⚒, C (20 ton), ⚓, Gaz, ⬛, ⬛.

MEDEMBLIK: Ent on 232°, Dir lt Oc 5s between FR/G. Thence Oosterhaven (P & D) into Middenhaven (short stay) and via bridge to Westerhaven. **Pekelharinghaven** (120) HM ☎ (0227) 542175; ent is to port by Castle, ⬛, ⬛, R. **Middenhaven** HM ☎ 541686, ⚒. **Stichting Jachthaven** HM ☎ 541681 in Westerhaven, ⬛, C. **Town** ⓑ, ⬛, ⚒, ⬛, ⚒, ⬛, Dr, ⬛, R, ⬛. **Regatta Centre** 0·5M S of hbr entr. HM ☎ (0227) 547781, ⬛ 450, C (20 ton), ⬛, ⬛, R.

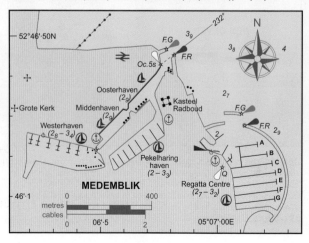

2.16 IJMUIDEN

N Holland **52°27'·94N 04°32'·39E** (Hbr ent) SPM ❄❄⚓⚓⚓✿✿

CHARTS AC 1631, 124; Zeekaart 1450, 1543, 1035, 1350; DYC 1801.8; Imray C25

TIDES +0400 Dover; ML 1·0. Noordzeekanaal level may be above or below sea level

Standard Port VLISSINGEN (→)

Times				Height (metres)			
High Water		Low Water		MHWS	MHWN	MLWN	MLWS
0300	0900	0400	1000	4·9	4·1	1·0	0·5
1500	2100	1600	2200				
Differences IJMUIDEN							
+0145	+0140	+0305	+0325	−2·8	−2·4	−0·7	−0·3
PETTEN (SOUTH) 18M N of IJmuiden							
+0210	+0215	+0345	+0500	−2·8	−2·3	−0·5	−0·2

SHELTER Very good at Seaport (SPM) marina (2·9m-4·8m).

NAVIGATION WPT 52°28'·10N 04°30'·94E, 100°/0·9M to ent. Beware strong tidal streams across hbr ent, scend inside Buitenhaven and commercial tfc – do not impede. Keep a good lookout, especially astern. 3 knots max speed in marina.

Marina access chan is buoyed/lit as per the chartlet.

LOCKS In IJmuiden the 4 locks are North, Middle, South and Small. Yachts normally use the S'most Small lock (Kleine Sluis) which opens H24 on request Ch 22; wait W or E of it.
Lock signals shown W and E from each lock are standard, ie:

● ● ● = Lock not in use; no entry.   ● = No entry/exit.

● ● = Prepare to enter/exit.   ● = Enter or exit.

Tidal & sluicing sigs may be shown from or near the conspic Hbr Ops Centre (HOC) bldg, near the front 100·5° ldg lt:

Tidal signals: ● over Ⓦ = rising tide;   Ⓦ over ● = falling tide.

Sluicing sigs are a △ of 3 horiz lts and 1 lt at the apex. The sluices are N of the N lock, so unlikely to affect yachts.

LIGHTS AND MARKS Both ldg lt ho's 100·5° for Zuider Buitenkanaal are dark R twrs. The HOC bldg is conspic next to front lt; so are 6 chimneys (138-166m high) 7ca N and ENE of Small lock.

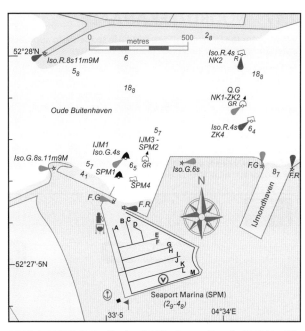

COMMUNICATIONS (Code 0255) Coast Guard 537644; Tfc Centre IJmuiden 564500, VHF Ch 07, see also VTS overleaf; Police 0900 8844; ⊜ 020 5813614; British Consul (020) 6764343; Ⓗ (023) 5453200; Hbr Ops 523934; Seaport Marina call *SPM* VHF Ch 74; Pilot 564503.

FACILITIES Seaport Marina (SPM) ☎ 560300. www.marinaseaport. nl info@ marinaseaport.nl ⚓ 600 inc Ⓥ, €2·20 inc shwr & ⏚. Berth as directed, or on M pontoon in a slot with green tally. D & P, ⏃, Ⓔ, BH (70 ton), ⏏, Gas, ⎌, ⚓, ✖, ✎, R, ⏠, ▣, ⛟. Buses to Amsterdam and Haarlem in summer.

Town Gaz, ⛟, R, ⏠, @, ✉, Ⓑ, ⇌ (bus to Beverwijk), ✈ Amsterdam. Ferry: IJmuiden-Newcastle.

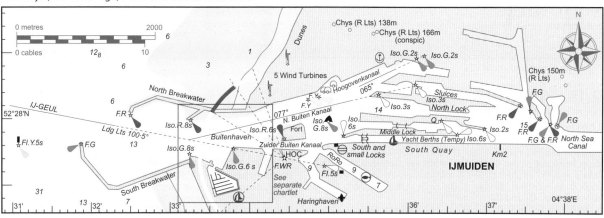

Netherlands

2.17   NOORDZEEKANAAL

VTS Monitor the following VTS stns (H24) in sequence to approach, enter and transit the canal (see diagram opposite):

• *IJmuiden Traffic Centre*	Ch 07	W of IJM C buoy
• *IJmuiden Port Control*	Ch 61	IJM buoy to locks
• *IJmuiden Locks*	Ch 22	at the locks
• *Noordzeekanaal Traffic Centre*	Ch 03	Locks to km 11
• *Amsterdam Port Control*	Ch 68	Km 11 – Amsterdam
• *Sector Schellingwoude*	Ch 60	City centre (04°55'E) to Buiten IJ

Radar surveillance is available on request Ch 07. Visibility reports are broadcast on all VHF chans every H+00 when vis <1000m.

NAVIGATION Canal speed limit is 9 knots. The 13·5M transit is simple, but there is much commercial traffic. Keep as far to stbd as possible. Keep a good lookout for vessels emerging from dock basins and side canals. The banks and ents to basins and side canals are well lit, so night navigation need be no problem apart from the risk of not being seen by other vessels against shore lights.

FACILITIES There are small marinas at IJmond beyond lifting bridge (Ch 18) in Zijkanaal C, km 10 (S bank); and at Nauerna (Zijkanaal D, km 12) (N bank).

WV IJmond ✿✿✿⚓⚓✿. Ch 31, HM ☎ (023) 5375003. ⌿ €1.10. ⏚, D, BY, C (20 ton), 🛢, 🛒, R.

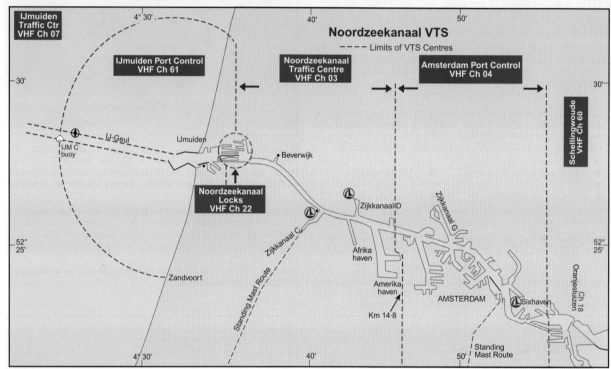

Fig 2.17A Noordzeekanaal VTS

2.18   AMSTERDAM

Noord Holland 52°22'·97N 04°53'·92E   Marinas ✿✿✿✿⚓⚓✿✿✿

CHARTS AC 124; DYC 1801.8, 1810.2; ANWB G, I

NAVIGATION Het IJ (pronounced eye) is the well lit/buoyed chan through the city centre. From IJ 10/11 to IJ 14/15 buoys yachts must keep out of Het IJ, using a yacht chan between the lateral buoys and RW (N side) or GW (S side) buoys further outboard. A second recreational fairway, 100m wide and 5.5m deep (NAP), runs between IJ2 and IJ6.

Two yacht crossing points by YM 14-15 lead to Oranjesluizen, use the N lock, marked 'SPORT'; Ch 18, H24. Waiting piers/jetties either side. The Schellingwoude bridge (9m) opens on the hour and ±20 min, except Mon-Fri 0600-0900 and 1600-1800; VHF Ch 18.

COMMUNICATIONS (Code 020) Emergency 112; Police 0900 8844; ⊖ 5867511; Brit Consul 6764343; Dr 0880 030600; Traffic Info VHF Ch 68; Port Control (East) 6221515; Port Control (West) 0255 514457; Port Info VHF Ch 14; Westerdoks-brug 6241457, VHF Ch 22,69; Oranjesluizen VHF Ch 18; Amsterdam Marina VHF Ch 31.

FACILITIES Complete shelter in all yacht hbrs/marinas.

Amsterdam Marina (52°24'·12N 04°53'·10E), VHF Ch31,☎ 6310767. 250+100Ⓥ, max LOA 30m. €2·50 inc ⏚; 🛢, 🛒, R, 🛒. info@ marinaamsterdam.com   www.marinaamsterdam.com

Marina Het Realeneiland 52°23'·16N 04°53'·26E, located in the Westerdok, there are two bridges which open simultaneously on request. Booking is required. No VHF. ☎ 6238855. 50 inc Ⓥ, max LOA 20m. €2·50. hetrealeneiland@upcmail.nl Marina only has showers/toilets, but all other facilities within easy walking distance (<8 mins). Reports welcome.

WVDS Sixhaven 52°22'·90N 04°54'·40E, close NE of IJ8 buoy and NE of conspic Central ⇌ Stn, is small and popular, so in season is often full and log-jammed 1800-1100. ☎ 6329429. 100 + Ⓥ, max LOA 15m. €1·50 inc ⏚, 🛒 (w/e), 🛢, 🛒. www.sixhaven.nl WIP, due to end 2017, on adjacent new Metro N-S line detracts only slightly. Free ferries to N bank (ditto for next entry WV Aeolus).

WV Aeolus 52°22'·91N 04°55'·17E. Few Ⓥ berths and rafting is strictly controlled. ☎ 6360791. Often full in season, no pre-booking, berth as directed. 45 + 8 Ⓥ, €1·10. ⏚, YC, 🛒, 🛒.

Aquadam Twellegea 52°23'·04N 04°56'·63E, ent to Zijkanaal K. ☎ 6320616. €2·50, ✗, P, C (30 ton). www.aquadam.nl Full BY facilities. Bus to city centre.

WV Zuiderzee 52°22'·95N 04°57'·77E, 140m NE of Oranjesluizen. ☎ 6946884, www.wsv-dezuiderzee.nl €1·10, YC.

City All needs; Gaz, Ⓔ, ACA, DYC Agent, Ⓑ, @, ✉, ⇌, ✈. Amsterdam gives access to the N Holland and Rijn canals.

AMSTERDAM *continued*

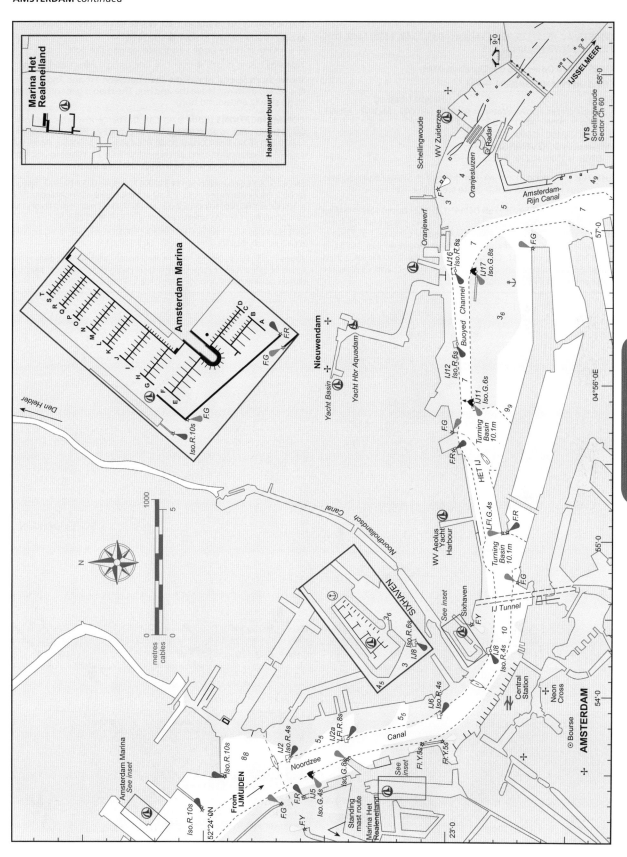

Netherlands

2.19 SCHEVENINGEN

Zuid Holland 52°06'·24N 04°15'·26E ✤✤⊕♢♢♢✿✿

CHARTS AC 1630, 125, 122; Zeekaart 1035, 1349, 1350, 1449; DYC 1801.7; ANWB H/J; Imray C25

TIDES +0320 Dover; ML 0·9; Duration 0445

Standard Port VLISSINGEN (→)

Times				Height (metres)			
High Water		Low Water		MHWS	MHWN	MLWN	MLWS
0300	0900	0400	1000	4·9	4·1	1·0	0·5
1500	2100	1600	2200				
Differences SCHEVENINGEN							
+0105	+0100	+0220	+0245	−2·7	−2·3	−0·7	−0·2

SHELTER Very good in marina. Ent difficult in SW-N F6 winds, and dangerous in NW F6-8 which cause scend in outer hbr.

NAVIGATION WPT 52°07'·75N 04°14'·12E (SCH buoy) 156°/1·6M to ent; access H24. Close west of the 156° leading line and 1M from the hbr ent, outfalls are marked by E and W cardinal light buoys and by 2 SPM buoys (off chartlet). The promenade pier, Iso 5s, is 1·2M NE of the hbr ent. Caution: Strong tidal streams set across the ent. Slack water is about HW Scheveningen –2 and +3. Beware large ships and FVs entering/leaving.

LIGHTS AND MARKS Daymarks include: the reddish-brown lt ho (5ca E of hbr ent); twr bldgs in Scheveningen and Den Haag.

Traffic signals (from signal mast, N side of ent to Voorhaven):

● over ○ = No entry. ○ over ● = No exit.
Fl ● = One or more large vessels are leaving the port.

Tide sigs (same mast): ● over ○ = tide rising. ○ over ● = tide falling.

Shown from SE end of narrow chan between 1st and 2nd Hbrs: ● = vessels must not leave the 2nd Hbr. The chan is generally blind, so go slowly and sound horn.

COMMUNICATIONS (Code 070) Call *Traffic Centre Scheveningen* Ch 21 (H24) prior to entry/departure to avoid FVs; Police 0900 8844; ⊖ 020 5813614; Brit Consul (020) 6764343; Dr 3450650; Port HM 3527711; Radar (info only) on request VHF Ch 21; When in 2nd Hbr call *Yacht Club Scheveningen* VHF Ch 31 for a berth.

FACILITIES **YC Scheveningen** ☎ 3520017, mobile 0653 293137. www.jachtclubscheveningen.com info@jachtclubscheveningen.com 223 + 100 ⓥ, €1·66 plus tax €1·27 per adult. Visitors *must* turn to berth/raft bows NE, for fire safety reasons. ⬚, ⬛, R ☎ 3520308.

2nd Harbour Fuel barge GEO (0630-1600), D only. ⬛, DYC agent; BY, C, ⬚, ⬚, ✎, ✂, ⬚.

Town P, ☷, R, ⬚, ✉, Ⓑ, ⇌, ✈ Rotterdam and Amsterdam. The town is effectively merged with Den Haag (The Hague), seat of Dutch government and well worth a visit by bus.

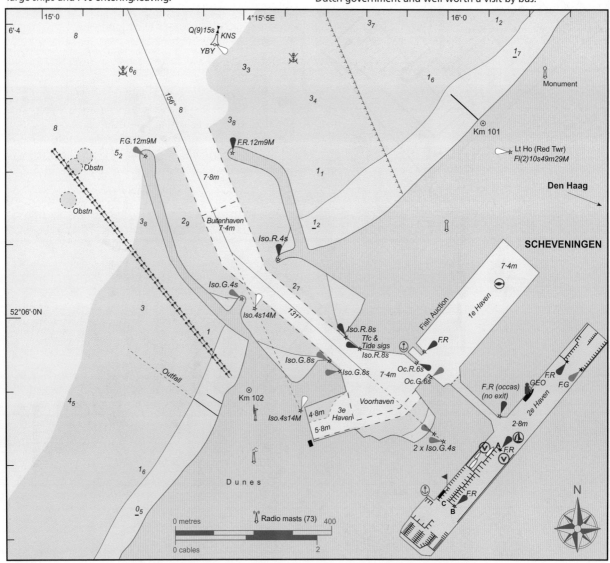

DEN HELDER TO SCHEVENINGEN

South of Den Helder the coast is low, and, like most of the Dutch coast, not readily visible from seaward. Conspic landmarks include: chimneys of nuclear power station 1·5M NNE of Petten; Egmond aan Zee light house; chimneys of steelworks N of IJmuiden; two light houses at IJmuiden; big hotels at Zandvoort; Noordwijk aan Zee light house; and Scheveningen light house and big hotels.

A wind farm centred on 52°36'·2N 04°26'·4E (about 6·7M W of Egmond aan Zee) contains a No Entry area marked by 5 peripheral turbines, each L Fl Y 15s 15m 5M, Horn Mo (U) 30s. A second No Entry wind farm is 8M further W, centred on 52°35'·4N 04°13'·2E and marked by 6 cardinal lt buoys (2W, 2E, 1N, 1S); see AC 1631.

▶*3M W of IJmuiden the N-going stream begins at HW Hoek van Holland –0120, and the S-going at HW Hoek van Holland +0430, sp rates about 1·5kn. Off ent to IJmuiden the stream turns about 1h earlier and is stronger, and in heavy weather there may be a dangerous sea.*◀ From **IJmuiden** the **Noordzeekanaal** leads east to **Amsterdam** and the **IJsselmeer**.

HOEK VAN HOLLAND TO THE WESTERSCHELDE

Off Hoek van Holland at the ent to Europoort and **Rotterdam** shipping is very dense and fast-moving. Yachts must go up-river via the Nieuwe Waterweg which near Vlaardingen becomes the Nieuwe Maas.

The Slijkgat (lit) is the approach chan to **Stellendam** and entry to the Haringvliet. The Schaar, Schouwenbank, Middelbank and Steenbanken lie parallel to the coast off the approaches to Oosterschelde. From the N, Geul van de Banjaard (partly lit) joins Westgat and leads to Oude Roompot, which with Roompot (unlit) are the main, well marked channels to the **Roompotsluis**,

in S half of the barrage. Here the Oosterschelde (AC 192) is entered.

Rounding Walcheren via the Oostgat, close inshore, Westkapelle lt ho is conspic with two smaller lts nearby: Molenhoofd 5ca WSW and Noorderhoofd 7ca NNW. The Oostgat is the inshore link between Oosterschelde and Westerschelde and also the N approach to the latter.

Deurloo and Spleet are unlit secondary channels parallel to Oostgat and a mile or so to seaward. By day they keep yachts clear of commercial traffic in the Oostgat.

All channels converge between **Vlissingen** and **Breskens**. This bottleneck is declared a Precautionary Area in which yachts have no rights of way over other vessels and therefore must keep an above average lookout, staying clear of all traffic. Vessels <20m must give way to larger craft; and yachts <12m should stay just outside the main buoyed chans.

The main approach chan to the Westerschelde from the W is the Scheur, which yachts may follow just outside the fairway. From **Zeebrugge** and the SW use the Wielingen chan, keeping close to S side of estuary until past **Breskens**.

If crossing the Scheur there are two recommended routes. The W route runs to the W of Songa with a dogleg at W10 towards SG-W. The E route from Breskens, head up channel from ARV-VH, staying S of the G bys, turning N to cross the mini-TSS which runs E/W close off Vlissingen. Ensure you cross at right angles. The tide runs hard in the estuary, causing a bad sea in chans and overfalls on some banks in strong winds. There is shoaling.

The passage up-river to **Antwerpen** is best made in one leg, starting from Breskens, Vlissingen or **Terneuzen** in order to get the tidal timing right.

2.20   TSS AND VTS OFF SOUTH NETHERLANDS AND BELGIUM

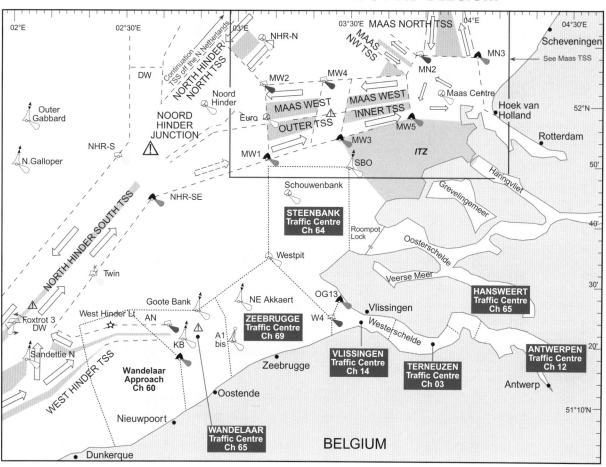

Netherlands

STANDARD TIME UT –01
Subtract 1 hour for UT
For Dutch Summer Time add
ONE hour in **non-shaded areas**

HOEK VAN HOLLAND   LAT 51°59'N   LONG 4°07'E
TIMES AND HEIGHTS OF HIGH AND LOW WATERS

Dates in **red** are **SPRINGS**
Dates in **blue** are **NEAPS**

YEAR 2015

JANUARY

	Time	m		Time	m
1 TH	0705 1140 1700	0.5 1.9 0.3	**16** F	0440 1101 1640 2336	0.5 1.9 0.4
2 F	0016 0817 1236 1805	2.1 0.5 2.0 0.4	**17** SA	0540 1205 1744	0.4 2.0 0.4
3 SA	0104 0920 1325 1844	2.1 0.4 2.1 0.4	**18** SU	0038 0614 1306 1823	2.1 0.4 2.1 0.4
4 SU	0154 1005 1410 1934	2.1 0.4 2.2 0.5	**19** M	0125 0656 1346 1904	2.1 0.3 2.2 0.4
5 M ○	0243 0755 1455 2300	2.1 0.4 2.2 0.5	**20** TU ●	0215 0845 1431 1950	2.2 0.3 2.3 0.5
6 TU	0325 0824 1536 2345	2.1 0.3 2.3 0.5	**21** W	0257 0806 1515 2025	2.2 0.2 2.4 0.5
7 W	0406 0905 1611	2.1 0.3 2.3	**22** TH	0339 0842 1557	2.2 0.1 2.4
8 TH	0025 0434 0934 1648	0.5 2.1 0.3 2.3	**23** F	0000 0425 0925 1646	0.5 2.2 0.1 2.4
9 F	0105 0515 1015 1729	0.5 2.1 0.2 2.2	**24** SA	0035 0508 1016 1729	0.5 2.2 0.1 2.4
10 SA	0110 0545 1055 1805	0.5 2.1 0.2 2.2	**25** SU	0135 0555 1105 1818	0.5 2.1 0.1 2.3
11 SU	0130 0625 1145 1845	0.5 2.0 0.2 2.1	**26** M	0220 0649 1206 1915	0.5 2.1 0.2 2.2
12 M	0150 0700 1224 1914	0.5 2.0 0.2 2.0	**27** TU ◗	0134 0746 1309 2014	0.5 2.0 0.1 2.1
13 TU ◗	0150 0756 1315 2020	0.5 1.9 0.2 2.0	**28** W	0205 0844 1415 2123	0.5 2.0 0.2 2.0
14 W	0230 0856 1425 2126	0.5 1.9 0.3 2.0	**29** TH	0304 0954 1545 2245	0.5 1.9 0.3 1.9
15 TH	0314 1001 1525 2230	0.5 1.8 0.4 1.9	**30** F	0420 1116 1644	0.5 1.9 0.3
			31 SA	0005 0515 1225 1749	1.9 0.5 2.0 0.4

FEBRUARY

	Time	m		Time	m
1 SU	0105 0916 1315 2140	2.0 0.4 2.1 0.4	**16** M	0004 0556 1235 2106	1.9 0.3 2.0 0.4
2 M	0206 1000 1405 2224	2.0 0.3 2.1 0.4	**17** TU	0108 0625 1327 2155	2.0 0.3 2.2 0.4
3 TU	0234 1046 1445 2254	2.1 0.3 2.2 0.5	**18** W	0156 0705 1412 1928	2.1 0.2 2.3 0.4
4 W ○	0320 0815 1518 2335	2.1 0.3 2.2 0.5	**19** TH ●	0238 0745 1455 2006	2.1 0.1 2.4 0.5
5 TH	0345 0845 1555 2347	2.1 0.3 2.3 0.5	**20** F	0322 0825 1539 2045	2.2 0.1 2.4 0.5
6 F	0419 0911 1629	2.1 0.2 2.3	**21** SA	0405 0906 1626	2.2 0.1 2.4
7 SA	0007 0449 0949 1705	0.5 2.1 0.2 2.2	**22** SU	0024 0447 0949 1709	0.5 2.2 0.1 2.4
8 SU	0037 0526 1025 1738	0.4 2.1 0.2 2.2	**23** M	0114 0535 1039 1755	0.4 2.2 0.1 2.3
9 M	0125 0556 1059 1808	0.4 2.1 0.2 2.1	**24** TU	0210 0621 1139 1849	0.4 2.2 0.1 2.1
10 TU	0155 0621 1145 1839	0.5 2.1 0.2 2.1	**25** W ◖	0020 0711 1244 1950	0.4 2.1 0.1 2.0
11 W	0005 0700 1224 1925	0.5 2.0 0.2 2.1	**26** TH	0124 0816 1405 2055	0.4 2.0 0.2 1.8
12 TH ◗	0140 0745 1345 2025	0.5 2.0 0.2 2.0	**27** F	0246 0936 1526 2220	0.4 1.9 0.3 1.7
13 F	0235 0855 1455 2156	0.4 1.9 0.3 1.9	**28** SA	0345 1044 1624 2346	0.4 1.8 0.3 1.8
14 SA	0340 1026 1555 2300	0.4 1.8 0.4 1.9			
15 SU	0454 1135 1726	0.5 1.9 0.4			

MARCH

	Time	m		Time	m
1 SU	0454 1205 1950	0.4 1.9 0.4	**16** M	0415 1116 1644 2346	0.3 1.9 0.4 1.8
2 M	0044 0553 1306 2120	1.9 0.3 2.0 0.3	**17** TU	0515 1216 2045	0.3 2.0 0.4
3 TU	0139 0945 1355 2216	2.0 0.2 2.1 0.3	**18** W	0046 0559 1308 2135	1.9 0.2 2.2 0.3
4 W	0225 1030 1425 2245	2.0 0.2 2.1 0.4	**19** TH	0132 0639 1352 2210	2.0 0.2 2.3 0.3
5 TH ○	0255 0800 1459 2310	2.0 0.3 2.2 0.4	**20** F ●	0217 0720 1435 1945	2.1 0.1 2.4 0.4
6 F	0326 0814 1528 2310	2.1 0.3 2.2 0.4	**21** SA	0259 0800 1516 2026	2.2 0.1 2.4 0.4
7 SA	0351 0844 1605 2327	2.1 0.2 2.2 0.4	**22** SU	0342 0841 1603	2.2 0.1 2.4
8 SU	0421 0919 1635	2.1 0.2 2.2	**23** M	0020 0427 0928 1646	0.4 2.3 0.1 2.3
9 M	0004 0451 1234 1708	0.3 2.1 0.2 2.2	**24** TU	0110 0508 1018 1732	0.3 2.2 0.1 2.2
10 TU	0044 0521 1024 1736	0.3 2.1 0.2 2.1	**25** W	0206 0556 1115 1821	0.3 2.2 0.2 2.1
11 W	0136 0556 1105 1807	0.3 2.1 0.2 2.1	**26** TH	0245 0646 1240 1915	0.3 2.0 0.2 1.9
12 TH	0205 0630 1145 1849	0.3 2.1 0.2 2.1	**27** F ◖	0100 0734 1344 2015	0.3 2.0 0.2 1.7
13 F ◗	0005 0708 1250 1938	0.3 2.1 0.2 2.0	**28** SA	0215 0844 1454 2144	0.3 1.9 0.3 1.6
14 SA	0147 0816 1435 2055	0.3 1.9 0.3 1.8	**29** SU	0334 1036 1605 2325	0.3 1.8 0.3 1.6
15 SU	0254 0956 1535 2225	0.3 1.8 0.3 1.7	**30** M	0456 1146 1730	0.3 1.9 0.4
			31 TU	0025 0535 1245 2040	1.7 0.2 2.0 0.3

APRIL

	Time	m		Time	m
1 W	0111 0630 1325 2141	1.9 0.2 2.0 0.3	**16** TH	0019 0529 1245 2110	1.8 0.2 2.1 0.3
2 TH	0200 1006 1359 2226	1.9 0.2 2.1 0.3	**17** F	0111 0615 1329 2135	1.9 0.1 2.3 0.4
3 F	0224 0745 1431 2235	2.0 0.2 2.1 0.4	**18** SA ●	0156 0656 1415 2225	2.1 0.1 2.3 0.4
4 SA	0255 0759 1505 2250	2.0 0.3 2.2 0.4	**19** SU ○	0237 0740 1459 1959	2.2 0.1 2.3 0.4
5 SU	0321 0825 1535 2255	2.1 0.3 2.2 0.3	**20** M	0322 0819 1543	2.2 0.1 2.3
6 M	0355 1114 1607 2344	2.1 0.3 2.2 0.3	**21** TU	0001 0405 0905 1627	0.3 2.3 0.2 2.2
7 TU	0425 1204 1639	2.1 0.2 2.1	**22** W	0057 0447 1335 1716	0.3 2.3 0.2 2.1
8 W	0024 0455 1250 1708	0.2 2.1 0.2 2.1	**23** TH	0146 0530 1416 1759	0.2 2.2 0.2 2.0
9 TH	0115 0527 1324 1745	0.2 2.1 0.3 2.1	**24** F	0226 0619 1455 1844	0.2 2.1 0.3 1.8
10 F	0155 0605 1124 1830	0.2 2.2 0.3 2.0	**25** SA	0014 0715 1340 1944	0.2 2.0 0.3 1.7
11 SA	0000 0649 1310 1919	0.2 2.1 0.3 1.9	**26** SU ◖	0140 0820 1555 2044	0.2 1.9 0.3 1.6
12 SU ◗	0110 0744 1436 2035	0.2 2.0 0.3 1.7	**27** M	0305 0934 1555 2245	0.2 1.8 0.4 1.5
13 M	0235 0920 1536 2159	0.2 1.9 0.4 1.7	**28** TU	0414 1116 1645 2343	0.2 1.8 0.4 1.6
14 TU	0346 1045 1624 2326	0.2 1.9 0.4 1.7	**29** W	0526 1203 1930	0.2 1.9 0.3
15 W	0433 1149 2016	0.3 2.0 0.3	**30** TH	0035 0604 1249 2056	1.7 0.2 2.0 0.3

Chart Datum is 0·92 metres below NAP Datum. HAT is 2·5 metres above Chart Datum.

》 **FREE** monthly updates from 《
www.reedsalmanac.co.uk

STANDARD TIME UT –01
Subtract 1 hour for UT
For Dutch Summer Time add
ONE hour in **non-shaded areas**

HOEK VAN HOLLAND   LAT 51°59'N   LONG 4°07'E
TIMES AND HEIGHTS OF HIGH AND LOW WATERS

Dates in red are **SPRINGS**
Dates in blue are NEAPS

YEAR 2015

MAY

Time	m		Time	m
1 0115	1.8	**16** 0045	1.9
0645	0.3	0555	0.1
F 1325	2.0	SA 1308	2.2
2140	0.3	2105	0.3
2 0149	1.9	**17** 0135	2.0
0715	0.3	0635	0.2
SA 1359	2.1	SU 1357	2.2
2205	0.3	2200	0.3
3 0219	2.0	**18** 0217	2.1
0735	0.3	0726	0.2
SU 1436	2.1	M 1440	2.2
2250	0.3	● 1945	0.3
4 0251	2.1	**19** 0306	2.2
0754	0.3	0810	0.2
M 1505	2.2	TU 1527	2.2
○ 2250	0.3	2345	0.3
5 0322	2.1	**20** 0345	2.2
1055	0.3	1155	0.3
TU 1546	2.2	W 1607	2.1
2325	0.2		
6 0359	2.2	**21** 0036	0.2
1135	0.3	0427	2.2
W 1616	2.1	TH 1254	0.3
		1655	2.0
7 0004	0.2	**22** 0115	0.2
0432	2.2	0510	2.2
TH 1215	0.3	F 1350	0.3
1651	2.1	1738	1.9
8 0100	0.2	**23** 0205	0.1
0507	2.2	0559	2.1
F 1304	0.3	SA 1435	0.3
1728	2.0	1825	1.9
9 0146	0.2	**24** 0240	0.1
0549	2.2	0650	2.1
SA 1334	0.3	SU 1510	0.4
1816	1.9	1915	1.8
10 0220	0.1	**25** 0044	0.1
0635	2.1	0746	1.9
SU 1410	0.3	M 1420	0.4
1905	1.8	◑ 2005	1.7
11 0045	0.1	**26** 0230	0.2
0735	2.0	0845	1.8
M 1427	0.4	TU 1515	0.4
◑ 2015	1.7	2104	1.6
12 0205	0.1	**27** 0405	0.2
0855	2.0	0955	1.8
TU 1505	0.4	W 1614	0.4
2140	1.7	2225	1.6
13 0316	0.1	**28** 0455	0.2
1016	2.0	1104	1.8
W 1805	0.4	TH 1726	0.3
2244	1.7	2355	1.6
14 0404	0.1	**29** 0534	0.2
1126	2.0	1210	1.9
TH 1940	0.4	F 1805	0.3
2355	1.8		
15 0505	0.1	**30** 0036	1.7
1225	2.1	0625	0.3
F 2025	0.3	SA 1256	2.0
		2050	0.3
		31 0109	1.9
		0655	0.3
		SU 1325	2.1
		2145	0.3

JUNE

Time	m		Time	m
1 0146	2.0	**16** 0200	2.1
0704	0.3	0713	0.3
M 1405	2.1	TU 1428	2.1
2225	0.3	● 1935	0.3
2 0221	2.1	**17** 0246	2.2
0740	0.3	0806	0.4
TU 1439	2.2	W 1515	2.1
○ 1954	0.3	2015	0.3
3 0255	2.2	**18** 0328	2.2
0816	0.4	1146	0.4
W 1516	2.2	TH 1555	2.1
2035	0.2		
4 0335	2.2	**19** 0016	2.1
1115	0.4	0415	2.2
TH 1555	2.1	F 1240	0.4
		1638	2.0
5 0000	0.2	**20** 0055	0.2
0412	2.2	0455	2.2
F 1155	0.4	SA 1326	0.4
1636	2.1	1725	2.0
6 0046	0.2	**21** 0147	0.1
0456	2.2	0539	2.2
SA 1255	0.3	SU 1411	0.4
1717	2.0	1758	1.9
7 0125	0.1	**22** 0220	0.2
0537	2.2	0618	2.1
SU 1335	0.3	M 1440	0.4
1805	1.9	1846	1.9
8 0210	0.1	**23** 0004	0.1
0625	2.2	0710	2.0
M 1426	0.4	TU 1410	0.4
1900	1.8	1924	1.8
9 0014	0.1	**24** 0054	0.2
0726	2.1	0800	1.9
TU 1500	0.4	W 1450	0.4
◑ 2005	1.8	◑ 2025	1.7
10 0125	0.1	**25** 0155	0.2
0834	2.0	0856	1.9
W 1500	0.4	TH 1550	0.4
2116	1.8	2120	1.7
11 0240	0.1	**26** 0420	0.2
0945	2.0	0955	1.8
TH 1534	0.4	F 1637	0.4
2215	1.8	2226	1.7
12 0340	0.2	**27** 0525	0.3
1056	2.0	1055	1.9
F 1857	0.4	SA 1725	0.3
2326	1.8	2336	1.7
13 0434	0.2	**28** 0610	0.3
1158	2.1	1154	1.9
SA 1955	0.4	SU 1805	0.3
14 0025	1.9	**29** 0030	1.9
0540	0.2	0700	0.4
SU 1256	2.1	M 1256	2.0
2050	0.4	1844	0.3
15 0116	2.0	**30** 0115	2.0
0629	0.2	0635	0.4
M 1341	2.1	TU 1336	2.1
1855	0.3	1904	0.3

JULY

Time	m		Time	m
1 0155	2.1	**16** 0235	2.2
0713	0.4	0754	0.5
W 1418	2.1	TH 1505	2.1
1934	0.2	● 2004	0.3
2 0235	2.2	**17** 0315	2.2
0756	0.4	1115	0.5
TH 1457	2.2	F 1549	2.1
○ 2016	0.2	2046	0.2
3 0316	2.3	**18** 0356	2.2
0835	0.4	1216	0.5
F 1539	2.1	SA 1626	2.1
2049	0.2	2119	0.2
4 0356	2.3	**19** 0435	2.2
1156	0.4	1300	0.5
SA 1621	2.1	SU 1659	2.1
2128	0.1	2159	0.2
5 0437	2.3	**20** 0515	2.2
1235	0.4	1346	0.5
SU 1706	2.0	M 1738	2.0
2212	0.1	2246	0.1
6 0522	2.3	**21** 0555	2.2
1314	0.4	1400	0.5
M 1748	2.0	TU 1809	2.0
2306	0.1	2325	0.2
7 0615	2.2	**22** 0636	2.1
1355	0.4	1400	0.5
TU 1845	1.9	W 1850	1.9
2355	0.1		
8 0705	2.2	**23** 0015	0.2
1454	0.4	0716	2.0
W 1939	1.9	TH 1410	0.4
◐		1924	1.9
9 0105	0.1	**24** 0110	0.3
0815	2.1	0806	2.0
TH 1440	0.5	F 1420	0.4
2046	1.9	◑ 2030	1.8
10 0209	0.1	**25** 0205	0.2
0914	2.1	0906	1.9
F 1515	0.4	SA 1454	0.4
2155	1.9	2136	1.8
11 0315	0.1	**26** 0305	0.3
1030	2.0	1006	1.9
SA 1604	0.4	SU 1700	0.4
2254	1.9	2234	1.8
12 0436	0.2	**27** 0415	0.4
1135	2.0	1115	1.9
SU 1704	0.4	M 1750	0.4
		2350	1.9
13 0005	1.9	**28** 0600	0.4
0525	0.3	1216	2.0
M 1234	2.0	TU 1805	0.3
1805	0.4		
14 0059	2.0	**29** 0041	2.0
0624	0.3	0614	0.4
TU 1335	2.1	W 1310	2.0
1843	0.4	1839	0.3
15 0148	2.1	**30** 0136	2.1
0704	0.4	0654	0.4
W 1425	2.1	TH 1355	2.1
1929	0.3	1915	0.3
		31 0215	2.2
		0729	0.5
		F 1440	2.2
		○ 1950	0.2

AUGUST

Time	m		Time	m
1 0255	2.3	**16** 0339	2.3
0805	0.5	1156	0.6
SA 1518	2.2	SU 1601	2.1
2026	0.1	2100	0.3
2 0337	2.4	**17** 0415	2.3
0846	0.5	1224	0.5
SU 1602	2.2	M 1635	2.1
2105	0.1	2129	0.3
3 0421	2.4	**18** 0449	2.3
1220	0.5	1247	0.5
M 1645	2.2	TU 1709	2.1
2150	0.1	2210	0.3
4 0505	2.4	**19** 0527	2.2
1305	0.5	1307	0.5
TU 1731	2.1	W 1739	2.1
2236	0.1	2250	0.3
5 0550	2.3	**20** 0555	2.1
1355	0.5	1340	0.5
W 1819	2.1	TH 1809	2.1
2329	0.1	2325	0.3
6 0646	2.2	**21** 0625	2.1
1440	0.5	1154	0.5
TH 1908	2.1	F 1839	2.0
7 0034	0.1	**22** 0004	0.3
0746	2.1	0705	2.1
F 1400	0.5	SA 1310	0.4
◐ 2011	2.0	◐ 1925	2.0
8 0144	0.2	**23** 0120	0.3
0849	2.0	0744	2.0
SA 1440	0.5	SU 1415	0.4
2114	1.9	2024	1.9
9 0300	0.2	**24** 0236	0.4
1006	1.9	0916	1.9
SU 1535	0.5	M 1509	0.4
2241	1.9	2155	1.8
10 0415	0.3	**25** 0335	0.4
1125	1.9	1030	1.9
M 1645	0.4	TU 1700	0.4
2349	2.0	2304	1.9
11 0513	0.4	**26** 0455	0.5
1224	2.0	1145	1.9
TU 1745	0.4	W 1734	0.4
12 0049	2.1	**27** 0020	2.0
0916	0.4	0544	0.5
W 1324	2.0	TH 1245	2.0
2135	0.3	1805	0.3
13 0146	2.1	**28** 0105	2.2
1000	0.4	0936	0.5
TH 1415	2.1	F 1335	2.1
1915	0.3	1845	0.3
14 0225	2.2	**29** 0155	2.3
1025	0.5	0704	0.5
F 1454	2.1	SA 1415	2.2
● 1949	0.3	○ 1926	0.2
15 0305	2.2	**30** 0236	2.4
1115	0.5	0746	0.6
SA 1536	2.1	SU 1458	2.2
2025	0.3	1959	0.1
		31 0317	2.5
		0822	0.5
		M 1542	2.3
		2039	0.1

Netherlands

Chart Datum is 0·92 metres below NAP Datum. HAT is 2·5 metres above Chart Datum.

STANDARD TIME UT –01
Subtract 1 hour for UT
For Dutch Summer Time add
ONE hour in **non-shaded areas**

HOEK VAN HOLLAND   LAT 51°59'N   LONG 4°07'E
TIMES AND HEIGHTS OF HIGH AND LOW WATERS

Dates in red are **SPRINGS**
Dates in blue are **NEAPS**

YEAR 2015

SEPTEMBER

Time	m		Time	m
1 0359	2.5	**16** 0421	2.3
0859	0.5	1157	0.5
TU 1626	2.3	W 1639	2.2
2125	0.1	2134	0.4
2 0445	2.4	**17** 0451	2.2
0948	0.6	1240	0.5
W 1707	2.3	TH 1710	2.2
2212	0.1	2215	0.4
3 0529	2.4	**18** 0525	2.2
1345	0.5	1326	0.5
TH 1756	2.2	F 1738	2.2
2301	0.2	2245	0.4
4 0618	2.2	**19** 0555	2.2
1435	0.5	1105	0.4
F 1841	2.2	SA 1808	2.2
		2324	0.4
5 0005	0.2	**20** 0628	2.2
0716	2.1	1145	0.4
SA 1245	0.5	SU 1845	2.2
◑ 1939	2.1		
6 0135	0.3	**21** 0026	0.4
0814	2.0	0716	2.1
SU 1416	0.5	M 1300	0.4
2044	2.0	◐ 1940	2.1
7 0234	0.3	**22** 0200	0.4
0945	1.8	0814	1.9
M 1520	0.4	TU 1435	0.4
2215	1.9	2104	1.9
8 0355	0.4	**23** 0304	0.5
1105	1.8	0950	1.8
TU 1646	0.4	W 1534	0.4
2333	2.0	2233	1.9
9 0714	0.5	**24** 0424	0.5
1219	1.9	1110	1.8
W 1724	0.4	TH 1644	0.4
		2350	2.1
10 0039	2.1	**25** 0805	0.5
0845	0.4	1215	1.9
TH 1315	2.0	F 1735	0.4
2125	0.3		
11 0129	2.2	**26** 0045	2.2
0956	0.4	0910	0.5
F 1405	2.1	SA 1309	2.1
2216	0.3	1815	0.3
12 0209	2.2	**27** 0128	2.4
1036	0.5	0945	0.5
SA 1435	2.1	SU 1356	2.2
1940	0.4	1855	0.5
13 0245	2.3	**28** 0212	2.5
1100	0.6	0719	0.5
SU 1504	2.1	M 1437	2.3
● 2010	0.3	○ 1935	0.2
14 0318	2.3	**29** 0255	2.5
0824	0.6	0755	0.5
M 1539	2.2	TU 1516	2.3
2029	0.3	2016	0.2
15 0349	2.3	**30** 0338	2.5
0849	0.6	0835	0.5
TU 1610	2.2	W 1600	2.4
2106	0.3	2106	0.2

OCTOBER

Time	m		Time	m
1 0423	2.4	**16** 0425	2.3
0922	0.5	1205	0.5
TH 1645	2.4	F 1642	2.3
2145	0.3	2145	0.5
2 0508	2.3	**17** 0455	2.2
1009	0.5	1255	0.5
F 1729	2.3	SA 1708	2.3
2245	0.3	2214	0.5
3 0555	2.2	**18** 0525	2.2
1106	0.5	1039	0.4
SA 1818	2.3	SU 1745	2.3
2344	0.4	2254	0.5
4 0645	2.1	**19** 0605	2.2
1205	0.4	1126	0.3
SU 1909	2.2	M 1826	2.2
◐		2343	0.5
5 0114	0.4	**20** 0649	2.1
0744	1.9	1214	0.3
M 1330	0.4	TU 1916	2.1
2015	2.0	◐	
6 0225	0.5	**21** 0150	0.5
0904	1.8	0749	1.9
TU 1445	0.4	W 1355	0.4
2156	1.9	2023	2.0
7 0346	0.5	**22** 0244	0.6
1057	1.8	0915	1.8
W 1614	0.4	TH 1505	0.4
2315	2.0	2205	2.0
8 0640	0.5	**23** 0354	0.6
1155	1.9	1040	1.8
TH 1709	0.4	F 1605	0.4
		2315	2.1
9 0019	2.1	**24** 0730	0.6
0820	0.5	1145	1.9
F 1255	2.0	SA 1706	0.3
2037	0.4		
10 0105	2.2	**25** 0015	2.2
0926	0.5	0845	0.5
SA 1333	2.1	SU 1241	2.1
2146	0.4	1750	0.3
11 0145	2.2	**26** 0106	2.4
1006	0.5	0936	0.5
SU 1416	2.1	M 1329	2.2
1915	0.4	1836	0.3
12 0216	2.3	**27** 0151	2.5
1035	0.5	0659	0.5
M 1439	2.2	TU 1415	2.3
1944	0.4	○ 1915	0.2
13 0249	2.3	**28** 0236	2.5
0804	0.5	0738	0.5
TU 1505	2.2	W 1455	2.4
● 2009	0.4	1958	0.2
14 0326	2.3	**29** 0319	2.4
0824	0.5	0819	0.5
W 1537	2.3	TH 1539	2.4
2034	0.4	2046	0.3
15 0355	2.3	**30** 0403	2.4
1130	0.5	0901	0.4
TH 1609	2.3	F 1623	2.4
2116	0.4	2129	0.4
		31 0447	2.3
		0949	0.4
		SA 1707	2.4
		2226	0.5

NOVEMBER

Time	m		Time	m
1 0535	2.2	**16** 0034	0.5
1039	0.4	0509	2.2
SU 1755	2.3	M 1023	0.3
		1727	2.3
2 0246	0.5	**17** 0120	0.5
0625	2.0	0550	2.1
M 1134	0.4	TU 1104	0.3
1845	2.2	1808	2.3
3 0054	0.5	**18** 0200	0.6
0714	1.9	0638	2.0
TU 1254	0.4	W 1205	0.3
◑ 1944	2.1	1858	2.2
4 0200	0.5	**19** 0210	0.6
0824	1.8	0735	1.9
W 1405	0.4	TH 1314	0.3
2105	2.0	◑ 2016	2.1
5 0305	0.6	**20** 0235	0.6
1010	1.7	0856	1.8
TH 1556	0.4	F 1436	0.3
2246	1.9	2136	2.1
6 0414	0.6	**21** 0335	0.6
1120	1.8	1010	1.8
F 1644	0.4	SA 1530	0.3
2345	2.0	2245	2.1
7 0707	0.5	**22** 0657	0.6
1215	1.9	1118	1.9
SA 1735	0.4	SU 1635	0.3
		2350	2.2
8 0035	2.1	**23** 0805	0.5
0830	0.5	1216	2.0
SU 1255	2.0	M 1725	0.3
1824	0.4		
9 0111	2.2	**24** 0041	2.3
0925	0.5	0900	0.5
M 1340	2.0	TU 1305	2.2
1905	0.4	1816	0.3
10 0145	2.2	**25** 0128	2.4
1005	0.5	0645	0.5
TU 1410	2.1	W 1352	2.3
1935	0.5	○ 1859	0.3
11 0219	2.3	**26** 0217	2.4
0744	0.5	0725	0.5
W 1435	2.2	TH 1437	2.4
● 1954	0.5	1945	0.4
12 0256	2.3	**27** 0306	2.3
0809	0.5	0808	0.4
TH 1515	2.3	F 1522	2.4
2019	0.5	2029	0.4
13 0326	2.3	**28** 0347	2.3
0834	0.4	0850	0.4
F 1545	2.3	SA 1607	2.4
2056	0.5	2116	0.5
14 0402	2.3	**29** 0432	2.2
0911	0.4	0936	0.4
SA 1616	2.3	SU 1648	2.4
2046	0.3		
15 0006	0.5	**30** 0125	0.5
0436	2.2	0518	2.1
SU 0950	0.4	M 1021	0.3
1651	2.3	1736	2.3

DECEMBER

Time	m		Time	m
1 0215	0.5	**16** 0116	0.5
0605	2.0	0539	2.1
TU 1115	0.3	W 1055	0.2
1825	2.2	1759	2.3
2 0306	0.6	**17** 0155	0.5
0656	2.0	0625	2.0
W 1214	0.3	TH 1146	0.2
1914	2.1	1849	2.2
3 0130	0.6	**18** 0230	0.6
0745	1.9	0718	2.0
TH 1314	0.3	F 1245	0.2
◑ 2020	2.0	◑ 1956	2.2
4 0225	0.6	**19** 0240	0.6
0845	1.8	0829	1.9
F 1504	0.3	SA 1345	0.2
2125	1.9	2105	2.1
5 0350	0.6	**20** 0254	0.6
0955	1.7	0940	1.9
SA 1620	0.4	SU 1506	0.2
2235	1.9	2216	2.1
6 0445	0.6	**21** 0354	0.6
1125	1.7	1046	1.9
SU 1715	0.4	M 1605	0.3
2350	2.0	2319	2.1
7 0534	0.5	**22** 0734	0.6
1226	1.8	1149	2.0
M 1814	0.4	TU 1705	0.3
8 0040	2.0	**23** 0025	2.2
0830	0.5	0830	0.5
TU 1300	1.9	W 1246	2.1
1904	0.4	1806	0.4
9 0115	2.1	**24** 0116	2.2
0925	0.4	0629	0.5
W 1336	2.0	TH 1337	2.2
2020	0.5	1856	0.4
10 0156	2.2	**25** 0205	2.2
1016	0.4	0716	0.4
TH 1409	2.2	F 1425	2.3
1934	0.5	○ 1939	0.4
11 0229	2.2	**26** 0256	2.2
0755	0.4	0755	0.4
F 1445	2.2	SA 1507	2.3
● 1954	0.5	2026	0.5
12 0302	2.3	**27** 0335	2.2
0826	0.4	0835	0.3
SA 1521	2.3	SU 1555	2.4
2033	0.5		
13 0338	2.2	**28** 0016	0.5
0900	0.3	0900	0.5
SU 1557	2.3	M 0914	0.3
2324	0.5	1637	2.4
14 0419	2.2	**29** 0106	0.5
0929	0.3	0500	2.1
M 1636	2.3	TU 1001	0.2
		1719	2.3
15 0025	0.5	**30** 0144	0.5
0456	2.2	0545	2.1
TU 1009	0.2	W 1049	0.2
1715	2.3	1801	2.3
		31 0224	0.5
		0625	2.0
		TH 1145	0.2
		1845	2.2

Chart Datum is 0·92 metres below NAP Datum. HAT is 2·5 metres above Chart Datum.

》》 FREE monthly updates from **《《**
www.reedsalmanac.co.uk

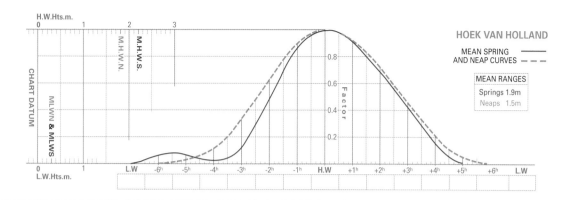

HOEK VAN HOLLAND

MEAN SPRING AND NEAP CURVES

MEAN RANGES	
Springs	1.9m
Neaps	1.5m

2.21 MAAS TSS

Large ships bound up-Channel for Europoort route via the Dover Strait and the Noord Hinder South TSS to Noord Hinder Junction (a large pentagon roughly centred on 52°N 02°51'·1E). Here ships enter the MAAS TRAFFIC SEPARATION SCHEME.

Maas West Outer TSS starts some 33M offshore and funnels large ships 083°/27M via the TSS lanes or Eurogeul (DW route dredged 24·5m) towards a second pentagon 'Maas Precautionary Area' clear of Maas West Inner TSS and 10M offshore. When abeam Maas Centre SWM buoy, ships enter the Maasgeul (Maas narrows) and track inbound 5·5M on the 112° leading lights to the Maasmond (Maas mouth, ie the harbour entrance).

Yachts should avoid the whole complex by using the ITZ and/or crossing the Maasgeul via the recommended track (see Hoek van Holland and www.maasvlakte2.com/uploads/crossing_route.pdf). Knowing the above is to be aware of what you are avoiding.

HOEK VAN HOLLAND TO THE SOUTH EAST UK

Yachts out of Rotterdam/Hoek van Holland bound for the southern Thames Estuary should route 254°/52M from MV-N buoy to NHR-SE buoy, passing MW5, Goeree tower, MW3 and MW1 buoys. Cross the Noord Hinder South TSS between NHR-SE and NHR-S buoys. Thence depending on destination, set course 242°/44M to Outer Tongue for the River Thames; or 228°/46M to NE Goodwin for Ramsgate or points south.

If bound for the River Orwell or adjacent rivers, it may be best to pass north (rather than south) of the large and busy Sunk Outer and Inner Precautionary Areas and their associated TSS. From NHR-S buoy route via West Gabbard, North Inner Gabbard, S Shipwash and Rough buoys to pick up the recommended yacht track at Cork Sand Yacht beacon; it is a less direct route than going south via Galloper, but it avoids the worst of the commercial traffic.

2.21A MAAS TSS, PRECAUTIONARY AREA AND MAASGEUL

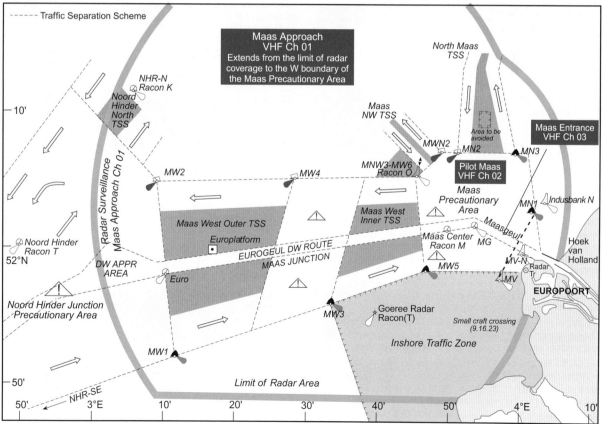

Netherlands

2.22 HOEK VAN HOLLAND AND NIEUWE WATERWEG VTS

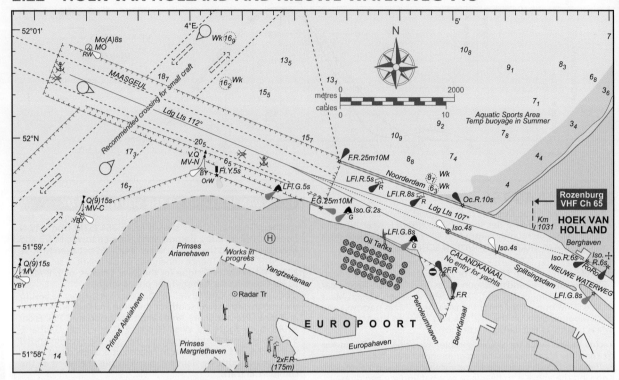

CROSSING THE MAASGEUL To cross the entrance (ie seaward of the bkwtrs), coasting yachts should advise *Maas Ent* Ch 03 of position/course/speed, then monitor Ch 03. Cross on the recommended track, 046° (226°) under power; see chartlet. Beware strong cross tides. Keep a keen lookout for fast moving merchantmen; Rules 18 d (ii) and 28.

HOEK VAN HOLLAND

CHARTS AC 122, 132; Zeekaart 1540, 1349, 1350, 1449; DYC 1801.6, 1801.7; Imray C30, Y5

TIDES +0251 Dover; ML 0·9; Duration 0505. HOEK VAN HOLLAND is a Standard Port (←), but has no Secondary ports; see also Rotterdam. Double LWs occur, more obviously at sp; in effect a LW stand. The 1st LW is about 5½ hrs after HW and the 2nd LW about 4¼ hrs before the next HW. Predictions are for the *lower* LW. Prolonged NW gales can raise levels by up to 3m.

SHELTER Entry safe, but in strong on-shore winds heavy seas/swell develop. The first adequate shelter is 6M up river at Maassluis (3m). Complete shelter 10-19M further E at Rotterdam.

NAVIGATION From N, WPT 52°02'·89N 04°03'·57E (Indusbank NCM lt buoy, Q), 190°/3·2M to Noorderdam lt, FR.

From S, WPT 51°59'·61N 04°00'·20E (MV-N buoy), 101°/3·0M to ent to Nieuwe Waterweg. *Yachts must on no account enter the Calandkanaal or Europoort. Stay in the Nieuwe Waterweg.* Maasvlakte 2 is due to open around Autumn 2014.

LIGHTS AND MARKS See chartlet and Lights, buoys & waypoints for details. Outer ldg lts 112° to ent; then 107° Red (ie keep to port) ldg lts into Nieuwe Waterweg, both R trs, W bands.

Hbr patrol vessels show a Fl Bu lt; additionally a Fl R lt = 'Stop'.

COMMUNICATIONS (Code 0174) TC/Port Authority (010) 2522801; Police (0900) 8844; Brit Consul (020) 6764343; ⊞ 4112800.

FACILITIES Berghaven is currently closed to yachts, use only in emergencies, HM 638850.

Hoek van Holland P, D, ✉, Ⓑ, ⇌, 🛒, R, ⌂, ✈ (Rotterdam). Ferries: Hook-Harwich; Rotterdam (Vlaardingen)-Hull.

Maasluis Marina No longer accessible due to a damaged lock.

NIEUWE WATERWEG VTS

Arrival procedure for yachts First report to *Maas Approach* or *Pilot Maas*, depending on distance offshore (or *Maas Ent* if within 4M of hbr ent), stating name/type of vessel, position and destination. Obey any instructions, monitoring the relevant Radar Ch's (limits as shown by W ☐ signboards on the river banks; Km signs are similar).

Rules for yachts in Nieuwe Waterweg/Nieuwe Maas: Monitor VTS channels (see below); transmit only in emergency or if obliged to deviate from the usual traffic flow. Keep to extreme stbd limit of buoyed line, avoiding debris between buoys and bank. No tacking/beating; no ⚓. Engine ready for instant start. Able to motor at 3·24kn (6km/hr). Hoist a radar reflector, esp in poor vis or at night. Cross chan quickly at 90°. All docks are prohib to yachts, except to access a marina. *Keep a good lookout, especially astern.*

The 3 **Traffic Centres (TC)** oversee their Radar surveillance stations and sub-sectors *(italics)*, on dedicated VHF chans below:

- **TC Hoek van Holland (VCH)** Ch 11. (See diagram above)

Maas Approach	Ch 01	38 – 11M W of Hoek;
Pilot Maas	Ch 02	11 – 4M W of Hoek;
Maas Entrance	Ch 03	4M – km 1031.

  English is the primary language on Ch 01, 02 and 03.

Rozenburg	Ch 65	km 1031 – 1028;
Maasluis	Ch 80	km 1028 – 1017.

- **Botlek Information & Tracking system** Ch 14.

Botlek	Ch 61	km 1017 – 1011;
Eemhaven	Ch 63	km 1011 – 1007.

- **TC Rotterdam (VCR)** Ch 11.

Waalhaven	Ch 60	km 1007 – 1003·5;
Maasbruggen	Ch 81	km 1003·5 – 998;
Brienenoord	Ch 81	km 998 – 993.

Harbour Coordination Centre (HCC) administers and controls Rotterdam port, Ch 19 (H24).

MSI broadcasts by TCs Ch 11 and on request by Radar stns.

Nieuwe Waterweg VTS and Nieuwe Maas into central Rotterdam *continued*

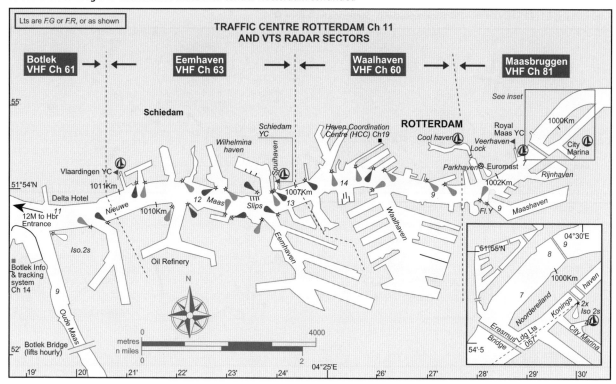

2.23   ROTTERDAM

Zuid Holland **51°54'·00N 04°28'·00E** (610m S of Euromast)
❀❀❀♤♤♤♧♧♧

CHARTS AC 122, 132, 133; Zeekaart 1540/1/2; DYC 1809.4, 1809.5

TIDES +0414 Dover; ML 0·9; Duration 0440

Standard Port VLISSINGEN (→)

Times				Height (metres)			
High Water		Low Water		MHWS	MHWN	MLWN	MLWS
0300	0900	0400	1000	4·9	4·1	1·0	0·5
1500	2100	1600	2200				

Differences EUROPLATFORM (30M W of Hoek van Holland)

+0005	−0005	−0030	−0055	−2·7	−2·3	−0·5	−0·1

MAASSLUIS (Km 1019)

+0155	+0115	+0100	+0310	−2·9	−2·4	−0·8	−0·3

VLAARDINGEN (Km 1011)

+0150	+0120	+0130	+0330	−2·8	−2·3	−0·7	−0·2

NOTE: Double LWs occur. Maasluis and Vlaardingen are referenced to Vlissingen, in UK ATT as above. The Dutch HP33 *Tidal heights and streams in Dutch coastal waters* shows the time differences below, relative to HW and the first LW at Hoek van Holland:

HOEK VAN HOLLAND	HW	1st LW
Maasluis	+0102	+0308
Vlaardingen	+0103	+0333
Rotterdam	+0111	+0341

SHELTER Good in the yacht hbrs where visitors are welcome (see Facilities). There is always a considerable chop/swell in the river due to constant heavy traffic to/from Europoort and Rotterdam.

NAVIGATION See 2.22 for WPTs (to enter Nieuwe Waterweg) and Yacht Rules. From the hbr ent to the conspic Euromast (51°54'·33N 04°28'·00E) is about 18M (33km). 6M W of the Euromast, the very busy Oude Maas joins at km 1013, giving access to Dordrecht and the Delta network of canals/lakes.

COMMUNICATIONS (Code 010) See chartlet above for VTS in central Rotterdam. In emergency call Rotterdam Tfc Centre Ch 11; Police (0900) 8844; ⊜ 2442266; Brit Consul (020) 676 4343; Ⓗ 4112800; Hbr Coordination Centre (HCC) 2522601, also Emergency; see Facilities for VHF Chans at locks/bridges, English is the second language.

FACILITIES Marinas/yacht harbours from seaward:

Vlaardingen YC, 51°53'·98N 04°20'·93E, 400m E of Delta Hotel. Berth in Buitenhaven (3·6-4·4m) or lock (Ch 20) into Oude Haven (2·7m). HM ☎ 2484333, P, D, M, BY, ⚒, △, Gaz, ⌁.

Spuihaven, 51°54'·00N 04°24'·00E, immediately E of the ent to Wilhelmina Haven. €1·25/m. No lock/bridge to transit. Schiedam YC ☎ mob 0644326722, ⌑ (1·6-2·8m), D, ⚒, ⓑ, ⚓, ⌂, ⌁.

Coolhaven Yacht Hbr, 51°54'·12N 04°28'·00E; next to Euromast 185m. Access through Parkhaven via lock (Ch 22). ☎ 4764146, ⌑ (2·7m), P, D, M, ⚒, ⓑ, ⚓, C, ⛝, ⌂, ▦, R, ⎙.

Veerhaven. 51°54'·39N 04°28'·76E, 5ca E of Euromast. ☎ 4365446, Mob 0653536107, www.veerhavenrotterdam.nl info@ veerhavenrotterdam.nl Centre for traditional sea-going vessels. ⓥ welcome, €1·80. ⌑ (3·9m), ⚒, ⓑ, △, ⌂, ▦ 350m N, Water taxi to S bank. **Royal Maas YC** ☎ 4137681, (clubhouse, members only).

City Marina, 51°54'·64N 04°29'·76E. Go under Erasmus bridge (Ch 18) via lifting section at SE end which only opens 1000, 1100, 1330, 1530 & 1900LT or on request Ch 18 2030-0700 one hour before req'd (11m clearance under fixed span). Ldg lts 056·7°, both Iso 2s; then 2nd ent to stbd, via lifting bridge. ☎ 4854096, Mob 0622 215761, www.citymarinarotterdam.nl info@citymarinarotterdam. nl 130 ⌑ +40 ⓥ in 4m. €1·85/m/night for 2 nights; €1·50 3rd-7th nights; €1·25 7 nights. YC, Water taxi to N bank, @, ▦.

WSV IJsselmonde, 51°54'·24N 04°33'·34E, on S bank at km 994, 800m E of Brienenoordbrug, Ch 20 (off chartlet). ☎ 4828333, ⌑ (1·3-2·1m).

City all facilities, ACA, DYC Agent. Ferry: Rotterdam (Vlaardingen) –Hull; Hook–Harwich.

2.24 HARINGVLIET (Stellendam and Hellevoetsluis)

Zuid Holland 51°49'·46N 04°02'·29E (Goereesesluis). Stellendam ✻✵⚓⚓✿

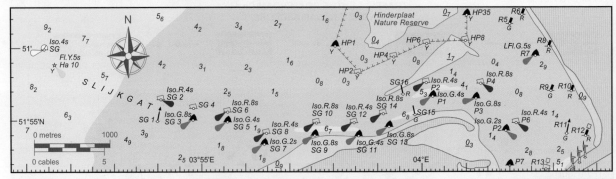

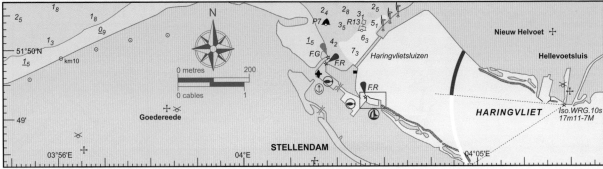

CHARTS AC 1630, 110; Zeekaart 1447, 1448; DYC 1801.6, 1807.6; Imray C30

TIDES +0300 Dover; ML 1·2; Duration 0510

Standard Port VLISSINGEN (→)

Times				Height (metres)			
High Water		Low Water		MHWS	MHWN	MLWN	MLWS
0300	0900	0400	1000	4·9	4·1	1·0	0·5
1500	2100	1600	2200				
Differences HARINGVLIETSLUIZEN							
+0015	+0015	+0015	−0020	−1·9	−1·9	−0·6	−0·2

NOTE: Double LWs occur. The rise after the 1st LW is called the Agger. Water levels on this coast are much affected by weather. Prolonged NW gales can raise levels by up to 3m. Water levels in the Haringvliet can drop by 0·5m an hour when the sluices are open.

SHELTER Good in all the marinas. The entrance to the Slijkgat can be rough in W/NW winds stronger than Force 6, and also with wind against tide. When there is heavy swell, entry into the Slijkgat is not advisable. Call Post Ouddorp, VHF Ch 25 if in doubt.

NAVIGATION WPT 51°51'·95N 03°51'·42E (SG SWM buoy, Iso 4s), 110°/2·7M to SG5/6 chan buoys. Note 1·4m shoal close N bys SG5/8, 7/8 and 9/10. Call Post Ouddorp VHF (see Comms) for latest silting info. Thence 2·4M via the well buoyed/lit Slijkgat chan to SG15/16 bns. Follow Pampus chan P1,3,5,7,9 SHM buoys SSE for 2·2M to the Buitenhaven, avoiding the no-entry sluicing area, marked by 4 SPM buoys.

Access is via a lock which operates 24/7 and has recessed bollards. 2 bridges lift in sequence to minimise road tfc delays. Note: the W bridge has 14m vertical clearance when down (with digital clearance gauge outside), the E bridge only 5·4m.

Hellevoetsluis is 2·6M E of Stellendam marina on the N bank. Three hbrs from W: Heliushaven, Het Groote Dok and Koopvaardijhaven, a LtHo (see below) marks ent to Groote Dok.

LIGHTS AND MARKS Haringvlietsluizen: 3 ● in △ are shown from pier heads on dam when sluicing in progress. Groote Dok LtHo: Iso WRG 10s 16m W11M, R8M, G7M; W tower, R top; 266°-G-275°-W-294°-R-316°-W036°-G-058°-W-095°-R-140°.

COMMUNICATIONS Post Ouddorp (lighthouse) VHF Ch 25 for weather, advice & assistance (H+30); ⊖ Rotterdam (010) 4298088 or Vlissingen (0118) 484600; Emergencies 112; Brit Consul (020) 676 4343; Stellendam Port HM 0187 491000; Lock (Walcheren Canal) (0118) 412840; Lock 0187 497350, *Goereese Sluis* VHF Ch 20 for bridges and lock; Hellevoetsluis HM (and locks) VHF Ch 74.

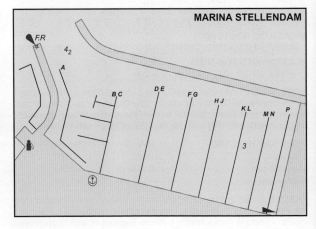

FACILITIES Stellendam Marina ☎ 0187 493769, VHF Ch 31. www. marinastellendam.nl info@marinastellendam.nl 200 ⌣ inc ♥, €2·00 inc tourist tax & shower. Berth as directed in 3m; all pontoons have fingers. D&P, ⌂, ⚓, ⬚, C (20 ton), ▢, ⬚, R ☎ 0187 492344, bike hire.

Town (4½ km) ⬚, R, ⬚, ✉. ✈ (Rotterdam). Bus to Vlissingen & Spijkenisse. Ferry: Hoek of Holland-Harwich; Rotterdam-Hull.

Heliushaven On the E side is **Marina Cape Helius** ☎ 0181 310056, mob 0613181974. www.marina-capehelius.nl havenkantoor@ marina-capehelius.nl €1·50 + €0·70 per person tourist tax; D. Reports welcome.

There are also 3 YCs situated on the W side of Heliushaven which may be able to help with berthing. **YC Helius** ☎ 0181 316563, mob 0616756515; €1·40 + €0·70 per person tourist tax; D. **YC Hellevoetsluis** ☎ 0181 315868, €1·40 + €0·70 per person tourist tax. **YC Haringvliet** ☎ 0181 314748, €1·35 + €0·70 per person tourist tax.

Groote Dok. ♥ AB before the bridge, ⬚, ⚓, Shwrs. In summer the bridge opens every hour. After the bridge is **Marina Hellevoetsluis** ☎ 0181 312166. www.marina-capehelius.nl info@marina-capehelius.nl €1·50 + €0·70 per person tourist tax; D. Reports welcome.

Koopvaardijhaven. ♥ berths with ⬚ on the W side, though there can also be a lot of commercial traffic here. Reports welcome.

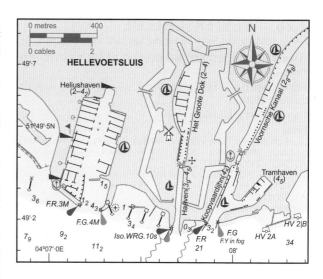

Yagra BY (E bank) ☎ 0181 314748, mob 0629403177 www. jachtservice-reparatie.nl Reports welcome.

Town ⬚, R, ⬚, ✉.

2.25 ROOMPOTSLUIS (for Oosterschelde)

Zeeland **51°37'·11N 03°41'·08E** Roompot Lock

CHARTS AC 1630, 110; Zeekaart 1448; DYCs 1805.8, 1801.5; Imray C30

TIDES +0230 Dover

Standard Port VLISSINGEN (⟶)

Times				Height (metres)			
High Water		Low Water		MHWS	MHWN	MLWN	MLWS
0300	0900	0400	1000	4·9	4·1	1·0	0·5
1500	2100	1600	2200				
Differences ROOMPOT BUITEN							
–0015	+0005	+0005	–0020	–1·2	–1·1	–0·3	–0·1

SHELTER An approach in strong SW through NW winds is not advised. The Buitenhaven's inner part is sheltered.

NAVIGATION WPT 51°39'·35N 03°33'·65E (abeam OR1 SHM buoy), 122°/4·2M via Oude Roompot chan to the 073·5° ldg line, both Oc G 5s, into the Buitenhaven. The flood sets E from HW Vlissingen –3 to +1. See Passage information for the several offshore banks.

Alternatively Roompot chan, buoyed but unlit, is further south and closer inshore.

Keep clear of the buoyed areas, W and E of the storm-surge barrier, which are very dangerous due to strong tidal streams and many obstructions.

Roompotsluis lock (☎ 0111 659265). Lock hrs: H24. Waiting pontoons are W and E of the lock with intercom phones to the remote control centre. Customs can be cleared at the lock in season.

The fixed bridge has 18·2m least clearance. At LW clearance is approx 21m. Check with tide gauges or lock-keeper if in doubt. Small bollards, fixed at vertical intervals, are recessed into the lock walls. Ent to/exit from the lock is controlled by R/G traffic lights.

LIGHTS AND MARKS See Lights, buoys & waypoints & chartlet.

COMMUNICATIONS Lock *Roompotsluis* Ch 18. Roompot Marina Ch 31. Monitor Ch 68 which broadcasts local forecasts at H+15.

FACILITIES Roompot Marina ❄❄⌂⚓⚓✿✿ Good shelter, 1·5M SE of lock. ☎ (0113) 374125, marina@roompot.nl. 250 + 80 ♥, €2·00 + €1·60pp tourist tax, D, P, ⚓, Gas, Gaz, ▢, ⬚, ⬚, R, ⑧. Dr ☎ 372565; ⊖ 0118 484600.

Alternatively, follow G3-G17 buoys into **Betonhaven** about 1M NE of the lock. ⚓ in 3-6m, good holding in sticky black mud, or ⌣ on a pontoon (Roompot marina II). €1·00, plus €1·60 tourist tax, for 3 days max stay; no ⚓, no ⬚. Easy walk to the Delta Expo.

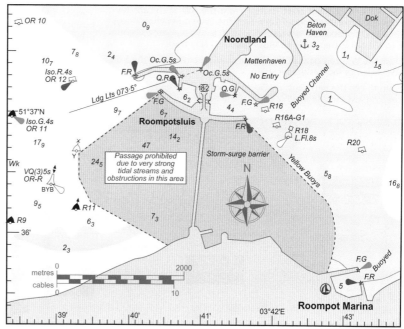

2.26 WESTERSCHELDE

Zeeland mostly, but Belgium for the last 12M to Antwerpen

CHARTS AC 1874, 120, 128; Zeekaart 1443; BE 103, 104; DYC 1803; Imray C30

TIDES +0200 Dover; ML Hansweert 2·7, Westkapelle 2·0, Bath 2·8; Duration 0555

Standard Port VLISSINGEN (→)

Times				Height (metres)			
High Water		Low Water		MHWS	MHWN	MLWN	MLWS
0300	0900	0400	1000	4·9	4·1	1·0	0·5
1500	2100	1600	2200				
Differences WESTKAPELLE (8M NW of Vlissingen)							
−0025	−0015	−0010	−0025	−0·6	−0·6	−0·1	−0·1
HANSWEERT							
+0100	+0050	+0040	+0100	+0·7	+0·6	+0·1	0·0
BATH							
+0125	+0115	+0115	+0140	+1·2	+1·0	+0·2	+0·1

SHELTER In strong winds a bad sea can be met in the estuary mouth. Conditions become easier further up-river. See Facilities.

NAVIGATION Westerschelde is the waterway to Antwerpen (and via canal to Gent), very full of ships and barges, especially in the last 15M. The main channel winds through a mass of well marked sand-banks. It is essential to work the tides, which average 2½kn, more at springs. Best timing is most easily achieved by starting from Vlissingen, Breskens or Terneuzen. Yachts should keep to the edge of main chan. Use alternative chans with caution; Vaarwater langs Hoofdplat and de Paulinapolder/Thomasgeul are buoyed shortcuts popular with yachtsmen, but note that channels shift regularly.

Commercial shipping: Yachts should keep just outside the busy shipping chans, ie Wielingen from the SW, Scheur from the W, and Oostgat from the NW. A listening watch on Ch 10 (ship-to-ship) is compulsory above buoy 100 (near Antwerpen).

Be aware of large ship anchorages: Wielingen Noord and Zuid, either side of the fairway, as defined by buoys W6-Trawl-WN6 and W9-Songa. Further E, Flushing Roads anchorage is defined by Songa, SS1, SS5 and ARV-VH buoys. Ocean-going ships often manoeuvre off Vlissingen to transfer pilots.

S of Vlissingen (see Breskens) an E-W TSS (part of a Precautionary area) is best avoided by yachts who should cross the fairway via the recommended N-S track between Buitenhaven and ARV3 SPM lt buoy. Fast ferries, which have right of way, ply half-hourly from Vlissingen Buitenhaven to Breskens. *Keep a sharp lookout.*

Recommended small craft routes: From the SW there are few dangers. After Zeebrugge, keep S of the Wielingen chan buoys (W1-9). Off Breskens avoid fast ferries to/from Vlissingen; continue E to SS1 buoy, then cross to Vlissingen on a N'ly track.

From the W, keep clear of the Scheur chan by crossing to the S of Wielingen as soon as practicable.

From the N, the narrow, busy Oostgat can be used with caution, keeping just outside the SW edge of the buoyed/lit chan.

Three lesser, unlit day-only N'ly routes which avoid Oostgat are:

- From Kaloo or DR1 buoys, follow the Geul van de Rassen, Deurloo & Spleet chans to SP4 buoy. Thence E via WN6 buoy.
- Or continue down Deurloo from DL5 by to join Oostgat at OG19 by; thence cross to the N shore when Oostgat tfc permits.
- Another route, slightly further offshore, is to skirt the NW side of Kaloo bank to Botkil-W buoy, thence SE via Geul de Walvischstaart (PHM buoys only) to Trawl SCM buoy.

LIGHTS AND MARKS The apprs are well lit by lighthouses: on the S shore at Nieuwe Sluis, and on the N shore at Westkapelle; see Lights, buoys & waypoints. The main fairways are, for the most part, defined by ldg lts and by the W sectors of the many Dir lts.

SCHELDEMOND VTS (www.vts-scheldt.net) covers from the North Sea outer approaches up-river to Antwerpen; see the diagram below and TSS off S Netherlands. Yachts should monitor at all times the VHF Ch for the area in which they are, so as to be aware of other shipping and to be contactable if required. Do not transmit, unless called. 7 **Traffic Centres** control the Areas below, within which Radar stations provide radar, weather and hbr info, as shown below:

Outer approaches: (*Traffic Centre* is the callsign prefix)		
Wandelaar	Ch 65	*Zeebrugge Radar* Ch 04.
Zeebrugge	Ch 69	*Radar* as in line above.
Steenbank	Ch 64	*Radar* also on Ch 64.
In the Westerschelde: (*Centrale* is the callsign prefix)		
Vlissingen	Ch 14	*Radar* Ch 21. Vlissingen to E2A/PvN SPR buoys (51°24'N 03°44'E).
Terneuzen	Ch 03	*Radar* Ch 03. Thence to Nos 32/35 buoys (51°23'N 03°57'E). Ch 11 Terneuzen-Gent Canal.
Hansweert	Ch 65	*Radar* Ch 65. Thence to Nos 46/55 buoys (51°21'N 04°02'E).
Zandvliet	Ch 12	Thence to Antwerpen. *Radar Waarde* 19; *Saeftinge* 21; *Zandvliet* 04; *Kruisschans* 66.

In **emergency**, call initially on the working channel in use; state yacht's name, position and the nature of the problem. You may then be switched to Ch **67 (Emergency)** or another VHF channel.

Broadcasts of visibility, Met, tidal data and ship movements are made in Dutch at: H +00 by *Terneuzen* Ch 11; H +10 by *Zeebrugge* Ch 69; H +30 by *Zandvliet* Ch 12; H +50 by *Centrale Vlissingen* Ch 14; H +55 by *Radar Vlissingen* Ch 21 in English.

FACILITIES Some minor hbrs from Terneuzen to Antwerpen (38M) are listed below. They may be useful in emergency or offer shelter, but most dry. Yachts usually go non-stop to Antwerpen.

ELLEWOUTSDIJK, 51°23'·10N 03°49'·05E. BE 103; DYC 1803.2. HW +2 and +0·3m on Vlissingen; ML 2·6m. Small, unlit hbr, 27 ⌂, voluntary donation. 1·5m at MLWS. Strong cross eddy on ebb. HM ☎ (0113) 548431/06 251154766. C (10 ton), Gaz, @, YC.

HOEDEKENSKERKE, 51°25'·11N 03°54'·90E. BE 103; DYC 1803.3. Disused ferry hbr (dries) abeam MG13 SHM buoy (Iso.G.4s).

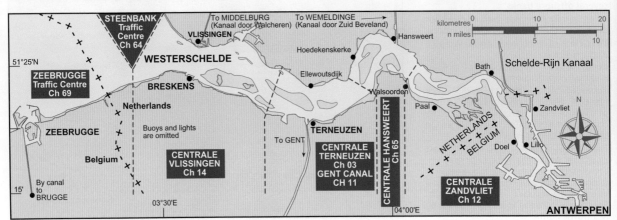

€1·00/m (min €8·00/night) inc ⏻, ⚓. **YC WV Hoedekenskerke** ☎ (0113) 639278, mob 0653 794069. 33 + 6 Ⓥ, Gaz, ⚓, ⚠, Shwrs at campsite 400m. **Town** ✉, Ⓑ, ⇌ (Goes).

HANSWEERT, 51°26'·37N 04°00'·66E. BE 103; DYC 1803.3. Tidal differences above. Temporary stop, but it is the busy ent to Zuid Beveland canal, lock Ch 22. Lt Oc WRG 10s, R lattice tr, W band, at ent. Waiting berths outside lock on E side. **No smoking or naked flames in, or near lock. Services:** ✎, BY, P, D, C (17 ton), ⌿, R. **Town** ✉, Ⓑ, ⇌ (Kruiningen-Yerseke).

WALSOORDEN, 51°22'·93N 04°02'·10E. BE 103; DYC 1803.3. HW is +0110 and +0·7m on Vlissingen; ML 2·6m. Prone to swell. SHM buoy 57, Iso G 8s, is 500m N of ent where 16 silos are conspic. Ldg lts 220° both Oc 3s. Unmarked stone pier just outside E hbr pier, partly dries at LW. Yacht basin dead ahead on ent to hbr, depths 2 to 2·8m. 4/5 ⚓, €0·30/m, max stay H24. *Zandvliet Radio* VHF Ch 12. WSV d'Ouwe Haven ☎ (0114) 681235, ⚓, ⚓, Gas, P, D, BY, C (16 ton), ✎, ⌕, ⌑. **Town** R, ⌑, ✉.

PAAL, 51°21'·25N 04°06'·65E. BE 103; DYC 1803.3. HW +0120 and +0·8m on Vlissingen; ML 2·7m. Appr via No. 63 SHM buoy and tide gauge, across drying Speelmansgat. Unlit, drying yacht hbr on S bank at river mouth, ent marked by withy. HM ☎ (0114) 314974, 0611 028174. *Zandvliet Radio* Ch 12. **Jachthaven** 150 ⚓, Shwr €0·50, Gaz, ✎, ⌕, ⌑, R, @ in YC. ⌕, ⌑ (10 mins walk). **Yachtclub** ☎ (0114) 315548; www.wv-saeftinghe.nl

DOEL, 51°18'·67N 04°16'·11E. BE 103; DYC 1803.5. HW +0100 and +0·7m on Vlissingen. Small drying hbr next to 'ghost town' on W bank. Ldg lts 188·5°: front Fl WR 3s on N pier hd; rear Fl 3s, synch. HM ☎ (03) 5758103; **YC de Noord** ☎ 7733669, open to visitors, useful in extremis. R, ⌑, ⚓.

LILLO, 51°18'·16N 04°17'·30E. BE 103; DYC 1803.5. 1M SE of Doel on opp bank; small drying hbr for shoal-draft only; Customs base. T-jetty has Oc WRG 10s. HM (035) 686456; **YC Scaldis.**

2.27 VLISSINGEN (FLUSHING)

Zeeland **51°26'·31N 03°34'·61E** Koopmanshaven ✲✲☀♁♦♦♦✿✿✿

CHARTS AC 1872, 1874, 120; Zeekaart 1442, 1443, 1533; BE 103; DYC 1803.2, 1801.4; Imray C30

TIDES +0210 Dover; ML 2·3; Duration 0555. Note: Vlissingen is a Standard Port (→)

SHELTER Very good in both yacht hbrs.

NAVIGATION WPT 51°25'·16N 03°33'·66E (Songa SHM buoy, QG), 027°/1·29M to Koopmanshaven ent. Keep to W pier side, strong crossflow until piers. Study Westerschelde.

LIGHTS AND MARKS From North West, Oostgat 117° ldg lts: Front RW pile; rear Sardijngeul, Oc WRG 5s, R/W banded mast, R △.

Note: Conspic radar twr (close NW of Koopmanshaven) shows a Fl Y lt to warn when ships are approaching in the blind NW arc from Oostgat-Sardijngeul.

A conspic, floodlit R/W metal framework tr (50m) near de Ruyter Marina indicates the appr. Buitenhaven traffic signals from mole W side of ent: R flag or extra ● near FR on W mole hd = No entry.

COMMUNICATIONS (Code 0118) Emergency 112; Schelde Traffic Coordination Centre 424760; Police 0900-8844; ⊖ 484600; Brit Consul (020) 676 4343; Dr 412233; Port HM 0115 647400, VHF Ch 14; Sealock VHF Ch 18; Canal bridges VHF Ch 22, see also Westerschelde; Michiel de Ruyter and Schelde Marinas: nil VHF; use mouse.

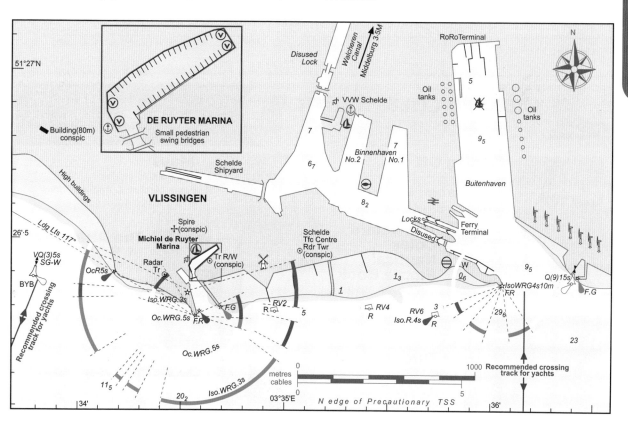

FACILITIES

Michiel de Ruyter Marina (2·9m) ☎ 414498, mob 0653537181. *Pre-booking in season is strongly advised.* 100 + 40 Ⓥ, €2·00/m + €1·00 tax/head. ▢, ⏛, R, @. info@montparnasse.nl www.montparnasse.nl

Ent is 6m narrow, over a sill with 1·0m water at MLWS. Access HW±4. Check depth gauge on outer wall or with HM. 2 small footbridges (R/G tfc lts) are swiftly swung open by HM 0800-2200LT. They stay open 2200–0800LT, but only for yachts to leave; ●● (vert) tfc lts prohibit arrival from sea. Storm barrier is open 1/4-1/11. Pilot boats use the adjacent inlet at high speed with scant regard for safety.

VVW Schelde (2·8-4·1m) ☎ 465912, mob 0638195369. www.vvwschelde.nl 90 + 50 Ⓥ, €1·50 + €1·00 tax/head. ⏛ €1·00/4kWh. 500m by road from ferry. D, ▢, ⏛, R, ⚓, ▬ (12 ton max), @, bike hire.

At ent to the Buitenhaven beware ferries; keep to port, pass S of the ferry terminal for the most N'ly and smallest sealock, which operates H24. Waiting possible on piles to SE.

Town ▢, ▢, ⏛, ⏛, R, ⏛, ⊠, Ⓑ, ⇌, ✈ (Antwerpen). Foot ferry to Breskens; road tunnel to Terneuzen. At Middelburg: BY, ⚒, ⚒, △.

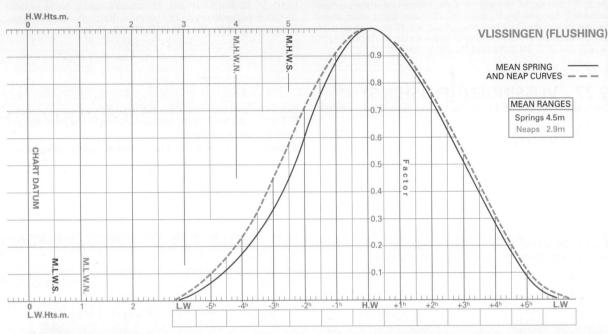

VLISSINGEN (FLUSHING)

MEAN SPRING AND NEAP CURVES

MEAN RANGES
Springs 4.5m
Neaps 2.9m

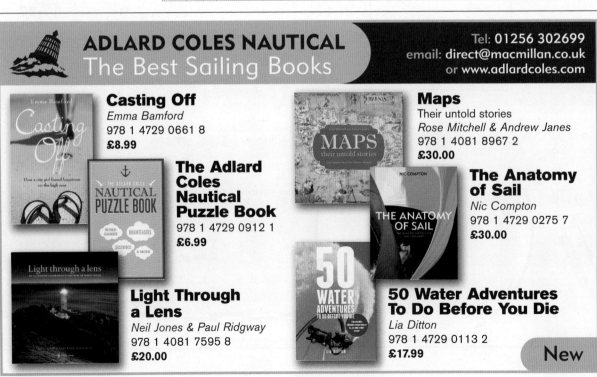

STANDARD TIME UT –01
Subtract 1 hour for UT
For Dutch Summer Time add
ONE hour in **non-shaded areas**

VLISSINGEN LAT 51°27′N LONG 3°36′E
TIMES AND HEIGHTS OF HIGH AND LOW WATERS

Dates in red are **SPRINGS**
Dates in blue are **NEAPS**

YEAR 2015

JANUARY

Day	Time m	Time m	Time m	Time m	Day	Time m	Time m	Time m	Time m
1 TH	0445 1.2	1048 4.4	1725 0.9	2330 4.5	**16** F	0355 1.2	1015 4.2	1636 1.1	2250 4.3
2 F	0556 1.0	1149 4.5	1822 0.8		**17** SA	0505 1.1	1116 4.4	1741 1.0	2350 4.5
3 SA	0025 4.6	0650 0.9	1246 4.7	1910 0.8	**18** SU	0605 0.9	1211 4.6	1836 0.8	
4 SU	0116 4.7	0735 0.7	1335 4.8	1952 0.8	**19** M	0039 4.7	0706 0.7	1258 4.9	1922 0.7
5 M ○	0159 4.8	0816 0.7	1416 4.9	2029 0.8	**20** TU ●	0125 4.9	0752 0.6	1345 5.1	2010 0.6
6 TU	0239 4.8	0858 0.6	1452 4.9	2108 0.8	**21** W	0209 5.0	0840 0.4	1428 5.2	2057 0.6
7 W	0316 4.8	0935 0.6	1528 4.9	2146 0.9	**22** TH	0253 5.1	0927 0.3	1513 5.3	2142 0.6
8 TH	0347 4.8	1015 0.6	1607 4.9	2216 0.9	**23** F	0336 5.1	1016 0.2	1556 5.3	2228 0.6
9 F	0420 4.8	1050 0.7	1641 4.8	2252 0.9	**24** SA	0421 5.1	1102 0.2	1645 5.2	2311 0.7
10 SA	0458 4.7	1122 0.7	1718 4.7	2322 1.0	**25** SU	0509 5.0	1148 0.3	1737 5.0	
11 SU	0536 4.6	1155 0.8	1756 4.5	2355 1.1	**26** M	0000 0.8	0559 4.9	1236 0.4	1831 4.8
12 M	0610 4.5	1226 0.9	1836 4.4		**27** TU ☽	0051 0.9	0658 4.7	1326 0.6	1936 4.6
13 TU ☽	0029 1.1	0656 4.3	1306 1.0	1925 4.3	**28** W	0146 1.0	0800 4.5	1420 0.8	2035 4.4
14 W	0126 1.2	0755 4.2	1354 1.1	2032 4.2	**29** TH	0244 1.1	0910 4.3	1536 1.0	2155 4.2
15 TH	0235 1.3	0906 4.1	1514 1.1	2139 4.2	**30** F	0404 1.2	1027 4.2	1700 1.0	2309 4.3
					31 SA	0536 1.1	1138 4.4	1806 0.9	

FEBRUARY

Day	Time m	Time m	Time m	Time m	Day	Time m	Time m	Time m	Time m
1 SU	0011 4.4	0636 0.9	1235 4.5	1855 0.9	**16** M	0539 0.9	1147 4.5	1816 0.9	
2 M	0105 4.6	0725 0.8	1325 4.7	1936 0.9	**17** TU	0017 4.6	0646 0.7	1241 4.8	1909 0.7
3 TU	0148 4.7	0805 0.7	1405 4.8	2015 0.8	**18** W	0106 4.8	0735 0.5	1326 5.0	1951 0.6
4 W ○	0222 4.8	0845 0.6	1439 4.8	2048 0.8	**19** TH ●	0150 5.0	0826 0.3	1413 5.2	2041 0.6
5 TH	0258 4.8	0918 0.6	1511 4.9	2122 0.8	**20** F	0233 5.1	0912 0.2	1455 5.3	2126 0.5
6 F	0325 4.8	0956 0.5	1542 4.9	2155 0.8	**21** SA	0316 5.2	0956 0.1	1537 5.3	2210 0.5
7 SA	0359 4.9	1026 0.6	1617 4.9	2225 0.8	**22** SU	0359 5.2	1040 0.1	1625 5.2	2255 0.6
8 SU	0428 4.8	1101 0.6	1647 4.8	2255 0.8	**23** M	0446 5.1	1122 0.2	1712 5.0	2335 0.6
9 M	0501 4.7	1125 0.7	1716 4.7	2326 0.9	**24** TU	0536 5.0	1206 0.4	1806 4.8	
10 TU	0533 4.6	1156 0.7	1748 4.6	2355 0.9	**25** W ◑	0026 0.7	0628 4.8	1256 0.6	1902 4.5
11 W	0605 4.5	1225 0.8	1831 4.5		**26** TH	0109 0.9	0731 4.5	1348 0.8	2006 4.2
12 TH ☽	0046 0.9	0656 4.4	1316 0.9	1935 4.3	**27** F	0213 1.1	0840 4.2	1453 1.0	2126 4.0
13 F ☽	0134 1.0	0810 4.2	1426 1.0	2056 4.1	**28** SA	0339 1.2	1006 4.1	1630 1.1	2250 4.0
14 SA	0306 1.1	0936 4.1	1543 1.1	2210 4.2					
15 SU	0430 1.1	1045 4.3	1705 1.0	2326 4.3					

MARCH

Day	Time m	Time m	Time m	Time m	Day	Time m	Time m	Time m	Time m
1 SU	0516 1.1	1126 4.2	1751 1.0	2356 4.2	**16** M	0354 1.0	1021 4.2	1640 1.1	2256 4.2
2 M	0620 0.9	1226 4.5	1840 0.9		**17** TU	0520 0.9	1126 4.5	1750 0.9	2357 4.5
3 TU	0050 4.5	0704 0.7	1309 4.6	1914 0.9	**18** W	0626 0.6	1221 4.8	1846 0.8	
4 W	0129 4.6	0745 0.7	1348 4.7	1956 0.8	**19** TH	0045 4.7	0718 0.4	1306 5.0	1937 0.6
5 TH ○	0206 4.7	0819 0.6	1416 4.8	2026 0.8	**20** F ●	0129 5.0	0806 0.3	1350 5.2	2020 0.5
6 F	0231 4.8	0856 0.6	1446 4.9	2058 0.8	**21** SA	0212 5.1	0850 0.2	1433 5.3	2105 0.5
7 SA	0301 4.9	0925 0.5	1517 4.9	2132 0.7	**22** SU	0255 5.2	0935 0.1	1518 5.3	2148 0.5
8 SU	0331 4.9	1000 0.5	1547 4.9	2206 0.7	**23** M	0339 5.2	1018 0.2	1603 5.2	2236 0.5
9 M	0402 4.9	1029 0.5	1617 4.8	2235 0.7	**24** TU	0425 5.2	1100 0.3	1649 5.0	2315 0.5
10 TU	0432 4.8	1100 0.6	1647 4.8	2302 0.7	**25** W	0509 5.0	1139 0.4	1739 4.7	
11 W	0501 4.8	1126 0.7	1718 4.7	2336 0.7	**26** TH	0001 0.6	0559 4.8	1226 0.6	1829 4.5
12 TH	0537 4.7	1206 0.7	1759 4.6		**27** F ◑	0045 0.8	0655 4.5	1315 0.9	1932 4.1
13 F ☽	0016 0.8	0621 4.6	1245 0.8	1856 4.4	**28** SA	0144 1.0	0810 4.2	1425 1.1	2055 3.9
14 SA	0116 0.9	0726 4.3	1349 1.0	2015 4.1	**29** SU	0304 1.1	0936 4.0	1555 1.2	2226 3.9
15 SU	0223 1.0	0901 4.1	1516 1.1	2136 4.0	**30** M	0440 1.1	1056 4.1	1715 1.1	2330 4.1
					31 TU	0556 0.9	1158 4.4	1804 1.0	

APRIL

Day	Time m	Time m	Time m	Time m	Day	Time m	Time m	Time m	Time m
1 W	0025 4.3	0639 0.8	1241 4.5	1856 0.9	**16** TH	0605 0.6	1159 4.8	1826 0.8	
2 TH	0058 4.5	0725 0.7	1317 4.7	1928 0.8	**17** F	0021 4.7	0658 0.4	1245 5.0	1916 0.6
3 F	0135 4.6	0756 0.6	1349 4.8	2000 0.7	**18** SA ●	0106 4.9	0746 0.3	1333 5.1	2002 0.5
4 SA ○	0206 4.7	0821 0.6	1417 4.9	2032 0.7	**19** SU	0150 5.1	0827 0.2	1415 5.2	2045 0.4
5 SU	0232 4.8	0855 0.5	1449 4.9	2109 0.6	**20** M	0236 5.2	0913 0.2	1458 5.2	2130 0.4
6 M	0302 4.9	0930 0.5	1519 4.9	2139 0.6	**21** TU	0318 5.2	0956 0.3	1546 5.1	2213 0.4
7 TU	0335 4.9	1001 0.5	1551 4.9	2216 0.6	**22** W	0403 5.1	1036 0.4	1626 4.9	2256 0.5
8 W	0405 4.9	1035 0.6	1622 4.8	2245 0.6	**23** TH	0449 5.0	1115 0.6	1716 4.7	2338 0.6
9 TH	0436 4.8	1108 0.6	1657 4.7	2320 0.6	**24** F	0537 4.7	1156 0.8	1805 4.4	
10 F	0516 4.8	1147 0.7	1737 4.6		**25** SA	0026 0.7	0636 4.5	1246 1.0	1854 4.1
11 SA	0002 0.7	0601 4.6	1828 4.4		**26** SU ◑	0136 0.9	0735 4.2	1356 1.1	2006 3.9
12 SU ☽	0100 0.8	0705 4.4	1329 1.0	1950 4.1	**27** M	0240 1.0	0856 4.0	1510 1.2	2141 3.8
13 M	0209 0.9	0835 4.2	1449 1.1	2110 4.0	**28** TU	0350 1.0	1015 4.0	1615 1.2	2244 3.9
14 TU	0336 0.9	0956 4.3	1604 1.1	2228 4.1	**29** W	0506 0.9	1120 4.2	1725 1.1	2341 4.1
15 W	0456 0.8	1106 4.5	1725 0.9	2328 4.4	**30** TH	0600 0.8	1205 4.4	1816 0.9	

Chart Datum is 2·56 metres below NAP Datum. HAT is 5·4 metres above Chart Datum.

Netherlands

STANDARD TIME UT −01
Subtract 1 hour for UT
For Dutch Summer Time add
ONE hour in **non-shaded areas**

VLISSINGEN   LAT 51°27'N   LONG 3°36'E
TIMES AND HEIGHTS OF HIGH AND LOW WATERS

Dates in red are **SPRINGS**
Dates in blue are NEAPS

YEAR **2015**

MAY

Day	Time	m		Day	Time	m
1 F	0026	4.3		**16** SA	0638	0.4
	0642	0.7			1227	4.9
	1246	4.6			1855	0.6
	1849	0.8				
2 SA	0100	4.5		**17** SU	0045	4.8
	0721	0.7			0723	0.3
	1318	4.7			1313	5.0
	1931	0.7			1946	0.5
3 SU	0128	4.7		**18** M	0131	5.0
	0749	0.6			0807	0.3
	1347	4.8			1356	5.1
	2002	0.6		●	2028	0.4
4 M	0201	4.8		**19** TU	0216	5.1
	0825	0.6			0849	0.3
	1422	4.9			1443	5.0
○	2041	0.6			2112	0.4
5 TU	0235	4.9		**20** W	0300	5.1
	0900	0.5			0932	0.4
	1453	5.0			1526	5.0
	2116	0.5			2157	0.4
6 W	0306	4.9		**21** TH	0345	5.0
	0938	0.5			1016	0.6
	1526	4.9			1610	4.8
	2156	0.5			2238	0.5
7 TH	0345	4.9		**22** F	0427	4.9
	1016	0.6			1052	0.7
	1603	4.8			1655	4.7
	2236	0.5			2326	0.6
8 F	0421	4.9		**23** SA	0520	4.7
	1052	0.7			1136	0.8
	1643	4.7			1742	4.5
	2315	0.6				
9 SA	0501	4.8		**24** SU	0006	0.7
	1136	0.8			0605	4.5
	1725	4.6			1220	1.0
					1825	4.3
10 SU	0005	0.6		**25** M	0055	0.8
	0548	4.6			0659	4.3
	1222	0.9			1309	1.1
	1818	4.4		◐	1915	4.1
11 M	0056	0.7		**26** TU	0153	0.9
	0655	4.4			0800	4.1
	1320	1.0			1414	1.2
◐	1936	4.2			2025	3.9
12 TU	0155	0.7		**27** W	0300	0.9
	0816	4.4			0909	4.0
	1436	1.1			1525	1.2
	2046	4.1			2146	3.8
13 W	0316	0.7		**28** TH	0406	1.0
	0926	4.4			1026	4.1
	1545	1.0			1636	1.1
	2156	4.2			2250	4.0
14 TH	0436	0.7		**29** F	0506	0.9
	1035	4.5			1120	4.3
	1700	0.9			1726	1.0
	2306	4.4			2340	4.2
15 F	0540	0.6		**30** SA	0555	0.8
	1136	4.7			1201	4.5
	1806	0.8			1816	0.9
	2357	4.6				
				31 SU	0020	4.4
					0640	0.8
					1241	4.6
					1856	0.8

JUNE

Day	Time	m		Day	Time	m
1 M	0056	4.6		**16** TU	0116	4.9
	0715	0.7			0748	0.5
	1317	4.8			1345	4.9
	1936	0.7		●	2011	0.5
2 TU	0136	4.8		**17** W	0206	4.9
	0756	0.7			0829	0.5
	1352	4.9			1430	4.9
○	2016	0.6			2055	0.4
3 W	0206	4.9		**18** TH	0247	5.0
	0836	0.6			0912	0.6
	1429	5.0			1512	4.9
	2055	0.5			2139	0.4
4 TH	0246	5.0		**19** F	0330	5.0
	0916	0.6			0949	0.7
	1508	4.9			1555	4.8
	2141	0.4			2222	0.5
5 F	0326	5.0		**20** SA	0415	4.9
	0955	0.6			1028	0.8
	1548	4.9			1636	4.7
	2222	0.4			2306	0.5
6 SA	0405	4.9		**21** SU	0455	4.8
	1038	0.7			1110	0.9
	1632	4.8			1716	4.6
	2310	0.4			2345	0.6
7 SU	0450	4.9		**22** M	0539	4.6
	1121	0.8			1145	1.0
	1716	4.6			1755	4.4
8 M	0001	0.5		**23** TU	0026	0.7
	0542	4.7			0621	4.4
	1216	0.8			1224	1.1
	1811	4.5			1839	4.3
9 TU	0056	0.5		**24** W	0116	0.8
	0645	4.6			0709	4.3
	1305	0.9			1336	1.2
◐	1915	4.4		◐	1930	4.1
10 W	0144	0.5		**25** TH	0216	0.9
	0756	4.5			0805	4.1
	1409	1.0			1436	1.2
	2025	4.3			2030	4.0
11 TH	0250	0.6		**26** F	0310	1.0
	0859	4.5			0910	4.1
	1515	1.0			1546	1.2
	2130	4.3			2135	4.0
12 F	0406	0.7		**27** SA	0405	1.0
	1008	4.5			1016	4.1
	1624	1.0			1636	1.1
	2236	4.4			2246	4.1
13 SA	0509	0.6		**28** SU	0505	0.9
	1111	4.6			1116	4.3
	1740	0.9			1724	1.0
	2336	4.6			2338	4.3
14 SU	0616	0.5		**29** M	0555	0.9
	1209	4.8			1205	4.5
	1836	0.7			1825	0.9
15 M	0027	4.7		**30** TU	0025	4.5
	0702	0.5			0642	0.8
	1259	4.9			1249	4.7
	1928	0.6			1905	0.7

JULY

Day	Time	m		Day	Time	m
1 W	0107	4.7		**16** TH	0157	4.9
	0725	0.7			0811	0.7
	1328	4.9			1417	4.9
	1949	0.6		●	2045	0.5
2 TH	0147	4.9		**17** F	0239	4.9
	0808	0.6			0852	0.7
	1409	5.0			1458	4.9
○	2035	0.5			2121	0.5
3 F	0228	5.0		**18** SA	0315	4.9
	0855	0.6			0930	0.8
	1452	5.0			1535	4.9
	2122	0.4			2202	0.5
4 SA	0309	5.1		**19** SU	0356	4.9
	0938	0.6			1005	0.8
	1533	5.0			1616	4.8
	2209	0.3			2239	0.5
5 SU	0353	5.1		**20** M	0431	4.8
	1023	0.7			1046	0.9
	1616	4.9			1647	4.7
	2258	0.3			2321	0.6
6 M	0436	5.0		**21** TU	0507	4.7
	1109	0.7			1120	0.9
	1703	4.8			1726	4.6
	2348	0.3			2355	0.7
7 TU	0527	4.9		**22** W	0546	4.6
	1200	0.8			1149	1.0
	1756	4.7			1806	4.5
8 W	0035	0.4		**23** TH	0026	0.8
	0626	4.6			0625	4.4
	1250	0.9			1230	1.1
◐	1855	4.6			1846	4.4
9 TH	0128	0.4		**24** F	0100	0.9
	0729	4.7			0712	4.3
	1346	0.9			1310	1.1
	1955	4.5		◐	1936	4.2
10 F	0222	0.4		**25** SA	0144	1.0
	0832	4.6			0810	4.2
	1456	1.0			1414	1.2
	2102	4.4			2046	4.1
11 SA	0325	0.7		**26** SU	0306	1.1
	0941	4.5			0916	4.1
	1600	1.0			1545	1.2
	2210	4.4			2145	4.1
12 SU	0445	0.8		**27** M	0426	1.1
	1051	4.5			1026	4.1
	1726	1.0			1656	1.1
	2315	4.5			2301	4.2
13 M	0556	0.7		**28** TU	0520	1.0
	1156	4.6			1132	4.4
	1826	0.8			1750	0.9
					2355	4.5
14 TU	0018	4.6		**29** W	0615	0.9
	0646	0.7			1225	4.6
	1248	4.7			1846	0.8
	1915	0.7				
15 W	0111	4.8		**30** TH	0042	4.7
	0732	0.7			0706	0.8
	1337	4.8			1307	4.8
	2000	0.6			1929	0.6
				31 F	0126	5.0
					0751	0.7
					1350	5.0
				○	2018	0.5

AUGUST

Day	Time	m		Day	Time	m
1 SA	0209	5.1		**16** SU	0257	5.0
	0836	0.7			0908	0.8
	1433	5.1			1516	4.9
	2107	0.3			2138	0.5
2 SU	0251	5.2		**17** M	0329	5.0
	0920	0.6			0946	0.8
	1516	5.1			1547	4.9
	2153	0.3			2216	0.6
3 M	0335	5.2		**18** TU	0406	4.9
	1006	0.6			1015	0.9
	1558	5.1			1619	4.9
	2240	0.2			2245	0.6
4 TU	0422	5.2		**19** W	0438	4.8
	1052	0.7			1050	0.9
	1646	5.0			1652	4.8
	2325	0.3			2315	0.7
5 W	0506	5.1		**20** TH	0507	4.7
	1141	0.7			1121	1.0
	1732	4.9			1721	4.7
					2345	0.8
6 TH	0012	0.3		**21** F	0539	4.6
	0600	4.9			1146	1.0
	1225	0.8			1755	4.6
	1826	4.8				
7 F	0100	0.7		**22** SA	0016	0.9
	0701	4.7			0618	4.5
	1321	0.9			1221	1.0
◐	1925	4.6		◐	1836	4.4
8 SA	0156	0.7		**23** SU	0055	1.0
	0806	4.5			0716	4.3
	1415	1.0			1316	1.1
	2031	4.4			1947	4.2
9 SU	0256	0.8		**24** M	0156	1.0
	0916	4.3			0826	4.2
	1529	1.1			1425	1.2
	2148	4.3			2102	4.1
10 M	0420	1.0		**25** TU	0325	1.2
	1037	4.3			0940	4.1
	1700	1.1			1616	1.2
	2306	4.4			2219	4.2
11 TU	0536	0.9		**26** W	0446	1.1
	1146	4.5			1055	4.3
	1805	1.0			1720	1.0
					2330	4.5
12 W	0009	4.6		**27** TH	0550	1.0
	0636	0.9			1155	4.5
	1241	4.6			1820	0.8
	1859	0.7				
13 TH	0101	4.8		**28** F	0021	4.8
	0718	0.8			0646	0.9
	1328	4.8			1246	4.8
	1945	0.6			1916	0.6
14 F	0148	4.9		**29** SA	0107	5.0
	0758	0.8			0728	0.7
	1408	4.8			1329	5.0
●	2026	0.6		○	2000	0.4
15 SA	0222	4.9		**30** SU	0149	5.2
	0831	0.8			0816	0.7
	1441	4.9			1410	5.2
	2105	0.6			2047	0.3
				31 M	0233	5.3
					0902	0.6
					1455	5.3
					2132	0.5

Chart Datum is 2·56 metres below NAP Datum. HAT is 5·4 metres above Chart Datum.

STANDARD TIME UT –01
Subtract 1 hour for UT
For Dutch Summer Time add
ONE hour in **non-shaded areas**

VLISSINGEN   LAT 51°27'N   LONG 3°36'E

TIMES AND HEIGHTS OF HIGH AND LOW WATERS

Dates in red are SPRINGS
Dates in blue are NEAPS

YEAR 2015

SEPTEMBER

Day	Time	m	Time	m	Time	m	Time	m
1	0315	5.4	0945	0.6	TU 1535	5.3	2216	0.2
16	0336	5.0	0950	0.8	W 1547	5.0	2219	0.7
2	0359	5.3	1030	0.6	W 1621	5.2	2302	0.3
17	0405	4.9	1020	0.8	TH 1617	4.9	2245	0.8
3	0446	5.2	1116	0.7	TH 1706	5.1	2345	0.4
18	0436	4.8	1045	0.9	F 1647	4.8	2310	0.8
4	0536	4.9	1159	0.8	F 1757	4.9		
19	0506	4.7	1116	0.9	SA 1717	4.7	2346	0.9
5	0030	0.6	0636	4.7	SA 1244	0.9	◑ 1856	4.7
20	0537	4.6	1156	0.9	SU 1757	4.6		
6	0119	0.8	0738	4.4	SU 1349	1.1	2011	4.4
21	0020	1.0	0626	4.5	M 1246	1.0	◑ 1849	4.4
7	0225	1.0	0849	4.2	M 1504	1.2	2125	4.3
22	0115	1.1	0736	4.2	TU 1356	1.2	2025	4.2
8	0355	1.2	1016	4.1	TU 1647	1.1	2249	4.3
23	0234	1.3	0902	4.1	W 1524	1.2	2148	4.2
9	0514	1.1	1130	4.3	W 1756	0.9	2355	4.6
24	0410	1.2	1026	4.2	TH 1645	1.0	2259	4.5
10	0615	1.0	1226	4.6	TH 1845	0.8		
25	0525	1.1	1129	4.5	F 1756	0.8	2356	4.8
11	0050	4.8	0705	0.9	F 1309	4.7	1935	0.7
26	0614	0.9	1221	4.8	SA 1856	0.6		
12	0129	4.9	0735	0.9	SA 1348	4.8	2005	0.6
27	0043	5.1	0711	0.8	SU 1305	5.0	1938	0.4
13	0205	4.9	0809	0.9	SU 1417	4.9	● 2036	0.6
28	0126	5.3	0756	0.7	M 1347	5.2	○ 2025	0.3
14	0232	5.0	0846	0.8	M 1445	4.9	2109	0.6
29	0210	5.4	0838	0.6	TU 1431	5.3	2108	0.3
15	0306	5.0	0915	0.8	TU 1517	5.0	2146	0.6
30	0253	5.4	0925	0.6	W 1515	5.4	2155	0.3

OCTOBER

Day	Time	m	Time	m	Time	m	Time	m
1	0337	5.3	1008	0.6	TH 1557	5.3	2236	0.4
16	0337	5.0	0959	0.8	F 1549	5.0	2216	0.8
2	0426	5.2	1052	0.7	F 1646	5.2	2318	0.6
17	0407	4.9	1028	0.8	SA 1621	4.9	2246	0.9
3	0512	4.9	1135	0.8	SA 1732	5.0	2359	0.7
18	0437	4.8	1101	0.8	SU 1655	4.9	2321	0.9
4	0606	4.6	1225	0.9	SU 1829	4.7	◑	
19	0517	4.7	1136	0.9	M 1735	4.7		
5	0049	1.0	0706	4.4	M 1326	1.1	1946	4.4
20	0000	1.0	0602	4.5	TU 1226	1.0	◑ 1826	4.5
6	0156	1.2	0826	4.1	TU 1439	1.2	2106	4.2
21	0056	1.2	0705	4.3	W 1335	1.1	1956	4.3
7	0314	1.3	0950	4.0	W 1604	1.2	2226	4.3
22	0205	1.3	0836	4.1	TH 1455	1.1	2115	4.3
8	0456	1.3	1106	4.2	TH 1736	1.0	2331	4.5
23	0335	1.3	0950	4.2	F 1615	1.0	2230	4.5
9	0556	1.1	1200	4.4	F 1825	0.9		
24	0450	1.2	1100	4.4	SA 1736	0.8	2329	4.8
10	0026	4.7	0640	1.0	SA 1246	4.6	1905	0.8
25	0556	1.0	1152	4.7	SU 1825	0.6		
11	0101	4.8	0716	1.0	SU 1317	4.7	1941	0.7
26	0019	5.1	0645	0.8	M 1241	5.0	1919	0.5
12	0136	4.9	0741	0.9	M 1347	4.8	2011	0.7
27	0105	5.2	0736	0.7	TU 1326	5.2	○ 2002	0.4
13	0206	4.9	0816	0.8	TU 1417	4.9	● 2042	0.7
28	0149	5.3	0816	0.6	W 1409	5.3	2047	0.4
14	0235	5.0	0851	0.8	W 1447	5.0	2116	0.7
29	0234	5.3	0906	0.6	TH 1453	5.4	2130	0.4
15	0305	5.0	0925	0.8	TH 1519	5.0	2146	0.7
30	0319	5.2	0951	0.6	F 1536	5.3	2213	0.5
31	0405	5.1	1033	0.6	SA 1625	5.2	2253	0.7

NOVEMBER

Day	Time	m	Time	m	Time	m	Time	m
1	0452	4.9	1118	0.7	SU 1715	5.0	2336	0.9
16	0421	4.8	1051	0.7	M 1640	4.9	2306	0.9
2	0546	4.6	1206	0.8	M 1808	4.7		
17	0502	4.7	1135	0.8	TU 1721	4.8	2345	1.0
3	0025	1.1	0636	4.4	TU 1255	1.0	◐ 1910	4.4
18	0547	4.6	1220	0.8	W 1816	4.6		
4	0120	1.3	0740	4.1	W 1403	1.1	2019	4.2
19	0040	1.1	0650	4.4	TH 1320	0.9	◐ 1930	4.4
5	0235	1.4	0900	4.0	TH 1525	1.2	2145	4.2
20	0150	1.2	0805	4.2	F 1424	0.9	2048	4.4
6	0406	1.4	1026	4.0	F 1645	1.1	2256	4.3
21	0305	1.3	0916	4.3	SA 1546	0.9	2158	4.5
7	0516	1.3	1122	4.2	SA 1746	1.0	2345	4.5
22	0415	1.2	1026	4.4	SU 1700	0.8	2301	4.7
8	0600	1.2	1210	4.4	SU 1836	0.9		
23	0526	1.1	1125	4.7	M 1805	0.7	2357	4.9
9	0030	4.6	0640	1.0	M 1245	4.6	1905	0.9
24	0625	0.9	1217	4.9	TU 1855	0.6		
10	0106	4.8	0711	0.9	TU 1318	4.7	1936	0.8
25	0045	5.1	0716	0.7	W 1305	5.1	○ 1942	0.5
11	0136	4.9	0745	0.9	W 1347	4.9	● 2011	0.8
26	0133	5.2	0802	0.6	TH 1351	5.2	2027	0.5
12	0206	5.0	0822	0.8	TH 1422	5.0	2039	0.7
27	0218	5.2	0848	0.5	F 1436	5.2	2108	0.5
13	0239	5.0	0901	0.7	F 1456	5.0	2118	0.7
28	0306	5.1	0933	0.5	SA 1523	5.2	2152	0.6
14	0312	5.0	0936	0.7	SA 1526	5.0	2156	0.8
29	0349	5.0	1015	0.6	SU 1607	5.1	2229	0.8
15	0345	4.9	1009	0.7	SU 1601	5.0	2226	0.9
30	0436	4.9	1100	0.6	M 1655	5.0	2309	0.9

DECEMBER

Day	Time	m	Time	m	Time	m	Time	m
1	0518	4.7	1145	0.7	TU 1746	4.7	2355	1.1
16	0451	4.8	1131	0.6	W 1712	4.9	2340	0.9
2	0608	4.5	1229	0.9	W 1838	4.5		
17	0537	4.7	1215	0.6	TH 1802	4.7		
3	0041	1.2	0700	4.3	TH 1336	1.0	◑ 1936	4.3
18	0024	1.0	0636	4.5	F 1304	0.7	◑ 1910	4.6
4	0150	1.4	0755	4.1	F 1424	1.1	2034	4.1
19	0126	1.1	0740	4.4	SA 1410	0.8	2020	4.5
5	0255	1.4	0916	3.9	SA 1535	1.2	2206	4.1
20	0230	1.2	0846	4.4	SU 1515	0.8	2128	4.5
6	0354	1.4	1025	4.0	SU 1646	1.1	2306	4.2
21	0340	1.2	0956	4.4	M 1626	0.9	2232	4.6
7	0516	1.3	1126	4.2	M 1734	1.1	2350	4.4
22	0506	1.1	1059	4.5	TU 1738	0.8	2338	4.7
8	0555	1.1	1208	4.4	TU 1825	1.0		
23	0607	1.0	1157	4.7	W 1838	0.7		
9	0029	4.6	0634	1.0	W 1246	4.6	1902	0.9
24	0031	4.8	0700	0.8	TH 1251	4.9	1926	0.6
10	0105	4.7	0720	0.9	TH 1322	4.7	1941	0.8
25	0120	4.9	0750	0.6	F 1337	5.0	○ 2010	0.6
11	0141	4.9	0755	0.8	F 1355	4.9	● 2015	0.8
26	0207	5.0	0836	0.5	SA 1425	5.1	2052	0.7
12	0217	5.0	0838	0.7	SA 1430	5.0	2052	0.7
27	0252	5.0	0920	0.5	SU 1511	5.1	2132	0.7
13	0252	5.0	0915	0.7	SU 1509	5.0	2136	0.8
28	0336	5.0	0958	0.6	M 1556	5.1	2212	0.8
14	0329	5.0	1000	0.7	M 1546	5.0	2212	0.8
29	0415	4.9	1041	0.6	TU 1637	5.0	2251	0.9
15	0409	4.9	1046	0.6	TU 1626	5.0	2256	0.9
30	0455	4.8	1119	0.6	W 1719	4.8	2325	1.0
31	0538	4.6	1206	0.7	TH 1802	4.6		

Chart Datum is 2·56 metres below NAP Datum. HAT is 5·4 metres above Chart Datum.

Netherlands

2.28 BRESKENS

Zeeland **51°24'·00N 03°34'·08E** ❁❁❁◊◊◊✿✿✿

CHARTS AC 1874, 1872, 120; Zeekaart 120, 101; BE 103; DYC 1801.4, 1803.2; Imray C30

TIDES +0210 Dover; ML no data; Duration 0600

Standard Port VLISSINGEN (⟵) Use Vlissingen data.

SHELTER Good in all winds except N/NW. In fine weather ⚓ off Plaat van Breskens or in peaceful Vaarwater langs Hoofdplaat; no ⚓ in commercial/fishing hbr.

NAVIGATION WPT 51°24'·71N 03°33'·90E [ARV-VH NCM buoy, Q], 170°/7ca to hbr ent. Beware fast ferries and strong tides across the ent. Do not confuse the ent with the ferry port ent, 0·7M WNW, where yachts are prohib.

LIGHTS AND MARKS Large bldg/silo on centre pier in hbr and three apartment blocks (30m) SE of marina are conspic. See chartlet and Lights, buoys & waypoints. Nieuwe Sluis disused lt ho, 28m B/W banded 8-sided twr, is 1·8M W of marina.

COMMUNICATIONS (Code 0117); Police 0900 8844; ⊜ (0118) 484614/484624; British Consul (020) 676 4343; Ⓗ (0117) 459000; Dr 384010, at night/weekends (0115) 643000; Marina VHF Ch 31.

FACILITIES Marina jachthavenbreskens@zonnet.nl ☎ 381902. www.jachthavenbreskens.nl 580 ⌓ inc Ⓥ, €1·90 + €1·15 tourist tax. Enter marina between two wavebreak barges; access H24, 5m at ent. Berth on 1st pontoon where HM assigns a berth via an intercom ☎. ⊡, ♂, ⛵, ⊡, D & P (fuel berth in FV hbr), Gaz, ACA, BY, C (30T), BH (70T), ⊡, Ⓔ, ⚒, ⚒, ▬, ♿. **YC Breskens** ☎ 383278, ⊡, R (book early), @.

Town ⊡, R, ⊡, ✉, Ⓑ, Gas, ✈ (Oostende, Antwerp or Brussels). Pedestrian & bike ferry or car tunnel to Vlissingen for ⇌.

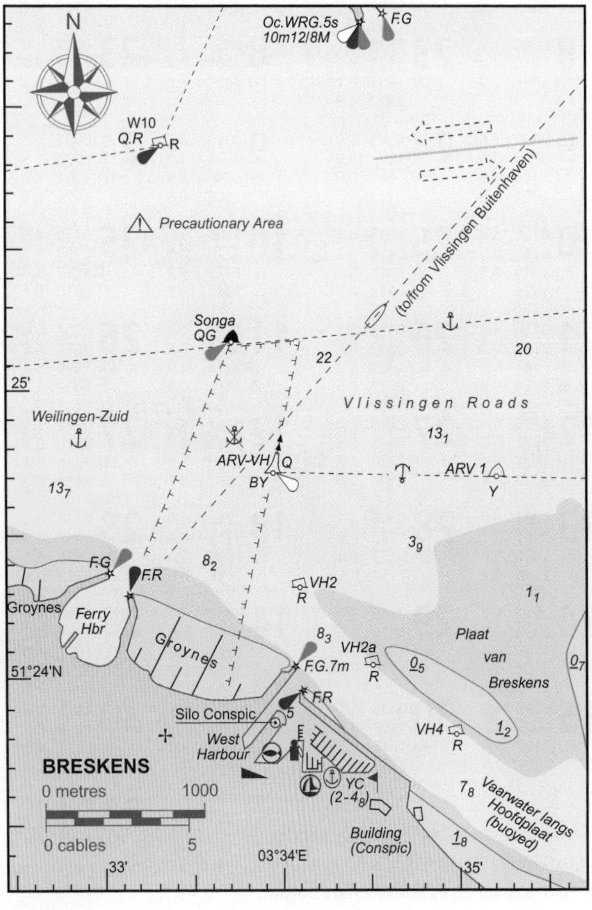

2.29 TERNEUZEN

Zeeland **51°20'·58N 03°49'·69E** ❁❁❁◊◊◊✿✿

CHARTS AC 120; Zeekaart 1443; BE 103, 105; DYC 1803.2; Imray C30

TIDES +0230 Dover; ML 2·5; Duration 0555

Standard Port VLISSINGEN (⟵)

Times				Height (metres)			
High Water		Low Water		MHWS	MHWN	MLWN	MLWS
0300	0900	0400	1000	4·9	4·1	1·0	0·5
1500	2100	1600	2200				
Differences TERNEUZEN							
+0020	+0020	+0020	+0030	+0·4	+0·3	+0·1	0·0

SHELTER Very good except in strong N'lies. Exposed ⚓ on N side of fairway between buoys WPT4, WPT6, PvT-ZE & ZE5. Strong currents.

NAVIGATION WPT 51°20'·82N 03°47'·96E [25B SHM buoy], 101°/1M hugging S bank to hbr ent. Fairway only 500m wide; big ships pass very close; lookout E/W and call *Traffic Centre Terneuzen*. Ch 03, when leaving. Very busy traffic from/to the locks; call *Port Control Terneuzen*, Ch 11. If S-bound via Gent Canal transit the E lock to berth in Zijkanaal A. Strong eddy during ebb at Veerhaven ent.

LIGHTS AND MARKS Dow Chemical works and storage tanks are conspic 2M W of hbr. Lt Oc WRG 5s, B/W post, on W mole is a conspic mark for the Veerhaven.

When entry to E Buitenhaven is prohib, a second ● is shown below FR on E mole. For E lock: ● = no entry; ●● (vert) = get ready; ● = go. No yachts in W Buitenhaven, Middle and W locks.

COMMUNICATIONS (Code 0115) Police 0900 8844; ⊜ (0118) 484600; British Consul (020) 676 4343; Ⓗ 688000; Dr 616262; Port HM 612161, call *Port Control* Ch 11 (H24) for locks and Gent canal; also info broadcasts every H+00; East lock VHF Ch 18; No marina VHF.

FACILITIES Two marinas in SE corner of former Veerhaven: **WV Honte Marina** where Ⓥ berths more likely. ☎ 697089, mobile 0651 168987. www.jachthaventerneuzen.nl 130 ⌓ €1·40. ⊡ (230v) €1·25, ♂, C (6 ton), ⊡.

WV Neusen Marina is close ESE (and in Zijkanaal A) ☎ 696331; www.wvneusen.nl 100 ⌓, €1.00; ♂, no wi-fi, ⊡. Boatyards (full services): **Aricom** www.aricom.nl ☎ 614577, €1·00/m. ♂, ⚒, ⊡, C (50 ton), ⚒, Gaz. **Vermeulen's Yachtwerf** ☎ 612716. ⌓, €0.75, C (50 ton).

Town P, D, ⊡, ⊡, R, ⊡, ✉, Ⓑ, ✈ (Antwerpen). Foot ferry Breskens to Vlissingen. Cars by Schelde tunnel Terneuzen-Ellewoutsdijk.

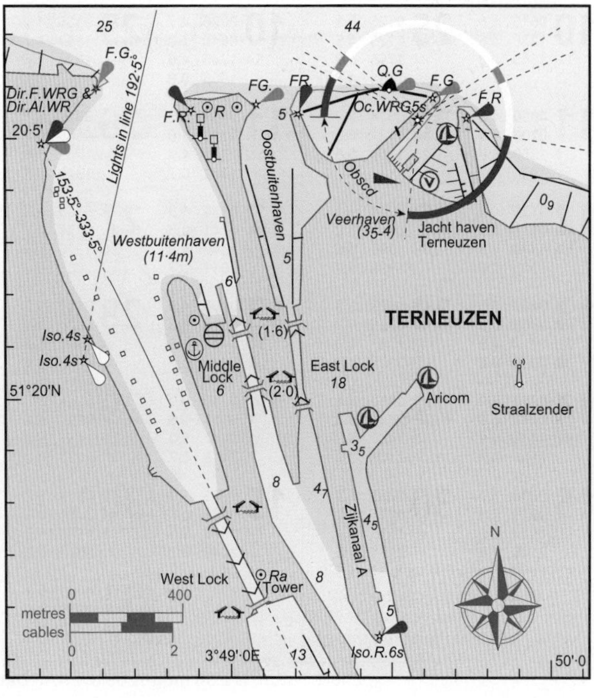

2.30 SPECIAL NOTES FOR BELGIUM

PROVINCES are given in lieu of UK 'counties'.

LANGUAGES Flemish, ie Dutch as spoken in Flanders, is the 1st language along the coast and N of Brussels. English is also widely spoken. French, the 2nd language, is spoken in and S of Brussels.

CURRENCY is the Euro €. VAT (BTW/TVA) is 21%.

CHARTS 'Vlaamse Banken' (BE) issued by the Hydrografische Dienst der Kust are most widely used. Dutch yacht charts (DYC 1800 series) cover all Belgian ports. Imray C30 is also popular.

TIME ZONE is –0100, which is allowed for in tidal predictions but no provision is made for daylight saving schemes.

HARBOURS Ports of entry are Nieuwpoort, Oostende and Zeebrugge; plus Blankenberge, early April – late Sep. Berths and moorings are administered by local YCs and municipal authorities.

SIGNALS At Oostende and Zeebrugge IPTS are used, and small craft wind warnings (also at Nieuwpoort and Blankenberge). They apply only to craft <6m LOA and indicate onshore wind >F3; offshore wind >F4. Day, 2 ▼s, points together; night, Fl Bu lt.

TELEPHONE To call UK from Belgium, dial 00 44 then the UK area code minus the prefix 0, followed by the number called. To call Belgium from UK, dial 00 32 then the code and 6/7 digit number. **Emergency**: ☎ 101 Police; ☎ 100 Fire, Ambulance and Marine. ☎ 112 (EU emergency number) is also operational.

BRITISH CONSULS Contact British Embassy, Brussels (consular) 02 287 6248.

MRCC Oostende coordinates SAR operations (5.14). If no contact, call *Oostende Radio* VHF Ch 16 or ☎ 100. For medical advice call *Radiomédical Oostende* on Ch 16.

PUBLIC HOLIDAYS New Year's Day, Easter Mon, Labour Day (1 May), Ascension Day, Whit Mon, National Day (21 July), Feast of the Assumption (15 Aug), All Saints' Day (1 Nov), Armistice Day (11 Nov), King's Birthday (15 Nov), Christmas Day.

RULES A ▼ when motor-sailing and a black ball ● at ⚓ are strictly enforced. Navigation within 200m of shore (MLWS) is prohib. Carry red diesel with caution, even if purchased abroad, see 2.5.

INLAND WATERWAYS At www.mobilit.fgov.be download CEVNI-based regulations in French or Dutch. Licence plates (*Immatriculatieplaat*) are required on Belgian waterways. Helmsman's Competence criteria are as for the Netherlands.

THE BELGIAN COAST

Long shoals lie roughly parallel to this 36M long coast (AC 1872). Mostly the deeper, buoyed channels run within 3M of shore, where the outer shoals can give some protection from strong W or SW winds. Strong W to NE winds can create dangerous conditions especially with wind against tide. Before reaching shoal water get a good fix, so as to correctly identify the required channel.

▶*Off the Belgian coast the E-going stream begins at HW Vlissingen –0320 (HW Dover –0120), and the W-going at HW Vlissingen +0240 (HW Dover +0440), sp rates 2kn. Mostly the streams run parallel with the coast.*◀

From **Zeebrugge** stay a mile offshore inside Wenduine Bank to pass **Oostende**, thence via Kleine Rede or Grote Reede into West Diep off **Nieuwpoort**. At the French border West Diep becomes the narrower, buoyed Passe de Zuydcoote. Thence the very well buoyed route runs close inshore for 25M to Dyck PHM buoy.

Conversely, E-bound from the Thames, if bound for Oostende or the Westerschelde, identify W Hinder lt. From further N, route via NHR-S and NHR-SE buoys or the N Hinder lt buoy. Enter the buoyed channels at Dyck.

Leave Oostende about ▶*HW Vlissingen –0300 on a fair tide*◀. Keep 2M off **Blankenberge**, and 1M or more off Zeebrugge's huge claw-like breakwaters, staying S of the Scheur channel to avoid much commercial traffic. Beware the strong tidal stream and possibly dangerous seas off Zeebrugge.

2.31 ANTWERPEN

Belgium, Antwerpen 51°13'·66N 04°23'·79E ❀❀⚓⚓☆☆☆

CHARTS AC 128; Zeekaart 1443; BE 103, 104; DYC 1803.5

TIDES +0342 Dover; ML 2·9; Duration 0605

Standard Port VLISSINGEN (◄—)

Times				Height (metres)			
High Water		Low Water		MHWS	MHWN	MLWN	MLWS
0300	0900	0400	1000	4·9	4·1	1·0	0·5
1500	2100	1600	2200				
Differences ANTWERPEN							
+0128	+0116	+0121	+0144	+1·2	+1·0	+0·1	+0·1

SHELTER Excellent in both marinas. ⚓ in the river is not advised.

NAVIGATION See Westerschelde. Best to check off the buoys coming up-river. There is a gap of 1·4M between No 116 PHM buoy and No 107 SHM buoy. Entrance to the Willemdok marina via Royersluis and Siberia bridge is permitted, but not recommended. Use the Kattendijksluis (abeam buoy 107). VHF 69, operating if tide between TAW 2.2–5.0m, or approximately 3±HW.

COMMUNICATIONS (Code 03) VTS, Zandvliet Centre VHF Ch 12, lock Ch 79; Radar VHF Ch 04, 66 ⊖ 2292004; Police 5460730; Ⓗ 2852000 (W Bank), 234111 (E Bank); Antwerp Port Ops Ch 74 (H24); Royerssluis VHF Ch 22; Access bridges VHF Ch 62; Willemdok VHF Ch 23; Linkeroever VHF Ch 09 (HW±1).

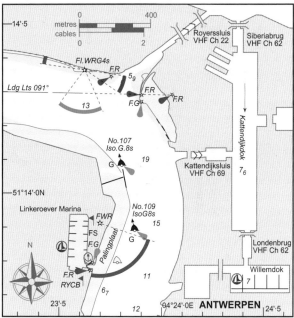

FACILITIES from seaward: **Willemdok Marina** 51°13'·78N 04°24'·43E. ☎ 2315066, Mobile 0495 535455. www.jachthaven-antwerpen.be jaw@pandora.be Wait on inshore side of T-shaped ferry pontoon S of No. 107 buoy. H24 access via Royerssluis, or from canals/docks. Siberia and Londen bridges open 0630, 0830, 1000, 1130, 1245, 1415, 1515, 1615*, 1730, 1845, 2015, 2145, 2245LT.*Sat/Sun/Public hols. To enter the Dock areas and marina, pre-arrange an FD number via ☎, e-mail or fax to Willemdok (0500-2300). 200 + Ⓥ, €1·50, €8·00 week. D, 🛒, ▨, 🅿.

Linkeroever Marina (W bank); Lat/Long under title. Access by gate HW ±1, 0800–2200 (1800 in winter). Y waiting buoy is off the ent. ☎ 2190895, Mobile 0475 643957. www.jachthaven-antwerpen.be jachthaven_linkeroever@skynet.be 200+Ⓥ, €1·50, €8·00 week. D, Gaz, 🅿, ✕, C (1·5 ton), BH (38 ton), ▨, ▬, R, 🛒.

Royal YC van België ☎ 2195231. www.rycb.be rycb@rycb.be. M, D, P, ▨ BY, ▬, 🗔, R.

Kon. Liberty YC ☎ 2191147. **Services:** ✕, BH, ACA, DYC Agent.

City centre is ¾M from Linkeroever via St. Annatunnel (pedestrian), 51°13'·22N. All facilities, @, ⇌, ✈.

2.32 ZEEBRUGGE

Belgium, West Flanders 51°21'·83N 03°11'·39E ⚙⚙⚙♦♦♦❀❀

CHARTS AC 2449, 3371, 1872, 1874; Zeekaart 1441; BE 104; DYC 1801.3, 1803; Imray C30

TIDES +0135 Dover; ML 2·4; Duration 0535. Note: Zeebrugge is a Standard Port (⟶).

SHELTER Very good in the marina, access H24.

NAVIGATION WPT 51°22'·48N 03°09'·95E [Z SHM buoy, QG], 129°/1·1M to ent (lat/long under title). Lts on outer bkwtr heads show high-vis strip lts to seaward. Beware strong currents in hbr apprs (up to 4kn at HW –1). Caution on ent/dep due to limited vis; give all jetties a wide berth. A busy commercial, naval and fishing port and a ferry terminal. An inner WPT 51°20'·85N 03°12'·29E off Leopold II Dam head is useful to avoid getting 'lost' inside the vast outer hbr, especially in poor vis; see chartlet.

LIGHTS AND MARKS Big ship ldg marks (hard to see by day) & lts (as chartlet) lead in sequence to Vissershaven and the marina:

- 136°: Both W cols, R bands.
- 154°: Front, W pylon, R bands; rear, W bldg, R bands.
- 220°: Both W cols, B bands. • 193°: Both W cols, R bands.

IPTS are shown from E outer bkwtr and Leopold II Dam. Extra sigs: 3 Fl Y lts (vert) + IPTS No 2 or 5 = LNG tanker entering/leaving. No exit/entry without specific permission.

COMMUNICATIONS (Code 050) Coast Guard 545072; Sea Saving Service 544007; Police 544148; ⊖ 545455; British Consul 02 287 6248; Dr 544590; Port HM 543241; Port Control 546867/550801, VHF Ch 71 (H24); Lock Mr 543231, VHF Ch 68; Marina, nil VHF.

FACILITIES Royal Belgian SC (VZW) ☎ 544903, mob 0496 789053. havenmeester@rbsc.be ☎ 100 + 100 ⓥ, €2·64. 🗲 (on coin meter), ▬, ✕, ⚒, D (0830-1200, 1300-1800), ✎, 🔧, ⬚, ⬚, R (Clubhouse Alberta) ☎ 544197. Completion of the new **BZYC** marina nearby due Summer 2014, reports welcome.

Town P, D, ✕, Gaz, 🛒, R, ⬚, ✉, Ⓑ. ⇌ 15 mins to Brugge. Tram to Oostende for ✈. Ferries to Hull and Rosyth (Edinburgh).

BRUGGE Masted yachts can transit Zeebrugge's eastern sealock to go 6M S via the Boudewijnkanaal (Ch 68) & 2 lifting bridges to Brugge docks. **Brugse Zeil en Yacht Club (BZYC)** is on the E bank: ☎ (0478) 711301. www.bzyc.be info@bzyc.be €1·00/m; 🗲 & 🗲 €2·00/da. 15 mins walk to city centre. Unmasted boats can go clockwise on the Oostende-Gent Canal (Ch 18) to **Flandria Marina** (S of city): ☎ 380866, mob 0477 384456. www.yachtclubflandria.be 10 mins walk to city centre; close to ⇌ (a visit by train is quick and easy).

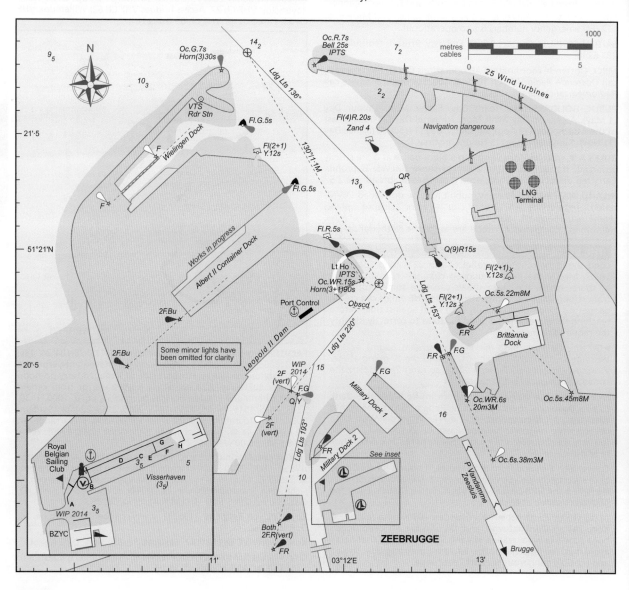

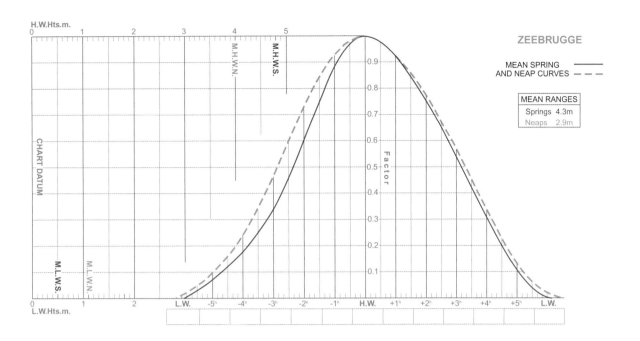

H.W.Hts.m.

ZEEBRUGGE

MEAN SPRING AND NEAP CURVES

MEAN RANGES

| Springs | 4.3m |
| Neaps | 2.9m |

CHART DATUM

M.H.W.N. M.H.W.S.

Factor

M.L.W.S. M.L.W.N.

L.W.Hts.m.

L.W. -5ʰ -4ʰ -3ʰ -2ʰ -1ʰ H.W. +1ʰ +2ʰ +3ʰ +4ʰ +5ʰ L.W.

1	*Borkum*	**1**																										
2	**Delfzijl**	22	**2**																									
3	Lauwersoog	30	46	**3**																								
4	Terschelling	65	85	43	**4**																							
5	Vlieland	72	92	52	7	**5**																						
6	Harlingen	80	102	67	19	18	**6**																					
7	Kornwerderzand	86	106	70	24	19	7	**7**																				
8	Den Oever	90	110	88	34	33	21	13	**8**																			
9	Oudeschild	94	114	79	38	34	25	18	10	**9**																		
10	**Den Helder**	95	115	81	39	33	30	24	11	5	**10**																	
11	Medemblik	104	124	99	39	40	27	20	12	22	24	**11**																
12	Enkhuizen	112	132	106	47	41	28	23	18	28	29	10	**12**															
13	Amsterdam	139	159	123	83	84	81	47	62	52	51	38	26	**13**														
14	IJmuiden	126	146	109	70	71	68	57	49	38	38	58	37	13	**14**													
15	Scheveningen	151	171	132	95	96	93	79	74	60	63	80	62	38	25	**15**												
16	Rotterdam	185	205	159	129	130	127	113	108	94	97	114	96	72	59	34	**16**											
17	Hook of Holland	165	185	146	109	110	107	93	88	74	77	94	76	52	39	14	20	**17**										
18	Stellendam	181	201	157	125	126	123	109	104	90	93	110	92	68	55	30	36	16	**18**									
19	**Roompotsluis**	193	204	177	128	124	129	118	109	110	97	130	112	90	63	50	49	29	27	**19**								
20	**Vlissingen**	211	222	190	146	143	147	137	128	121	115	141	123	108	82	61	67	47	45	21	**20**							
21	Terneuzen	220	240	202	164	165	162	152	143	133	132	153	135	111	98	73	79	59	57	36	12	**21**						
22	Antwerpen	249	269	221	193	194	191	181	172	162	161	182	164	140	127	102	108	88	86	65	41	31	**22**					
23	Breskens	202	230	192	154	155	152	142	133	123	122	143	125	101	88	63	69	49	47	21	3	12	45	**23**				
24	**Zeebrugge**	219	239	194	163	164	161	147	142	128	131	148	130	106	93	68	74	54	50	25	16	28	57	13	**24**			
25	Blankenberge	224	244	196	168	169	166	152	147	133	136	153	135	111	98	73	79	59	55	33	21	33	62	18	5	**25**		
26	Oostende	233	239	205	163	164	161	160	142	141	131	161	143	110	106	81	87	67	72	36	27	41	70	26	13	9	**26**	
27	Nieuwpoort	242	262	215	186	187	184	170	165	151	154	171	153	129	116	91	97	77	83	46	39	51	80	36	23	18	9	**27**
28	*Dunkerque*	257	277	228	201	202	199	185	180	166	169	186	168	144	131	106	112	92	90	57	50	67	96	52	40	35	26	15	**28**

DISTANCE TABLE
Approximate distances in nautical miles are by the most direct route while avoiding dangers and allowing for TSS. Places in *italics* are in adjoining areas; places in **bold** are in 0.31, Distances across the North Sea.

Belgium

STANDARD TIME UT –01
Subtract 1 hour for UT
For Belgian Summer Time add
ONE hour in **non-shaded areas**

ZEEBRUGGE LAT 51°21'N LONG 3°12'E
TIMES AND HEIGHTS OF HIGH AND LOW WATERS

Dates in red are **SPRINGS**
Dates in blue are **NEAPS**

YEAR 2015

JANUARY

Day	Time	m	Day	Time	m
1 TH	0416 / 1027 / 1650 / 2308	1.1 / 4.3 / 0.8 / 4.4	16 F	0350 / 0947 / 1618 / 2225	1.3 / 4.0 / 1.1 / 4.1
2 F	0527 / 1133 / 1753	1.0 / 4.4 / 0.8	17 SA	0451 / 1051 / 1714 / 2324	1.2 / 4.2 / 1.0 / 4.3
3 SA	0006 / 0624 / 1227 / 1844	4.5 / 0.9 / 4.6 / 0.8	18 SU	0545 / 1147 / 1805	1.0 / 4.4 / 0.9
4 SU	0052 / 0709 / 1311 / 1926	4.6 / 0.7 / 4.6 / 0.8	19 M	0014 / 0634 / 1235 / 1852	4.5 / 0.8 / 4.6 / 0.8
5 M	0132 / 0749 / 1350 / 2004	4.6 / 0.7 / 4.7 / 0.9	20 TU	0058 / 0719 / 1319 / 1936	4.6 / 0.6 / 4.8 / 0.7
6 TU	0209 / 0826 / 1427 / 2038	4.6 / 0.6 / 4.7 / 0.9	21 W	0141 / 0804 / 1403 / 2021	4.8 / 0.5 / 5.0 / 0.6
7 W	0244 / 0901 / 1503 / 2111	4.6 / 0.6 / 4.7 / 0.9	22 TH	0223 / 0849 / 1447 / 2107	4.9 / 0.3 / 5.0 / 0.6
8 TH	0319 / 0936 / 1539 / 2143	4.6 / 0.6 / 4.6 / 0.9	23 F	0307 / 0935 / 1532 / 2153	4.9 / 0.2 / 5.1 / 0.6
9 F	0354 / 1010 / 1614 / 2216	4.6 / 0.6 / 4.6 / 0.9	24 SA	0352 / 1023 / 1620 / 2240	4.9 / 0.2 / 5.0 / 0.6
10 SA	0427 / 1044 / 1649 / 2249	4.5 / 0.7 / 4.5 / 1.0	25 SU	0440 / 1111 / 1710 / 2329	4.8 / 0.3 / 4.9 / 0.7
11 SU	0501 / 1119 / 1725 / 2326	4.4 / 0.8 / 4.4 / 1.1	26 M	0531 / 1201 / 1805	4.7 / 0.4 / 4.4
12 M	0538 / 1159 / 1806	4.3 / 0.9 / 4.3	27 TU	0020 / 0627 / 1256 / 1905	0.9 / 4.5 / 0.6 / 4.4
13 TU	0009 / 0624 / 1248 / 1859	1.2 / 4.2 / 1.0 / 4.2	28 W	0119 / 0731 / 1400 / 2014	1.0 / 4.3 / 0.8 / 4.2
14 W	0106 / 0722 / 1400 / 2005	1.3 / 4.1 / 1.2 / 4.1	29 TH	0231 / 0845 / 1513 / 2131	1.2 / 4.1 / 1.0 / 4.1
15 TH	0233 / 0835 / 1516 / 2118	1.4 / 4.0 / 1.2 / 4.0	30 F	0353 / 1006 / 1629 / 2251	1.2 / 4.1 / 1.0 / 4.1
			31 SA	0512 / 1122 / 1740 / 2354	1.1 / 4.2 / 1.0 / 4.3

FEBRUARY

Day	Time	m	Day	Time	m
1 SU	0613 / 1218 / 1834	0.9 / 4.4 / 0.9	16 M	0521 / 1124 / 1742 / 2352	1.0 / 4.3 / 0.9 / 4.3
2 M	0041 / 0659 / 1300 / 1915	4.4 / 0.6 / 4.5 / 0.9	17 TU	0614 / 1216 / 1832	0.8 / 4.6 / 0.8
3 TU	0119 / 0737 / 1336 / 1948	4.5 / 0.7 / 4.6 / 0.9	18 W	0039 / 0702 / 1301 / 1919	4.5 / 0.5 / 4.8 / 0.7
4 W	0152 / 0810 / 1410 / 2018	4.6 / 0.6 / 4.6 / 0.9	19 TH	0122 / 0747 / 1345 / 2004	4.7 / 0.3 / 5.0 / 0.5
5 TH	0225 / 0842 / 1442 / 2047	4.6 / 0.5 / 4.7 / 0.8	20 F	0204 / 0832 / 1429 / 2049	4.9 / 0.2 / 5.1 / 0.5
6 F	0256 / 0913 / 1515 / 2118	4.6 / 0.5 / 4.7 / 0.8	21 SA	0248 / 0918 / 1514 / 2135	5.0 / 0.1 / 5.1 / 0.4
7 SA	0328 / 0944 / 1547 / 2150	4.6 / 0.5 / 4.7 / 0.8	22 SU	0333 / 1003 / 1600 / 2220	5.1 / 0.1 / 5.1 / 0.5
8 SU	0358 / 1016 / 1618 / 2223	4.6 / 0.5 / 4.6 / 0.8	23 M	0419 / 1050 / 1648 / 2306	5.0 / 0.2 / 4.9 / 0.6
9 M	0429 / 1049 / 1651 / 2257	4.6 / 0.6 / 4.6 / 0.8	24 TU	0508 / 1137 / 1738 / 2354	4.8 / 0.4 / 4.7 / 0.7
10 TU	0504 / 1124 / 1728 / 2335	4.6 / 0.7 / 4.5 / 0.9	25 W	0600 / 1228 / 1834	0.6 / 0.6 / 4.4
11 W	0545 / 1203 / 1812	4.4 / 0.8 / 4.4	26 TH	0049 / 0659 / 1330 / 1940	1.0 / 4.3 / 0.9 / 4.0
12 TH	0019 / 0634 / 1255 / 1909	1.1 / 4.3 / 1.0 / 4.1	27 F	0202 / 0814 / 1447 / 2101	1.2 / 4.0 / 1.1 / 3.8
13 F	0121 / 0739 / 1417 / 2024	1.3 / 4.1 / 1.2 / 4.0	28 SA	0327 / 0941 / 1604 / 2226	1.2 / 3.9 / 1.2 / 3.9
14 SA	0304 / 0902 / 1542 / 2146	1.4 / 3.9 / 1.2 / 3.9			
15 SU	0420 / 1020 / 1646 / 2256	1.2 / 4.0 / 1.1 / 4.1			

MARCH

Day	Time	m	Day	Time	m
1 SU	0445 / 1101 / 1718 / 2332	1.1 / 4.1 / 1.2 / 4.1	16 M	0349 / 0952 / 1619 / 2229	1.2 / 4.0 / 1.1 / 4.0
2 M	0551 / 1158 / 1816	0.9 / 4.3 / 1.1	17 TU	0454 / 1100 / 1718 / 2328	0.9 / 4.3 / 1.0 / 4.2
3 TU	0020 / 0640 / 1241 / 1857	4.3 / 0.8 / 4.4 / 1.0	18 W	0551 / 1155 / 1812	0.7 / 4.6 / 0.8
4 W	0058 / 0718 / 1315 / 1928	4.4 / 0.7 / 4.5 / 0.9	19 TH	0017 / 0641 / 1241 / 1900	4.5 / 0.5 / 4.8 / 0.6
5 TH	0130 / 0748 / 1347 / 1954	4.5 / 0.6 / 4.6 / 0.8	20 F	0101 / 0727 / 1325 / 1945	4.8 / 0.3 / 5.0 / 0.5
6 F	0200 / 0816 / 1418 / 2021	4.6 / 0.5 / 4.7 / 0.7	21 SA	0144 / 0812 / 1409 / 2030	5.0 / 0.1 / 5.1 / 0.4
7 SA	0230 / 0845 / 1448 / 2052	4.7 / 0.5 / 4.7 / 0.6	22 SU	0227 / 0857 / 1453 / 2115	5.1 / 0.0 / 5.1 / 0.3
8 SU	0300 / 0916 / 1518 / 2124	4.7 / 0.4 / 4.7 / 0.6	23 M	0312 / 0942 / 1538 / 2159	5.1 / 0.1 / 5.0 / 0.4
9 M	0330 / 0948 / 1548 / 2158	4.7 / 0.4 / 4.7 / 0.6	24 TU	0358 / 1027 / 1625 / 2244	5.0 / 0.2 / 4.8 / 0.5
10 TU	0401 / 1021 / 1621 / 2232	4.7 / 0.5 / 4.7 / 0.7	25 W	0445 / 1112 / 1713 / 2329	4.8 / 0.4 / 4.6 / 0.7
11 W	0435 / 1055 / 1657 / 2308	4.7 / 0.6 / 4.6 / 0.8	26 TH	0534 / 1200 / 1804	4.6 / 0.5 / 4.3
12 TH	0515 / 1133 / 1739 / 2349	4.4 / 0.7 / 4.4 / 0.9	27 F	0021 / 0631 / 1300 / 1906	0.9 / 4.3 / 1.0 / 3.9
13 F	0602 / 1219 / 1831	4.4 / 0.9 / 4.2	28 SA	0135 / 0742 / 1418 / 2025	1.1 / 4.0 / 1.3 / 3.7
14 SA	0044 / 0702 / 1329 / 1941	1.1 / 4.2 / 1.2 / 3.9	29 SU	0257 / 0908 / 1532 / 2148	1.2 / 3.8 / 1.3 / 3.7
15 SU	0221 / 0826 / 1508 / 2113	1.3 / 4.0 / 1.2 / 3.8	30 M	0408 / 1027 / 1641 / 2257	1.1 / 3.9 / 1.3 / 3.9
			31 TU	0515 / 1126 / 1743 / 2348	1.0 / 4.1 / 1.1 / 4.1

APRIL

Day	Time	m	Day	Time	m
1 W	0608 / 1211 / 1828	0.8 / 4.3 / 1.0	16 TH	0524 / 1132 / 1749 / 2353	0.6 / 4.6 / 0.8 / 4.5
2 TH	0028 / 0648 / 1247 / 1900	4.3 / 0.7 / 4.5 / 0.9	17 F	0617 / 1220 / 1839	0.4 / 4.8 / 0.6
3 F	0102 / 0719 / 1319 / 1926	4.4 / 0.6 / 4.6 / 0.8	18 SA	0039 / 0706 / 1305 / 1925	4.8 / 0.3 / 4.9 / 0.5
4 SA	0132 / 0746 / 1350 / 1954	4.6 / 0.5 / 4.7 / 0.7	19 SU	0124 / 0751 / 1349 / 2010	4.9 / 0.2 / 5.0 / 0.4
5 SU	0202 / 0815 / 1420 / 2026	4.6 / 0.5 / 4.7 / 0.6	20 M	0208 / 0836 / 1433 / 2054	5.0 / 0.1 / 5.0 / 0.3
6 M	0231 / 0848 / 1450 / 2100	4.7 / 0.4 / 4.8 / 0.5	21 TU	0252 / 0920 / 1518 / 2138	5.0 / 0.2 / 4.9 / 0.4
7 TU	0302 / 0922 / 1521 / 2135	4.7 / 0.4 / 4.7 / 0.5	22 W	0338 / 1004 / 1603 / 2222	4.9 / 0.4 / 4.7 / 0.5
8 W	0335 / 0956 / 1555 / 2211	4.7 / 0.5 / 4.7 / 0.6	23 TH	0424 / 1047 / 1649 / 2307	4.8 / 0.6 / 4.5 / 0.6
9 TH	0412 / 1032 / 1632 / 2248	4.7 / 0.6 / 4.6 / 0.7	24 F	0512 / 1133 / 1737 / 2356	4.5 / 0.8 / 4.3 / 0.8
10 F	0452 / 1110 / 1714 / 2330	4.6 / 0.8 / 4.4 / 0.8	25 SA	0604 / 1227 / 1833	4.2 / 1.1 / 3.9
11 SA	0539 / 1157 / 1805	4.5 / 0.9 / 4.2	26 SU	0106 / 0709 / 1342 / 1944	1.0 / 4.0 / 1.3 / 3.7
12 SU	0025 / 0639 / 1305 / 1915	1.0 / 4.2 / 1.1 / 3.9	27 M	0222 / 0826 / 1453 / 2101	1.1 / 3.8 / 1.4 / 3.7
13 M	0154 / 0802 / 1438 / 2045	1.1 / 4.1 / 1.2 / 3.8	28 TU	0327 / 0940 / 1556 / 2210	1.1 / 3.8 / 1.2 / 3.8
14 TU	0320 / 0927 / 1551 / 2201	1.1 / 4.1 / 1.1 / 4.0	29 W	0428 / 1042 / 1656 / 2306	1.0 / 4.0 / 1.2 / 4.0
15 W	0425 / 1036 / 1653 / 2302	0.8 / 4.3 / 1.0 / 4.2	30 TH	0523 / 1132 / 1746 / 2351	0.9 / 4.2 / 1.1 / 4.2

Chart Datum is 0·23 metres below TAW Datum. HAT is 5·6 metres above Chart Datum.

STANDARD TIME UT –01
Subtract 1 hour for UT
For Belgian Summer Time add
ONE hour in **non-shaded** areas

ZEEBRUGGE   LAT 51°21′N   LONG 3°12′E
TIMES AND HEIGHTS OF HIGH AND LOW WATERS

Dates in red are **SPRINGS**
Dates in blue are **NEAPS**

YEAR **2015**

MAY

Time	m		Time	m
1 F	0608 0.8 / 1212 4.4 / 1823 0.9	**16** SA	0554 0.4 / 1200 4.7 / 1819 0.7	
2 SA	0028 4.4 / 0642 0.7 / 1248 4.5 / 1854 0.8	**17** SU	0020 4.7 / 0645 0.4 / 1247 4.8 / 1907 0.6	
3 SU	0101 4.5 / 0713 0.6 / 1320 4.6 / 1926 0.7	**18** M	0106 4.8 / 0731 0.3 / 1332 4.8 / ● 1952 0.5	
4 M	0132 4.6 / 0745 0.5 / 1351 4.7 / ○ 2000 0.6	**19** TU	0151 4.9 / 0816 0.4 / 1416 4.8 / 2036 0.4	
5 TU	0204 4.7 / 0820 0.5 / 1423 4.7 / 2037 0.5	**20** W	0235 4.9 / 0859 0.4 / 1459 4.7 / 2119 0.4	
6 W	0238 4.7 / 0857 0.5 / 1457 4.7 / 2115 0.5	**21** TH	0320 4.8 / 0941 0.6 / 1543 4.5 / 2202 0.5	
7 TH	0314 4.7 / 0934 0.6 / 1534 4.6 / 2153 0.6	**22** F	0405 4.7 / 1023 0.7 / 1627 4.4 / 2246 0.6	
8 F	0353 4.7 / 1013 0.7 / 1613 4.5 / 2233 0.6	**23** SA	0450 4.5 / 1105 0.9 / 1712 4.3 / 2333 0.7	
9 SA	0436 4.6 / 1055 0.8 / 1657 4.4 / 2319 0.7	**24** SU	0538 4.3 / 1151 1.1 / 1801 4.1	
10 SU	0525 4.5 / 1145 0.9 / 1750 4.2	**25** M	0031 0.9 / 0633 4.1 / 1253 1.3 / ☽ 1859 3.9	
11 M	0017 0.8 / 0626 4.3 / 1251 1.1 / ☽ 1858 4.0	**26** TU	0140 1.0 / 0738 3.9 / 1406 1.4 / 2008 3.8	
12 TU	0135 0.9 / 0743 4.2 / 1411 1.1 / 2019 4.0	**27** W	0242 1.1 / 0846 3.9 / 1508 1.4 / 2114 3.8	
13 W	0250 0.8 / 0901 4.2 / 1521 1.1 / 2132 4.1	**28** TH	0340 1.0 / 0949 3.9 / 1605 1.3 / 2214 3.9	
14 TH	0356 0.7 / 1009 4.4 / 1625 1.0 / 2235 4.3	**29** F	0433 1.0 / 1044 4.1 / 1658 1.2 / 2306 4.1	
15 F	0457 0.6 / 1108 4.6 / 1725 0.8 / 2330 4.5	**30** SA	0521 0.8 / 1132 4.3 / 1743 1.0 / 2350 4.2	
		31 SU	0602 0.8 / 1213 4.4 / 1822 0.9	

JUNE

Time	m		Time	m
1 M	0028 4.4 / 0639 0.7 / 1250 4.6 / 1859 0.7	**16** TU	0054 4.7 / 0715 0.6 / 1319 4.6 / ● 1938 0.6	
2 TU	0104 4.5 / 0716 0.6 / 1325 4.6 / ○ 1937 0.6	**17** W	0138 4.7 / 0758 0.6 / 1402 4.6 / 2021 0.5	
3 W	0140 4.6 / 0755 0.6 / 1400 4.7 / 2016 0.6	**18** TH	0221 4.7 / 0839 0.7 / 1443 4.6 / 2102 0.5	
4 TH	0217 4.7 / 0834 0.6 / 1437 4.7 / 2057 0.5	**19** F	0303 4.7 / 0919 0.7 / 1524 4.6 / 2143 0.5	
5 F	0256 4.7 / 0915 0.6 / 1517 4.6 / 2139 0.5	**20** SA	0345 4.6 / 0958 0.8 / 1604 4.5 / 2224 0.5	
6 SA	0338 4.7 / 0958 0.7 / 1559 4.6 / 2223 0.6	**21** SU	0427 4.5 / 1036 0.9 / 1645 4.4 / 2306 0.6	
7 SU	0424 4.7 / 1043 0.8 / 1645 4.5 / 2312 0.6	**22** M	0510 4.4 / 1115 1.0 / 1727 4.3 / 2350 0.8	
8 M	0515 4.6 / 1135 0.9 / 1738 4.4	**23** TU	0555 4.3 / 1157 1.2 / 1812 4.1	
9 TU	0009 0.6 / 0614 4.5 / 1235 1.0 / ☽ 1841 4.3	**24** W	0043 0.9 / 0645 4.1 / 1252 1.3 / ☽ 1906 4.0	
10 W	0115 0.7 / 0723 4.4 / 1343 1.0 / 1952 4.2	**25** TH	0146 1.0 / 0745 4.0 / 1406 1.4 / 2010 3.9	
11 TH	0221 0.7 / 0834 4.4 / 1451 1.0 / 2102 4.2	**26** F	0247 1.1 / 0848 4.0 / 1512 1.3 / 2114 3.9	
12 F	0326 0.6 / 0942 4.4 / 1557 0.9 / 2209 4.3	**27** SA	0343 1.1 / 0950 4.0 / 1610 1.2 / 2214 4.0	
13 SA	0431 0.6 / 1046 4.5 / 1703 0.9 / 2310 4.4	**28** SU	0435 1.0 / 1046 4.2 / 1703 1.1 / 2308 4.1	
14 SU	0533 0.6 / 1143 4.5 / 1802 0.8	**29** M	0524 0.9 / 1137 4.3 / 1750 0.9 / 2356 4.3	
15 M	0005 4.6 / 0627 0.6 / 1234 4.6 / 1853 0.7	**30** TU	0608 0.8 / 1221 4.4 / 1834 0.8	

JULY

Time	m		Time	m
1 W	0038 4.5 / 0650 0.7 / 1301 4.6 / 1916 0.7	**16** TH	0128 4.6 / 0743 0.8 / 1348 4.6 / ● 2006 0.6	
2 TH	0119 4.6 / 0732 0.7 / 1340 4.6 / ○ 1958 0.6	**17** F	0207 4.7 / 0820 0.8 / 1426 4.6 / 2044 0.5	
3 F	0159 4.8 / 0814 0.6 / 1420 4.7 / 2041 0.5	**18** SA	0245 4.7 / 0856 0.8 / 1503 4.6 / 2122 0.5	
4 SA	0241 4.9 / 0858 0.6 / 1501 4.7 / 2126 0.4	**19** SU	0324 4.7 / 0932 0.8 / 1540 4.6 / 2159 0.5	
5 SU	0325 4.9 / 0944 0.7 / 1545 4.7 / 2212 0.4	**20** M	0401 4.7 / 1006 0.9 / 1616 4.6 / 2236 0.6	
6 M	0411 4.9 / 1031 0.7 / 1632 4.7 / 2302 0.4	**21** TU	0439 4.6 / 1041 0.9 / 1652 4.5 / 2312 0.7	
7 TU	0501 4.8 / 1121 0.8 / 1723 4.6 / 2354 0.4	**22** W	0515 4.5 / 1117 1.0 / 1728 4.4 / 2349 0.8	
8 W	0556 4.7 / 1215 0.9 / 1819 4.5 / ☽	**23** TH	0554 4.4 / 1156 1.1 / 1809 4.3	
9 TH	0051 0.5 / 0658 4.5 / 1314 1.0 / 1923 4.4	**24** F	0032 0.9 / 0640 4.2 / 1244 1.2 / ☽ 1900 4.1	
10 F	0152 0.6 / 0805 4.4 / 1420 1.0 / 2032 4.3	**25** SA	0130 1.1 / 0738 4.1 / 1356 1.3 / 2006 4.0	
11 SA	0258 0.7 / 0914 4.3 / 1531 1.1 / 2144 4.3	**26** SU	0248 1.2 / 0849 4.0 / 1522 1.3 / 2119 4.0	
12 SU	0407 0.8 / 1026 4.3 / 1643 1.0 / 2254 4.3	**27** M	0353 1.1 / 0959 4.0 / 1626 1.2 / 2227 4.1	
13 M	0515 0.8 / 1131 4.4 / 1749 0.9 / 2355 4.5	**28** TU	0450 1.0 / 1101 4.2 / 1721 1.0 / 2325 4.3	
14 TU	0613 0.8 / 1225 4.5 / 1842 0.8	**29** W	0540 0.9 / 1153 4.4 / 1810 0.9	
15 W	0045 4.6 / 0701 0.8 / 1309 4.5 / 1926 0.7	**30** TH	0014 4.5 / 0627 0.8 / 1238 4.5 / 1856 0.7	
		31 F	0058 4.7 / 0712 0.7 / 1320 4.7 / ○ 1940 0.5	

AUGUST

Time	m		Time	m
1 SA	0141 4.9 / 0756 0.6 / 1401 4.8 / 2024 0.4	**16** SU	0225 4.8 / 0832 0.8 / 1440 4.7 / 2058 0.5	
2 SU	0224 5.0 / 0841 0.6 / 1444 4.9 / 2110 0.3	**17** M	0259 4.8 / 0905 0.8 / 1514 4.8 / 2131 0.5	
3 M	0308 5.1 / 0927 0.5 / 1528 5.0 / 2157 0.2	**18** TU	0334 4.8 / 0937 0.7 / 1547 4.7 / 2204 0.5	
4 TU	0354 5.1 / 1015 0.6 / 1614 4.9 / 2245 0.2	**19** W	0407 4.7 / 1011 0.8 / 1619 4.7 / 2237 0.6	
5 W	0442 5.0 / 1102 0.6 / 1703 4.9 / 2334 0.3	**20** TH	0439 4.7 / 1044 0.8 / 1651 4.6 / 2310 0.7	
6 TH	0534 4.8 / 1152 0.7 / 1755 4.7	**21** F	0513 4.6 / 1119 0.9 / 1728 4.5 / 2346 0.8	
7 F	0026 0.5 / 0631 4.6 / 1246 0.9 / ☽ 1855 4.5	**22** SA	0552 4.5 / 1159 1.1 / 1812 4.4 / ☽	
8 SA	0124 0.7 / 0734 4.4 / 1350 1.1 / 2003 4.3	**23** SU	0030 1.0 / 0642 4.3 / 1251 1.2 / 1909 4.2	
9 SU	0232 0.9 / 0847 4.2 / 1507 1.1 / 2121 4.2	**24** M	0137 1.2 / 0749 4.1 / 1424 1.4 / 2027 4.0	
10 M	0346 1.0 / 1007 4.1 / 1626 1.1 / 2241 4.2	**25** TU	0312 1.3 / 0914 4.0 / 1552 1.3 / 2150 4.1	
11 TU	0459 1.0 / 1119 4.2 / 1736 0.9 / 2346 4.4	**26** W	0419 1.2 / 1028 4.1 / 1653 1.1 / 2258 4.3	
12 W	0601 1.0 / 1213 4.4 / 1830 0.8	**27** TH	0515 1.0 / 1127 4.3 / 1747 0.8 / 2352 4.6	
13 TH	0035 4.6 / 0649 0.9 / 1255 4.5 / 1913 0.7	**28** F	0605 0.8 / 1215 4.6 / 1835 0.6	
14 F	0114 4.7 / 0727 0.9 / 1331 4.6 / ● 1950 0.6	**29** SA	0038 4.9 / 0652 0.7 / 1258 4.8 / ○ 1920 0.4	
15 SA	0150 4.7 / 0800 0.9 / 1406 4.7 / 2024 0.5	**30** SU	0121 5.1 / 0737 0.6 / 1341 5.0 / 2006 0.2	
		31 M	0204 5.2 / 0823 0.5 / 1424 5.2 / 2051 0.1	

Chart Datum is 0·23 metres below TAW Datum. HAT is 5·6 metres above Chart Datum.

Belgium

STANDARD TIME UT –01
Subtract 1 hour for UT
For Belgian Summer Time add
ONE hour in **non-shaded areas**

ZEEBRUGGE   LAT 51°21'N   LONG 3°12'E
TIMES AND HEIGHTS OF HIGH AND LOW WATERS

Dates in red are **SPRINGS**
Dates in blue are **NEAPS**

YEAR 2015

SEPTEMBER

Time m	Time m
1 0249 5.3 / 0909 0.4 / TU 1508 5.2 / 2137 0.1	**16** 0305 4.9 / 0910 0.6 / W 1517 4.9 / 2134 0.5
2 0334 5.2 / 0955 0.5 / W 1553 5.2 / 2224 0.2	**17** 0336 4.8 / 0943 0.7 / TH 1548 4.8 / 2206 0.6
3 0421 5.1 / 1041 0.5 / TH 1641 5.0 / 2311 0.3	**18** 0406 4.8 / 1016 0.7 / F 1620 4.8 / 2238 0.7
4 0510 4.9 / 1128 0.7 / F 1731 4.8	**19** 0439 4.7 / 1050 0.8 / SA 1656 4.7 / 2313 0.8
5 0000 0.6 / 0603 4.6 / SA 1219 0.9 / ☽ 1827 4.6	**20** 0518 4.6 / 1128 1.0 / SU 1739 4.6 / 2354 1.0
6 0056 0.8 / 0705 4.3 / SU 1323 1.1 / 1936 4.3	**21** 0604 4.4 / 1216 1.1 / M 1833 4.3 ☾
7 0208 1.1 / 0820 4.0 / M 1446 1.2 / 2059 4.1	**22** 0052 1.2 / 0914 4.1 / TU 1332 1.3 / 1948 4.1
8 0325 1.2 / 0945 4.0 / TU 1605 1.2 / 2224 4.2	**23** 0232 1.3 / 0835 4.0 / W 1519 1.3 / 2119 4.1
9 0439 1.2 / 1059 4.1 / W 1715 1.0 / 2329 4.4	**24** 0350 1.2 / 0958 4.1 / TH 1625 1.1 / 2231 4.4
10 0543 1.1 / 1154 4.4 / TH 1811 0.8	**25** 0450 1.1 / 1100 4.3 / F 1722 0.8 / 2328 4.7
11 0017 4.6 / 0631 1.0 / F 1235 4.5 / 1853 0.7	**26** 0543 0.9 / 1151 4.6 / SA 1812 0.5
12 0055 4.7 / 0707 0.9 / SA 1310 4.7 / 1928 0.6	**27** 0016 5.0 / 0632 0.7 / SU 1236 4.9 / 1900 0.3
13 0129 4.8 / 0738 0.9 / SU 1343 4.8 / ● 2000 0.5	**28** 0100 5.2 / 0718 0.5 / M 1319 5.1 / ○ 1945 0.2
14 0201 4.8 / 0807 0.8 / M 1415 4.8 / 2030 0.5	**29** 0144 5.3 / 0804 0.4 / TU 1403 5.3 / 2031 0.1
15 0234 4.9 / 0837 0.7 / TU 1447 4.9 / 2102 0.5	**30** 0228 5.3 / 0849 0.4 / W 1447 5.3 / 2116 0.1

OCTOBER

Time m	Time m
1 0313 5.3 / 0934 0.4 / TH 1533 5.2 / 2202 0.2	**16** 0307 4.9 / 0918 0.6 / F 1521 4.9 / 2138 0.6
2 0359 5.1 / 1020 0.5 / F 1619 5.1 / 2247 0.4	**17** 0339 4.8 / 0953 0.7 / SA 1554 4.8 / 2212 0.7
3 0447 4.8 / 1105 0.7 / SA 1708 4.8 / 2335 0.7	**18** 0413 4.7 / 1028 0.8 / SU 1632 4.8 / 2248 0.9
4 0537 4.5 / 1155 0.9 / SU 1803 4.5 ☽	**19** 0452 4.6 / 1107 0.9 / M 1715 4.6 / 2330 1.0
5 0029 1.0 / 0636 4.2 / M 1259 1.1 / 1910 4.2	**20** 0538 4.4 / 1155 1.0 / TU 1809 4.4 ☾
6 0143 1.3 / 0751 4.0 / TU 1422 1.2 / 2033 4.1	**21** 0027 1.2 / 0639 4.2 / W 1308 1.2 / 1923 4.2
7 0259 1.4 / 0914 3.9 / W 1536 1.2 / 2155 4.1	**22** 0159 1.3 / 0805 4.0 / TH 1448 1.2 / 2052 4.2
8 0410 1.3 / 1028 4.0 / TH 1644 1.0 / 2301 4.3	**23** 0320 1.3 / 0928 4.1 / F 1556 1.0 / 2204 4.4
9 0515 1.2 / 1125 4.3 / F 1742 0.9 / 2350 4.5	**24** 0423 1.1 / 1032 4.3 / SA 1655 0.7 / 2303 4.7
10 0606 1.1 / 1209 4.5 / SA 1827 0.7	**25** 0520 0.9 / 1126 4.6 / SU 1749 0.5 / 2354 5.0
11 0030 4.7 / 0643 1.0 / SU 1245 4.7 / 1903 0.6	**26** 0612 0.7 / 1214 4.9 / M 1839 0.4
12 0104 4.8 / 0713 0.9 / M 1318 4.8 / 1933 0.6	**27** 0040 5.1 / 0700 0.6 / TU 1259 5.1 / ○ 1925 0.2
13 0136 4.9 / 0741 0.8 / TU 1349 4.8 / ● 2002 0.5	**28** 0125 5.2 / 0746 0.5 / W 1344 5.2 / 2011 0.2
14 0207 4.9 / 0812 0.7 / W 1420 4.9 / 2033 0.5	**29** 0209 5.2 / 0831 0.4 / TH 1428 5.2 / 2056 0.3
15 0238 4.9 / 0844 0.6 / TH 1450 4.9 / 2105 0.6	**30** 0254 5.1 / 0915 0.4 / F 1514 5.2 / 2140 0.4
	31 0339 5.0 / 1000 0.5 / SA 1601 5.0 / 2225 0.6

NOVEMBER

Time m	Time m
1 0426 4.7 / 1045 0.6 / SU 1649 4.8 / 2311 0.9	**16** 0353 4.7 / 1012 0.7 / M 1614 4.8 / 2231 0.9
2 0514 4.5 / 1134 0.8 / M 1741 4.5 / 2359 1.1	**17** 0434 4.6 / 1054 0.8 / TU 1700 4.7 / 2316 1.0
3 0609 4.2 / 1236 1.0 / TU 1843 4.3 ◖	**18** 0522 4.4 / 1145 0.9 / W 1754 4.5 ◖
4 0111 1.4 / 0717 4.0 / W 1352 1.1 / 1958 4.1	**19** 0013 1.4 / 0622 4.2 / TH 1255 1.0 / ◖ 1904 4.4
5 0226 1.5 / 0833 3.9 / TH 1501 1.1 / 2114 4.1	**20** 0132 1.3 / 0739 4.1 / F 1417 1.0 / 2025 4.3
6 0332 1.4 / 0946 4.0 / F 1605 1.1 / 2221 4.2	**21** 0249 1.2 / 0857 4.2 / SA 1525 0.9 / 2136 4.5
7 0435 1.3 / 1046 4.2 / SA 1704 1.0 / 2315 4.4	**22** 0354 1.1 / 1003 4.3 / SU 1627 0.7 / 2238 4.6
8 0531 1.2 / 1135 4.4 / SU 1753 0.8 / 2359 4.6	**23** 0456 1.0 / 1102 4.6 / M 1726 0.6 / 2333 4.8
9 0614 1.0 / 1216 4.5 / M 1832 0.8	**24** 0552 0.8 / 1154 4.8 / TU 1819 0.5
10 0037 4.7 / 0647 0.9 / TU 1251 4.6 / 1903 0.7	**25** 0023 4.9 / 0643 0.7 / W 1242 4.9 / ○ 1908 0.4
11 0111 4.8 / 0716 0.8 / W 1323 4.7 / ● 1933 0.7	**26** 0109 5.0 / 0730 0.6 / TH 1328 5.0 / 1954 0.4
12 0142 4.8 / 0748 0.7 / TH 1354 4.8 / 2006 0.6	**27** 0154 5.0 / 0815 0.5 / F 1414 5.1 / 2038 0.5
13 0212 4.8 / 0822 0.6 / F 1425 4.8 / 2040 0.6	**28** 0238 4.9 / 0859 0.5 / SA 1459 5.0 / 2121 0.6
14 0243 4.7 / 0857 0.6 / SA 1459 4.8 / 2115 0.6	**29** 0322 4.8 / 0943 0.5 / SU 1544 4.9 / 2204 0.8
15 0317 4.7 / 0934 0.7 / SU 1534 4.8 / 2152 0.8	**30** 0407 4.7 / 1028 0.6 / M 1630 4.7 / 2247 0.9

DECEMBER

Time m	Time m
1 0453 4.5 / 1115 0.7 / TU 1719 4.5 / 2334 1.1	**16** 0422 4.6 / 1046 0.7 / W 1648 4.7 / 2306 0.9
2 0542 4.3 / 1209 0.9 / W 1813 4.3	**17** 0510 4.5 / 1138 0.7 / TH 1742 4.6 / 2359 1.1
3 0031 1.3 / 0638 4.1 / TH 1315 1.0 / ◖ 1916 4.1	**18** 0606 4.4 / 1239 0.8 / F 1845 4.5 ◖
4 0141 1.4 / 0745 3.9 / F 1420 1.1 / 2025 4.0	**19** 0106 1.1 / 0713 4.3 / SA 1347 0.8 / 1956 4.4
5 0248 1.5 / 0854 3.9 / SA 1521 1.1 / 2131 4.1	**20** 0216 1.2 / 0825 4.3 / SU 1454 0.8 / 2106 4.4
6 0350 1.4 / 0957 4.0 / SU 1619 1.1 / 2231 4.2	**21** 0325 1.1 / 0934 4.5 / M 1600 0.8 / 2214 4.5
7 0448 1.3 / 1054 4.1 / M 1712 1.0 / 2322 4.3	**22** 0432 1.1 / 1040 4.4 / TU 1704 0.7 / 2316 4.5
8 0538 1.1 / 1141 4.3 / TU 1756 0.9	**23** 0537 0.9 / 1139 4.6 / W 1803 0.7
9 0006 4.5 / 0618 1.0 / W 1222 4.4 / 1833 0.8	**24** 0011 4.6 / 0632 0.8 / TH 1232 4.7 / 1854 0.6
10 0044 4.6 / 0652 0.9 / TH 1258 4.6 / 1907 0.8	**25** 0059 4.7 / 0719 0.7 / F 1319 4.8 / ○ 1940 0.6
11 0118 4.7 / 0726 0.8 / F 1331 4.7 / ● 1941 0.7	**26** 0143 4.7 / 0803 0.6 / SA 1403 4.9 / 2022 0.7
12 0150 4.7 / 0802 0.7 / SA 1405 4.8 / 2018 0.7	**27** 0225 4.7 / 0845 0.5 / SU 1445 4.9 / 2103 0.7
13 0224 4.7 / 0840 0.6 / SU 1441 4.8 / 2056 0.7	**28** 0306 4.7 / 0927 0.6 / M 1528 4.8 / 2143 0.8
14 0300 4.7 / 0919 0.6 / M 1520 4.8 / 2136 0.8	**29** 0348 4.7 / 1010 0.5 / TU 1611 4.7 / 2224 0.9
15 0339 4.7 / 1001 0.6 / TU 1602 4.8 / 2219 0.9	**30** 0430 4.6 / 1053 0.6 / W 1655 4.7 / 2304 1.0
	31 0513 4.4 / 1138 0.6 / TH 1740 4.4 / 2347 1.3

Chart Datum is 0·23 metres below TAW Datum. HAT is 5·6 metres above Chart Datum.

》》 **FREE** monthly updates from 《《
www.reedsalmanac.co.uk

2.33 BLANKENBERGE

Belgium, West Flanders **51°18'·90N 03°06'·48E** ✳✳✳✿✿✿✿✿✿

CHARTS AC 2449, 1872, 1874; DYC 1801.3; Imray C30

TIDES +0130 Dover; ML 2·5; Duration 0535
Standard Port ZEEBRUGGE (←)

Times				Height (metres)			
High Water		Low Water		MHWS	MHWN	MLWN	MLWS
0300	0900	0300	0900	4·8	3·9	1·1	0·5
1500	2100	1500	2100				
Differences BLANKENBERGE							
−0007		−0002		+0·1	+0·1	−0·1	−0·1

SHELTER Good, but entry is dangerous in NW'lies F6 and above.

NAVIGATION WPT 51°19'·60N 03°05'·31E, 134°/1M to pierheads. Caution: 4 unlit Y SPM buoys and one Fl (3) Y 20s lie E and W of hbr ent about 400m offshore. Beware strong tides (& fishing lines) across ent. Said to be dredged 2·5m during the season; but out of season it silts badly between piers and dries at LW. Do not try to ent/exit around low water, especially at springs and from Oct–end May, unless depths have been pre-checked. Call dredger Ch 10 for clearance to pass.

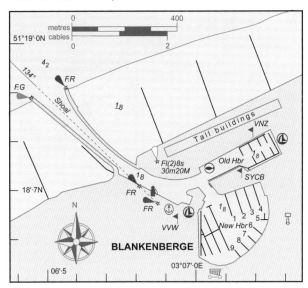

LIGHTS AND MARKS Conspic high-rise blocks E of lt ho, W twr B top. Ldg lts 134°, both FR, (Red X on front mast) show the best water. FG on W pier is more visible than FR (E pier). A water twr is conspic on E side of new Hbr. See also Lights, buoys & waypoints and chartlet.

COMMUNICATIONS (Code (0)50) *Blankenberge Rescue* Ch 08 or relay via Zeebrugge Traffic Centre VHF Ch 69; ⊖ 544223; Police 429842; Dr 333668; Ⓗ 413701; Brit Consul (02) 287 6248; VNZ, SYCB and VVW marinas VHF Ch 23; Dredger VHF Ch 10.

FACILITIES A Port of Entry, with Customs early Apr–late Sept.

Keep to port, past the FV hbr, for the old Yacht Hbr (1·8m); VNZ pontoons are on N side and SYCB to the E. Or turn 90° stbd into new Hbr/marina (2·5m); 12 pontoons, run by VNZ, SYCB & VVW.

Fees (same for all berths): Beam <9m €17·00; <11m €21·00; <13m €26·00; <15m €40·00.

VNZ (YC Vrije Noordzeezeilers) ☎ 425292, mobile 0497 565565. www.vnzblankenberge.be vnz@skynet.be ⌗, R.

SYCB (Scarphout YC) www.scarphout.be scarphout@skynet.be ☎ 411420, mobile 0476 971692. C (10/2½ ton), ▬, ⌗, R, ⌑.

VVW (Marina) www.vvwblankenberge.be ☎ 417536, mobile 0495 527536 info@vvwblankenberge.be. ⚓, ⌗, Ⓞ, ▬, P, D (hose, duty free), ⚒, ✗, Ⓔ, ⌱, ⚠, ⌑, C (20 ton).

Town Gaz, R, ⌗, ✉, Ⓑ, ⇌, ✈ Ostend.

2.34 OOSTENDE

Belgium, West Flanders **51°14'·35N 02°55'·09E** ✳✳✳✿✿✿✿✿✿✿

CHARTS AC 2449, 1872, 1874, 1873; SHOM 7214; Navi 1010; DYC 1801.2; Imray C30; BE D11

TIDES +0115 Dover; ML 2·79; Duration 0530
Standard Port ZEEBRUGGE (←)

Times				Height (metres)			
High Water		Low Water		MHWS	MHWN	MLWN	MLWS
0300	0900	0300	0900	4·8	4·0	1·1	0·5
1500	2100	1500	2100				
Differences OOSTENDE							
−0019	−0019	−0008	−0008	+0·4	+0·2	+0·2	+0·1

SHELTER Wash can enter RNSYC (2·2m). Very good in Mercator Marina (5·0m). RYCO (2·7m) may be exposed in strong W/NW'lies.

NAVIGATION WPT 51° 15'·2N 02° 54'·23E, 143°/1M to ent. Avoid the offshore banks esp in bad weather: From the NE stay to seaward of Wenduinebank, except in calm weather. From the NW keep S of W Hinder TSS and approach from MBN buoy. From the SW appr via West Diep and Kleine Rede, inside Stroombank. Note size of Montgomerydok entrance reduced to decrease wash.

LIGHTS AND MARKS Europa Centrum bldg (105m; twice as high as other bldgs) is conspic 4ca SSW of ent. W lt ho, 5ca ESE of the ent, is conspic with 2 sinusoidal blue bands. 143° ldg marks are lattice masts with R/W bands and X topmarks. See chartlet and Lights, buoys & waypoints for lt details.

IPTS from E pier, plus QY = hbr closed, ferry moving. At blind exit from Montgomerydok, QY lts = no exit, ferry/ship moving.

COMMUNICATIONS (Code 059) ⚓ VHF Ch 27 at 0820 & 1720 UT (English and Dutch); Police 701111; ⊖ 242070; Brit Consul (02) 287 6248; Ⓗ 552000; HM 321687, Ch 09 (H24); Mercator lock 705762, VHF Ch 14; Marina VHF Ch 14 (lock hrs); Demey lock (VHF 10) gives access to Oostende-Brugge canal.

FACILITIES from seaward: **Royal North Sea YC** (RNSYC), ☎ 430694 HM 505912. www.rnsyc.be robert@rnsyc.be No VHF. 150+50 Ⓥ, much rafting, €3·00 inc ⌁ & shwr (M/Cruisers €4·10/m). Grid, Ⓞ, ⚒, ⌱, ✗, ⌲, ⚠, R, ⌑.

Mercator lock Must pre-call Ch 14 for lock-in time and berth. Waiting pontoon N of lock. No freeflow. R/G tfc lts. Hrs (times in brackets are Fri-Sun & public hols): May/Jun 0800-2000 (2100); Jul/ Aug 0700-2200, 7/7; Sep 0800-1800 (2000). Oct–Apr, see web.

Mercator Marina ☎705762.www.mercatormarina.be 300+50 Ⓥ, €2·20, (vessels >13.75m, +€1·10/m p/d surcharge) , ⌁, ⚓, and shwrs not included; pay cash/card before entering lock outbound.

Royal YC Oostende (RYCO) ☎ 32477 676391(Dockmaster). ryco@ skynet.be www.ryco.be No VHF. 160 + 35 Ⓥ, €2·60 inc shwr. ⌁ €3·50/day. ▬ (10 ton), Grid, C (½ ton), R, ⌑.

Town All needs, ⇌, ✈.

CROSSING THE NORTH SEA FROM BELGIUM

(AC 1406, 323) There are so many permutations that it is better to try to apply just four broad principles:

- Avoid the N Hinder-Maas and W Hinder-Sandettie complexes.
- Cross TSS at their narrowest parts, ie between NHR-SE and Fairy W; and SW of Sandettie.
- Plan to cross the many offshore ridges at their extremities, zigzagging as necessary to achieve this.
- If bound for Dover up down-Channel use the coastal passage W to Dyck, then via MPC to SW Goodwin buoy. Or route via Sandettie to NE Goodwin buoy and into the southern Thames Estuary.

From the Scheur chan off Zeebrugge a fairly direct course via Track Ferry and S Galloper leads into the N Thames Estuary or towards the Suffolk ports. Avoid shoals, particularly in rough weather when the sea-state and under-keel clearance may be crucial problems. For N Sea distances see 0.31.

Belgium

OOSTENDE *continued*

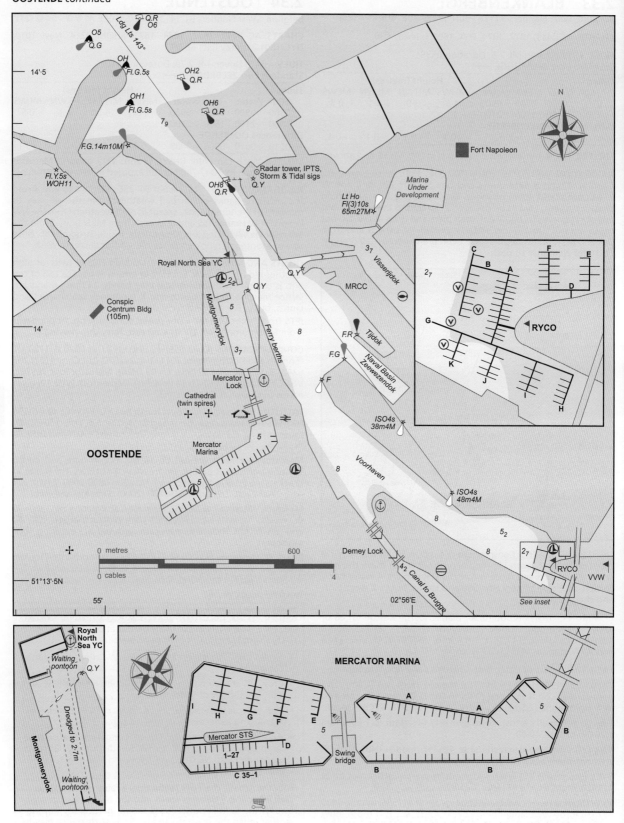

O5
Q.G

Q.R
O6

Ldg Lts 143°

OH
Fl.G.5s

OH2
Q.R

14'·5

OH1
Fl.G.5s

OH6
Q.R

7₉

F.G.14m10M

Fl.Y.5s
WOH11

OH8
Q.R

Radar tower, IPTS,
Storm & Tidal sigs
Q.Y

Fort Napoleon

Marina
Under
Development

N

Lt Ho
Fl(3)10s
65m27M

8

Visserijdok

2₇

C
B
A

F
E
D

Royal North Sea YC

Q.Y

MRCC

Conspic
Centrum Bldg
(105m)

2₇

Q.Y

G

V
V

V

RYCO

5

8

F.R

Tijdok

V

14'

Montgomerydok

3₇

F.G

Naval Basin
Zeewezendok

K

J

I

H

Mercator
Lock

F

Cathedral
(twin spires)

ISO4s
38m4M

OOSTENDE

Mercator
Marina

5

5

Voorhaven

8

ISO4s
48m4M

8

5₂

8

2₇

RYCO

VVW

See inset

Demey Lock

4₂ Canal to Brugge

51°13'·5N

55'

02°56'E

0 metres   600

0 cables   4

Ferry berths

Royal
North
Sea YC

Waiting
pontoon

Q.Y

Montgomerydok

Dredged to 2·7m

Waiting
pontoon

N

MERCATOR MARINA

I
H
G
F
E

A
A

A

5

Mercator STS

5

B

1–27

D

Swing
bridge

B

B

C 35–1

B

2.35 NIEUWPOORT

Belgium, W Flanders **51°09'·38N 02°43'·04E** ❀❀❀☙☙☙❁❁❁

CHARTS AC 2449, 1872, 1873; Belgian 101, D11; DYC 1801.2; SHOM 7214; Navicarte 1010; Imray C30

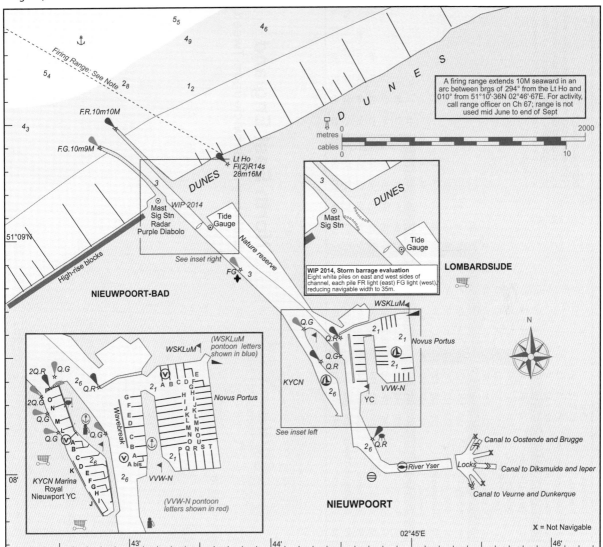

X = Not Navigable

TIDES +0105 Dover; ML 2·96; Duration 0515

Standard Port ZEEBRUGGE (←)

Times				Height (metres)			
High Water		Low Water		MHWS	MHWN	MLWN	MLWS
0300	0900	0300	0900	4·8	4·0	1·1	0·5
1500	2100	1500	2100				
Differences NIEUWPOORT							
–0031	–0031	–0010	–0010	+0·7	+0·5	+0·3	+0·1

SHELTER Good except in strong NW'lies. Access H24.

NAVIGATION WPT 51°10'·08N 02°41'·90E, 134°/1M to ent. The bar (1·5m) is liable to silt up but there is usually sufficient water for all but the deepest draught yachts. At sp the stream reaches 2kn across the ent. WIP 2014, inner approach chan, to evaluate a storm barrage, has reduced the navigable width to 35m; (see chartlet). The 1M long access chan to the marinas is marked by white-topped piles and coloured coded arrows for guidance to each of the 3 marinas (WSKLuM–blue; VVW-N–yellow; KYCN–grey). The chan is dredged 3·1m. Speed limit 5kts in hbr.

LIGHTS AND MARKS The high-rise blocks W of the entrance are in stark contrast to the sand dunes and flatlands to the E. The lt ho is a conspic 28m R twr, W bands; see chartlet and Lights, buoys & waypoints.

The central, pyramidal white HM bldg at VVW-N is conspic.

COMMUNICATIONS (Code 058) MRCC Oostende VHF Ch 16,67; VTS Wandelaar appr VHF Ch 60; Coast Guard/Marine Police 224030; Police 234246; ⊖ 233451; Brit Consul (02) 287 6248; Dr 233089; Port VHF Ch 60 (H24); Canal locks 233050; *Air Force Yacht Club* (WSKLuM): VHF Ch 72. KYCN: VHF Ch 23. VVW-N: VHF Ch 08.

FACILITIES The 3 marinas are: **WSKLuM**, N & E sides of Novus Portus. ☎ 233641, www.wsklum.be info@wsklm.be 370 inc ♥ on pontoons A & B, €1·80, ⟐ (16A). H24, ⌂, BH (25 ton), ⚓, ⬚, Ice, bike hire, R, ⬚; ⛬ 800m NE at Lombardsijde.

VVW-N, S & W sides of Novus Portus. ☎ 235232, www.vvwnieuwpoort.be info@vvwnieuwpoort.be ④ 1000 + ♥. ⟐ (16A) €1·70. ⌂, Ⓔ, BH (50t), ⚓, ⬚, ⚓, ⚒, ⚓, ⬚, R, ⬚, free bikes.

KYCN (Royal Nieuwpoort YC). info@kycn.be www.kycn.be ☎ 234413. 440 + 75 ♥, €2·58 Jul/Aug, €2·53 Apr/May/Jun/Sep/Oct; ⟐ €2·14/day. M, BH (25 ton) pier 'N' reserved for D, BH, ⚓, ⌂, ⚒, ⌂, ⚒, ⛬, ⬚, R, ⬚.

Fuel P, D, available alongside S of VVW-N on the E bank of the river, see inset, D, at KYCN. The river accesses the N Belgian canals.

Town P, D, Gaz, ⛬, R, ⬚, ⊠, Ⓑ, ⇒, ✈ (Oostende).

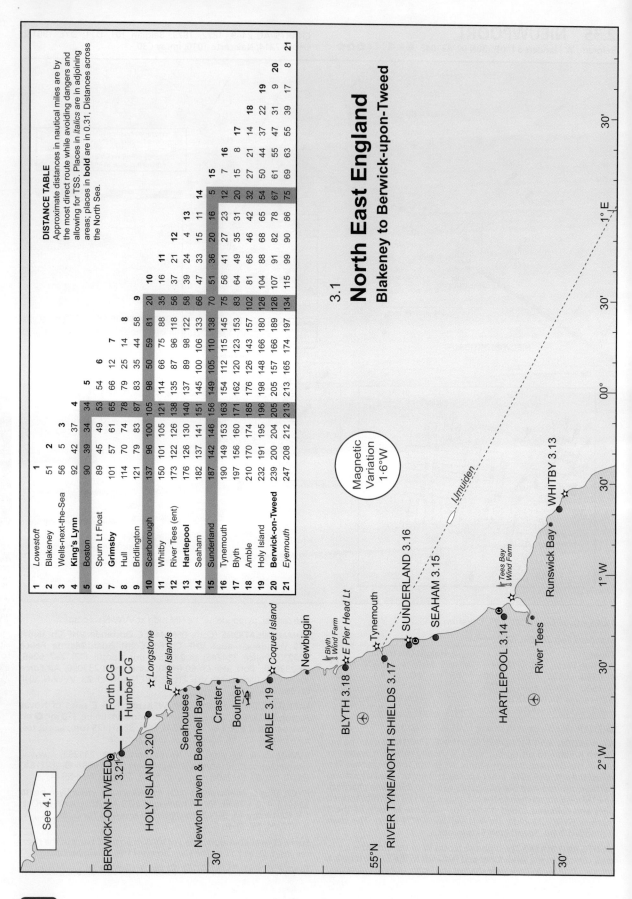

3.1

North East England
Blakeney to Berwick-upon-Tweed

DISTANCE TABLE

Approximate distances in nautical miles are by the most direct route while avoiding dangers and allowing for TSS. Places in *italics* are in adjoining areas; places in **bold** are in 0.31, Distances across the North Sea.

	1	2	3	4	5	6	7	8	9	10	11	12	13	14	15	16	17	18	19	20	21
1 *Lowestoft*	**1**																				
2 Blakeney	51	**2**																			
3 Wells-next-the-Sea	56	5	**3**																		
4 **King's Lynn**	92	42	37	**4**																	
5 Boston	90	39	34	34	**5**																
6 Spurn Lt Float	89	45	49	53	54	**6**															
7 **Grimsby**	101	57	61	65	66	12	**7**														
8 Hull	114	70	74	78	79	25	14	**8**													
9 Bridlington	121	79	83	87	83	35	44	58	**9**												
10 Scarborough	137	96	100	105	98	50	59	81	20	**10**											
11 Whitby	150	101	105	121	114	66	75	88	35	16	**11**										
12 River Tees (ent)	173	122	126	130	135	87	96	118	56	37	21	**12**									
13 **Hartlepool**	176	126	130	140	137	89	98	122	58	39	24	4	**13**								
14 Seaham	182	137	141	151	145	100	106	133	66	47	33	15	11	**14**							
15 Sunderland	187	142	146	156	149	105	110	138	70	51	36	20	16	5	**15**						
16 Tynemouth	190	149	153	163	154	112	115	145	75	56	41	27	23	12	7	**16**					
17 Blyth	197	156	160	171	162	120	123	153	83	64	49	35	31	20	15	8	**17**				
18 Amble	210	170	174	185	176	126	143	157	102	81	65	46	42	32	27	14	21	**18**			
19 Holy Island	232	191	195	196	198	148	166	180	126	104	88	68	65	54	50	37	44	22	**19**		
20 **Berwick-on-Tweed**	239	200	204	205	205	157	166	189	126	107	91	82	78	67	61	47	55	37	9	**20**	
21 *Eymouth*	247	208	212	213	213	165	174	197	134	115	99	90	86	75	69	63	55	39	17	8	**21**

Magnetic Variation 1·6°W

See 4.1

BERWICK-ON-TWEED 3.21

Forth CG

Humber CG

HOLY ISLAND 3.20

Longstone

☆ *Farne Islands*

Seahouses ☆

Newton Haven & Beadnell Bay ●

Craster ●

Boulmer ●

AMBLE 3.19 ☆ *Coquet Island*

Newbiggin ●

Blyth Wind Farm

BLYTH 3.18 ☆ *E Pier Head Lt*

RIVER TYNE/NORTH SHIELDS 3.17 ● Tynemouth

SUNDERLAND 3.16

SEAHAM 3.15

Tees Bay Wind Farm

HARTLEPOOL 3.14

● River Tees

IJmuiden

Runswick Bay ●

WHITBY 3.13

2°W   1°W   30′   30′   00°   30′   1°E   30′

55°N   30′   30′

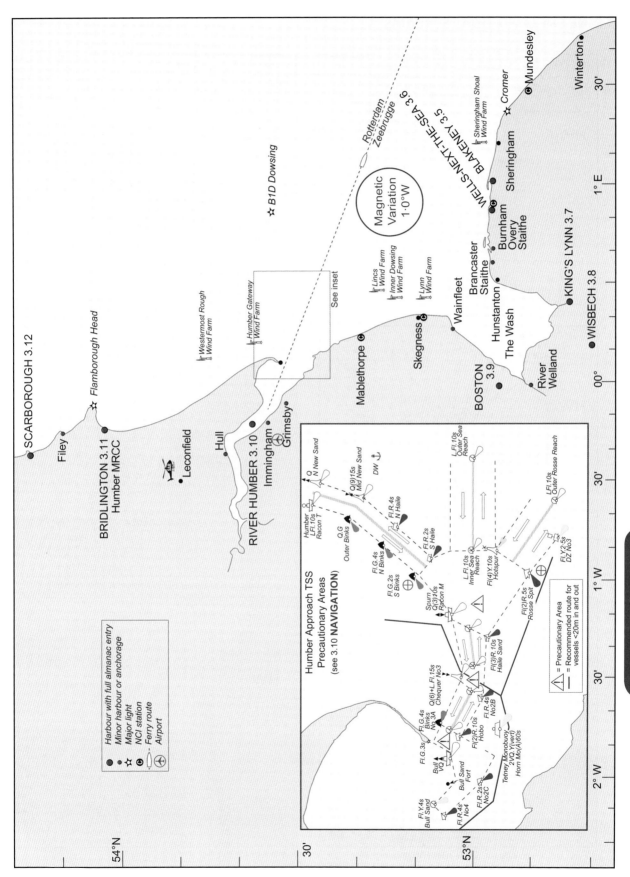

3.2 NE ENGLAND TIDAL STREAMS

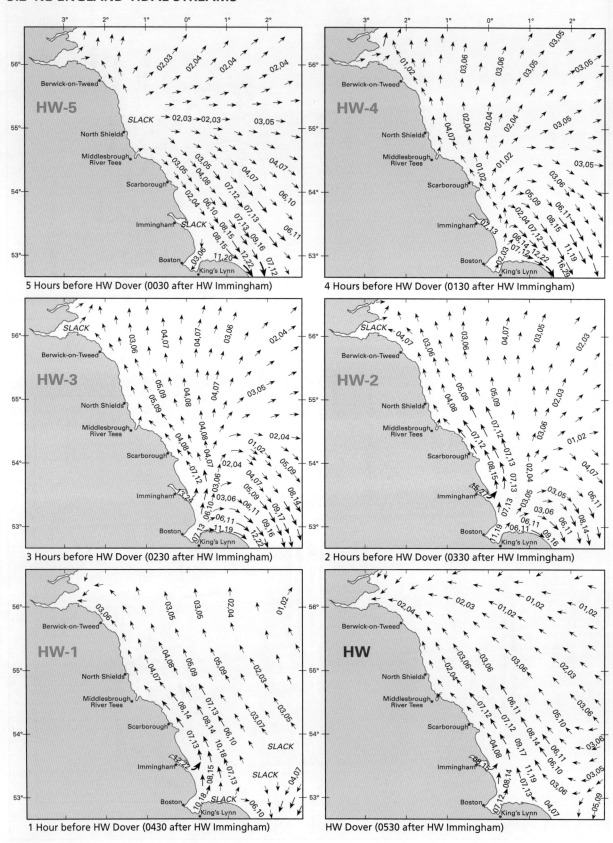

5 Hours before HW Dover (0030 after HW Immingham)

4 Hours before HW Dover (0130 after HW Immingham)

3 Hours before HW Dover (0230 after HW Immingham)

2 Hours before HW Dover (0330 after HW Immingham)

1 Hour before HW Dover (0430 after HW Immingham)

HW Dover (0530 after HW Immingham)

Northward 4.2   Southward 1.2

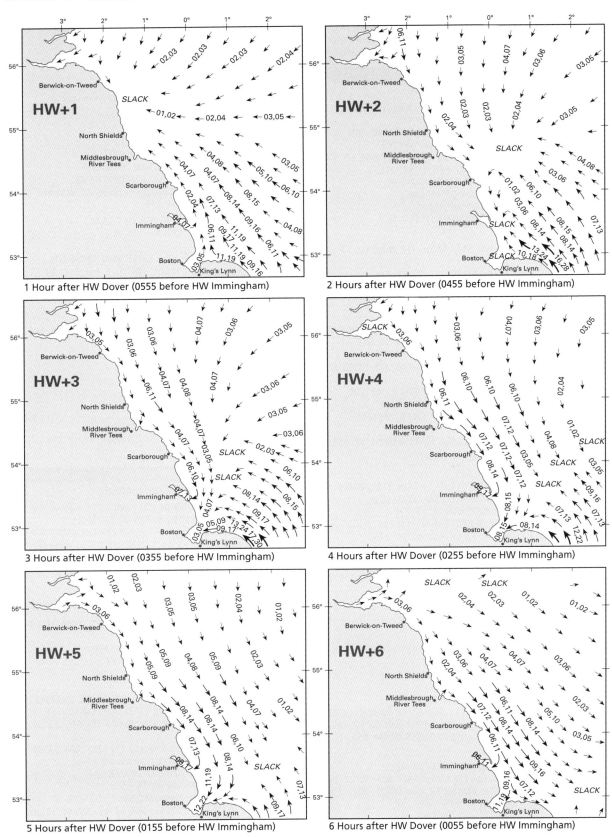

1 Hour after HW Dover (0555 before HW Immingham)

2 Hours after HW Dover (0455 before HW Immingham)

3 Hours after HW Dover (0355 before HW Immingham)

4 Hours after HW Dover (0255 before HW Immingham)

5 Hours after HW Dover (0155 before HW Immingham)

6 Hours after HW Dover (0055 before HW Immingham)

NE England

3.3 LIGHTS, BUOYS AND WAYPOINTS

Bold print = light with a nominal range of 15M or more. CAPITALS = place or feature. *CAPITAL ITALICS* = light-vessel, light float or Lanby. *Italics* = Fog signal. ***Bold italics*** = Racon. Some marks/buoys are fitted with AIS (<u>MMSI No</u>); see relevant charts.

GREAT YARMOUTH TO THE WASH

(Direction of buoyage ⇧ South to North)

YARMOUTH and CAISTER ROADS/COCKLE GATEWAY
SW Scroby ⬥ Fl G 2·5s; 52°35'·13N 01°46'·69E.
Scroby Elbow ⬥ Fl (2) G 5s; *Bell*; 52°36'·55N 01°46'·26E.
Yarmouth Outfall ⬤ Q R; 52°37'·58N 01°45'·70E.
Mid Caister ⬤ Fl (2) R 5s; *Bell*; 52°38'·99N 01°45'·66E.
NW Scroby ⬥ Fl (3) G 10s; 52°40'·36N 01°46'·31E.
N Caister ⬤ Fl (3) R 10s; 52°40'·77N 01°45'·65E.
Hemsby ⬤ Fl R 2·5s; 52°41'·80N 01°46'·00E.
N Scroby ⚑ VQ; 52°41'·39N 01°46'·47E.
Cockle ⚑ VQ (3) 5s; *Bell*; 52°44'·03N 01°43'·59E.

OFFSHORE ROUTE
Cross Sand ⚑ L Fl 10s 6m 5M; ***Racon (T) 10M***; 52°37'·03N 01°59'·14E.
E Cross Sand ⬤ Fl (4) R 15s; 52°38'·55N 01°53'·55E.
NE Cross Sand ⚑ VQ (3) 5s; 52°44'·22N 01° 53'·80E.
Smith's Knoll ⚑ Q (6) + L Fl 15s 7M; ***Racon (T) 10M***; 52°43'·52N 02°17'·89E.
S Winterton Ridge ⚑ Q (6) + L Fl 15s; 52°47'·21N 02°03'·44E.
E Hammond Knoll ⚑ Q (3) 10s; 52°52'·32N 01°58'·64E.
Hammond Knoll ⚑ Q (9) 15s; 52°49'·68N 01°57'·54E.
Newarp ⚑ L Fl 10s 7M; ***Racon (O) 10M***; 52°48'·37N 01°55'·69E; <u>992351118</u>.
S Haisbro ⚑ Q (6) + L Fl 15s; *Bell*; 52°50'·82N 01°48'·29E.
Mid Haisbro ⬥ Fl (2) G 5s; 52°54'·22N 01°41'·59E.
N Haisbro ⚑ Q; ***Racon (T) 10M***; 53°00'·22N 01°32'·29E; <u>992351031</u>.
Happisburgh ☆ Fl (3) 30s 41m 14M; 52°49'·21N 01°32'·18E.

(Direction of buoyage ⇧ East to West)

CROMER
Cromer ☆ 52°55'·45N 01°19'·01E; Fl 5s 84m **21M**; W 8-sided twr; vis: 102°-307° H24; ***Racon (O) 25M***; <u>992351015</u>.
Tayjack Wk ⬤ Fl R 2·5s; 52°57'·61N 01°15'·37E.
E Sheringham ⚑ Q (3) 10s; 53°02'·21N 01°14'·84E.
W Sheringham ⚑ Q (9) 15s; 53°02'·95N 01°06'·72E.

BLAKENEY
Blakeney Fairway (SWM) ⬤; 52°59'·31N 00°57'·83E (approx).
Blakeney Overfalls ⬤ Fl (2) R 5s; *Bell*; 53°03'·01N 01°01'·37E.

WELLS-NEXT-THE-SEA/BRANCASTER STAITHE
Wells WCM ⚑ Q(9) 15s; 52°59'·64N 00°51'·00E.
Bridgirdle ⬤ Fl R 2·5s; 53°01'·73N 00°43'·95E.

APPROACHES TO THE WASH
S Race ⚑ Q (6) + L Fl 15s; *Bell*; 53°07'·81N 00°57'·34E.
E Docking ⬤ Fl R 2·5s; 53°09'·82N 00°50'·39E.
N Race ⬥ Fl G 5s; *Bell*; 53°14'·98N 00°43'·87E.
N Docking ⚑ Q; 53°14'·82N 00°41'·49E.
Scott Patch ⚑ VQ (3) 5s; 53°11'·12N 00°36'·39E.
S Inner Dowsing ⚑ Q (6) + L Fl 15s; *Bell*; 53°12'·12N 00°33'·69E.
Boygrift Tower ⚑ Fl (2) 10s 12m 5M; 53°17'·63N 00°19'·24E.
Burnham Flats ⚑ Q (9) 15s; *Bell*; 53°07'·53N 00°34'·89E.

THE WASH
West Ridge ⚑ Q (9) 15s; 53°19'·06N 00°44'·47E.
N Well ⚑ L Fl 10s; *Bell*; ***Racon (T) 10M***; 53°03'·02N 00°27'·90E.
Roaring Middle L Fl 10s 7m 8M; 52°58'·64N 00°21'·08E.

CORK HOLE/KING'S LYNN
Sunk ⚑ Q (9) 15s; 52°56'·29N 00°23'·40E.
Seal Sand ⚑ Q; *Bell*; 52°56'·00N 00°20'·00E.

WISBECH CHANNEL/RIVER NENE
Beacons are moved as required.

FREEMAN CHANNEL
Boston Roads ⬤ L Fl 10s; 52°57'·61N 00°16'·29E.
Boston No. 1 ⬥ Fl G 3s; 52°57'·88N 00°15'·16E.
Alpha ⬤ Fl R 3s; 52°57'·65N 00°14'·99E.
No. 3 ⬥ Fl G 6s; 52°58'·08N 00°14'·07E.
No. 5 ⬥ Fl G 3s; 52°58'·51N 00°12'·72E.
Freeman Inner ⚑ Q (9) 15s; 52°58'·59N 00°11'·36E.
Delta ⬤ Fl R 6s; 52°58'·38N 00°11'·25E.

BOSTON LOWER ROAD
Echo ⬤ Fl R 3s; 52°58'·38N 00°10'·13E.
Foxtrot ⬤ Fl R 3s; 52°57'·60N 00°08'·94E.
Boston No. 9 ⬥ Fl G 3s; 52°57'·58N 00°08'·36E.
Black Buoy ⬤ Fl (2) R 6s; 52°56'·82N 00°07'·74E.
Tabs Head ⚑ Q WG 4m 1M; R □ on W mast; vis: W shore - 251°; G - shore; 52°56'·00N 00°04'·91E.

BOSTON, NEW CUT AND RIVER WITHAM
Ent N side, Dollypeg ⚑ QG 4m 1M; B △ on Bn; 52°56'·13N 00°05'·03E.
New Cut ⚑ Fl G 3s; △ on pile; 52°55'·98N 00°04'·67E.
New Cut Ldg Lts 240°. Front, No. 1, F 5m 5M; 52°55'·85N 00°04'·40E. Rear, 90m from front, F 8m 5M.

WELLAND CUT/RIVER WELLAND
SE side ⚐ Iso R 2s; NW side Iso G 2s. Lts QR (to port) and QG (to stbd) mark the chan upstream; 52°55'·72E 00°04'·68E.

(Direction of buoyage ⇧ North to South)

BOSTON DEEP/WAINFLEET ROADS
Scullridge ⬥; 52°59'·76N 00°13'·86E.
Friskney ⬥; 53°00'·59N 00°16'·76E.
Long Sand ⬥; 53°01'·27N 00°18'·30E.
Pompey ⬥; 53°02'·19N 00°19'·26E.
Swatchway ⬥; 53°03'·81N 00°19'·70E.
Off Ingoldmells Point ⚐ Fl Y 5s 22m 5M; Mast; *Mo (U) 30s*; 53°12'·49N 00°25'·85E.

THE WASH TO THE RIVER HUMBER

(Direction of buoyage ⇧ South to North)

Dudgeon ⚑ Q (9) 15s 7M; ***Racon (O) 10M;*** 53°16'·62N 01°16'·90E.
E Dudgeon ⚑ Q (3) 10s; 53°19'·72N 00°58'·69E.
Mid Outer Dowsing ⬥ Fl (3) G 10s; 53°24'·82N 01°07'·79E.
N Outer Dowsing ⚑ Q; 53°33'·52N 00°59'·59E; ***Racon (T) 10M***; <u>992351031</u>.
B.1D Platform Dowsing ⬗ 53°33'·68N 00°52'·63E; Fl (2) 10s 28m **22M**; Morse (U) R 15s 28m 3M; *Horn (2) 60s*.

RIVER HUMBER APPROACHES
W Ridge ⚑ Q (9) 15s; 53°19'·04N 00°44'·50E.
Inner Dowsing ⚑ Q (3) 10s 7M, ***Racon (T) 10M***; *Horn 60s*; 53°19'·10N 00°34'·80E.
Protector ⬤ Fl R 2·5s; 53°24'·84N 00°25'·12E.
DZ No. 4 ⬗ Fl Y 5s; 53°27'·15N 00°19'·06E.
DZ No. 3 ⬗ Fl Y 2·5s 53°29'·30N 00°19'·21E.
Rosse Spit ⬤ Fl (2) R 5s 53°30'·56N 00°16'·60E.
Outer Sand ⚑ Q (3) 10s; 53°36'·41N 00°29'·39E; <u>992351119</u>.
Haile Sand No. 2 ⬤ Fl (3) R 10s; 53°32'·42N 00°13'·18E.
Humber lt float L Fl G 10s 5M; ***Racon (T) 7M***; 53°38'·70N 00°21'·24E.
Humber Gateway Met Mast ⬗ Mo(U) 15s 12m 10M; 53°38'·24N 00°15'·73E; *Horn Mo(U) 30s*; Y framework mast.
N Binks ⬥ Fl G 4s; 53°36'·01N 00°18'·28E.
S Binks ⬥ Fl G 2s 53°34'·74N 00°16'·55E.
SPURN Q (3) 10s 10m 8M; ***Racon (M) 5M***; 53°33'·49N 00°14'·20E.
SE CHEQUER VQ (6)+L Fl 10s 6m 6M; 53°33'·27N 00°12'·33E.
Chequer No. 3 ⚑ Q (6) + L Fl 15s; 53°33'·07N 00°10'·63E.
No 2B ⬤ Fl R 4s; 53°32'·33N 00°09'·10E.

Tetney ⌖ 2 VQ Y (vert); *Horn Mo (A)60s*; QY on 290m floating hose; 53°32'·35N 00°06'·76E.

RIVER HUMBER/GRIMSBY/HULL
Binks No. 3A ▲ Fl G 4s; 53°33'·92N 00°07'·43E.
Spurn Pt ⌕ Fl G 3s 11m 5M; 53°34'·37N 00°06'·47E.
BULL ⌕ VQ 8m 6M; 53°33'·54N 00°05'·70E.
Bull Sand ⌀ Q R ; 53°34'·45N 00°03'·69E.
North Fort ⌕ Q; 53°33'·80N 00°04'·19E.
South Fort ⌕ Q (6) + L Fl 15s; 53°33'·65N 00°03'·96E.
Haile Sand Fort ⚲ Fl R 5s 21m 3M; 53°32'·07N 00°01'·99E.
Haile Chan No. 4 ⌀ Fl R 4s; 53°33'·64N 00°02'·84E.
Middle No. 7 VQ (6) + L Fl 10s; 53°35'·80N 00°01'·50E.

Grimsby Royal Dock ent E side ⚲ Fl (2) R 6s 10m 8M; Dn; 53°35'·08N 00°04'·04W.
Killingholme Lts in line 292°. Front, Iso R 2s 10m 14M. 53°38'·78N 00°12'·96W. Rear, 215m from front, F WRG 22m 3M; vis: 289·5°-G-290·5°-G/W-291·5°-W-292·5°-R/W-293·5° -R-294·5° (H24).

RIVER HUMBER TO WHITBY
Canada & Giorgios Wreck ⌕ VQ (3) 5s; 53°42'·37N 00°07'·16E.

BRIDLINGTON
SW Smithic ⌕ Q (9) 15s; 54°02'·41N 00°09'·21W.
N Pier Hd ⚲ Fl 2s 12m 9M; *Horn 60s*; (Tidal Lts) Fl R or Fl G; 54°04'·77N 00°11'·19W.
N Smithic ⌕ VQ; *Bell*; 54°06'·22N 00°03'·90W.
Flamborough Hd ☆ 54°06'·98N 00°04'·96W; Fl (4) 15s 65m **24M**; W ○ twr; *Horn (2) 90s*.

FILEY/SCARBOROUGH/WHITBY
Filey Brigg ⌕ Q (3) 10s; *Bell*; 54°12'·74N 00°14'·60W.
Scarborough E Pier Hd ⚲ QG 8m 3M; 54°16'·88N 00°23'·36W.
Scarborough Pier ⚲ Iso 5s 17m 9M; W ○ twr; vis: 219°- 039° (tide sigs); *Dia 60s*; 54°16'·91N 00°23'·40W.
Whitby ⌕ Q; *Bell*; 54°30'·33N 00°36'·58W.

Whitby High ☆ 54°28'·67N 00°34'·10W; Fl WR 5s 73m **18M**, R16M; W 8-sided twr & dwellings; vis:128°-R-143°-W- 319°.

Whitby E Pier ⚲ Fl(2) R 4s 16m 5M; 54°29'·57N 00°36'·71W; Masonry Twr.
Whitby E Pier Ext Hd ⚲ Q R 12m 5M; 54°29'·65N 00°36'·74W.
Whitby W Pier ⚲ Fl(2) G 4s 24m 5M; 54°29'·57N 00°36'·78W; Masonry Twr.
Whitby W Pier Ext Hd ⚲ Q G 12m 5M; 54°29'·65N 00°36'·80W.

WHITBY TO THE RIVER TYNE
RUNSWICK/REDCAR
Salt Scar ⌕ 54°38'·12N 01°00'·12W VQ; *Bell*.
Luff Way Ldg Lts 197°. Front, on Esplanade, FR 8m 7M; vis: 182°-212°; 54°37'·10N 01°03'·71W. Rear, 115m from front, FR 12m 7M; vis: 182°-212°.
High Stone. Lade Way Ldg Lts 247°. Front, Oc R 2·5s 9m 7M; 54°37'·15N 01°03'·92W. Rear, 43m from front, Oc R 2·5s 11m 7M; vis: 232°-262°.

TEES APPROACHES/HARTLEPOOL
Tees Fairway ⌕ Iso 4s 8m 8M; *Racon (B) unknown range*; *Horn (1) 5s*; 54°40'·94N 01°06'·48W.
Bkwtr Hd S Gare ☆ 54°38'·85N 01°08'·25W; Fl WR 12s 16m **W20M, R17M**; W ○ twr; vis: 020°-W-240°-R-357°; Sig Stn.
Ldg Lts 210·1° Front, FR 18m 13M; 54°37'·22N 01°10'·20W. **Rear**, 560m from front, FR 20m **16M**.
Longscar ⌕ Q (3) 10s; *Bell*; 54°40'·86N 01°09'·89W.
The Heugh ☆ 54°41'·79N 01°10'·56W; Fl (2) 10s 19m **19M**; W twr.

Hartlepool Marina Lock Dir Lt 308° Dir Fl WRG2s 6m 3M; vis: 305·5°-G-307°-W-309°-R-310·5°; 54°41'·45N 01°11'·92W.

SEAHAM/SUNDERLAND
Seaham N Pier Hd ⚲ Fl G 10s 12m 5M; W col, B bands; 54°50'·26N 01°19'·26W.

Sunderland Roker Pier Hd ☆ 54°55'·28N 01°21'·15W; Fl 5s 25m **18M**; W □ twr, 3 R bands and cupola: vis: 211°- 357°; *Siren 20s*.

Old N Pier Hd ⚲ QG 12m 8M; metal column; 54°55'·13N 01°21'·61W.

DZ ⌀ 54°57'·04N 01°18'·90W and ⌀ 54°58'·61N 01°19'·90W; both Fl Y 2·5s.

TYNE ENTRANCE/NORTH SHIELDS
Ent North Pier Hd ☆ 55°00'·88N 01°24'·18W; Fl (3) 10s 26m **26M**; Gy □ twr, W lantern; *Horn 10s*.
Herd Groyne Hd Dir Ldg Lt 249°, Oc 10s 14m **19M**; vis: 246·5°-W-251·5°; R pile structure, R&W lantern. Same structure Oc RG 10s 13m, 11M; vis: 224°-G-246·5, 251·5°-R-277°; sync with Dir lt FR (unintens) 080°-224°. *Bell (1) 5s*; 55°00'·49N 01°25'·44W.

RIVER TYNE TO BERWICK-UPON-TWEED
CULLERCOATS and BLYTH
Cullercoats Ldg Lts 256°. Front, FR 27m 3M; 55°02'·06N 01°25'·91W. Rear, 38m from front, FR 35m 3M.
Blyth Ldg Lts 324°. Front ⌕, F Bu 11m 10M; 55°07'·42N 01°29'·82W. Rear ⌕, 180m from front, F Bu 17m 10M. Both Or ⌕ on twr.
Blyth E Pier Hd ☆ 55°06'·98N 01°29'·21W; Fl(4) 10s 19m **21M**, W twr; same structure FR 13m 13M, vis:152°-249°; *Horn (3) 30s*.
Met Mast ⚲; Mo(U)15s 17m 10M; 55°08'·78N 01°25'·25W; Aero 3 FR (107m), *Horn 30s*.

COQUET ISLAND, AMBLE and WARKWORTH
Coquet ☆ 55°20'·03N 01°32'·39W; Fl (3) WR 20s 25m **W19M, R15M**; W□twr, turreted parapet, lower half Gy; vis: 330°-R-140°-W-163°-R-180°-W-330°; sector boundaries are indeterminate and may appear as Alt WR; *Horn 30s*.
Amble N Pier Head ⚲ Fl G 6s 12m 6M; 55°20'·39N 01°34'·25W.

SEAHOUSES, BAMBURGH and FARNE ISLANDS
N Sunderland ⌀ Fl R 2·5s; 55°34'·62N 01°37'·12W.
Bamburgh Black Rocks Point ☆ 55°36'·99N 01°43'·45W; Oc(2) WRG 8s 12m **W14M**, R11M, G11M; W bldg; vis: 122°-G-165°-W-175°-R-191°-W- 238°-R- 275°-W- 289°-G-300°.

Inner Farne ⚲ Fl (2) WR 15s 27m W10M, R7M; W ○ twr; vis: 119°- R - 280° - W -119°; 55°36'·92N 01°39'·35W.
Longstone ☆ **W side** 55°38'·63N 01°36'·66W; Fl 20s 23m **24M**; R twr, W band.
Swedman ▲ Fl G 2·5s; 55°37'·65N 01°41'·63W.

HOLY ISLAND
Ridge ⌕ Q (3) 10s; 55°39'·70N 01°45'·97W.
Plough Rock ⌕ Q (9) 15s; 55°40'·24N 01°46'·00W.
Old Law E Bn ⚲ (Guile Pt) Oc WRG 6s 9m 4M; vis: 180·5°-G-258·5°-W-261·5°-R-300°, 55°39'·49N 01°47'·59W; stone obelisk.
Heugh ⚲ Oc WRG 6s 24m 5M; vis: 135°-G-308°-W-311-R- shore; 55°40'·09N 01°47'·99W.
Plough Seat ⌀ QR; 55°40'·37N 01°44'·97W.
Goldstone ◢ QG; 55°40'·25N 01°43'·64W.

BERWICK-UPON-TWEED
Bkwtr Hd ⚲ Fl 5s 15m 6M; vis: 201°-009°, (obscured 155°-201°); W ○ twr, R cupola and base; FG (same twr) 8m 1M; vis 009°-G-155°; 55°45'·88N 01°59'·06W.

3.4 PASSAGE INFORMATION

For directions and pilotage refer to *Tidal Havens of the Wash and Humber* (Imray/Irving) which carefully documents the hbrs of this little-frequented cruising ground. N from R Humber see the Royal Northumberland YC's *Sailing Directions, Humber to Rattray Head*. The Admiralty *North Sea (West) Pilot* covers the whole coast. *North Sea Passage Pilot* (Imray/Navin) goes as far N as Cromer and across to Den Helder. Admiralty Leisure Folio 5614 covers the area Orford Ness to Whitby, and 5615 from Whitby to Berwick-upon-Tweed. More Passage Information is threaded between the harbours of this Area.

NORTH SEA PASSAGES

See 0.31 for distances across the North Sea. There is further Passage Information in Area 1 for the southern North Sea, in Area 4 for crossing to Norway and the Baltic, and in Area 2 for crossings from the Frisian Islands, German Bight, Belgium and the Netherlands.

OIL AND GAS INSTALLATIONS

Any craft going offshore in the N Sea is likely to encounter oil or gas installations. These are shown on Admiralty charts, where scale permits; the position of mobile rigs is updated in weekly NMs. Safety zones of radius 500m are established round all permanent platforms, mobile exploration rigs, and tanker loading moorings, as described in the Annual Summary of Admiralty Notices to Mariners No 20. Some of these platforms are close together or inter-linked. Unauthorised vessels, including yachts, must not enter these zones except in emergency or due to stress of weather.

Platforms show a main lt, Fl Mo (U) 15s 15M. In addition secondary lts, Fl Mo (U) R 15s 2M, synchronised with the main lt, may mark projections at each corner of the platform if not marked by a W lt. The fog signal is Horn Mo (U) 30s. See the Admiralty List of Lights and Fog Signals, Vol A.

NORTH NORFOLK COAST

(AC 1503, 108) The coast of N Norfolk is unfriendly in bad weather, with no hbr accessible when there is any N in the wind. The hbrs all dry, and seas soon build up in the entrances or over the bars, some of which are dangerous even in a moderate breeze and an ebb tide. But in settled weather and moderate offshore winds it is a peaceful area to explore, particularly for boats which can take the ground. At Blakeney and Wells chans shift almost every year, so local knowledge is essential and may best be acquired in advance from the HM, or possibly by following a friendly FV of suitable draft.

Haisborough Sand (buoyed) lies parallel to and 8M off the Norfolk coast at Happisburgh lt ho, with depths of less than 1m in many places, and drying 0·4m near the mid-point. The shoal is steep-to, on its NE side in particular, and there are tidal eddies. Even a moderate sea or swell breaks on the shallower parts. There are dangerous wks near the S end. Haisborough Tail and Hammond Knoll (with wk depth 1.6m) lie to the E of S end of Haisborough Sand. Newarp lt F is 5M SE. Similar banks lie parallel to and up to 60M off the coast.

▶ *The streams follow the generally NW/SE direction of the coast and offshore chans. But in the outer chans the stream is somewhat rotatory: when changing from SE-going to NW-going it sets SW, and when changing from NW-going to SE-going it sets NE, across the shoals. Close S of Haisborough Sand the SE-going stream begins at HW Immingham –0030; the NW-going at HW Immingham +0515, sp rates up to 2·5kn. It is possible to carry a fair tide from Gt Yarmouth to the Wash.* ◀

▶ *If proceeding direct from Cromer to the Humber, pass S of Sheringham Shoal (buoyed) where the ESE-going stream begins at HW Immingham –0225, and the WNW-going at +0430.* ◀ Proceed to NE of Blakeney Overfalls and Docking Shoal, and to SW of Race Bank, so as to fetch Inner Dowsing lt tr (lt, fog sig). Thence pass E of Protector Overfalls, and steer for Rosse Spit buoy at SE ent to R Humber.

3.5 BLAKENEY

Norfolk **52°59'·19N 00°57'·90E** (ent shifts) ❄💧⚓⚓⚓✿

CHARTS AC 1190, 108; Imray C29, C28, Y9

TIDES –0445 Dover; ML Cromer 2·8; Duration 0530; Zone 0 (UT)

Standard Port IMMINGHAM (→)

Times				Height (metres)			
High Water		Low Water		MHWS	MHWN	MLWN	MLWS
0100	0700	0100	0700	7·3	5·8	2·6	0·9
1300	1900	1300	1900				
Differences BLAKENEY BAR (approx 52°59'N 00°59'E)							
+0035	+0025	+0030	+0040	–1·6	–1·3	ND	ND
BLAKENEY (approx 52°57'N 01°01'E)							
+0115	+0055	ND	ND	–3·9	–3·8	ND	ND
CROMER							
+0044	+0032	+0108	+0059	–2·3	–1·8	–0·7	0·0

SHELTER Very good but limited access over shallow bar. In fresh on-shore winds conditions at the entrance deteriorate quickly, especially on the ebb. Moorings in The Pit area dry out.

NAVIGATION WPT 53°00'·00N 00°58'·20E, approx 225°/1M to Fairway RW buoy which is moved as required.

- Hjordis lit IDM buoy marks large dangerous wreck, close E of entrance.
- The bar is shallow, shifts often and the channel is marked by unlit SHM and PHM buoys, relaid each spring.
- Strangers are best advised to follow local boats in. Beware mussel lays, drying, off Blakeney Spit. Speed limit 8kn.

LIGHTS AND MARKS Conspic marks: Blakeney and Langham churches; a chimney on the house on Blakeney Point neck; TV mast (R lts) approx 2M S of entrance.

COMMUNICATIONS (Code 01263) MRCC (01262) 672317; Police 101; Dr 740314.

FACILITIES Quay ⌷ (Free), ◣, M, D, ⚓, C (15 ton); **Services:** 🏠 (Stratton Long) ☎ 740362, ⌷, BY, M, 🛢 & 🛢, ⚓, ✎, 🛢, ✗, ⚓, Gaz, ⛽. **Village** 🛒, ✗, ⌂, ✉, ®, ⇌ (Sheringham), ✈ (Norwich).

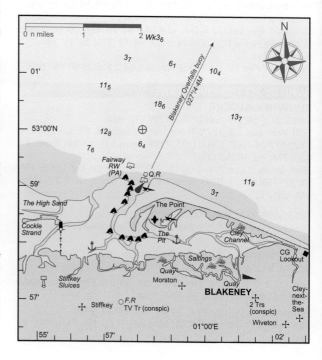

3.6 WELLS-NEXT-THE-SEA

Norfolk **52°59′·30N 00°49′·75E** (ent shifts) ⚓🌟💧💧💧🌸🌸🌸

CHARTS AC 1190, 108; Imray C29, C28, Y9

TIDES –0445 Dover; ML 1·2 Duration 0540

Standard Port IMMINGHAM (→)

Times				Height (metres)			
High Water		Low Water		MHWS	MHWN	MLWN	MLWS
0100	0700	0100	0700	7·3	5·8	2·6	0·9
1300	1900	1300	1900				
Differences WELLS BAR (approx 52°59′N 00°49′E)							
+0020	+0020	+0020	+0020	–1·3	–1·0	ND	ND
WELLS-NEXT-THE-SEA (approx 52°58′N 00°51′E)							
+0035	+0045	+0340	+0310	–3·8	–3·8	CD+	CD+
BURNHAM OVERY STAITHE							
+0045	+0055	ND	ND	–5·0	–4·9	ND	ND
HUNSTANTON							
+0010	+0020	+0105	+0025	+0·1	–0·2	–0·1	0·0

NOTE: LW time differences at Wells are for the end of a LW stand which lasts about 4 hrs at sp and about 5 hrs at nps.

SHELTER Good, but entrance difficult in strong on-shore winds. Outer Harbour is mainly for commercial wind farm tenders and survey vessels, but with HM prior permission, vessels <2m draft may shelter in adverse conditions. Limited access (max draft 3m at springs); best attempted on the flood. Quay berths mostly dry, pontoon berths at W end of Town Quay with 1·5m at LW.

NAVIGATION WPT Wells, WCM 52°59′·64N 00°51′·00E. Ent varies in depth and position; buoys are altered to suit. Initially keep to W side of chan to counter E-going tide; and to E side of chan from No 12 PHM lt buoy to Quay.

Obtain HM's advice, Hbr Launch often available to escort visitors into hbr & up to Quay. Spd limits: No 6 buoy to Quay 8kn; above this 5kn. See www.wellsharbour.co.uk for latest harbour chart.

LIGHTS AND MARKS From WCM Q (9) 15s the channel is well marked by lateral buoys, all Fl.3s, R to port, G to stbd. The lifeboat house (W with R roof) at N end of harbour is conspicuous.

COMMUNICATIONS (Code 01328) MRCC (01262) 672317; Police 101; Dr 710741; Ⓗ 710097. HM 711646, mob 07775 507284.

Call '*Wells Harbour*' Ch 12 16 before entering, listens HW–2 to HW+2 and when vessels expected.

FACILITIES Main Quay ⚓ on pontoons or quay, £18-£22/night; ⚡, Showers, 🚾, 🗑, 🔧, ⚓, 🛒, ✖, BH (9 ton), C (25 ton mobile), 🏪, 🛢, ✕, 🗑; **E Quay** Slips (£6/craft/day), M, L; **Wells SC** ☎ 710622, ⚓, 🗑; **Services:** Ⓔ, ACA, 🔩, LB. **Town:** 🏪 & 🏪 (Hbr fuelling stn HW-2 to HW+3; supply up to 500 galls), Gas, 🗑, 🛢, R, 🗑, ✉, Ⓑ, ⇌ (bus to Norwich/King's Lynn), ✈ (Norwich).

ADJACENT HARBOURS
BURNHAM OVERY STAITHE, Norfolk, **52°58′·95N 00°46′·55E** ⚓💧🌸🌸🌸. AC 1190, 108. HW –0420 on Dover. See 3.7. Small drying hbr; ent chan has 0·3m MLWS. ⚓ off the Staithe only suitable in good weather. No lts. Scolt Hd is conspic to W and Gun Hill to E; Scolt Hd Island is conspic 3M long sandbank which affords some shelter. Chan varies constantly and buoys are moved to suit. Local knowledge advisable.

Facilities: Burnham Overy Staithe SC ☎ (01328) 738348, M, L.
Services: 🏪, M, 🔧, ✖, ⚓, ⚓.
Burnham Market EC Wed; 🗑, 🏪 & 🏪, ✕, 🛢.

BRANCASTER STAITHE, Norfolk, **52°59′·02N 00°37′·65E** ⚓💧🌸🌸🌸. AC 1190, 108. HW –0425 on Dover; as Burnham. Small drying hbr, dangerous to enter except by day in settled weather. Spd limit 6kn. Appr from due N. Conspic golf club house when in, Fl 5s 8m 3M, is 0·5M S of chan ent and Fairway buoy. Beware wk shown on chart. Sandbanks shift; buoys changed to suit. Scolt Hd conspic to E. Local knowledge or Pilot advised. Possible ⚓ in The Hole. HM ☎ (01485) 210638.

Facilities: Brancaster Staithe SC ☎ 210249, ✕, 🗑;
Hunstanton SC ☎ (01485) 534705

Services: BY, 🏪, 🕮, ⚓, 🏪 & 🏪, 🔧, ✕, ✖, 🗑, 🛢.

THE WASH

(AC 108,1200) The Wash is formed by the estuaries of the rivers Great Ouse, Nene, Welland and Witham; it is an area of shifting sands, most of which dry. Important features are the strong tidal streams, the low-lying shore, and the often poor vis. Watch the echo sounder carefully, because buoys may have been moved to accommodate changes in the channel. ▶*Near North Well, the in-going stream begins at HW Immingham –0430, and the out-going at HW Immingham +0130, sp rates about 2kn. The in-going stream is usually stronger than the out-going, but its duration is less. Prolonged NE winds cause an in-going current, which can increase the rate and duration of the in-going stream and raise the water level at the head of the estuary. Do not attempt entry to the rivers too early on the flood, which runs hard in the rivers.* ◀

North Well SWM lt buoy and Roaring Middle lt F are the keys to entering the Wash from N or E. But from the E it is also possible to appr via a shallow route N of Stiffkey Overfalls and Bridgirdle PHM buoy; thence via Sledway and Woolpack PHM lt buoy to North Well and into Lynn Deeps. Near north end of Lynn Deeps there are overfalls over Lynn Knock at sp tides. Approach King's Lynn via the buoyed/lit Bulldog chan. For R Nene (Wisbech) follow the Wisbech Chan. Boston and R Welland are reached via Freeman Chan, westward from Roaring Middle; or via Boston Deep, all lit.

The NW shore of The Wash is fronted by mudflats extending 2–3M offshore and drying more than 4m; a bombing range is marked by Y bns and buoys. Wainfleet Swatchway should only be used in good vis; the buoyed chan shifts constantly, and several shoals (charted depths unreliable) off Gibraltar Pt obstruct access to Boston Deep. In an emergency Wainfleet offers good shelter (dries).

Wisbech Cut provides access inland to the Fens Middle Levels, which are navigable by narrow boat and river cruisers. Dog in a Doublet Lock above Wisbech is the practical limit of sea going vessels.

The Gt Ouse is navigable as far as Ely 24M upstream. There is a lock half-way at Denver Sluice ☎ (01366) 382340/VHF Ch 73, and low bridges beyond.

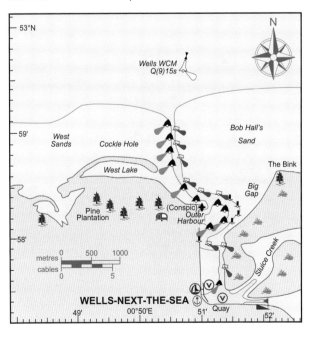

WELLS-NEXT-THE-SEA

3.7 KING'S LYNN

Norfolk 52°49´·72N 00°21´·14E (W Stones Bn) ✿✿⚓☸✿✿

CHARTS AC 1190, 108, 1200, 5614. Imray C29, Y9

TIDES −0443 Dover, +0030 Immingham; ML 3·6; Duration 0340

Standard Port IMMINGHAM (→)

Times				Height (metres)			
High Water		Low Water		MHWS	MHWN	MLWN	MLWS
0100	0700	0100	0700	7·3	5·8	2·6	0·9
1300	1900	1300	1900				
Differences KING'S LYNN							
+0030	+0030	+0305	+0140	−0·5	−0·8	−0·8	+0·1
WEST STONES							
+0025	+0025	+0115	+0040	−0·3	−0·4	−0·3	+0·2

SHELTER Port is well sheltered; entry only recommended HW−3½. A busy commercial and fishing port. 3 Visitors pontoons on S quay. River moorings available from local clubs; keep clear of FV moorings.

NAVIGATION WPT Sunk WCM 52° 56'.29N 00° 23'.40E follow Bulldog chan buoyed/lit apprs to King's Lynn. Upstream to Denver Sluice (ent to inland routes) 6 bridges span river, min cl 9·15m less ht of tide above dock sill at King's Lynn. Allow 1½H for passage. The sandbanks regularly shift and extend several miles into the Wash; buoyage is altered accordingly. Contact HM a week beforehand for info or see www.sailthewash.com.

LIGHTS AND MARKS See 3.3 and chartlet.

COMMUNICATIONS Code (01553) MRCC (01262) 672317; Police 101; HM ☎ 0773411 Docks ☎ 691555.

Kings Lynn Hbr Radio Ch **14** 11 (M-F: 0800-1730 LT. Other times: HW −4 to HW+1.) (ABP) Ch **14** 16 11 (HW−2½ to HW).

FACILITIES � £42 (<9m/48hrs), ⚓, C (32 ton), ⛽, ⚒, ⚓, 🔧, Ⓔ, D. **Town** 🅟 & ⛽, 🛒, ✕, 🏦, ✉, Ⓑ, ⇄, ✈ (Norwich).

Ely Marina 24M up the Great Ouse River, ☎ (01353) 664622, ◣, M, P, D, ⚓, ⚒, 🔧, ✕, C (10 ton), ⛽.

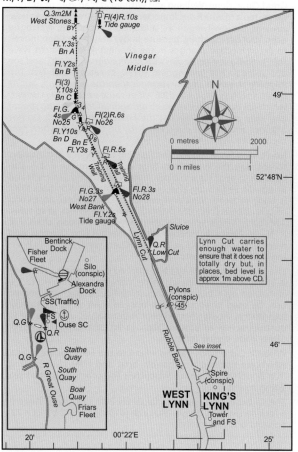

3.8 WISBECH

Cambridgeshire 52°40´·02N 00°09´·55E✿✿⚓☸✿✿

CHARTS AC 1190, 108, 1200, 5614. Imray C29, Y9

TIDES −0443 Dover, +0030 Immingham; ML 3·6; Duration 0340

Standard Port IMMINGHAM (→)

Times				Height (metres)			
High Water		Low Water		MHWS	MHWN	MLWN	MLWS
0100	0700	0100	0700	7·3	5·8	2·6	0·9
1300	1900	1300	1900				
OUTER WESTMARK KNOCK							
+0010	+0015	+0040	+0020	−0·2	−0·5	−0·6	−0·4
WISBECH CUT							
+0020	+0010	+0120	+0055	−0·3	−0·7	−0·4	ND
WISBECH							
+0055	+0040	DR	DR	−0·2	−0·6	DR	DR

SHELTER Excellent in river with Wisbech Yacht Harbour pontoon berths and facilities immediately below Freedom Br in Wisbech. Vessels of 4·8m draft can reach Wisbech at sp (3·4m at nps).

NAVIGATION WPT Roaring Middle Lt Flt 52° 58'.64N 00° 21'.08E 220°/7M to Wisbech No 1 SHM Fl G 5s. Call HM at RAF No 4 ECM (⚓s for waiting) to check commercial traffic and Cross Keys Sw Br. Red flags and lights shown when Holbeach Firing Range in use. Chan to R Nene well marked with lit buoys/bns. Best ent HW−3. Given 24H notice of visit Cross Keys Sw Br in river opens by request. Waiting pontoon 0.5M below bridge thence 6M to Wisbech. Departure best at HW; if draught >3m, clear Kerr NCM by HW+3. For pilotage notes ☎ Hbr Office or visit www.fenland.gov.uk.

LIGHTS AND MARKS See 3.3 and chartlet.

COMMUNICATIONS Code (01945) MRCC (01262) 672317; Police 101; Dr 582133; Ⓗ 585781; HM ☎ 588059 (24H); Cross Keys Swing Bridge ☎ 01406 350364.

HM *Wisbech Harbour* Ch **09** call HM and Cross Keys Sw Br HW±3.

FACILITIES **Yacht Hbr** (102 ⌐ + 15♥), £0.90, min charge £5, ⚓, ◔, 🔧, ⒺⒸ, @. D (barge). **Town** 🅟, ⛽, 🛒, Gas, 🏦, ✕.

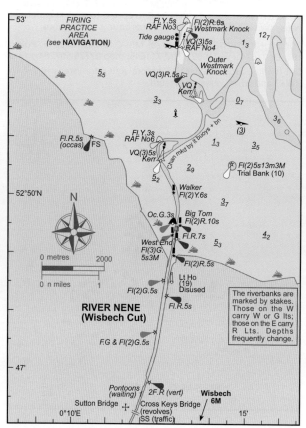

3.9 BOSTON

Lincs **52°56'·00N 00°04'·92E** (Tabs Head bn) 🌼🌸⬡⬡🌸🌸

CHARTS AC 108, 1200, 5614; Imray C29, Y9

TIDES –0415 Dover; ML 3·3; Duration Flood 0500, Ebb 0700

Standard Port IMMINGHAM (→)

Times				Height (metres)			
High Water		Low Water		MHWS	MHWN	MLWN	MLWS
0100	0700	0100	0700	7·3	5·8	2·6	0·9
1300	1900	1300	1900				
Differences BOSTON							
0000	+0010	+0140	+0050	–0.5	–1.0	–0.9	–0.5
TABS HEAD (WELLAND RIVER)							
0000	+0005	+0125	+0020	+0.2	–0.2	–0.2	–0.2
SKEGNESS							
+0010	+0015	+0030	+0020	–0.4	–0.5	–0.1	0.0
INNER DOWSING LIGHT TOWER							
0000	0000	+0010	+0010	–0.9	–0.7	–0.1	+0.3

SHELTER Very good. Except in emergency, berthing in the Dock is prohib wthout HM permission. Yachts secure just above Dock ent and see HM. The port is administered by Port of Boston Ltd.

Yachts capable of lowering masts can pass through the Grand Sluice (**24 hrs notice required**) into fresh water. Sluice dimensions 16m x 9m and opens twice a tide at approx HW±2. It leads into the R Witham Navigation which goes 31M to Lincoln. Marina is to stbd immediately beyond the sluice. British Waterways have 50 moorings, with 🛥 and ⊡▷, beyond Grand Sluice.

NAVIGATION WPT Boston Rds SWM lt buoy, 52°57'·61N 00°16'·29E, 282°/0·75M to Freeman Chan ent. Thence Bar Chan is well marked, but liable to change. SW of Clay Hole a new chan has formed which dries 0.6m at entr; it is marked by SHM lt buoys Nos 11N, 13N, and 15. Tabs Head marks the ent to the river; it should be passed not earlier than HW–3 to enable the Grand Sluice to be reached before the start of the ebb. Beware rocky bottom within 100m of the Sluice. On reaching Boston Dock, masts should be lowered to negotiate swing bridge (cannot always be opened) and three fixed bridges. Chan through town is un-navigable at LW.

LIGHTS AND MARKS St Boltoph's ch tr (the Boston Stump) is conspic from afar. New Cut and R Witham are marked by bns with topmarks. FW lts mark ldg lines: three pairs going upstream and six pairs going downstream.

COMMUNICATIONS (Code 01205) MRCC (01262) 672317; Police 101; Ⓗ 364801. Dock office ☎ 365571 (H24 & emergency); HM ☎ 362328; Grand Sluice Control ☎ 364864 (not always manned but has answerphone) mob 07712 010920.

All vessels between No 9 buoy and Grand Sluice must listen Ch 12 (also advisable to maintain watch while in local tidal waters). Call: *Boston Port Control* VHF Ch 12 (HW –2½ to HW +1½ when commercial shipping is moving). Ch 11 used by dock staff as required. *Grand Sluice* Ch 74.

FACILITIES **Boston Marina** (48 + some Ⓥ) ☎ 364420, £7 per night any size inc ⊡▷; 🛥, D, ⛽, ACA, C in dock, see HM (emergency); **Grand Sluice** showers and toilets; **BWB** moorings: 1st night free, then £5·00. **Services:** Ⓑⓒ, ✎, ⚒, Gas. **Town** Thurs; 🛒, ✗, 🗐, ✉, Ⓑ, ⇌, ✈ (Humberside).

ADJACENT HARBOURS

RIVER WELLAND, Lincolnshire, **52°56'·00N 00°04'·92E** (Tabs Head bn). AC 1190, 1200. At Welland Cut HW –0440 on Dover; ML 0·3m; Duration 0520. See 3.9. At Tabs Head bn HW ±3, ent Welland Cut which is defined by training walls and lt bns. Beware sp flood of up to 5kn. Berth 6M up at **Fosdyke Yacht Haven** ☎ 01205 260240. (50 + 6Ⓥ 2m depth); ⊡▷, Showers, Ⓦ, D by prior arrangement, 🛥, ✎, BH (50 ton – only one between R. Humber & Lowestoft), ✗, 🗐.

WAINFLEET, Lincolnshire, **53°04'·79N 00°19'·89E** (chan ent). AC 108. Skegness HW +0500 on Dover. See 3.9 (Skegness). ML 4·0m; Duration 0600. Shelter good. Recommended max boat length 10m, draught 1·5m. Lit PHM indicates entrance to drying channel close S of Gibraltar Point. Chan through saltings marked by buoys and bns with lateral topmarks but no lts. Enter HW ±1½. Facilities: M, ⚓ (larger boats at fishing jetties, smaller at YC), 🛥 at YC ⚓. **Town** All facilities at Skegness (3½ miles).

Skegness YC skegnessyachtclub.co.uk ☎ 0779 941856 (Commodore) on the R Steeping inside Gibraltar Pt has a membership of about 65 with a small clubhouse. M, L, ⚓, 🛥 at ⚓, Showers, Ⓦ.

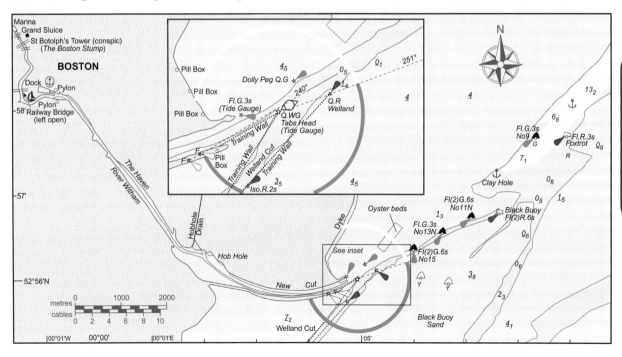

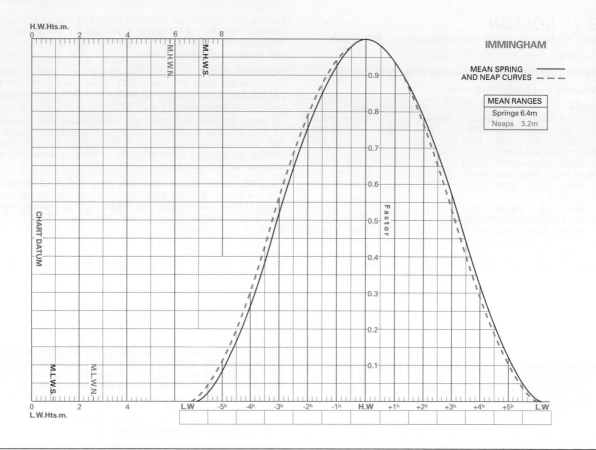

H.W.Hts.m.

IMMINGHAM

MEAN SPRING ──────
AND NEAP CURVES ─ ─ ─

MEAN RANGES
Springs 6·4m
Neaps 3·2m

M.H.W.N.
M.H.W.S.
CHART DATUM
M.L.W.S.
M.L.W.N.

Factor

L.W.Hts.m.

THE WASH TO THE RIVER HUMBER

(AC 108, 107) Inner Dowsing is a narrow N/S sandbank with a least depth of 1·2m, 8M offshore between Skegness and Mablethorpe. There are overfalls off the W side of the bank at the N end. Inner Dowsing ECM (Q(3) 10s, Racon T) is to the NE of the bank, S Inner Dowsing and Scott Patch indicate its southernmost extent. Inshore of the bank lie three wind farms: Lynn (27 turbines), Inner Dowsing (27 turbines) and Lincs Offshore (under construction). The extremities of the windfarms are indicated by a series of cardinal marks and selected turbines are marked by lights and fog signals.

In the outer approaches to The Wash and R. Humber there are many offlying banks, but few of them are of direct danger to yachts. The sea however breaks on some of them in bad weather, when they should be avoided. Fishing vessels may be encountered, and there are many oil/gas installations offshore.

RIVER HUMBER

(AC 104, 1188, 3497) The Humber is formed by the Ouse and the Trent, which meet 13M above Kingston-upon-Hull. The river is commercially important and gives access to these rivers and inland waterways; it also drains most of Yorkshire and the Midlands. Where the Humber estuary reaches the sea between Northcoates Pt and Spurn Hd it is 4M wide. A VTS scheme is in operation to regulate commercial shipping in the Humber, Ouse and Trent and provide full radar surveillance. Yachts are advised to monitor the appropriate Humber VTS frequency.

Approaching from the S, a yacht should make good Rosse Spit and then Haile Sand No 2, both PHM lt buoys, before altering westward leading SW of Bull Channel.

If bound to/from the N, avoid The Binks, a shoal (dries 1·6m in places) extending 3M E from Spurn Hd, with a rough sea when wind is against tide. Depths offshore are irregular and subject to frequent change; it would be best to round the S Binks SPM buoy, unless in calm conditions and with local knowledge.

Haile Sand and Bull Sand Forts are both conspic to the SW of Spurn Head; beyond them it is advisable to keep just outside one of the buoyed chans, since shoals are liable to change. Hawke Chan (later Sunk) is the main dredged chan to the N. Haile Chan favours the S side and Grimsby. Bull Chan takes a middle course before merging with Haile Chan. There are good yachting facilities at Grimsby and Hull. ⚓ inside Spurn Head.

▶ *Streams are strong, even fierce at sp; local info suggests that they are stronger than shown in Tidal Streams based upon NP 251 (Admiralty Tidal Stream Atlas). 5ca S of Spurn Hd the flood sets NW from about HW Immingham –0520, sp rate 3·5kn; the ebb sets SE from about HW Immingham, sp rate 4kn. The worst seas are experienced in NW gales against a strong flood tide. 10M E of Spurn Hd the tidal streams are not affected by the river; relative to HW Immingham, the S-going stream begins at –0455, and the N-going at +0130. Nearer the entrance the direction of the S-going stream becomes more W'ly, and that of the N-going stream more E'ly. ◀*

IMMINGHAM   LAT 53°38′N   LONG 0°11′W

TIMES AND HEIGHTS OF HIGH AND LOW WATERS

STANDARD TIME (UT)
For Summer Time add ONE hour in **non-shaded areas**

Dates in red are SPRINGS
Dates in blue are NEAPS

YEAR 2015

JANUARY

Day	Time	m	Day	Time	m
1 TH	0212 / 0845 / 1500 / 2115	6.3 / 2.0 / 6.3 / 2.1	**16** F	0129 / 0753 / 1420 / 2018	5.8 / 2.3 / 5.9 / 2.5
2 F	0318 / 0944 / 1556 / 2214	6.4 / 1.9 / 6.5 / 1.8	**17** SA	0242 / 0859 / 1520 / 2127	6.0 / 2.1 / 6.2 / 2.1
3 SA	0417 / 1036 / 1644 / 2306	6.6 / 1.7 / 6.7 / 1.5	**18** SU	0344 / 0959 / 1612 / 2229	6.4 / 1.8 / 6.6 / 1.7
4 SU	0508 / 1122 / 1726 / 2353	6.7 / 1.6 / 6.9 / 1.3	**19** M	0439 / 1054 / 1700 / 2325	6.7 / 1.5 / 7.0 / 1.3
5 M ○	0553 / 1205 / 1806	6.8 / 1.5 / 7.1	**20** TU ●	0530 / 1145 / 1745	7.0 / 1.2 / 7.3
6 TU	0036 / 0634 / 1244 / 1843	1.2 / 6.9 / 1.5 / 7.1	**21** W	0017 / 0618 / 1234 / 1829	0.9 / 7.3 / 1.0 / 7.6
7 W	0116 / 0711 / 1319 / 1917	1.2 / 6.8 / 1.5 / 7.1	**22** TH	0107 / 0704 / 1321 / 1912	0.6 / 7.4 / 0.9 / 7.7
8 TH	0151 / 0745 / 1351 / 1949	1.3 / 6.8 / 1.6 / 7.1	**23** F	0153 / 0749 / 1405 / 1955	0.5 / 7.4 / 0.8 / 7.8
9 F	0223 / 0816 / 1420 / 2019	1.4 / 6.7 / 1.7 / 6.9	**24** SA	0238 / 0832 / 1447 / 2039	0.5 / 7.3 / 1.0 / 7.7
10 SA	0253 / 0847 / 1449 / 2051	1.6 / 6.5 / 1.9 / 6.7	**25** SU	0321 / 0917 / 1530 / 2125	0.7 / 7.1 / 1.2 / 7.4
11 SU	0324 / 0922 / 1521 / 2125	1.8 / 6.3 / 2.0 / 6.5	**26** M	0406 / 1006 / 1615 / 2216	1.1 / 6.7 / 1.6 / 7.0
12 M	0359 / 1001 / 1559 / 2205	2.0 / 6.1 / 2.3 / 6.2	**27** TU ☽	0454 / 1102 / 1706 / 2317	1.5 / 6.4 / 2.0 / 6.5
13 TU ☽	0443 / 1049 / 1649 / 2256	2.2 / 5.9 / 2.5 / 6.0	**28** W	0550 / 1207 / 1811	2.0 / 6.0 / 2.4
14 W	0539 / 1152 / 1752	2.4 / 5.7 / 2.7	**29** TH	0030 / 0700 / 1318 / 1934	6.1 / 2.3 / 5.9 / 2.5
15 TH	0005 / 0644 / 1309 / 1905	5.8 / 2.4 / 5.7 / 2.7	**30** F	0149 / 0817 / 1428 / 2055	6.0 / 2.4 / 5.9 / 2.4
			31 SA	0303 / 0923 / 1531 / 2159	6.0 / 2.3 / 6.2 / 2.0

FEBRUARY

Day	Time	m	Day	Time	m
1 SU	0408 / 1017 / 1624 / 2251	6.3 / 2.0 / 6.5 / 1.7	**16** M	0327 / 0935 / 1549 / 2209	6.2 / 1.9 / 6.5 / 1.7
2 M	0459 / 1104 / 1708 / 2337	6.5 / 1.8 / 6.8 / 1.4	**17** TU	0426 / 1035 / 1640 / 2309	6.5 / 1.5 / 7.0 / 1.2
3 TU ○	0541 / 1147 / 1747	6.6 / 1.6 / 7.0	**18** W ●	0518 / 1129 / 1727	7.0 / 1.1 / 7.4
4 W	0019 / 0617 / 1226 / 1823	1.2 / 6.8 / 1.5 / 7.1	**19** TH	0003 / 0606 / 1219 / 1812	0.7 / 7.3 / 0.8 / 7.7
5 TH	0057 / 0651 / 1301 / 1857	1.2 / 6.8 / 1.4 / 7.1	**20** F	0052 / 0650 / 1305 / 1856	0.4 / 7.5 / 0.6 / 7.9
6 F	0132 / 0721 / 1333 / 1928	1.2 / 6.8 / 1.4 / 7.1	**21** SA	0138 / 0732 / 1349 / 1939	0.2 / 7.6 / 0.6 / 7.9
7 SA	0203 / 0750 / 1400 / 1958	1.2 / 6.8 / 1.5 / 7.0	**22** SU	0220 / 0813 / 1431 / 2022	0.3 / 7.5 / 0.7 / 7.8
8 SU	0231 / 0819 / 1427 / 2026	1.4 / 6.7 / 1.6 / 6.9	**23** M	0301 / 0853 / 1511 / 2106	0.6 / 7.2 / 0.9 / 7.5
9 M	0256 / 0849 / 1454 / 2055	1.5 / 6.6 / 1.7 / 6.7	**24** TU	0340 / 0936 / 1551 / 2153	1.0 / 6.9 / 1.4 / 7.0
10 TU	0324 / 0922 / 1526 / 2129	1.7 / 6.4 / 1.9 / 6.5	**25** W ☽	0421 / 1024 / 1635 / 2250	1.6 / 6.4 / 1.9 / 6.4
11 W	0357 / 1000 / 1606 / 2211	2.0 / 6.1 / 2.2 / 6.2	**26** TH	0508 / 1125 / 1731	2.1 / 6.0 / 2.3
12 TH ☾	0445 / 1050 / 1702 / 2307	2.2 / 5.9 / 2.4 / 5.9	**27** F	0002 / 0613 / 1240 / 1855	5.9 / 2.6 / 5.7 / 2.6
13 F	0552 / 1159 / 1818	2.5 / 5.7 / 2.6	**28** SA	0127 / 0745 / 1356 / 2034	5.7 / 2.8 / 5.7 / 2.5
14 SA	0028 / 0710 / 1333 / 1939	5.7 / 2.5 / 5.7 / 2.5			
15 SU	0213 / 0826 / 1449 / 2058	5.8 / 2.3 / 6.1 / 2.2			

MARCH

Day	Time	m	Day	Time	m
1 SU	0246 / 0901 / 1504 / 2140	5.8 / 2.6 / 5.9 / 2.1	**16** M	0153 / 0800 / 1419 / 2035	5.8 / 2.4 / 6.0 / 2.0
2 M	0353 / 0957 / 1600 / 2230	6.0 / 2.3 / 6.3 / 1.7	**17** TU	0313 / 0913 / 1524 / 2150	6.2 / 2.0 / 6.5 / 1.5
3 TU	0443 / 1044 / 1646 / 2314	6.3 / 1.9 / 6.6 / 1.4	**18** W	0412 / 1015 / 1618 / 2250	6.7 / 1.5 / 7.0 / 1.0
4 W	0522 / 1125 / 1725 / 2355	6.6 / 1.6 / 6.8 / 1.2	**19** TH	0503 / 1110 / 1707 / 2343	7.1 / 1.1 / 7.4 / 0.6
5 TH ○	0556 / 1204 / 1800	6.7 / 1.5 / 7.0	**20** F ●	0549 / 1200 / 1753	7.4 / 0.8 / 7.7
6 F	0032 / 0626 / 1240 / 1832	1.1 / 6.8 / 1.4 / 7.0	**21** SA	0031 / 0631 / 1247 / 1838	0.3 / 7.5 / 0.5 / 7.9
7 SA	0107 / 0654 / 1312 / 1903	1.1 / 6.9 / 1.3 / 7.1	**22** SU	0117 / 0711 / 1331 / 1921	0.3 / 7.6 / 0.5 / 7.9
8 SU	0138 / 0722 / 1340 / 1934	1.2 / 6.9 / 1.4 / 7.0	**23** M	0158 / 0750 / 1412 / 2004	0.3 / 7.5 / 0.6 / 7.8
9 M	0206 / 0751 / 1405 / 2003	1.3 / 6.8 / 1.4 / 6.9	**24** TU	0237 / 0828 / 1451 / 2047	0.6 / 7.3 / 0.8 / 7.4
10 TU	0230 / 0820 / 1432 / 2031	1.4 / 6.8 / 1.5 / 6.8	**25** W	0314 / 0907 / 1529 / 2133	1.1 / 6.9 / 1.2 / 6.9
11 W	0255 / 0850 / 1502 / 2102	1.6 / 6.6 / 1.7 / 6.6	**26** TH	0350 / 0950 / 1610 / 2226	1.6 / 6.5 / 1.7 / 6.3
12 TH	0325 / 0925 / 1539 / 2143	1.8 / 6.4 / 1.9 / 6.3	**27** F ☽	0432 / 1044 / 1701 / 2337	2.2 / 6.0 / 2.2 / 5.8
13 F ☾	0407 / 1012 / 1631 / 2237	2.1 / 6.1 / 2.2 / 6.0	**28** SA	0529 / 1200 / 1815	2.7 / 5.7 / 2.6
14 SA	0512 / 1114 / 1747 / 2354	2.4 / 5.8 / 2.4 / 5.7	**29** SU	0102 / 0655 / 1322 / 2002	5.5 / 3.0 / 5.6 / 2.5
15 SU	0636 / 1245 / 1912	2.6 / 5.7 / 2.4	**30** M	0219 / 0830 / 1432 / 2110	5.6 / 2.8 / 5.8 / 2.2
			31 TU	0324 / 0929 / 1530 / 2201	5.9 / 2.4 / 6.1 / 1.8

APRIL

Day	Time	m	Day	Time	m
1 W	0414 / 1016 / 1617 / 2244	6.2 / 2.0 / 6.5 / 1.5	**16** TH	0352 / 0953 / 1553 / 2226	6.7 / 1.5 / 7.0 / 1.0
2 TH	0454 / 1058 / 1656 / 2324	6.5 / 1.7 / 6.7 / 1.3	**17** F	0442 / 1048 / 1644 / 2319	7.0 / 1.1 / 7.3 / 0.6
3 F	0527 / 1137 / 1731	6.7 / 1.5 / 6.8	**18** SA ●	0527 / 1138 / 1732	7.3 / 0.8 / 7.6
4 SA ○	0001 / 0556 / 1214 / 1804	1.2 / 6.8 / 1.4 / 6.9	**19** SU	0008 / 0609 / 1226 / 1818	0.4 / 7.5 / 0.6 / 7.7
5 SU	0038 / 0625 / 1247 / 1837	1.1 / 6.9 / 1.3 / 7.0	**20** M	0053 / 0649 / 1311 / 1904	0.4 / 7.5 / 0.5 / 7.7
6 M	0110 / 0655 / 1317 / 1909	1.1 / 6.9 / 1.3 / 7.0	**21** TU	0135 / 0728 / 1353 / 1948	0.5 / 7.4 / 0.6 / 7.5
7 TU	0140 / 0725 / 1345 / 1941	1.2 / 6.9 / 1.3 / 6.9	**22** W	0213 / 0805 / 1433 / 2031	0.8 / 7.2 / 0.9 / 7.2
8 W	0206 / 0755 / 1414 / 2012	1.3 / 6.9 / 1.4 / 6.8	**23** TH	0249 / 0843 / 1511 / 2115	1.2 / 6.9 / 1.2 / 6.8
9 TH	0234 / 0826 / 1446 / 2046	1.5 / 6.8 / 1.5 / 6.6	**24** F	0324 / 0922 / 1551 / 2204	1.7 / 6.5 / 1.6 / 6.2
10 F	0306 / 0903 / 1526 / 2129	1.7 / 6.5 / 1.7 / 6.4	**25** SA ☽	0402 / 1010 / 1638 / 2308	2.2 / 6.1 / 2.1 / 5.8
11 SA	0349 / 0949 / 1619 / 2225	2.0 / 6.3 / 2.0 / 6.0	**26** SU	0453 / 1117 / 1740	2.6 / 5.8 / 2.4
12 SU ☾	0451 / 1051 / 1732 / 2343	2.3 / 6.0 / 2.2 / 5.8	**27** M	0027 / 0601 / 1240 / 1902	5.5 / 2.9 / 5.6 / 2.5
13 M	0612 / 1215 / 1854	2.5 / 5.9 / 2.1	**28** TU	0140 / 0730 / 1351 / 2023	5.6 / 2.9 / 5.7 / 2.3
14 TU	0137 / 0736 / 1349 / 2015	5.8 / 2.4 / 6.1 / 1.8	**29** W	0243 / 0846 / 1451 / 2118	5.8 / 2.6 / 6.0 / 2.0
15 W	0253 / 0850 / 1457 / 2127	6.2 / 2.0 / 6.5 / 1.4	**30** TH	0335 / 0939 / 1540 / 2204	6.1 / 2.2 / 6.2 / 1.7

Chart Datum: 3·90 metres below Ordnance Datum (Newlyn). HAT is 8·0 metres above Chart Datum.

NE England

STANDARD TIME (UT)
For Summer Time add ONE hour in **non-shaded areas**

IMMINGHAM   LAT 53°38'N   LONG 0°11'W
TIMES AND HEIGHTS OF HIGH AND LOW WATERS

Dates in red are SPRINGS
Dates in blue are NEAPS

YEAR 2015

MAY

Time	m		Time	m
1 0417	6.4		**16** 0418	6.9
1023	1.9		1025	1.3
F 1621	6.5		SA 1622	7.1
2246	1.5		2254	0.9
2 0451	6.6		**17** 0504	7.1
1104	1.6		1117	1.0
SA 1657	6.6		SU 1713	7.3
2327	1.3		2344	0.8
3 0523	6.8		**18** 0547	7.3
1143	1.5		1206	0.8
SU 1734	6.8		M 1802	7.4 ●
4 0005	1.2		**19** 0030	0.8
0555	6.9		0628	7.3
M 1220	1.3		TU 1253	0.7
○ 1810	6.9		1849	7.4
5 0041	1.2		**20** 0112	0.9
0629	7.0		0707	7.3
TU 1254	1.3		W 1337	0.8
1847	6.9		1933	7.2
6 0114	1.2		**21** 0151	1.1
0703	7.0		0745	7.2
W 1328	1.3		TH 1418	0.9
1924	6.9		2016	7.0
7 0146	1.3		**22** 0227	1.4
0736	7.0		0823	6.9
TH 1402	1.2		F 1456	1.2
2000	6.8		2059	6.7
8 0219	1.4		**23** 0301	1.7
0811	6.9		0900	6.8
F 1440	1.3		SA 1534	1.5
2039	6.7		2143	6.3
9 0257	1.6		**24** 0338	2.1
0850	6.7		0941	6.3
SA 1523	1.5		SU 1616	1.9
2125	6.4		2234	5.9
10 0342	1.9		**25** 0421	2.4
0938	6.5		1033	6.0
SU 1617	1.7		M 1707	2.2
2223	6.1		☽ 2337	5.7
11 0441	2.2		**26** 0516	2.7
1038	6.2		1143	5.8
M 1724	1.8		TU 1807	2.3
☽ 2341	6.0			
12 0554	2.3		**27** 0046	5.6
1155	6.1		0622	2.8
TU 1838	1.8		W 1256	5.7
			1913	2.3
13 0114	6.0		**28** 0149	5.7
0711	2.3		0735	2.7
W 1319	6.3		TH 1359	5.8
1952	1.6		2019	2.2
14 0226	6.3		**29** 0245	5.9
0824	2.0		0844	2.5
TH 1429	6.6		F 1453	6.0
2101	1.4		2115	1.9
15 0326	6.6		**30** 0332	6.2
0928	1.6		0939	2.2
F 1529	6.9		SA 1540	6.2
2201	1.1		2204	1.7
			31 0412	6.4
			1026	1.9
			SU 1623	6.5
			2250	1.5

JUNE

Time	m		Time	m
1 0450	6.7		**16** 0527	7.0
1110	1.6		1150	1.0
M 1705	6.6		TU 1750	7.0
2332	1.4		●	
2 0528	6.9		**17** 0009	1.2
1152	1.4		0609	7.1
TU 1747	6.8		W 1238	0.9
○			1837	7.0
3 0013	1.3		**18** 0053	1.2
0606	7.0		0649	7.2
W 1234	1.2		TH 1323	0.9
1829	6.9		1921	7.0
4 0053	1.2		**19** 0132	1.3
0644	7.1		0728	7.1
TH 1315	1.1		F 1404	1.0
1910	7.0		2001	6.8
5 0131	1.3		**20** 0208	1.5
0722	7.1		0804	7.0
F 1355	1.1		SA 1441	1.2
1952	6.9		2040	6.6
6 0210	1.3		**21** 0241	1.7
0801	7.1		0839	6.8
SA 1438	1.1		SU 1516	1.4
2036	6.8		2116	6.4
7 0251	1.4		**22** 0314	1.9
0843	7.0		0915	6.6
SU 1524	1.2		M 1552	1.7
2124	6.7		2155	6.1
8 0337	1.6		**23** 0351	2.2
0931	6.8		0956	6.3
M 1616	1.4		TU 1633	1.9
2220	6.4		2240	5.9
9 0431	1.9		**24** 0434	2.4
1028	6.6		1047	6.0
TU 1715	1.5		W 1722	2.2
☽ 2329	6.2		☽ 2336	5.7
10 0535	2.1		**25** 0528	2.6
1136	6.4		1150	5.8
W 1820	1.6		TH 1817	2.3
11 0045	6.2		**26** 0040	5.7
0645	2.1		0630	2.7
TH 1252	6.4		F 1258	5.8
1928	1.6		1918	2.3
12 0155	6.3		**27** 0144	5.8
0756	2.0		0738	2.6
F 1402	6.5		SA 1401	5.9
2035	1.5		2021	2.2
13 0257	6.4		**28** 0242	6.0
0904	1.8		0845	2.4
SA 1506	6.7		SU 1459	6.0
2136	1.4		2120	2.0
14 0353	6.7		**29** 0334	6.3
1004	1.5		0945	2.1
SU 1605	6.8		M 1552	6.3
2232	1.3		2213	1.7
15 0443	6.9		**30** 0420	6.6
1059	1.2		1039	1.8
M 1659	7.0		TU 1641	6.6
2322	1.2		2303	1.5

JULY

Time	m		Time	m
1 0504	6.8		**16** 0552	7.0
1129	1.5		1224	1.1
W 1728	6.8		TH 1826	6.9
2349	1.3		●	
2 0547	7.0		**17** 0035	1.4
1217	1.2		0631	7.1
TH 1815	7.0		F 1307	1.0
○			1905	6.9
3 0034	1.2		**18** 0114	1.4
0628	7.2		0709	7.1
F 1304	1.0		SA 1347	1.0
1900	7.1		1942	6.8
4 0118	1.1		**19** 0149	1.5
0710	7.4		0744	7.1
SA 1349	0.8		SU 1422	1.2
1944	7.1		2015	6.7
5 0201	1.1		**20** 0220	1.6
0751	7.4		0816	7.0
SU 1433	0.8		M 1454	1.4
2029	7.1		2046	6.6
6 0244	1.2		**21** 0250	1.7
0834	7.4		0848	6.8
M 1519	0.8		TU 1525	1.6
2116	7.0		2118	6.4
7 0328	1.3		**22** 0320	1.9
0921	7.2		0922	6.5
TU 1606	1.0		W 1558	1.8
2207	6.7		2154	6.2
8 0417	1.6		**23** 0355	2.2
1013	6.9		1001	6.3
W 1658	1.3		TH 1636	2.0
☽ 2305	6.5		2238	6.0
9 0512	1.9		**24** 0439	2.4
1115	6.7		1050	6.0
TH 1756	1.6		F 1725	2.3
			☽ 2335	5.8
10 0012	6.2		**25** 0535	2.6
0616	2.1		1154	5.8
F 1225	6.4		SA 1825	2.4
1901	1.8			
11 0121	6.2		**26** 0046	5.7
0729	2.2		0643	2.7
SA 1338	6.3		SU 1311	5.7
2010	1.9		1931	2.4
12 0228	6.2		**27** 0158	5.8
0843	2.1		0755	2.6
SU 1448	6.4		M 1424	5.9
2116	1.8		2039	2.2
13 0330	6.4		**28** 0300	6.1
0948	1.8		0907	2.3
M 1553	6.5		TU 1527	6.2
2214	1.7		2141	2.0
14 0423	6.6		**29** 0354	6.5
1045	1.5		1011	1.9
TU 1651	6.7		W 1623	6.5
2305	1.6		2237	1.7
15 0510	6.8		**30** 0442	6.8
1136	1.2		1109	1.4
W 1741	6.8		TH 1714	6.8
2352	1.5		2329	1.4
			31 0528	7.2
			1201	1.0
			F 1802	7.1
			○	

AUGUST

Time	m		Time	m
1 0017	1.1		**16** 0053	1.4
0611	7.4		0646	7.2
SA 1251	0.7		SU 1324	1.0
1848	7.3		1916	6.9
2 0104	1.0		**17** 0127	1.4
0654	7.6		0719	7.1
SU 1337	0.5		M 1357	1.1
1932	7.4		1946	6.8
3 0148	0.9		**18** 0157	1.5
0737	7.7		0750	7.1
M 1421	0.5		TU 1427	1.3
2015	7.4		2014	6.8
4 0231	0.9		**19** 0224	1.6
0820	7.7		0821	6.9
TU 1504	0.6		W 1454	1.5
2058	7.2		2043	6.6
5 0313	1.1		**20** 0250	1.8
0905	7.5		0851	6.7
W 1548	0.8		TH 1521	1.7
2144	6.9		2115	6.5
6 0358	1.4		**21** 0320	2.0
0954	7.2		0923	6.5
TH 1634	1.3		F 1551	2.0
2236	6.6		2151	6.2
7 0447	1.8		**22** 0357	2.2
1051	6.7		1002	6.2
F 1727	1.7		SA 1633	2.2
☽ 2337	6.2		☽ 2237	5.9
8 0547	2.2		**23** 0448	2.5
1200	6.3		1055	5.9
SA 1832	2.1		SU 1733	2.5
			2343	5.7
9 0047	6.0		**24** 0558	2.7
0703	2.4		1217	5.7
SU 1318	6.1		M 1847	2.6
1947	2.3			
10 0159	6.0		**25** 0113	5.7
0826	2.3		0716	2.6
M 1435	6.1		TU 1355	5.8
2058	2.3		2003	2.5
11 0307	6.2		**26** 0229	5.7
0936	2.0		0835	2.6
TU 1547	6.3		W 1508	6.1
2158	2.1		2114	2.2
12 0405	6.5		**27** 0329	6.4
1032	1.6		0949	1.9
W 1644	6.5		TH 1607	6.5
2248	1.8		2215	1.8
13 0451	6.8		**28** 0420	6.9
1121	1.3		1050	1.4
TH 1730	6.7		F 1659	6.9
2334	1.6		2309	1.4
14 0532	7.0		**29** 0507	7.3
1205	1.1		1143	0.9
F 1809	6.8		SA 1746	7.3
●			○ 2359	1.4
15 0015	1.5		**30** 0551	7.6
0610	7.1		1232	0.5
SA 1247	1.0		SU 1831	7.5
1844	6.9			
			31 0045	0.8
			0635	7.9
			M 1318	0.3
			1914	7.6

Chart Datum: 3·90 metres below Ordnance Datum (Newlyn). HAT is 8·0 metres above Chart Datum.

STANDARD TIME (UT)
For Summer Time add ONE hour in **non-shaded areas**

IMMINGHAM LAT 53°38'N LONG 0°11'W
TIMES AND HEIGHTS OF HIGH AND LOW WATERS

Dates in red are **SPRINGS**
Dates in blue are **NEAPS**

YEAR **2015**

SEPTEMBER

Time	m	Time	m
1 0130 0.7 0718 8.0 TU 1402 0.3 1954 7.6		**16** 0132 1.4 0723 7.1 W 1357 1.3 1943 6.9	
2 0212 0.7 0801 7.9 W 1443 0.5 2035 7.4		**17** 0158 1.5 0753 7.0 TH 1423 1.5 2011 6.8	
3 0254 0.9 0846 7.7 TH 1524 0.9 2117 7.1		**18** 0223 1.7 0822 6.8 F 1447 1.7 2040 6.7	
4 0335 1.3 0933 7.2 F 1605 1.4 2204 6.7		**19** 0251 1.8 0852 6.6 SA 1514 1.9 2112 6.4	
5 0421 1.7 1028 6.7 SA 1653 2.0 ☽ 2301 6.2		**20** 0325 2.1 0929 6.3 SU 1551 2.2 2154 6.1	
6 0517 2.2 1137 6.2 SU 1755 2.5		**21** 0413 2.4 1019 6.0 M 1648 2.5 ☽ 2252 5.8	
7 0014 5.9 0636 2.5 M 1300 5.9 1920 2.7		**22** 0523 2.6 1135 5.7 TU 1807 2.8	
8 0131 5.8 0810 2.5 TU 1421 5.9 2040 2.6		**23** 0022 5.7 0645 2.6 W 1331 5.7 1932 2.7	
9 0242 6.0 0920 2.1 W 1534 6.1 2139 2.3		**24** 0157 6.0 0808 2.3 TH 1449 6.1 2048 2.3	
10 0341 6.4 1013 1.7 TH 1628 6.4 2228 2.0		**25** 0301 6.4 0925 1.8 F 1548 6.6 2152 1.8	
11 0428 6.7 1059 1.4 F 1709 6.7 2311 1.7		**26** 0354 6.9 1026 1.3 SA 1639 7.0 2246 1.4	
12 0508 7.0 1140 1.2 SA 1745 6.8 2351 1.5		**27** 0442 7.4 1119 0.8 SU 1726 7.4 2336 1.0	
13 0545 7.1 1219 1.1 SU 1817 6.9 ●		**28** 0528 7.7 1208 0.5 M 1809 7.6 ○	
14 0028 1.4 0619 7.2 M 1255 1.1 1846 7.0		**29** 0023 0.7 0613 7.9 TU 1254 0.3 1850 7.7	
15 0102 1.4 0652 7.2 TU 1328 1.2 1915 7.0		**30** 0109 0.6 0657 8.0 W 1337 0.4 1930 7.6	

OCTOBER

Time	m	Time	m
1 0152 0.7 0742 7.9 TH 1418 0.6 2009 7.5		**16** 0133 1.5 0728 7.0 F 1353 1.5 1943 7.0	
2 0233 0.9 0826 7.6 F 1457 1.0 2049 7.2		**17** 0200 1.6 0759 6.9 SA 1419 1.6 2012 6.8	
3 0314 1.2 0913 7.2 SA 1535 1.6 2133 6.7		**18** 0230 1.7 0831 6.7 SU 1448 1.9 2044 6.6	
4 0356 1.7 1006 6.6 SU 1617 2.2 ☽ 2226 6.3		**19** 0305 1.9 0909 6.4 M 1526 2.2 2125 6.4	
5 0448 2.2 1114 6.1 M 1713 2.7 2338 5.9		**20** 0352 2.2 1000 6.1 TU 1620 2.5 ☽ 2221 6.1	
6 0604 2.6 1237 5.8 TU 1839 3.0		**21** 0500 2.4 1113 5.8 W 1736 2.7 2340 5.9	
7 0058 5.8 0743 2.5 W 1355 5.8 2010 2.9		**22** 0621 2.4 1304 5.8 TH 1901 2.7	
8 0210 6.0 0853 2.2 TH 1504 6.0 2112 2.6		**23** 0118 6.1 0742 2.1 F 1423 6.2 2018 2.4	
9 0310 6.3 0944 1.9 F 1558 6.4 2201 2.2		**24** 0229 6.5 0856 1.7 SA 1524 6.6 2124 1.9	
10 0359 6.6 1029 1.6 SA 1639 6.6 2243 1.8		**25** 0326 6.9 0958 1.2 SU 1615 7.0 2221 1.4	
11 0440 6.9 1109 1.3 SU 1714 6.8 2323 1.6		**26** 0417 7.4 1052 0.9 M 1702 7.4 2312 1.1	
12 0516 7.0 1147 1.2 M 1746 7.0		**27** 0505 7.7 1142 0.6 TU 1745 7.6 ○	
13 0000 1.5 0550 7.1 TU 1223 1.2 ● 1814 7.0		**28** 0001 0.8 0552 7.8 W 1229 0.5 1826 7.6	
14 0034 1.4 0623 7.1 W 1257 1.2 1844 7.1		**29** 0048 0.7 0638 7.9 TH 1312 0.6 1906 7.6	
15 0105 1.4 0656 7.1 TH 1327 1.3 1914 7.1		**30** 0132 0.7 0724 7.7 F 1353 0.8 1946 7.5	
		31 0214 0.9 0809 7.5 SA 1431 1.2 2025 7.2	

NOVEMBER

Time	m	Time	m
1 0254 1.2 0855 7.0 SU 1508 1.7 2106 6.8		**16** 0217 1.5 0818 6.7 M 1432 1.8 2027 6.8	
2 0336 1.6 0946 6.5 M 1546 2.2 2153 6.4		**17** 0255 1.7 0900 6.5 TU 1512 2.0 2109 6.6	
3 0423 2.1 1049 6.1 TU 1634 2.7 ☽ 2257 6.0		**18** 0343 1.9 0951 6.2 W 1604 2.3 2202 6.4	
4 0526 2.4 1204 5.8 W 1741 3.0		**19** 0445 2.1 1059 6.0 TH 1711 2.5 ☽ 2311 6.2	
5 0017 5.8 0651 2.6 TH 1317 5.7 1912 3.1		**20** 0558 2.1 1231 6.0 F 1829 2.6	
6 0130 5.9 0809 2.4 F 1422 5.9 2030 2.8		**21** 0037 6.2 0714 2.0 SA 1350 6.2 1946 2.4	
7 0232 6.1 0905 2.1 SA 1517 6.2 2125 2.4		**22** 0154 6.5 0826 1.7 SU 1453 6.5 2055 2.0	
8 0324 6.4 0950 1.8 SU 1602 6.5 2209 2.1		**23** 0257 6.8 0929 1.4 M 1548 6.9 2155 1.6	
9 0407 6.6 1032 1.6 M 1640 6.7 2250 1.8		**24** 0353 7.2 1025 1.1 TU 1637 7.2 2249 1.2	
10 0444 6.8 1111 1.4 TU 1712 6.9 2328 1.6		**25** 0445 7.4 1116 0.9 W 1722 7.4 ○ 2340 1.0	
11 0520 6.9 1149 1.3 W 1744 7.0 ●		**26** 0535 7.5 1204 0.9 TH 1805 7.5	
12 0005 1.5 0555 7.0 TH 1225 1.3 1816 7.1		**27** 0029 0.8 0623 7.6 F 1250 0.9 1846 7.5	
13 0039 1.4 0631 7.0 F 1258 1.4 1849 7.1		**28** 0115 0.8 0709 7.5 SA 1331 1.1 1926 7.4	
14 0111 1.4 0707 7.0 SA 1328 1.4 1921 7.1		**29** 0158 0.9 0755 7.3 SU 1409 1.3 2005 7.2	
15 0143 1.5 0742 6.9 SU 1358 1.6 1953 7.0		**30** 0239 1.2 0839 6.9 M 1445 1.7 2044 7.0	

DECEMBER

Time	m	Time	m
1 0318 1.5 0925 6.6 TU 1521 2.1 2125 6.6		**16** 0251 1.4 0853 6.7 W 1504 1.7 2059 6.9	
2 0359 1.9 1016 6.2 W 1601 2.4 2214 6.3		**17** 0337 1.5 0942 6.5 TH 1551 2.0 2148 6.7	
3 0448 2.2 1117 5.9 TH 1652 2.8 ☽ 2320 6.0		**18** 0431 1.7 1041 6.3 F 1649 2.2 ☽ 2249 6.5	
4 0546 2.4 1224 5.7 F 1756 3.0		**19** 0534 1.8 1155 6.1 SA 1758 2.4	
5 0034 5.8 0654 2.5 SA 1328 5.8 1910 3.0		**20** 0002 6.4 0644 1.9 SU 1312 6.2 1912 2.3	
6 0141 5.9 0803 2.4 SU 1427 5.9 2026 2.7		**21** 0120 6.4 0755 1.8 M 1420 6.3 2025 2.1	
7 0238 6.1 0900 2.1 M 1517 6.2 2125 2.4		**22** 0230 6.6 0902 1.7 TU 1521 6.6 2132 1.8	
8 0328 6.3 0949 1.9 TU 1600 6.5 2212 2.1		**23** 0333 6.8 1002 1.5 W 1614 6.9 2231 1.5	
9 0411 6.5 1033 1.7 W 1638 6.7 2255 1.8		**24** 0430 7.0 1055 1.3 TH 1703 7.1 2324 1.2	
10 0451 6.7 1115 1.5 TH 1715 6.9 2336 1.6		**25** 0523 7.2 1145 1.2 F 1748 7.3 ○	
11 0531 6.8 1154 1.4 F 1752 7.1 ●		**26** 0014 1.0 0612 7.2 SA 1231 1.2 1829 7.3	
12 0015 1.4 0611 6.9 SA 1232 1.4 1828 7.1		**27** 0101 0.9 0658 7.2 SU 1313 1.2 1910 7.3	
13 0054 1.3 0651 7.0 SU 1309 1.4 1904 7.2		**28** 0144 1.0 0741 7.1 M 1351 1.4 1948 7.3	
14 0132 1.3 0730 7.0 M 1345 1.4 1940 7.2		**29** 0223 1.1 0821 6.9 TU 1425 1.6 2024 7.1	
15 0210 1.3 0810 6.9 TU 1422 1.5 2017 7.1		**30** 0259 1.4 0900 6.6 W 1457 1.8 2059 6.8	
		31 0334 1.6 0937 6.4 TH 1531 2.1 2136 6.5	

NE England

Chart Datum: 3·90 metres below Ordnance Datum (Newlyn). HAT is 8·0 metres above Chart Datum.

3.10 RIVER HUMBER

S bank: NE and N Lincolnshire. N bank: E Riding of Yorks and City of Kingston-upon-Hull.
Hull marina: **53°44′·24N 00°20′·15W** ❀❀◊◊◊◊❀❀❀

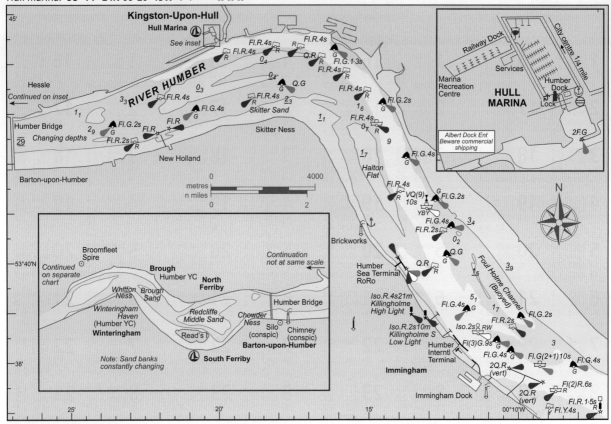

CHARTS AC 1190, 107, 104, 1188, 3496, 3497, 5614; Imray C29; ABP

TIDES –0510 Immingham, –0452 Hull, Dover; ML 4·1; Duration 0555
Standard Port IMMINGHAM (⟵)

Times				Height (metres)			
High Water		Low Water		MHWS	MHWN	MLWN	MLWS
0100	0700	0100	0700	7·3	5·8	2·6	0·9
1300	1900	1300	1900				
Differences BULL SAND FORT							
–0020	–0030	–0035	–0015	–0.4	–0.3	+0.1	+0.2
GRIMSBY							
–0012	–0014	–0015	–0013	–0.3	–0.2	+0.1	+0.4
HULL (ALBERT DOCK)							
+0019	+0019	+0033	+0027	+0.3	+0.1	–0.1	–0.2
HUMBER BRIDGE							
+0027	+0022	+0049	+0039	–0.1	–0.4	–0.7	–0.6
BURTON STATHER (R Trent)*							
+0105	+0050	+0240	+0205	–2.0	–2.7	–2.2	–1.1
KEADBY (R Trent)*							
+0135	+0120	+0425	+0410	–2.8	–3.3	–2.3	–0.9
BLACKTOFT (R Ouse)†							
+0100	+0055	+0325	+0255	–1.6	–1.8	–2.2	–1.1
GOOLE (R Ouse)†							
+0130	+0115	+0355	+0350	–1.6	–2.1	–1.9	–0.6

* Normal river level at Burton Stather is about 0·1m below CD, and at Keadby 0·1m to 0·2m below CD.

† Heights of LW can increase by up to 0·3m at Blacktoft and 0·6m at Goole when river in spate. HW hts are little affected.

SHELTER R Humber is the estuary of the rivers Ouse and Trent. The estuary has strong tidal streams: a strong NW'ly against a spring flood of 3-4kn causes a short steep sea, as does a SE'ly over the ebb stream. Off Hull Marina it can be very choppy with fresh winds over spring tidal streams.

Anchorages Inside Spurn Hd only with winds from NE to ESE, or close off Haile Sand Fort in fair weather. In S to W winds there is a good ⚓ off the SW bank 8ca above N Killingholme Oil jetty, well out of main chan. In N'lies ⚓ off Hawkin's Pt, N of S9 buoy.

Marinas at Hull, S Ferriby and the docks at Goole are all entered by lock access HW±3, and Grimsby also by lock HW±2. Immingham should only be used in emergency. S Ferriby should not be attempted without up-to-date ABP charts for the ever-changing buoyed chan above Hull. Waiting pontoon at S Ferriby.

Do not attempt entry to Winteringham or Brough Havens without contacting Humber Yawl Club for details of approach channel and mooring availability. Both dry to soft mud. Winteringham is prone to heavy silting, but is dredged.

NAVIGATION Note TSS on chartlet 3.1 and on AC 109, guidance at www.humber.com/Yachting_and_Leisure/Pleasure_Craft_Navigation
From S, WPT 53°30′·50N 00°16′·50E, 1ca SW of Rosse Spit PHM buoy, Fl (2) R 5s. Thence pass S of Haile Sand No 2, then via No 2B, Tetney monobuoy and No 2C into Haile Chan.

From N, WPT 53°34′·74N 00°16′·55E, S Binks SHM buoy, Fl G 2s. Thence passing N of Spurn Lt Float, SE Chequer to Chequer No 3 crossing to S of Bull Chan at this point. This avoids strong tidal streams off Spurn Hd. Best arrival is LW. Sp tides are fierce: 4·4kn ebb off Spurn Head and Immingham. There is a big ship ⚓ S of Spurn Hd. Keep clear of large commercial vessels using Hawke (8·4m) and Sunk (8·8m) Chans; these are marked by S1-S9 SHM buoys, all Fl G 1·5s (S8 is a SHM bn, Fl G 1·5s with tide gauge); and by P2-P9 PHM buoys, all Fl R 1·5s. Foul Holme Chan (SHM buoys FH1 to FH9) off Immingham is recommended for small craft.

For **Grimsby,** the lock into Fish Docks is 255°/1·35M from Lower Burcom No 6 Lt Float, Fl R 4s. The jetty off the W entr to Royal Dock has been extended further into Grimsby Road.

Off **Kingston-upon-Hull** a tidal eddy and streams can be rotatory: the flood makes W up Hull Roads for ¾hr whilst the ebb is already running down-river over Skitter Sand on the opposite bank (reaches 2½kn at sp). Humber Bridge (conspic) has 29m clearance.

LIGHTS AND MARKS The Humber is well marked. At Grimsby a conspic tr (94m with 'minaret' on top) is 300m W of Fish Dock lock. IPTS at to Grimsby, Immingham, Killingholme, Hull and Goole. A number of jetties with F lts have additional FL lts shown in fog.

COMMUNICATIONS (Codes: Grimsby 01472; Hull 01482) Police 101; Humber HM 01482 327171; see also: www.humber.com

Advise *VTS Humber* on Ch 14 (or ☎ 01482 212191) position and intentions on appr from seaward of Clee Ness lt float; listen on Ch 14 / 12 when W of the float and Ch 15 upstream fm the Humber Bridge to Gainsborough (R Trent) and Goole (R Ouse). ⚓, nav & tidal information is broadcast on Ch 12/14 every odd H+03; more detailed info, including height of tide, is available on request.

GRIMSBY Port Director 327171; MRCC (01262) 672317.

HULL Lock ☎ 330508; MRCC (01262) 672317; ⊖ 782107.

Other VHF stns: *Grimsby Docks Radio* Ch **74** (H24) 18 79 call Humber Cruising for marina staff or *Fishdock Island* for lock keeper. Immingham *Docks Radio* Ch 19 68 (H24). R Hull Port Ops Service call *Drypool Radio* Ch 22 (Mon-Fri HW–2 to HW+1; Sat 0900-1100 LT). *Hull Marina* Ch M **80** (H24); *Albert Dock Radio* Ch 09. *Ferriby Sluice* (R Ancholme Lock) Ch 74. Humber YC, Ch M (if racing). *Goole Docks Radio* Ch 14 (H24) 09 19. Boothferry Bridge Ch 09 (H24). Selby Railway and Toll Bridges Ch 09. Br Waterways locks Ch 74. *Brough and Winteringham Havens, Humber Yawl Club* Ch M.

FACILITIES

Humber Mouth YC ☎ (01472) 812063, M drying at Tetney Haven.

GRIMSBY NE Lincs (01472) **Fish Docks** Lock access (R/G tfc lts) HW±3 £10 locking fee for Ⓥ, both gates open for free flow HW±2, enter free of charge with authorisation by *Fish Dock Island*, Ch 74. Gates may close at extreme HW springs to prevent flooding.

Meridian Quay Marina www.hca grimsby.co.uk ☎ 268424, 200⚲+30 Ⓥ, £3·00 inc ⚡, ▣, D, ⚒, ⚲, ▣, BY, BH (35ton), ▯, wi-fi.

Grimsby and Cleethorpes YC ☎ 356678; enter via ABP Royal Dock, avoiding the extended piers enclosing tidal basin to N and W, limited ⚲; M, ♆, ▣, ✕, ▯. **Town** all facilities.

Hull Marina ⚓ www.bwml.co.uk/hull_marina ☎ (01482) 609960; (312+20 Ⓥ £2·75), access HW±3 via lock (width 8·5m) 150m to the E. 1 Apr-31 Oct H24, 1 Nov-31 Mar 0700-2100 – otherwise 24hrs notice. **No** shelter from W through S to E when waiting outside lock in river especially in strong W winds or if marina shut. The pontoon in basin for craft awaiting lock in dries, *do not settle into the mud*. Marina office open 0900-1700 daily; D, ▣, Gas, ⊖, ⚲, ♺, ⚲, ▣, BH (50 ton), C (2 ton), ▣, ⚴, ACA. **City** All facilities.

Ferries: Rotterdam/Zeebrugge daily; 10 hrs; www.poferries.com.

South Ferriby Marina N Lincs. southferribymarina.com ☎ (01652) 635620; access HW±3, 100+20Ⓥ £10/craft<10m<+£1/m max LOA 12m. Lock fee £7. VHF 80; D, ⚡, ♆, ▣, Gas, C (20 ton). **Village** 🛒, ▯.

S Ferriby Lock ☎ 01652 635219. River Authority Ⓥ berths £8/48hrs. Lock Fee £7 (70' LOA, 18' beam, 6' draft); ♺. VHF 74: 0730-1600.

Humber Yawl Club has two facilities: **Brough Haven** E Riding, ☎ (01482) 667224, entry HW±1½; Ch 37/M1 limited ⚲; ⚓, ♆, ▯. **Winteringham Haven** N Lincs ☎ (01724) 734452. Limited access, dredging in progress; Ch 37/M1. BH (10 ton), ✉.

GOOLE Take the flood up the River Humber, follow the buoyed channel past Hull, Brough and when approaching Trent Falls Apex alter course to stbd and follow the River Ouse to Goole. Situated off the Aire and Calder Navigation and accessed via the commercial lock for Goole Docks (Ch 14) are two havens, limited Ⓥ.

Goole Boathouse ☎ 01405 763985 ⚲ £5 <40' LOA, max draft 6ft.

Viking Marina www.vikingmarine.com ☎ 01405 765737, ⚲ £8·00, <80' LOA, 20' beam, 9' draft; ⚓, ⚴, D, Gas, ⚒, ⚲, ▣, BH (18 ton).

NABURN follow R Ouse, 4M S of York and 80M above Spurn Pt; **Naburn Marina** ☎ (01904) 621021; 300+50Ⓥ max draft 1·1m £3·00 ▣, P, D, ♆, showers, 🚾, ♺, ⚡ (£2·00), ⚒, ⚲, BH (16 ton), ✕.

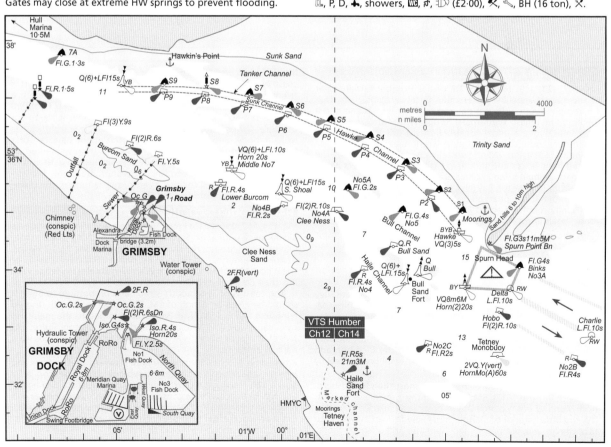

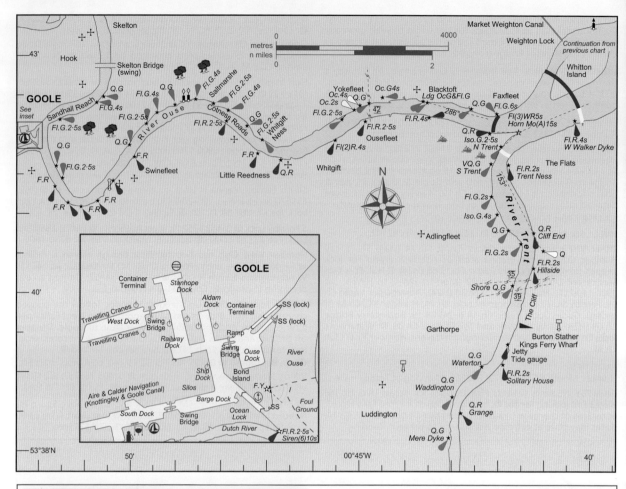

RIVER HUMBER TO HARTLEPOOL

(AC 107, 121, 129, 134, 5615) NE of the Humber Estuary clear of the main channel lies the Humber Gateway Wind Farm. Due for completion in 2015 it is marked by 5 cardinal buoys and a 79m high mast. Westernmost Rough Wind Farm, marked by 4 cardinal buoys, is under construction 3M off Withernsea on the inshore route to Bridlington. A wreck hazardous to surface navigation lies in 8m, 2M off Tunstall. Navigation is aided by the disused light house and prominent church spires/towers along the coast. A small firing practice area lies inshore off the beach at Royston. Bridlington Bay (chart 1882) is clear of dangers apart from Smithic Shoals (marked by N and S cardinal lt buoys), lying S of Flamborough Hd about 2½M off Bridlington; seas break on these shoals in strong N or E winds even at HW.

Flamborough Head (lt, fog sig, RG) is a steep, W cliff with conspic light house on summit. The light may be obscured by cliffs when close inshore. An old lt ho, also conspic, is 2½ca WNW.

▶ *Tides run hard around the Head which, in strong winds against a sp tide, is best avoided by 2M.* ◀

From here the coast runs NW, with no offshore dangers until Filey Brigg where rocky ledges extend 5ca ESE, marked by a lit ECM. ⚓ in Filey B in N or offshore winds. NW of Filey Brigg beware Old Horse Rks and foul ground 5ca offshore; maintain this offing past Scarborough to Whitby High Lt. Off Whitby beware Whitby Rk and The Scar (dries in places) to the E of hbr, and Upgang Rks (dries in places) 1M to WNW; swell breaks heavily on all these rocks.

From Whitby to Hartlepool dangers lie no more than 1M offshore. Runswick Bay (AC 1612), 5M NW of Whitby, provides ⚓ in winds from S and W but is dangerous in onshore winds. 2½M further NW the little harbour of Staithes is suitable for yachts which can take the ground, but only in good weather and offshore winds.

Redcliff, dark red and 205m high, is a conspic feature of this coast which, along to Hunt Cliff, is prone to landslides and is fringed with rky ledges which dry for about 3ca off. There is a conspic radio mast 4ca SSE of Redcliff. Off Redcar and Coatham beware Salt Scar and West Scar, drying rky ledges lying 1– 8ca offshore. Other ledges lie close SE and S of Salt Scar which has NCM lt buoy. Between R. Tees and Hartlepool beware Long Scar, detached rky ledge (dries 2m) with extremity marked by ECM lt buoy. Tees and Hartlepool Bays are exposed to strong E/SE winds. The R. Tees and Middlesbrough are highly industrialised. At Hartlepool there is a centre specialising in the maintenance and restoration of Tall Ships.

HARTLEPOOL TO COQUET ISLAND

(AC 134, 152, 156, 5615) From The Heugh an offing of 1M clears all dangers until past Seaham and approaching Sunderland, where White Stones, rky shoals with depth 1·8m, lie 1·75M SSE of Roker Pier lt ho, and Hendon Rk, depth 0·9m, lies 1·25M SE of the lt ho. 1M N of Sunderland is Whitburn Steel, a rky ledge with less than 2m over it; a dangerous wreck (buoyed) lies 1ca SE of it. The coast N of Tynemouth is foul, and on passage to Blyth it should be given an offing of 1M. St Mary's Island (with disused conspic lt ho) is 3·5M N of Tynemouth, joined to the mainland by a causeway. The tiny drying harbour of Seaton Sluice, 1M NW of St Mary's Island, is accessible only in offshore winds via a narrow entrance.

Proceeding N from Blyth, keep well seaward of The Sow and Pigs rks, and set course to clear Newbiggin Pt and Beacon Pt by about 1M. Newbiggin church spire is prominent from N and S, and NW of Beacon Pt are conspic chys of aluminium smelter and power stn. 2M NNW of Beacon Pt is Snab Pt where rks extend 3ca seaward. Further offshore Cresswell Skeres, rky patches with depth 3m, lie about 1·5M NNE of Snab Pt.

3.11 BRIDLINGTON

E Riding of Yorkshire 54°04'·78N 00°11'·21W ✿✿⌂⌂⌂✿✿

CHARTS AC 1191, 1190, 129, 121, 1882, 5614; Imray C29

TIDES +0553 Dover; ML 3·6; Duration 0610

Standard Port RIVER TEES (→)

Times				Height (metres)			
High Water		Low Water		MHWS	MHWN	MLWN	MLWS
0000	0600	0000	0600	5·5	4·3	2·0	0·9
1200	1800	1200	1800				
Differences BRIDLINGTON							
+0100	+0050	+0055	+0050	+0·6	+0·4	+0·3	+0·2
FILEY BAY							
+0042	+0042	+0047	+0034	+0·3	+0·6	+0·4	+0·1

SHELTER Good, except in E, SE and S winds. Hbr dries completely to soft black mud. Berth on S pier or near HM's Office as directed. A marina is planned but agreement not yet reached.

NAVIGATION WPT SW Smithic WCM, Q (9) 15s, 54°02'·41N 00°09'·21W, 333°/2·6M to ent. Close-in appr is with N pier hd lt on brg 002° to keep W of drying patch (The Canch). Beware bar, 1m at MLWN, could dry out at MLWS.

LIGHTS AND MARKS Hbr is 4M WSW of Flamborough Hd lt, Fl (4) 15s 65m 24M. Y racing marks are laid in the Bay, Apr-Oct. Tidal sigs, by day from S pier: R flag = >2·7m in hbr; No flag = < 2·7m. At night from N pier: Fl ● = >2·7m in hbr; Fl ● = < 2·7m.

COMMUNICATIONS (Code 01262) MRCC 672317; Police 101; Ⓗ 606666. HM 670148/9, watchkeeper 409011, mob 0860 275150. Call on VHF Ch 16, then Ch 12 for working.

FACILITIES **S Pier** ⚓, ⚲ £2.64 /sq m/week or £20/yacht <3days, D (tank/hose ☎ 500227), C (3 ton), BH (75 ton), ⚓; M, see HM; **Royal Yorks YC** ☎ 672041, L, ⚓, ✕, ⌂. **Town** 🅿, 🛈, ✎, 🖾, 🛒, ✕, ⌂, ✉, Ⓑ, ⇌, ✈ (Humberside).

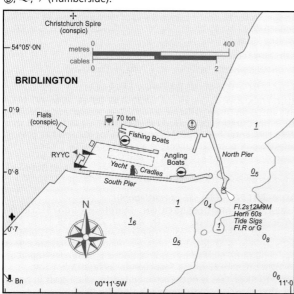

+
Christchurch Spire
(conspic)

BRIDLINGTON

ADJACENT ANCHORAGE (7M SE of Scarborough)
FILEY, N Yorkshire, 54°12'·80N 00°16'·20W, AC 1882, 129. HW +0532 on Dover; ML 3·5m; Duration 0605. See 3.11. Good ⚓ in winds from S to NNE in 4 – 5m on hard sand. Lt on cliff above CG Stn, G metal column, FR 31m 1M vis 272° 308°. Filey Brigg, a natural bkwtr, is marked by ECM buoy, Q(3)10s, Bell. Beware Old Horse Rks, 2M WNW of Filey Brigg, foul ground extending ½M offshore. An unmarked Historic Wreck (see 0.29) lies at 54°11'·51N 00°13'·48W.
Facilities: 🛒, ✕, ⌂, L, Ⓗ ☎ (01723) 68111, ✉, Ⓑ, ⇌.

3.12 SCARBOROUGH

N. Yorkshire 54°16'·88N 00°23'·36W ✿✿⌂⌂⌂✿✿✿

CHARTS AC 1191, 129, 1612, 5614; Imray C29

TIDES +0527 Dover; ML 3·5; Duration 0615

Standard Port RIVER TEES (→)

Times				Height (metres)			
High Water		Low Water		MHWS	MHWN	MLWN	MLWS
0000	0600	0000	0600	5·5	4·3	2·0	0·9
1200	1800	1200	1800				
Differences SCARBOROUGH							
+0040	+0040	+0030	+0030	+0·2	+0·3	+0·3	0·0

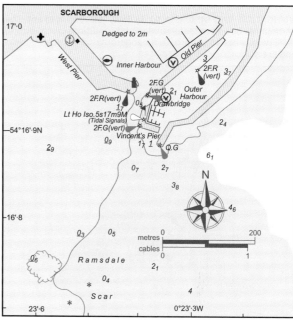

SCARBOROUGH

SHELTER Good in Outer Harbour (dries) for local residents, access via narrow (10m) entrance by East pier, but not in strong E/SE'lies. In winter months access to Outer Hbr is via the drawbridge only.

Ⓥ ⚲ on SE side of pontoons in Inner Harbour, dredged to 2m.

NAVIGATION WPT 54°16'·50N 00°22'·00W, 302°/0·83M to E pier lt. Appr from the E to avoid Ramsdale Scar, rky shoal 0·9m. Keep careful watch for salmon nets E & SE of ent. Beware rks extending approx 20m SW of E pier head. Give Castle Headland close N of hbr a wide berth due to coastal defences. Min depths in approach and entrance to Inner Harbour approx 0·1m.

LIGHTS AND MARKS Lt ho (conspic), Iso 5s, Dia 60s, on Vincent Pier is shown by night or B ● by day when there is more than 3·7m over bar in entrance. A Y SPM Fl Y 4s, 113° E pier 1·6NM marks the end of an outfall; another, N of the harbour 0·7NM NE of Scalby Ness is marked by a PHM Fl R 5s. Scarbourough YC sets lit Y SPM. Other lts as shown on chartlet.

COMMUNICATIONS (Code 01723) MRCC (01262) 672317; Police 101; Ⓗ 368111. Port Control 373877, Call *Scarborough Port Control* VHF Ch 12 16 (H24). Watchkeeper will offer guidance to approaching visitors.

FACILITIES HM www.scarboroughbc.gov.uk ☎ 373530 (HO); ⚲ £10/night, inner harbour pontoon berth £24·60/night <10m LOA, M, ⚓, ⊞, D, C (4 ton), ⚓; **Scarborough YC** ☎ 3/3821, ⚲, ⚓, M, ⚓, ✎, 🛈, ⌂.

Services ✎, 🛈, ✕, 🛈, 🅿 & 🛈, Ⓔ.

Town 🅿 & 🛈, ⚓ (£11·50) 🛒, ✕, ⌂, ✉, Ⓑ, ⇌, ✈ (Humberside).

3.13 WHITBY

N. Yorkshire 54°29'·65N 00°36'·78W ✦❂◊◊◊✿✿✿

CHARTS AC 129, 134, 1612, 5614, 5615; Imray C29, C24

TIDES +0500 Dover; ML 3·3; Duration 0605

Standard Port RIVER TEES (→)

Times				Height (metres)			
High Water		Low Water		MHWS	MHWN	MLWN	MLWS
0000	0600	0000	0600	5·5	4·3	2·0	0·9
1200	1800	1200	1800				
Differences WHITBY							
+0020	+0020	+0018	+0017	+0·1	+0·1	+0·2	+0·1

SHELTER Good, except in lower hbr in strong NW to NE winds.

NAVIGATION WPT 54°30'·21N 00°36'96W, 169°/0·57M to ent. The harbour can be entered safely under most conditions except during N-NE gales when the approach is dangerous due to breaking seas and entry should not be attempted.

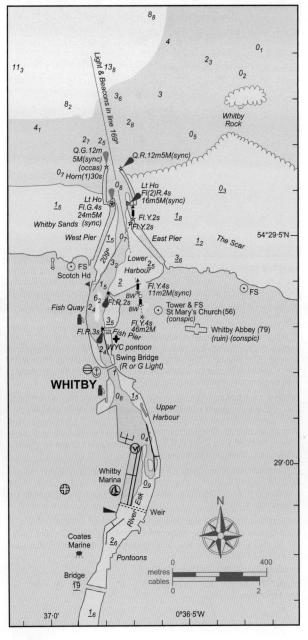

- From the SE beware Whitby Rk; leave Whitby NCM lit buoy to port.
- Beware strong set to E from HW –2 to HW, when nearing piers.

Vessels >37m LOA must embark pilot; via HM. All vessels must proceed at a safe speed within the Harbour and sailing vessels are to use auxiliary power if so equipped.

Min depth in entrance approx 1·0m. Bridge opens on request HW±2 every H and H+30. Additional openings at w/e and BH: May-Sep 0930 and1730; Aug 1300 (irrespective of tides). FG lts = open; FR lts = shut. Wait on pontoon at Fish Pier if necessary. If alongside Fish Quay or FVs, craft must not be left unattended.

Priority for Swing Bridge passage:
1. Commercial vessels with pilot embarked (keep well clear);
2. Large vessels; 3. Vessels inbound fm seaward; 4. When both bridge sections open 2-way traffic in single file keeping to stbd. Establish comms with Whitby Bridge Ch **11** prior to transit.

LIGHTS AND MARKS See Lights, buoys & waypoints and chartlet. Ruins of Whitby Abbey are to the E of the entrance. Whitby High Lt ho (white 8-sided tower) is 2M ESE of harbour entrance, which is marked on either side by 5m high R and G wooden towers respectively lit with QR and QG lts. The E Pier Lt Ho Fl (2)R 4s on a 16m masonry tower has been re-commissioned. This together with The W Pier Lt Ho Fl(2)G 4s 24m, are synchronised with lts on the pier extensions. Leading lines for entering hbr:

2 bns (W △, and W ○ with B stripe) seen between the outer pierheads (Q Fl R and Q Fl G) lead 169° into hbr. At night the Fwd bn sync Fl Y 4s, aligns with a lt sync Fl Y 4s (46m) on a lamp post. Maintain this line until bns on E pier (2 sync Fl Y 2s) are abeam. Thence keep these same bns in transit astern bearing 029°.

COMMUNICATIONS (Code 01947) MRCC (01262) 672317; Police 101; Dr 820888. HM www.yorkshireports.co.uk ☎ 602354/602272.

Hbr and Marina VHF Ch **11** 16 12 (H24). Whitby Bridge Ch **11** 16 06 (listens on Ch 16 HW–2 to HW+2).

FACILITIES Whitby Marina (dredged 1.5m) is 2ca beyond swing bridge; visitor berths at seaward end of long pontoon. ☎ 600165. 240+10 Ⓥ, £2.20; ⬛, 📱, ⚒, ⊞, ✗, C, ⬛, △, ▬, BH, ACA, Gas, Gaz. **Whitby YC** ☎ 603623, M, L, 🚽.

Fish Quay D (in commercial quantities only, ☎ 602255), C (1 ton).

Town All domestic facilities, ✗, 🚽, ≋, ✈ (Teesside).

ADJACENT ANCHORAGE (5M WNW of Whitby)

RUNSWICK BAY, N. Yorkshire, **54°32'·11N 00°44'·20W.** AC 1612. HW +0505 on Dover: Differences on R Tees are approx as Whitby; ML 3·1m; Duration 0605. Good shelter in all winds from SSE thru W to NW. Enter bay at 225° keeping clear of many rks at base of cliffs. Two W posts (2FY by night when required by lifeboat) 18m apart are ldg marks 270° to LB ho and can be used to lead into ⚓. Good holding in 6m to 9m in middle of bay. Facilities: **Runswick Bay Rescue Boat Station** ☎ (01947) 840965. **Village** 🚽, ✗, 🛒.

ADJACENT PORT (3M SSE of Hartlepool)

RIVER TEES / MIDDLESBROUGH, Middlesbrough/Stockton, **54°38'·94N 01°08'·48W.** ✦❂◊✿. AC 152, 2567, 2566; Imray C29; OS 93. HW +0450 Dover; Standard Port River Tees. ML 3·1; Duration 0605. R. Tees & Middlesbrough are a major industrial area. Tees Bay wind farm, marked by cardinal buoys, is being developed up to 1½M offshore SE of the Tees channel as far as West Scar.

Entry to River Tees is not recommended for small craft in heavy weather, especially in strong winds from NE to SE.

Tees Fairway SWM buoy, Iso 4s 8m 8M, Horn 5s, Racon, is at 54°40'·93N 01°06'·38W, 030°/2·4M from S Gare bkwtr. The channel is well buoyed from the Fairway buoy to beyond Middlesbrough. Ldg lts 210°, both FR on framework trs. At Old CG stn a Q lt, or 3 ● (vert), = no entry without HM's consent. Call: *Tees Port Control* VHF Ch **14** 22 16 12 (H24). Monitor Ch 14; also info Ch 14 22. *Tees Barrage Radio* Ch M (37). HM ☎ (01642) 277201; Police 248184.

South Gare Marine Club ☎ 491039 (occas), M, ⚓, ▬; **Castlegate Marine Club** ☎ 583299 ▬, M, ⚓, ⚒, ✗, ⬛, ⬛; **Tees Motor Boat Club** M; **Services:** ⊞, ⚒, Ⓔ, ACA. **City** All domestic facilities, ≋, ✈. Hartlepool Marina (3.13) lies 3M to the NNW with all yacht facilities.

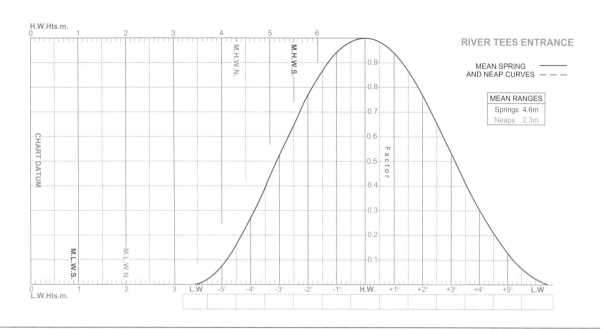

H.W.Hts.m.

RIVER TEES ENTRANCE

MEAN SPRING ——————
AND NEAP CURVES – – – –

MEAN RANGES
Springs 4.6m
Neaps   2.3m

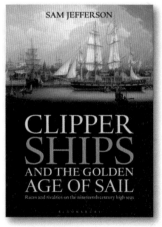

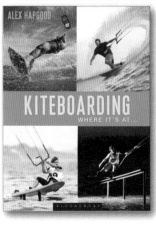
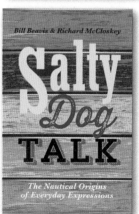
NE England

STANDARD TIME (UT)
For Summer Time add ONE hour in **non-shaded areas**

RIVER TEES LAT 54°38'N LONG 1°09'W
TIMES AND HEIGHTS OF HIGH AND LOW WATERS

Dates in red are **SPRINGS**
Dates in blue are **NEAPS**

YEAR 2015

JANUARY

Day	Time	m	Day	Time	m
1 TH	0637	1.5	**16** F	0547	1.9
	1246	4.7		1154	4.4
	1905	1.7		1819	2.0
2 F	0105	4.8	**17** SA	0022	4.5
	0737	1.5		0651	1.7
	1344	4.9		1254	4.7
	2002	1.4		1921	1.7
3 SA	0204	4.9	**18** SU	0123	4.7
	0826	1.4		0747	1.4
	1432	5.1		1347	4.9
	2051	1.2		2016	1.3
4 SU	0252	5.0	**19** M	0218	5.0
	0909	1.3		0838	1.2
	1513	5.2		1436	5.2
	2133	1.1		2106	1.0
5 M	0334	5.1	**20** TU	0308	5.3
	0948	1.3		0926	1.0
	1551	5.3		1522	5.5
	○ 2212	1.0		● 2155	0.6
6 TU	0413	5.1	**21** W	0355	5.5
	1023	1.3		1012	0.8
	1625	5.3		1607	5.7
	2249	1.0		2241	0.4
7 W	0449	5.1	**22** TH	0442	5.6
	1056	1.3		1057	0.7
	1658	5.3		1651	5.8
	2324	1.0		2326	0.3
8 TH	0525	5.1	**23** F	0529	5.6
	1128	1.4		1141	0.7
	1731	5.3		1736	5.8
	2358	1.1			
9 F	0600	5.0	**24** SA	0011	0.3
	1159	1.5		0615	5.5
	1806	5.2		1225	0.8
				1822	5.7
10 SA	0031	1.2	**25** SU	0057	0.9
	0636	4.9		0704	5.3
	1232	1.6		1311	1.0
	1844	5.0		1911	5.5
11 SU	0107	1.3	**26** M	0144	0.8
	0716	4.7		0755	5.0
	1308	1.8		1400	1.3
	1925	4.8		2004	5.2
12 M	0145	1.5	**27** TU	0236	1.2
	0800	4.6		0851	4.8
	1351	1.9		1457	1.6
	2012	4.6		◑ 2105	4.9
13 TU	0230	1.7	**28** W	0337	1.5
	0849	4.4		0954	4.5
	1442	2.1		1606	1.9
	◑ 2105	4.5		2214	4.6
14 W	0327	1.9	**29** TH	0451	1.8
	0948	4.3		1105	4.4
	1549	2.2		1728	1.9
	2208	4.4		2332	4.4
15 TH	0436	2.0	**30** F	0614	1.9
	1051	4.3		1221	4.5
	1707	2.2		1849	1.8
	2315	4.4			
			31 SA	0052	4.5
				0721	1.8
				1327	4.7
				1951	1.6

FEBRUARY

Day	Time	m	Day	Time	m
1 SU	0154	4.7	**16** M	0058	4.6
	0813	1.6		0725	1.5
	1417	4.9		1321	4.8
	2040	1.3		1956	1.3
2 M	0242	4.8	**17** TU	0159	5.0
	0855	1.5		0821	1.2
	1459	5.1		1415	5.2
	2120	1.1		2051	0.8
3 TU	0322	5.0	**18** W	0251	5.3
	0932	1.4		0910	0.9
	1536	5.2		1503	5.5
	○ 2156	1.0		● 2140	0.5
4 W	0357	5.0	**19** TH	0339	5.5
	1005	1.3		0957	0.7
	1609	5.3		1549	5.8
	2230	0.9		2226	0.2
5 TH	0431	5.1	**20** F	0425	5.7
	1036	1.2		1041	0.5
	1640	5.3		1634	5.9
	2301	0.9		2310	0.1
6 F	0502	5.1	**21** SA	0510	5.7
	1106	1.2		1124	0.5
	1709	5.3		1718	6.0
	2332	0.9		2353	0.1
7 SA	0533	5.1	**22** SU	0555	5.6
	1135	1.2		1206	0.6
	1740	5.2		1803	5.8
8 SU	0002	1.0	**23** M	0035	0.4
	0605	5.0		0639	5.4
	1206	1.3		1249	0.8
	1813	5.1		1850	5.6
9 M	0034	1.1	**24** TU	0119	0.7
	0640	4.9		0727	5.1
	1239	1.5		1334	1.1
	1850	5.0		1940	5.2
10 TU	0109	1.3	**25** W	0205	1.2
	0720	4.7		0818	4.8
	1316	1.6		1426	1.5
	1932	4.8		◐ 2038	4.8
11 W	0149	1.5	**26** TH	0301	1.7
	0806	4.5		0917	4.4
	1359	1.8		1532	1.8
	2020	4.6		2146	4.4
12 TH	0238	1.8	**27** F	0415	2.0
	0900	4.3		1028	4.2
	1454	2.0		1658	2.0
	◑ 2121	4.4		2307	4.2
13 F	0342	2.0	**28** SA	0546	2.1
	1003	4.2		1151	4.3
	1611	2.1		1829	1.9
	2233	4.3			
14 SA	0502	2.0			
	1112	4.3			
	1738	2.0			
	2348	4.4			
15 SU	0620	1.8			
	1220	4.5			
	1854	1.7			

MARCH

Day	Time	m	Day	Time	m
1 SU	0034	4.3	**16** M	0553	1.9
	0700	2.0		1150	4.5
	1303	4.5		1829	1.6
	1933	1.6			
2 M	0138	4.5	**17** TU	0037	4.6
	0753	1.8		0702	1.6
	1356	4.7		1256	4.8
	2021	1.4		1935	1.1
3 TU	0224	4.7	**18** W	0139	5.0
	0835	1.6		0800	1.2
	1438	4.9		1352	5.2
	2059	1.2		2031	0.7
4 W	0302	4.9	**19** TH	0231	5.3
	0910	1.4		0850	0.9
	1515	5.1		1442	5.5
	2133	1.0		2120	0.3
5 TH	0336	5.0	**20** F	0319	5.5
	0943	1.2		0937	0.6
	1547	5.2		1528	5.8
	○ 2205	0.9		● 2206	0.1
6 F	0407	5.1	**21** SA	0404	5.7
	1013	1.1		1021	0.4
	1617	5.3		1613	5.9
	2235	0.8		2249	0.1
7 SA	0435	5.1	**22** SU	0447	5.7
	1042	1.1		1104	0.4
	1645	5.3		1658	5.9
	2304	0.8		2331	0.2
8 SU	0504	5.1	**23** M	0530	5.6
	1111	1.1		1145	0.5
	1714	5.2		1743	5.8
	2333	0.9			
9 M	0534	5.1	**24** TU	0011	0.4
	1141	1.1		0613	5.4
	1745	5.2		1227	0.7
				1829	5.5
10 TU	0004	1.0	**25** W	0053	0.8
	0607	5.0		0658	5.1
	1214	1.2		1311	1.0
	1819	5.0		1918	5.1
11 W	0039	1.2	**26** TH	0136	1.3
	0645	4.8		0746	4.8
	1249	1.4		1401	1.4
	1859	4.8		2014	4.7
12 TH	0117	1.4	**27** F	0227	1.8
	0727	4.6		0842	4.5
	1329	1.6		1503	1.7
	1947	4.6		◑ 2119	4.3
13 F	0203	1.7	**28** SA	0337	2.1
	0819	4.4		0951	4.2
	1421	1.8		1625	1.9
	◑ 2048	4.4		2237	4.1
14 SA	0303	1.9	**29** SU	0507	2.3
	0924	4.3		1111	4.2
	1534	2.0		1754	1.9
	2202	4.3			
15 SU	0427	2.0	**30** M	0001	4.2
	1037	4.3		0626	2.2
	1707	1.9		1228	4.3
	2322	4.3		1900	1.7
			31 TU	0108	4.3
				0722	1.9
				1324	4.6
				1948	1.4

APRIL

Day	Time	m	Day	Time	m
1 W	0155	4.6	**16** TH	0117	4.9
	0805	1.7		0735	1.2
	1408	4.8		1328	5.2
	2028	1.2		2006	0.7
2 TH	0233	4.8	**17** F	0209	5.2
	0842	1.4		0826	0.9
	1446	5.0		1419	5.5
	2103	1.0		2056	0.4
3 F	0307	5.0	**18** SA	0257	5.5
	0915	1.2		0914	0.6
	1519	5.1		1507	5.7
	2136	0.9		● 2143	0.2
4 SA	0338	5.1	**19** SU	0341	5.6
	0946	1.1		0959	0.5
	1550	5.2		1553	5.8
	○ 2206	0.8		2226	0.2
5 SU	0406	5.1	**20** M	0424	5.6
	1016	1.0		1043	0.4
	1618	5.2		1638	5.7
	2235	0.8		2308	0.4
6 M	0435	5.2	**21** TU	0506	5.5
	1047	1.0		1125	0.5
	1648	5.2		1724	5.6
	2306	0.8		2348	0.6
7 TU	0506	5.2	**22** W	0548	5.4
	1118	1.0		1207	0.7
	1720	5.2		1810	5.3
	2338	0.9			
8 W	0539	5.1	**23** TH	0028	1.0
	1152	1.1		0631	5.1
	1756	5.0		1251	0.9
				1858	5.0
9 TH	0013	1.1	**24** F	0110	1.4
	0616	4.9		0716	4.8
	1229	1.2		1339	1.3
	1838	4.9		1951	4.7
10 F	0053	1.3	**25** SA	0156	1.8
	0659	4.8		0808	4.5
	1311	1.4		1437	1.6
	1928	4.7		◐ 2051	4.3
11 SA	0139	1.6	**26** SU	0258	2.1
	0751	4.6		0911	4.3
	1405	1.6		1547	1.8
	2030	4.5		2200	4.1
12 SU	0239	1.9	**27** M	0418	2.3
	0855	4.4		1025	4.2
	1516	1.7		1704	1.8
	◑ 2143	4.3		2315	4.1
13 M	0402	2.0	**28** TU	0537	2.2
	1008	4.4		1138	4.3
	1644	1.7		1813	1.7
	2301	4.4			
14 TU	0526	1.9	**29** W	0022	4.3
	1122	4.5		0638	2.0
	1804	1.4		1240	4.4
				1905	1.5
15 W	0015	4.6	**30** TH	0115	4.5
	0636	1.6		0727	1.8
	1230	4.8		1329	4.6
	1910	1.0		1949	1.3

Chart Datum: 2·85 metres below Ordnance Datum (Newlyn). HAT is 6·1 metres above Chart Datum.

FREE monthly updates from
www.reedsalmanac.co.uk

STANDARD TIME (UT)
For Summer Time add ONE hour in **non-shaded areas**

RIVER TEES LAT 54°38'N LONG 1°09'W

TIMES AND HEIGHTS OF HIGH AND LOW WATERS

Dates in **red** are **SPRINGS**
Dates in blue are NEAPS

YEAR 2015

MAY

Time	m	Time	m
1 0157 / 0807 / F 1410 / 2028	4.7 / 1.5 / 4.8 / 1.2	**16** 0147 / 0803 / SA 1359 / 2033	5.1 / 1.0 / 5.3 / 0.6
2 0233 / 0843 / SA 1447 / 2103	4.9 / 1.3 / 5.0 / 1.0	**17** 0236 / 0853 / SU 1449 / 2121	5.3 / 0.8 / 5.5 / 0.5
3 0305 / 0917 / SU 1520 / 2135	5.0 / 1.1 / 5.1 / 0.9	**18** 0321 / 0940 / M 1537 / ● 2205	5.4 / 0.6 / 5.5 / 0.6
4 0336 / 0950 / M 1552 / ○ 2208	5.1 / 1.0 / 5.1 / 0.9	**19** 0404 / 1025 / TU 1623 / 2247	5.5 / 0.6 / 5.5 / 0.7
5 0407 / 1024 / TU 1625 / 2241	5.2 / 0.9 / 5.2 / 0.9	**20** 0445 / 1108 / W 1708 / 2327	5.4 / 0.6 / 5.4 / 0.9
6 0441 / 1059 / W 1701 / 2317	5.2 / 0.9 / 5.1 / 0.9	**21** 0526 / 1150 / TH 1753	5.3 / 0.7 / 5.2
7 0517 / 1136 / TH 1742 / 2355	5.2 / 0.9 / 5.1 / 1.1	**22** 0007 / 0607 / F 1234 / 1838	1.1 / 5.1 / 0.9 / 5.0
8 0557 / 1216 / F 1827	5.1 / 1.0 / 4.9	**23** 0046 / 0649 / SA 1319 / 1926	1.4 / 4.9 / 1.2 / 4.7
9 0037 / 0640 / SA 1303 / 1919	1.3 / 4.9 / 1.2 / 4.8	**24** 0128 / 0736 / SU 1408 / 2018	1.7 / 4.7 / 1.4 / 4.4
10 0125 / 0733 / SU 1358 / 2019	1.5 / 4.8 / 1.3 / 4.6	**25** 0217 / 0830 / M 1505 / ◑ 2117	2.0 / 4.5 / 1.7 / 4.3
11 0225 / 0834 / M 1507 / ◑ 2128	1.8 / 4.6 / 1.4 / 4.5	**26** 0322 / 0933 / TU 1609 / 2220	2.2 / 4.3 / 1.8 / 4.2
12 0341 / 0944 / TU 1623 / 2240	1.9 / 4.6 / 1.4 / 4.5	**27** 0435 / 1041 / W 1715 / 2325	2.3 / 4.3 / 1.8 / 4.2
13 0459 / 1057 / W 1737 / 2350	1.8 / 4.7 / 1.3 / 4.7	**28** 0543 / 1146 / TH 1814	2.1 / 4.3 / 1.7
14 0608 / 1204 / TH 1843	1.6 / 4.9 / 1.0	**29** 0023 / 0639 / F 1242 / 1904	4.4 / 2.0 / 4.5 / 1.4
15 0053 / 0708 / F 1305 / 1941	4.9 / 1.3 / 5.1 / 0.8	**30** 0112 / 0727 / SA 1330 / 1949	4.6 / 1.7 / 4.7 / 1.4
		31 0154 / 0809 / SU 1412 / 2028	4.8 / 1.5 / 4.8 / 1.2

JUNE

Time	m	Time	m
1 0231 / 0848 / M 1451 / 2106	4.9 / 1.3 / 5.0 / 1.1	**16** 0305 / 0925 / TU 1525 / ● 2148	5.3 / 0.8 / 5.3 / 0.9
2 0307 / 0926 / TU 1529 / ○ 2144	5.1 / 1.1 / 5.1 / 1.0	**17** 0348 / 1010 / W 1611 / 2230	5.3 / 0.8 / 5.3 / 1.0
3 0344 / 1004 / W 1608 / 2222	5.2 / 0.9 / 5.2 / 0.9	**18** 0428 / 1053 / TH 1654 / 2309	5.3 / 0.7 / 5.2 / 1.1
4 0421 / 1044 / TH 1648 / 2302	5.3 / 0.8 / 5.2 / 0.9	**19** 0507 / 1134 / F 1736 / 2346	5.3 / 0.8 / 5.1 / 1.2
5 0500 / 1125 / F 1732 / 2343	5.3 / 0.8 / 5.2 / 1.0	**20** 0545 / 1214 / SA 1817	5.2 / 0.9 / 5.0
6 0542 / 1210 / SA 1819	5.3 / 0.8 / 5.1	**21** 0022 / 0623 / SU 1254 / 1858	1.4 / 5.1 / 1.1 / 4.8
7 0027 / 0627 / SU 1258 / 1911	1.2 / 5.2 / 0.9 / 5.0	**22** 0059 / 0705 / M 1335 / 1942	1.6 / 4.9 / 1.3 / 4.6
8 0117 / 0719 / M 1352 / 2008	1.4 / 5.1 / 1.0 / 4.8	**23** 0138 / 0751 / TU 1420 / 2030	1.8 / 4.7 / 1.5 / 4.4
9 0214 / 0817 / TU 1453 / ◑ 2110	1.6 / 4.9 / 1.2 / 4.7	**24** 0225 / 0843 / W 1512 / ◑ 2124	2.0 / 4.5 / 1.7 / 4.3
10 0320 / 0922 / W 1600 / 2217	1.7 / 4.8 / 1.2 / 4.6	**25** 0326 / 0942 / TH 1611 / 2223	2.2 / 4.3 / 1.8 / 4.2
11 0430 / 1031 / TH 1709 / 2324	1.7 / 4.8 / 1.3 / 4.7	**26** 0437 / 1046 / F 1714 / 2324	2.2 / 4.3 / 1.8 / 4.3
12 0539 / 1140 / F 1817	1.6 / 4.8 / 1.2	**27** 0544 / 1149 / SA 1814	2.1 / 4.4 / 1.7
13 0029 / 0644 / SA 1245 / 1919	4.8 / 1.4 / 5.0 / 1.1	**28** 0021 / 0642 / SU 1247 / 1908	4.4 / 1.9 / 4.5 / 1.6
14 0127 / 0743 / SU 1344 / 2014	5.0 / 1.2 / 5.1 / 0.9	**29** 0113 / 0733 / M 1338 / 1956	4.6 / 1.6 / 4.7 / 1.4
15 0219 / 0837 / M 1437 / 2104	5.1 / 1.0 / 5.2 / 0.9	**30** 0159 / 0820 / TU 1424 / 2041	4.9 / 1.4 / 4.9 / 1.2

JULY

Time	m	Time	m
1 0241 / 0904 / W 1508 / 2124	5.1 / 1.1 / 5.1 / 1.0	**16** 0335 / 0958 / TH 1559 / ● 2213	5.3 / 0.9 / 5.2 / 1.1
2 0323 / 0948 / TH 1552 / ○ 2207	5.3 / 0.9 / 5.3 / 0.9	**17** 0413 / 1037 / F 1638 / 2250	5.3 / 0.8 / 5.2 / 1.2
3 0404 / 1032 / F 1636 / 2250	5.4 / 0.7 / 5.4 / 0.9	**18** 0448 / 1114 / SA 1715 / 2323	5.3 / 0.9 / 5.1 / 1.2
4 0446 / 1116 / SA 1721 / 2334	5.5 / 0.6 / 5.4 / 0.9	**19** 0523 / 1150 / SU 1751 / 2356	5.3 / 0.9 / 5.1 / 1.3
5 0529 / 1202 / SU 1809	5.5 / 0.6 / 5.3	**20** 0557 / 1225 / M 1827	5.2 / 1.1 / 5.0
6 0018 / 0614 / M 1249 / 1858	1.0 / 5.5 / 0.6 / 5.2	**21** 0028 / 0634 / TU 1300 / 1905	1.4 / 5.1 / 1.2 / 4.8
7 0106 / 0704 / TU 1339 / 1951	1.1 / 5.4 / 0.8 / 5.0	**22** 0102 / 0714 / W 1337 / 1947	1.6 / 4.9 / 1.4 / 4.6
8 0157 / 0758 / W 1434 / ◑ 2048	1.3 / 5.2 / 1.0 / 4.8	**23** 0141 / 0759 / TH 1419 / 2034	1.8 / 4.7 / 1.6 / 4.5
9 0255 / 0859 / TH 1535 / 2150	1.5 / 5.0 / 1.2 / 4.7	**24** 0228 / 0851 / F 1511 / ◑ 2128	2.0 / 4.5 / 1.8 / 4.3
10 0402 / 1007 / F 1642 / 2257	1.7 / 4.8 / 1.4 / 4.6	**25** 0330 / 0951 / SA 1615 / 2229	2.2 / 4.3 / 2.0 / 4.3
11 0513 / 1118 / SA 1754	1.7 / 4.7 / 1.5	**26** 0445 / 1058 / SU 1724 / 2333	2.2 / 4.3 / 1.9 / 4.3
12 0006 / 0625 / SU 1231 / 1902	4.7 / 1.6 / 4.8 / 1.4	**27** 0558 / 1206 / M 1830	2.0 / 4.4 / 1.8
13 0111 / 0731 / M 1336 / 2001	4.8 / 1.4 / 4.9 / 1.3	**28** 0034 / 0701 / TU 1307 / 1928	4.5 / 1.8 / 4.6 / 1.6
14 0206 / 0827 / TU 1430 / 2051	5.0 / 1.2 / 5.0 / 1.3	**29** 0129 / 0755 / W 1401 / 2019	4.8 / 1.4 / 4.9 / 1.3
15 0254 / 0915 / W 1517 / 2134	5.1 / 1.0 / 5.1 / 1.2	**30** 0217 / 0845 / TH 1449 / 2107	5.1 / 1.1 / 5.2 / 1.1
		31 0303 / 0933 / F 1535 / ○ 2152	5.3 / 0.8 / 5.4 / 0.9

AUGUST

Time	m	Time	m
1 0346 / 1019 / SA 1621 / 2237	5.6 / 0.5 / 5.5 / 0.7	**16** 0427 / 1050 / SU 1650 / 2258	5.4 / 0.9 / 5.2 / 1.2
2 0429 / 1104 / SU 1706 / 2320	5.7 / 0.3 / 5.6 / 0.7	**17** 0458 / 1121 / M 1722 / 2328	5.3 / 0.9 / 5.2 / 1.2
3 0513 / 1148 / M 1752	5.8 / 0.3 / 5.6	**18** 0529 / 1152 / TU 1754 / 2357	5.3 / 1.0 / 5.1 / 1.3
4 0004 / 0557 / TU 1233 / 1839	0.7 / 5.8 / 0.4 / 5.5	**19** 0602 / 1223 / W 1829	5.3 / 1.2 / 5.0
5 0048 / 0645 / W 1320 / 1928	0.9 / 5.6 / 0.6 / 5.2	**20** 0029 / 0638 / TH 1258 / 1907	1.4 / 5.2 / 1.4 / 4.8
6 0136 / 0737 / TH 1410 / 2022	1.1 / 5.4 / 1.0 / 5.0	**21** 0105 / 0719 / F 1336 / 1951	1.6 / 4.8 / 1.6 / 4.6
7 0229 / 0836 / F 1507 / ◐ 2121	1.4 / 5.0 / 1.3 / 4.7	**22** 0146 / 0807 / SA 1423 / ◐ 2042	1.8 / 4.6 / 1.8 / 4.4
8 0334 / 0943 / SA 1616 / 2229	1.7 / 4.7 / 1.7 / 4.5	**23** 0238 / 0905 / SU 1524 / 2142	2.1 / 4.4 / 2.0 / 4.3
9 0450 / 1100 / SU 1735 / 2345	1.8 / 4.6 / 1.8 / 4.5	**24** 0352 / 1015 / M 1641 / 2250	2.2 / 4.3 / 2.1 / 4.3
10 0613 / 1222 / M 1851	1.8 / 4.6 / 1.8	**25** 0518 / 1130 / TU 1758 / 2358	2.1 / 4.4 / 2.0 / 4.5
11 0057 / 0723 / TU 1330 / 1950	4.7 / 1.5 / 4.7 / 1.6	**26** 0633 / 1240 / W 1903	1.8 / 4.6 / 1.7
12 0154 / 0818 / W 1422 / 2037	4.9 / 1.3 / 4.9 / 1.5	**27** 0100 / 0733 / TH 1339 / 1958	4.8 / 1.4 / 4.9 / 1.4
13 0240 / 0903 / TH 1505 / 2118	5.1 / 1.1 / 5.1 / 1.4	**28** 0153 / 0826 / F 1429 / 2047	5.1 / 1.0 / 5.3 / 1.1
14 0320 / 0941 / F 1543 / ● 2154	5.2 / 1.0 / 5.2 / 1.3	**29** 0241 / 0915 / SA 1516 / ○ 2134	5.5 / 0.6 / 5.5 / 0.8
15 0355 / 1017 / SA 1618 / 2227	5.3 / 0.9 / 5.2 / 1.2	**30** 0326 / 1001 / SU 1601 / 2218	5.7 / 0.3 / 5.7 / 0.6
		31 0409 / 1045 / M 1645 / 2301	5.9 / 0.2 / 5.8 / 0.5

Chart Datum: 2·85 metres below Ordnance Datum (Newlyn). HAT is 6·1 metres above Chart Datum.

》 FREE monthly updates from 《
www.reedsalmanac.co.uk
159

NE England

STANDARD TIME (UT)
For Summer Time add ONE hour in **non-shaded areas**

RIVER TEES   LAT 54°38'N   LONG 1°09'W
TIMES AND HEIGHTS OF HIGH AND LOW WATERS

Dates in red are SPRINGS
Dates in blue are NEAPS

YEAR 2015

SEPTEMBER

Day	Time	m	Day	Time	m
1 TU	0453 / 1129 / 1730 / 2344	6.0 / 0.2 / 5.8 / 0.6	**16** W	0501 / 1120 / 1721 / 2329	5.3 / 1.0 / 5.2 / 1.2
2 W	0538 / 1212 / 1816	5.9 / 0.3 / 5.6	**17** TH	0532 / 1150 / 1754	5.2 / 1.1 / 5.1
3 TH	0027 / 0624 / 1256 / 1902	0.7 / 5.7 / 0.6 / 5.3	**18** F	0001 / 0606 / 1224 / 1831	1.3 / 5.1 / 1.3 / 5.0
4 F	0113 / 0715 / 1344 / 1953	1.0 / 5.4 / 1.1 / 5.0	**19** SA	0035 / 0645 / 1301 / 1913	1.5 / 4.9 / 1.5 / 4.8
5 SA	0204 / 0813 / 1439 / 2051	1.4 / 5.0 / 1.5 / 4.7	**20** SU	0115 / 0731 / 1346 / 2002	1.7 / 4.7 / 1.8 / 4.5
6 SU	0308 / 0921 / 1548 / 2200	1.7 / 4.6 / 1.9 / 4.4	**21** M	0203 / 0829 / 1443 / 2102	1.9 / 4.4 / 2.1 / 4.4
7 M	0430 / 1042 / 1715 / 2320	1.9 / 4.4 / 2.1 / 4.4	**22** TU	0312 / 0941 / 1603 / 2212	2.1 / 4.3 / 2.2 / 4.3
8 TU	0600 / 1210 / 1835	1.8 / 4.4 / 2.0	**23** W	0444 / 1100 / 1728 / 2325	2.0 / 4.4 / 2.1 / 4.5
9 W	0037 / 0709 / 1318 / 1933	4.6 / 1.6 / 4.6 / 1.8	**24** TH	0606 / 1214 / 1838	1.7 / 4.6 / 1.8
10 TH	0135 / 0801 / 1406 / 2018	4.8 / 1.4 / 4.8 / 1.6	**25** F	0031 / 0710 / 1316 / 1934	4.8 / 1.3 / 5.0 / 1.4
11 F	0220 / 0842 / 1446 / 2056	5.0 / 1.2 / 5.0 / 1.5	**26** SA	0127 / 0804 / 1407 / 2025	5.2 / 0.9 / 5.3 / 1.1
12 SA	0258 / 0918 / 1521 / 2130	5.2 / 1.0 / 5.2 / 1.3	**27** SU	0217 / 0853 / 1454 / 2112	5.5 / 0.5 / 5.6 / 0.8
13 SU	0332 / 0950 / 1553 / 2201	5.3 / 0.9 / 5.2 / 1.2	**28** M	0303 / 0939 / 1538 / 2156	5.8 / 0.3 / 5.8 / 0.6
14 M	0403 / 1021 / 1623 / 2231	5.4 / 0.9 / 5.3 / 1.1	**29** TU	0347 / 1023 / 1622 / 2240	6.0 / 0.2 / 5.9 / 0.5
15 TU	0432 / 1051 / 1651 / 2300	5.4 / 0.9 / 5.3 / 1.1	**30** W	0432 / 1106 / 1706 / 2323	6.0 / 0.2 / 5.8 / 0.5

OCTOBER

Day	Time	m	Day	Time	m
1 TH	0517 / 1148 / 1750	5.9 / 0.4 / 5.6	**16** F	0506 / 1121 / 1724 / 2337	5.2 / 1.1 / 5.2 / 1.2
2 F	0006 / 0604 / 1232 / 1836	0.7 / 5.7 / 0.8 / 5.4	**17** SA	0540 / 1155 / 1801	5.1 / 1.3 / 5.1
3 SA	0052 / 0655 / 1317 / 1925	0.9 / 5.3 / 1.2 / 5.1	**18** SU	0012 / 0620 / 1234 / 1842	1.4 / 4.9 / 1.5 / 4.9
4 SU	0142 / 0752 / 1410 / 2021	1.3 / 4.9 / 1.7 / 4.7	**19** M	0053 / 0707 / 1317 / 1930	1.6 / 4.7 / 1.8 / 4.7
5 M	0244 / 0859 / 1518 / 2128	1.7 / 4.6 / 2.1 / 4.5	**20** TU	0142 / 0805 / 1413 / 2030	1.7 / 4.5 / 2.0 / 4.5
6 TU	0404 / 1018 / 1644 / 2247	1.9 / 4.3 / 2.3 / 4.4	**21** W	0248 / 0916 / 1531 / 2139	1.9 / 4.4 / 2.2 / 4.5
7 W	0533 / 1144 / 1806	1.9 / 4.3 / 2.2	**22** TH	0415 / 1033 / 1657 / 2252	1.9 / 4.4 / 2.1 / 4.6
8 TH	0005 / 0641 / 1252 / 1904	4.5 / 1.7 / 4.5 / 2.0	**23** F	0536 / 1147 / 1808	1.6 / 4.7 / 1.8
9 F	0105 / 0732 / 1340 / 1950	4.7 / 1.5 / 4.8 / 1.8	**24** SA	0000 / 0642 / 1250 / 1907	4.8 / 1.3 / 5.0 / 1.5
10 SA	0151 / 0812 / 1419 / 2028	4.9 / 1.3 / 5.0 / 1.6	**25** SU	0100 / 0738 / 1343 / 2000	5.2 / 0.9 / 5.3 / 1.1
11 SU	0230 / 0848 / 1453 / 2102	5.1 / 1.1 / 5.1 / 1.4	**26** M	0152 / 0828 / 1431 / 2048	5.5 / 0.6 / 5.6 / 0.8
12 M	0304 / 0920 / 1525 / 2134	5.2 / 1.0 / 5.2 / 1.2	**27** TU	0240 / 0915 / 1516 / 2135	5.8 / 0.4 / 5.8 / 0.6
13 TU	0336 / 0951 / 1553 / 2204	5.3 / 1.0 / 5.3 / 1.1	**28** W	0327 / 1000 / 1600 / 2220	5.9 / 0.3 / 5.8 / 0.5
14 W	0406 / 1021 / 1621 / 2234	5.3 / 1.0 / 5.3 / 1.1	**29** TH	0413 / 1044 / 1643 / 2304	5.9 / 0.4 / 5.8 / 0.5
15 TH	0435 / 1050 / 1651 / 2304	5.3 / 1.0 / 5.3 / 1.1	**30** F	0500 / 1126 / 1727 / 2348	5.8 / 0.6 / 5.6 / 0.7
			31 SA	0548 / 1209 / 1811	5.6 / 1.0 / 5.4

NOVEMBER

Day	Time	m	Day	Time	m
1 SU	0033 / 0637 / 1253 / 1858	0.9 / 5.2 / 1.4 / 5.1	**16** M	0605 / 1214 / 1820	5.0 / 1.5 / 5.1
2 M	0123 / 0731 / 1341 / 1950	1.2 / 4.9 / 1.8 / 4.8	**17** TU	0040 / 0653 / 1259 / 1907	1.3 / 4.8 / 1.7 / 4.9
3 TU	0219 / 0833 / 1442 / 2051	1.6 / 4.5 / 2.2 / 4.6	**18** W	0130 / 0750 / 1353 / 2004	1.5 / 4.7 / 1.9 / 4.8
4 W	0328 / 0943 / 1559 / 2202	1.8 / 4.3 / 2.4 / 4.4	**19** TH	0232 / 0855 / 1503 / 2109	1.6 / 4.5 / 2.1 / 4.7
5 TH	0447 / 1059 / 1719 / 2317	1.9 / 4.3 / 2.4 / 4.4	**20** F	0347 / 1007 / 1623 / 2220	1.6 / 4.5 / 2.1 / 4.7
6 F	0557 / 1208 / 1824	1.8 / 4.4 / 2.2	**21** SA	0503 / 1118 / 1735 / 2329	1.5 / 4.7 / 1.9 / 4.9
7 SA	0021 / 0651 / 1302 / 1913	4.6 / 1.6 / 4.6 / 2.0	**22** SU	0611 / 1222 / 1839	1.3 / 4.9 / 1.6
8 SU	0113 / 0735 / 1344 / 1955	4.7 / 1.4 / 4.8 / 1.7	**23** M	0032 / 0711 / 1319 / 1935	5.1 / 1.0 / 5.2 / 1.3
9 M	0156 / 0814 / 1421 / 2032	4.9 / 1.3 / 5.0 / 1.5	**24** TU	0129 / 0805 / 1409 / 2027	5.4 / 0.8 / 5.4 / 1.0
10 TU	0234 / 0849 / 1454 / 2106	5.1 / 1.2 / 5.2 / 1.3	**25** W	0222 / 0854 / 1456 / 2116	5.6 / 0.7 / 5.6 / 0.8
11 W	0308 / 0922 / 1524 / 2138	5.2 / 1.1 / 5.3 / 1.2	**26** TH	0311 / 0941 / 1541 / 2203	5.7 / 0.6 / 5.7 / 0.6
12 TH	0341 / 0953 / 1554 / 2211	5.2 / 1.1 / 5.3 / 1.1	**27** F	0359 / 1025 / 1624 / 2248	5.7 / 0.7 / 5.6 / 0.6
13 F	0413 / 1025 / 1626 / 2244	5.2 / 1.1 / 5.3 / 1.1	**28** SA	0446 / 1108 / 1707 / 2333	5.6 / 0.9 / 5.6 / 0.7
14 SA	0446 / 1058 / 1701 / 2319	5.2 / 1.1 / 5.3 / 1.1	**29** SU	0533 / 1149 / 1750	5.4 / 1.1 / 5.4
15 SU	0523 / 1135 / 1738 / 2357	5.1 / 1.3 / 5.2 / 1.2	**30** M	0017 / 0620 / 1231 / 1833	0.9 / 5.2 / 1.4 / 5.2

DECEMBER

Day	Time	m	Day	Time	m
1 TU	0102 / 0709 / 1313 / 1919	1.1 / 4.9 / 1.7 / 5.0	**16** W	0031 / 0642 / 1247 / 1850	1.0 / 5.0 / 1.5 / 5.2
2 W	0151 / 0801 / 1402 / 2011	1.4 / 4.6 / 2.0 / 4.7	**17** TH	0120 / 0735 / 1337 / 1942	1.1 / 4.9 / 1.7 / 5.0
3 TH	0246 / 0859 / 1502 / 2111	1.7 / 4.4 / 2.3 / 4.5	**18** F	0215 / 0834 / 1438 / 2043	1.3 / 4.7 / 1.8 / 4.9
4 F	0349 / 1003 / 1615 / 2218	1.9 / 4.3 / 2.4 / 4.4	**19** SA	0319 / 0939 / 1548 / 2150	1.4 / 4.6 / 1.9 / 4.8
5 SA	0457 / 1109 / 1727 / 2325	1.9 / 4.3 / 2.3 / 4.4	**20** SU	0429 / 1047 / 1701 / 2259	1.4 / 4.6 / 1.9 / 4.8
6 SU	0600 / 1210 / 1828	1.8 / 4.4 / 2.2	**21** M	0540 / 1154 / 1811	1.4 / 4.7 / 1.9
7 M	0025 / 0653 / 1301 / 1917	4.5 / 1.7 / 4.6 / 1.9	**22** TU	0008 / 0647 / 1257 / 1915	4.9 / 1.3 / 5.0 / 1.4
8 TU	0117 / 0737 / 1344 / 1959	4.7 / 1.5 / 4.8 / 1.7	**23** W	0112 / 0747 / 1352 / 2012	5.1 / 1.1 / 5.2 / 1.2
9 W	0201 / 0817 / 1422 / 2038	4.8 / 1.4 / 5.0 / 1.5	**24** TH	0210 / 0839 / 1442 / 2104	5.2 / 1.0 / 5.3 / 1.0
10 TH	0241 / 0854 / 1457 / 2115	5.0 / 1.2 / 5.2 / 1.3	**25** F	0302 / 0927 / 1528 / 2152	5.4 / 1.0 / 5.5 / 0.8
11 F	0318 / 0929 / 1531 / 2152	5.1 / 1.2 / 5.3 / 1.1	**26** SA	0350 / 1011 / 1611 / 2236	5.4 / 1.1 / 5.5 / 0.7
12 SA	0355 / 1005 / 1606 / 2229	5.2 / 1.1 / 5.4 / 1.0	**27** SU	0435 / 1052 / 1651 / 2318	5.4 / 1.1 / 5.5 / 0.7
13 SU	0432 / 1042 / 1643 / 2307	5.2 / 1.1 / 5.4 / 1.0	**28** M	0519 / 1131 / 1730 / 2359	5.3 / 1.2 / 5.4 / 0.8
14 M	0512 / 1121 / 1722 / 2348	5.2 / 1.2 / 5.4 / 1.0	**29** TU	0601 / 1208 / 1809	5.2 / 1.4 / 5.3
15 TU	0555 / 1202 / 1804	5.1 / 1.3 / 5.3	**30** W	0039 / 0642 / 1244 / 1849	1.0 / 5.0 / 1.6 / 5.1
			31 TH	0119 / 0725 / 1321 / 1933	1.2 / 4.8 / 1.8 / 4.9

Chart Datum: 2·85 metres below Ordnance Datum (Newlyn). HAT is 6·1 metres above Chart Datum.

3.14 HARTLEPOOL

Hartlepool **54°41'·26N 01°11'·90W** (West Hbr ent) ⊛⊛♤♤♤♧♧

CHARTS AC 152, 2567, 2566, 5615; Imray C24

TIDES +0437 Dover; ML 3·0; Duration 0600

Standard Port RIVER TEES (←—)

Times				Height (metres)			
High Water		Low Water		MHWS	MHWN	MLWN	MLWS
0000	0600	0000	0600	5·5	4·3	2·0	0·9
1200	1800	1200	1800				
Differences HARTLEPOOL							
–0004	–0004	–0006	–0006	–0·1	–0·1	–0·2	–0·1
MIDDLESBROUGH							
0000	+0002	0000	–0003	+0·1	+0·2	+0·1	–0·1

SHELTER Excellent in marina (5m) 4Ca SW of port. Strong E/SE winds raise broken water and swell in the bay, making ent channel hazardous, but possible. In such conditions, ask marina's advice.

NAVIGATION WPT 54°40'·86N 01°09'·90W, Longscar ECM buoy, 295°/1·06M to W Hbr ent. (For Victoria Hbr, 308°/0·65M to Nos 1/2 buoys.) From S, beware Longscar Rks, 4ca WSW of WPT. Tees Fairway SWM buoy, (54°40'·94N 01°06'·47W) is 2M E of Longscar ECM buoy and may assist the landfall. Tees Bay Wind Farm, consists of 27 turbines (extremities Fl Y 5s 13m 5M) up to 1½M offshore SE of the Tees channel as far as West Scar. Speed limit 4kn in W Hbr.

LIGHTS AND MARKS Tees Fairway Iso 4s 8m 8M, Horn(1) 5s. Longscar ECM buoy Q(3), bell, lies off the entrance. Steetly Works chimney, 1·4M NW of marina ent, and St Hilda's Church tower on The Heugh, are both prominent. Entry to commercial port on ldg lt Dir Iso WRG 324° following clearly buoyed channel. Dir lt Fl WRG leads 308° to marina lock, between W Hbr outer piers, Oc R and Oc G, and inner piers, FR and FG; bright street lts on S pier.

Lock sigs: ● = Proceed; ● = Wait; ● ● = Lock closed.

Dir lt, Iso WRG, leads 325° via lit buoyed chan to Victoria Hbr.

COMMUNICATIONS (Code 01429) MRCC (01262) 672317; ⊜ (0191) 257 9441; Police 101; Dr 272679; Tees Port Authority (01642) 277205; Marina Lock Ch M, 80. Marina Ch **M**, 80. *Tees Port Control* info Ch 14, 22 (H24). *Hartlepool Dock Radio* Ch 12, only for ship docking.

FACILITIES

Hartlepool Marina Access via channel dredged to CD and lock (max beam 8.5m), over tidal cill 0.8m below CD, (HW± 5), (H24). www.hartlepool-marina.com ☎ 865744, 500+100 ♥, £2.16. D (H24), LPG, BY, ⊡, ⚒, ◿, ⚠, ⚒, ◻, ⚓, ⛴, BH (40 and 300 tons), C (13 tons), Gas, Gaz.

Victoria Hbr (commercial dock, not normally for yachts), access H24. Call *Tees Port Control* Ch 14 for short-stay.

Tees & Hartlepool YC ☎ 233423, ⌨, ◣.

Town ⌕ & ⌕, ⛟, (H24), R, ⌨, ✉, ⑧, ⇌, ✈ (Teesside).

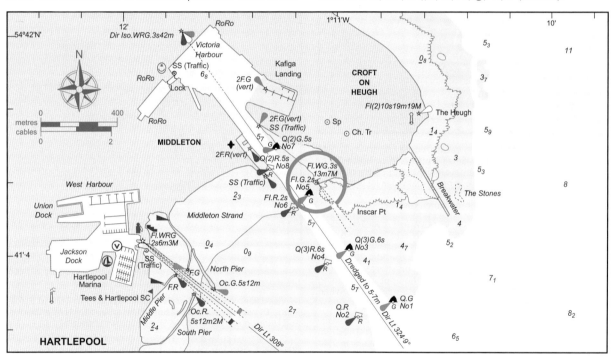

HARTLEPOOL TO SOUTHERN NETHERLANDS

(AC 2182A, 1191, 1190, 1503, 1408, 1610, 3371, 110) From abeam Whitby the passage can, theoretically, be made on one direct course, but this would conflict with oil/gas activities and platforms including Rough and Amethyst fields off Humber, Hewett off Cromer and very extensive fields further offshore. Commercial, oil-rig support and fishing vessels may be met S of Flamborough Hd and particularly off NE Norfolk where it is advisable to follow an inshore track.

After passing Flamborough Hd, Dowsing B1D, Dudgeon lt buoy and Newarp lt F, either:

Proceed SE'ly to take departure from the Outer Gabbard; thence cross N Hinder South TSS at right angles before heading for Roompotsluis via Middelbank and subsequent buoyed chan.

Or set course ESE from the vicinity of Cross Sand lt buoy and Smith's Knoll, so as to cross the N/S deep-water traffic routes to the E. Thence alter SE towards Hoek van Holland, keeping N of Maas Approaches TSS.

HARTLEPOOL TO THE GERMAN BIGHT

(AC 2182A, 1191, 266, 1405) Taking departure eastward from abeam Whitby High lt, skirt the SW Patch off Dogger Bank, keeping clear S of Gordon Gas Field and then N of German Bight W Approach TSS. Thence head for the Elbe or Helgoland; the latter may also serve as a convenient haven in order to adjust the passage for Elbe tides and streams, without greatly increasing passage distance. ▶ *Tidal streams are less than 1kn away from the coast and run E/W along much of the route.* ◀

NE England

3.15 SEAHAM

Durham **54°50'·24N 01°19'·28W** ❄❄❄

CHARTS AC 152, 1627, 5615; Imray C24

TIDES +0435 Dover; ML 3·0; Duration 0600

Standard Port RIVER TEES (←—)

Times				Height (metres)			
High Water		Low Water		MHWS	MHWN	MLWN	MLWS
0000	0600	0000	0600	5·5	4·3	2·0	0·9
1200	1800	1200	1800				
Differences SEAHAM							
–0015	–0015	–0015	–0015	–0·3	–0·2	0·0	–0·2

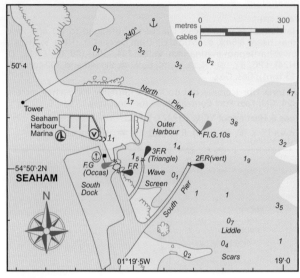

SHELTER Prior to arrival visiting yachts should confirm with HM availability/suitability of berth. Small craft berth in North Dock, now a marina with an automatic gate maintaining 1.5m min depth near the entrance. South Dock is not usually available to non-commercial vessels. Speed limit 5kn. Or ⚓ 2½ca offshore with clock tower in transit 240° with St John's church tower.

NAVIGATION WPT 54°50'·36N 01°18'·60W (off chartlet), 256°/ 0·40M to N breakwater lighthouse. Shoals and rocks to S of S breakwater (Liddle Scars). Outer harbour is shallow, min depth 1.2m, and the harbour can be subject to considerable swell; entrance should not be attempted in strong on-shore winds. The N Dock lies to the right of S Dock gates, the appr chan leading between small drying basins. Automatic gate opens/shuts when HoT 2.5m above CD (approx HW ±3½).

LIGHTS AND MARKS No leading lights, but harbour is easily identified by lighthouse (W with B bands) on N pier, Fl G 10s 12m 5M. FS at NE corner of S dock on with N lighthouse leads in 256° clear of Tangle Rocks. 3FR lts on wave screen are in form of a △.

Traffic sigs at S Dock: ● = Vessels enter: ● = Vessels leave.

Traffic sigs at N Dock gate: 3 ● (vert) = shut : 3 ● (vert) = open.

COMMUNICATIONS (Code 0191) MRCC (01262) 672317; Police 101; Dr 5812332. HM 07801 215236.

VHF Ch **12** 16 06 0800–1700 (Mon-Fri), *Seaham Marina* Ch 80.

FACILITIES S Dock (Seaham Hbr Dock Co) ☎ 516 1700, ➰ £5 but normally no charge for the odd night, L, ⚓, C (40 ton), ➰; **N Dock** Marina (78 inc 3 Ⓥ up to 10m).

Town (½M) 🅿 & 🅿, ⚓ and 🅗. ✎ and 🅛 available out of town (about 5M). 🍴, ✕, 🛒, ✉, Ⓑ, ⇌, ✈ (Teesside or Newcastle).

3.16 SUNDERLAND

Tyne and Wear **54°55'·23N 01°21'·15W** ❄❄❄❄❄❄

CHARTS AC 152, 1627, 5615; Imray C24

TIDES +0430 Dover; ML 2·9; Duration 0600; Zone 0 (UT)

Standard Port RIVER TEES (←—)

Times				Height (metres)			
High Water		Low Water		MHWS	MHWN	MLWN	MLWS
0000	0600	0000	0600	5·5	4·3	2·0	0·9
1200	1800	1200	1800				
Differences SUNDERLAND							
–0017	–0017	–0016	–0016	–0·2	–0·1	0·0	0·0

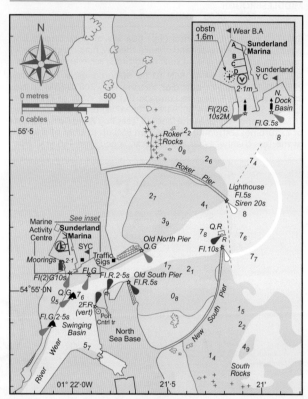

SHELTER Very good, but strong Easterlies cause heavy swell in entrance and outer harbour. Marina is protected by a fixed breakwater; access H24.

NAVIGATION WPT 54°55'·21N 01°20'·10W, 278°/0·61M to Roker Pier lt. Beware wreck at Whitburn Steel, about 1M N of entrance, and Hendon Rk (0·9m), 1·2M SE of harbour entrance.

Appr to marina ent is marked by SHM dolphin, Fl G 5s, and E jetty, Fl (2) G 10s. Close (4m) SSW of end of pontoon D, beware substantial obst'n (1·6m) in surrounding depth 2·1m, see chartlet.

LIGHTS AND MARKS 3 Fl ● at Pilot Stn (Old N Pier) = danger in harbour; no entry/departure.

COMMUNICATIONS (Code 0191) MRCC (01262) 672317; ⊖ (0191) 257 9441; Police 101; 🄷 565 6256. HM 567 2626 (HO), 567 0161 (OT).

Sunderland Marina Ch M, 80. Port VHF Ch **14** (H24); tide and visibility reports on request.

FACILITIES Sunderland Marina 120 pontoon berths in 2·1m, max LOA 13m; and 110 moorings. ☎ 5144721. Ⓥ (if available) £2.05/m; M £10/craft, ⚓, D (H24), ⚓, ⚓, ⚓.

Sunderland YC ☎ 567 5133, ⚓, ➰, 🛒, ⚓ (dinghy).

Wear Boating Association ☎ 567 5313, ➰.

Services: 🅛, 🅗, ✎, ⚓,

Town 🅿, Gas, Gaz, 🍴, ✕, 🛒, ✉, 🗓, Ⓑ, ⇌, ✈ (Newcastle).

3.17   R TYNE/NORTH SHIELDS

Tyne and Wear **55°00'·89N 01°24'·10W** ❀❀❀⚓⚓⚓❁❁

CHARTS AC 152, 1191, 1934, 5615; Imray C24

TIDES +0430 Dover; ML 3·0; Duration 0604

Standard Port NORTH SHIELDS (→)

Times				Height (metres)			
High Water		Low Water		MHWS	MHWN	MLWN	MLWS
0200	0800	0100	0800	5·0	3·9	1·8	0·7
1400	2000	1300	2000				
Differences NEWCASTLE-UPON-TYNE							
+0003	+0003	+0008	+0008	+0·3	+0·2	+0·1	+0·1

SHELTER Good in all weather. Access H24, but in strong E and NE winds appr may be difficult for smaller craft due to much backwash off the piers. Confused seas can build at the ent in severe weather, and a large steep swell can break dangerously when meeting an ebb tide up to half a mile inside the harbour. In emergency or as a refuge yachts may berth on Fish Quay; contact HM.

NAVIGATION WPT 55°01'·00N 01°23'·00W, 250°/0·7M to hbr ent following recommended route in Ldg lt Oc sector. Outbound keep S of hbr ent centreline. From S, no dangers. From N, beware Bellhues Rk (approx 1M N of hbr and ¾M off shore); give N pier a wide berth. Dredged chan in Lower Hbr is buoyed. 6kn speed limit in the river west of Herd Groyne Lt Ho. In river proceed under power keeping to the starboard side. Tacking across the channel is prohibited. The 7 bridges at Newcastle have least clearance above HAT of 25m, or 4·5m when Millennium Bridge is closed.

LIGHTS AND MARKS See 3.3 and chartlet. W Lt LFl 10s shows from centre span of the Millennium Bridge when fully open.

COMMUNICATIONS (Code 0191) MRCC (01262) 672317; Met 2326453; Police 101; Ⓗ (Tynemouth) 2596660; Ⓗ (Newcastle) 2325131. HM 2570407; Tyne VTS 2572080. *Tyne VTS* Ch **12**, 11 (H24). Marinas: Royal Quays Ch 80. St Peter's Ch 80 M.

FACILITIES Notes: A conservancy fee (£10) may be levied by the Port Authority on all visiting craft. Craft waiting to enter the marinas should do so outside the fairway.

Royal Quays Marina ⚓ 54°59'·79N 01°26'·84W, in former Albert Edward Dock, is 2M upriver from pierheads. ☎ 2728282; 302 berths inc Ⓥ, 7·9m depth; £2.30. Lock (42.5m x 7.5m) departures H and H+30; arrivals H+15 and H+45, or on request at quiet times, H24. Waiting pontoon outside lock. BY, BH (30 ton), D, P (H24), ⚓, Ⓞ, Ⓑ, Gas, Gaz, ▯, ⛟.

St Peter's Marina 54°57'·94N 01°34'·35W, 8M upriver, and 1M E of city. ☎ 2654472; 140 + 20 Ⓥ, £2.27. Access approx HW±3½ over sill, dries 0·8m, which retains 2·5m within. Traffic lights at ent. P on pontoon outside ent in 2m, Ⓞ. **Services.** ✎, ✗, ◣, C, ACA, Ⓔ.

Millennium Bridge in city centre, limited pontoon berthing below the bridge; pre-book ☎ 2211363.

Newcastle City Marina enquiries@newcastlecitymarina.co.uk ☎ 2211348, mob 07435 788426; Boats <26m: price on sliding scale 5m £10 → £30 >14m, short stay < 5hrs free. Ⓓ, ⚓.

City. All amenities, ⇌ (Newcastle/S Shields), ✈ (Newcastle). **Ferries:** Ijmuiden; daily; 16 hrs; DFDS (www.dfdsseaways.co.uk).

ADJACENT HARBOUR

CULLERCOATS, 55°02'·08N 01°25'·81W. AC 1191. +0430 Dover. Tides as 3.16. Small drying hbr 1·6M N of R Tyne ent. Appr on ldg line 256°, two bns (FR lts), between drying rks. An occas fair weather ‡ or dry against S pier. Facilities at Tynemouth.

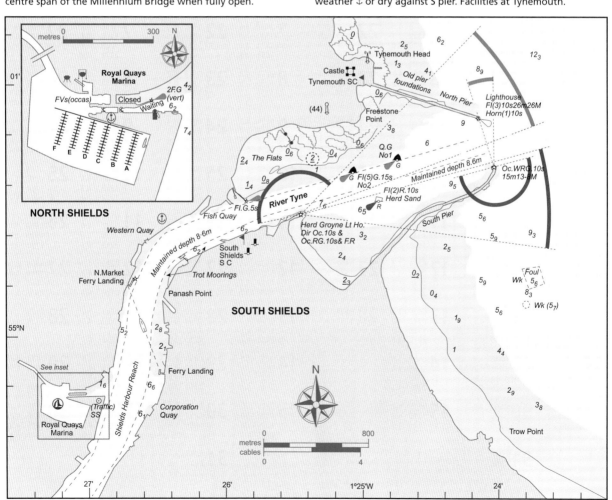

STANDARD TIME (UT)
For Summer Time add ONE hour in **non-shaded areas**

RIVER TYNE/NORTH SHIELDS   LAT 55°00'N   LONG 1°26'W
TIMES AND HEIGHTS OF HIGH AND LOW WATERS

Dates in red are **SPRINGS**
Dates in blue are **NEAPS**

YEAR 2015

JANUARY

Day	Time	m	Day	Time	m
1 TH	0624 / 1233 / 1854	1.5 / 4.5 / 1.6	16 F	0536 / 1146 / 1809	1.8 / 4.2 / 1.9
2 F	0054 / 0724 / 1329 / 1951	4.6 / 1.4 / 4.7 / 1.4	17 SA	0013 / 0640 / 1248 / 1911	4.2 / 1.6 / 4.4 / 1.6
3 SA	0151 / 0814 / 1416 / 2041	4.7 / 1.3 / 4.8 / 1.2	18 SU	0116 / 0736 / 1340 / 2005	4.5 / 1.4 / 4.7 / 1.3
4 SU	0238 / 0857 / 1457 / 2124	4.8 / 1.3 / 4.9 / 1.0	19 M	0208 / 0826 / 1425 / 2054	4.8 / 1.2 / 4.9 / 0.9
5 M	0320 / 0935 / 1535 / 2202	4.9 / 1.2 / 5.0 / 0.9	20 TU	0255 / 0913 / 1508 / 2142	5.0 / 0.9 / 5.2 / 0.6
6 TU	0359 / 1010 / 1610 / 2238	4.9 / 1.2 / 5.1 / 0.9	21 W	0340 / 0958 / 1551 / 2228	5.2 / 0.8 / 5.4 / 0.4
7 W	0435 / 1043 / 1644 / 2312	4.9 / 1.2 / 5.0 / 0.9	22 TH	0425 / 1043 / 1634 / 2314	5.3 / 0.7 / 5.5 / 0.3
8 TH	0511 / 1114 / 1717 / 2345	4.8 / 1.3 / 5.0 / 1.0	23 F	0511 / 1126 / 1718 / 2359	5.3 / 0.7 / 5.5 / 0.3
9 F	0546 / 1145 / 1752	4.7 / 1.4 / 4.9	24 SA	0558 / 1210 / 1805	5.2 / 0.8 / 5.4
10 SA	0019 / 0622 / 1218 / 1828	1.1 / 4.6 / 1.5 / 4.8	25 SU	0045 / 0647 / 1255 / 1855	0.5 / 5.0 / 1.0 / 5.2
11 SU	0055 / 0701 / 1254 / 1908	1.3 / 4.4 / 1.7 / 4.6	26 M	0133 / 0740 / 1345 / 1950	0.8 / 4.7 / 1.3 / 4.9
12 M	0134 / 0744 / 1335 / 1953	1.5 / 4.3 / 1.8 / 4.4	27 TU	0226 / 0838 / 1443 / 2054	1.1 / 4.5 / 1.6 / 4.6
13 TU	0221 / 0833 / 1426 / 2046	1.6 / 4.1 / 2.0 / 4.2	28 W	0329 / 0942 / 1556 / 2206	1.4 / 4.3 / 1.8 / 4.4
14 W	0317 / 0932 / 1534 / 2150	1.8 / 4.0 / 2.1 / 4.1	29 TH	0442 / 1055 / 1718 / 2326	1.7 / 4.2 / 1.8 / 4.3
15 TH	0426 / 1037 / 1655 / 2301	1.9 / 4.0 / 2.1 / 4.1	30 F	0600 / 1209 / 1838	1.8 / 4.3 / 1.7
			31 SA	0041 / 0709 / 1313 / 1941	4.3 / 1.7 / 4.4 / 1.5

FEBRUARY

Day	Time	m	Day	Time	m
1 SU	0142 / 0802 / 1403 / 2030	4.4 / 1.6 / 4.6 / 1.3	16 M	0052 / 0714 / 1315 / 1945	4.4 / 1.5 / 4.5 / 1.2
2 M	0229 / 0844 / 1445 / 2111	4.5 / 1.4 / 4.8 / 1.1	17 TU	0150 / 0809 / 1405 / 2038	4.7 / 1.2 / 4.9 / 0.8
3 TU	0309 / 0921 / 1521 / 2147	4.7 / 1.3 / 4.9 / 0.9	18 W	0239 / 0857 / 1450 / 2126	5.0 / 0.9 / 5.2 / 0.4
4 W	0344 / 0953 / 1553 / 2219	4.8 / 1.2 / 5.0 / 0.9	19 TH	0324 / 0943 / 1533 / 2212	5.2 / 0.6 / 5.5 / 0.2
5 TH	0416 / 1024 / 1625 / 2250	4.8 / 1.1 / 5.0 / 0.8	20 F	0408 / 1026 / 1616 / 2257	5.4 / 0.5 / 5.6 / 0.1
6 F	0448 / 1053 / 1655 / 2321	4.8 / 1.1 / 5.0 / 0.8	21 SA	0452 / 1109 / 1700 / 2340	5.4 / 0.5 / 5.6 / 0.1
7 SA	0519 / 1122 / 1726 / 2352	4.7 / 1.1 / 5.0 / 0.9	22 SU	0537 / 1151 / 1746	5.3 / 0.6 / 5.5
8 SU	0551 / 1152 / 1759	4.7 / 1.2 / 4.9	23 M	0024 / 0622 / 1234 / 1834	0.4 / 5.1 / 0.8 / 5.2
9 M	0024 / 0625 / 1224 / 1834	1.1 / 4.6 / 1.4 / 4.7	24 TU	0108 / 0711 / 1320 / 1927	0.7 / 4.8 / 1.1 / 4.9
10 TU	0058 / 0701 / 1259 / 1913	1.2 / 4.4 / 1.6 / 4.5	25 W	0155 / 0805 / 1414 / 2028	1.1 / 4.5 / 1.4 / 4.5
11 W	0137 / 0744 / 1341 / 1959	1.5 / 4.3 / 1.7 / 4.3	26 TH	0252 / 0907 / 1523 / 2140	1.6 / 4.2 / 1.7 / 4.2
12 TH	0224 / 0836 / 1438 / 2059	1.7 / 4.1 / 1.9 / 4.1	27 F	0407 / 1020 / 1650 / 2302	1.9 / 4.1 / 1.8 / 4.0
13 F	0329 / 0942 / 1558 / 2215	1.9 / 4.0 / 2.0 / 4.0	28 SA	0534 / 1141 / 1819	2.0 / 4.1 / 1.7
14 SA	0451 / 1058 / 1728 / 2339	1.9 / 4.0 / 1.9 / 4.1			
15 SU	0609 / 1213 / 1844	1.7 / 4.2 / 1.6			

MARCH

Day	Time	m	Day	Time	m
1 SU	0024 / 0651 / 1251 / 1924	4.1 / 1.9 / 4.2 / 1.5	16 M	0542 / 1141 / 1818	1.8 / 4.2 / 1.5
2 M	0127 / 0745 / 1344 / 2012	4.3 / 1.7 / 4.4 / 1.3	17 TU	0030 / 0652 / 1248 / 1923	4.4 / 1.5 / 4.5 / 1.1
3 TU	0213 / 0826 / 1426 / 2051	4.4 / 1.5 / 4.6 / 1.1	18 W	0130 / 0749 / 1342 / 2018	4.7 / 1.2 / 4.9 / 0.7
4 W	0250 / 0901 / 1501 / 2124	4.6 / 1.3 / 4.8 / 0.9	19 TH	0219 / 0838 / 1429 / 2106	5.0 / 0.8 / 5.2 / 0.3
5 TH	0323 / 0932 / 1532 / 2155	4.7 / 1.1 / 4.9 / 0.8	20 F	0304 / 0923 / 1513 / 2152	5.2 / 0.6 / 5.5 / 0.1
6 F	0353 / 1002 / 1602 / 2225	4.8 / 1.0 / 5.0 / 0.8	21 SA	0347 / 1007 / 1556 / 2236	5.4 / 0.4 / 5.6 / 0.1
7 SA	0422 / 1030 / 1631 / 2254	4.8 / 1.0 / 5.0 / 0.8	22 SU	0430 / 1049 / 1641 / 2318	5.4 / 0.4 / 5.6 / 0.2
8 SU	0451 / 1059 / 1701 / 2324	4.8 / 1.0 / 5.0 / 0.8	23 M	0513 / 1131 / 1727	5.3 / 0.5 / 5.4
9 M	0521 / 1128 / 1733 / 2355	4.8 / 1.0 / 4.9 / 0.9	24 TU	0000 / 0556 / 1214 / 1815	0.4 / 5.1 / 0.7 / 5.2
10 TU	0553 / 1159 / 1806	4.7 / 1.1 / 4.7	25 W	0041 / 0642 / 1259 / 1907	0.8 / 4.8 / 0.9 / 4.8
11 W	0027 / 0627 / 1231 / 1843	1.1 / 4.6 / 1.3 / 4.6	26 TH	0125 / 0733 / 1349 / 2006	1.2 / 4.5 / 1.3 / 4.4
12 TH	0103 / 0707 / 1313 / 1929	1.3 / 4.4 / 1.5 / 4.4	27 F	0217 / 0832 / 1453 / 2114	1.7 / 4.2 / 1.6 / 4.1
13 F	0147 / 0756 / 1406 / 2028	1.6 / 4.2 / 1.7 / 4.2	28 SA	0328 / 0942 / 1617 / 2232	2.0 / 4.0 / 1.8 / 3.9
14 SA	0249 / 0901 / 1522 / 2146	1.8 / 4.1 / 1.8 / 4.0	29 SU	0458 / 1102 / 1746 / 2354	2.1 / 4.0 / 1.7 / 4.0
15 SU	0415 / 1020 / 1656 / 2313	1.9 / 4.0 / 1.8 / 4.1	30 M	0620 / 1217 / 1854	2.0 / 4.1 / 1.6
			31 TU	0058 / 0717 / 1314 / 1942	4.1 / 1.8 / 4.3 / 1.3

APRIL

Day	Time	m	Day	Time	m
1 W	0145 / 0759 / 1358 / 2020	4.3 / 1.6 / 4.5 / 1.1	16 TH	0108 / 0725 / 1317 / 1954	4.7 / 1.2 / 4.8 / 0.6
2 TH	0222 / 0834 / 1434 / 2054	4.5 / 1.3 / 4.7 / 1.0	17 F	0158 / 0815 / 1406 / 2044	5.0 / 0.9 / 5.1 / 0.3
3 F	0255 / 0906 / 1506 / 2125	4.7 / 1.2 / 4.8 / 0.8	18 SA	0242 / 0902 / 1452 / 2130	5.2 / 0.6 / 5.4 / 0.2
4 SA	0325 / 0936 / 1536 / 2156	4.8 / 1.0 / 4.9 / 0.8	19 SU	0325 / 0946 / 1537 / 2213	5.3 / 0.4 / 5.4 / 0.2
5 SU	0354 / 1006 / 1606 / 2226	4.8 / 0.9 / 4.9 / 0.7	20 M	0407 / 1030 / 1623 / 2255	5.3 / 0.4 / 5.4 / 0.4
6 M	0423 / 1036 / 1637 / 2257	4.9 / 0.9 / 4.9 / 0.8	21 TU	0449 / 1113 / 1709 / 2336	5.2 / 0.4 / 5.2 / 0.6
7 TU	0454 / 1107 / 1709 / 2329	4.8 / 0.9 / 4.8 / 0.9	22 W	0532 / 1156 / 1757	5.0 / 0.6 / 5.0
8 W	0526 / 1140 / 1745	4.8 / 1.0 / 4.7	23 TH	0016 / 0616 / 1240 / 1848	1.0 / 4.8 / 0.9 / 4.7
9 TH	0002 / 0601 / 1216 / 1824	1.1 / 4.7 / 1.1 / 4.6	24 F	0058 / 0704 / 1328 / 1943	1.3 / 4.6 / 1.2 / 4.4
10 F	0039 / 0642 / 1258 / 1912	1.3 / 4.5 / 1.3 / 4.4	25 SA	0144 / 0758 / 1424 / 2044	1.7 / 4.3 / 1.5 / 4.1
11 SA	0125 / 0732 / 1353 / 2013	1.5 / 4.4 / 1.5 / 4.2	26 SU	0245 / 0902 / 1535 / 2152	2.0 / 4.1 / 1.7 / 3.9
12 SU	0226 / 0835 / 1505 / 2129	1.7 / 4.2 / 1.6 / 4.1	27 M	0406 / 1013 / 1655 / 2306	2.1 / 4.0 / 1.7 / 3.9
13 M	0349 / 0952 / 1633 / 2252	1.9 / 4.1 / 1.5 / 4.2	28 TU	0529 / 1128 / 1805	2.1 / 4.0 / 1.6
14 TU	0516 / 1111 / 1753	1.8 / 4.3 / 1.3	29 W	0013 / 0632 / 1231 / 1858	4.0 / 1.9 / 4.2 / 1.4
15 W	0007 / 0626 / 1221 / 1859	4.4 / 1.5 / 4.5 / 1.0	30 TH	0105 / 0720 / 1319 / 1941	4.2 / 1.7 / 4.3 / 1.3

Chart Datum: 2·60 metres below Ordnance Datum (Newlyn). HAT is 5·7 metres above Chart Datum.

》》 **FREE** monthly updates from 《《
www.reedsalmanac.co.uk

STANDARD TIME (UT)
For Summer Time add ONE hour in **non-shaded areas**

RIVER TYNE/NORTH SHIELDS LAT 55°00′N LONG 1°26′W

TIMES AND HEIGHTS OF HIGH AND LOW WATERS

Dates in red are **SPRINGS**
Dates in blue are **NEAPS**

YEAR 2015

MAY

Time	m	Time	m
1 0146 0800 F 1359 2018	4.4 1.5 4.5 1.1	**16** 0135 0752 SA 1346 2021	4.9 1.0 5.0 0.6
2 0222 0835 SA 1435 2052	4.6 1.2 4.7 1.0	**17** 0221 0842 SU 1435 2108	5.0 0.7 5.2 0.5
3 0254 0909 SU 1508 2125	4.7 1.1 4.8 0.9	**18** 0305 0929 M 1521 ● 2152	5.1 0.8 5.2 0.5
4 0325 0941 M 1541 ○ 2159	4.8 1.0 4.8 0.8	**19** 0347 1013 TU 1608 2234	5.2 0.5 5.2 0.7
5 0357 1015 TU 1615 2232	4.9 0.9 4.9 0.8	**20** 0429 1057 W 1654 2314	5.1 0.5 5.1 0.9
6 0430 1049 W 1651 2307	4.9 0.8 4.9 0.9	**21** 0511 1139 TH 1741 2352	5.0 0.7 4.9 1.1
7 0504 1126 TH 1730 2344	4.9 0.9 4.8 1.0	**22** 0553 1221 F 1828	4.8 0.9 4.6
8 0542 1206 F 1813	4.8 1.0 4.7	**23** 0031 0637 SA 1305 1917	1.4 4.7 1.1 4.4
9 0025 0625 SA 1252 1903	1.2 4.7 1.1 4.5	**24** 0113 0725 SU 1353 2010	1.6 4.4 1.3 4.2
10 0113 0716 SU 1347 2004	1.4 4.5 1.2 4.4	**25** 0202 0820 M 1449 ◐ 2107	1.9 4.3 1.5 4.0
11 0213 0817 M 1454 ◐ 2115	1.6 4.4 1.3 4.3	**26** 0305 0921 TU 1554 2209	2.1 4.1 1.7 3.9
12 0328 0929 TU 1612 2230	1.7 4.3 1.3 4.3	**27** 0420 1027 W 1701 2314	2.1 4.0 1.7 4.0
13 0448 1044 W 1727 2341	1.7 4.4 1.2 4.4	**28** 0531 1133 TH 1802	2.0 4.1 1.6
14 0558 1153 TH 1833	1.5 4.6 0.9	**29** 0013 0630 F 1231 1853	4.1 1.8 4.2 1.4
15 0042 0659 F 1253 1930	4.7 1.2 4.8 0.7	**30** 0103 0719 SA 1320 1938	4.3 1.6 4.3 1.3
		31 0145 0801 SU 1401 2018	4.5 1.4 4.5 1.1

JUNE

Time	m	Time	m
1 0222 0840 M 1440 2056	4.7 1.2 4.7 1.0	**16** 0249 0915 TU 1511 ● 2134	5.0 0.8 5.0 0.9
2 0258 0917 TU 1517 ○ 2133	4.8 1.0 4.8 0.9	**17** 0331 1000 W 1556 2215	5.1 0.7 5.0 0.9
3 0333 0955 W 1556 2212	4.9 0.9 4.9 0.9	**18** 0412 1043 TH 1640 2254	5.1 0.6 4.9 1.0
4 0409 1035 TH 1636 2251	5.0 0.8 4.9 0.9	**19** 0452 1123 F 1722 2330	5.0 0.7 4.8 1.2
5 0447 1116 F 1718 2332	5.0 0.7 4.9 1.0	**20** 0531 1201 SA 1804	4.9 0.8 4.7
6 0528 1159 SA 1804	5.0 0.7 4.8	**21** 0006 0611 SU 1240 1846	1.3 4.8 1.0 4.5
7 0015 0613 SU 1247 1855	1.1 4.9 0.8 4.7	**22** 0042 0652 M 1320 1931	1.5 4.6 1.2 4.3
8 0104 0703 M 1340 1953	1.3 4.8 0.9 4.5	**23** 0123 0738 TU 1404 2019	1.7 4.4 1.4 4.2
9 0159 0801 TU 1440 2057	1.4 4.7 1.1 4.4	**24** 0210 0830 W 1456 ◐ 2113	1.9 4.3 1.6 4.0
10 0304 0907 W 1549 2205	1.6 4.6 1.1 4.4	**25** 0310 0927 TH 1557 2212	2.0 4.2 1.7 4.0
11 0418 1017 TH 1700 2314	1.6 4.5 1.1 4.4	**26** 0421 1030 F 1701 2314	2.1 4.0 1.7 4.0
12 0529 1127 F 1806	1.5 4.6 1.1	**27** 0532 1135 SA 1802	2.0 4.1 1.6
13 0018 0634 SA 1233 1907	4.6 1.3 4.7 1.0	**28** 0014 0633 SU 1236 1856	4.2 1.7 4.2 1.5
14 0114 0733 SU 1331 2002	4.7 1.1 4.8 0.9	**29** 0106 0725 M 1328 1945	4.4 1.6 4.4 1.3
15 0204 0827 M 1423 2050	4.9 0.9 4.9 0.9	**30** 0151 0812 TU 1414 2029	4.6 1.3 4.6 1.1

JULY

Time	m	Time	m
1 0232 0855 W 1456 2112	4.8 1.1 4.8 1.0	**16** 0318 0948 TH 1544 ● 2159	5.0 0.8 4.9 1.1
2 0311 0938 TH 1538 ○ 2154	5.0 0.8 4.9 0.9	**17** 0356 1027 F 1623 2234	5.0 0.7 4.9 1.1
3 0350 1021 F 1621 2237	5.1 0.6 5.0 0.8	**18** 0433 1103 SA 1701 2307	5.0 0.7 4.8 1.1
4 0431 1105 SA 1706 2320	5.2 0.5 5.1 0.8	**19** 0508 1137 SU 1737 2339	5.0 0.8 4.7 1.2
5 0513 1150 SU 1752	5.2 0.5 5.0	**20** 0543 1211 M 1813	4.9 0.9 4.6
6 0004 0558 M 1237 1841	0.9 5.2 0.5 4.9	**21** 0011 0619 TU 1246 1851	1.3 4.8 1.1 4.5
7 0050 0648 TU 1327 1935	1.1 5.1 0.7 4.7	**22** 0046 0659 W 1323 1932	1.5 4.6 1.3 4.3
8 0141 0742 W 1421 2034	1.2 4.9 0.9 4.6	**23** 0126 0742 TH 1406 2019	1.7 4.4 1.5 4.2
9 0239 0844 TH 1523 2138	1.4 4.7 1.1 4.4	**24** 0213 0833 F 1458 ◐ 2113	1.9 4.2 1.7 4.1
10 0348 0953 F 1632 2246	1.6 4.6 1.3 4.4	**25** 0314 0933 SA 1602 2216	2.0 4.1 1.8 4.0
11 0502 1106 SA 1743 2355	1.6 4.5 1.3 4.4	**26** 0431 1041 SU 1712 2323	2.1 4.0 1.8 4.1
12 0615 1218 SU 1850	1.5 4.5 1.3	**27** 0547 1153 M 1818	1.9 4.1 1.7
13 0057 0721 M 1322 1948	4.6 1.3 4.6 1.3	**28** 0027 0651 TU 1258 1916	4.3 1.7 4.3 1.5
14 0151 0817 TU 1416 2037	4.7 1.1 4.7 1.2	**29** 0121 0746 W 1351 2007	4.5 1.4 4.6 1.2
15 0237 0905 W 1502 2120	4.9 0.9 4.8 1.1	**30** 0207 0835 TH 1437 2053	4.8 1.0 4.8 1.0
		31 0250 0921 F 1521 ○ 2137	5.0 0.7 5.1 0.8

AUGUST

Time	m	Time	m
1 0331 1006 SA 1605 2221	5.3 0.4 5.2 0.7	**16** 0411 1039 SU 1635 2242	5.1 0.7 4.9 1.1
2 0413 1051 SU 1649 2304	5.4 0.3 5.3 0.6	**17** 0442 1109 M 1707 2312	5.1 0.8 4.8 1.1
3 0456 1136 M 1734 2347	5.5 0.2 5.2 0.7	**18** 0514 1140 TU 1739 2342	5.0 0.9 4.7 1.2
4 0541 1220 TU 1821	5.4 0.3 5.1	**19** 0548 1212 W 1813	4.9 1.0 4.6
5 0032 0629 W 1307 1911	0.9 5.3 0.6 4.9	**20** 0014 0623 TH 1246 1850	1.3 4.7 1.2 4.5
6 0119 0722 TH 1358 2007	1.1 5.1 0.9 4.6	**21** 0049 0702 F 1323 1931	1.5 4.5 1.4 4.3
7 0214 0822 F 1456 ◑ 2109	1.3 4.8 1.2 4.4	**22** 0130 0747 SA 1408 ◑ 2021	1.7 4.3 1.7 4.2
8 0321 0931 SA 1605 2219	1.6 4.5 1.5 4.3	**23** 0223 0844 SU 1508 2122	1.9 4.1 1.9 4.1
9 0440 1049 SU 1722 2333	1.7 4.3 1.7 4.3	**24** 0337 0956 M 1625 2235	2.0 4.0 1.9 4.1
10 0602 1208 M 1837	1.6 4.3 1.6	**25** 0504 1116 TU 1744 2349	2.0 4.1 1.8 4.2
11 0042 0712 TU 1315 1937	4.4 1.4 4.5 1.5	**26** 0621 1230 W 1851	1.7 4.3 1.6
12 0139 0808 W 1408 2025	4.6 1.2 4.6 1.4	**27** 0052 0722 TH 1329 1945	4.5 1.3 4.6 1.3
13 0224 0853 TH 1451 2105	4.8 1.0 4.7 1.3	**28** 0143 0814 F 1417 2033	4.8 0.9 4.9 1.0
14 0303 0932 F 1529 ● 2140	4.9 0.8 4.8 1.2	**29** 0227 0902 SA 1501 ○ 2118	5.2 0.6 5.2 0.7
15 0338 1006 SA 1603 2212	5.0 0.8 4.9 1.1	**30** 0310 0947 SU 1544 2202	5.4 0.3 5.4 0.6
		31 0352 1032 M 1628 2245	5.6 0.1 5.4 0.5

Chart Datum: 2·60 metres below Ordnance Datum (Newlyn). HAT is 5·7 metres above Chart Datum.

NE England

》 FREE monthly updates from 《
www.reedsalmanac.co.uk
165

STANDARD TIME (UT)
For Summer Time add ONE hour in **non-shaded areas**

RIVER TYNE/NORTH SHIELDS   LAT 55°00'N   LONG 1°26'W
TIMES AND HEIGHTS OF HIGH AND LOW WATERS

Dates in red are **SPRINGS**
Dates in blue are **NEAPS**

YEAR 2015

SEPTEMBER

Time	m	Time	m
1 0435	5.7	**16** 0446	5.0
1115	0.1	1109	0.9
TU 1711	5.4	W 1707	4.9
2328	0.6	2315	1.1
2 0520	5.6	**17** 0518	4.9
1159	0.3	1139	1.0
W 1757	5.2	TH 1739	4.8
		2346	1.2
3 0011	0.7	**18** 0552	4.8
0608	5.4	1211	1.2
TH 1244	0.6	F 1813	4.7
1845	4.8		
4 0058	1.0	**19** 0019	1.4
0701	5.1	0629	4.6
F 1331	1.0	SA 1247	1.4
1938	4.7	1851	4.5
5 0150	1.3	**20** 0059	1.6
0801	4.7	0713	4.4
SA 1426	1.4	SU 1329	1.7
☽ 2040	4.4	1938	4.3
6 0256	1.6	**21** 0149	1.8
0911	4.4	0809	4.2
SU 1537	1.8	M 1425	1.9
2151	4.2	☽ 2039	4.2
7 0420	1.7	**22** 0300	1.9
1032	4.2	0922	4.1
M 1702	1.9	TU 1545	2.0
2310	4.2	2154	4.1
8 0548	1.7	**23** 0429	1.9
1155	4.2	1047	4.1
TU 1823	1.9	W 1713	2.0
		2313	4.2
9 0024	4.4	**24** 0552	1.6
0659	1.5	1205	4.3
W 1303	4.4	TH 1825	1.7
1923	1.7		
10 0121	4.6	**25** 0022	4.5
0752	1.3	0657	1.3
TH 1354	4.5	F 1306	4.7
2008	1.5	1922	1.4
11 0206	4.8	**26** 0117	4.9
0834	1.1	0751	0.9
F 1433	4.7	SA 1355	5.0
2045	1.4	2011	1.0
12 0243	4.9	**27** 0203	5.2
0909	0.9	0839	0.5
SA 1507	4.8	SU 1440	5.3
2117	1.2	2057	0.7
13 0316	5.0	**28** 0247	5.5
0940	0.8	0925	0.2
SU 1538	4.9	M 1522	5.5
● 2147	1.1	○ 2141	0.5
14 0346	5.1	**29** 0330	5.7
1010	0.8	1009	0.1
M 1608	4.9	TU 1604	5.5
2217	1.1	2224	0.5
15 0416	5.1	**30** 0414	5.7
1040	0.8	1053	0.2
TU 1637	4.9	W 1647	5.5
2246	1.1	2307	0.5

OCTOBER

Time	m	Time	m
1 0500	5.6	**16** 0454	5.0
1135	0.4	1111	1.0
TH 1732	5.3	F 1710	4.9
2351	0.7	2324	1.2
2 0549	5.4	**17** 0528	4.8
1218	0.8	1143	1.2
F 1818	5.0	SA 1744	4.8
		2359	1.3
3 0037	0.9	**18** 0606	4.7
0641	5.0	1219	1.4
SA 1304	1.2	SU 1823	4.7
1909	4.8		
4 0130	1.3	**19** 0039	1.5
0741	4.7	0651	4.5
SU 1357	1.6	M 1301	1.7
☽ 2009	4.5	1909	4.5
5 0233	1.6	**20** 0130	1.6
0851	4.3	0747	4.3
M 1505	2.0	TU 1357	1.9
2119	4.3	☽ 2007	4.3
6 0355	1.8	**21** 0236	1.8
1008	4.1	0859	4.2
TU 1633	2.2	W 1513	2.0
2238	4.2	2120	4.3
7 0522	1.7	**22** 0400	1.8
1130	4.1	1021	4.2
W 1757	2.1	TH 1642	2.0
2354	4.3	2239	4.3
8 0634	1.6	**23** 0522	1.5
1238	4.3	1137	4.4
TH 1858	1.9	F 1756	1.8
		2350	4.6
9 0054	4.5	**24** 0630	1.2
0725	1.4	1240	4.7
F 1328	4.5	SA 1856	1.4
1942	1.7		
10 0140	4.7	**25** 0049	4.9
0805	1.2	0725	0.9
SA 1407	4.7	SU 1332	5.0
2018	1.5	1947	1.1
11 0217	4.8	**26** 0139	5.2
0839	1.1	0815	0.6
SU 1440	4.8	M 1417	5.3
2051	1.3	2035	0.8
12 0250	5.0	**27** 0226	5.5
0910	0.9	0902	0.4
M 1510	4.9	TU 1500	5.4
2121	1.2	○ 2120	0.6
13 0320	5.0	**28** 0311	5.6
0940	0.9	0947	0.3
TU 1539	5.0	W 1542	5.5
● 2151	1.1	2205	0.5
14 0350	5.1	**29** 0356	5.6
1010	0.9	1030	0.4
W 1609	5.0	TH 1625	5.4
2221	1.1	2249	0.5
15 0421	5.0	**30** 0443	5.6
1040	0.9	1113	0.7
TH 1639	5.0	F 1708	5.3
2252	1.1	2334	0.7
		31 0532	5.3
		1155	1.0
		SA 1754	5.1

NOVEMBER

Time	m	Time	m
1 0020	0.9	**16** 0551	4.8
0624	4.9	1201	1.4
SU 1239	1.2	M 1803	4.8
1842	4.8		
2 0110	1.2	**17** 0028	1.3
0721	4.6	0637	4.6
M 1327	1.7	TU 1245	1.6
1938	4.6	1849	4.7
3 0208	1.5	**18** 0118	1.4
0824	4.3	0732	4.5
TU 1426	2.1	W 1338	1.8
☽ 2042	4.3	1944	4.5
4 0319	1.7	**19** 0220	1.5
0933	4.1	0839	4.3
W 1546	2.3	TH 1447	1.9
2154	4.2	☽ 2052	4.5
5 0437	1.8	**20** 0334	1.5
1047	4.1	0954	4.3
TH 1709	2.2	F 1608	1.9
2308	4.2	2206	4.5
6 0549	1.7	**21** 0451	1.4
1156	4.2	1107	4.5
F 1816	2.1	SA 1723	1.8
		2318	4.6
7 0013	4.3	**22** 0600	1.2
0644	1.6	1212	4.7
SA 1251	4.4	SU 1828	1.5
1906	1.9		
8 0104	4.5	**23** 0022	4.9
0727	1.4	0659	1.0
SU 1333	4.6	M 1308	4.9
1946	1.6	1923	1.2
9 0145	4.7	**24** 0118	5.1
0804	1.3	0753	0.8
M 1409	4.7	TU 1356	5.1
2021	1.4	2015	1.0
10 0221	4.8	**25** 0208	5.3
0838	1.1	0842	0.7
TU 1441	4.9	W 1441	5.3
2055	1.3	○ 2103	0.8
11 0255	4.9	**26** 0256	5.4
0911	1.0	0928	0.6
W 1512	5.0	TH 1524	5.4
● 2127	1.2	2150	0.6
12 0327	5.0	**27** 0343	5.4
0943	1.0	1011	0.7
TH 1543	5.0	F 1606	5.4
2200	1.1	2235	0.6
13 0400	5.0	**28** 0430	5.3
1015	1.0	1054	0.9
F 1614	5.0	SA 1649	5.3
2233	1.1	2320	0.7
14 0434	4.9	**29** 0518	5.1
1048	1.1	1134	1.2
SA 1647	5.0	SU 1733	5.1
2308	1.1		
15 0511	4.9	**30** 0004	0.9
1123	1.2	0606	4.9
SU 1723	4.9	M 1215	1.4
2346	1.2	1817	4.9

DECEMBER

Time	m	Time	m
1 0050	1.1	**16** 0020	1.0
0657	4.6	0625	4.8
TU 1257	1.7	W 1233	1.4
1906	4.7	1833	4.9
2 0138	1.4	**17** 0108	1.1
0750	4.4	0717	4.6
W 1344	2.0	TH 1323	1.6
2000	4.5	1925	4.8
3 0232	1.6	**18** 0203	1.2
0848	4.2	0817	4.5
TH 1443	2.2	F 1421	1.7
☽ 2101	4.3	☽ 2026	4.7
4 0336	1.8	**19** 0307	1.3
0951	4.1	0924	4.4
F 1558	2.3	SA 1532	1.8
2208	4.2	2135	4.6
5 0444	1.8	**20** 0419	1.4
1057	4.2	1035	4.4
SA 1713	2.2	SU 1649	1.8
2316	4.2	2247	4.6
6 0547	1.8	**21** 0530	1.3
1159	4.2	1143	4.5
SU 1817	2.1	M 1759	1.6
		2358	4.7
7 0017	4.3	**22** 0636	1.2
0640	1.6	1245	4.7
M 1252	4.4	TU 1904	1.4
1907	1.9		
8 0108	4.4	**23** 0101	4.9
0726	1.5	0734	1.1
TU 1335	4.6	W 1339	4.9
1950	1.6	2001	1.1
9 0151	4.6	**24** 0157	5.0
0806	1.3	0827	1.0
W 1412	4.7	TH 1427	5.1
2029	1.4	2052	0.9
10 0230	4.7	**25** 0248	5.1
0843	1.2	0914	0.9
TH 1447	4.9	F 1511	5.2
2105	1.2	○ 2140	0.8
11 0306	4.8	**26** 0335	5.2
0919	1.1	0957	0.8
F 1520	5.0	SA 1553	5.2
● 2141	1.1	2225	0.7
12 0342	4.9	**27** 0420	5.1
0955	1.1	1037	1.0
SA 1554	5.1	SU 1633	5.2
2218	1.0	2307	0.7
13 0419	5.0	**28** 0503	5.0
1032	1.1	1115	1.2
SU 1629	5.1	M 1714	5.1
2256	0.9	2347	0.9
14 0458	5.0	**29** 0546	4.9
1110	1.1	1151	1.3
M 1707	5.1	TU 1754	5.0
2337	0.9		
15 0540	4.9	**30** 0025	1.0
1149	1.2	0628	4.7
TU 1748	5.0	W 1227	1.5
		1835	4.8
		31 0105	1.2
		0712	4.5
		TH 1305	1.7
		1919	4.6

Chart Datum: 2·60 metres below Ordnance Datum (Newlyn). HAT is 5·7 metres above Chart Datum.

》》 **FREE** monthly updates from 《《
www.reedsalmanac.co.uk

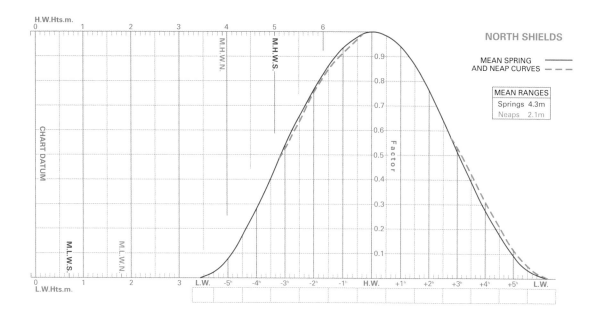

NORTH SHIELDS

MEAN SPRING ——————
AND NEAP CURVES – – – –

MEAN RANGES	
Springs	4.3m
Neaps	2.1m

3.18 BLYTH

Northumberland 55°06'·98N 01° 29'·27W ✿✿✿⬦⬦✿✿

CHARTS AC 152, 156, 1626, 5615; Imray C24

TIDES +0430 Dover; ML 2·8; Duration 0558

Standard Port NORTH SHIELDS (←)

Times				Height (metres)			
High Water		Low Water		MHWS	MHWN	MLWN	MLWS
0200	0800	0100	0800	5·0	3·9	1·8	0·7
1400	2000	1300	2000				
Differences BLYTH							
+0005	−0007	−0001	+0009	0·0	0·0	−0·1	+0·1

SHELTER Very good. Access H24 but at LW in strong SE winds, seas break across entrance.

NAVIGATION WPT 55°06'·57N 01°28'·74W, 324°/0·5M to harbour entrance. From N, beware The Pigs, The Sow and Seaton Sea Rks. A meteorological mast is 3M offshore and 2 wind turbines on North Spit (1·2M N of hbr ent) centred on 55°08'·16N 01°29'·41W. No dangers from S. See RNYC Sailing Directions, £28·75 inc P&P, from RNYC, House Yacht Tyne, S Hbr, Blyth NE24 3PB (website below).

LIGHTS AND MARKS Blyth E Pier Hd, W twr on S end. Outer ldg lts 324°, Or ◇ on framework trs. Inner ldg lts 338°, front W 6-sided tr; rear W △ on mast. See chartlet and 3.3 for lt details.

COMMUNICATIONS (Code 01670) MRCC (01262) 672317; Police 101. HM 352678, Call *Blyth Hbr Control* Ch **12** 11 (H24) for clearance to enter/ leave.

FACILITIES R Northumberland YC www.rnyc.org.uk ☎ 353636. In SE part of South Hbr, E side of Middle Jetty, ❶ berth on N side of RNYC pontoons in 4·4m least depth. 123 ⌂ £1·50, 🚽, C (1½ ton for trailer sailers), BH (20 ton),⚒ (www.millermarine.co.uk), @, 🖨. **South Hbr** ☎ 352678, ⚓, C (50 ton).

Town 📞 & 📠 (07836 677730), 🛒, ✕, 🖥, ✉, Ⓑ, Gas, Gaz, bus to Newcastle ⇌, ✈.

ADJACENT ANCHORAGE
NEWBIGGIN, Northumberland, **55°10'·75N 01°30'·10W**. AC 156. Tides approx as for Blyth, 3·5M to the S. Temp, fair weather ⚓ in about 4m in centre of the bay, off the conspic sculptures on the

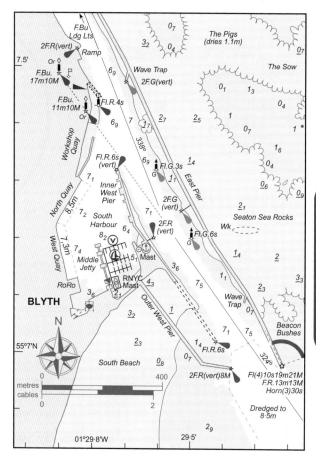

breakwater; sheltered from SW to N winds. Caution: offlying rky ledges to N and S. Conspic church on N side of bay; bkwtr lt Fl G 10s 4M. Facilities: **SC** (dinghies). **Town** 🛒, ✕, 🖥.

3.19 AMBLE

Northumberland 55°20'·37N 01°34'·25W ✿✿✿♨♨♨✿✿

CHARTS AC 156, 1627, 5615; Imray C24

TIDES +0412 Dover; ML 3·1; Duration 0606

Standard Port NORTH SHIELDS (←—)

Times				Height (metres)			
High Water		Low Water		MHWS	MHWN	MLWN	MLWS
0200	0800	0100	0800	5·0	3·9	1·8	0·7
1400	2000	1300	2000				
Differences AMBLE							
–0013	–0013	–0016	–0020	0·0	0·0	+0·1	+0·1
COQUET ISLAND							
–0010	–0010	–0020	–0020	+0·1	+0·1	0·0	+0·1

SHELTER The Hbr (alias Warkworth Hbr) is safe in all winds. But ent is dangerous in strong N to E winds or in swell, when heavy seas break on Pan Bush shoal and on the bar at hbr ent, where least depth is 0·8m. ⚓ in Coquet Road or NNE of North Pier.

NAVIGATION WPT 55°21'·00N 01°33'·10W, 225° to hbr ent, 0·9M. Ent recommended from NE, passing N and W of Pan Bush. The S-going stream sets strongly across ent. Once inside the N

bkwtr, beware drying banks to stbd, ie on N side of channel; keep close (15m) to S quays. 4kn speed limit in hbr.

- In NE'ly gales broken water can extend to Coquet Island, keep E of island and go to Blyth where appr/ent may be safer.
- Coquet Chan (min depth 0·3m) is not buoyed and is only advised with caution, by day, in good vis/weather, slight sea state and with adequate rise of tide, ie HW–2.

LIGHTS AND MARKS Coquet Island lt ho, (conspic) W☐tr, turreted parapet, lower half grey; horn 30s. See chartlet and 3.3.

COMMUNICATIONS (Code 01665) HM ☎ 710306; MRCC (01262) 672317; local CG 710575; Police 101; Ⓗ (01670) 521212.

Amble Marina Ch 80 (7/7, 0900-1700). HM Ch 16, works Ch 14 (Mon-Fri 0900-1700 LT). Coquet YC Ch M (occas).

FACILITIES **Amble Marina** marina@ amble.co.uk ☎ 712168, is about 5ca from hbr ent. Tidal gauge shows depth over sill, 0·8m above CD; access between PHM buoy and old jetty, both unlit. Pontoons are 'A' to 'F' from sill; ⓥ berth on 'B' initially. 200 ⌑+40 ⓥ, £2·50. ⚓,▣,⚓,D, ✕, ✎, ⊞, Ⓔ, ⚐, ⚑, BY, BH (50t), C, ✕, ☐, ☷, Gas, Gaz. Hbr D, ⌑. **Coquet YC** ☎ 711179 ◣, ☐, M, ⚓, L.

Town ☷, ✕, ☐, ✉, ⇌ (Alnmouth), ✈ (Newcastle).

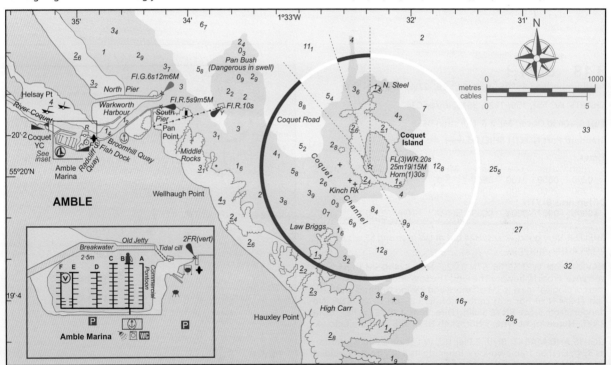

HBRS AND ANCHORAGES BETWEEN AMBLE AND HOLY ISLAND

BOULMER, Northumberland, **55°25'·00N 01°33'·90W.** AC 156. Tides approx as for Amble, 4·6M to the S. A small haven almost enclosed by N and S Rheins, rky ledges either side of the narrow (30m) ent, Marmouth; only advised in settled offshore weather. 2 FW bns (lit when req'd by LB or FVs) lead approx 257° through the ent, leaving close to stbd a bn on N Rheins. ⚓ just inside in about 1·5m or dry out on sand at the N end. Few facilities: Pub, ✉ in village. Alnwick is 4M inland.

CRASTER, Northumberland, **55°28'·40N 01°35'·30W.** AC 156. Tidal differences: interpolate between Amble (3.19) and N Sunderland (3.20). Strictly a fair weather ⚓ in offshore winds, 1M S of the conspic Dunstanburgh Castle (ru). The ent, 40m wide, is N of Muckle Carr and S of Little Carr which partly covers and has a bn on its S end. ⚓ in about 3·5m just inshore of these 2 rocky outcrops; or berth at the E pier on rk/sand inside the tiny drying hbr. Facilities: ☷, ✕, ☐.

NEWTON HAVEN and BEADNELL BAY, Northumberland, **55°30'·90N 01° 36'·70W.** AC 156. HW +0342 on Dover; Tidal differences: interpolate between Amble (3.19) and N Sunderland (3.20). ML 2·6m; Duration 0625. A safe ⚓ in winds from NNW to SE via S but susceptible to swell. Ent to S of Newton PHM buoy and Newton Pt. Beware Fills Rks. ⚓ between Fills Rks and Low Newton by the Sea in 4/5m. A very attractive ⚓ with no lts, marks or facilities except a pub. Further ⚓ S of Beadnell Pt (1M N of Newton Pt) in 4–6m; small, fishing hbr whose wall is newly rebuilt; Beadnell SC. Village 0·5M.

SEAHOUSES (North Sunderland), Northumberland, **55°35'·04N 01°38'·91W.** AC 1612. HW +0340 on Dover; ML No data; Duration 0618. See 3.20. Good shelter except in on-shore winds when swell makes outer hbr berths (0·7m) very uncomfortable and dangerous. Inner hbr has excellent berths but usually full of FVs. Beware The Tumblers (rks) to the W of ent and rks protruding NE from bkwtr hd Fl R 2·5s 6m; NW pier hd

FG 11m 3M; vis 159°-294°, on W tr; traffic sigs; Siren 90s when vessels expected. Good facilities. When it is dangerous to enter, a ● is shown over the FG lt (or R flag over a Bu flag) on NW pier hd.

FARNE ISLANDS, Northumberland, **55°37′·15N 01°39′·37W**. AC 160, 156, 111. HW +0345 on Dover; ML 2·6m; Duration 0630. See 3.20. The islands are a NT nature reserve in a beautiful area; they should only be attempted in good weather. Landing is only allowed on Farne Is, Staple Is and Longstone. In the inner group, ⚓ in The Kettle on the NE side of Inner Farne; near the Bridges (connecting Knocks Reef to West Wideopen); or to the S of West Wideopen. In the outer group, ⚓ in Pinnacle Haven (between Staple Is/Brownsman). Beware turbulence over Knivestone and Whirl Rks and eddy S of Longstone during NW tidal streams. Lts and marks: Black Rocks Pt, Oc (2) WRG 8s 12m 14/11M;122°-G-165°-W-175°-R-191°-W-238°-R-275°-W-289°-G-300°. Bamburgh Castle is conspic 6ca to the SE. Farne Is lt ho at SW Pt, Fl (2) WR 15s 27m

8/6M; W ○ tr; 119°-R-280°-W-119°. Longstone Fl 20s 23m 24M, R tr with W band (conspic), RC. Caution: reefs extend about 7ca seaward. No facilities.

NATIONAL NATURE RESERVE (Holy Island) A National Nature Reserve (NNR) extends from Budle Bay (**55°37′N 01°45′·W**, close to Black Rocks Point lt ho) along the coast to Cheswick Black Rocks, 3M SE of Berwick-upon-Tweed. The NNR extends seaward from the HW shoreline to the drying line; it includes Holy Island and the adjacent islets.

Visiting craft are asked to respect two constraints:

- Landing is prohibited on the small island of Black Law (55°39′·68N 01°47′·50W) from April to August inclusive.
- Boats should not be landed or recovered anywhere in the NNR except at the designated and buoyed watersports zone on the SE side of Budle Bay.

COQUET ISLAND TO FARNE ISLANDS

(AC 156) Coquet Is (lt, fog sig) lies about 5ca offshore at SE end of Alnmouth B, and nearly 1M NNE of Hauxley Pt, off which dangerous rks extend 6ca offshore, drying 1·9m. On passage, normally pass 1M E of Coquet Is in the W sector of the lt. Coquet chan may be used in good vis by day; but it is only 2ca wide, not buoyed, has least depth of 0·9m near the centre. ▶*The stream runs strongly: S-going from HW Tyne −0515 and N-going from HW Tyne +0045.* ◀ In S or W winds, there are good anchs in Coquet Road, W and NW of the Island.

Amble (Warkworth) Hbr ent is about 1M W of Coquet Is, and 1·5M SE of Warkworth Castle (conspic). 4ca NE and ENE of ent is Pan Bush, rky shoal with least depth of 0·9m on which dangerous seas can break in any swell. The bar has varying depths, down to less than 1m. The entrance is dangerous in strong winds from N/E when broken water may extend to Coquet Is. Once inside, the hbr is safe.

Between Coquet Is and the Farne Is, 19M to N, keep at least 1M offshore to avoid various dangers. To seaward, Craster Skeres lie 5M E of Castle Pt, and Dicky Shad and Newton Skere lie 1·75M and 4·5M E of Beadnell Pt; these are three rky banks on which the sea breaks heavily in bad weather.

FARNE ISLANDS

(AC 111, 160) The coast between N Sunderland Pt (Snook) and Holy Island, 8M NW, has fine hill (Cheviots) scenery fronted by dunes and sandy beaches. The Farne Is and offlying shoals extend 4·5M offshore, and are a mini-cruising ground well worth visiting in good weather. The islands are a bird sanctuary, owned and operated by the National Trust, with large colonies of sea birds and grey seals. The R Northumberland YC's Sailing Directions (see 3.18) are useful; AC 111 is essential.

Inner Sound separates the islands from the mainland. In good conditions it is a better N/S route than keeping outside the whole group; but the stream runs at 3kn at sp, and with strong wind against tide there is rough water. If course is set outside the Farne Islands, pass 1M E of Longstone (lit) to clear Crumstone Rk 1M

to S, and Knivestone (dries 3·6m) and Whirl Rks (depth 0·6m) respectively 5 and 6ca NE of Longstone lt ho. The sea breaks on these rocks.

The islands, rks and shoals are divided by Staple Sound, running NW/SE, into an inner and outer group. The former comprises Inner Farne, W and E Wideopens and Knock's Reef. Inner Farne (lt) is the innermost Is; close NE there is anch called The Kettle, sheltered except from NW, but anch out of stream close to the Bridges connecting Knock's Reef and W Wideopen. 1M NW of Inner Farne Is and separated by Farne Sound, which runs NE/SW, lies the Megstone, a rk 5m high. Beware Swedman reef (dries 0·5m), marked by SHM buoy 4ca WSW of Megstone.

The outer group of Islands comprises Staple and Brownsman Islands, N and S Wamses, the Harcars and Longstone. There is occas anch between Staple and Brownsman Is. ▶ *Piper Gut and Crafords Gut may be negotiated in calm weather and near HW, stemming the S-going stream.* ◀

HOLY ISLAND TO BERWICK

(AC 1612, 111, 160) ▶ *Near the Farne Is and Holy Is the SE-going stream begins at HW Tyne −0430, and the NW-going at HW Tyne +0130. Sp rates are about 2.5kn in Inner Sound, 4kn in Staple Sound and about 3.5kn 1M NE of Longstone, decreasing to seaward. There is an eddy S of Longstone on NW-going stream.* ◀

Holy Is (or Lindisfarne) lies 6M WNW of Longstone, and is linked to mainland by a causeway covered at HW. There is a good anch on S side (AC 1612) with conspic daymarks and dir lts. The castle and a W obelisk at Emmanuel Head are also conspic. ▶ *The stream runs strongly in and out of hbr, W-going from HW Tyne +0510, and E-going from HW Tyne −0045. E of Holy Is, Goldstone chan runs N/S between Goldstone Rk (dries) SHM buoy on E side and Plough Seat Reef and Plough Rk (both dry) on W side, with PHM buoy.* ◀

Berwick Bay has some offlying shoals. Berwick-upon-Tweed is easily visible against the low shoreline, which rises again to high cliffs further north. The hbr entrance is restricted by a shallow bar, dangerous in onshore winds.

3.20 HOLY ISLAND

Northumberland 55°39′·57N 01°46′·81W ❄❄⚓❄❄❄❄

TIDES +0344 Dover; ML No data; Duration 0630

Standard Port NORTH SHIELDS (←)

Times				Height (metres)			
High Water		Low Water		MHWS	MHWN	MLWN	MLWS
0200	0800	0100	0800	5·0	3·9	1·8	0·7
1400	2000	1300	2000				
Differences HOLY ISLAND							
−0043	−0039	−0105	−0110	−0·2	−0·2	−0·3	−0·1
NORTH SUNDERLAND (Seahouses)							
−0048	−0044	−0058	−0102	−0·2	−0·2	−0·2	0·0

CHARTS AC 111, 1612, 5615; Imray C24

SHELTER Good S of The Heugh in 3-6m, but ⚓ is uncomfortable in fresh W/SW winds esp at sp flood, and foul in places; trip-line advised. Better shelter in The Ouse on sand/mud if able to dry out; but not in S/SE winds. For detailed information for trailer sailers see www.dca.uk.com.

NAVIGATION WPT 55°39′·76N 01°44′·88W, 260°/1·55M to Old Law E bn. From N identify Emmanuel Hd, conspic W △ bn, then appr via Goldstone Chan leaving Plough Seat PHM buoy to stbd. From S, clear Farne Is thence to WPT. Outer ldg bns lead 260° close past Ridge ECM and Triton SHM buoys. Possible overfalls in chan across bar (1·6m) with sp ebb up to 4kn. Inner ldg marks lead 310° to ⚓. Inshore route, round Castle Pt via Hole Mouth and The Yares, may be more sheltered, but is not for strangers.

Continued overleaf

HOLY ISLAND *continued*

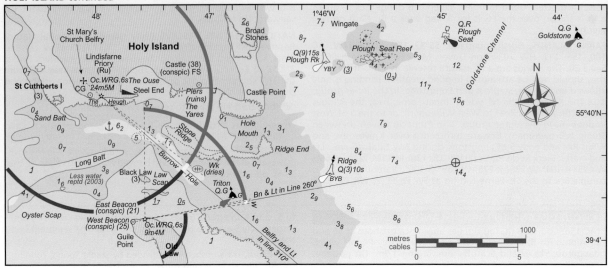

LIGHTS AND MARKS See 3.3 and chartlet above. Outer leading marks/lts are Old Law beacons (conspic), 2 reddish obelisks 21/25m on 260°; E beacon has directional light, Oc WRG 6s. Inner leading marks/lights are The Heugh tower, B △, on with St Mary's church belfry 310°. The Heugh has directional light, Oc WRG 6s. Directional lights Oc WRG are aligned on 260° and 309·5° respectively.

COMMUNICATIONS (Code 01289) MRCC (01262) 672317; HM 389248.

FACILITIES Limited. ⏚ on village green, ⏚ (contact HM prior to launching) £5.00, ✗, ⌂, limited ▦, ☏ & ☏ from Beal (5M); bus (occas) to Berwick. Note Lindisfarne is ancient name; Benedictine Abbey (ruins) and Castle (NT) are worth visiting. Causeway to mainland, covers at HW, is useable approx HW+3½ to HW-2.

3.21 BERWICK-UPON-TWEED

Northumberland 55°45'·87N 01°59'·05W ❄❄❄❄❄❄

CHARTS AC 111, 160, 1612, 5615; Imray C24

TIDES +0348 Dover; ML 2·5; Duration 0620
Standard Port NORTH SHIELDS (←)

Times				Height (metres)			
High Water		Low Water		MHWS	MHWN	MLWN	MLWS
0200	0800	0100	0800	5·0	3·9	1·8	0·7
1400	2000	1300	2000				
Differences BERWICK-UPON-TWEED							
−0053	−0053	−0109	−0109	−0·3	−0·1	−0·5	−0·1

SHELTER Good shelter or ⚓ except in strong E/SE winds. ⌂ may be available in Tweed Dock (no dock gates) which is primarily used by commercial shipping. If possible contact HM beforehand to avoid disappointment. Alternative temporary ⌂ possible at W end of Fish Jetty (1·2m).

NAVIGATION WPT 55°45'·62N 01°58'·0W, 294°/0·65M to breakwater lighthouse.

- On-shore winds and ebb tides cause very confused seas over the bar, minimum depth 0·6m. From HW−2 to HW+1 strong flood tide sets S across the entrance; keep well up to breakwater.
- The sands at the mouth of the Tweed shift so frequently that local knowledge is essential to enter the harbour.

Town Hall Spire and Lt ho in line at 294°. Keep close to breakwater to avoid Sandstell Point. When past PHM buoy and S of Crabwater Rk, keep Spittal Bns (Or ▽ on B Or Bn) in line brg 207°; best water may be further W. Berwick Bridge (first/lowest) has about 3m clearance.

LIGHTS AND MARKS See 3.3 and chartlet.

COMMUNICATIONS (Code 01289) MRCC (01262) 672317; Police 101; Dr 307484. HM 307404.

VHF Ch 12 16 (0800-1700).

FACILITIES Tweed Dock ☎ 307404, ⌂ £8.00, M, ☏ & ☏, ⏚, Showers, ⚒, ☐, ✗, C (Mobile 3 ton), ⏚, ⛽. **Town** ☏, ▦, ✗, ⌂, ⊠, Ⓑ, ⇌ and ✈ (Newcastle or Edinburgh).

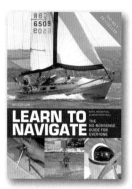

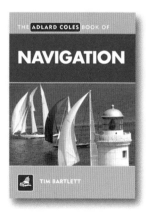
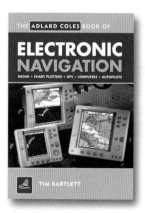

East Scotland

Eyemouth to Shetland Islands

AREA 4 – SOUTH EAST SCOTLAND

4.1 Area map and Distance table – Eyemouth to Peterhead **172**

4.2 Tidal stream charts **174**

4.3 Lights, buoys and waypoints **176**

4.4 Passage information **178**

4.5 Eyemouth **178**
Burnmouth • St Abbs

4.6 Dunbar **179**
N Berwick

4.7 Firth of Forth (Rosyth tide tables/curves) **181**
Port Edgar • Granton • Aberdour • Elie •
St Monans • North Berwick • Fisherrow •
Cramond

4.8 Forth and Clyde Canal **183**
Minor harbours and ⚓s in the Firth of Forth
Leith, Tide tables and curves

4.9 Anstruther **187**
Kirkcaldy • Pittenweem • Crail • Isle of May

4.10 River Tay **189**
Perth • St Andrews

4.11 Arbroath **190**

4.12 Montrose **190**

4.13 Stonehaven **191**
Johnshaven • Gourdon

4.14 Aberdeen,
Tide tables and curves **192**

AREA 5 – NORTH EAST SCOTLAND

5.1 Area map and Distance table –
Fraserburgh to Lerwick **196**

5.2 Tidal stream charts **198**

5.3 Lights, buoys and waypoints **200**

5.4 Passage information **202**

5.5 Peterhead **203**
Boddam

5.6 Fraserburgh **204**
Rosehearty

5.7 Macduff and Banff **205**
Portsoy

5.8 Whitehills **205**
Cullen • Portknockie • Findochty

5.9 Buckie **206**

5.10 Lossiemouth **206**

5.11 Hopeman **207**

5.12 Burghead **207**

5.13 Findhorn **208**

5.14 Nairn **208**
Invergordon, Tide tables and curves **209**

5.15 Inverness **213**
Fortrose • Avoch • Caledonian Canal

5.16 Portmahomack **215**
Cromarty Firth • Dornoch Firth •
Golspie • Lybster

5.17 Helmsdale **216**

5.18 Wick,
Tide tables and curves **216**

5.19 Scrabster **221**
Kyle of Tongue • Loch Eriboll

5.20 Orkney Islands **222**
Houton Bay • Shapinsay • Auskerry • Pierowall

5.21 Stromness **224**

5.22 Kirkwall **224**

5.23 Stronsay **225**

5.24 Shetland Islands **226**
Foula • Balta Sound • Scalloway •
Vaila Sound (Walls) • Fair Isle

5.25 Lerwick,
Tide tables and curves **227**

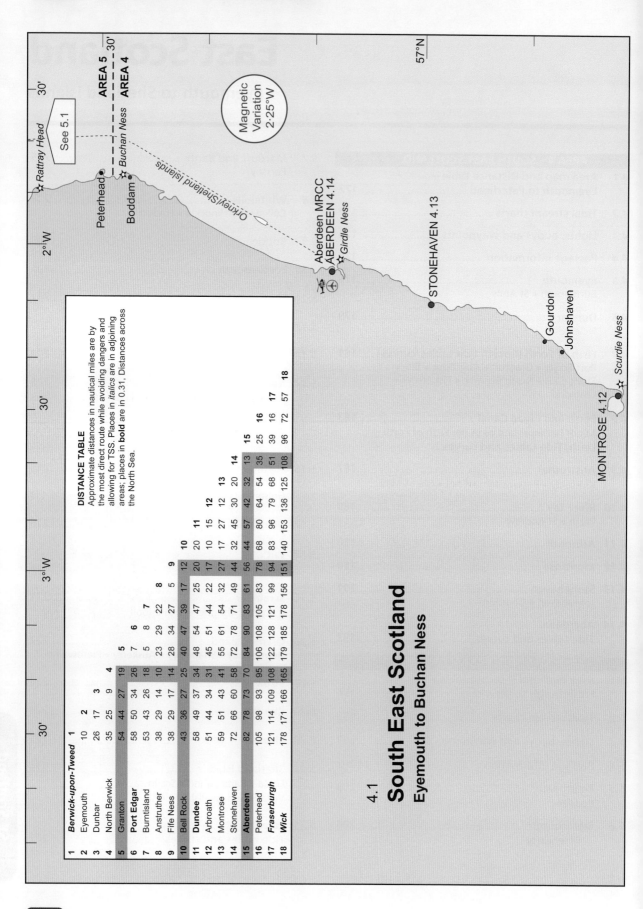

Rattray Head

See 5.1

AREA 5

30'

30'

Buchan Ness

AREA 4

Peterhead

Boddam

Orkney/Shetland Islands

Magnetic Variation 2·25°W

2°W

57°N

Aberdeen MRCC
ABERDEEN 4.14

Girdle Ness

STONEHAVEN 4.13

Gourdon

Johnshaven

Scurdie Ness

MONTROSE 4.12

30'

3°W

30'

DISTANCE TABLE
Approximate distances in nautical miles are by the most direct route while avoiding dangers and allowing for TSS. Places in *italics* are in adjoining areas; places in **bold** are in 0.31. Distances across the North Sea.

1	*Berwick-upon-Tweed*	**1**																
2	Eyemouth	10	**2**															
3	Dunbar	26	17	**3**														
4	North Berwick	35	25	9	**4**													
5	**Port Edgar**	54	44	27	19	**5**												
6	Burntisland	58	50	34	26	7	**6**											
7	Anstruther	53	43	26	18	5	8	**7**										
8	Fife Ness	38	29	14	10	23	29	22	**8**									
9	Bell Rock	38	29	17	14	28	34	27	5	**9**								
10	**Dundee**	43	36	27	25	40	47	39	17	12	**10**							
11	Arbroath	58	49	37	34	48	54	47	25	20	20	**11**						
12	Montrose	51	44	34	31	45	51	44	22	17	10	15	**12**					
13	Stonehaven	59	51	43	41	55	61	54	27	17	10	27	12	**13**				
14	**Aberdeen**	72	66	60	58	72	78	71	49	44	32	45	30	20	**14**			
15	Peterhead	82	78	73	70	84	90	83	61	56	44	57	42	32	13	**15**		
16	*Fraserburgh*	105	98	93	95	106	108	105	83	78	68	80	64	54	35	25	**16**	
17	*Wick*	121	114	109	108	122	128	121	99	94	83	96	79	68	51	39	16	**17**
18		178	171	166	165	179	185	178	156	151	140	153	136	125	108	96	72	57	**18**

4.1

South East Scotland
Eyemouth to Buchan Ness

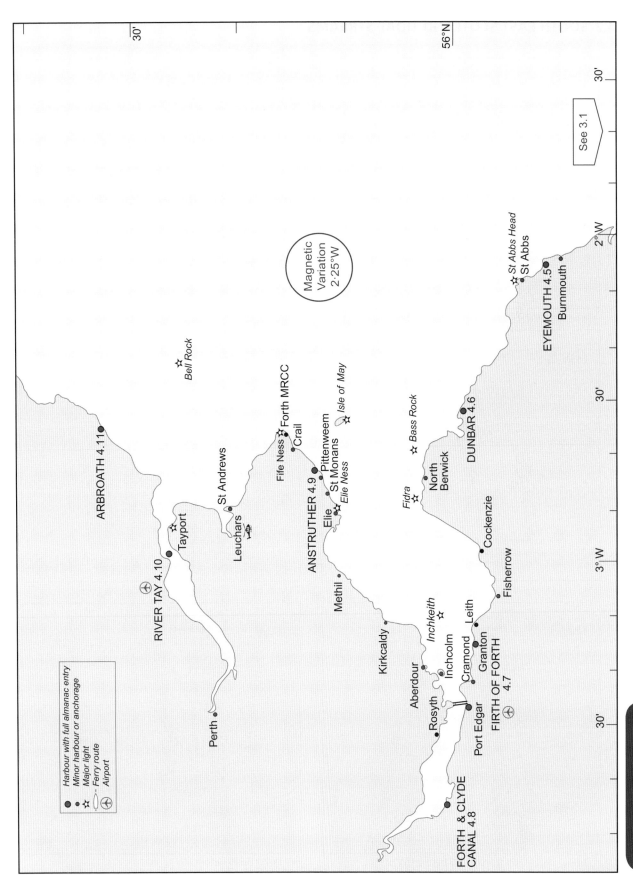

30'

56°N

30'

See 3.1

Magnetic
Variation
2·25°W

2°W

St Abbs Head
St Abbs

EYEMOUTH 4.5
Burnmouth

Bell Rock

Forth MRCC
Fife Ness
Crail

DUNBAR 4.6

Pittenweem
St Monans
ANSTRUTHER 4.9
Elie
Elie Ness

Isle of May

Bass Rock

North
Berwick

ARBROATH 4.11

St Andrews

Fidra

Cockenzie

Leuchars

Tayport

Fisherrow

RIVER TAY 4.10

Methil

Inchkeith

Perth

Kirkcaldy

Leith
Cramond
Granton

Aberdour

Inchcolm

FIRTH OF FORTH
4.7

Rosyth

Port Edgar

FORTH & CLYDE
CANAL 4.8

30'

3°W

30'

- Harbour with full almanac entry
- Minor harbour or anchorage
☆ Major light
-- Ferry route
⊕ Airport

4.2 SOUTH EAST SCOTLAND TIDAL STREAMS

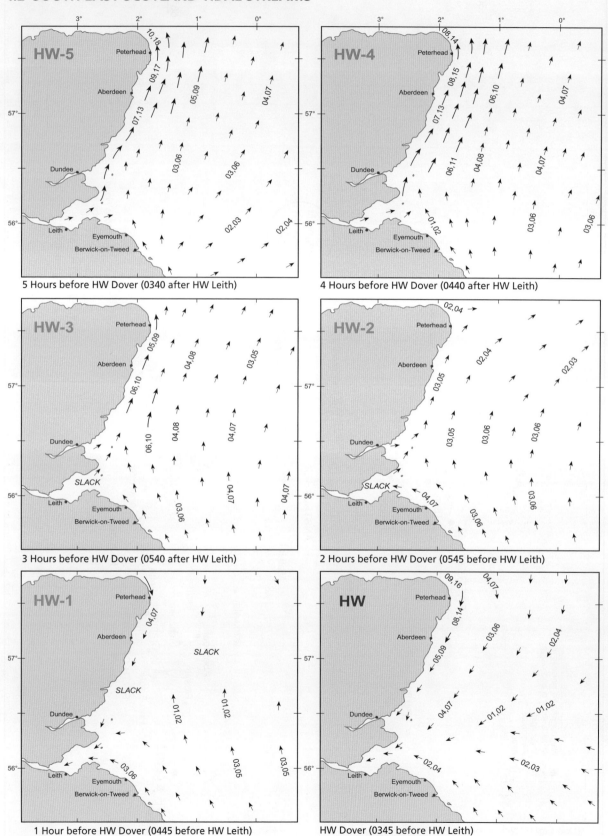

5 Hours before HW Dover (0340 after HW Leith)

4 Hours before HW Dover (0440 after HW Leith)

3 Hours before HW Dover (0540 after HW Leith)

2 Hours before HW Dover (0545 before HW Leith)

1 Hour before HW Dover (0445 before HW Leith)

HW Dover (0345 before HW Leith)

Northward 5.2   Southward 3.2

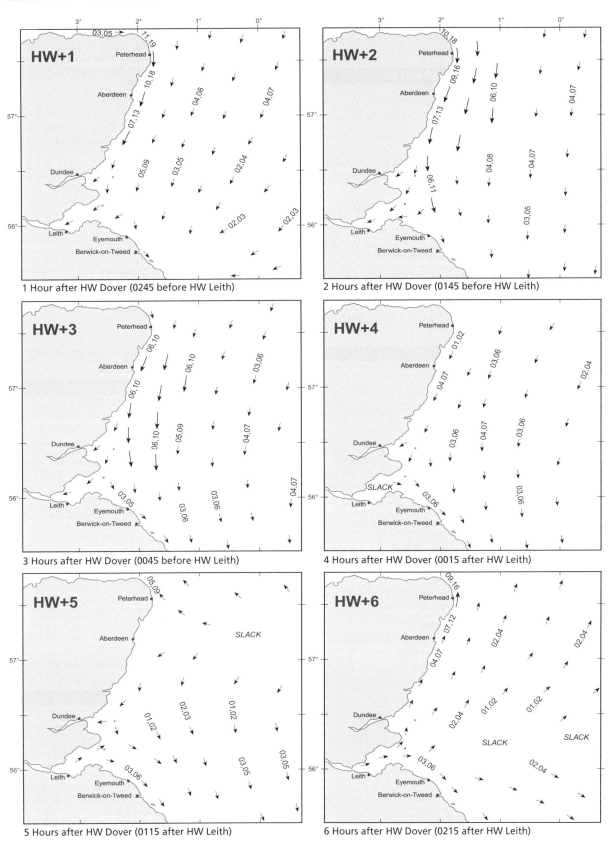

1 Hour after HW Dover (0245 before HW Leith)

2 Hours after HW Dover (0145 before HW Leith)

3 Hours after HW Dover (0045 before HW Leith)

4 Hours after HW Dover (0015 after HW Leith)

5 Hours after HW Dover (0115 after HW Leith)

6 Hours after HW Dover (0215 after HW Leith)

SE Scotland

4.3 LIGHTS, BUOYS AND WAYPOINTS

Bold print = light with a nominal range of 15M or more. CAPITALS = place or feature. *CAPITAL ITALICS* = light-vessel, light float or Lanby. *Italics* = Fog signal. ***Bold italics*** = Racon. Some marks/buoys are fitted with AIS; see relevant charts.

BERWICK-UPON-TWEED TO BASS ROCK

BURNMOUTH
Ldg lts 241°. Front, FR 29m 4M; 55°50'·53N 02°04'·25W. Rear, 45m from front, FR 35m 4M. Both on W posts (unclear by day).

EYEMOUTH
Blind Buss ⚲ Q; 55°52'·80N 02°05'·25E.
Ldg Lts 174°. Front, W Bkwtr Hd ⚲, FG 9m 6M; 55°52'·47N 02°05'·29W. Rear, elbow 55m from front, FG 10m 6M.

ST ABBS to DUNBAR and BASS ROCK
St Abbs Hd ☆ 55°54'·96N 02°08'·29W; Fl 10s 68m **26M**; W twr; ***Racon (T) 18M***.
Barns Ness Tower (Lt ho disused 36m); 55°59'·22N 02°26'·76W.
Torness Pwr Stn Ldg Lts 215°. Front, Iso G 4s 6m 6M; W □ with B vert stripe on plinth; 55°58'·27N 02°24'·86W. Rear, Iso G 4s 22m 3M; W □ with B vert stripe on post; sync with front.
Dunbar Hbr Ldg Lts (Bayswell Hill) 198°. Front, Oc G 6s 15m 3M; 3 Or △ on col; 56°00'·26N 02°31'·21W. Rear, Oc G 6s 22m 3M; 3 Or ▽; sync with front; both lts 188°-G(intens)-208°.
Bass Rock, S side, ⚲ Fl (3) 20s 46m 10M; W twr; vis: 241°-107°; 56°04'·61N 02°38'·48W.

FIRTH OF FORTH AND SOUTH SHORE

(Direction of buoyage East to West)

NORTH BERWICK
Outfall ⚲ Fl Y; 56°04'·29N 02°40'·89W.

Fidra ☆ 56°04'·39N 02°47'·13W; Fl (4) 30s 34m **15M**; W twr; obsc by Bass Rock, Craig Leith and Lamb Island.

PORT SETON, COCKENZIE, FISHERROW and S CHANNEL
Port Seton, E Pier Hd ⚲ Iso WR 4s 10m W9M, R6M; vis: shore - R - 105°- W - 225°- R - shore; *Bell (occas);* 55°58'·40N 02°57'·23W.
Fisherrow E Pier Hd ⚲ Oc 6s 5m 6M; 55°56'·79N 03°04'·11W.
Narrow Deep ⚲ Fl (2) R 10s; 56°01'·46N 03°04'·59W.
Herwit ⚲ Fl (3) G 10s; 56°01'·05N 03°06'·52W.
North Craig ⚲ Q (3) 10s 56°01'·02N 03°03'·52W.
Craigh Waugh ⚲ Fl (2) 10s;56°00'·26N 03°04'·47W.
Diffuser Hds (Outer) ⚲ 55°59'·81N 03°07'·84W.

LEITH and GRANTON
Leith Approach ⚲Fl R 3s; 55°59'·95N 03°11'·51W.
East Bkwtr Hd ⚲ Iso R 4s 7m 9M; 55°59'·48N 03°10'·94W.
GrantonE Pier Head ⚲ Fl R 2s 5m 6M; 55°59'·28N 03°13'·27W.

NORTH CHANNEL and MIDDLE BANK
Inchkeith Fairway ⚲ Iso 2s; ***Racon (T) 5M***; 56°03'·49N 03°00'·10W.
No. 1 ⚲ Fl G 9s; 56°03'·22N 03°03'·71W.
No. 2 ⚲ Fl R 9s; 56°02'·90N 03°03'·72W.
No. 3 ⚲ Fl G 6s; 56°03'·22N 03°06'·10W.
No. 4 ⚲ Fl R 6s; 56°02'·89N 03°06'·11W.
No. 5 ⚲ Fl G 3s; 56°03'·18N 03°07'·88W.
No. 6 ⚲ Fl R 3s; 56°03'·05N 03°08'·44W.
No. 8 ⚲ Fl R 9s 56°02'·95N 03°09'·62W.
Inchkeith ⚲ 56°02'·01N 03°08'·17W; Fl 15s 67m 14M; stone twr.
Pallas Rock ⚲ VQ (9) 10s 56°01'·50N 03°09'·30W.
East Gunnet ⚲ Q (3) 10s; 56°01'·41N 03°10'·38W.
West Gunnet ⚲ Q (9) 15s 56°01'·34N 03°11'·06W.
No. 7 ⚲ QG; ***Racon (T) 5M***; 56°02'·80N 03°10'·97W.
No. 9 ⚲ Fl G 6s; 56°02'·32N 03°13'·48W.
No. 10 ⚲ Fl R 6s; 56°02'·07N 03°13'·32W.

No. 11 ⚲ Fl G 3s 56°02'·08N 03°15'·26W.
No. 12 ⚲ Fl R 3s; 56°01'·78N 03°15'·15W.
No. 13 ⚲ Fl G 9s; 56°01'·77N 03°16'·94W.
No. 14 ⚲ Q R; 56°01'·51N 03°16'·90W.
Oxcars ⚲ Fl (2) WR 7s 16m W13M, R12M; W twr; R band; vis: 072°-W-087°- R-196°-W-313°-R-072°; 56°01'·36N 03°16'·84W.
Inchcolm E Pt ⚲ Fl (3) 15s 20m 10M; Gy twr; part obsc by land 075°-145·5°; 56°01'·72N 03°17'·83W.
No. 15 ⚲ Fl G 6s; 56°01'·39N 03°18'·95W.

MORTIMER'S DEEP
Hawkcraig Point Ldg Lts 292°. Front, Iso 5s 12m 14M; W twr; vis: 282°-302°; 56°03'·03N 03°17'·07W. Rear, 96m from front, Iso 5s 16m 14M; W twr; vis: 282°-302°.
Inchcolm S Lts in line 066°. Front, 84m from rear, Q 7m 7M; W twr; vis: 062·5°-082·5°; 56°01'·78N 03°18'·28W. Common Rear, Iso 5s 11m 7M; W twr; vis: 062·5°-082·5°; 56°01'·80N 03°18'·13W. N Lts in line 076·7°. Front, 80m from rear, Q 7m 7M; W twr; vis: 062·5°-082·5°.

APPROACHES TO FORTH BRIDGES
No. 17 ⚲ Fl G 3s; 56°01'·23N 03°19'·84W.
No. 16 ⚲ Fl R 3s; 56°00'·87N 03°19'·60W.
No. 19 ⚲ Fl G 9s; 56°00'·71N 03°22'·47W.
Beamer Rk W ⚲ Fl 3s 5m 9M; W post; vis: 050°-230°; 56°00'·30N 03°24'·79W.
Beamer Rk E ⚲ Fl 3s 5m 9M; W post; vis: 230°-050°; 56°00'·27N 03°24'·72W.

PORT EDGAR
W Bkwtr Hd ⚲ Fl R 4s 4m 8M; 55°59'·86N 03°24'·78W. W blockhouse.

FIRTH OF FORTH – NORTH SHORE (INWARD)

BURNTISLAND
W Pier Outer Hd ⚲ Fl (2) R 6s 7m; W twr; 56°03'·22N 03°14'·26W.
E Pier Outer Hd ⚲ Fl (2) G 6s 7m 5M; 56°03'·24N 03°14'·17W.

ABERDOUR, BRAEFOOT BAY and INCHCOLM
Hawkcraig Pt ⚲ (see **MORTIMER'S DEEP** above).
Braefoot Bay Terminal, W Jetty. Ldg Lts 247·3°. **Front**, Fl 3s 6m **15M**; W △ on E dolphin; vis: 237·2°-257·2°; 56°02'·16N 03°18'·71W; 4 dolphins with 2 FG (vert). **Rear**, 88m from front, Fl 3s 12m **15M**; W ▽ on appr gangway; vis: 237·2°-257·2°; sync with front.

INVERKEITHING BAY
St David's ⚲ Fl G 5s 3m 7M; Or □, on pile; 56°01'·37N 03°22'·29W.
Channel ⚲ QG; 56°01'·43N 03°23'·02W.

ROSYTH
Main Chan Dir lt 323·5°. Bn 'A' Oc WRG 7m 4M; R □ on W post with R bands; vis: 318°-G-321°-321°-W-326°-R-328° (H24); 56°01'·19N 03°25'·61W.
Dir lt 115°, Bn 'C' Oc WRG 6s 7m 4M; W ▽ on W Bn; vis: 110°- R -113° W -116·5° - G -120°; 56°00'·61N 03°24'·25W.
S Arm Jetty Hd ⚲ L Fl (2) WR 12s 5m W9M; R6M; vis: 010°-W-280°-R-010°; 56°01'·09N 03°26'·58W.

RIVER FORTH

ROSYTH to GRANGEMOUTH
Dhu Craig ⚲ Fl G 5s; 56°00'·74N 03°27'·23W.
Blackness ⚲ QR; 56°01'·06N 03°30'·30W.
Tancred Bank ⚲ Fl (2) R 10s; 56°01'·58N 03°31'·91W.
Dods Bank ⚲ Fl R 3s; 56°02'·03N 03°34'·07W.
Bo'ness ⚲ Fl R 10s; 56°02'·23N 03°35'·38W.
Torry ⚲ Fl G 10s 5m 7M; G ○ structure; 56°02'·46N 03°35'·28W.
Bo'ness Bcns ⚲ 2 QR 3m 2M; 56°01'·85N 03°36'·22W.
Bo'ness Hbr ⚲ ; 56°01'·26N 03°36'·46W.

GRANGEMOUTH

Grangemouth App No. 1 ⚓ Fl (3) 10s 4m 6M;56°02'·12N 03°38'·10W.

Hen & Chickens ⚓ Fl (3) G 10s; 56°02'·35N 03°38'·08W.

FIRTH OF FORTH – NORTH SHORE (OUTWARD)

KIRKCALDY and METHIL

Kirkaldy E. Pier Hd ⚓ Fl WG 10s 12m 8M; vis: 156°-G-336°-W-156°; 56°06'·78N 03°08'·90W.

Methil Outer Pier Hd ⚓ Oc G 6s 8m 5M; W twr; vis: 280°-100°; 56°10'·76N 03°00'·48W.

ELIE and ST MONANS

Elie Ness ☆ 56°11'·04N 02°48'·77W; Fl 6s 15m **17M**; W twr.

St Monans Bkwtr Hd ⚓ Oc WRG 6s 5m W7M, R4M, G4M; vis: 282°-G-355°-W-026°-R-038°; 56°12'·20N 02°45'·94W.

PITTENWEEM and ANSTRUTHER EASTER

Pittenweem, Ldg Lts 037° Middle Pier Hd. Front, FR 4m 5M. Rear, FR 8m 5M. Both Gy Cols, Or stripes; 56°12'·69N 02°43'·69W.

Pittenweem, E Bkwtr Hd ⚓ Fl (2) RG 5s 9m R9M, G6M; vis: 265°-R-345°-G-055°; *Horn 90s (occas)*; 56°12'·63N 02°43'·74W.

Anstruther, Ldg Lts 019°. Front FG 7m 4M; 56°13'·28N 02°41'·76W. Rear, 38m from front, FG 11m 4M, (both W masts).

MAY I, CRAIL, ST ANDREWS and FIFE NESS to MONTROSE

Isle of May ☆ 56°11'·12N 02°33'·46W(Summit); Fl (2) 15s 73m **22M**; □ twr on stone dwelling.

Crail, Ldg Lts 295°. Front, FR 24m 6M (not lit when hbr closed); 56°15'·46N 02°37'·84W. Rear, 30m from front, FR 30m 6M.

Fife Ness ☆ 56°16'·74N 02°35'·19W; Iso WR 10s 12m **W21M, R20M**; W bldg; vis: 143°-W-197°-R-217°-W-023°; 002320798.

N Carr ⚓ Q (3) 10s 3m 5M; 56°18'·05N 02°32'·94W.

St Andrews ⚓ 56°20'·38N 02°47'·07W; Dir lt 277·7; Iso WRG 2s 17m 9M; vis: 272°-G-276°-AlWG-277°-W-278°-AlWR-279°-R-283°.

St Andrews N Bkwtr Bn ⚓ Fl G 3M 56°20'·36N 02°46'·77W.

Bell Rk ☆ 56°26'·08N 02°23'·21W; Fl 5s 28m **18M**; *Racon (M) 18M*.

RIVER TAY, TAYPORT, DUNDEE and PERTH

Tay Fairway ⚓ L Fl 10s; *Bell*; 56°28'·30N 02°36'·60W.

Middle ⚓ Fl G 3s; 56°28'·08N 02°38'·24W.

Middle ⚓ Fl (2) R 6s 56°27'·82N 02°37'·97W.

Abertay N ⚓ Q (3) 10s; *Racon (T) 8M*; 56°27'·39N 02°40'·36W.

Abertay S (Elbow) ⚓ Fl R 6s 56°27'·13N 02°39'·83W.

Tayport High Lt ⚓ 56°27'·17N 02°53'·95W; Dir lt 269°; Iso WRG 3s 24m W14M, R14M, G14M; W twr vis: 267°-G-268°-W-270°-R-271°.

ARBROATH

Ldg lts 299·2°. Front , FR 7m 5M; W col; 56°33'·29N 02°35'·16W. Rear, 50m from front, FR 13m 5M; W col.

MONTROSE

Scurdie Ness ☆ 56°42'·10N 02°26'·24W; Fl (3) 20s 38m **23M**; W twr; *Racon (T) 14-16M*.

Outer Ldg Lts 271·5°; Front, FR 11m 5M; W twin pillars, R bands; 56°42'·21N 02°27'·41W; Rear, 272m from front, FR 18m 5M; W twr, R cupola.

Inner Ldg Lts 265°; Front FG 21m 5M; Rear FG 33m 5M.

MONTROSE TO RATTRAY HEAD

JOHNSHAVEN and GOURDON HARBOUR

Johnshaven, Ldg Lts 316°. Front, FR 5m; 56°47'·62N 02°20'·26W. Rear, 85m from front, FG 20m; shows R when unsafe to ent hbr. Gourdon Hbr, Ldg Lts 358°. Front, FR 5m 5M; W twr; shows G when unsafe to enter; *Siren (2) 60s* (occas); 56°49'·69N 02°17'·24W. Rear, 120m from front, FR 30m 5M; W twr. Todhead Lighthouse (disused), white tower, 13m.

STONEHAVEN to GIRDLE NESS

Outer Pier Hd ⚓ Iso WRG 4s 7m 5M; vis: 214°-G-246°-W-268°-R-280°; 56°57'·59N 02°12'·00W.

Girdle Ness ☆ Fl (2) 20s 56m **22M**; obsc by Greg Ness when brg more than about 020°; *Racon (G) 25M*; 57°08'·34N 02°02'·91W.

ABERDEEN

Fairway ⚓ Mo (A) 5s; *Racon (T) 7M*; 57°09'·31N 02°01'·95W.

Torry Ldg lts 237·2°, Front FR or G 14m 5M; R when ent safe, FG when dangerous to navigate; W twr; 57°08'·38N 02°04'·50W. Rear, 220m from front, FR or G 19m 5M; R when ent safe, FG when dangerous to navigate; W twr; 57°08'·31N 02°04'·68W.

Aberdeen Harbour Ent ⚓ 57°08'·38N 02°04'·48W; Dir lt 237·2° Fl WRG 1s 7m 9M; metal post; vis: 235·2°-QG-236·2°-AlQGW-236·7°-QW-237·7°-AlQRW-238·2°-QR-239·2°.

S Bkwtr Hd ⚓ Fl (3) R 8s 23m 7M; 57°08'·69N 02°03'·34W.

N Pier Hd ⚓ Iso G 4s 11m 10M; W twr; 57°08'·74N 02°03'·69W. In fog FY 10m (same twr) vis: 136°-336°; *Bell (3) 12s*.

S Skates Nose Jetty Hd ⚓ Q R 4m 4M; 57°08'·49N 02°04'·06W.

Abercrombie Jetty Hd ⚓ Oc G 4s 5m 4M; 57°08'·53N 02°04'·15W.

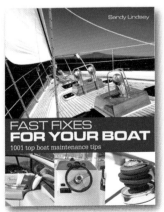
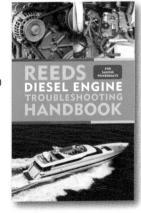

4.4 PASSAGE INFORMATION

For these waters refer to the Admiralty *North Sea (West) Pilot*; R Northumberland YC's *Sailing Directions Humber to Rattray Head*, and the *Forth Yacht Clubs Association Pilot Handbook*, which covers the Firth of Forth in detail. Admiralty Leisure Folios 5615 and 5617 cover the area from Eyemouth to Peterhead.

A 'Rover Ticket', £50 from Aberdeenshire and Moray Councils allows berthing (subject to availability) for one week from the date of arrival at the first harbour. Scheme includes, Johnshaven, Gourdon, Stonehaven, Rosehearty, Banff, Portsoy, Cullen, Portknockie, Findochty, Hopeman and Burghead. More Passage Information is threaded between the harbours of this Area.

BERWICK-UPON-TWEED TO BASS ROCK

(AC 160,175) From Berwick-upon-Tweed to the Firth of Forth there is no good hbr which can be approached with safety in strong onshore winds. So, if on passage with strong winds from N or E, plan accordingly and keep well to seaward. In late spring and early summer fog (haar) is likely in onshore winds.

The coast N from Berwick is rocky with cliffs rising in height to Burnmouth, then diminishing gradually to Eyemouth. Keep 5ca offshore to clear outlying rks. Burnmouth, although small, has more alongside space than Eyemouth, which is a crowded fishing hbr. 2·1M NW is St Abbs Hbr, with temp anchorage in offshore winds in Coldingham B close to the S.

St Abbs Hd (lt) is a bold, steep headland, 92m high, with no offlying dangers. ▶ *The stream runs strongly round the Hd, causing turbulence with wind against tide; this can be largely avoided by keeping close inshore. The ESE-going stream begins at HW Leith –0345, and the WNW-going at HW Leith +0240.* ◀ There is a good anch in Pettico Wick, on NW side of Hd, in S winds, but dangerous if the wind shifts onshore. There are no off-lying dangers between St Abbs Hd and Fast Castle Hd, 3M WNW. Between Fast Castle Hd and Barns Ness, about 8M NW, is the attractive little hbr of Cove; but it dries and should only be approached in ideal conditions.

Torness Power Station (conspic, lt on bkwtr) is 1·75M SE of Barns Ness (lt) which lies 2·5M ESE of Dunbar and is fringed with rks; tidal streams as for St Abbs Hd. Conspic chys are 7½ca WSW inland of Barns Ness. Between here and Dunbar keep at least 2½ca offshore to clear rky patches. Sicar Rk (7·9m depth) lies about 1·25M ENE of Dunbar, and sea breaks on it in onshore gales.

The direct course from Dunbar to Bass Rk (lt) is clear of all dangers; inshore of this line beware Wildfire Rks (dry) on NW side of Bellhaven Bay. In offshore winds there is anch in Scoughall Road. Great Carr is a ledge of rks, nearly covering at HW, 1M ESE of Gin Hd, with Carr bn (stone tr surmounted by cross) at its N end. Drying ledges of rks extend 1M SE of Great Carr, up to 3ca offshore. Keep at least 5ca off Carr bn in strong onshore winds. Tantallon Castle (ruins) is on cliff edge 1M W of Great Car. Bass Rk (lt) lies 1·25M NNE of Gin Hd, and is a sheer, conspic rk (115m) with no offlying dangers; landing difficult due to swell.

4.5 EYEMOUTH

Borders 55°52'·52N 02°05'·29W ✿❀⚓⚓⚓⚓

CHARTS AC 160, 1612, 5615; Imray C24

TIDES +0330 Dover; ML No data; Duration 0610

Standard Port LEITH (➝)

Times				Height (metres)			
High Water		Low Water		MHWS	MHWN	MLWN	MLWS
0300	0900	0300	0900	5·6	4·4	2·0	0·8
1500	2100	1500	2100				
Differences EYEMOUTH							
–0005	+0007	+0012	+0008	–0·4	–0·3	0·0	+0·1

SHELTER Good in all weathers except uncomfortable surge in N over F5. Busy FV hbr which encourages yachtsman to visit. Berth as directed by HM. The options are:

- Middle Quay (100m pontoon), depth 0.9m bottom soft mud.
- On the W wall of the N-pointing jetty by the LB.
- On W wall of the centre jetty W of Gunsgreen House (conspic).
- ⚓ in bay only in offshore winds.

NAVIGATION WPT 55°52'·80N 02°05'·34W, 174°/3ca to E bkwtr lt.

- Entry should not be attempted in strong N to E winds. F.R (occas) lt ● or R flag = unsafe to enter indicates unsafe to enter bay or hbr.
- Caution, the entrance is 17m wide and is maintained to 2m depth with soundings taken monthly due to frequent sand movement and silting.
- Appr can be made N or S of Hurkars; from the N, beware Blind Buss 1·2m, marked by NCM lit buoy about 200m ENE of WPT.
- From the S, approach on 250° midway between Hurkars and Hettle Scar (no ldg marks).
- Approaching vessels are advised to contact HM (mob 07885 742505) for latest information.

LIGHTS AND MARKS St Abbs Hd lt ho Fl 10s 68m 26M is 3M NW. Ldg lts 174° both FG 9/10m 6M, orange columns on W pier.

COMMUNICATIONS (Code 01890) MRCC (01224) 592334; Police 101; Dr 750599, Ⓗ (0131) 536 1000. HM 750223, Mobile 07885 742505.

VHF Ch 16 **12** (HO). Advisable to listen to VHF Ch 6 for FVs entering/leaving port.

FACILITIES Hbr ⌂ (quay) £14.80, (pontoon) £18.90 (charges based

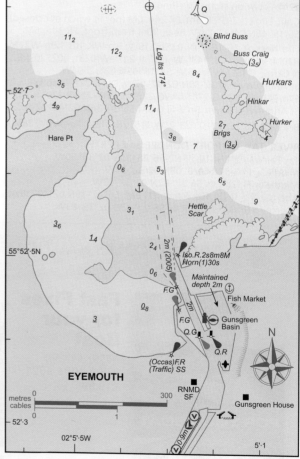

EYEMOUTH

on 10m LOA; discount for more than 3 nights), ⚓, ⛽, ▯, showers (2x50p), ☎ (at harbour building), ▬, BY, ✎, ⚒, C (12 ton mobile), Ⓔ, wi-fi. See www.eyemouth-harbour.co.uk

Town LB, ☎, ▯, ☰, ✕, ⌂, ✉, ▯, Gas, Gaz, Ⓑ. ⇌ (bus to Berwick-on-Tweed and Edinburgh), ✈ (Edinburgh).

ADJACENT HARBOURS

BURNMOUTH, Borders, **55°50′·61N 02°04′·10W**. AC 160. HW +0315 on Dover, –0025 on Leith; Duration 0615. Use Eyemouth tides 4.5. From S beware Quarry Shoal Rks; and E & W Carrs from N. 2 W posts (unclear by day, FR 29/35m 4M) 45m apart, lead 253° to close N of the hbr; as hbr mouth opens, enter on about 185° with outer hbr ent in line with 2FG (vert). Min depth at ent at LWS is 0·6m. Shelter is good especially in inner hbr (dries). With on-shore winds, swell makes outer hbr uncomfortable. HM (018907) 81283 (home). Facilities: 🍺 £10 (all LOA), ⚓, limited 🛒.

ST ABBS, Borders, **55°54′·10N 02°07′·74W**. AC 175. HW +0330 on Dover, –0017 on Leith; HW –0·6m on Leith; Duration 0605. Ldg line (about 228°) S face of Maw Carr on village hall (conspic R roof) leads SW until the hbr ent opens to port and the 2nd ldg line (about 176°) can be seen 2FR 2/4m 1M, or Y LB ho visible through ent. On E side of ent chan, beware Hog's Nose and on W side the Maw Carr. Shelter good. In strong on-shore winds outer hbr suffers from waves breaking over E pier. Inner hbr (dries) is best but often full of FVs. HM (0775 1136758) directs visitors. Facilities: 🍺 £15 (all LOA), 🛥 (launching £15), ⚓, 🔧, at quay, ✕, ✉, 🛒, more facilities & bar at Coldingham.

4.6 DUNBAR

East Lothian 56°00′·39N 02°31′·09W ❀❀⌑⌑❁❁❁

CHARTS AC 175, 734, 5615; Imray C24, C23, C27

TIDES +0330 Dover; ML 3·0; Duration 0600

Standard Port LEITH (⟶)

Times				Height (metres)			
High Water		Low Water		MHWS	MHWN	MLWN	MLWS
0300	0900	0300	0900	5·6	4·4	2·0	0·8
1500	2100	1500	2100				
Differences DUNBAR							
–0005	+0003	+0003	–0003	–0·3	–0·3	0·0	+0·1
FIDRA							
–0001	0000	–0002	+0001	–0·2	–0·2	0·0	0·0

SHELTER Outer (Victoria) Hbr is subject to surge in strong NW to NE winds. N side dries; ♥ berth on E wall on N side of bridge, dries approx HW±2. Contact HM. Keep steps clear. Inner (Old or Cromwell) Hbr dries and is safe in strong onshore conditions; entry is through a bridge, lifted on request to HM.

NAVIGATION WPT 56°00′·60N 02°31′·49W, 132°/3ca to hbr ent, preferable entry in marginal conditions.

- Entry is dangerous in heavy on-shore swell with no access in strong winds from NW to E.
- Beware Wallace's Head Rock, Half Ebb Rock (2‚m), 1½ca from ent. and Outer Buss 4ca E of ent.
- Min depth at ent 0·5m, but may be much less in abnormal circumstances.
- Keep to port on entry to avoid rockfall off castle.

LIGHTS AND MARKS Church and Castle ruin both conspic. From NE, ldg lts, Oc G 6s 15/22m 3M, synch, intens 188°-208°, 2 W △ on Or cols, lead 198° through the outer rks to the Roads; thence narrow ent opens with QR brg 132°. From NW, appr on brg 132° between bns on Wallaces Head and Half Ebb Rk.

COMMUNICATIONS (01368) MRCC (01224) 592334; Police 101; Dr 863704; Ⓗ (0131) 536 1000. HM 865404, Mobile 07958754858, harbourmaster@talktalk.net.

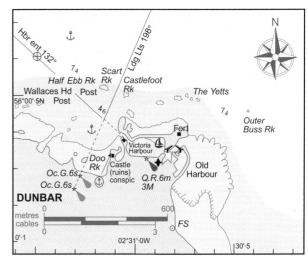

FACILITIES **Quay** 🍺 £16 (£20 over 12m LOA), ⚓, D, 🛥; **N Wall** M, 🍺; **Inner Hbr** 🛥, 🍺. **Town** LB, 🅿, 🔧, Gas, Gaz, ▣, 🛒, ✕, 🏧, ✉, Ⓑ, ⇌, ✈ Edinburgh.

ADJACENT HARBOUR

NORTH BERWICK, East Lothian, **56°03′·74N 02°43′·04W**. AC 734. Fidra HW +0344 on Dover; ML 3·0m; Duration 0625. See 4.6 Fidra. Shelter good with winds from S to W but dangerous with on-shore winds. Very small drying harbour with entrance 8m wide. Max LOA normally 30′; LOA >40′ only in emergency. From E or W, from position 0·25M S of Craigleith, steer S for Plattock Rks, thence SSW 40m off harbour wall (beware Maiden Rocks to the W) before turning 180° to port into hbr. Galloway Pier extends N from hbr wall.

Breakwater light F R 7m 3M (2 F R (vert) when harbour closed) and FG 6m 3M (about 1ca S) in transit 188°. Facilities: 🍺 £14.50, L, ⚓ on pier, HM www.nbharbour.org.uk ☎ (01620) 893333, Mob 0777 6467373,

East Lothian YC ☎ (01620) 892698, M, ⚓s, 🅿.
Town 🅿 & 🅿, 🛒, Gas, Ⓑ, ✉, ⇌ and bus Edinburgh.

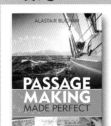

SE Scotland

FIRTH OF FORTH – SOUTH SHORE

(AC 734, 735) Westward of Bass Rk, Craigleith (51m), Lamb Is (24m) and Fidra (31m) lie 5ca or more offshore, while the coast is generally foul. Craigleith is steep-to, and temporary anchorage can be found on SE and SW sides; if passing inshore of it keep well to N side of chan. N Berwick hbr (dries) lies S of Craigleith, but is unsafe in onshore winds. Between Craigleith and Lamb Is, beware drying rks up to 3ca from land. Lamb Is is 1·5M WNW of N Berwick and has a rky ledge extending 2½ca SW. Fidra Is (lt) is a bird reserve, nearly connected to the shore by rky ledges, and should be passed to the N; passage and anchorage on S side are tricky. Anchor on E or W sides, depending on wind, in good weather.

In the bay between Fidra and Edinburgh some shelter can be found in SE winds in Aberlady Bay and Gosford Bay. The best anchorage is SW of Craigielaw Pt. Port Seton is a drying fishing harbour 7½ca E of the conspic chys of Cockenzie Power Station; entry is not advisable in strong onshore winds. Cockenzie (dries) is close to power station; beware Corsik Rk 400m to E. No attractions except boatyard.

There are no dangers on the direct course from Fidra to Inchkeith (lt), which stands between the buoyed deep water chans. Rks extend 7½ca SE from Inchkeith, and 5ca off the W side where there is a small hbr below the lt ho; landing is forbidden without permission. N Craig and Craig Waugh (least depth 0·2m) are buoyed shoals 2·5M SE from Inchkeith lt ho.

▶*In N Chan, close to Inchkeith the W-going (flood) stream begins about HW Leith –0530, and the E-going at HW Leith +0030, sp rates about 1kn. The streams gather strength towards the Forth bridges, where they reach 2·25kn and there may be turbulence.*◀

Leith is wholly commercial; Granton has yacht moorings in the E hbr; Port Edgar has a major yacht hbr close W of Forth Road Bridge. Hound Point oil terminal is an artificial 'island-jetty' almost in mid-stream, connected to the shore by underwater pipeline (no ⚓). Yachts may pass the terminal on either side at least 30m off keeping well clear of manoeuvring ships.

▶*Tidal streams are quite weak in the outer part of the Firth, apart from the stream in the Tay, which attains 5kn in most places. Coastwise tidal streams between Fife Ness and Arbroath are weak.*

Northbound. *Leave before HW (Dover +0400) to be at N Carr at Dover +0600. Bound from Forth to Tay aim to arrive at Abertay By at LW slack (Dover –0200).*

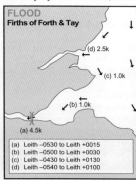

FLOOD	
Firths of Forth & Tay	

(d) 2.5k
(c) 1.0k
(b) 1.0k
(a) 4.5k

| (a) Leith –0530 to Leith +0015 |
| (b) Leith –0500 to Leith +0030 |
| (c) Leith –0430 to Leith +0130 |
| (d) Leith –0540 to Leith +0100 |

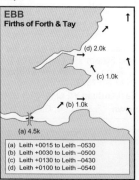

EBB	
Firths of Forth & Tay	

(d) 2.0k
(c) 1.0k
(b) 1.0k
(a) 4.5k

| (a) Leith +0015 to Leith –0530 |
| (b) Leith +0030 to Leith –0500 |
| (c) Leith +0130 to Leith –0430 |
| (d) Leith +0100 to Leith –0540 |

Southbound. *Leave before LW (Dover –0200) to be at Bass Rk at HW Dover. If bound from Tay to Forth, leave late in ebb to pick up early flood off St Andrews to N Carr and into Forth.*◀

RIVER FORTH TO KINCARDINE

(AC 736, 737, 738) The main shipping chan under the N span of the rail bridge is busy with commercial traffic for Grangemouth and Rosyth. W of Beamer Rk the Firth widens as far as Bo'ness (small drying hbr) on the S shore where the chan narrows between drying mudbanks.

▶*Forth Replacement Crossing construction continues to the W of the Forth Road Bridge between 56° 00'·76N, 3° 24'·44W (shore) and 55° 59'·61N, 3° 25'·16W (shore). There are now 3 pillars, one on Beamer Rk and two clear of the main navigable routes. Works will be ongoing until the end of 2016 and numerous craft will be operating in the vicinity. Forth and Tay Navigation Service will broadcast information and vessels should maintain a listening watch on VHF Ch 71.*◀

Charlestown (N bank) dries, but is a secure hbr. Grangemouth is industrially conspicuous. Beware of gas carriers, tankers and other cargo vessels; there are no facilities for yachts. Few yachts go beyond Kincardine swing bridge, clearance 6·5m, which is no longer opened. Clackmannanshire Bridge, clearance 6·5m, is about 4ca further up-river.

FIRTH OF FORTH – NORTH SHORE

(AC 734, 190) From Burntisland the N shore of Firth of Forth leads E to Kinghorn Ness. 1M SSW of Kinghorn Ness Blae Rk (SHM lt buoy) has least depth of 4·1m, and seas break on it in E gales.

▶ *Rost Bank lies halfway between Kinghorn Ness and Inchkeith, with tide rips at sp tides or in strong winds.* ◀

From Kinghorn Ness to Kirkcaldy, drying rks lie up to 3ca offshore. Kirkcaldy Hbr is effectively closed, but yachts can enter inner dock near HW by arrangement; ent is dangerous in strong E'lies, when seas break a long way out.

Between Kirkcaldy and Methil the only dangers more than 2ca offshore are The Rockheads, extending 4ca SE of Dysart, and marked by 2 SHM buoys. Largo B is anch, well sheltered from N and E, but avoid gaspipes near E side. Close SW of Elie, beware W Vows (dries) and E Vows (dries, bn). There is anch close W of Elie Ness (4.7). Ox Rk (dries 2m) lies 5ca ENE of Elie Ness, and 2½ca offshore; otherwise there are no dangers more than 2ca offshore past St Monance, Pittenweem and Anstruther, but in bad weather the sea breaks on Shield Rk 4ca off Pittenweem. From Anstruther to Crail and on to Fife Ness keep 3ca offshore to clear Caiplie Rk and other dangers.

May Island (lt) lies about 5M S of Fife Ness; its shores are bold except at NW end where rks extend 1ca off. Anch near N end at E or W Tarbert, on lee side according to winds; in good weather it is possible to land. Lt ho boats use Kirkhaven, close SE of lt ho.

FORTH TO NORWAY AND THE BALTIC

(AC 2182B, 2182C) Heading ENE'ly from the Firth of Forth the main hazards result from offshore industrial activities and their associated traffic. Particularly in summer months oil/gas exploration, movement of drilling rigs and pipe laying create potentially hazardous situations for small craft. Rig movements and many of the more intense activities are published in Notices to Mariners, but even so it is wise to avoid the gas and oil fields where possible and never to approach within 500m of installations. There are TSS to be avoided off the S and SW coast of Norway. Strong currents and steep seas may be experienced in the approaches to the Skagerrak.

4.7 FIRTH OF FORTH
E and W Lothian/City of Edinburgh/Fife

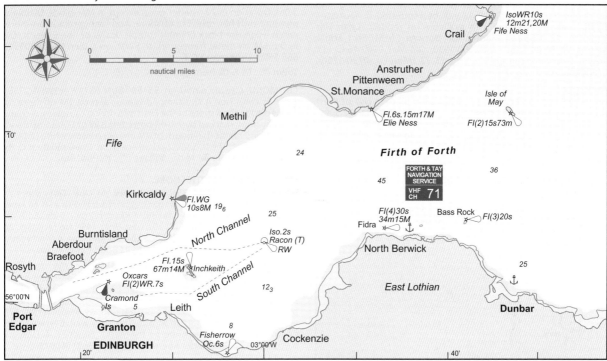

CHARTS AC 734, 735, 736, 737, 741, 5615; Imray C23, C27

TIDES +0350 (Granton) Dover; ML 3·3; Duration 0620

Standard Port LEITH (→)

Times				Height (metres)			
High Water		Low Water		MHWS	MHWN	MLWN	MLWS
0300	0900	0300	0900	5·6	4·4	2·0	0·8
1500	2100	1500	2100				
Differences COCKENZIE							
–0007	–0015	–0013	–0005	–0·2	0·0	ND	ND

GRANTON: Same as LEITH

SHELTER Port Edgar offers good shelter, but surge at LW esp in E winds. Silting in centre of entrance and close to wavebreak. Granton mostly dries but is open to violent swell in N'lies. Pontoons on E side of Middle Pier in about 2m and RFYC welcomes visitors. Pilot launches berth at seaward end. Leith is purely commercial. Rosyth should only be used in emergency. Forth Navigation Service controls Firth of Forth, Granton Hbr and all commercial docks.

NAVIGATION Port Edgar 56°N 03°24'·3W, 244°/3ca to W bkwtr. Do not enter E of wavebreak, beware of shallows at W end; 3kn sp limit. Granton WPT 56°00'·00N 03°13'·31W, 180°/0·72M to entry.

- Beware Hound Pt terminal; Forth Railway and Road Bridges; vessels bound to/from Rosyth and Grangemouth especially in local fog (haar). 12kn speed limit W of Forth Rly Bridge.
- On N shore, no vessel may enter Mortimer's Deep (Braefoot gas terminal) without approval from Forth Navigation Service.
- Protected chan runs from Nos 13 & 14 buoys (NNW of Oxcars) under the bridges (N of Inch Garvie and Beamer Rk), to Rosyth. When activated (occas) via Forth Ports plc, other vessels must clear the chan for Rosyth traffic.
- Caution: strong tidal streams.

LIGHTS AND MARKS See 4.3 and chartlets. Granton: R flag with W diagonal cross (or ● lt) on signal mast at middle pier hd = Entry prohibited.

COMMUNICATIONS (Code 0131) MRCC (01224) 592334; Police 101; ⊞ Edinburgh Royal Infirmary 2292477; Forth and Tay Navigation Service (01324) 98584; QHM Rosyth (01383) 425050.

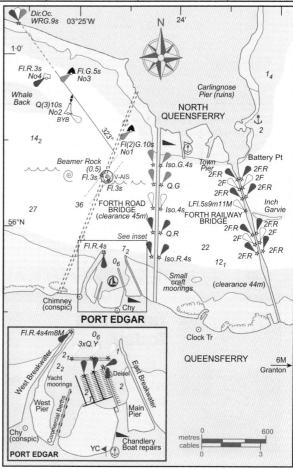

HMNB CLYDE (01436) 674321 ext 3206, for naval activity off Scotland; Forth Yacht Clubs Ass'n 5523452.

Call *Forth Navigation* (at Grangemouth) Ch **71** (calling and short messages, H24) 16; **20** 12 will be requested if necessary. Traffic, nav and weather info available on request. Leith Hbr Radio Ch 12. Granton Marina, call *Boswell* Ch M. Port Edgar Marina Ch M **80** (Apr-Sept 0900-1930; Oct-Mar 0900-1630 LT). Rosyth Dockyard, call *QHM* Ch 74 13 73 (Mon-Fri: 0730-1700). Grangemouth Docks Ch 14 (H24).

FACILITIES

GRANTON Extensive development is taking place in NW of West Hrbr. HM via Leith, ☎ 555 8866, 🚰, ⛴; **Royal Forth YC** ☎ 552 3006, ⛴, M, L, 🚰, C (5 ton), D, ⛽, 🍸; **Forth Corinthian YC** ☎ 552 5939, ⛴, M, L, 🍸; **Services:** Gas, Gaz, ⚒, 🛥, 🔧. **Town** ⛽ & ⛽ 🛒, ✕, 🍸, ✉, Ⓑ, ⇄, ✈ (Buses to Edinburgh).

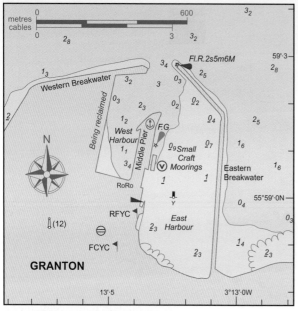

SOUTH QUEENSFERRY Port Edgar Marina ☎ 313330, admin. PE@edinburghleisure.co.uk, (301 ⚓ +8Ⓥ) £1.95, Access H24; M, ⛴, 🛥, 🔧, D, C (5 ton) on N end of main pier, ⛽, Ⓔ, 🔧, ⚒, ⛵, Gas, Gaz, 🚰, ✕; Port Edgar YC, 🍸. **Town** ⛽, 🛒, ✕, 🍸, ✉, Ⓑ, ⇄ (Dalmeny), ✈ Edinburgh.

ROSYTH Dockyard and ferry port; no facilities for yachts except in emergency. **Ferries:** Zeebrugge; 3/week; 17 Hrs; Superfast (www.superfast.com).

GRANGEMOUTH HM ☎ 01324 498566 (H24); Port Office ☎ 498597 (HO). VHF Ch 14 16. Commercial port.

FIRTH OF FORTH SOUTH SHORE

FISHERROW, East Lothian, **55°56′·79N 03°04′·09W.** AC 734, 735. HW +0345 on Dover, –0005 on Leith; HW –0·1m on Leith; ML 3·0m; Duration 0620. Shelter good except in NW winds. Mainly a pleasure craft hbr, dries 5ca offshore. Appr dangerous in on-shore winds. High-rise block (38m) is conspic 9ca W of hbr. E pier lt, Oc 6s 5m 6M on metal framework tr. Berth on E pier. HM ☎ (0131) 665 5900; **Fisherrow YC** 🚰.

Town 🛒, ⛽ & ⛽ from garage, ✕, 🍸, Ⓑ, ✉, ⛵.

CRAMOND, City of Edinburgh, **55°59′·80N 03°17′·49W.** AC 736. Tides as Leith (see 4.7). Cramond Island, approx 1M offshore, is connected to the S shore of the Firth by a drying causeway. A chan, virtually dries, marked by 7 SHM posts, leads W of Cramond Island to Cramond hbr at the mouth of R Almond, conspic white houses. ⚓ free or ⚓ off the Is. Seek local advice from: **Cramond Boat Club** ☎ (0131) 336 1356, 🚰, M, 🍸. **Village** 🛒, ✕, Pub, Bus.

FIRTH OF FORTH NORTH SHORE

INCHCOLM, Fife, **56°01′·85N 03°17′·89W.** AC 736. Tides see 4.7. Best ⚓ in 4m, N of abbey (conspic); appr from NW or ESE, to land at pier close E (small fee). Meadulse Rks (dry) on N side. Ends of island foul. At SE end, lt Fl (3) 15s, obsc 075°-145°. No facilities. ☎ 0131-244 3101. Keep clear of large ships under way in Mortimer's Deep, which is well marked with ldg lts and lit lateral buoys.

ABERDOUR, Fife, **56°03′·00N 03°17′·49W.** AC 735, 736. HW +0345 on Dover; +0005 on Leith; HW 0·5m on Leith; ML 3·3m; Duration 0630. See 4.7. Good shelter except in SE winds when a swell occurs. The ⚓ between The Little Craigs and the disused pier is good but exposed to winds from E to SW. Temp berths, £7, are available in hbr (dries) alongside the quay wall. Beware Little Craigs (dries 2·2m). There are no lts/ marks. Facilities: 🚰 (tap on pier), ✕, 🛒, 🍸 in village; **Aberdour BC** ☎ (01383) 860029.

ELIE, Fife, **56°11′·20N 02°49′·29W.** AC 734. HW +0325 on Dover, –0015 on Leith; HW –0·1m on Leith; ML 3·0m; Duration 0620; Elie B provides good shelter from N winds for small craft but local knowledge is needed. Hbr dries; 3 short term waiting buoys available. Beware ledge off end of pier which dries. From E beware Ox Rk (dries 1m) 5M ENE of Elie Ness; from W beware rks off Chapel Ness, W Vows, E Vows (surmounted by cage bn) and Thill Rk, marked by PHM buoy. Lt: Elie Ness Fl 6s 15m 17M, W tr. HM (01333) 330219; ⚓ (3) drying £10/night, M, ⛽, 🚰, 🛥, SC, ⛴. Police 08456 005702. Dr ☎ 330302; **Services:** D (tanker), Gas, Gaz. ⛽. In Elie & Earlsferry: ✕, 🛒, 🍸, ✉, Ⓑ.

ST MONANS, Fife, **56°12′·25 N 02°45′·94W.** AC 734. HW +0335 on Dover, –0020 on Leith; HW –0·1m on Leith; ML 3·0m; Duration 0620. Shelter good except in strong SE to SW winds when scend occurs in the hbr (dries). Berth alongside E pier until contact with HM. From NE keep at least 2½ca from coast. Bkwtr hd Oc WRG 6s 5m 7/4M; E pier hd 2 FG (vert) 6m 4M. W pier hd 2 FR (vert)6m4M. **Facilities** HM ☎ 07930 869538 (part time) if no reply, 01333 310836 (Anstruther HM assists); ⚓ (example for 10m LOA) £17.20 then £8.60/day thereafter, 🚰, ⛽, ⛽; **Services:** Gas, D (tanker ☎ 730622), AC. Police ☎ 08456 005702. **Village** R, 🍸, 🛒, ✉, Ⓑ.

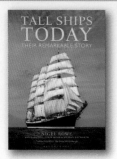

4.8 FORTH AND CLYDE CANAL

Lowland Carron River Ent. **51°02'·30N 03°41'·46W** ✴⚓⚓⚘⚘

These notes are for the convenience of those entering the canal at Grangemouth. The eastern extension, by-passing low bridges on the R Carron, was completed autumn 2013, opened Mar 2014.

CHARTS AC 737, 741, 5615; Imray C27; *The Skipper's Guide* Forth & Clyde and Union Canal essential. Obtain from, Lowland Canals Office, Canal House, Applecross Street, Glasgow, G4 9SP. ☎ (0141) 332 6936, www.scottishcanals.co.uk or www.waterscape.com.

TIDES Carron River +0325 Dover, 0030 Leith.

SHELTER Carron Sea Lock operates HW–4 to HW+1½, 0800-2000 and daylight hours. Temporary berthing at Grangemouth YC or at nearby Refuge Posts. Temporary ⚓s close WNW of Carron PHM and close SSW of Carron Bn SHM dependent on depth.

NAVIGATION Carron River entrance approached from Grangemouth Roads via Small Craft Recommended Tracks close N of Ship Manoeuvring Area.

- Canal passage has to be booked in advance, call *Carron Sea Lock* VHF Ch 74, ☎ (01324)483034/07810 0794468.
- The canal is about 30M long with 39 locks. Allow a minimum of 21 hours underway for a passage to Bowling Sea Lock. Transit of the canal can be achieved in 2 days by reaching the Summit Pound at Lock 20 Wyndford on the first day.
- Canal can take vessels 20m LOA, 6m beam, 1.8m draft (add 0.1m/4inches to draft for freshwater), mast ht 3.0m. Masts should be unstepped before passing through Kerse Bridge which is equipped with air draft gauges calibrated for the canal dimensions.
- Mast craneage at Bowling, Grangemouth YC and Port Edgar for larger yachts.
- Vessels should have a reliable engine and be capable of a minimum speed through the water of 4kn against adverse conditions. Ebb tide attains rates of up to 6kn in Carron River after heavy rainfall. 4mph speed limit throughout the canal.
- Access via Falkirk Wheel to Union Canal and Edinburgh, refer to *Scottish Canals Skipper's Guide.*

LOCKS Carron Sea Lock and Bowling Sea Lock are operated by canal staff. At other locks staff available to assist. 5 day passage licence costs £5/m for boats with crew to assist at locks and £15/m without, including access to the Falkirk Wheel, Union Canal and Edinburgh.

LIGHTS AND MARKS Carron River channel is marked by lighted By PHM & Bn SHM and unlit By(s) PHM & SHM. Bkwtr/Training Bank to W & N of channel marked with Bn(s) & Bol(s).

BOAT SAFETY SCHEME *The Skipper's Guide* refers. At Carron Sea Lock transient/visiting craft staying no more than 28 days will be subject to a Dangerous Boat Check of gas and fuel systems. Also required to complete a boat condition declaration and provide evidence of insurance for £1M third party liability.

COMMUNICATIONS Carron Sea Lock (01324) 483034/07810794468. *Carron Sea Lock* VHF Ch **74**.

FACILITIES Carron Sea Lock ⚓, P, 🚾, ⚐, ⛴. **Falkirk Wheel (on Forth & Clyde)** ⚓, P, D, 🚾, ⚐. For details throughout the canal refer to *The Skipper's Guide* (using maps).

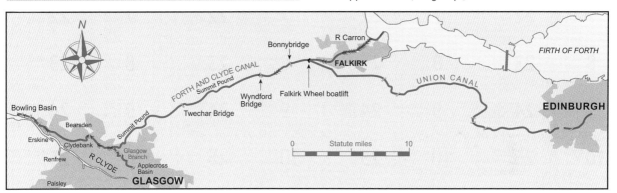

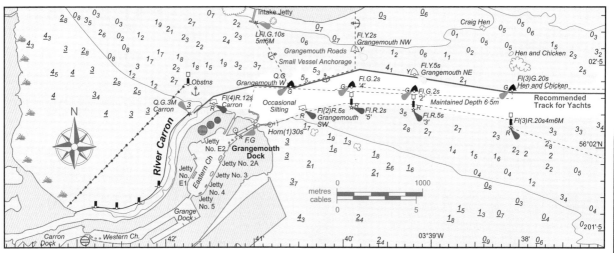

STANDARD TIME (UT)
For Summer Time add ONE hour in **non-shaded areas**

LEITH   LAT 55°59'N   LONG 3°11'W
TIMES AND HEIGHTS OF HIGH AND LOW WATERS

Dates in red are **SPRINGS**
Dates in blue are **NEAPS**

YEAR 2015

JANUARY

Time m	Time m
1 0519 1.7 / 1133 5.0 / TH 1737 1.7 / 2359 5.0	**16** 0423 2.0 / 1047 4.6 / F 1700 2.1 / 2322 4.6
2 0619 1.6 / 1232 5.1 / F 1838 1.5	**17** 0531 1.8 / 1151 4.8 / SA 1759 1.8
3 0057 5.1 / 0707 1.5 / SA 1324 5.3 / 1930 1.3	**18** 0025 4.9 / 0624 1.5 / SU 1248 5.1 / 1852 1.4
4 0147 5.2 / 0748 1.4 / SU 1408 5.4 / 2015 1.1	**19** 0119 5.2 / 0714 1.3 / M 1337 5.4 / 1943 1.0
5 0231 5.3 / 0824 1.3 / M 1449 5.5 / ○ 2055 1.0	**20** 0206 5.5 / 0803 1.0 / TU 1421 5.7 / ● 2035 0.7
6 0310 5.3 / 0855 1.2 / TU 1527 5.5 / 2129 0.9	**21** 0250 5.8 / 0852 0.8 / W 1503 5.9 / 2124 0.4
7 0348 5.3 / 0923 1.2 / W 1603 5.4 / 2157 1.0	**22** 0333 5.9 / 0939 0.6 / TH 1546 6.0 / 2212 0.3
8 0423 5.3 / 0949 1.3 / TH 1638 5.3 / 2223 1.1	**23** 0418 5.9 / 1025 0.6 / F 1631 6.0 / 2258 0.3
9 0458 5.2 / 1017 1.4 / F 1712 5.2 / 2251 1.2	**24** 0504 5.8 / 1109 0.8 / SA 1718 5.9 / 2342 0.5
10 0534 5.0 / 1047 1.5 / SA 1748 5.1 / 2322 1.3	**25** 0553 5.6 / 1151 1.0 / SU 1807 5.7
11 0613 4.9 / 1119 1.7 / SU 1827 4.9 / 2359 1.6	**26** 0025 0.8 / 0645 5.3 / M 1234 1.3 / 1902 5.4
12 0655 4.7 / 1156 1.9 / M 1911 4.7	**27** 0110 1.3 / 0744 5.0 / TU 1324 1.7 / ◐ 2008 5.1
13 0043 1.8 / 0742 4.6 / TU 1247 2.2 / ◐ 2001 4.6	**28** 0206 1.6 / 0850 4.8 / W 1436 1.9 / 2119 4.8
14 0140 2.0 / 0837 4.5 / W 1405 2.3 / 2104 4.5	**29** 0329 1.9 / 0958 4.7 / TH 1604 2.0 / 2231 4.7
15 0256 2.1 / 0941 4.5 / TH 1541 2.3 / 2214 4.5	**30** 0455 2.0 / 1109 4.7 / F 1726 1.9 / 2344 4.7
	31 0606 1.9 / 1217 4.8 / SA 1835 1.6

FEBRUARY

Time m	Time m
1 0048 4.9 / 0656 1.7 / SU 1313 5.1 / 1925 1.4	**16** 0606 1.6 / 1222 5.0 / M 1837 1.4
2 0139 5.0 / 0734 1.5 / M 1358 5.2 / 2006 1.2	**17** 0057 5.2 / 0658 1.3 / TU 1316 5.3 / 1931 0.9
3 0220 5.2 / 0805 1.4 / TU 1437 5.4 / ○ 2040 1.0	**18** 0147 5.5 / 0748 0.9 / W 1401 5.7 / ● 2023 0.5
4 0256 5.2 / 0834 1.2 / W 1512 5.4 / 2109 0.9	**19** 0231 5.8 / 0837 0.6 / TH 1444 6.0 / 2111 0.2
5 0328 5.3 / 0903 1.1 / TH 1544 5.4 / 2137 0.9	**20** 0315 6.0 / 0923 0.4 / F 1528 6.1 / 2157 0.0
6 0359 5.3 / 0933 1.1 / F 1615 5.4 / 2204 0.9	**21** 0359 6.0 / 1008 0.4 / SA 1613 6.1 / 2241 0.1
7 0431 5.2 / 1001 1.3 / SA 1647 5.3 / 2231 1.0	**22** 0444 5.9 / 1051 0.5 / SU 1659 6.0 / 2322 0.4
8 0504 5.1 / 1026 1.3 / SU 1719 5.2 / 2257 1.1	**23** 0530 5.6 / 1130 0.8 / M 1748 5.7
9 0540 5.0 / 1048 1.4 / M 1754 5.1 / 2322 1.3	**24** 0000 0.8 / 0620 5.3 / TU 1207 1.1 / 1841 5.4
10 0618 4.9 / 1114 1.6 / TU 1832 4.9 / 2352 1.6	**25** 0036 1.3 / 0715 5.0 / W 1249 1.5 / ◐ 1943 5.0
11 0700 4.7 / 1149 1.8 / W 1916 4.7	**26** 0118 1.8 / 0818 4.7 / TH 1355 1.9 / 2052 4.7
12 0035 1.8 / 0749 4.6 / TH 1244 2.1 / ◐ 2012 4.5	**27** 0240 2.1 / 0927 4.5 / F 1541 2.0 / 2204 4.5
13 0145 2.1 / 0851 4.4 / F 1419 2.2 / 2126 4.4	**28** 0428 2.2 / 1040 4.5 / SA 1716 1.9 / 2323 4.5
14 0331 2.1 / 1004 4.5 / SA 1619 2.1 / 2246 4.5	
15 0503 2.0 / 1118 4.7 / SU 1737 1.8 / 2358 4.8	

MARCH

Time m	Time m
1 0547 2.1 / 1156 4.6 / SU 1825 1.7	**16** 0439 2.0 / 1046 4.6 / M 1716 1.7 / 2332 4.8
2 0034 4.7 / 0639 1.9 / M 1256 4.9 / 1912 1.4	**17** 0545 1.6 / 1156 4.9 / TU 1820 1.2
3 0124 4.9 / 0714 1.6 / TU 1341 5.1 / 1947 1.2	**18** 0035 5.1 / 0638 1.2 / W 1252 5.3 / 1914 0.8
4 0203 5.1 / 0743 1.4 / W 1418 5.2 / 2017 1.0	**19** 0125 5.5 / 0728 0.9 / TH 1339 5.7 / 2005 0.4
5 0235 5.2 / 0812 1.2 / TH 1451 5.3 / ○ 2045 0.9	**20** 0210 5.8 / 0816 0.5 / F 1423 6.0 / ● 2052 0.1
6 0305 5.3 / 0843 1.0 / F 1521 5.4 / 2112 0.8	**21** 0253 6.0 / 0903 0.3 / SA 1507 6.1 / 2137 0.0
7 0333 5.3 / 0914 1.0 / SA 1551 5.4 / 2141 0.8	**22** 0337 6.0 / 0948 0.2 / SU 1553 6.1 / 2219 0.1
8 0404 5.3 / 0943 1.0 / SU 1622 5.4 / 2209 0.9	**23** 0421 5.9 / 1031 0.4 / M 1640 6.0 / 2259 0.4
9 0436 5.2 / 1006 1.1 / M 1653 5.3 / 2232 1.0	**24** 0508 5.6 / 1111 0.7 / TU 1729 5.7 / 2335 0.9
10 0510 5.1 / 1022 1.2 / TU 1727 5.1 / 2249 1.2	**25** 0556 5.3 / 1146 1.0 / W 1821 5.3
11 0546 5.0 / 1044 1.4 / W 1804 5.0 / 2312 1.4	**26** 0003 1.4 / 0648 5.0 / TH 1223 1.4 / 1919 4.9
12 0626 4.8 / 1117 1.6 / TH 1847 4.8 / 2350 1.7	**27** 0039 1.8 / 0748 4.7 / F 1321 1.8 / ◐ 2023 4.6
13 0712 4.7 / 1206 1.8 / F 1941 4.6 / ◐	**28** 0147 2.2 / 0854 4.4 / SA 1512 2.0 / 2132 4.4
14 0055 2.0 / 0810 4.5 / SA 1331 2.0 / 2051 4.5	**29** 0349 2.4 / 1004 4.4 / SU 1649 1.9 / 2249 4.4
15 0256 2.2 / 0925 4.4 / SU 1546 2.0 / 2216 4.5	**30** 0508 2.2 / 1121 4.5 / M 1755 1.7
	31 0004 4.5 / 0602 2.0 / TU 1225 4.7 / 1841 1.5

APRIL

Time m	Time m
1 0057 4.8 / 0640 1.7 / W 1312 4.9 / 1915 1.3	**16** 0009 5.2 / 0612 1.2 / TH 1226 5.3 / 1851 0.7
2 0135 5.0 / 0713 1.4 / TH 1350 5.1 / 1945 1.1	**17** 0101 5.5 / 0703 0.9 / F 1315 5.6 / 1942 0.4
3 0207 5.1 / 0746 1.2 / F 1423 5.2 / 2014 0.9	**18** 0147 5.7 / 0753 0.6 / SA 1401 5.9 / ● 2029 0.3
4 0236 5.2 / 0819 1.0 / SA 1454 5.3 / ○ 2044 0.8	**19** 0231 5.9 / 0842 0.3 / SU 1448 6.0 / 2114 0.2
5 0306 5.3 / 0852 0.9 / SU 1525 5.4 / 2115 0.8	**20** 0315 5.9 / 0929 0.3 / M 1535 6.0 / 2157 0.3
6 0337 5.3 / 0923 0.9 / M 1557 5.3 / 2144 0.8	**21** 0400 5.8 / 1012 0.4 / TU 1622 5.8 / 2236 0.6
7 0410 5.3 / 0950 1.0 / TU 1629 5.3 / 2210 1.0	**22** 0446 5.6 / 1053 0.7 / W 1711 5.5 / 2309 1.1
8 0443 5.2 / 1007 1.1 / W 1704 5.2 / 2227 1.2	**23** 0533 5.3 / 1129 1.0 / TH 1802 5.2 / 2334 1.5
9 0520 5.1 / 1028 1.2 / TH 1743 5.1 / 2250 1.4	**24** 0623 5.0 / 1202 1.3 / F 1855 4.9
10 0600 5.0 / 1103 1.4 / F 1829 4.9 / 2330 1.7	**25** 0006 1.8 / 0718 4.7 / SA 1250 1.7 / ◐ 1952 4.6
11 0646 4.8 / 1156 1.6 / SA 1922 4.7	**26** 0103 2.2 / 0818 4.5 / SU 1416 1.9 / 2053 4.4
12 0043 2.0 / 0743 4.6 / SU 1326 1.8 / ◐ 2030 4.6	**27** 0243 2.4 / 0922 4.5 / M 1559 1.9 / 2158 4.3
13 0239 2.1 / 0856 4.5 / M 1525 1.8 / 2151 4.6	**28** 0414 2.3 / 1031 4.4 / TU 1703 1.8 / 2310 4.4
14 0412 1.9 / 1018 4.7 / TU 1653 1.5 / 2307 4.9	**29** 0511 2.1 / 1138 4.5 / W 1751 1.6
15 0518 1.6 / 1128 5.0 / W 1756 1.1	**30** 0011 4.6 / 0556 1.8 / TH 1232 4.7 / 1830 1.4

Chart Datum: 2·90 metres below Ordnance Datum (Newlyn). HAT is 6·3 metres above Chart Datum.

FREE monthly updates from
www.reedsalmanac.co.uk

STANDARD TIME (UT)
For Summer Time add ONE hour in **non-shaded areas**

LEITH LAT 55°59'N LONG 3°11'W
TIMES AND HEIGHTS OF HIGH AND LOW WATERS

Dates in red are **SPRINGS**
Dates in blue are **NEAPS**

YEAR 2015

MAY

Day	Time	m	Day	Time	m
1 F	0055 0636 1314 1904	4.8 1.5 4.9 1.2	**16** SA	0037 0638 1254 1917	5.4 1.0 5.5 0.7
2 SA	0131 0714 1350 1938	5.0 1.3 5.1 1.1	**17** SU	0125 0731 1343 2006	5.6 0.7 5.7 0.6
3 SU	0204 0751 1425 2012	5.2 1.1 5.2 0.9	**18** M	0211 0822 1431 ● 2052	5.7 0.5 5.8 0.5
4 M ○	0237 0827 1459 2046	5.3 1.0 5.3 0.9	**19** TU	0256 0911 1519 2134	5.7 0.5 5.7 0.7
5 TU	0311 0902 1533 2121	5.4 0.9 5.3 0.9	**20** W	0342 0955 1606 2212	5.6 0.5 5.6 0.9
6 W	0345 0936 1609 2154	5.4 0.9 5.3 1.0	**21** TH	0427 1036 1654 2244	5.5 0.7 5.4 1.2
7 TH	0421 1008 1646 2226	5.3 1.0 5.3 1.1	**22** F	0513 1111 1741 2307	5.3 1.0 5.2 1.5
8 F	0459 1039 1728 2259	5.2 1.1 5.2 1.4	**23** SA	0559 1141 1828 2337	5.1 1.2 4.9 1.8
9 SA	0541 1119 1815 2347	5.1 1.2 5.1 1.6	**24** SU	0648 1218 1917	4.8 1.5 4.7
10 SU ☽	0629 1218 1909	5.0 1.4 4.9	**25** M ☽	0024 0740 1312 2009	2.0 4.6 1.8 4.5
11 M ☽	0059 0725 1336 2014	1.8 4.8 1.5 4.8	**26** TU	0130 0836 1431 2105	2.2 4.5 1.9 4.4
12 TU	0222 0835 1505 2129	1.9 4.7 1.5 4.8	**27** W	0301 0935 1556 2203	2.3 4.4 1.9 4.4
13 W	0343 0952 1625 2241	1.8 4.8 1.3 4.9	**28** TH	0416 1036 1653 2304	2.2 4.4 1.8 4.5
14 TH	0448 1101 1728 2343	1.6 5.0 1.1 5.1	**29** F	0511 1136 1741	2.0 4.6 1.6
15 F	0545 1200 1825	1.3 5.3 0.9	**30** SA	0000 0558 1229 1822	4.7 1.7 4.8 1.4
			31 SU	0048 0641 1314 1902	4.9 1.5 4.9 1.2

JUNE

Day	Time	m	Day	Time	m
1 M	0130 0721 1355 1940	5.1 1.3 5.1 1.1	**16** TU	0156 0807 1419 ● 2031	5.5 0.8 5.5 0.9
2 TU ○	0209 0801 1434 2020	5.3 1.1 5.3 1.0	**17** W	0242 0856 1506 2112	5.5 0.7 5.5 0.9
3 W	0247 0842 1512 2100	5.4 0.9 5.4 0.9	**18** TH	0326 0939 1551 2148	5.5 0.6 5.4 1.0
4 TH	0324 0924 1550 2143	5.4 0.8 5.4 0.9	**19** F	0410 1018 1634 2217	5.4 0.8 5.3 1.2
5 F	0402 1007 1631 2226	5.5 0.8 5.4 1.0	**20** SA	0452 1050 1716 2241	5.3 0.9 5.2 1.4
6 SA	0443 1052 1715 2311	5.4 0.8 5.4 1.2	**21** SU	0533 1116 1758 2310	5.2 1.1 5.0 1.6
7 SU	0527 1139 1803 2359	5.4 0.9 5.3 1.4	**22** M	0615 1147 1840 2349	5.0 1.3 4.8 1.8
8 M	0615 1230 1856	5.2 1.1 5.1	**23** TU	0659 1228 1925	4.8 1.5 4.6
9 TU ☽	0054 0709 1330 1957	1.6 5.1 1.2 5.0	**24** W ☽	0038 0747 1321 2014	2.0 4.6 1.7 4.5
10 W	0159 0815 1440 2106	1.7 5.0 1.3 4.9	**25** TH	0143 0841 1426 2109	2.2 4.5 1.9 4.4
11 TH	0310 0928 1554 2214	1.7 4.9 1.3 4.9	**26** F	0304 0939 1544 2206	2.2 4.4 1.9 4.5
12 F	0418 1037 1701 2318	1.6 5.0 1.3 5.0	**27** SA	0420 1040 1650 2306	2.1 4.5 1.8 4.6
13 SA	0520 1139 1801	1.4 5.1 1.1	**28** SU	0519 1141 1743	1.9 4.6 1.6
14 SU	0015 0617 1237 1856	5.2 1.2 5.3 1.0	**29** M	0004 0608 1237 1829	4.8 1.7 4.8 1.4
15 M	0108 0714 1330 1945	5.4 1.0 5.4 0.9	**30** TU	0057 0654 1326 1914	5.0 1.4 5.1 1.2

JULY

Day	Time	m	Day	Time	m
1 W	0143 0739 1410 1958	5.2 1.1 5.3 1.1	**16** TH	0230 0843 1454 ● 2049	5.4 0.8 5.4 1.1
2 TH ○	0225 0825 1452 2044	5.4 0.9 5.5 0.9	**17** F	0312 0922 1534 2122	5.5 0.7 5.4 1.1
3 F	0305 0913 1533 2131	5.6 0.7 5.6 0.8	**18** SA	0351 0956 1612 2150	5.5 0.8 5.3 1.1
4 SA	0345 1001 1616 2217	5.7 0.5 5.7 0.8	**19** SU	0429 1024 1649 2216	5.4 0.9 5.2 1.2
5 SU	0427 1048 1700 2304	5.7 0.5 5.6 0.9	**20** M	0505 1049 1725 2244	5.3 1.0 5.1 1.4
6 M	0512 1134 1748 2349	5.6 0.6 5.5 1.1	**21** TU	0541 1117 1803 2315	5.1 1.2 5.0 1.5
7 TU	0600 1221 1839	5.5 0.8 5.3	**22** W	0619 1151 1844 2352	5.0 1.4 4.8 1.8
8 W ☽	0037 0652 1312 1936	1.3 5.3 1.0 5.1	**23** TH	0701 1232 1929	4.8 1.6 4.7
9 TH	0131 0754 1410 2041	1.5 5.1 1.3 4.9	**24** F ☽	0039 0749 1324 2019	2.0 4.6 1.8 4.5
10 F	0237 0905 1522 2149	1.7 5.0 1.5 4.9	**25** SA	0148 0846 1432 2118	2.2 4.5 2.0 4.5
11 SA	0351 1015 1636 2255	1.7 4.9 1.5 4.9	**26** SU	0315 0951 1557 2221	2.2 4.4 2.0 4.5
12 SU	0501 1123 1743 2358	1.6 5.0 1.5 5.0	**27** M	0439 1058 1709 2326	2.1 4.5 1.9 4.7
13 M	0607 1226 1841	1.4 5.1 1.4	**28** TU	0541 1203 1804	1.8 4.7 1.6
14 TU	0055 0706 1322 1929	5.2 1.2 5.2 1.3	**29** W	0026 0632 1300 1853	5.0 1.5 5.0 1.4
15 W	0146 0758 1411 2012	5.3 1.0 5.3 1.2	**30** TH	0118 0722 1349 1940	5.2 1.1 5.3 1.1
			31 F ○	0203 0811 1432 2028	5.5 0.8 5.6 0.8

AUGUST

Day	Time	m	Day	Time	m
1 SA	0245 0901 1514 2116	5.7 0.5 5.8 0.7	**16** SU	0330 0929 1547 2124	5.5 0.8 5.3 1.1
2 SU	0326 0949 1557 2203	5.9 0.3 5.9 0.6	**17** M	0403 0956 1619 2152	5.4 0.8 5.3 1.1
3 M	0409 1035 1642 2248	6.0 0.2 5.8 0.6	**18** TU	0435 1021 1653 2218	5.4 0.9 5.2 1.2
4 TU	0454 1120 1728 2332	5.9 0.3 5.7 0.8	**19** W	0509 1047 1728 2242	5.3 1.1 5.1 1.4
5 W	0542 1203 1818	5.8 0.6 5.5	**20** TH	0544 1114 1806 2308	5.1 1.3 5.0 1.6
6 TH	0015 0633 1248 1912	1.1 5.5 1.0 5.2	**21** F	0622 1144 1847 2341	4.9 1.5 4.8 1.8
7 F ☽	0103 0733 1338 2015	1.4 5.2 1.4 4.9	**22** SA ☽	0706 1224 1934	4.7 1.8 4.6
8 SA	0206 0844 1449 2124	1.7 4.9 1.7 4.8	**23** SU	0033 0759 1331 2031	2.1 4.5 2.1 4.5
9 SU	0329 0956 1616 2234	1.8 4.8 1.9 4.8	**24** M	0207 0906 1505 2140	2.2 4.4 2.2 4.5
10 M	0452 1109 1732 2344	1.8 4.8 1.8 4.9	**25** TU	0357 1021 1639 2251	2.2 4.5 2.0 4.6
11 TU	0606 1219 1832	1.6 4.9 1.7	**26** W	0517 1133 1743 2357	1.9 4.7 1.8 4.9
12 W	0045 0704 1316 1916	5.1 1.3 5.1 1.5	**27** TH	0615 1235 1835	1.5 5.1 1.4
13 TH	0136 0749 1401 1953	5.3 1.1 5.2 1.3	**28** F	0053 0706 1326 1922	5.3 1.0 5.4 1.1
14 F ●	0218 0827 1440 2025	5.4 0.9 5.3 1.2	**29** SA ○	0140 0756 1411 2010	5.6 0.6 5.7 0.7
15 SA	0255 0900 1514 2055	5.5 0.8 5.3 1.1	**30** SU	0222 0844 1453 2057	5.9 0.3 6.0 0.5
			31 M	0305 0931 1536 2144	6.1 0.1 6.0 0.4

Chart Datum: 2·90 metres below Ordnance Datum (Newlyn). HAT is 6·3 metres above Chart Datum.

SE Scotland

STANDARD TIME (UT)
For Summer Time add ONE hour in **non-shaded areas**

LEITH LAT 55°59'N LONG 3°11'W
TIMES AND HEIGHTS OF HIGH AND LOW WATERS

Dates in red are SPRINGS
Dates in blue are NEAPS

YEAR 2015

SEPTEMBER

Day	Time m	Time m	Time m	Time m
1 TU	0348 6.2	1016 0.1	1620 6.0	2228 0.5
16 W	0407 5.4	0952 0.9	1622 5.3	2153 1.1
2 W	0434 6.1	1059 0.3	1706 5.8	2311 0.7
17 TH	0439 5.3	1017 1.0	1656 5.2	2213 1.3
3 TH	0522 5.9	1141 0.6	1754 5.5	2353 1.0
18 F	0513 5.2	1037 1.2	1732 5.1	2234 1.5
4 F	0614 5.6	1220 1.1	1848 5.2	
19 SA	0551 5.0	1100 1.5	1811 4.9	2304 1.7
5 SA	0037 1.4	0713 5.2	1305 1.6	1950 4.9
20 SU	0633 4.8	1133 1.8	1856 4.8	2349 1.9
6 SU	0138 1.7	0823 4.9	1416 2.0	2059 4.7
21 M	0724 4.6	1231 2.1	1951 4.6	
7 M	0313 1.6	0937 4.7	1557 2.2	2211 4.7
22 TU	0112 2.2	0829 4.5	1425 2.3	2100 4.5
8 TU	0448 1.9	1053 4.6	1719 2.1	2325 4.8
23 W	0319 2.1	0948 4.5	1611 2.2	2218 4.6
9 W	0600 1.6	1207 4.8	1817 1.9	
24 TH	0453 1.8	1104 4.8	1720 1.8	2328 4.9
10 TH	0029 5.0	0652 1.4	1303 5.0	1858 1.7
25 F	0555 1.4	1209 5.1	1813 1.4	
11 F	0118 5.2	0732 1.2	1345 5.2	1929 1.5
26 SA	0026 5.3	0646 1.0	1302 5.5	1900 1.1
12 SA	0158 5.3	0803 1.0	1419 5.3	1957 1.3
27 SU	0114 5.7	0735 0.6	1347 5.8	1948 0.7
13 SU	0233 5.4	0831 0.9	1450 5.3	2028 1.1 ●
28 M	0158 6.0	0823 0.2	1429 6.0	2035 0.5 ○
14 M	0305 5.5	0858 0.8	1519 5.4	2058 1.0
29 TU	0242 6.2	0909 0.1	1512 6.1	2122 0.3
15 TU	0336 5.5	0925 0.8	1550 5.4	2128 1.0
30 W	0327 6.3	0954 0.1	1557 6.0	2208 0.4

OCTOBER

Day	Time m	Time m	Time m	Time m
1 TH	0414 6.1	1037 0.4	1643 5.8	2251 0.6
16 F	0413 5.4	0950 1.1	1627 5.3	2154 1.2
2 F	0503 5.9	1117 0.8	1731 5.6	2333 1.0
17 SA	0448 5.2	1010 1.3	1703 5.3	2215 1.4
3 SA	0555 5.5	1153 1.3	1824 5.2	
18 SU	0526 5.1	1032 1.5	1742 5.1	2245 1.5
4 SU	0016 1.4	0654 5.1	1231 1.8	1924 4.9
19 M	0610 4.9	1106 1.8	1826 4.9	2331 1.8
5 M	0114 1.8	0801 4.8	1336 2.2	2033 4.7
20 TU	0701 4.8	1202 2.1	1919 4.7	
6 TU	0253 2.0	0911 4.6	1526 2.4	2143 4.6
21 W	0053 2.0	0803 4.6	1359 2.3	2026 4.6
7 W	0428 1.9	1025 4.5	1649 2.3	2256 4.7
22 TH	0248 2.0	0920 4.6	1540 2.2	2146 4.7
8 TH	0537 1.7	1140 4.7	1746 2.1	
23 F	0424 1.7	1036 4.9	1651 1.9	2258 5.0
9 F	0001 4.9	0625 1.5	1237 4.9	1825 1.8
24 SA	0528 1.3	1141 5.2	1746 1.5	2357 5.3
10 SA	0052 5.1	0702 1.3	1319 5.1	1857 1.6
25 SU	0622 1.0	1235 5.5	1836 1.1	
11 SU	0132 5.3	0730 1.2	1352 5.2	1928 1.3
26 M	0048 5.7	0711 0.6	1322 5.8	1924 0.8
12 M	0206 5.4	0757 1.0	1422 5.3	2001 1.2
27 TU	0135 6.0	0800 0.4	1406 6.0	2013 0.5 ○
13 TU	0238 5.4	0825 0.9	1451 5.4	2033 1.1 ●
28 W	0221 6.1	0847 0.3	1450 6.1	2102 0.4
14 W	0309 5.5	0855 0.9	1521 5.4	2105 1.0
29 TH	0308 6.2	0932 0.4	1535 6.0	2149 0.5
15 TH	0340 5.4	0924 0.9	1553 5.4	2132 1.1
30 F	0356 6.0	1014 0.6	1621 5.8	2234 0.7
31 SA	0446 5.8	1053 1.0	1710 5.5	2316 1.0

NOVEMBER

Day	Time m	Time m	Time m	Time m
1 SU	0538 5.5	1125 1.5	1801 5.2	2357 1.3
16 M	0508 5.2	1028 1.5	1719 5.2	2251 1.4
2 M	0634 5.1	1155 1.9	1858 5.0	
17 TU	0552 5.1	1105 1.7	1804 5.1	2340 1.6
3 TU	0045 1.7	0734 4.8	1246 2.2	2001 4.7
18 W	0643 5.0	1206 2.0	1856 4.9	
4 W	0209 2.0	0837 4.6	1423 2.5	2106 4.6
19 TH	0053 1.7	0742 4.8	1337 2.1	1958 4.8
5 TH	0344 2.0	0943 4.5	1557 2.4	2213 4.6
20 F	0221 1.8	0853 4.8	1504 2.1	2115 4.9
6 F	0451 1.9	1053 4.6	1657 2.3	2319 4.7
21 SA	0348 1.6	1007 4.9	1618 1.9	2228 5.0
7 SA	0541 1.7	1155 4.7	1743 2.0	
22 SU	0457 1.4	1113 5.2	1717 1.6	2330 5.3
8 SU	0014 4.9	0619 1.5	1242 4.9	1822 1.7
23 M	0555 1.1	1209 5.4	1811 1.3	
9 M	0058 5.1	0651 1.4	1318 5.1	1858 1.5
24 TU	0025 5.6	0648 0.9	1300 5.7	1903 0.9
10 TU	0136 5.2	0722 1.2	1351 5.3	1934 1.3
25 W	0116 5.8	0738 0.7	1346 5.8	1955 0.7 ○
11 W	0210 5.3	0753 1.1	1423 5.4	2009 1.2 ●
26 TH	0205 5.9	0826 0.6	1431 5.9	2046 0.6
12 TH	0243 5.4	0826 1.0	1455 5.5	2043 1.1
27 F	0253 5.9	0911 0.7	1517 5.9	2134 0.6
13 F	0317 5.4	0858 1.0	1529 5.5	2116 1.1
28 SA	0342 5.8	0953 0.9	1604 5.7	2219 0.7
14 SA	0352 5.3	0930 1.1	1603 5.4	2147 1.1
29 SU	0430 5.7	1030 1.2	1651 5.5	2300 1.0
15 SU	0428 5.3	1000 1.3	1640 5.4	2217 1.2
30 M	0519 5.4	1058 1.5	1739 5.3	2336 1.2

DECEMBER

Day	Time m	Time m	Time m	Time m
1 TU	0609 5.1	1122 1.8	1829 5.1	
16 W	0537 5.3	1121 1.5	1747 5.3	2354 1.2
2 W	0009 1.5	0700 4.9	1202 2.1	1923 4.8
17 TH	0626 5.2	1210 1.7	1837 5.2	
3 TH	0057 1.8	0754 4.6	1302 2.3	2021 4.7
18 F	0046 1.4	0721 5.0	1312 1.9	1934 5.1
4 F	0212 2.0	0851 4.5	1431 2.5	2121 4.6
19 SA	0152 1.5	0826 4.9	1425 2.0	2044 5.0
5 SA	0340 2.1	0950 4.5	1556 2.4	2222 4.6
20 SU	0309 1.6	0937 4.9	1541 1.9	2159 5.0
6 SU	0441 2.0	1051 4.5	1656 2.2	2322 4.7
21 M	0425 1.5	1045 5.0	1649 1.6	2306 5.1
7 M	0529 1.8	1149 4.7	1745 2.0	
22 TU	0530 1.4	1146 5.2	1750 1.5	
8 TU	0015 4.8	0610 1.6	1237 4.9	1828 1.7
23 W	0007 5.3	0628 1.2	1242 5.4	1848 1.2
9 W	0102 5.0	0648 1.5	1318 5.1	1908 1.5
24 TH	0103 5.5	0721 1.1	1332 5.6	1944 0.9
10 TH	0142 5.2	0725 1.3	1356 5.3	1946 1.3
25 F	0154 5.6	0809 1.0	1419 5.7	2035 0.7 ○
11 F	0220 5.3	0802 1.2	1433 5.4	2024 1.1 ●
26 SA	0243 5.7	0854 1.0	1504 5.7	2122 0.7
12 SA	0257 5.4	0839 1.1	1508 5.5	2103 1.0
27 SU	0329 5.6	0934 1.0	1549 5.7	2205 0.7
13 SU	0334 5.4	0917 1.1	1544 5.5	2143 1.0
28 M	0414 5.5	1008 1.2	1633 5.6	2242 0.9
14 M	0412 5.5	0957 1.2	1622 5.5	2225 1.0
29 TU	0458 5.4	1033 1.4	1716 5.4	2311 1.1
15 TU	0453 5.4	1038 1.3	1702 5.4	2308 1.1
30 W	0541 5.2	1058 1.5	1758 5.3	2334 1.3
31 TH	0623 4.9	1127 1.8	1842 5.0	

Chart Datum: 2·90 metres below Ordnance Datum (Newlyn). HAT is 6·3 metres above Chart Datum.

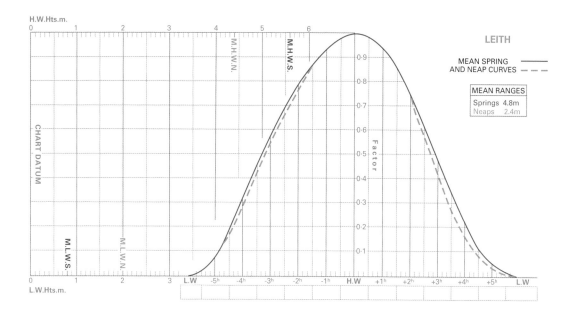

4.9 ANSTRUTHER

Fife **56°13'·15N 02°41'·82W** ✿✿✿⊕⊕⊕✿✿✿

CHARTS AC 175, 734, 5615; Imray C24, C23, C27

TIDES +0315 Dover; ML 3·1; Duration 0620

Standard Port LEITH (←—)

Times				Height (metres)			
High Water		Low Water		MHWS	MHWN	MLWN	MLWS
0300	0900	0300	0900	5·6	4·4	2·0	0·8
1500	2100	1500	2100				
Differences ANSTRUTHER EASTER							
–0018	–0012	–0006	–0008	–0·3	–0·2	0·0	0·0

SHELTER Good, but dangerous to enter in strong E to S winds. Hbr dries. Pontoon berths for bilge keel craft only, drying out soft mud.

NAVIGATION WPT 56°12'·59N 02°42'·20W, 019° to ent, 0·60M. Beware FVs and creels in the area. Do not go N of W Pier Lt due to rks extending N & W across the mouth of Dreel Burn.

LIGHTS AND MARKS Conspic tr on W pier. Ldg lts 019°, both FG 7/11m 4M. Pier lts as chartlet. Horn (3) 60s in conspic tr.

COMMUNICATIONS (Code 01333) MRCC 450666; Police: 101, Dr 310352; Ⓗ St Andrews 01334 472327, Kirkaldy 01592 643355; ⊖ 0800 595000. HM ☎ 310836 (HO).

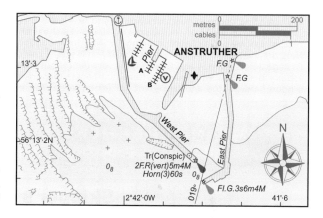

Anstruther Hbr VHF Ch 11 16 (HO) or Forth CG 16 (OT).

FACILITIES Harbour: wall � (22 + 8♥); for 10m LOA: entry £16.00 then £8.00 per day; pontoons (no fin keels, 100 + 8 ♥,check availability with HM) £18.00 then £10.45 per day; ◣, ⏚, ⬙, ⬙, Shwrs 0800-2100; **Services:** D (tanker ☎ 730622), Marine engineer (☎ 310134), ACA, Gas, Gaz,🗍, Ⓔ (☎ 311459), LB. **Town,** 🍴 & 🏨, ⚖ (☎ 01383 622444), SC (08456 0057023492) ▦, ✗, 🏠, ✉, Ⓑ, ⇌ (bus Cupar or Leuchars), ✈ Edinburgh/Dundee.

ADJACENT HARBOURS AND ANCHORAGE

KIRKCALDY, Fife, **56°06'·80N 03°08'·96W.** AC 741. HW +0345 on Dover, –0005 on Leith; HW –0·1m on Leith; ML 3·2m; Duration 0620. See 4.9. Shelter good except in strong E winds; an emergency refuge. Officially the hbr is closed (no commercial tfc, but some local FVs) and not manned; depths may be less than charted due to silting. The only hbr light is on E Pier head, Fl WG 10s 12m 8M. Small craft should contact Forth Ports Authority, ☎ 01383 421800, Forth Navigation Ch 71 (H24) for advice.

METHIL, Fife, **56°10'·75N 03°00'·55W.** AC 734,741. HW +0330 Dover; –0020 and –0·1 on Leith; ML 3m; Duration 0615. Commercial activity greatly reduced; infrastructure limited. Access at all states of the tide and provides shelter from E'lies, but dangerous to enter in bad weather. Dock ☎ (01333) 426725. Berthing by prior arrangement at Methil Boat Club ☎ (01333) 421110. In emergency call Forth Navigation Ch 71 (H24) or Forth Coastguard Ch 16.

PITTENWEEM, Fife, **56°12'·60N 02°43'·79W.** AC 734. HW +0325 Dover; –0015 and –0·1m on Leith; ML 3m; Duration 0620. Busy fishing hbr, dredged 1-2m, access all tides, but not in onshore winds; seek advice before entering at LW springs. Yachts not encouraged; contact HM for berth at W end of inner hbr, but only for emergency use. Outer hbr dries to rock; is only suitable for temp stop in calm weather. Appr 037° on ldg marks/lts, W cols, both FR 3/8m 5M. Rks to port marked by bn, Fl R 4s 3m 2M, and 3 unlit bns. E bkwtr lt Fl (2) RG 5s 9m 9/6M, 265°-R-345°-G-055°. **R/T** VHF Ch 11 (0700-2100, Mon-Fri) or Forth CG Ch 16 (other times). HM ☎ (01333) 312591. Facilities: ⚓, ▯, D (pump: contact HM; tanker: ☎ 730622), Gas, ▦, 🏠.

CRAIL, Fife, **56°15'·35N 02°37'·29W.** AC 175. HW +0320 on Dover, –0020 on Leith; HW –0·2m on Leith; ML 3·0m; Duration 0615. Good shelter but only for boats able to take the ground, but limited manoeuvring area. Appr between S pier and bn on rks to S following ldg line 295°, two W concrete pillars with FR lts, 24/30m 6M. Turn 150° to stbd for ent. Call Forth CG on VHF Ch 16 before entering. Beware FVs and creel ends. HM ☎ 07540 672809 (part-time, Mon-Fri). Facilities: ⌷, entry £16.00/craft then £8.00/ day, ⌷, ⚓, ⌷, ⌷. **Village** ⌷, ✕, ⌷, ✉, Ⓑ.

ISLE OF MAY, Fife, 56°11′·40N 02°33′·69W. AC 734. HW +0325 on Dover, –0025 on Leith. In settled weather only, and depending on the wind, ⚓ at E or W Tarbert in 4m; landing at Altarstanes. Near the SE tip there is a tiny hbr at Kirkhaven, with narrow, rky ent; yachts can moor fore-and-aft to rings in rks, in about 1-1·5m. SDs

are needed. Beware Norman Rk to N of Island, and Maiden Hair Rk to S. At the summit, a 3 tr on stone ho, Fl (2) 15s 73m 22M. The island is a National Nature Reserve managed by Scottish National Heritage (☎ 01334 654038). It is a bird/seal colony sanctuary. Sensitive seasons: (a) breeding birds April to September; (b) breeding seals October to January; (c) moulting seals January to March. Land only at Alterstanes or (where restrictions may apply) Kirkhaven. Warden in residence Easter to end October when visitor centre open 1000-1730 BST. Contact on VHF Ch 16 or 6, or on first landing. No overnight accommodation or camping. Avoid marked out areas to minimise disturbance to wildlife and ongoing conservation experiments.

FIFE NESS TO MONTROSE

(AC 190) Fife Ness is fringed by rky ledges, and a reef extends 1M NE to N Carr Rk (dries 1·4m, marked by bn). In strong onshore winds keep to seaward of N Carr ECM lt buoy. From here keep 5ca offshore to clear dangers entering St Andrews B, where there is anch; the little hbr dries, and should not be approached in onshore winds.

Northward from Firth of Forth to Rattray Hd the coast is mostly rky and steep-to, and there are no out-lying dangers within 2M of the coast except those off R Tay and Bell Rk. But in an onshore blow there are few safe havens; both yachts and crews need to be prepared for offshore cruising rather than coast-crawling.

R Tay (AC 1481) is approached from the NE via Fairway buoy; it is dangerous to cut corners from the S. The Bar, NE of Abertay lt buoy, is dangerous in heavy weather, particularly in strong onshore wind or swell. Abertay Sands extend nearly 4M E of Tentsmuir Pt on S side of chan (buoyed); Elbow is a shoal extension eastward. Gaa Sands, running 1·75M E from Buddon Ness, are marked by Abertay lt buoy (Racon) on N side of chan. Passage across Abertay and Gaa Sands is very dangerous. The estuary is shallow, with many shifting sandbanks; Tayport is a good passage stop and best yacht hbr (dries) in the Tay. ▶

S of Buddon Ness the W-going (flood) stream begins about HW Aberdeen –0400, and the E-going at about HW Aberdeen +0230, sp rates 2kn. ◀

Bell Rk (lt, Racon) lies about 11·5M E of Buddon Ness. ▶ *2M E of Bell Rk the S-going stream begins HW Aberdeen –0220, and the N-going at HW Aberdeen +0405, sp rates 1kn. W of Bell Rk the streams begin earlier.* ◀

N from Buddon Ness the coast is sandy. 1·25M SW of Arbroath beware Elliot Horses, rky patches with depth 1·9m, which extend about 5ca offshore. Between Whiting Ness and Scurdie Ness, 9·5M NNE, the coast is clear of out-lying dangers, but is mostly fringed with drying rks up to 1ca off. In offshore winds there is temp anch in SW of Lunan B, off Ethie Haven.

Scurdie Ness (lt, Racon) is conspic on S side of ent to Montrose. Scurdie Rks (dry) extend 2ca E of the Ness. On N side of chan Annat Bank dries up to about 5ca E of the shore, opposite Scurdie Ness (AC 1438). ▶ *The in-going stream begins at HW Aberdeen –0500, and the outgoing at HW Aberdeen +0115; both streams are very strong, up to 7kn at sp, and there is turbulence off the ent on the ebb. The ent is dangerous in strong onshore winds, with breaking seas extending to Scurdie Ness on the ebb. In marginal conditions the last quarter of the flood is best time to enter.* ◀

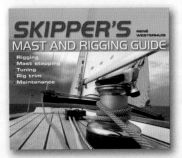

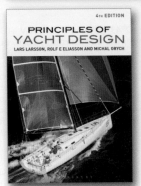
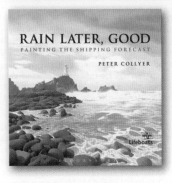

4.10 RIVER TAY

Fife/Angus Tayport (56°27'·10N 02°52'·87W) ✱✿⚓⚓✿✿

CHARTS AC 190, 1481, 5617; Imray C23

TIDES +0401 (Dundee) Dover; ML 3·1; Duration 0610

Standard Port ABERDEEN (→)

Times				Height (metres)			
High Water		Low Water		MHWS	MHWN	MLWN	MLWS
0000	0600	0100	0700	4·3	3·4	1·6	0·6
1200	1800	1300	1900				
Differences BAR							
+0100	+0100	+0050	+0110	+0·9	+0·8	+0·3	+0·1
DUNDEE							
+0140	+0120	+0055	+0145	+1·2	+1·0	+0·5	+0·4
NEWBURGH							
+0215	+0200	+0250	+0335	−0·2	−0·4	−1·1	−0·5
PERTH							
+0220	+0225	+0510	+0530	−0·9	−1·4	−1·2	−0·3

NOTE: At Perth LW time differences give the start of the rise, following a LW stand of about 4 hours.

SHELTER Good in Tay Estuary, but ent is dangerous in strong E/SE winds or on-shore swell. **Tayport** is best place for yachts on passage. Harbour partly dries except W side of NE pier; S side has many yacht moorings. **Dundee** Commercial harbour. Possible moorings off Royal Tay YC. ⚓s as chartlet: the ⚓ off the city is exposed/landing difficult. Off S bank good shelter at Woodhaven and ⚓s from Wormit BC. There are other ⚓s up-river at Balmerino, Newburgh and Inchyra.

NAVIGATION WPT Tay Fairway SWM buoy, 56°28'·30N 02°36'·60W, 239°/1M to Middle Bar buoys. Chan is well buoyed, least depth 5·2m. Keep N of Larick, a conspic disued lt bn.

> Beware strong tidal streams. No passage across Abertay or Gaa Sands; charted depths are unreliable.

LIGHTS AND MARKS See 4.3 and chartlet. 'Abertay' ECM buoy (Racon), at E end of Gaa Sands is a clear visual mark.

COMMUNICATIONS (Code 01382): MRCC (01224) 592334; Tayport Hbr Trust, Berthing Master 553799; Police 101; Dr 221976; ⊕ 660111. Forth & Tay Navigation Service (01324) 498584; HM (Dundee) 224121; HM (Perth) (01738) 624056.
Forth & Tay Navigation Service VHF Ch **71**; *Dundee Hbr Radio* VHF Ch **12** 16 (H24); local nav warnings, weather, vis and tides on request. Royal Tay YC, Ch M.

FACILITIES
N BANK: Royal Tay YC (Broughty Ferry) ☎ 477516, ⚓s free, ✕, 🛢;
Services: 🛢, M, L, ⚓, 🅱, ✕, C (2 ton), ACA.
Dundee City 🗃 & 🗃, 🛢, 🛒, ✕, 🛢, ✉, ⒷB, ≈, ✈.

S BANK: Tayport Hbr Access HW±4, hbr dries 0.6m above CD with soft mud. Ent SWM at edge of chan 50m from hbr; ldg marks (185°) R △ on slipway and post. R/Wpost, F W on East wall. ⌐ (88 + 7♥) £12·50 <35ft< £15·00 <45ft/ day; (phil.tayportharbour@gmail.com) ⚓, L, ⚓, 🗃, 🛒, ✕, 🛢, ✉, Ⓑ, bus to St Andrews/Dundee.
Wormit Boating Club ☎ 541400 ⚓s free, ⚓, L, ⚓, 🛒.

ADJACENT HARBOURS
PERTH, Perth & Kinross, **56°22'·89N 03°25'·74W**. AC 1481; OS 53, 58. Tides, see 4.11. FYCA Pilot Handbook needed. Leave Tay Rly bridge about HW Dundee −2 to carry the tide for 16·5M to Perth. Keep clear of coasters which have to travel at speed and are constrained by their draft. Lit chan favours S bank for 9M to Newburgh. ⚓ to N of chan at W of town in 2m, piers are to be refurbished and only used with caution, ⚓ newly repaired. Care is required due to mudbanks mid-stream; keep S of Mugdrum Is. Up-river, power cables clearance 33m and Friarton Bridge 26m. Keep S of Willow Is, past gasworks to Hbr on W bank. Hbr has approx 1·5m. See HM, ☎ (01738) 624056, for berth. VHF Ch 09 16. ⚓, 🗃 & 🗃, all city amenities, ≈, ✈.

ST ANDREWS, Fife, **56°20'·32N 02°46'·79W**. AC 190. HW −0015 Leith. Small drying hbr 7M S of Tay Estuary /8M NW of Fife Ness. In strong onshore winds breaking seas render appr/ent impossible. Appr near HW on 270°, N bkwtr bn in transit with cathedral twr; Dir Iso WRG 2s (277·5°) on lookout bldg. A recce by dinghy is useful. Best water is about 10m S of the bkwtr. 8m wide ent to inner hbr (drying 2·5m) has lock gates, usually open, and sliding footbridge; berth on W side. Facilities: ⚓, SC; all amenities of university town, inc golf course.

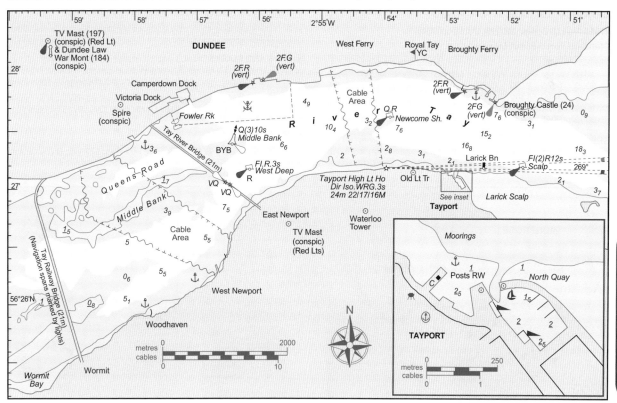

4.11 ARBROATH

Angus 56°33'·22N 02°34'·99W ✳✳💧💧🌸🌸

CHARTS AC 190, 1438, 5617; Imray C23

TIDES +0317 Dover; ML 2·9; Duration 0620

Standard Port ABERDEEN (→)

Times				Height (metres)			
High Water		Low Water		MHWS	MHWN	MLWN	MLWS
0000	0600	0100	0700	4·3	3·4	1·6	0·6
1200	1800	1300	1900				
Differences ARBROATH							
+0056	+0037	+0034	+0055	+1·0	+0·8	+0·4	+0·2

SHELTER Good, especially in Inner Basin with lock gates, afloat pontoon berths with 2.5m depth maintained. Ent can be dangerous in moderate SE swell. Inside the entrance, turn to starboard and then to starboard again. HM manned 0700 - 2000 (2200 on selected weekends), during which time lock opens approx HW±3.

NAVIGATION WPT 56°32'·98N 02°34'·21W, 299°/0·5M to ent.

Entry should not be attempted LW±2½. Beware Knuckle rks to stbd and Cheek Bush rks to port on entering.

LIGHTS AND MARKS Ldg lts 299°, both FR 7/13m 5M, or twin trs of St Thomas' ⌖ visible between N pier lt ho and W bkwtr bn. Hbr entry sigs: Fl G 3s on E pier = Entry safe. Same lt shows FR when hbr closed, entry dangerous. Siren (3) 60s at E pier lt is occas, for FVs. Inner Basin Lock Gates, FR = closed, FG = open >2.5m over sill.

COMMUNICATIONS (Code 01241) MRCC (01224) 592334 MRCC 01333 452000; Police 101; Dr 876836. HM 872166; VHF Ch 11 16; harbourmaster@angus.gov.uk.

FACILITIES **Inner Basin** 59 inc 🅥, £14·50/craft, showers, 🚻, **Pier** 🛒 £13/craft, ⚓, ⛽, 🅟; **Services:** D (on Oil Pier), BY, ⚓, L, ⚒, 🅗, C (8 ton) Ⓔ, M, Gas. **Town** 🏨, 🛒, ✕, 🏧, ✉, Ⓑ, ⇌, ✈ (Dundee).

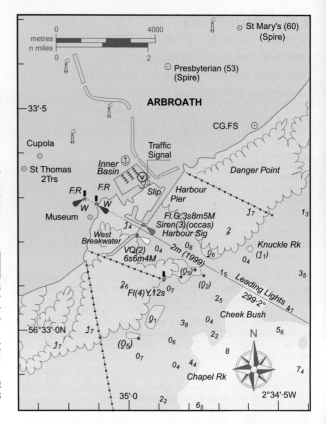

4.12 MONTROSE

Angus 56°42'·19N 02°26'·60W ✳✳💧💧🌸🌸

CHARTS AC 190, 1438, 5617; Imray C23

TIDES +0320 Dover; ML 2·9; Duration 0645

Standard Port ABERDEEN (→)

Times				Height (metres)			
High Water		Low Water		MHWS	MHWN	MLWN	MLWS
0000	0600	0100	0700	4·3	3·4	1·6	0·6
1200	1800	1300	1900				
Differences MONTROSE							
+0050	+0045	+0035	+0030	+0·6	+0·4	+0·3	+0·2

SHELTER Good; yachts are welcome in this busy commercial port. Contact HM for 🛒, usually available, but beware wash from other traffic. Double mooring lines advised due to strong tidal streams (up to 6kn).

NAVIGATION WPT 56°42'·18N 02°25'·11W, 271°/1·25M to front ldg lt. Beware Annat Bank to N and Scurdie Rks to S of ent chan. In quiet weather best access is LW to LW+1, but in strong onshore winds only safe access would be from HW –2 to HW.

Ent is dangerous with strong onshore winds against any ebb tide when heavy overfalls develop.

LIGHTS AND MARKS See 4.3 and chartlet two sets of ldg lts: Outer 271·5°, both FR 11/18m 5M, front W twin pillars, R bands; rear W tr, R cupola. Inner 265°, both FG 21/33m 5M, Orange △ front and ▽ rear.

COMMUNICATIONS (Code 01674) MRCC (01224) 592334; Police 101; Dr 672554. HM 672302.
VHF Ch 12 16 (H24).

FACILITIES **N Quay** ☎ 672302, 🛒 £11/24hrs, £27/wk; D (by tanker via HM), ⚓, ⚒, 🅗, C (1½ to 40 ton), 🅟, Gas. **Town** 🚂, ✕, 🏨, 🏧, ✉, Ⓑ, ⇌, ✈ (Aberdeen).

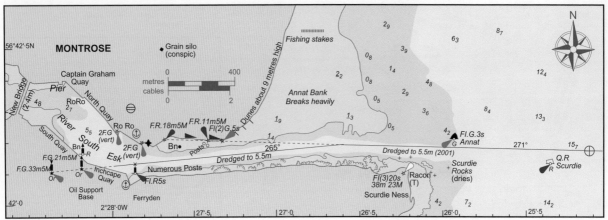

MONTROSE TO BUCHAN NESS

(AC 210) N from Montrose the coast is sandy for 5M to Milton Ness, where there is anch on S side in N winds. Johnshaven, 2M NE, is a small hbr (dries) with tight entrance, which should not be approached with onshore wind or swell. 5ca NE, off Brotherton Cas, drying rks extend 4ca offshore. Gourdon has a small hbr (mostly dries) approached on ldg line between rky ledges; inner hbr has storm gates. Outside the hbr rks extend both sides of entrance, and the sea breaks heavily in strong E winds. Keep a sharp lookout for lobster pot dan buoys between Montrose and Stonehaven.

North to Inverbervie the coast is fringed with rky ledges up to 2ca offshore. Just N of Todhead Pt is Catterline, a small B which forms a natural anch in W winds, but open to E. Downie Pt, SE of Stonehaven, should be rounded 1ca off. The Bay is encumbered by rky ledges up to 2ca from shore and exposed to the E; anch 6ca E of Bay Hotel or berth afloat in outer hbr.

From Garron Pt to Girdle Ness the coast is mostly steep-to. Fishing nets may be met off headlands during fishing season. Craigmaroinn and Seal Craig (dry) are parts of reef 3ca offshore.

HARBOURS SOUTH OF STONEHAVEN

JOHNSHAVEN, Aberdeenshire, 56°47'·60N 02°20'·07W. AC 210. HW +0245 on Dover; +0045 and +0.4m on Aberdeen; ML 2·7m; Duration 0626. Very small, attractive drying hbr 6·5M N of Montrose.

> Ent impossible in strong onshore winds; strictly a fair weather visit with great caution. Even in calm weather swell is a problem inside the hbr.

Appr from 5ca SE at near HW. Conspic W shed at N end of hbr. Ldg marks/lts on 316°: front, R structure with FR 5m; rear is G structure, 20m up the hill and 85m from front, with FG (FR when entry unsafe). Transit leads between rky ledges to very narrow (20m) ent. Turn 90° port into Inner Basin (dries 2·5m) and berth on outer wall or secure to mooring chains, rigged NE/SW. Stonehaven HM ☎ (01569) 762741 (part-time). Facilities: ⚓, ⚓£20/night, ⚒, C (5 ton), ⚓, ⚒, ✕, ⚒, ⌂, ✉. Bus to Montrose/Aberdeen.

For details of Rover Ticket see 4.4.

SE of Portlethen, a fishing village with landing sheltered by rks. Cove B has a very small fishing hbr, off which there is anch in good weather; Mutton Rk (dries 2·1m) lie 1½ca offshore. From Cove to Girdle Ness keep 5ca offshore, avoiding Hasman Rks (dries 3·4m) 1ca off Altens.

Greg Ness and Girdle Ness (lt, Racon), at SE corner of Aberdeen Bay, are fringed by rks. Girdlestone is a rocky patch, depth less than 2m, 2ca ENE of lt ho. A drying patch lies 2ca SE of lt ho.
▶ *Off Girdle Ness the S-going stream begins at HW Aberdeen –0430, and the N-going at HW Aberdeen +0130, sp rates 2·5kn. A race forms on S-going stream.* ◀

(AC 213) From Aberdeen there are few offshore dangers to Buchan Ness. Drums Links Firing Range lies 8¾M N of Aberdeen; red flags and lights are shown when firing is taking place. R Ythan, 1·75M SSW of Hackley Hd, is navigable by small craft, but chan shifts constantly. 3M North is the very small hbr of Collieston (mostly dries), only accessible in fine weather. 4·75M NNE of Hackley Head lie The Skares, rks (marked by PHM lt buoy) extending 3½ca from S point of Cruden B, where there is anch in offshore winds. On N side of Cruden B is Port Erroll (dries 2·5m).

GOURDON, Aberdeenshire, 56°49'·49N 02°17'·21W. AC 210. HW +0240 on Dover; +0035 on Aberdeen; HW +0·4m on Aberdeen; ML 2·7m; Duration 0620. Shelter good in inner W hbr (dries about 2m; protected by storm gates); access from about mid-flood. E (or Gutty) hbr is rky, with difficult access. Beware rky ledges marked by bn and extending 200m S from W pier end. **A dangerous rk dries on the ldg line** about 1½ca S of pier heads. Ldg marks/lts 358°, both FR 5/30m 5M, 2 W trs; front lt shows G when not safe to enter. W pier hd Fl WRG 3s 5m 9/7M, vis 180°-G-344°-W-354°-R-180°. Essential to keep in W sector until R Ldg Lts are aligned. E bkwtr hd Q 3m 7M. HM ☎ (01569) 762741 (part-time, same as 4.13). Facilities: ⚓, ⚓ from standpipe, D, ⚒, ⚒, M, ⚒, ✕, ⌂.

4.13 STONEHAVEN

Aberdeenshire 56°57'·57N 02°12'·02W ✲✲✲✲♦❀❀

CHARTS AC 210, 1438, 5617; Imray C23

TIDES +0235 Dover; ML 2·6; Duration 0620

Standard Port ABERDEEN (→)

Times				Height (metres)			
High Water		Low Water		MHWS	MHWN	MLWN	MLWS
0000	0600	0100	0700	4·3	3·4	1·6	0·6
1200	1800	1300	1900				
Differences STONEHAVEN							
+0013	+0008	+0013	+0009	+0·2	+0·2	+0·1	0·0

SHELTER Good, especially from offshore winds. Berth in Outer harbour on W side of breakwater (3m to 2m) or N wall; sandbank forms with varying depths (not <0.6m to date) in middle to W side. Or ⚓ outside in fair weather. Hbr speed limit 3kn. Inner hbr dries 3·4m and in bad weather is closed, indicated by FG(occas) lt as shown. Do not go S of leading line, to clear rocks close E of inner harbour wall.

NAVIGATION WPT 56°57'·69N 02°11'·11W, 258°/0·5M to bkwtr lt. Give Downie Pt a wide berth. ***Do not enter in strong on-shore winds.***

LIGHTS AND MARKS N pier Iso WRG 4s 7m 5M; appr in W sector, 246°-268°. Inner hbr ldg lts 273° only apply to inner hbr: front FW 6m 5M; rear FR 8m 5M. FG on SE pier is shown when inner hbr is closed by a boom in bad weather. Conspic monument on hill top to S of hbr.

COMMUNICATIONS (Code 01569) MRCC (01224) 592334; Police 101; Dr 762945; Maritime Rescue Institute 765768.

HM (part-time) 762741, Mobile 07741050210; VHF Ch 11.

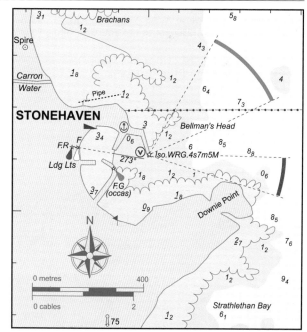

FACILITIES Hbr ⚓£20 /night, L, M, ⚒, ⚓, new heads and shwrs. ⚓ (£15, or craft < 3.1m £10), ⚒, C (1·5 ton), LB, D by tanker, Fri early am; **Aberdeen & Stonehaven SC** ⚓, ⌂.
Town ⚓, Gas, ⚒, ✕, ⌂, ⊞, ✉, ⑧, ⇌, ✈ (Aberdeen). Berthing Fees: *For details of a Rover Ticket see 4.4.*

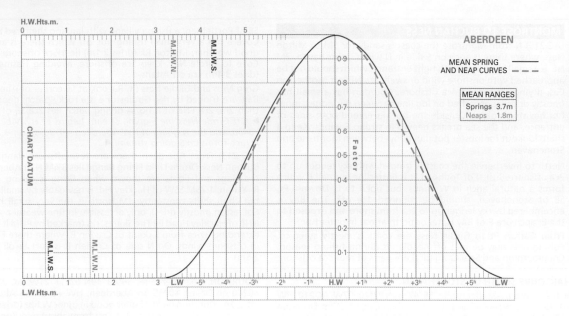

ABERDEEN

MEAN SPRING AND NEAP CURVES

MEAN RANGES	
Springs	3.7m
Neaps	1.8m

4.14 ABERDEEN

Aberdeenshire 57°08'·70N 02°03'·59W ✿✿✿◊✿✿

CHARTS AC 210, 1446, 5617; Imray C23

TIDES +0231 Dover; ML 2·5; Duration 0620

SHELTER Good in hbr; open at all tides, but do not enter in strong NE/ESE winds. Call Aberdeen VTS when 3M off for permission to enter VTS area and berthing availability.

Yachts are not encouraged in this busy commercial port, but usually lie on N side of Albert Basin alongside floating linkspan.

⚓ in Aberdeen Bay gives some shelter from S and W winds. Peterhead is 25M to N; Stonehaven is 13M S.

NAVIGATION WPT Fairway SWM buoy, Mo (A) 5s, Racon, 57°09'·31N 02°01'·96W, 236°/1M to hbr ent. Give Girdle Ness a berth of at least ¼M (more in bad weather). Do not pass close round pier hds. Strong tidal streams and, with river in spate, overfalls. Chan dredged to 6m on ldg line.

LIGHTS AND MARKS Dir lt 237·2° Fl WRG 1s 7m 9M. Ldg lts FR 237·2° 5M (FG when unsafe). Traffic sigs at root of N pier:

🔴	=	Entry prohib
⚫	=	Dep prohib
⚫ & 🔴	=	Port closed

COMMUNICATIONS (Code 01224) MRCC 592334; ⚓ 722334; Police 101.

Aberdeen VTS 597000; VHF Ch **12** 16 (H24).

FACILITIES Services: ⚲ £18/craft for up to 5 days , ▣, Ⓔ, ⚒, ACA. **City** all amenities, ⇌, ✈. **Ferries:** Kirkwall and Lerwick (www. northlinkferries.co.uk).

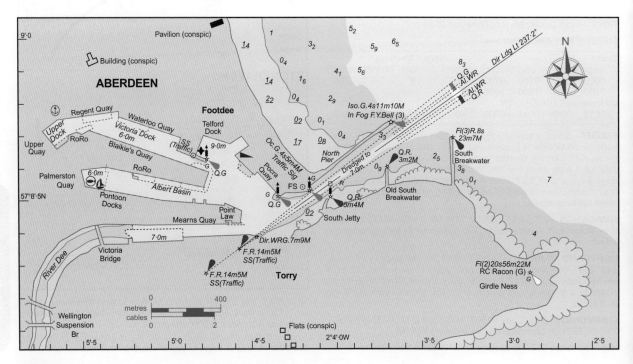

STANDARD TIME (UT)
For Summer Time add ONE hour in **non-shaded areas**

ABERDEEN   LAT 57°09'N   LONG 2°04'W

TIMES AND HEIGHTS OF HIGH AND LOW WATERS

Dates in red are SPRINGS
Dates in blue are NEAPS

YEAR 2015

JANUARY

#	Time	m	Time	m	#	Time	m	Time	m
1 TH	0404	1.4	1028	3.8	16 F	0312	1.6	0940	3.6
	1634	1.5	2249	3.9		1547	1.8	2208	3.6
2 F	0504	1.3	1123	4.0	17 SA	0418	1.5	1042	3.7
	1730	1.3	2344	4.0		1650	1.5	2310	3.8
3 SA	0552	1.3	1209	4.1	18 SU	0514	1.3	1133	4.0
	1817	1.1				1742	1.2		
4 SU	0032	4.1	0633	1.2	19 M	0001	4.0	0602	1.1
	1251	4.2	1858	1.0		1219	4.2	1829	0.9
5 M ○	0115	4.1	0710	1.2	20 TU ●	0049	4.2	0648	0.9
	1328	4.3	1937	0.9		1302	4.4	1915	0.6
6 TU	0154	4.1	0745	1.1	21 W	0134	4.4	0732	0.7
	1404	4.3	2013	0.9		1344	4.6	2001	0.6
7 W	0230	4.1	0819	1.2	22 TH	0219	4.5	0816	0.7
	1438	4.3	2047	0.9		1427	4.7	2046	0.3
8 TH	0306	4.0	0851	1.2	23 F	0305	4.5	0900	0.7
	1511	4.2	2121	0.9		1512	4.7	2132	0.4
9 F	0341	4.0	0923	1.3	24 SA	0352	4.4	0944	0.8
	1545	4.1	2155	1.0		1559	4.6	2220	0.5
10 SA	0417	3.9	0956	1.4	25 SU	0442	4.2	1031	1.0
	1621	4.0	2231	1.2		1649	4.4	2309	0.7
11 SU	0456	3.7	1032	1.5	26 M	0535	4.0	1123	1.2
	1702	3.9	2311	1.3		1746	4.2		
12 M	0541	3.6	1114	1.7	27 TU ☽	0004	1.0	0633	3.8
	1749	3.7	2358	1.5		1224	1.4	1849	3.9
13 TU ☽	0632	3.5	1207	1.8	28 W	0106	1.3	0737	3.6
	1844	3.6				1333	1.6	2000	3.7
14 W	0055	1.6	0729	3.4	29 TH	0218	1.5	0850	3.6
	1316	1.9	1947	3.5		1457	1.6	2121	3.6
15 TH	0202	1.7	0833	3.5	30 F	0342	1.6	1005	3.6
	1432	1.9	2056	3.5		1619	1.5	2237	3.7
					31 SA	0449	1.5	1107	3.8
						1719	1.4	2337	3.8

FEBRUARY

#	Time	m	Time	m	#	Time	m	Time	m
1 SU	0539	1.4	1156	3.9	16 M	0452	1.4	1107	3.8
	1806	1.2				1723	1.1	2343	3.9
2 M	0024	3.9	0619	1.3	17 TU	0545	1.1	1158	4.1
	1238	4.1	1845	1.0		1813	0.8		
3 TU ○	0103	4.0	0655	1.2	18 W ●	0032	4.2	0632	0.8
	1314	4.2	1921	0.9		1243	4.4	1859	0.4
4 W	0138	4.0	0728	1.1	19 TH	0118	4.4	0716	0.6
	1347	4.2	1954	0.8		1327	4.6	1944	0.2
5 TH	0211	4.1	0759	1.0	20 F	0202	4.5	0801	0.5
	1418	4.3	2026	0.8		1410	4.7	2029	0.1
6 F	0242	4.1	0829	1.0	21 SA	0246	4.5	0842	0.5
	1449	4.2	2056	0.8		1454	4.8	2113	0.2
7 SA	0313	4.1	0858	1.1	22 SU	0330	4.4	0925	0.6
	1520	4.2	2127	0.9		1540	4.7	2157	0.4
8 SU	0345	3.9	0929	1.1	23 M	0416	4.3	1009	0.8
	1552	4.1	2159	1.0		1629	4.4	2243	0.7
9 M	0419	3.8	1001	1.3	24 TU	0506	4.0	1058	1.0
	1628	4.0	2233	1.1		1723	4.1	2333	1.1
10 TU	0457	3.7	1037	1.4	25 W ☽	0601	3.8	1154	1.3
	1708	3.8	2312	1.3		1825	3.8		
11 W	0541	3.6	1120	1.6	26 TH	0031	1.4	0703	3.6
	1757	3.6				1303	1.5	1935	3.6
12 TH ☽	0001	1.5	0635	3.5	27 F	0142	1.7	0815	3.4
	1219	1.7	1900	3.5		1429	1.6	2058	3.4
13 F	0107	1.7	0741	3.4	28 SA	0316	1.8	0936	3.5
	1338	1.8	2013	3.4		1601	1.5	2221	3.5
14 SA	0226	1.7	0853	3.4					
	1505	1.7	2132	3.5					
15 SU	0346	1.6	1006	3.6					
	1623	1.5	2246	3.7					

MARCH

#	Time	m	Time	m	#	Time	m	Time	m
1 SU	0431	1.7	1045	3.6	16 M	0319	1.6	0932	3.5
	1702	1.4	2322	3.6		1558	1.3	2224	3.7
2 M	0521	1.5	1137	3.8	17 TU	0431	1.4	1041	3.8
	1748	1.2				1702	1.0	2324	3.9
3 TU	0007	3.7	0601	1.4	18 W ●	0526	1.1	1135	4.1
	1219	3.9	1825	1.0		1753	0.6		
4 W	0044	3.9	0635	1.2	19 TH	0013	4.2	0613	0.8
	1254	4.0	1859	0.9		1223	4.4	1840	0.3
5 TH ○	0117	4.0	0707	1.1	20 F ●	0058	4.4	0657	0.5
	1325	4.1	1930	0.8		1307	4.6	1924	0.1
6 F	0147	4.0	0737	1.0	21 SA	0141	4.5	0740	0.4
	1355	4.2	2000	0.7		1350	4.7	2008	0.1
7 SA	0216	4.1	0806	0.9	22 SU	0223	4.5	0822	0.4
	1425	4.2	2029	0.7		1435	4.7	2051	0.2
8 SU	0245	4.0	0834	0.9	23 M	0306	4.4	0905	0.4
	1455	4.2	2058	0.8		1521	4.6	2133	0.4
9 M	0315	4.0	0904	1.0	24 TU	0350	4.3	0949	0.6
	1526	4.1	2129	0.9		1609	4.3	2216	0.8
10 TU	0347	3.9	0934	1.0	25 W	0437	4.0	1035	0.9
	1601	4.0	2201	1.0		1703	4.0	2303	1.1
11 W	0422	3.8	1009	1.2	26 TH	0529	3.8	1129	1.1
	1639	3.8	2237	1.2		1803	3.7	2357	1.5
12 TH	0502	3.7	1050	1.3	27 F ●	0630	3.5	1234	1.4
	1726	3.7	2323	1.4		1911	3.5		
13 F ☽	0553	3.5	1144	1.5	28 SA	0105	1.8	0738	3.4
	1828	3.5				1355	1.6	2028	3.3
14 SA	0027	1.6	0700	3.4	29 SU	0236	1.9	0857	3.4
	1302	1.6	1945	3.4		1531	1.5	2152	3.3
15 SU	0152	1.7	0816	3.4	30 M	0403	1.8	1012	3.5
	1433	1.6	2106	3.5		1634	1.4	2255	3.5
					31 TU	0455	1.6	1108	3.6
						1720	1.2	2340	3.6

APRIL

#	Time	m	Time	m	#	Time	m	Time	m
1 W	0535	1.4	1150	3.8	16 TH	0504	1.1	1111	4.0
	1757	1.0				1731	0.6	2352	4.2
2 TH	0016	3.8	0610	1.2	17 F	0552	0.8	1200	4.3
	1226	3.9	1830	0.9		1819	0.4		
3 F	0049	3.9	0642	1.0	18 SA ●	0036	4.3	0637	0.6
	1259	4.0	1901	0.8		1247	4.5	1903	0.3
4 SA ○	0118	4.0	0712	0.9	19 SU	0119	4.4	0721	0.4
	1330	4.1	1931	0.7		1332	4.6	1946	0.3
5 SU	0148	4.1	0742	0.8	20 M	0200	4.4	0804	0.4
	1400	4.1	2001	0.7		1417	4.5	2028	0.4
6 M	0217	4.1	0811	0.8	21 TU	0242	4.4	0847	0.4
	1431	4.1	2031	0.8		1503	4.4	2109	0.6
7 TU	0247	4.1	0842	0.8	22 W	0325	4.2	0930	0.6
	1504	4.1	2102	0.8		1552	4.2	2151	0.9
8 W	0320	4.0	0914	0.9	23 TH	0411	4.0	1016	0.8
	1540	4.0	2135	1.0		1644	3.9	2235	1.2
9 TH	0355	3.9	0950	1.0	24 F	0500	3.8	1107	1.0
	1620	3.8	2213	1.2		1741	3.7	2325	1.5
10 F	0436	3.8	1033	1.1	25 SA ☽	0556	3.6	1205	1.3
	1709	3.7	2300	1.4		1842	3.4		
11 SA	0526	3.6	1129	1.3	26 SU	0027	1.8	0658	3.4
	1812	3.5				1315	1.5	1949	3.3
12 SU ☽	0005	1.6	0631	3.5	27 M	0143	1.9	0808	3.3
	1245	1.4	1927	3.5		1436	1.5	2104	3.3
13 M	0129	1.7	0747	3.5	28 TU	0311	1.9	0922	3.4
	1411	1.4	2044	3.5		1550	1.5	2211	3.4
14 TU	0254	1.6	0903	3.6	29 W	0416	1.7	1025	3.5
	1532	1.2	2201	3.7		1641	1.3	2301	3.5
15 W	0407	1.3	1013	3.8	30 TH	0501	1.5	1113	3.6
	1638	0.9	2302	3.9		1721	1.1	2341	3.7

Chart Datum: 2·25 metres below Ordnance Datum (Newlyn). HAT is 4·8 metres above Chart Datum.

SE Scotland

ABERDEEN LAT 57°09'N LONG 2°04'W
TIMES AND HEIGHTS OF HIGH AND LOW WATERS

STANDARD TIME (UT)
For Summer Time add ONE hour in **non-shaded areas**

Dates in red are SPRINGS
Dates in blue are NEAPS

YEAR **2015**

MAY

Day	Time	m	Time	m	Time	m	Time	m
1 F	0539	1.3	1153	3.8	1757	1.0		
2 SA	0015	3.8	0613	1.1	1229	3.9	1829	0.9
3 SU	0048	4.0	0645	1.0	1302	4.0	1901	0.8
4 M	0119	4.0	0717	0.9	1336	4.1	1934	0.8
5 TU	0151	4.1	0750	0.8	1410	4.1	2007	0.8
6 W	0223	4.1	0824	0.8	1446	4.1	2041	0.8
7 TH	0258	4.1	0900	0.8	1525	4.0	2118	1.0
8 F	0336	4.0	0940	0.9	1608	3.9	2200	1.1
9 SA	0418	3.9	1027	1.0	1700	3.8	2250	1.3
10 SU	0510	3.8	1123	1.1	1802	3.6	2352	1.5
11 M	0613	3.7	1233	1.2	1911	3.6		
12 TU	0108	1.5	0724	3.6	1350	1.1	2023	3.6
13 W	0227	1.5	0835	3.7	1505	1.0	2135	3.7
14 TH	0338	1.3	0945	3.8	1612	0.9	2237	3.9
15 F	0439	1.1	1047	4.0	1708	0.7	2329	4.1
16 SA	0532	0.9	1140	4.2	1758	0.6		
17 SU	0015	4.2	0619	0.7	1229	4.3	1843	0.5
18 M	0059	4.3	0704	0.5	1316	4.4	1926	0.5
19 TU	0140	4.3	0748	0.5	1402	4.3	2008	0.6
20 W	0222	4.3	0851	0.5	1449	4.2	2048	0.8
21 TH	0304	4.2	0914	0.6	1536	4.1	2128	1.0
22 F	0348	4.1	0958	0.8	1625	3.9	2209	1.2
23 SA	0433	3.9	1043	1.0	1715	3.7	2253	1.5
24 SU	0523	3.7	1133	1.2	1808	3.5	2345	1.7
25 M	0618	3.5	1230	1.3	1904	3.4		
26 TU	0048	1.8	0716	3.4	1334	1.4	2004	3.3
27 W	0200	1.9	0820	3.4	1442	1.5	2110	3.3
28 TH	0314	1.8	0928	3.4	1546	1.4	2210	3.4
29 F	0415	1.6	1027	3.5	1637	1.3	2258	3.6
30 SA	0501	1.4	1114	3.6	1719	1.1	2339	3.8
31 SU	0541	1.3	1156	3.8	1757	1.0		

JUNE

Day	Time	m	Time	m	Time	m	Time	m
1 M	0016	3.9	0617	1.1	1235	3.9	1832	0.9
2 TU	0052	4.0	0654	0.9	1313	4.0	1909	0.8
3 W	0127	4.1	0731	0.8	1351	4.1	1947	0.8
4 TH	0203	4.2	0810	0.7	1431	4.1	2026	0.8
5 F	0241	4.2	0851	0.7	1513	4.1	2107	0.9
6 SA	0321	4.2	0934	0.7	1600	4.0	2151	1.0
7 SU	0406	4.1	1022	0.8	1651	3.9	2241	1.2
8 M	0457	4.0	1117	0.8	1750	3.8	2339	1.3
9 TU	0556	3.9	1219	0.9	1853	3.7		
10 W	0046	1.4	0702	3.8	1327	1.0	1958	3.7
11 TH	0157	1.4	0810	3.8	1437	1.0	2107	3.7
12 F	0309	1.4	0920	3.8	1546	1.0	2213	3.8
13 SA	0416	1.2	1027	3.9	1648	0.9	2309	4.0
14 SU	0514	1.0	1125	4.0	1741	0.9	2358	4.1
15 M	0605	0.8	1217	4.1	1827	0.8		
16 TU	0042	4.2	0651	0.7	1306	4.2	1910	0.8
17 W	0125	4.2	0735	0.6	1351	4.2	1950	0.9
18 TH	0206	4.2	0817	0.6	1435	4.1	2029	0.9
19 F	0246	4.2	0858	0.7	1518	4.0	2106	1.1
20 SA	0326	4.1	0937	0.8	1601	3.9	2143	1.2
21 SU	0406	4.0	1017	0.9	1644	3.7	2221	1.3
22 M	0449	3.8	1058	1.1	1729	3.6	2303	1.5
23 TU	0535	3.7	1145	1.2	1817	3.5	2353	1.7
24 W	0626	3.6	1237	1.4	1909	3.4		
25 TH	0054	1.8	0722	3.4	1337	1.5	2006	3.3
26 F	0203	1.8	0824	3.4	1440	1.5	2109	3.4
27 SA	0313	1.8	0930	3.4	1543	1.5	2210	3.5
28 SU	0416	1.6	1032	3.5	1638	1.3	2301	3.7
29 M	0507	1.4	1124	3.7	1725	1.2	2345	3.8
30 TU	0551	1.2	1209	3.8	1807	1.1		

JULY

Day	Time	m	Time	m	Time	m	Time	m
1 W	0026	4.0	0632	1.0	1252	4.0	1848	0.9
2 TH	0105	4.2	0714	0.7	1334	4.1	1930	0.8
3 F	0145	4.3	0756	0.6	1417	4.2	2012	0.8
4 SA	0225	4.4	0840	0.5	1501	4.2	2055	0.8
5 SU	0307	4.4	0925	0.5	1547	4.2	2140	0.9
6 M	0353	4.3	1012	0.5	1637	4.1	2227	1.0
7 TU	0442	4.2	1103	0.6	1731	4.0	2320	1.1
8 W	0538	4.1	1200	0.8	1829	3.8		
9 TH	0020	1.3	0639	4.0	1302	1.0	1932	3.7
10 F	0128	1.4	0746	3.8	1409	1.1	2040	3.7
11 SA	0241	1.4	0859	3.8	1523	1.2	2150	3.7
12 SU	0358	1.3	1013	3.8	1632	1.2	2252	3.8
13 M	0502	1.2	1117	3.9	1728	1.1	2345	3.9
14 TU	0555	1.0	1211	4.0	1815	1.1		
15 W	0030	4.1	0641	0.8	1258	4.0	1856	1.0
16 TH	0112	4.2	0723	0.7	1340	4.1	1934	1.0
17 F	0151	4.2	0802	0.7	1419	4.1	2009	1.0
18 SA	0227	4.2	0838	0.7	1457	4.0	2043	1.0
19 SU	0303	4.2	0913	0.7	1533	3.9	2116	1.1
20 M	0338	4.1	0947	0.8	1609	3.8	2150	1.2
21 TU	0414	4.0	1023	1.0	1647	3.7	2225	1.3
22 W	0453	3.9	1101	1.1	1729	3.6	2305	1.5
23 TH	0538	3.7	1145	1.3	1817	3.5	2354	1.7
24 F	0631	3.5	1238	1.5	1911	3.4		
25 SA	0057	1.8	0730	3.4	1341	1.6	2011	3.4
26 SU	0212	1.8	0836	3.4	1449	1.6	2117	3.5
27 M	0327	1.7	0948	3.5	1558	1.5	2221	3.6
28 TU	0434	1.5	1053	3.6	1656	1.4	2315	3.8
29 W	0526	1.2	1146	3.8	1745	1.1		
30 TH	0001	4.0	0612	0.9	1233	4.0	1829	0.9
31 F	0044	4.2	0656	0.7	1317	4.2	1913	0.8

AUGUST

Day	Time	m	Time	m	Time	m	Time	m
1 SA	0126	4.4	0740	0.4	1400	4.4	1956	0.7
2 SU	0207	4.6	0825	0.3	1444	4.4	2039	0.6
3 M	0250	4.6	0909	0.3	1529	4.4	2123	0.7
4 TU	0335	4.6	0955	0.3	1616	4.3	2208	0.8
5 W	0423	4.5	1043	0.5	1707	4.1	2258	1.0
6 TH	0517	4.3	1135	0.8	1803	3.9	2354	1.2
7 F	0618	4.0	1234	1.1	1905	3.7		
8 SA	0101	1.4	0726	3.8	1342	1.4	2013	3.6
9 SU	0219	1.5	0843	3.7	1502	1.5	2128	3.6
10 M	0345	1.4	1004	3.7	1619	1.5	2237	3.8
11 TU	0453	1.3	1111	3.7	1716	1.4	2332	3.9
12 W	0545	1.1	1204	3.9	1802	1.3		
13 TH	0018	4.1	0628	0.9	1247	4.0	1840	1.2
14 F	0057	4.2	0706	0.8	1324	4.0	1915	1.1
15 SA	0132	4.2	0741	0.7	1358	4.1	1948	1.0
16 SU	0205	4.3	0814	0.7	1431	4.1	2019	1.0
17 M	0237	4.3	0845	0.7	1502	4.0	2049	1.0
18 TU	0309	4.2	0916	0.8	1534	4.0	2119	1.1
19 W	0342	4.1	0947	0.9	1608	3.9	2151	1.2
20 TH	0417	4.0	1021	1.1	1645	3.8	2227	1.4
21 F	0457	3.8	1059	1.3	1728	3.6	2309	1.5
22 SA	0545	3.6	1145	1.5	1820	3.5		
23 SU	0004	1.7	0645	3.5	1247	1.7	1922	3.4
24 M	0119	1.8	0754	3.5	1402	1.7	2031	3.5
25 TU	0244	1.8	0910	3.4	1522	1.7	2142	3.6
26 W	0403	1.5	1025	3.6	1630	1.5	2246	3.8
27 TH	0503	1.2	1124	3.9	1724	1.2	2337	4.1
28 F	0552	0.9	1212	4.1	1810	1.0		
29 SA	0022	4.3	0637	0.5	1257	4.4	1854	0.7
30 SU	0105	4.6	0721	0.3	1340	4.5	1937	0.6
31 M	0147	4.7	0805	0.2	1423	4.6	2019	0.8

Chart Datum: 2·25 metres below Ordnance Datum (Newlyn). HAT is 4·8 metres above Chart Datum.

STANDARD TIME (UT)	ABERDEEN LAT 57°09'N LONG 2°04'W	Dates in red are SPRINGS
For Summer Time add ONE hour in **non-shaded areas**	TIMES AND HEIGHTS OF HIGH AND LOW WATERS	Dates in blue are NEAPS
		YEAR **2015**

SEPTEMBER

Day	Time m	Time m	Time m	Time m
1 TU	0230 4.8	0849 0.2	1506 4.5	2102 0.6
16 W	0241 4.2	0845 0.8	1501 4.1	2051 1.0
2 W	0315 4.7	0933 0.3	1552 4.4	2147 0.7
17 TH	0313 4.2	0915 0.9	1533 4.1	2122 1.1
3 TH	0403 4.6	1019 0.6	1640 4.2	2235 0.9
18 F	0347 4.0	0946 1.1	1608 3.9	2156 1.3
4 F	0456 4.3	1109 0.9	1735 4.0	2330 1.2
19 SA	0425 3.9	1022 1.3	1647 3.8	2236 1.4
5 SA ◑	0558 4.0	1206 1.3	1837 3.7	
20 SU	0511 3.7	1105 1.5	1736 3.7	2327 1.6
6 SU	0037 1.4	0708 3.7	1315 1.6	1946 3.6
21 M ◐	0610 3.5	1203 1.7	1839 3.5	
7 M	0159 1.6	0827 3.6	1441 1.8	2105 3.6
22 TU	0040 1.7	0723 3.5	1324 1.8	1952 3.5
8 TU	0332 1.5	0953 3.6	1605 1.7	2218 3.7
23 W	0209 1.7	0841 3.5	1451 1.8	2106 3.6
9 W	0440 1.3	1100 3.7	1701 1.6	2315 3.9
24 TH	0332 1.5	0958 3.7	1605 1.6	2215 3.8
10 TH	0529 1.2	1149 3.8	1744 1.4	2359 4.0
25 F	0437 1.2	1100 4.0	1701 1.3	2310 4.1
11 F	0609 1.0	1228 3.9	1820 1.3	
26 SA	0529 0.8	1150 4.2	1749 1.0	2357 4.4
12 SA	0036 4.1	0644 0.9	1302 4.0	1853 1.1
27 SU	0615 0.5	1234 4.5	1833 0.7	
13 SU ●	0109 4.2	0716 0.8	1333 4.1	1923 1.0
28 M ○	0042 4.7	0659 0.3	1317 4.6	1915 0.5
14 M	0140 4.3	0746 0.7	1402 4.1	1953 1.0
29 TU	0125 4.8	0742 0.2	1359 4.7	1958 0.5
15 TU	0210 4.3	0816 0.8	1431 4.1	2022 1.0
30 W	0209 4.9	0826 0.2	1442 4.6	2041 0.5

OCTOBER

Day	Time m	Time m	Time m	Time m
1 TH	0255 4.8	0909 0.4	1526 4.5	2126 0.7
16 F	0248 4.2	0846 1.0	1504 4.2	2059 1.1
2 F	0344 4.5	0953 0.7	1613 4.3	2214 0.9
17 SA	0323 4.1	0918 1.1	1538 4.1	2134 1.2
3 SA	0438 4.3	1041 1.1	1706 4.0	2309 1.2
18 SU	0402 4.0	0954 1.3	1617 3.9	2214 1.3
4 SU ◐	0540 3.9	1136 1.5	1808 3.8	
19 M	0448 3.8	1037 1.5	1704 3.8	2306 1.5
5 M	0014 1.4	0648 3.7	1244 1.8	1916 3.6
20 TU ◐	0547 3.6	1135 1.7	1805 3.7	
6 TU	0133 1.6	0805 3.5	1409 1.9	2032 3.6
21 W	0015 1.6	0659 3.6	1254 1.8	1918 3.6
7 W	0306 1.6	0929 3.5	1538 1.9	2149 3.6
22 TH	0140 1.6	0814 3.6	1420 1.8	2032 3.7
8 TH	0415 1.4	1036 3.6	1636 1.7	2248 3.8
23 F	0301 1.4	0930 3.8	1536 1.6	2142 3.9
9 F	0503 1.3	1124 3.8	1719 1.5	2332 3.9
24 SA	0409 1.1	1034 4.0	1635 1.3	2242 4.1
10 SA	0542 1.1	1202 3.9	1755 1.4	
25 SU	0504 0.8	1126 4.3	1726 1.0	2333 4.4
11 SU	0009 4.1	0615 1.0	1234 4.0	1827 1.2
26 M	0552 0.6	1211 4.5	1812 0.8	
12 M	0043 4.3	0647 0.9	1304 4.1	1858 1.1
27 TU ○	0020 4.6	0637 0.4	1254 4.6	1856 0.6
13 TU ●	0114 4.2	0717 0.8	1333 4.2	1928 1.0
28 W	0106 4.8	0721 0.4	1336 4.7	1939 0.5
14 W	0145 4.3	0746 0.8	1402 4.2	1957 1.0
29 TH	0151 4.8	0804 0.5	1419 4.6	2024 0.5
15 TH	0216 4.2	0816 0.9	1432 4.2	2027 1.0
30 F	0238 4.7	0846 0.7	1502 4.5	2109 0.7
31 SA	0328 4.5	0930 0.9	1549 4.3	2156 0.9

NOVEMBER

Day	Time m	Time m	Time m	Time m
1 SU	0421 4.2	1015 1.3	1639 4.1	2248 1.1
16 M	0347 4.0	0937 1.3	1556 4.1	2203 1.2
2 M	0520 3.9	1106 1.6	1737 3.9	2348 1.4
17 TU	0433 3.9	1021 1.5	1642 4.0	2254 1.3
3 TU ◐	0623 3.7	1207 1.9	1840 3.7	
18 W	0530 3.8	1116 1.6	1739 3.9	2357 1.4
4 W	0057 1.5	0730 3.5	1322 2.0	1949 3.6
19 TH ◐	0638 3.7	1228 1.8	1849 3.8	
5 TH	0216 1.6	0845 3.5	1448 2.0	2103 3.6
20 F	0112 1.4	0748 3.7	1347 1.8	2000 3.8
6 F	0333 1.6	0955 3.6	1558 1.9	2208 3.7
21 SA	0228 1.3	0859 3.8	1502 1.6	2110 3.9
7 SA	0427 1.4	1047 3.7	1646 1.7	2257 3.8
22 SU	0338 1.1	1006 4.0	1607 1.4	2215 4.1
8 SU	0508 1.3	1128 3.9	1725 1.5	2338 3.9
23 M	0438 0.9	1102 4.2	1703 1.2	2312 4.3
9 M	0543 1.2	1202 4.0	1800 1.3	
24 TU	0531 0.8	1150 4.4	1753 0.9	
10 TU	0014 4.1	0616 1.1	1235 4.1	1832 1.2
25 W ○	0002 4.5	0618 0.7	1235 4.5	1839 0.7
11 W ●	0048 4.2	0648 1.0	1306 4.2	1904 1.1
26 TH	0051 4.6	0702 0.6	1317 4.6	1925 0.6
12 TH	0121 4.2	0719 1.0	1336 4.3	1936 1.0
27 F	0138 4.6	0745 0.7	1400 4.6	2010 0.6
13 F	0154 4.2	0751 1.0	1408 4.3	2008 1.0
28 SA	0225 4.5	0828 0.9	1443 4.5	2054 0.7
14 SA	0229 4.2	0824 1.0	1441 4.3	2043 1.0
29 SU	0313 4.4	0909 1.1	1527 4.3	2140 0.8
15 SU	0306 4.1	0858 1.2	1516 4.2	2121 1.1
30 M	0403 4.1	0951 1.3	1614 4.2	2226 1.0

DECEMBER

Day	Time m	Time m	Time m	Time m
1 TU	0455 3.9	1036 1.6	1704 4.0	2316 1.3
16 W	0421 4.1	1009 1.3	1626 4.2	2243 1.0
2 W	0549 3.7	1126 1.8	1759 3.8	
17 TH	0514 3.9	1100 1.4	1719 4.1	2340 1.1
3 TH ◗	0012 1.5	0646 3.5	1226 2.0	1858 3.6
18 F ◐	0614 3.8	1202 1.6	1822 4.0	
4 F	0115 1.6	0747 3.5	1336 2.0	2002 3.6
19 SA	0045 1.2	0719 3.8	1313 1.7	1929 3.9
5 SA	0223 1.7	0853 3.5	1452 2.0	2110 3.6
20 SU	0156 1.3	0827 3.8	1427 1.6	2040 3.9
6 SU	0331 1.6	0956 3.6	1600 1.9	2212 3.6
21 M	0307 1.2	0937 3.9	1539 1.5	2151 4.0
7 M	0425 1.5	1046 3.7	1650 1.7	2302 3.8
22 TU	0415 1.0	1039 4.1	1644 1.3	2255 4.1
8 TU	0508 1.4	1128 3.9	1730 1.5	2344 3.9
23 W	0514 1.0	1132 4.2	1740 1.1	2351 4.3
9 W	0546 1.3	1205 4.0	1807 1.3	
24 TH	0604 1.0	1220 4.3	1829 0.9	
10 TH	0023 4.0	0620 1.2	1240 4.2	1841 1.2
25 F ○	0041 4.3	0649 0.9	1304 4.4	1915 0.7
11 F ●	0100 4.1	0655 1.1	1313 4.2	1917 1.0
26 SA	0129 4.4	0731 0.9	1346 4.5	1959 0.7
12 SA	0136 4.2	0730 1.0	1347 4.3	1953 0.9
27 SU	0214 4.3	0811 1.0	1427 4.4	2041 0.7
13 SU	0213 4.2	0807 1.0	1422 4.3	2031 0.9
28 M	0259 4.3	0850 1.1	1508 4.4	2121 0.8
14 M	0252 4.2	0845 1.1	1500 4.3	2111 0.9
29 TU	0342 4.1	0927 1.2	1549 4.2	2201 0.9
15 TU	0334 4.1	0925 1.2	1540 4.3	2155 1.0
30 W	0426 4.0	1005 1.4	1631 4.1	2242 1.1
31 TH	0510 3.8	1045 1.6	1716 3.9	2326 1.3

Chart Datum: 2·25 metres below Ordnance Datum (Newlyn). HAT is 4·8 metres above Chart Datum.

》》 FREE monthly updates from 《《
www.reedsalmanac.co.uk

SE Scotland

Shetland Islands
(see 5.24)

Orkney Islands
(see 5.20)

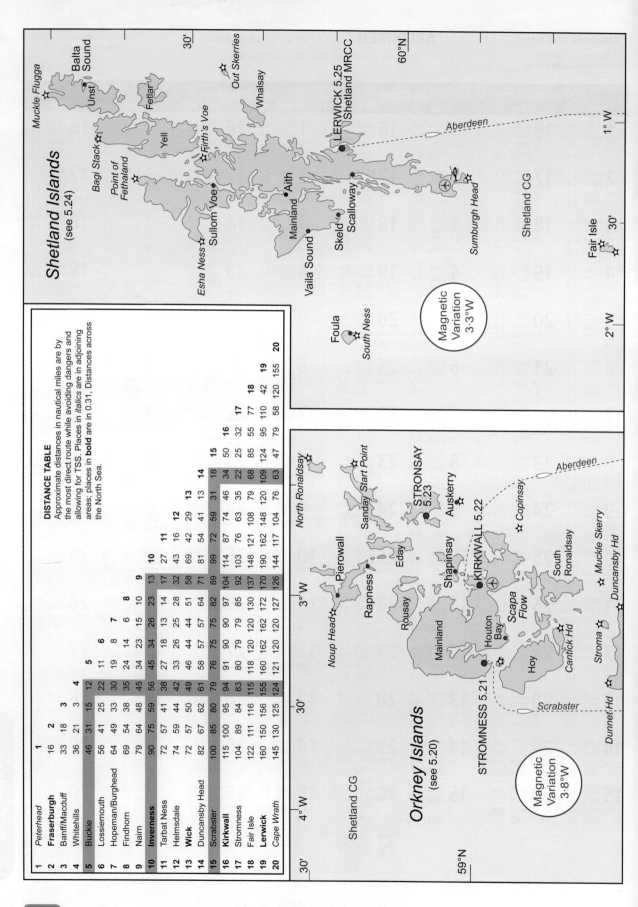

DISTANCE TABLE

Approximate distances in nautical miles are by the most direct route while avoiding dangers and allowing for TSS. Places in *italics* are in adjoining areas; places in **bold** are in 0.31. Distances across the North Sea.

	1	2	3	4	5	6	7	8	9	10	11	12	13	14	15	16	17	18	19	20
1 *Peterhead*	**1**																			
2 **Fraserburgh**	16	**2**																		
3 Banff/Macduff	33	18	**3**																	
4 Whitehills	36	21	3	**4**																
5 Buckie	46	31	15	12	**5**															
6 Lossiemouth	56	41	25	22	11	**6**														
7 Hopeman/Burghead	64	49	33	30	19	8	**7**													
8 Findhorn	69	54	38	35	24	14	6	**8**												
9 Nairn	79	64	48	45	34	23	15	10	**9**											
10 Inverness	90	75	59	56	45	34	26	23	13	**10**										
11 Tarbat Ness	72	57	41	38	27	18	13	14	17	27	**11**									
12 Helmsdale	74	59	44	42	33	26	25	28	32	43	16	**12**								
13 **Wick**	72	57	50	49	46	44	44	51	58	69	42	29	**13**							
14 Duncansby Head	82	67	62	61	58	57	57	64	71	81	54	41	13	**14**						
15 Scrabster	100	85	80	79	76	75	75	82	89	99	72	59	31	18	**15**					
16 **Kirkwall**	115	100	95	94	91	90	90	97	104	114	87	74	46	34	50	**16**				
17 Stromness	104	89	84	83	80	79	79	85	92	103	76	63	35	22	25	32	**17**			
18 Fair Isle	122	111	116	115	118	120	120	130	137	148	121	108	79	68	85	55	77	**18**		
19 **Lerwick**	160	150	156	155	160	162	162	172	170	190	162	148	120	109	124	95	110	42	**19**	
20 Cape Wrath	145	130	125	124	121	120	120	127	126	144	117	104	76	63	79	58	79	120	155	**20**

Magnetic Variation 3·3°W

Magnetic Variation 3·8°W

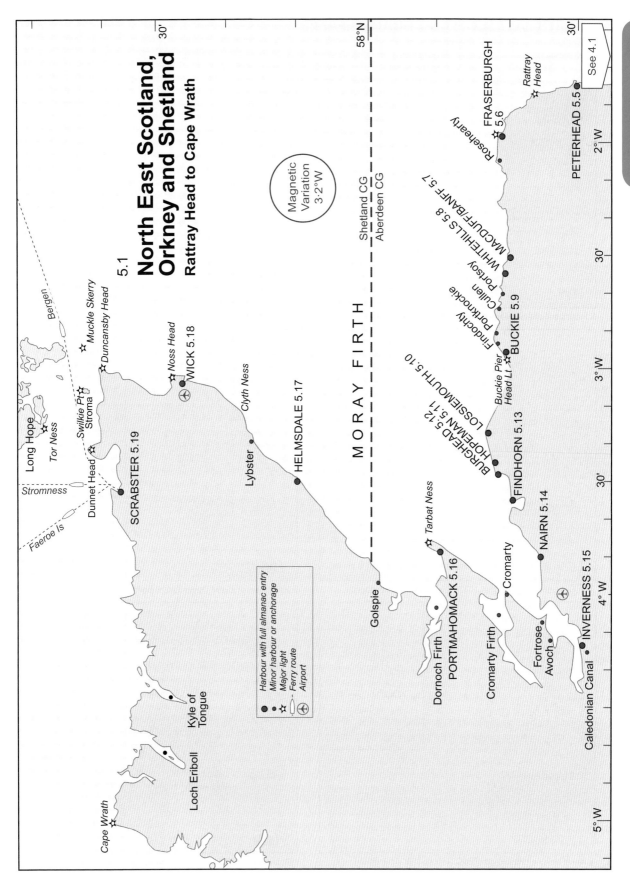

5.1

North East Scotland, Orkney and Shetland

Rattray Head to Cape Wrath

Magnetic Variation 3·2°W

58°N

Shetland CG
Aberdeen CG

MORAY FIRTH

Bergen

Muckle Skerry
Duncansby Head
Swilkie Pt
Stroma
Tor Ness
Long Hope
Stromness
Faeroe Is

Noss Head
WICK 5.18

Dunnet Head
SCRABSTER 5.19

Clyth Ness
Lybster

HELMSDALE 5.17

Golspie

Tarbat Ness
Dornoch Firth
PORTMAHOMACK 5.16

Cromarty
Cromarty Firth
Fortrose
Avoch
Caledonian Canal
INVERNESS 5.15

NAIRN 5.14

FINDHORN 5.13
BURGHEAD 5.12
HOPEMAN 5.11
LOSSIEMOUTH 5.10

Buckie Pier
Head Lt
BUCKIE 5.9
Findochty
Portknockie
Cullen
Portsoy
WHITEHILLS 5.8
MACDUFF/BANFF 5.7

Rosehearty
FRASERBURGH 5.6

Rattray Head
PETERHEAD 5.5

See 4.1

Kyle of Tongue
Loch Eriboll
Cape Wrath

Harbour with full almanac entry
Minor harbour or anchorage
Major light
Ferry route
Airport

2°W
3°W
30'
4°W
30'
5°W
30'
30'

5.2 NORTH EAST SCOTLAND TIDAL STREAMS

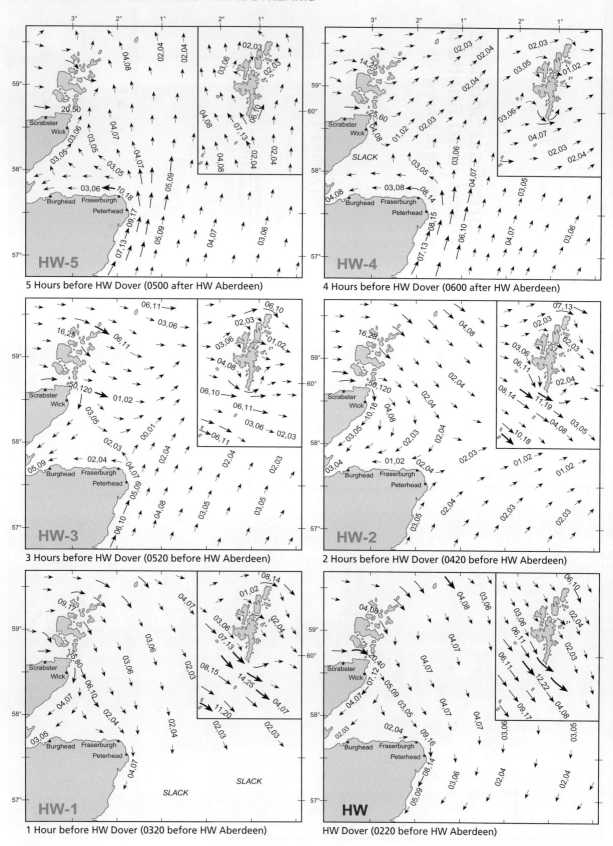

5 Hours before HW Dover (0500 after HW Aberdeen)

4 Hours before HW Dover (0600 after HW Aberdeen)

3 Hours before HW Dover (0520 before HW Aberdeen)

2 Hours before HW Dover (0420 before HW Aberdeen)

1 Hour before HW Dover (0320 before HW Aberdeen)

HW Dover (0220 before HW Aberdeen)

Southward 4.2

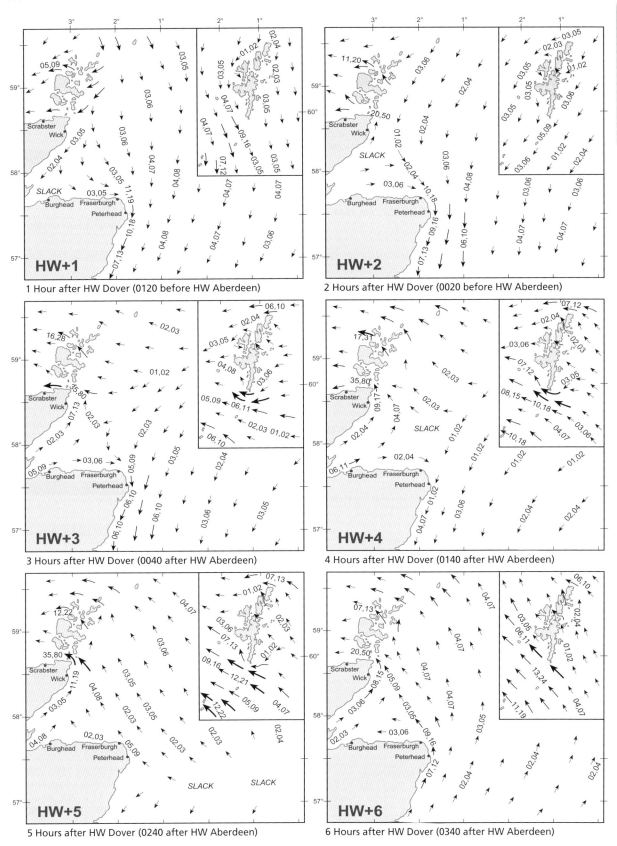

1 Hour after HW Dover (0120 before HW Aberdeen)

2 Hours after HW Dover (0020 before HW Aberdeen)

3 Hours after HW Dover (0040 after HW Aberdeen)

4 Hours after HW Dover (0140 after HW Aberdeen)

5 Hours after HW Dover (0240 after HW Aberdeen)

6 Hours after HW Dover (0340 after HW Aberdeen)

5.3 LIGHTS, BUOYS AND WAYPOINTS

Bold print = light with a nominal range of 15M or more. CAPITALS = place or feature. *CAPITAL ITALICS* = light-vessel, light float or Lanby. *Italics* = Fog signal. ***Bold italics*** = Racon. Some marks/buoys are fitted with AIS (MMSI No); see relevant charts.

BUCHAN NESS TO INVERNESS
PETERHEAD and RATTRAY HEAD
Buchan Ness ☆ Fl 5s 40m **18M**; W twr, R bands; ***Racon (O) 14-16M***; 57°28'·23N 01°46'·51W.
Kirktown Ldg lts 314°. Front, Oc R 6s 14m 10M; Or △ on lattice mast; 57°30'·22N 01°47'·21W. Rear, Oc R 6s 21m 10M (sync with front); Or ▽ on lattice mast.
S Bkwtr Hd ⚡ Fl (2) R 12s 24m 7M; 57°29'·79N 01°46'·54W.
N Bkwtr Hd ⚡ Iso RG 6s 19m 11M; W tripod; vis: 171°-R-236°-G-171°; *Horn 30s*; 57°29'·84N 01°46'·32W.

Rattray Hd ☆ 57°36'·61N 01°49'·03W Fl (3) 30s 28m **18M**; W twr; ***Racon (M) 15M***; *Horn (2) 45s*.

FRASERBURGH
Fraserburgh Ldg lt 291°; Iso R 2s 12m 9M; 57°41'·57N 02°00'·13W. Rear, 75m from front, Iso R 2s 17m 9M.
Fraserburgh, Balaclava Bkwtr Head ⚡ Fl (2) G 8s 26m 6M; dome on W twr; vis: 178°-326°; 57°41'·51N 01°59'·70W.

Kinnaird Hd ☆ 57°41'·87N 02°00'·26W Fl 5s 25m **22M**; vis: 092°-297°.

MACDUFF, BANFF and WHITEHILLS
Macduff Pier Hd ⚡ Fl (2) WRG 6s 12m W9M, R7M; W twr; vis: shore-G-115°-W-174°-R-210°; 57°40'·25N 02°30'·02W.
Macduff Ldg Lts 127°, Front FR 44m 3M; 57°40'·12N 02°29'·75W. Rear, 60m from front, FR 55m 3M; both Or △ on mast.
Banff Ldg Lts 295°, Front Fl R 4s; 57°40·30N 02°31·36W. Rear, QR; both vis: 210°-345°.

Whitehills Pier Hd ⚡ 57°40'·80N 02°34'·88W Fl WR 3s 7m W9M, R6M; W twr; vis: 132°-R-212°-W-245°.

PORTSOY and FINDOCHTY
Portsoy Pier Ldg Lts 173°, Front Fl G 4s 20m 3M; post; 57°41'·09N 02°41'·40W; Rear Q G 22m 3M; R △ on BW post.
Findochty Middle Pier Ldg Lts 166°, Front FR 6m 3M; 57°41'·90N 02°54'·20W. Rear FR 10m 3M.

BUCKIE
West Muck ⚡ QR 5m 7M; tripod; 57°41'·06N 02°58'·01W.
N Pier 60m from Hd ☆ 57°40'·9N 02°57'·5W Oc R 10s 15m **15M** W twr.

LOSSIEMOUTH, HOPEMAN and BURGHEAD
Lossiemouth S Pier Hd ⚡ Fl R 6s 11m 5M; 57°43'·42N 03°16'·69W.
Halliman Skerries ↯ Q; ***Racon M***, 57°44'·33N 03°18'·57W.
Hopeman Ldg Lts 081°, Front,FR 3m; 57°42'·71N 03°26'·18W. Rear, 10m from front, FR 4m.
Burghead N Bkwtr Hd ⚡ Oc 8s 7m 5M; 57°42'·09N 03°30'·03W.

FINDHORN, NAIRN and INVERNESS FIRTH
Findhorn Landfall ↯ LF 10s 57°40'·34N 03°38'·77W.
Nairn E Pier Hd ⚡ Oc WRG 4s 6m 5M; 8-sided twr; vis: shore-G-100°-W-207°-R-shore; 57°35'·62N 03°51'·65W.
Riff Bank E ⚬ Fl Y 10s 3m 5M 57°38'·38N 03°58'·18W; AIS.

SOUTH CHANNEL
Riff Bank S ↯ Q (6) + L Fl 15s; 57°36'·73N 04°00'·97W.
Chanonry ⚡ 57°34'·45N 04°05'·56W Oc 6s 12m 12M; W twr; vis: 148°-073°.
Munlochy ⚬ L Fl 10s; 57°32'·91N 04°07'·65W .
Petty Bank ⚭ Fl R 5s 57°31'·58N 04°08'·98W.
Meikle Mee ◣ Fl G 3s 57°30'·26N 04°12'·02W.

Longman Pt ↧ Fl WR 2s 7m W5M, R4M; vis: 078°-W-258°-R-078°; 57°29'·99N 04°13'·31W.
Craigton Point ⚡ Fl WRG 4s 6m W11M, R7M, G7M; vis: 312° - W - 048° - R - 064° - W - 085°- G - shore; 57°30'·05N 04°14'·09W.
Bridge Centre , Or △; ***Racon (K) 6M***; 57°29'·97N 04°13'·79W.

INVERNESS and CALEDONIAN CANAL
R. Ness Outer ↧ QR 3m 4M; 57°29'·83N 04°13'·93W.
Carnarc Pt ⚡ Fl G 2s 8m 4M; G lattice twr; 57°29'·72N 04°14'·25W.
Clachnaharry, S Tr'ng Wall Hd ↧ Iso G 4s 5m 2M; tfc sigs; 57°29'·43N 04°15'·86W.

INVERNESS TO DUNCANSBY HEAD
CROMARTY FIRTH and INVERGORDON
Fairway ⚬ L Fl 10s; ***Racon (M) 5M***; 57°39'·96N 03°54'·19W.
Cromarty Bank ◣ Fl (2) G 10s; 57°40'·66N 03°56'·78W.
Buss Bank ⚭ Fl R 3s 57°40'·97N 03°59'·54W.

Cromarty - The Ness (Lt ho disused W tr 13m); 57°40'·98N 04°02'·20W

Nigg Oil Terminal Pier Hd ⚡ Oc G 5s 31m 5M; Gy twr, floodlit; 57°41'·54N 04°02'·60W.

DORNOCH FIRTH to LYBSTER
Tarbat Ness ☆ 57°51'·88N 03°46'·76W Fl (4) 30s 53m **24M**; W twr, R bands; ***Racon (T) 14-16M***.
Lybster, S Pier Hd ⚡ Oc R 6s 10m 3M; 58°17'·79N 03°17'·41W.
Clyth Ness Lt Ho (unlit); W twr, R band; 58°18'·64N 03°12'·74W.

WICK
S Pier Hd ⚡ Fl WRG 3s 12m W12M, R9M, G9M; W 8-sided twr; vis: 253°-G-270°-W-286°-R-329°; *Bell (2) 10s* (occas); 58°26'·34N 03°04'·73W.

Dir lt 288.5° F WRG 9m W10M, R7M, G7M; col, N end of bridge; vis: 283·5°-G-287·2°-W-289·7°-R-293·5°; 58°26'·54N 03°05'·34W

Noss Hd ☆ 58°28'·71N 03°03'·09W Fl WR 20s 53m **W25M, R21M**; W twr; vis: shore-R-191°-W-shore.

DUNCANSBY HEAD TO CAPE WRATH
Duncansby Hd ☆ 58°38'·65N 03°01'·58W Fl 12s 67m **22M**; W twr; ***Racon (T)***.

Muckle Skerry ☆ 58°41'·41N 02°55'·49W Fl (3) 30s 52m **23M**; W twr; 992351086.

Lother Rock ⚡ Fl 2s 13m 6M; ***Racon (M) 10M***; 58°43'·79N 02°58'·69W.
Swona ⚡ Fl 8s 17m 9M; vis: 261°-210°; 58°44'·25N 03°04'·24W.
Swona N Hd ⚡ Fl (3) 10s 16m 10M; 58°45'·11N 03°03'·10W.

Stroma ☆, Swilkie Point 58°41'·75N 03°07'·01W Fl (2) 20s 32m **20M**; W twr.

Dunnet Hd ☆ 58°40'·28N 03°22'·60W Fl (4) 30s 105m **23M**.

THURSO, SCRABSTER and CAPE WRATH
Thurso Ldg Lts 195°. Front, FG 5m 4M; Gy post; 58°35'·96N 03°30'·76W. Rear, FG 6m 4M; Gy mast.
Scrabster Q. E. Pier Hd ⚡ Fl (2) 4s 8m 8M 58°36'·66N 03°32'·31W.
Strathy Pt Lt Ho (disused) W twr on W dwelling; 58°36'·04N 04°01'·12W.

Sule Skerry ☆ 59°05'·09N 04°24'·38W Fl (2) 15s 34m **21M**; W twr; ***Racon (T)***.

North Rona ☆ 59°07'·27N 05°48'·91W Fl (3) 20s 114m **22M**.
Sula Sgeir ⚡ Fl 15s 74m 11M; □ structure; 59°05'·61N 06°09'·57W.
Loch Eriboll, White Hd ⚡ Fl WR10s 18m W13M, R12M; W twr and bldg; vis: 030°-W-172°-R-191°-W-212°; 58°31'·01N 04°38'·90W.

Cape Wrath ☆ 58°37'·54N 04°59'·94W Fl (4) 30s 122m **22M**; W twr.

ORKNEY ISLANDS

Tor Ness ☆ 58°46'·78N 03°17'·86W Fl 5s 21m **17M**; W twr.
Cantick Hd (S Walls, SE end) ⚓ 58°47'·23N 03°07'·88W Fl 20s 35m 13M; W twr.

SCAPA FLOW and APPROACHES

Long Hope, S Ness Pier Hd ⚓ Fl WRG 3s 6m W7M, R5M, G5M; vis: 082°-G- 242°-W- 252°-R-082°; 58°48'·05N 03°12'·35W.

Hoxa Head ⚓ Fl WR 3s 15m W9M, R6M; W twr; vis: 026°-W-163°-R-201°-W-215°; 58°49'·31N 03°02'·09W.

Nevi Skerry ⚓ Fl (2) 6s 7m 6M; 58°50'·67N 03°02'·70W.
Flotta Grinds ⚓ Fl (2) R; 58°50'·97N 03°00'·77W; 992351083.
Rose Ness ⚓ 58°52'·33N 02°49'·97W Fl 6s 24m 8M; W twr.
Barrel of Butter ⚓ Fl (2) 10s 6m 7M; 58 53'·40N 03°07'·62W.
Cava ⚓ Fl WR 3s 11m W10M, R8M; W ○ twr; vis: 351°-W-143°-196°-W-251°-R-271°-R-298°; 58°53'·21N 03°10'·70W .

Houton Bay Ldg Lts 316°. Front ⚓ Fl G 3s 8m. Rear ⚓, 200m from front, FG 16m; vis: 312°- 320°; 58°54'·97N 03°11'·56W.

CLESTRAN SOUND and HOY SOUND

Graemsay Is Hoy Sound ☆ Ldg Lts 104°. Front Low, Iso 3s 17m 12M; W twr; vis: 070°-255°, 58°56'·42N 03°18'·60W. **High Rear**, 1·2M from front, Oc WR 8s 35m **W20M, R16M**; W twr; vis: 097°-R-112°-W-163°-R-178°-W-332°; obsc on Ldg line within 0·5M.

Skerry of Ness ⚓ Fl WG 4s 7m W7M, G4M; vis: shore -W-090°-G-shore; 58°56'·95N 03°17'·83W.

STROMNESS

Ldg Lts 317°. Front, FR 29m 11M; post on W twr; 58°57'·61N 03°18'·15W. Rear, 55m from front, FR 39m 11M; vis: 307°-327°; H24.

AUSKERRY

Copinsay ⚓ 58°53'·77N 02°40'·35W Fl (5) 30s 79m **21M**; W twr.

Auskerry ☆ 59°01'·51N 02°34'·34W Fl 20s 34m **20M**; W twr.

Helliar Holm, S end ⚓ Fl WRG 10s 18m W14M, R11M, G11M; W twr; vis: 256°-G-276°-W-292°-R-098°-W-116°-G-154°; 59°01'·13N 02°54'·09W.

Balfour Pier Shapinsay ⚓ Fl (2) WRG 5s 5m W3M, R2M, G2M; vis: 270°-G-010°-W-020°-R-090°; 59°01'·86N 02°54'·49W.

KIRKWALL

Thieves Holm, ⚓ Q R 8M; 59°01'·09N 02°56'·21W.

Pier N end ☆ 58°59'·29N 02°57'·72W Iso WRG 5s 8m **W15M**, R13M, G13M; W twr; vis: 153°-G-183°-W-192°-R-210°.

WIDE FIRTH

Linga Skerry ⚓ Q (3) 10s; 59°02'·39N 02°57'·56W.
Boray Skerries ⚓ Q (6) + L Fl 15s; 59°03'·65N 02°57'·66W.
Skertours ⚓ Q; 59°04'·11N 02°56'·72W.
Galt Skerry ⚓ Q; 59°05'·21N 02°54'·20W.
Brough of Birsay ☆ 59°08'·19W 03°20'·41W Fl (3) 25s 52m **18M**.

Papa Stronsay NE end, The Ness ⚓ Fl(4)20s 8m 9M; W twr; 59°09'·34N 02°34'·93W.

SANDAY ISLAND and NORTH RONALDSAY

Quiabow ⚓ Fl (2) G 12s; 59°09'·82N 02°36'·30W.
Start Pt ☆ 59°16'·69N 02°22'·71W Fl (2) 20s 24m **18M**.
Kettletoft Pier Hd ⚓ Fl WRG 3s 7m W7M, R5M, G5M; vis: 351°-W- 011°-R-180°-G-351°; 59°13'·80N 02°35'·86W.
N Ronaldsay ☆ NE end, 59°23'·34N 02°22'·91W Fl 10s 43m **24M**; R twr, W bands; *Racon (T) 14-17M.*

EDAY and EGILSAY

Calf Sound ⚓ Fl (3) WRG 10s 6m W8M, R6M, G6M; W twr; vis: shore-R-215°-W-222°-G-301°-W-305°; 59°14'·21N 02°45'·82W.
Backaland Pier ⚓ 59°09'·43N 02°44'·88W Fl R 3s 5m 4M; vis: 192°-250°.

Egilsay Graand ⚓ Q (6) + L Fl 15s; 59°06'·86N 02°54'·42W.

WESTRAY and PIEROWALL

Noup Head ☆ 59°19'·86N 03°04'·23W Fl 30s 79m **20M**; W twr; vis: about 335°-282° but partially obsc 240°-275°.

Pierowall E Pier Head ⚓ Fl WRG 3s 7m W11M, R7M, G7M; vis: 254°-G-276°-W-291°-R-308°-G-215°; 59°19'·35N 02°58'·53W.

Papa Westray, Moclett Bay Pier Head ⚓ Fl WRG 5s 7m W5M, R3M, G3M; vis: 306°-G-341°-W-040°-R-074°; 59°19'·60N 02°53'·52W.

SHETLAND ISLES

FAIR ISLE

Skadan South ☆, 59°30'·84N 01°39'·16W Fl (4) 30s 32m **22M**; W twr; vis: 260°-146°, obsc inshore 260°-282°.

Skroo ☆ N end 59°33'·13N 01°36'·58W Fl (2) 30s 80m **22M**; W twr; vis: 086·7°-358°.

MAINLAND, SOUTH

Sumburgh Head ☆ 59°51'·21N 01°16'·58W Fl (3) 30s 91m **23M**.
Mousa, Perie Bard ⚓ Fl 3s 20m 10M; 59°59'·84N 01°09'·51W.

BRESSAY and LERWICK

Bressay, Kirkabister Ness ⚓ 60°07'·20N 01°07'·31W; Fl (2) 10s 18m 10M. Adjacent Lt Ho disused.

Maryfield Ferry Terminal ⚓ Oc WRG 6s 5m 5M; vis: W008°-R013°-G-111°-008°; 60°09'·43N 01°07'·45W.

North Ness ⚓ Iso WG 4s 4m 5M; vis: shore-W-158°-G-216°-W-301°; 60°09'·57N 01°08'·77W

Loofa Baa ⚓ Q (6) + L Fl 15s 4m 5M; 60°09'·72N 01°08'·79W.
Soldian Rock ⚓ Q (6) + L Fl 15s 60°12'·51N 01°04'·73W.
N ent Dir lt 215°, Oc WRG 6s 27m 8M; Y △, Or stripe; vis: 211°-R-214°-W-216°-G-221°; 60°10'·47N 01°09'·53W.

Rova Hd ⚓ 60°11'·46N 01°08'·60W Fl (3) WRG 18s 12m W12M, R9M, G9M; W twr; vis: 090°-R-182°-W-191°-G-213°-R-241°-W-261·5°-G-009°-R-040°. Same structure and synchronised: Fl (3) WRG 18s 14m **W16M**, R13M, G13M; vis: 176·5°-R-182°-W-191°-G-196·5°.

Dales Voe ⚓ Fl (2) WRG 8s 5m W4M, R3M, G3M; vis: 220°-G-227°-W-233°-R-240°; 60°11'·79N 01°11'·23W.

Hoo Stack ⚓ Fl (4) WRG 12s 40m W7M, R5M, G5M; W pylon; vis: 169°-R-180°-W-184°-G-193°-W-169°. Same structure, Dir lt 182°. Fl (4) WRG 12s 33m W9M, R6M, G6M; vis: 177°- R-180°-W-184°-W-187°; synch with upper lt; 60°14'·96N 01°05'·38W.

Mull (Moul) of Eswick ⚓ Fl WRG 3s 50m W9M, R6M, G6M; W twr; vis: 028°-R-200°-W-207°-G-018°-W-028°; 60°15'·74N 01°05'·90W.

Inner Voder ⚓ Q (9) 15s; 60°16'·44N 01°05'·18W; AIS.

WHALSAY and SKERRIES

Symbister Ness ⚓ Fl (2) WG 12s 11m W8M, G6M; W twr; vis: shore-W-203°-G-shore; 60°20'·43N 01°02'·29W.

Suther Ness ⚓ Fl WRG 3s 10m W10M, R8M, G7M; vis: shore -W-038°-R-173°-W-206°-G-shore; 60°22'·12N 01°00'·20W.

Bound Skerry ☆ 60°25'·47N 00°43'·72W Fl 20s 44m **20M**; W twr.

South Mouth. Ldg Lts 014°. Front, FY3m 2M; 60°25'·33N 00°45'·01W. Rear, FY 12m 2M.

Muckle Skerry ⚓ Fl (2) WRG 10s 15m W7M, R5M, G5M; W twr; vis: 046°-W-192°-R-272°-G-348°-W-353°-R-046°; 60°26'·41N 00°51'·84W.

YELL SOUND

S ent, Lunna Holm ⚓ Fl (3) WRG 15s 19m W10M,R7M,G7M; W ○twr; vis: shore-R-090°-W-094°-G-209°-W-275°-R-shore; 60°27'·34N 01°02'·52W.

Firths Voe ☆, N shore 60°27'·21N 01°10'·63W Oc WRG 8s 9m **W15M**, R10M, G10M; W twr; vis: 189°-W-194°-G-257°-W-261°-R-339°-W-066°.

Linga Is. Dir lt 150° ⚓ Q (4) WRG 8s 10m W9M, R9M, G9M; vis: 145°-R-148°-W-152°-G-155°. Q (4) WRG 8s 10m W7M, R4M, G4M; same structure; vis: 052°-R-146°, 154°-G-196°-W-312°; synch; 60°26'·80N 01°09'·13W.

The Rumble Bn ⚓ R Bn; Fl 10s 8m 4M; *Racon (O)*; 60°28'·16N 01°07'·26W.

Yell, Ulsta Ferry Term. Bkwtr Hd ⚓ Oc RG 4s 7m R5M, G5M; vis: shore-G-354°, 044°-R-shore. Same structure; Oc WRG 4s 5m W8M, R5M, G5M; vis: shore-G-008°-W-036°-R-shore; 60°29'·74N 01°09'·52W.

Toft Ferry Terminal ☆,Dir lt 241° (H24); Dir Oc WRG 10s 8m **W16M**, R10M, G10M; vis: 236° -G-240°-W-242°-R-246°; by day W2M, R1M, G1M. 60°27'·96N 01°12'·34W.

Ness of Sound, W side ⚓ Fl (3) WRG 12s 18m W9M, R6M, G6M; vis: shore-G-345°-W-350°-R-160°-W-165°-G-shore; 60°31'·34N 01°11'·28W.

Brother Is. Dir lt 329°, Fl (4) WRG 8s 16m W10M, R7M, G7M; vis: 323·5°-G-328°-W-330°-R-333·5°; 60°30'·95N 01°14'·11W.

Mio Ness ⚓ Q (2) WR 10s 12m W7M, R4M; W ○ twr; vis: 282° - W - 238° - R - 282°; 60°29'·66N 01°13'·68W.

Tinga Skerry ⚓ Q(2)G 10s 9m 5M. W ○ twr; 60°30'·48N 01°14'·86W.

YELL SOUND, NORTH ENTRANCE

Bagi Stack ⚓ Fl (4) 20s 45m 10M; 60°43'·53N 01°07'·54W.

Gruney Is ⚓ Fl WR 5s 53m W8M, R6M; W twr; vis: 064°-R-180°-W-012°; *Racon (T) 14M*; 60°39'·15N 01°18'·17W.

Pt of Fethaland ☆ 60°38'·05N 01°18'·70W Fl (3) WR 15s 65m **W24M, R20M**; vis 080°-R-103°-W-160°-206°-W-340°.

Muckle Holm ⚓ Fl (4) 10s 32m 10M 60°34'·83N 01°16'·01W.

Little Holm ⚓ Iso 4s 12m 6M; W twr; 60°33'·42N 01°15'·88W.

Outer Skerry ⚓ Fl 6s 12m 8M; 60°33'·04N 01°18'·32W.

Quey Firth ⚓ Oc WRG 6s 22m W12M, R8M, G8M; W twr; vis: shore (through S & W)-W-290°-G-327°-W-334°-W-shore; 60°31'·43N 01°19'·58W.

Lamba, S side ⚓Fl WRG 3s 30m W8M, R5M, G5M; W twr; vis: shore-G-288°-W-293°-R-327°-W-044°-R-140°-W-shore. Dir lt 290·5° Fl WRG 3s 24m W10M, R7M, G7M; vis: 285·5°-G-288°-W-293°-W-295·5°; 60°30'·73N 01°17'·84W.

SULLOM VOE

Gluss Is ☆ Ldg Lts 194·7° (H24). **Front**, 60°29'·77N 01°19'·44W F 39m **19M**; □ on Gy twr; **Rear**, 0·75M from front, F 69m **19M**; □ on Gy twr; both Lts 9M by day.

Little Roe ⚓ Fl (3) WR 10s 16m W5M, R4M; W structure, Or band; vis: 036°-R-095·5°-W-036°; 60°29'·99N 01°16'·46W.

Skaw Taing ⚓ Ldg Lts 150·5°. Front, Oc WRG 5s 21m W8M, R5M, G5M; Or and W structure; vis: 049°-W-078°-G-147°-W-154°-R-169°-W-288°; 60°29'·10N 01°16'·86W. Rear, 195m from front, Oc 5s 35m 8M; vis: W145°-156°.

Ness of Bardister ⚓ Oc WRG 8s 20m W9M, R6M, G6M; Or &W structure; vis: 180·5°- W-240°- R-310·5°- W-314·5°- G-030·5°; 60°28'·19N 01°19'·63W.

Fugla Ness. Lts in line 212·3°. Rear, 60°27'·25N 01°19'·74W Iso 4s 45m 14M. Common front 60°27'·45N 01°19'·57W Iso 4s 27m 14M; synch with rear Lts. Lts in line 203°. Rear, 60°27'·26N 01°19'·81W Iso 4s 45m 14M.

Sella Ness ☆ Dir lt 133·5°; 60°26'·76N 01°16'·66W Oc WRG 10s 19m **W16M**, R3M, G3M; vis: 123·5° -G- 130·5°-Al WG (white phase increasing with brg)-132·5°-W-134·5°-Al WR(R phase inc with brg)-136·5°-R-143·5°; H24. By day Oc WRG 10s 19m W2M, R1M,G1M as above.

EAST YELL, UNST and BALTA SOUND

Whitehill ⚓ Fl WR 3s 24m W9M, R6M; W clad metal frame twr; vis: 147°-W-163°-R-211°-W-352°-R-003°; 60°34'·80N 01°00'·22W.

Fetlar. Hamars Ness ⚓ Iso G 6s 5m 3M; 60°37'·78N 00°55'·73W.

Balta Sound ⚓Fl WR 10s 17m 10M, R7M; vis: 249°-W-008°-R-058°-W-154°; 60°44'·43N 00°47'·68W.

Holme of Skaw ⚓ Fl 5s 8m 8M; white metal framework twr; 60°49'·87N 00°46'·30W.

Muckle Flugga ☆ 60°51'·32N 00°53'·13W Fl (2) 20s 66m **22M**.

Yell. Cullivoe Bkwtr Hd ⚓ Fl (2) WRG 10s 3m 4M; vis: 080°-G-294°-W-355°-R-080°; 60°41'·86N 00°59'·70W.

Unst. Head of Mula ⚓ Fl WRG 5s 48m W10M, G7M, R7M; metal framework twr; vis: 292°-G-357°-W-002°-R-157°-W-161·5; 60°40'·76N 00°57'·58W.

MAINLAND, WEST

Esha Ness ☆ 60°29'·34N 01°37'·65W Fl 12s 61m **25M**.

Ness of Hillswick ⚓ Fl (4) WR 15s 34m W9M, R6M; vis: 217°-W-093°-R-114°; 60°27'·21N 01°29'·80W.

Muckle Roe, Swarbacks Minn ⚓ Fl WR 3s 30m W9M, R6M; vis: 314°-W-041°-R-075°-W-137°; 60°20'·98N 01°27'·07W.

W Burra Firth Outer ⚓ Oc WRG 8s 27m W9M, R7M, G7M; vis: 136°-G-142°-W-150°-R-156°. H24; 60°17'·79N 01°33'·56W.

W Burra Firth Inner ☆ 60°17'·78N 01°32'·17W F WRG 9m **W15M**, R9M, G9M; vis: 095°-G-098°-W-102°-105°; H24.

Ve Skerries ⚓ Fl (2) 20s 17m 11M; W twr; *Racon (T) 15M*; 60°22'·36N 01°48'·78W.

Papa Stour Housa Voe Dir lt 228° ⚓ F WRG 2m W9M, R7M, G7M; vis: 219°- G-226°- W-230°-R-239°; 60°19'·58N 01°40'·47W.

Rams Head ⚓ Fl WRG 8s 16m W9M, R6M; G6M; W house; vis: 265°-G-355°-W-012°-R-090°-W-136°, obsc by Vaila I when brg more than 030°; 60°11'·96N 01°33'·47W.

North Havra ⚓ Fl(3) WRG 12s 24m W11M, R8M, G8M; W twr; vis: 001°-G-053·5°-W-060·5°-R-144°, 274°- G-334°-W-337·5°-R -001°; 60°09'·85N 01°20'·29W.

SCALLOWAY

Bullia Skerry ⚓ Fl 5s 5m 5M; stainless steel pillar & platform 60°06'·55N 01°21'·57W.

Point of the Pund ⚓ Fl WRG 5s 20m W7M, R5M, G5M; W GRP twr; vis: 267°-W-350°-R-090°-G-111°-R-135°-W-140°-G-177°; 60°07'·99N 01°18'·31W.

Whaleback Skerry ⚓ Q; 60°07'·95N 01°18'·90W.

Blacks Ness Pier SW corner ⚓ Oc WRG 10s 10m W11M, G8M, R8M; vis: 052°-G-063·5°-W-065·5°-R-077°; 60°08'·02N 01°16'·59W.

Fugla Ness ⚓ Fl (2) WRG 10s 20m W10M, R7M, G7M; W twr; vis: 014°-G-032°-W-082°-R-134°-W-shore; 60°06'·38N 01°20'·85W.

FOULA

South Ness ☆ 60°06'·75N 02°03'·86W Fl WR (3) 15s 36m **W18M** R14M; W twr; vis: 221°-W-255°-R-277°-W-123°-obscured-221°.

5.4 PASSAGE INFORMATION

Refer to the *N Coast of Scotland Pilot*; the CCC's SDs (3 vols) for N and NE coasts of Scotland; Orkney; and Shetland. Admiralty Leisure Folio 5617 covers the area from Fraserburgh to Inverness and the Caledonian Canal.

A 'Rover Ticket', £50 from Aberdeenshire and Moray Councils, allows berthing (subject to availability) for one week from arrival at the first harbour. The scheme includes: Johnshaven, Gourdon, Stonehaven, Rosehearty, Banff, Portsoy, Cullen, Portknockie, Findochty, Hopeman and Burghead.

Orkney Marinas levy the same charge for Kirkwall, Stromness, Westray and other places in the Orkney Islands, except St Margaret's Hope (5.20) which is independent. The 2014 tariffs are (per metre; 2% surcharge for card payment): £2/day, £12/week, £30/month, £80 for six months. Electricity is free for stays of less than 6 mths. More information is threaded between the following entries.

BUCHAN NESS TO RATTRAY HEAD

Buchan Ness (lt, fog sig, Racon) is a rky peninsula. 2ca N is Meikle Mackie islet, close W of which is the small hbr of Boddam (dries). 3ca NE of Meikle Mackie is The Skerry, a rk 6m high on S side of Sandford B; rks on which the sea breaks extend 2ca NNE. The chan between The Skerry and the coast is foul with rks and not advised. Peterhead is easy to enter in almost all conditions and is an excellent passage port with marina at SW corner of the Bay.

Numerous submarine pipelines lead ashore to St Fergus Terminal in Rattray Bay. **Notes on offshore installations, see 3.4.**

Rattray Hd (with lt, fog sig on The Ron, rk 2ca E of Hd) has rky foreshore, drying for 2ca off. Rattray Briggs is a detached reef, depth 0·2m, 2ca E of lt ho. Rattray Hard is a rky patch, depth 10·7m, 1·5M ENE of lt ho, which raises a dangerous sea during onshore gales. ▶ *Off Rattray Hd the S-going stream begins at HW Aberdeen –0420, and the N-going at HW Aberdeen +0110, sp rates 3kn. In normal conditions keep about 1M E of Rattray Hd, but pass 5M off in bad weather, preferably at slack water.* ◀ Conspic radio masts with red lights lie 2·5M WNW and 2·2M W of lighthouse.

MORAY FIRTH: SOUTH COAST

(AC 115, 222, 223) Crossing the Moray Firth from Rattray Hd (lt, fog sig) to Duncansby Hd (lt, Racon) heavy seas may be met in strong W winds. Most hbrs in the Firth are exposed to NE-E winds. For oil installations, see 3.4; the Beatrice Field is 20M S of Wick.

▶ *Tidal streams attain 3kn at sp close off Rattray Hd, but 5M NE of the Head the NE-going stream begins at HW Aberdeen +0140, and the SE-going stream at HW Aberdeen –0440, sp rates 2kn. Streams are weak elsewhere in the Moray Firth, except in the inner part.* ◀

In late spring/early summer fog (haar) is likely in onshore winds. In strong winds the sea breaks over Steratan Rk and Colonel Rk, respectively 3M E and 1M ENE of Fraserburgh. Banff B is shallow; N of Macduff beware Collie Rks. Banff hbr dries, and should not be approached in fresh NE-E winds, when seas break well offshore; Macduff is a possible alternative.

From Meavie Pt to Scar Nose dangers extend up to 3ca from shore in places. Beware Caple Rk (depth 0·2m) 7½ca W of Logie Hd.

Spey B is clear of dangers more than 7½ca from shore; anch here, but only in offshore winds. Beware E Muck (dries) 5ca SW of Craigenroan, an above-water rky patch 5ca SW of Craig Hd, and Middle Muck and W Muck in approach to Buckie; Findochty & Portknockie are 2 and 3.5M ENE. Halliman Skerries (dry; bn) lie 1·5M WNW of Lossiemouth. Covesea Skerries (dry) lie 5ca NW of their lt ho (disused).

To the SW of a line between Helmsdale and Lossiemouth is a EU Special Area of Conservation to protect a vulnerable population of bottlenose dolphins. Mariners are advised to proceed at a safe, constant speed through the area and avoid disturbing them.

Inverness Firth is approached between Nairn and S Sutor. In heavy weather there is a confused sea with overfalls on Guillam Bank, 9M S of Tarbat Ness. The sea also breaks on Riff Bank (S of S Sutor) which dries in places. Chans run both N and S of Riff Bank.

▶ *Off Fort George, on E side of ent to Inverness Firth (AC1078), the SW-going stream begins at HW Aberdeen +0605, sp rate 2·5kn; the NE-going stream begins at HW Aberdeen –0105, sp rate 3·5kn. There are eddies and turbulence between Fort George and Chanonry Pt when stream is running hard. Tidal streams in the Inverness Firth and approaches are not strong, except in the Cromarty Firth Narrows, the Fort George Narrows and the Kessock Road, including off the entrance to the Caledonian Canal.* ◀

There is a firing range between Nairn and Inverness marked, when in operation, by flags at Fort George. Much of Inverness Firth is shallow, but a direct course from Chanonry Pt to Kessock Bridge, via Munlochy SWM and Meikle Mee SHM lt buoys, carries a least depth of 2·1m. Meikle Mee bank dries 0·2m.

5.5 PETERHEAD

Aberdeenshire **57°29'·81N 01°46'·42W** ✵✵✵✵⚓⚓✿✿

CHARTS AC 213, 1438, 5617; Imray C23

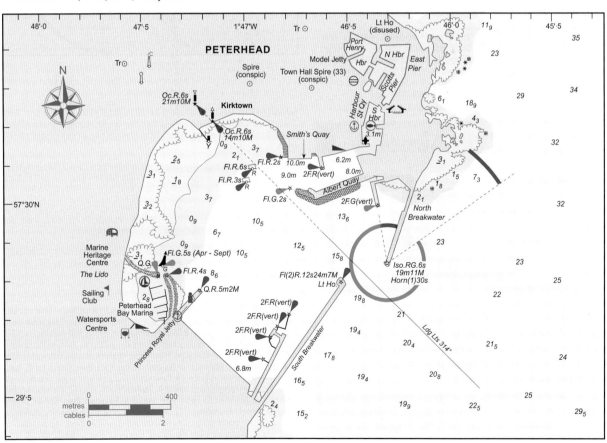

Continued overleaf

PETERHEAD *continued*

TIDES +0140 Dover; ML 2·3; Duration 0620

Standard Port ABERDEEN (←)

Times				Height (metres)			
High Water		Low Water		MHWS	MHWN	MLWN	MLWS
0000	0600	0100	0700	4·3	3·4	1·6	0·6
1200	1800	1300	1900				
Differences PETERHEAD							
−0035	−0045	−0035	−0040	−0·3	−0·2	0·0	+0·1

SHELTER Good in marina (2·8m). A useful passage hbr, also a major fishing and oil/gas industry port. Access any weather/tide.

NAVIGATION WPT 57°29′·44N 01°45′·75W, 314°/0·5M to ent. No dangers. 5kn speed limit in Bay; 4kn in marina. Chan between marina bkwtr and SHM lt buoy is <30m wide.

LIGHTS AND MARKS Power stn chy (183m) is conspic 1·25M S of entrance. Ldg marks 314°, front Or △, rear Or ▽, on lattice masts; lights as chartlet. Marina E bkwtr ☆ Fl R 4s 6m 2M; W bkwtr hd, QG 5m 2M, vis 185°-300°. Buchan Ness ☆ Fl 5s 40m 28M is 1·6M S of entrance.

COMMUNICATIONS (Code 01779) MRCC (01224) 592334; Police 101; Dr 474841; Ⓗ 472316. Marina Manager (Bay Authority: www. peterheadport.co.uk) 477868; Hr Control (H24) 483630.

All vessels, including yachts, **must** call *Peterhead Harbour Radio* VHF Ch **14** for clearance to enter/depart the Bay.

FACILITIES Peterhead Bay Marina marina@peterheadport.co.uk ☎ 477868, access all tides, 2·3m at ent, max LOA 20m. Pontoons are 'E' to 'A' from entrance.150 ⌷, £13 up to 6m LOA + £1/m (7 days for price of 5); Ⓓ, Gaz, Gas, Ⓛ; D from bowser at end of Princess Royal jetty (☆ Q R);R, ⚒ and Ⓓ at caravan site. **Peterhead SC** ☎ (01358) 751340 (Sec); **Services:** ⚓, ✎, Ⓑ, Ⓔ, ✗, C, Gas. **Town** ⚫, ⚒, ✗, ✉, bus to Aberdeen for ⇌ & ✈.

ADJACENT HARBOUR

BODDAM, Aberdeenshire, **57°28′·47N 01°46′·56W.** AC 213. HW +0145 on Dover; Tides as 5.5. Good shelter in the lee of Meikle Mackie, the island just N of Buchan Ness, Fl 5s 40m 28M Horn (3) 60s. Inner hbr dries/unlit. Beware rks around Meikle Mackie and to the SW of it. Appr from 1½ca NW of The Skerry. Yachts on S side of outer hbr. All facilities at Peterhead, 2M N.

5.6 FRASERBURGH

Aberdeenshire **57°41′·50N 01°59′·79W** ✿✿⚓⚓✿✿

CHARTS AC 115, 222, 1462, 5617; Imray C23

TIDES +0120 Dover; ML 2·3; Duration 0615

Standard Port ABERDEEN (←)

Times				Height (metres)			
High Water		Low Water		MHWS	MHWN	MLWN	MLWS
0000	0600	0100	0700	4·3	3·4	1·6	0·6
1200	1800	1300	1900				
Differences FRASERBURGH							
−0122	−0118	−0115	−0115	−0·5	−0·4	−0·1	+0·2

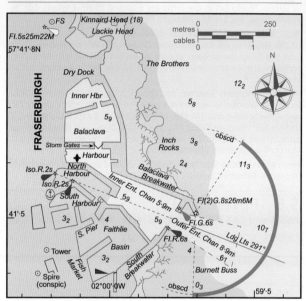

SHELTER A safe refuge, but ent is dangerous in NE/SE gales. A very busy fishing hbr; yachts are not encouraged but may find a berth in S Hbr (3.2m). FVs come and go H24.

NAVIGATION WPT 57°41′·30N 01°58′·80W, 291°/0·57M to ent. The Outer Ent Chan is maintained to 8·9m and Inner Ent Chan 5·9m. Good lookout on entering/leaving. Yachts can enter under radar control in poor vis.

LIGHTS AND MARKS Kinnairds Hd lt ho, Fl 5s 25m 22M, is 0·45M NNW of ent. Cairnbulg Briggs bn, Fl (2) 10s 9m 6M, is 1·8M ESE of ent. Ldg lts 291°: front Iso R 2s 12m 9M; rear Iso R 2s 17m 9M.

COMMUNICATIONS (Code 01346) MRCC (01224) 592334; Police 101; Dr 518088. Port Office 515858; Watch Tr 515926. Call on approach VHF Ch **12 16** (H24) for directions/berth.

FACILITIES **Port** ☎ 515858, ⌷ £10 (in S Hbr) any LOA, ⚓, Ⓟ, D, ⚓, Ⓛ, ✎, Ⓑ, ✗, C (30 ton & 70 ton mobile), ⚐, ⚒, ✗, ✉; **Town** ✉, Ⓑ, ⇌, ✈ (bus to Aberdeen).

ADJACENT HARBOURS

ROSEHEARTY, Aberdeen, **57°42′·08N 02°06′·87W.** ✿✿⚓⚓✿✿ AC 222, 213. HW Aberdeen −1. E pier and inner hbr dry, but end of W pier is accessible at all tides. Ent exposed in N/E winds; in E/SE winds hbr can be uncomfortable. Ldg lts, 219°, on BW metal poles; rks E of ldg line. When 30m from pier, steer midway between ldg line and W pier (W round tower), Fl 4s. Port Rae, close to E, has unmarked rks; local knowledge req'd. ⌷ £10 any LOA. *For details of Rover berthing ticket see 5.4.* **Town** ⚒, ✗, ✉, ✉. Firing range: for info ☎ (01346) 571634; see also 5.4. **Pennan Bay**, 5M W: ⚓ on sand between Howdman (2·9m) and Tamhead (2·1m) rks, 300m N of hbr (small craft only). **Gardenstown** (Gamrie Bay). Appr from E of Craig Dagerty rk (4m, conspic). Harbour dries, or ⚓ off.

5.7 MACDUFF/BANFF

Aberdeenshire Macduff **57°40'·25N 02°30'·03W** ⚓⚓⚓⚓
Banff **57°40'·22N 02°31'·27W** ⚓⚓⚓⚓

CHARTS AC 115, 222, 1462, 5617; Imray C23

TIDES + 0055 Dover; ML 2·0; Duration 0615

Standard Port ABERDEEN (←—)

Times				Height (metres)			
High Water		Low Water		MHWS	MHWN	MLWN	MLWS
0200	0900	0400	0900	4·3	3·4	1·6	0·6
1400	2100	1600	2100				
Differences BANFF							
–0100	–0150	–0150	–0050	–0·4	–0·2	–0·1	+0·2

SHELTER Macduff: Reasonably good, but ent not advised in strong NW winds. Slight/moderate surge in outer hbr with N/NE gales. Hbr ent is 17m wide with 3 basins; approx 2·6m in outer hbr and 2m inner hbr. A busy cargo/fishing port with limited space for yachts. **Banff**: Popular hbr which dries. When Macduff ent is very rough in strong NW/N winds, Banff can be a safe refuge; pontoon berths in both basins. Best to contact HM beforehand. In strong E/ENE winds Banff is unusable.

NAVIGATION WPT 57°40'·48N 02°30'·59W, 127°/0·4M to **Macduff** ent. WPT 57°40'·11N 02°30'·85W, 115°/0·25M to **Banff** ent. Beware Feachie Craig, Collie Rks and rky coast N and S of hbr ent.

LIGHTS AND MARKS Macduff: Ldg lts/marks 127° both FR 44/55m 3M, orange △s. Pier hd lt, Fl (2) WRG 6s 12m 9/7M, W tr; shore-G-115°-W-174°-R-210°, Horn (2) 20s. **Banff**: Fl 4s end of New Quay and ldg lts 295° rear Fl R 2s, front Fl R 4s.

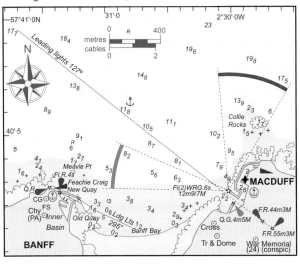

COMMUNICATIONS (Code 01261) MRCC (01224) 592334; Police 101; Dr (Banff) 812027. HM (Macduff) 832236, Watch tr 833962; HM (Banff) 815544.

Macduff Ch 12 16 (H24); **Banff** Ch 12.

FACILITIES Macduff: Hbr £10 any LOA; ⚓, ⚓, ⚓, 🅱, ⚒, 🅰. **Town** 🏠 & 🏠, ⚒, ✕, 🏠, ✉, ⚓ (bus to Keith).

Banff: Hbr www.banffmarina.com ● in Inner Hbr marina, £10 any LOA, *Rover berthing ticket see 5.4*; ⚓, ⚓, 🔌, 🅾, 🆚; **Banff SC**: showers. **Town**, 🏠 & 🏠, Gas, ⚒, ✕, 🏠, ⚓, Ⓑ, ✈ (Aberdeen).

ADJACENT HARBOURS

PORTSOY, Aberdeenshire, **57°41'·34N 02°41'·59W**. ⚓⚓⚓⚓. AC 222. HW +0047 on Dover; –0132 and Ht –0·3m on Aberdeen. Small drying hbr; ent exposed to NW/NE'lies. New Hbr to port of ent partially dries; Inner Hbr dries to clean sand. Ldg lts 173°, front Fl G 4s 20m 3M, metal post; rear Q G 22m 3M, R △ on BW post. HM ☎ (01261) 815544. Facilities: few but hosts Scottish Traditional Boat Festival late June/early July. ⚓ £10, *for details of Rover berthing ticket see 5.4*, ⚓, ⚓, ⚒, ✕, 🏠, ✉. **Sandend Bay**, 1·7M W (57°41'N 02°44'·5W). ⚓ on sand E of hbr.

5.8 WHITEHILLS

Aberdeenshire **57°40'·80N 02°34'·87W** ⚓⚓⚓⚓⚓

CHARTS AC 115, 222, 5617; Imray C23

TIDES +0050 Dover; ML 2·4; Duration 0610

Standard Port ABERDEEN (←—)

Times				Height (metres)			
High Water		Low Water		MHWS	MHWN	MLWN	MLWS
0200	0900	0400	0900	4·3	3·4	1·6	0·6
1400	2100	1600	2100				
Differences WHITEHILLS							
–0122	–0137	–0117	–0127	–0·4	–0·3	+0·1	+0·1

SHELTER Safe. In strong NW/N winds beware surge in the narrow ent and outer hbr, when ent is best not attempted. See HM for vacant pontoon berth.

NAVIGATION WPT 57°41'·98N 02°34'·89W, 180°/1·2M to bkwtr lt. Reefs on S side of chan marked by 2 rusty/white SHM bns. Beware fishing floats. Narrow entrance 1·7m below CD, Outer Hbr pontoon berths 2m and Inner Hbr 1.5m–1·8m.

LIGHTS AND MARKS Fl WR 3s on pier hd, vis 132°-R-212°-W-245°; approach in R sector.

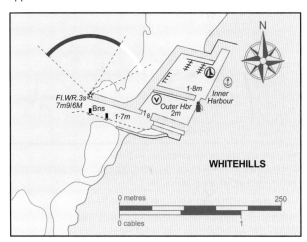

COMMUNICATIONS (Code 01261) MRCC (01224) 592334; Police 101; Dr 812027. HM www.whitehillsharbour.co.uk ☎ 861291, mobile 07906 135786.

Whitehills Hbr Radio VHF Ch **14** 16.

FACILITIES Marina (47 + ●), £15 (decreasing to £30/3nights), Quayside £12, @, D, 🅾, showers, 🔧, 🅱, 🅰; **Town** ⚒, ✕, 🏠, ✉, ⚓ (bus to Keith), ✈ (Aberdeen).

ADJACENT HARBOURS

CULLEN, Moray, **57°41'·63N 02°49'·29W**. ⚓⚓⚓. AC 222. HW +0045 on Dover, HW –0135 & –0·3m on Aberdeen; Duration 0555; ML 2·4m. Shelter good, but ent hazardous in strong W/N winds. Appr on 180° toward conspic viaduct and W bn on N pier. Caple Rk, 0·2m, is 5ca NE of hbr. Small drying hbr, best for shoal draft. Moor S of Inner jetty if < 1m draft with F G bn close S of the root of N pier. Beware moorings across inner basin ent. Pontoons in inner hbr (1·8m at HW Np). *For Rover berthing ticket see 5.4.* HM ☎ (01542) 831700. **Town** Gas, Gaz (hardware store), ⚒, R, 🏠, ✉.

PORTKNOCKIE, Moray, **57°42'·28N 02°51'·79W**. ⚓⚓⚓⚓. AC 222. HW +0045 on Dover; –0135 and ht –0·3m Aberdeen; ML 2·3m; Duration 0555; access H24. Good shelter in one of the safest hbrs on S side of Moray Firth, but scend is often experienced; care needed in strong NW/N winds. FW ldg lts, on white-topped poles, lead approx 151°, to ent. Orange street lts surround the hbr. Limited ABs on N Quay; most of inner hbr dries. HM ☎ (01542) 840833 (home, p/time); Facilities: ⚓, ⚓; *for details of Rover berthing ticket see 5.4*, ⚓, ✕; Dr ☎ 840272. **Town** Ⓑ, ✉, ⚒, 🏠.

5.9 BUCKIE

Moray **57°40'·84N 02°57'·63W** ✿✿✿❄❄❄❄✿✿

CHARTS AC 223, 1462, 5617; Imray C23

TIDES +0040 Dover; ML 2·4; Duration 0550
Standard Port ABERDEEN (←—)

Times				Height (metres)			
High Water		Low Water		MHWS	MHWN	MLWN	MLWS
0200	0900	0400	0900	4·3	3·4	1·6	0·6
1400	2100	1600	2100				
Differences BUCKIE							
–0130	–0145	–0125	–0140	–0·2	–0·2	0·0	+0·1

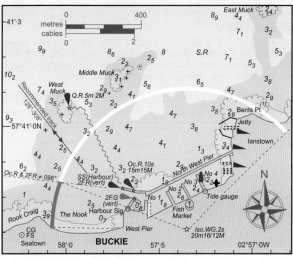

SHELTER Good in all weathers.

In strong NNW to NE winds there is a dangerous swell over the bar at hbr ent, which is 24m wide.

Access H24. Berth in No 4 basin as directed by HM.

NAVIGATION Beware W, Middle and E Muck Rks, 3ca off shore. WPT 57°41'·3N 02°59'·0W, 125°/0·8M to ent. The recommended track from the WPT to the hbr ent is 128° until the 2FR (vert) and the Oc R 10s on the N breakwater are in line (096°). The N bkwtr lt aligned with the Iso WG 2s behind the hbr leads clear of W Muck on a hdg of 120°. Traffic is controlled by VHF.

LIGHTS AND MARKS W Muck QR 5m 2M (tripod); N bkwtr, Oc R 10s 15m 15M (W twr), N bwtr hd 2FR(vert), S bwtr hd 2FG(vert). Harbour Lt Iso WG 2s 20m 16/12M, (W tr, R top inshore of hbr).

COMMUNICATIONS (Code 01542) MRCC (01224) 592334; Police 101; Dr 831555. HM 831700, mob 07842 532360.

VHF Ch 12 16 (H24).

FACILITIES ⌂ £17·50 or £8·50 <12hrs, ⏚, ⚓; **Services:** D & P (delivery), ✎, ✗, ⓑ, ▣, ◣, BY, BH (50 tons), C (15 ton), Gas. **Town** ☕, ▢, Ⓑ, ✉, ▢ at Strathlene caravan site 1·5M E, ⇌ (bus to Elgin), ✈ (Aberdeen or Inverness).

ADJACENT HARBOUR (2M ENE OF BUCKIE)

FINDOCHTY, Moray, **57°41'·94N 02°54'·29W**. AC 222. HW +0045 on Dover, HW –0135 & ht –0·2m on Aberdeen; ML 2·3m; Duration 0550. Ent is about 2ca W of conspic church belfry. 1ca N of ent, leave Beacon Rock (3m high) to stbd. Ldg lts, FR, lead 166° into Outer Basin which dries 0·2m and has many rky outcrops. Ent faces N and is 20m wide; unlit white bn at hd of W pier. Good shelter in inner basin for 100 small craft/yachts on 3 pontoons (the 2 W'ly pontoons dry); possible ⌂ on Sterlochy Pier in 2m; ◣ (£10) *for details of Rover berthing ticket see 5.4.* HM mob 07900 920445. **Town** ☕, ✗, ▢, ✉, Ⓑ.

5.10 LOSSIEMOUTH

Moray **57°43'·41N 03°16'·63W** ✿✿❄❄❄✿✿✿

CHARTS AC 223, 1462, 5617; Imray C23

TIDES +0040 Dover; ML 2·3; Duration 0605
Standard Port ABERDEEN (←—)

Times				Height (metres)			
High Water		Low Water		MHWS	MHWN	MLWN	MLWS
0200	0900	0400	0900	4·3	3·4	1·6	0·6
1400	2100	1600	2100				
Differences LOSSIEMOUTH							
–0125	–0200	–0130	–0130	–0·2	–0·2	0·0	0·0

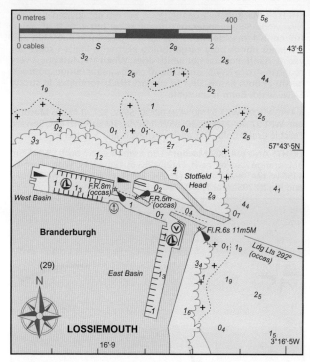

SHELTER Very good in winds from SSE to NW. Pontoon berths in both basins, dredged 2m. West Basin also used by FVs.

- In N to SE winds >F6 appr can be dangerous, with swell tending to break across hbr mouth and in outer hbr. Residual swell from E to SE can be particularly hazardous.

- Near ent, beware current from R Lossie setting in N'ly direction, causing confused water in N to SE winds at sp.

- Vessels drawing >2m would have little clearance at LWS ±2.

NAVIGATION WPT 57°43'·38N 03°16'·09W, 277°/0·3M to ent. Rks to N and S of hbr ent; appr from E. Approx 0·4m in entrance at LWS.

LIGHTS AND MARKS Halliman Skerries (drying) 1NM W of harbour entrance are marked by NCM, Q; *Racon M*. Ldg lts 292°, both FR 5/8m; S pier hd Fl R 6s 11m 5M.

COMMUNICATIONS (Code 01343) MRCC (01224) 592334; Police 101; Dr 812277.

VHF Ch 12 16 HO.

FACILITIES **Lossiemouth Marina** ☎ 813066 (95 inc Ⓥ) ⌂ £20 for first 24hrs and £15 thereafter/craft, ▣, &, wi-fi.

Hbr ◣ (£50 pa), ✗, ✎, ⓑ, BH (25 ton), C (1 ton).
Hbr Service Stn ☎ 813001, Mon-Fri 0800-2030, Sat 0800-1930, Sun 0930-1900, ▣ & ▢, Gas, Gaz.
Town ☕, ✗, ▢, ✉, Ⓑ/Ⓒ, ⇌ (bus to Elgin), ✈ (Inverness).

5.11 HOPEMAN

Moray **57°42'·70N 03°26'·31W** ❄☀◊◊❀❀

CHARTS AC 223, 1462, 5617; Imray C23

TIDES +0050 Dover; ML 2·4; Duration 0610

Standard Port ABERDEEN (←)

Times				Height (metres)			
High Water		Low Water		MHWS	MHWN	MLWN	MLWS
0200	0900	0400	0900	4·3	3·4	1·6	0·6
1400	2100	1600	2100				
Differences HOPEMAN							
–0120	–0150	–0135	–0120	–0·2	–0·2	0·0	0·0

SHELTER Once in Inner Basin, shelter good from all winds; but hbr dries. Ent is difficult in winds from NE to SE. A popular yachting hbr with ⌐.

NAVIGATION WPT 57°42'·66N, 03°26'·59W, 083° to ent, 0·17M.

Dangerous rks lie off hbr ent. Do not attempt entry in heavy weather. Beware lobster pot floats E and W of hbr (Mar-Aug).

LIGHTS AND MARKS See 5.3 and chartlet.

COMMUNICATIONS (Code 01343) MRCC (01224) 592334; Police 101; Dr 543141. HM 835337 (part-time).
Burghead Radio Ch 14 (HX).

FACILITIES Hbr ⌐ £9, *for details of Rover Ticket see 5.4*, ⚓, ⚓
⚒, ⚔, ☎.
Town 🛒, ✕, ⌂, ✉, ⑧, ⚏ (bus to Elgin), ✈ (Inverness).

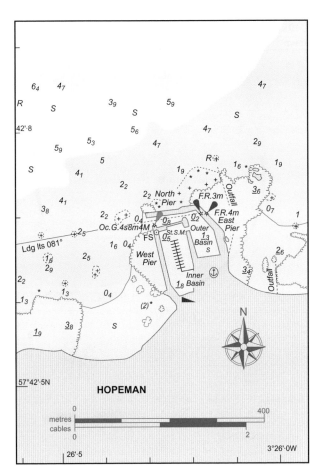

HOPEMAN

5.12 BURGHEAD

Moray **57°42'·06N 03°30'·02W** ❄☀◊◊❀❀

CHARTS AC 223, 1462, 5617; Imray C23

TIDES +0035 Dover; ML 2·4; Duration 0610

Standard Port ABERDEEN (←)

Times				Height (metres)			
High Water		Low Water		MHWS	MHWN	MLWN	MLWS
0200	0900	0400	0900	4·3	3·4	1·6	0·6
1400	2100	1600	2100				
Differences BURGHEAD							
–0120	–0150	–0135	–0120	–0·2	–0·2	0·0	0·0

SHELTER One of the few Moray Firth hbrs accessible in strong E winds. Go alongside where available and contact HM. Can be very busy with FVs.

NAVIGATION WPT 57°42'·28N 03°30'·39W, 137°/0·28M to N pier lt QR. 0·6m in ent chan and 1·4m in hbr, but depths variable due to sand movement. Advisable to contact HM if entering near LW. 3kn speed limit.

LIGHTS AND MARKS No ldg lts but night ent is safe after identifying the N pier lts: QR 3m 5M and Oc 8s 7m 5M.

COMMUNICATIONS (Code 01343) MRCC (01224) 592334; Police 101; Dr 812277. HM 835337.
Burghead Radio VHF Ch **14** 12 (HO and when vessel due).

FACILITIES Hbr ⌐ £9, *for details of Rover Ticket see 5.4*, ⚓, ⌐,
C (50 ton mobile), L, ⚓, BY, ⚔.
Town ⌂, ✉, 🛒, ⑧, ⚏ (bus to Elgin), ✈ (Inverness).

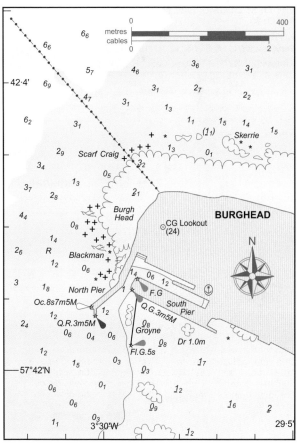

BURGHEAD

5.13 FINDHORN

Moray **57°39'·64N 03°37'·47W** ❀❀❀☆☆ ✿✿✿

CHARTS AC 223, 5617; Imray C23

TIDES +0110 Dover; ML 2·5; Duration 0615

Standard Port ABERDEEN (←)

Times				Height (metres)			
High Water		Low Water		MHWS	MHWN	MLWN	MLWS
0200	0900	0400	0900	4·3	3·4	1·6	0·6
1400	2100	1600	2100				
Differences FINDHORN							
–0120	–0150	–0135	–0130	0·0	–0·1	0·0	+0·1

SHELTER ⚓ in pool off boatyard or off N pier or dry out alongside, inside piers and ask at YC; or pick up Y ⚓ off N pier.

Do not attempt entry in strong NW/NE winds or with big swell running; expect breakers/surf either side of entrance.

NAVIGATION From the SWM Landfall Buoy the bar, which dries, is marked (Fl R marker); thence follow marked chan to entrance.

- Bar and sands shift frequently esp following bad weather.
- Buoys (inc SWM) often move to follow channel into the bay.
- Marks may be lifted Nov to early Apr.

Once past The Ee, turn port inside G buoys. The S part of Findhorn Bay dries extensively.

LIGHTS AND MARKS Unlit. There is a windsock on FS by The Ee. Boatyard building is conspic.

COMMUNICATIONS (Code 01309) MRCC (01224) 592334; Police 101; Dr 678866/678888; Findhorn Pilot (Derek Munro) 690802, mob 07747 840916; Findhorn BY 690099. Fairways Committee (via BY) 690099.

VHF Ch M *Chadwick Base* (when racing in progress). Findhorn BY: Ch 80.

FACILITIES **Royal Findhorn YC** ☎ 690247, M, ⚓ (free), ⚓, ⬚; Services: BY, L, M, ⬚, ⚓, ⬛, C (16 ton), ⬚, ⚒, ⬚, ACA, ⚒. **Kinloss** (2½M) ⬚ & ⬚, Gas, Gaz.

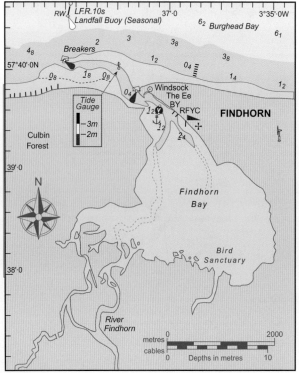

5.14 NAIRN

Highland **57°35'·61N 03°51'·65W** ❀❀❀☆☆ ✿✿✿

CHARTS AC 223, 1462, 5617; Imray C23

TIDES +0110 Dover; ML 2·2; Duration 0615

Standard Port INVERGORDON (→)

Times				Height (metres)			
High Water		Low Water		MHWS	MHWN	MLWN	MLWS
0100	0700	0000	0700	4·3	3·3	1·6	0·7
1300	1900	1200	1900				
Differences NAIRN							
+0005	–0015	0000	–0015	0·0	0·0	0·0	0·0
McDERMOTT BASE							
+0015	–0005	+0015	0000	–0·1	0·0	+0·1	+0·2

SHELTER Good, but entry difficult in fresh NNE'ly. Pontoons in hbr with ❶ berths. Best entry HW ± 1½. No commercial shipping.

NAVIGATION The beach dries to 100m off the pierheads. A mark is laid in the deepest water off the entrance to indicate line of approach. Inside, the best water is to the E side of the river chan which dries approx 1·9m.

- Buoy and sands shift frequently esp following bad weather.
- Mark may be lifted Nov to early Apr.

LIGHTS AND MARKS Lt ho on E pier hd, Oc WRG 4s 6m 5M, vis shore-G-100°-W-207°-R-shore. Keep in W sector.

COMMUNICATIONS (Code 01667) MRCC (01224) 592334; Police 101; Clinic 452096; Dr 453421. Hbr Office 452453, mob 07851 635088.

VHF Ch M (weekends only).

FACILITIES **Nairn Basin** ⚓ £15.28 - 48hrs, ⬛ (launching £6), AC (110 volts), ⬚ & ⬚; **Nairn SC** ☎ 453897, ⬚. **Town** ⬛, ✗, ⬚, ✉, Ⓑ, ⇌, ✈ (Inverness).

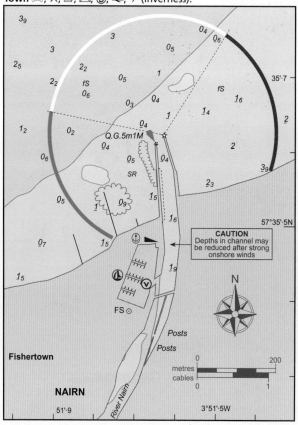

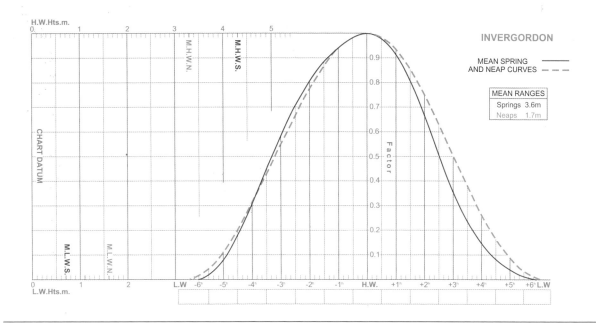

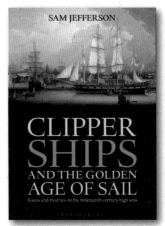

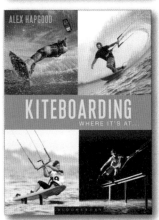
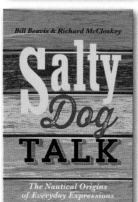

Invergordon tides

STANDARD TIME (UT)
For Summer Time add ONE hour in **non-shaded** areas

INVERGORDON LAT 57°41'N LONG 4°10'W
TIMES AND HEIGHTS OF HIGH AND LOW WATERS

Dates in red are **SPRINGS**
Dates in blue are **NEAPS**

YEAR 2015

JANUARY

Day	Time	m	Time	m	Time	m	Time	m
1 TH	0312	1.4	0853	3.8	1539	1.4	2114	3.8
2 F	0410	1.3	0959	3.9	1634	1.2	2223	3.9
3 SA	0458	1.3	1053	4.1	1721	1.1	2316	4.1
4 SU	0536	1.3	1138	4.3	1801	0.9	2325	4.3
5 M ○	0000	4.1	0603	1.2	1218	4.3	1835	0.9
6 TU	0038	4.1	0622	1.2	1253	4.4	1906	0.9
7 W	0112	4.1	0647	1.2	1327	4.3	1938	0.9
8 TH	0145	4.0	0714	1.2	1400	4.2	2011	1.0
9 F	0219	3.9	0735	1.3	1434	4.1	2043	1.1
10 SA	0252	3.8	0751	1.4	1504	3.9	2058	1.2
11 SU	0323	3.7	0818	1.5	1531	3.8	2117	1.4
12 M	0357	3.6	0853	1.6	1606	3.6	2201	1.5
13 TU ◐	0439	3.5	0939	1.8	1652	3.5	2310	1.7
14 W	0532	3.4	1100	1.9	1752	3.4		
15 TH	0100	3.4	0640	3.4	1339	1.9	1914	3.4
16 F	0207	1.6	0751	3.5	1450	1.7	2028	3.6
17 SA	0300	1.4	0854	3.7	1546	1.4	2130	3.8
18 SU	0355	1.3	0953	4.0	1640	1.2	2229	4.0
19 M	0452	1.1	1049	4.2	1731	0.9		
20 TU ●	0543	0.9	1142	4.5	1818	0.6		
21 W	0016	4.4	0630	0.8	1232	4.7	1903	0.4
22 TH	0105	4.5	0714	0.7	1319	4.8	1947	0.3
23 F	0152	4.6	0756	0.7	1405	4.8	2031	0.3
24 SA	0239	4.5	0837	0.8	1451	4.7	2114	0.5
25 SU	0325	4.3	0917	0.9	1537	4.5	2158	0.8
26 M	0411	4.1	0957	1.2	1624	4.2	2243	1.1
27 TU ◐	0458	3.9	1043	1.4	1715	4.0	2336	1.4
28 W	0550	3.7	1146	1.6	1816	3.7		
29 TH	0135	1.6	0651	3.5	1409	1.7	1927	3.6
30 F	0256	1.6	0806	3.5	1523	1.5	2054	3.6
31 SA	0357	1.5	0929	3.7	1623	1.3	2212	3.7

FEBRUARY

Day	Time	m	Time	m	Time	m	Time	m
1 SU	0448	1.5	1032	3.9	1711	1.1	2306	3.9
2 M	0527	1.4	1120	4.1	1750	1.0	2347	4.0
3 TU ○	0549	1.3	1159	4.2	1820	0.9		
4 W	0022	4.0	0557	1.2	1233	4.3	1845	0.8
5 TH	0052	4.0	0626	1.1	1305	4.3	1913	0.8
6 F	0122	4.0	0701	1.0	1337	4.3	1945	0.8
7 SA	0152	4.0	0733	1.1	1408	4.2	2017	0.9
8 SU	0221	3.9	0748	1.1	1436	4.0	2041	1.0
9 M	0249	3.8	0748	1.2	1503	3.9	2048	1.2
10 TU	0322	3.7	0810	1.3	1535	3.7	2053	1.4
11 W	0401	3.6	0843	1.5	1617	3.6	2125	1.5
12 TH	0449	3.5	0928	1.7	1710	3.4	2343	1.7
13 F ◐	0548	3.4	1148	1.8	1820	3.3		
14 SA	0131	1.7	0700	3.4	1413	1.7	1948	3.4
15 SU	0236	1.5	0812	3.6	1518	1.4	2103	3.7
16 M	0334	1.3	0918	3.9	1619	1.1	2210	3.9
17 TU	0434	1.1	1022	4.2	1714	0.7	2311	4.2
18 W ●	0527	0.8	1121	4.5	1802	0.4		
19 TH	0003	4.5	0613	0.6	1214	4.7	1846	0.2
20 F	0051	4.6	0656	0.5	1302	4.9	1929	0.1
21 SA	0136	4.7	0738	0.4	1349	4.9	2010	0.2
22 SU	0220	4.6	0818	0.5	1434	4.8	2052	0.4
23 M	0304	4.4	0858	0.7	1519	4.6	2132	0.7
24 TU	0347	4.2	0937	1.0	1605	4.3	2212	1.1
25 W ◑	0431	3.9	1021	1.3	1655	3.9	2257	1.5
26 TH	0520	3.6	1123	1.6	1753	3.6		
27 F	0104	1.8	0617	3.5	1347	1.7	1902	3.4
28 SA	0237	1.8	0723	3.4	1504	1.5	2029	3.4

MARCH

Day	Time	m	Time	m	Time	m	Time	m
1 SU	0340	1.7	0839	3.5	1604	1.3	2157	3.5
2 M	0432	1.6	1004	3.7	1653	1.1	2250	3.7
3 TU	0511	1.4	1057	3.9	1731	1.0	2329	3.9
4 W	0531	1.3	1135	4.1	1756	0.9		
5 TH ○	0000	4.0	0533	1.2	1209	4.2	1817	0.8
6 F	0028	4.0	0605	1.0	1240	4.3	1845	0.7
7 SA	0056	4.1	0642	0.9	1312	4.2	1918	0.7
8 SU	0125	4.1	0717	0.9	1342	4.2	1950	0.8
9 M	0153	4.0	0745	1.0	1411	4.1	2019	0.9
10 TU	0223	3.9	0726	1.1	1441	3.9	2031	1.1
11 W	0257	3.8	0741	1.1	1515	3.8	2007	1.3
12 TH	0335	3.7	0814	1.3	1555	3.6	2041	1.4
13 F ◐	0420	3.5	0856	1.4	1646	3.5	2132	1.7
14 SA	0517	3.4	1000	1.7	1754	3.3		
15 SU	0052	1.7	0626	3.4	1340	1.5	1920	3.4
16 M	0214	1.6	0738	3.6	1453	1.3	2041	3.6
17 TU	0317	1.3	0846	3.8	1557	0.9	2153	3.9
18 W	0416	1.0	0954	4.1	1654	0.6	2255	4.2
19 TH	0508	0.8	1059	4.4	1742	0.3	2347	4.5
20 F ●	0555	0.5	1154	4.7	1826	0.1		
21 SA	0033	4.7	0637	0.4	1244	4.9	1907	0.0
22 SU	0117	4.7	0718	0.3	1330	4.9	1948	0.2
23 M	0159	4.6	0759	0.4	1415	4.7	2028	0.4
24 TU	0241	4.4	0839	0.6	1500	4.5	2106	0.8
25 W	0323	4.2	0919	0.9	1546	4.2	2141	1.2
26 TH	0406	3.9	1004	1.2	1636	3.8	2213	1.6
27 F ◑	0454	3.6	1110	1.5	1731	3.5	2315	1.9
28 SA	0548	3.5	1320	1.6	1835	3.3		
29 SU	0209	1.9	0649	3.4	1435	1.5	1949	3.3
30 M	0312	1.8	0754	3.4	1535	1.3	2123	3.4
31 TU	0404	1.6	0902	3.6	1624	1.2	2220	3.6

APRIL

Day	Time	m	Time	m	Time	m	Time	m
1 W	0444	1.5	1012	3.8	1701	1.1	2258	3.8
2 TH	0504	1.3	1058	4.0	1724	0.9	2329	3.9
3 F	0511	1.2	1136	4.1	1745	0.8	2358	4.0
4 SA ○	0545	1.0	1210	4.2	1816	0.7		
5 SU	0028	4.1	0622	0.9	1244	4.2	1850	0.7
6 M	0059	4.1	0658	0.8	1317	4.2	1924	0.7
7 TU	0129	4.1	0730	0.9	1349	4.1	1956	0.9
8 W	0202	4.0	0746	1.0	1423	4.0	2019	1.1
9 TH	0237	3.9	0725	1.0	1500	3.8	1946	1.2
10 F	0316	3.8	0758	1.1	1543	3.7	2022	1.4
11 SA	0401	3.6	0843	1.3	1635	3.5	2119	1.6
12 SU ◐	0457	3.5	1121	1.5	1740	3.4		
13 M	0013	1.7	0602	3.5	1312	1.4	1859	3.4
14 TU	0150	1.6	0712	3.6	1430	1.1	2020	3.6
15 W	0258	1.3	0819	3.8	1535	0.8	2135	3.9
16 TH	0357	1.1	0928	4.1	1632	0.6	2236	4.2
17 F	0449	0.8	1036	4.3	1721	0.3	2328	4.5
18 SA ●	0536	0.5	1135	4.6	1806	0.2		
19 SU	0013	4.6	0619	0.4	1226	4.7	1846	0.2
20 M	0057	4.6	0700	0.3	1312	4.7	1926	0.4
21 TU	0138	4.6	0741	0.4	1357	4.6	2004	0.6
22 W	0219	4.4	0822	0.6	1442	4.4	2040	1.0
23 TH	0300	4.2	0905	0.9	1528	4.1	2105	1.3
24 F	0343	3.9	0952	1.2	1616	3.8	2107	1.6
25 SA ◑	0429	3.7	1059	1.4	1708	3.5	2154	1.9
26 SU	0521	3.5	1241	1.5	1805	3.3		
27 M	0128	2.0	0618	3.4	1356	1.5	1906	3.3
28 TU	0233	1.9	0718	3.4	1454	1.4	2011	3.4
29 W	0324	1.7	0817	3.5	1541	1.3	2116	3.5
30 TH	0404	1.6	0914	3.7	1617	1.2	2207	3.7

Chart Datum: 2·10 metres below Ordnance Datum (Local). HAT is 5·0 metres above Chart Datum.

STANDARD TIME (UT)		
For Summer Time add ONE hour in **non-shaded areas**		

INVERGORDON LAT 57°41'N LONG 4°10'W
TIMES AND HEIGHTS OF HIGH AND LOW WATERS

Dates in red are **SPRINGS**
Dates in blue are NEAPS

YEAR **2015**

MAY

Day	Time m	Time m	Time m	Time m		Day	Time m	Time m	Time m	Time m
1 F	0427 1.4	1009 3.8	1641 1.1	2248 3.9		16 SA	0430 0.9	1016 4.2	1702 0.5	2307 4.3
2 SA	0447 1.2	1057 4.0	1710 0.9	2325 4.0		17 SU	0519 0.7	1117 4.4	1747 0.5	2354 4.5
3 SU	0523 1.0	1139 4.1	1747 0.8	2359 4.1		18 M ●	0604 0.5	1209 4.5	1828 0.5	
4 M ○	0602 0.9	1217 4.1	1824 0.8			19 TU	0037 4.5	0645 0.5	1256 4.5	1906 0.6
5 TU	0033 4.2	0639 0.8	1254 4.2	1901 0.8		20 W	0119 4.5	0727 0.5	1341 4.4	1942 0.8
6 W	0108 4.2	0715 0.8	1330 4.1	1936 0.9		21 TH	0159 4.4	0808 0.6	1425 4.2	2013 1.1
7 TH	0144 4.1	0748 0.9	1409 4.0	2008 1.0		22 F	0240 4.2	0851 0.8	1509 4.0	2023 1.3
8 F	0222 4.0	0814 1.0	1450 3.9	2027 1.2		23 SA	0322 4.0	0937 1.1	1554 3.8	2033 1.5
9 SA	0303 3.9	0802 1.1	1536 3.8	2026 1.4		24 SU	0406 3.8	1031 1.3	1641 3.6	2115 1.7
10 SU	0349 3.8	0954 1.2	1629 3.6	2221 1.5		25 M ◑	0454 3.6	1140 1.4	1731 3.4	2213 1.9
11 M ◑	0443 3.7	1114 1.2	1730 3.5	2338 1.6		26 TU	0546 3.5	1254 1.5	1825 3.3	2341 2.0
12 TU	0543 3.7	1243 1.2	1840 3.5			27 W	0643 3.4	1354 1.5	1922 3.3	
13 W	0110 1.5	0648 3.7	1406 1.0	1957 3.6		28 TH	0226 1.8	0740 3.5	1441 1.4	2018 3.4
14 TH	0235 1.4	0755 3.8	1512 0.9	2111 3.9		29 F	0308 1.7	0835 3.5	1517 1.3	2112 3.6
15 F	0336 1.1	0904 4.0	1611 0.7	2214 4.1		30 SA	0341 1.5	0928 3.7	1553 1.2	2203 3.8
						31 SU	0419 1.3	1020 3.8	1635 1.1	2248 4.0

JUNE

Day	Time m	Time m	Time m	Time m		Day	Time m	Time m	Time m	Time m
1 M	0500 1.1	1108 4.0	1719 1.0	2330 4.1		16 TU ●	0552 0.7	1155 4.3	1812 0.8	
2 TU ○	0542 1.0	1151 4.1	1801 0.9			17 W	0019 4.4	0633 0.6	1242 4.3	1847 0.9
3 W	0009 4.2	0623 0.8	1233 4.2	1841 0.9		18 TH	0101 4.4	0714 0.6	1325 4.2	1918 1.0
4 TH	0049 4.2	0703 0.8	1315 4.2	1921 0.9		19 F	0140 4.3	0753 0.7	1407 4.1	1945 1.1
5 F	0129 4.2	0745 0.7	1358 4.1	2000 1.0		20 SA	0219 4.2	0832 0.8	1447 4.0	1959 1.3
6 SA	0210 4.2	0827 0.8	1443 4.1	2039 1.1		21 SU	0259 4.1	0912 1.0	1528 3.8	2012 1.4
7 SU	0254 4.1	0913 0.8	1531 3.9	2121 1.2		22 M	0339 3.9	0950 1.2	1609 3.6	2046 1.5
8 M	0340 4.0	1004 0.9	1621 3.8	2210 1.4		23 TU	0421 3.7	1023 1.3	1651 3.5	2131 1.7
9 TU ◑	0431 3.9	1102 1.0	1716 3.7	2309 1.5		24 W ◑	0506 3.6	1036 1.5	1737 3.4	2229 1.8
10 W	0526 3.9	1212 1.1	1818 3.6			25 TH	0558 3.4	1238 1.6	1832 3.3	2347 1.9
11 TH	0018 1.5	0626 3.8	1311 1.1	1928 3.7		26 F	0658 3.4	1339 1.5	1931 3.4	
12 F	0206 1.4	0733 3.8	1451 1.0	2043 3.8		27 SA	0208 1.8	0756 3.4	1429 1.5	2027 3.5
13 SA	0316 1.2	0844 3.9	1553 0.9	2150 4.0		28 SU	0300 1.6	0851 3.5	1515 1.3	2120 3.7
14 SU	0414 1.0	0959 4.0	1646 0.9	2246 4.2		29 M	0348 1.4	0945 3.7	1602 1.2	2211 3.9
15 M	0506 0.8	1103 4.2	1732 0.8	2335 4.3		30 TU	0436 1.2	1038 3.9	1652 1.1	2300 4.1

JULY

Day	Time m	Time m	Time m	Time m		Day	Time m	Time m	Time m	Time m
1 W	0523 1.0	1128 4.1	1740 1.0	2345 4.2		16 TH ●	0003 4.3	0622 0.7	1229 4.2	1828 1.1
2 TH ○	0609 0.8	1215 4.2	1825 0.9			17 F	0043 4.4	0657 0.7	1309 4.1	1851 1.1
3 F	0029 4.4	0653 0.6	1301 4.3	1908 0.8		18 SA	0120 4.3	0731 0.7	1345 4.1	1916 1.1
4 SA	0114 4.4	0737 0.5	1347 4.3	1950 0.8		19 SU	0156 4.3	0804 0.8	1421 4.0	1942 1.2
5 SU	0158 4.5	0822 0.5	1434 4.3	2031 0.9		20 M	0232 4.2	0838 0.9	1456 3.9	2000 1.3
6 M	0243 4.4	0908 0.6	1521 4.2	2113 1.0		21 TU	0307 4.0	0907 1.1	1529 3.7	2020 1.4
7 TU	0329 4.3	0954 0.7	1608 4.1	2155 1.2		22 W	0340 3.8	0908 1.2	1558 3.6	2052 1.5
8 W	0417 4.2	1043 0.9	1658 3.9	2244 1.3		23 TH	0407 3.6	0935 1.4	1628 3.5	2135 1.7
9 TH	0508 4.0	1141 1.1	1753 3.7	2344 1.5		24 F ◑	0442 3.5	1029 1.6	1713 3.4	2240 1.8
10 F	0606 3.9	1308 1.2	1857 3.6			25 SA	0535 3.4	1243 1.7	1820 3.3	
11 SA	0135 1.5	0713 3.7	1432 1.3	2012 3.7		26 SU	0026 1.9	0701 3.3	1353 1.6	1936 3.4
12 SU	0259 1.4	0828 3.7	1538 1.2	2125 3.8		27 M	0224 1.7	0813 3.4	1446 1.5	2037 3.6
13 M	0402 1.2	0947 3.8	1634 1.2	2227 4.0		28 TU	0318 1.5	0913 3.6	1535 1.3	2133 3.8
14 TU	0457 1.0	1053 4.0	1721 1.1	2319 4.2		29 W	0411 1.2	1011 3.9	1628 1.2	2228 4.1
15 W	0543 0.8	1145 4.1	1759 1.1			30 TH	0504 0.9	1107 4.1	1721 1.0	2320 4.3
						31 F ○	0553 0.7	1158 4.3	1808 0.8	

AUGUST

Day	Time m	Time m	Time m	Time m		Day	Time m	Time m	Time m	Time m
1 SA	0009 4.5	0639 0.4	1247 4.5	1852 0.7		16 SU	0056 4.4	0701 0.7	1320 4.1	1849 1.1
2 SU	0056 4.7	0723 0.3	1333 4.5	1934 0.6		17 M	0128 4.3	0731 0.7	1350 4.1	1922 1.1
3 M	0142 4.7	0807 0.3	1419 4.5	2016 0.7		18 TU	0200 4.2	0804 0.8	1419 4.0	1949 1.1
4 TU	0228 4.7	0851 0.4	1504 4.4	2057 0.8		19 W	0230 4.1	0832 1.0	1444 3.9	1958 1.3
5 W	0314 4.6	0934 0.6	1549 4.2	2138 1.0		20 TH	0256 3.9	0841 1.2	1509 3.7	2013 1.4
6 TH	0400 4.4	1019 0.9	1636 4.0	2223 1.2		21 F	0324 3.8	0847 1.3	1542 3.6	2042 1.5
7 F	0450 4.1	1111 1.2	1726 3.8	2321 1.5		22 SA	0401 3.6	0915 1.5	1626 3.5	2126 1.7
8 SA	0547 3.8	1235 1.4	1827 3.6			23 SU	0449 3.4	1044 1.7	1721 3.4	2329 1.9
9 SU	0116 1.6	0655 3.6	1418 1.5	1941 3.6		24 M	0554 3.3	1317 1.7	1834 3.4	
10 M	0246 1.5	0816 3.6	1527 1.5	2101 3.7		25 TU	0150 1.7	0728 3.4	1421 1.6	1951 3.6
11 TU	0352 1.3	0940 3.7	1624 1.4	2209 3.9		26 W	0250 1.5	0843 3.6	1514 1.4	2056 3.8
12 W	0447 1.1	1044 3.9	1711 1.3	2302 4.1		27 TH	0346 1.2	0947 3.9	1608 1.2	2156 4.1
13 TH	0531 0.9	1133 4.0	1746 1.3	2345 4.3		28 F	0443 0.8	1047 4.2	1710 1.0	2254 4.4
14 F ●	0607 0.8	1213 4.1	1805 1.2			29 SA ○	0534 0.5	1141 4.4	1749 0.7	2347 4.7
15 SA	0022 4.4	0634 0.7	1248 4.1	1820 1.1		30 SU	0620 0.3	1229 4.5	1833 0.6	
						31 M	0036 4.9	0703 0.1	1314 4.7	1915 0.5

Chart Datum: 2·10 metres below Ordnance Datum (Local). HAT is 5·0 metres above Chart Datum.

STANDARD TIME (UT)
For Summer Time add ONE hour in **non-shaded areas**

INVERGORDON LAT 57°41'N LONG 4°10'W
TIMES AND HEIGHTS OF HIGH AND LOW WATERS

Dates in **red** are **SPRINGS**
Dates in **blue** are **NEAPS**

YEAR 2015

SEPTEMBER

Time	m		Time	m
1 0123	4.9	**16** 0127	4.3
0746	0.1	0731	0.8
TU 1359	4.7	W 1342	4.1
1957	0.5	1931	1.1
2 0209	4.9	**17** 0156	4.2
0829	0.3	0801	0.9
W 1443	4.6	TH 1408	4.0
2038	0.7	1945	1.2
3 0255	4.7	**18** 0225	4.0
0911	0.6	0818	1.1
TH 1526	4.4	F 1437	3.9
2119	0.9	1941	1.3
4 0341	4.4	**19** 0257	3.9
0954	1.0	0802	1.3
F 1612	4.1	SA 1512	3.8
2205	1.2	2008	1.4
5 0431	4.1	**20** 0336	3.7
1041	1.4	0827	1.5
SA 1701	3.8	SU 1555	3.7
◑ 2305	1.5	2048	1.6
6 0528	3.8	**21** 0424	3.5
1200	1.7	0911	1.7
SU 1759	3.6	M 1649	3.5
		◐ 2303	1.8
7 0107	1.6	**22** 0526	3.4
0636	3.6	1225	1.9
M 1404	1.8	TU 1756	3.5
1909	3.6		
8 0233	1.5	**23** 0115	1.7
0801	3.5	0650	3.4
TU 1512	1.7	W 1357	1.7
2034	3.7	1912	3.6
9 0337	1.3	**24** 0224	1.4
0930	3.6	0816	3.6
W 1609	1.6	TH 1455	1.5
2147	3.9	2022	3.8
10 0430	1.1	**25** 0322	1.1
1030	3.8	0925	3.9
TH 1655	1.4	F 1549	1.2
2241	4.1	2125	4.2
11 0513	1.0	**26** 0420	0.8
1114	4.0	1027	4.2
F 1727	1.4	SA 1642	1.0
2322	4.2	2227	4.5
12 0544	0.9	**27** 0512	0.5
1151	4.1	1121	4.5
SA 1738	1.3	SU 1730	0.7
2356	4.3	2324	4.7
13 0604	0.8	**28** 0559	0.2
1221	4.2	1208	4.8
SU 1751	1.1	M 1814	0.5
●		○	
14 0026	4.4	**29** 0015	4.9
0627	0.8	0642	0.1
M 1249	4.2	TU 1254	4.8
1824	1.0	1856	0.4
15 0057	4.3	**30** 0103	5.0
0658	0.7	0724	0.2
TU 1316	4.2	W 1337	4.8
1900	1.0	1938	0.5

OCTOBER

Time	m		Time	m
1 0149	4.9	**16** 0128	4.2
0806	0.4	0735	1.0
TH 1420	4.7	F 1341	4.2
2019	0.6	1936	1.1
2 0235	4.7	**17** 0201	4.1
0846	0.8	0759	1.2
F 1503	4.4	SA 1413	4.0
2102	0.9	1924	1.3
3 0322	4.4	**18** 0238	3.9
0927	1.2	0735	1.3
SA 1547	4.1	SU 1450	3.9
2150	1.2	1948	1.4
4 0413	4.1	**19** 0319	3.8
1009	1.6	0802	1.5
SU 1636	3.9	M 1533	3.8
◑ 2253	1.5	2030	1.5
5 0509	3.7	**20** 0408	3.6
1112	1.9	0849	1.7
M 1732	3.7	TU 1626	3.7
		◑ 2251	1.7
6 0051	1.6	**21** 0509	3.5
0613	3.5	1133	1.9
TU 1342	2.0	W 1730	3.6
1837	3.6		
7 0211	1.6	**22** 0035	1.6
0733	3.5	0624	3.5
W 1449	1.8	TH 1324	1.8
1953	3.6	1841	3.7
8 0312	1.4	**23** 0156	1.3
0903	3.6	0747	3.7
TH 1544	1.7	F 1433	1.6
2111	3.8	1951	3.9
9 0404	1.2	**24** 0258	1.1
1003	3.8	0901	3.9
F 1629	1.6	SA 1529	1.3
2208	4.0	2057	4.2
10 0445	1.1	**25** 0356	0.8
1045	4.0	1004	4.3
SA 1702	1.5	SU 1622	1.0
2249	4.1	2201	4.4
11 0512	1.1	**26** 0450	0.5
1119	4.1	1059	4.5
SU 1710	1.3	M 1711	0.8
2322	4.2	2302	4.7
12 0527	0.9	**27** 0538	0.4
1149	4.2	1147	4.7
M 1726	1.2	TU 1756	0.6
2353	4.3	○ 2355	4.8
13 0553	0.9	**28** 0622	0.3
1216	4.3	1232	4.8
TU 1802	1.0	W 1839	0.5
●			
14 0025	4.3	**29** 0043	4.9
0627	0.8	0703	0.4
W 1244	4.3	TH 1316	4.8
1838	1.0	1921	0.5
15 0057	4.3	**30** 0130	4.8
0702	0.9	0744	0.6
TH 1312	4.2	F 1358	4.6
1912	1.0	2004	0.7
		31 0216	4.6
		0823	1.0
		SA 1441	4.4
		2048	0.9

NOVEMBER

Time	m		Time	m
1 0304	4.3	**16** 0224	4.0
0859	1.3	0738	1.4
SU 1525	4.2	M 1434	4.1
2137	1.2	1952	1.3
2 0353	4.1	**17** 0308	3.9
0921	1.7	0753	1.5
M 1612	3.9	TU 1518	3.9
2240	1.5	2121	1.4
3 0446	3.7	**18** 0358	3.8
0946	2.0	0845	1.7
TU 1704	3.7	W 1609	3.8
◐		2239	1.4
4 0017	1.6	**19** 0455	3.6
0543	3.5	1058	1.8
W 1303	2.1	TH 1708	3.8
1803	3.6	◐ 2357	1.4
5 0136	1.6	**20** 0601	3.6
0647	3.5	1220	1.8
TH 1414	2.0	F 1813	3.8
1907	3.6		
6 0237	1.5	**21** 0122	1.3
0758	3.5	0715	3.7
F 1510	1.9	SA 1401	1.6
2011	3.7	1922	3.9
7 0327	1.4	**22** 0232	1.1
0908	3.7	0831	3.9
SA 1556	1.7	SU 1506	1.4
2109	3.8	2030	4.1
8 0407	1.3	**23** 0334	0.9
0957	3.8	0938	4.2
SU 1629	1.6	M 1603	1.1
2159	4.0	2138	4.3
9 0429	1.2	**24** 0430	0.8
1036	4.0	1036	4.4
M 1644	1.4	TU 1655	0.9
2242	4.1	2243	4.5
10 0445	1.1	**25** 0519	0.7
1110	4.2	1127	4.6
TU 1707	1.2	W 1742	0.7
2320	4.2	○ 2338	4.6
11 0520	1.0	**26** 0604	0.6
1144	4.3	1213	4.7
W 1743	1.1	TH 1826	0.6
● 2356	4.3		
12 0559	0.9	**27** 0028	4.7
1216	4.3	0645	0.7
TH 1821	1.0	F 1256	4.7
		1909	0.6
13 0031	4.3	**28** 0115	4.6
0637	1.0	0724	0.9
F 1248	4.3	SA 1339	4.6
1856	1.0	1952	0.7
14 0107	4.2	**29** 0200	4.4
0713	1.0	0800	1.1
SA 1321	4.3	SU 1420	4.4
1929	1.1	2036	0.9
15 0144	4.1	**30** 0245	4.2
0745	1.2	0829	1.4
SU 1356	4.2	M 1503	4.2
1957	1.2	2122	1.1

DECEMBER

Time	m		Time	m
1 0332	4.0	**16** 0259	4.0
0828	1.6	0849	1.3
TU 1547	4.0	W 1509	4.1
2212	1.3	2133	1.1
2 0419	3.8	**17** 0348	3.9
0859	1.8	0933	1.5
W 1635	3.8	TH 1556	4.0
2313	1.5	2226	1.2
3 0508	3.6	**18** 0440	3.8
0951	2.0	1030	1.6
TH 1727	3.7	F 1649	3.9
◐		◐ 2325	1.2
4 0032	1.6	**19** 0537	3.7
0600	3.5	1134	1.7
F 1104	2.1	SA 1748	3.9
1824	3.6		
5 0142	1.7	**20** 0038	1.3
0658	3.5	0641	3.7
SA 1419	2.0	SU 1257	1.6
1923	3.6	1854	3.9
6 0233	1.6	**21** 0204	1.2
0756	3.5	0754	3.8
SU 1509	1.9	M 1441	1.5
2020	3.7	2005	3.9
7 0308	1.5	**22** 0315	1.1
0852	3.7	0909	4.0
M 1546	1.7	TU 1546	1.3
2113	3.8	2119	4.1
8 0330	1.4	**23** 0414	1.0
0943	3.9	1014	4.2
TU 1615	1.5	W 1642	1.0
2203	3.9	2230	4.2
9 0406	1.3	**24** 0506	1.0
1030	4.1	1108	4.4
W 1649	1.3	TH 1732	0.8
2249	4.0	2327	4.4
10 0451	1.2	**25** 0550	0.9
1112	4.2	1156	4.5
TH 1727	1.2	F 1816	0.7
2330	4.1	○	
11 0535	1.1	**26** 0017	4.4
1150	4.3	0629	0.9
F 1807	1.1	SA 1240	4.6
●		1858	0.6
12 0010	4.2	**27** 0102	4.4
0617	1.0	0704	1.0
SA 1228	4.3	SU 1322	4.5
1846	1.0	1939	0.7
13 0050	4.2	**28** 0144	4.3
0658	1.0	0736	1.1
SU 1306	4.3	M 1402	4.4
1925	1.0	2019	0.8
14 0131	4.2	**29** 0225	4.1
0737	1.1	0801	1.3
M 1344	4.3	TU 1441	4.3
2005	1.0	2058	1.0
15 0214	4.1	**30** 0306	4.0
0813	1.2	0808	1.4
TU 1425	4.2	W 1521	4.1
2047	1.0	2135	1.2
		31 0346	3.8
		0830	1.6
		TH 1602	3.9
		2208	1.4

Chart Datum: 2·10 metres below Ordnance Datum (Local). HAT is 5·0 metres above Chart Datum.

MORAY FIRTH: NORTH WEST COAST

(AC 115) Cromarty Firth (AC 1889, 1890) is entered between the North and South Sutors, both fringed by rks, some of which dry.

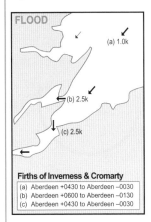

FLOOD

(a) 1.0k

(b) 2.5k

(c) 2.5k

Firths of Inverness & Cromarty

(a)	Aberdeen +0430 to Aberdeen –0030
(b)	Aberdeen +0600 to Aberdeen –0130
(c)	Aberdeen +0430 to Aberdeen –0030

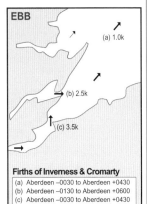

EBB

(a) 1.0k

(b) 2.5k

(c) 3.5k

Firths of Inverness & Cromarty

(a)	Aberdeen –0030 to Aberdeen +0430
(b)	Aberdeen –0130 to Aberdeen +0600
(c)	Aberdeen –0030 to Aberdeen +0430

▶ *Off the entrance the in-going stream starts at HW Aberdeen +0600, and the out-going at HW Aberdeen –0130, sp rates 1·5 kn, stronger in the narrows between Nigg and Cromarty* ◀ Buss Bank buoy, Fl R 3s, marks the entrance, and there is good sheltered anchorages within the firth. Keep 100m clear of the Nigg Oil Terminal on the north side. A buoyed deep-water channel runs to Invergordon; outside the channel there are shallows and drying banks. Beware large ships and tugs using Invergordon.

The coast NE to Tarbat Ness (lt) is fringed with rocks. Beware Three Kings (dries) about 3M NE of N Sutor. ▶ *Culloden Rk, a shoal with depth of 1·8m, extends 2½ca NE of Tarbat Ness, where stream is weak.*◀

Beware salmon nets between Tarbat Ness and Portmahomack. Dornoch Firth is shallow, with shifting banks, and in strong E'lies the sea breaks heavily on the bar E of Dornoch Pt.

At Lothbeg Pt, 5M SW of Helmsdale, a rocky ledge extends 5ca offshore. Near Berriedale, 7M NE of Helmsdale, The Pinnacle, a detached rk 61m high, stands close offshore. The Beatrice oil field lies on Smith Bank, 28M NE of Tarbat Ness, and 11M off Caithness coast. Between Dunbeath and Lybster there are no dangers more than 2ca offshore. Clyth Ness is fringed by detached and drying rks. From here to Wick the only dangers are close inshore. There is anch in Sinclair's B in good weather, but Freswick B further N is better to await the tide in Pentland Firth (beware wreck in centre of bay). Stacks of Duncansby and Baxter Rk (depth 2·7m) lie 1M and 4ca S of Duncansby Hd.

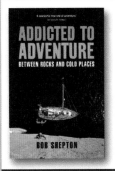
5.15 INVERNESS

Highland 57°29'·73N 04°14'·17W ✲✲🌢🌢🌢🌢✿✿

CHARTS AC 223, 1077, 1078, 5617; Imray C23

TIDES +0100 Dover; ML 2·7; Duration 0620

Standard Port INVERGORDON (←—)

Times				Height (metres)			
High Water		Low Water		MHWS	MHWN	MLWN	MLWS
0100	0700	0000	0700	4·3	3·3	1·6	0·7
1300	1900	1200	1900				
Differences INVERNESS							
+0010	+0015	+0015	+0010	+0·3	+0·2	+0·1	+0·1
FORTROSE							
0000	+0010	+0010	–0010	0·0	+0·1	ND	ND
CROMARTY							
–0005	0000	0000	–0005	0·0	0·0	0·0	0·0
DINGWALL							
+0020	+0015	ND	ND	0·0	+0·1	ND	ND

SHELTER Good in all weathers. Berth at Inverness Marina (2.5m at CD) or at one of the 2 marinas in the Caledonian Canal, entr to which can be difficult in strong tidal streams. The sea lock is normally available HW±4 in canal hours; the gates cannot be opened LW±2.

NAVIGATION WPT Meikle Mee SHM By Fl G 3s, 57°30'·25N 04°12'·03W, 250°/0·74M to Longman Pt bn. Inverness Firth is deep from Chanonry Pt to Munlochy SWM buoy, but shoal (2·1m) to Meikle Mee buoy. Meikle Mee partly dries. Beware bird rafts S of Avoch (off chartlet). Tidal streams are strong S of Craigton Pt (E-going stream at sp exceeds 5kn). Ent to R Ness is narrow, dredged to 3m CD. For the entrance to the Caledonian Canal, keep to N Kessock bank until clear of unmarked shoals on S bank. Care must be taken to avoid Carnarc Pt W of R mouth.

LIGHTS AND MARKS Longman Pt bn Fl WR 2s 7m 5/4M, vis 078°-W-258°-R-078°. Craigton Pt lt, Fl WRG 4s 6m 11/7M vis 312°-W-048°-R-064°-W-085°-G-shore. Caledonian Canal ent marked by QR and Iso G 4s on ends of training walls.

COMMUNICATIONS (Code 01463) MRCC (01224) 592334; Police 101; Dr 234151. HM 715715; Clachnaharry Sea Lock 713896; Canal Office 233140.

Inverness Hbr Office VHF Ch 12 (Mon-Fri: 0800 -1700 LT). *Inverness Marina* Ch 12. Caledonian Canal: Ch 74 is used by all stations. Call: *Clachnaharry Sea Lock;* or for office: *Caledonian Canal.*

FACILITIES **Inverness Marina** www.invernessmarina.com ☎ 220501 150 inc 20✇, £2.00, D, BH (45 ton), BY, 🛢, 🛒, ⚒, 🗑, dredged to 3m below CD, full disabled access. **City** All domestic facilities, ⇌, ✈.

MINOR HARBOURS IN INVERNESS FIRTH

FORTROSE, Highland, 57°34'·71N 04°08'·04W. AC 1078. Tides 5.15. HW +0055 on Dover; ML 2·5m; Duration 0620. Small drying unlit hbr, soft silt bottom, well protected by Chanonry Ness to E, limited space. Follow ldg line 296°, Broomhill Ho (conspic on hill to NW) in line with school spire until abeam SPM buoy; then turn W to avoid Craig an Roan rks (1·8m) ESE of ent. Chanonry Pt lt, Oc 6s 12m 15M, obscd 073°-shore. HM ☎ (01381) 620311; Dr ☎ 622000. **Facilities:** ⚓ £5, 4 ⚓, L, M, P, D, ⚓, scrubbing grid, Gas, ✗, 🛒, ✉, Ⓑ; **Chanonry SC** (near pier) ☎ 01381 621973.

AVOCH, Highland, 57°34'·03N 04°09'·94W. AC 1078. Tides as Fortrose (1·25M to the ENE). Hbr dries, mostly on the N side, but is bigger than Fortrose. Small craft may stay afloat at neaps against the S pier (2FR (vert)). ⚓ may be available on drying pontoons; one ⚓ (max 35ft LOA) off hbr ent. HM ☎ (mobile) 07779 833951. **Facilities:** ⚓ £7, ⚓, ⚓. **Village:** ✉, 🛒, ✗, 🍺, 🏪 & 🏪, ⚒.

NORTH KESSOCK PIER, Highlands, 57°30'·06N 4°14'·87W. AC 1078. Tides as Inverness (1 M to the ESE). Unlit tidal slipway, suitable for leisure craft up to 20 meters. 2m depth at MLWS. Mud and rounded stones bottom, sheltered from SW by Bkwtr. Ideal if awaiting sea lock at Caledonian Canal. Approach on N shore to avoid shallows at Inverness Harbour and South Kessock. **Facilities** ⚓, ⚓ (tidal), ⚓ (by arrangement). **Village** LB(inshore), Ⓑ, 🛒, ✗, 🍺, Dolphin & Seal Centre, Bus. Jim Prentice ☎ 07802 915741.

INVERNESS *continued*

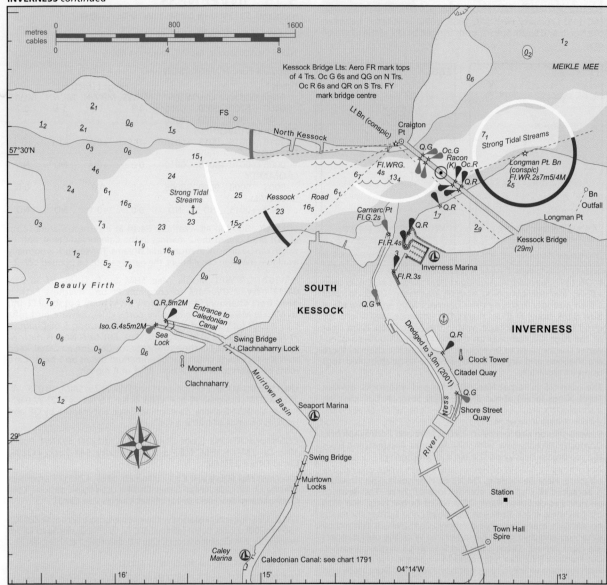

CALEDONIAN CANAL

Clachnaharry Sea Lock 57°29'·44N 04°15'·84W. These notes are for the convenience of those entering the Canal at Inverness.

CHARTS AC 1791, 1078, 5617. *Scottish Canals Skipper's Guide* essential.

TIDES Differences: Clachnaharry +0116 on Dover.

SHELTER Clachnaharry sea lock operates HW±4 (sp) within canal hours. The road and rail swing bridges may cause delays up to 25 mins. Seaport and Caley marinas: see Facilities.

NAVIGATION The 60M Caledonian Canal consists of 38M through three lochs (Lochs Ness, Oich and Lochy), connected by 22M through canals. It can take vessels 45m LOA, 10m beam, 4m draft and max mast ht 27·4m. The passage normally takes two full days, possibly longer in the summer; 13 hrs is absolute minimum.

Speed limit is 5kn in canal sections. There are 10 swing bridges; road tfc has priority at peak hrs. Do not pass bridges without the keeper's instructions. From Clachnaharry sea lock to Loch Ness (Bona Ferry lt ho) is approx 7M, via Muirtown and Dochgarroch locks.

LOCKS All 29 locks are manned and operate early May to early Oct, 0800-1800LT daily. For regulations and *Scottish Canals Skipper's Guide* apply: Canal Manager, Muirtown Wharf, Inverness IV3 5LS, www. scottishcanals.co.uk ☎ 01463 725500.

BOAT SAFETY SCHEME Visiting vessels will be checked for apparent dangerous defects eg leaking gas or fuel, damaged electrical cables, taking in water, risk of capsize. £1M 3rd party insurance is required.

LIGHTS AND MARKS Chans are marked by posts, cairns and unlit buoys, PHM on the NW side of the chan and SHM on the SE side.

COMMUNICATIONS Clachnaharry sea lock (01463) 713896; Canal Office, Inverness (01463) 233140.

Sea locks and main lock flights operate VHF Ch **74** (HO).

FACILITIES Seaport Marina www.scottishcanals.co.uk ☎ (01463) 725500, (80+20Ⓥ), ⚓, ⛽, D, Gas, Gaz, ⟁, ▣, ⚒, ⚒, 🛢, C (40t), 🅱.
Caley Marina www.caleymarina.com ☎ (01463) 236539, (25+25 Ⓥ £1.50), D, 🅿, ⚒, ⚒, 🛢, C (20t), ACA.

MINOR HARBOURS FROM CROMARTY FIRTH TO WICK

CROMARTY FIRTH, Highland, **57°41'·18N 04°02'·09W**. AC 1889, 1890. HW +0100 on Dover –0135 on Aberdeen; HW height 0.0m on Aberdeen; ML 2·5m; Duration 0625. See 5.15. Excellent hbr extending 7·5M W, past Invergordon, then 9M SW. Good shelter always available, depending on wind direction. Beware rks and reefs round N and S Sutor at the ent; many unlit oil rig mooring buoys. *Cromarty Firth Port Control* VHF Ch 11 16 13 (H24) ☎ (01349) 852308.

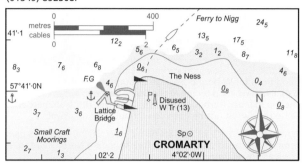

CROMARTY HARBOUR, Highland. **57°41'·00N 04°02'·35W**. From WPT 57°41'·10N 04°02'·50W, 142°/1.3ca to entrance. When inside harbour beware of set towards lattice bridge, tide runs at up to 4kts. Sheltered from N through E to S. Approx 20 ⌒ on 50m central pontoon, £20 o/n, depths range from 1·6m to 1m at inner end. 2 ⚓ 2ca W of S pier hd, or ⚓ in approx 6m with good holding but exposed to the West. Facility administered by Cromarty Harbour Trust, www.cromartyharbour.org. Barry Pickles ☎ (07453 695648) (office not normally manned) or call Ch M/16. D, ⊥, 🔌 available. **Cromarty Boat Club**, www.cromartyboatclub.org, 2 ⚓ in 0·5m to 1·5m; showers, 🚾, 🔲 (owned by Boat Club; key held at Royal Hotel). ✉, 🍴. Local ferry to Nigg.

INVERGORDON WEST HARBOUR, Highland. **57°41'·12N 04°10'·05W**. ⌒ on pontoons, 🔲, C (3 ton), D, ⊥, ✉, P, ✗, 🍴, Gas, L. Dinghy landing at Invergordon Boat Club (1·5M W), ☎ (01349) 893772.

DORNOCH FIRTH, Highland. **57°51'·28N 03°59'·39W**. AC 115, 223. HW +0115 on Dover; ML 2·5m; Duration 0605; see 5.16. Excellent shelter but difficult ent. There are many shifting sandbanks, especially near the ent, from N edge of Whiteness Sands to S edge of Gizzen Briggs. ⚓s in 7m ¾M ESE of Dornoch Pt (sheltered from NE swell by Gizzen Briggs); in 7m 2ca SSE of Ard na Cailc; in 3·3m 1M below Bonar Bridge. Firth extends 15M inland, but AC coverage ceases ¼M E of Ferry Pt. The A9 road bridge, 3·3M W of Dornoch Pt, with 11m clearance, has 3 spans lit on both sides; span centres show Iso 4s, N bank pier Iso G 4s, S bank pier Iso R 4s and 2 midstream piers QY. Tarbat Ness lt ho Fl (4) 30s 53m 24M. Fl R 5s lt shown when Tain firing range active. Very limited facilities at Ferrytown and Bonar Bridge. MRCC ☎ 01224 592334. **Dornoch:** 🍴, 🏧, ✉, Dr, Ⓑ, ✗, 🍴.

GOLSPIE, Highland, **57°58'·71N 03°56'·79W**. AC 223. HW +0045 on Dover; ML 2·3m; Duration 068. See 5.16. Golspie pier projects 60m SE across foreshore with arm projecting SW at the head, giving shelter during NE winds. Beware The Bridge, a bank (0·3m to 1·8m) running parallel to the shore ¼M to seaward of pier hd. Seas break heavily over The Bridge in NE winds. There are no lts. To enter, keep Duke of Sutherland's Memorial in line 316° with boathouse SW of pier, until church spire in village is in line 006° with hd of pier, then keep on those marks. Hbr gets very congested; good ⚓ off pier. HM ☎ 01431 821692. **Town** 🔲, 🏧, Dr, Ⓗ, L, M, 🏧, Gas, ✉, ✗, ⇌, 🍴, Ⓑ.

LYBSTER, Highland, **58°17'·72N 03°17'·39W**. AC 115. HW +0020 on Dover; HW -0150 sp, -0215 np; HW ht -0·6m on Aberdeen; ML 2·1m; Duration 0620. Excellent shelter in SW corner of inner hbr; ⌒ on W side of pier in about 1·2m. Most of hbr dries to sand/mud and is much used by FVs; no bollards on N wall. Appr on about 350°. Beware rks close on E side of ent; narrow (10m) ent is difficult in strong E to S winds. Min depth 2·5m in ent. S pier hd, Oc R 6s 10m 3M, occas in fishing season. ⌒ £7.00 per week, ⊥ on W quay. Showers/🔲 at Waterlines Visitor Centre, 01593 721520. **Town** 🔲, ✗, 🍴.

5.16 PORTMAHOMACK

Highland **57°50'·25N 03°50'·00W** ❀❀⚓⚓✿✿

CHARTS AC 115, 223; Imray C23

TIDES +0035 Dover; ML 2·5; Duration 0600

Standard Port ABERDEEN (←—)

Times				Height (metres)			
High Water		Low Water		MHWS	MHWN	MLWN	MLWS
0300	0800	0200	0800	4·3	3·4	1·6	0·6
1500	2000	1400	2000				
Differences PORTMAHOMACK							
–0120	–0210	–0140	–0110	–0·2	–0·1	+0·1	+0·1
MEIKLE FERRY (Dornoch Firth)							
–0100	–0140	–0120	–0055	+0·1	0·0	–0·1	0·0
GOLSPIE							
–0130	–0215	–0155	–0130	–0·3	–0·3	–0·1	0·0

SHELTER Good, but uncomfortable in SW/NW winds. Hbr dries, access only at HW, but good ⚓ close SW of pier.

NAVIGATION WPT 57°53'·00N 03°50'·00W, 180°/2.7M to 1ca W of hbr ent. Beware Curach Rks which lie from 2ca SW of pier to the shore. Rks extend N and W of the pier. Beware lobster pot floats and salmon nets N of hbr. Tain firing & bombing range is about 3M to the W, S of mouth of Dornoch Firth; R flags, R lts, shown when active.

LIGHTS AND MARKS Tarbert Ness lt ho Fl (4) 30s 53m 24M, W twr R bands, is 2·6M to NE of hbr. Pier hd 2 FR (vert) 7m 5M.

COMMUNICATIONS (Code 01862) MRCC (01224) 592334; Dr 892759. No HM; enquiries: harbours@highland.gov.uk ☎ (01571) 844807.

FACILITIES **Hbr,** ⌒ <5m £9, 5-7m £12, 7-10m £16, some drying pontoon berths, M, L, ⊥, 🚾. **Town** ✉, 🍴, 🔲, ✗, ⇌ (bus to Tain), ✈ (Inverness).

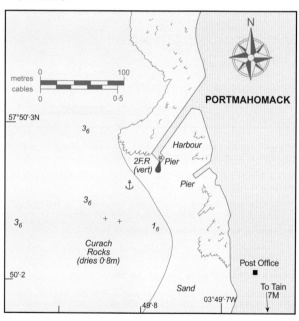

5.17 HELMSDALE

Highland 58°06'·83N 03°38'·89W ✪✪⚓⚓✿✿

CHARTS AC 115, 1462; Imray C23

TIDES +0035 Dover; ML 2·2; Duration 0615

Standard Port WICK (→)

Times				Height (metres)			
High Water		Low Water		MHWS	MHWN	MLWN	MLWS
0000	0700	0200	0700	3·5	2·8	1·4	0·7
1200	1900	1400	1900				
Differences HELMSDALE							
+0025	+0015	+0035	+0030	+0·5	+0·3	+0·1	−0·1

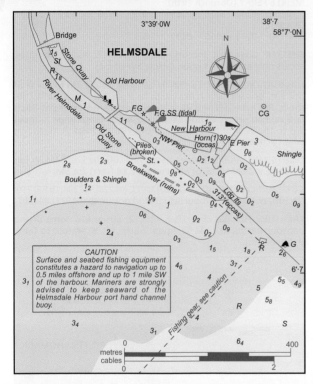

CAUTION
Surface and seabed fishing equipment constitutes a hazard to navigation up to 0.5 miles offshore and up to 1 mile SW of the harbour. Mariners are strongly advised to keep seaward of the Helmsdale Harbour port hand channel buoy.

SHELTER Good, except in strong E/SE'lies. ⌓ on NW pier, approx 1m. 80m of pontoon berths through HM.

NAVIGATION WPT 58°06'·59N 03°38'·39W, 313°/0·35M to ent; ldg marks are black masts with Or □ topmarks.

• Surface and seabed fishing gear, hazardous to navigation, extends up to 0.5M offshore and 1.0M SW of hbr.

• Essential to pass seaward of Hbr Chan PHM.

• Beware spate coming down river after heavy rain. Shoals both sides of chan and bar build up when river in spate.

LIGHTS AND MARKS See 5.3 and chartlet.

COMMUNICATIONS (Code 01431) MRCC (01224) 592334; Police 101; Dr 821221, or 821225 (Home). HM ☎ 821692 (Office).

VHF Ch 13 16.

FACILITIES ⌓ <5m £9, 5m-7m £12, 7m-10m £16, M (See HM), D ⚓, ◣.

Town Gas, Gaz (hardware store), 🛒, ✕, 🏧, ✉, Ⓑ (Brora), ⇌.

5.18 WICK

Highland 58°26'·38N 03°04'·72W ✪✪✪⚓✿

CHARTS AC 115, 1462; Imray C23, C68

TIDES +0010 Dover; ML 2·0; Duration 0625. Wick is a Standard Port. Daily tidal predictions are given below.

Standard Port WICK (→)

Times				Height (metres)			
High Water		Low Water		MHWS	MHWN	MLWN	MLWS
0000	0700	0200	0700	3·5	2·8	1·4	0·7
1200	1900	1400	1900				
Differences DUNCANSBY HEAD							
−0115	−0115	−0110	−0110	−0·4	−0·4	ND	ND

SHELTER Good, except in strong NNE to SSE winds, to await right conditions for W-bound passage through the Pentland Firth (see 5.4). Berth where directed in the Outer Harbour, approx 2m, or in marina in Inner Harbour, 2·0m. NB: The River Hbr (commercial) is leased and must not be entered without prior approval.

NAVIGATION WPT 58°26'·18N 03°03'·39W, 284°/0·72M to S pier. From the N, open up hbr ent before rounding North Head so as to clear drying Proudfoot Rks.

Hbr ent is dangerous in strong E'lies as craft have to turn 90° to port at the end of S pier.

On S side of bay, unlit NCM, 300m ENE of LB slip, marks end of ruined bkwtr.

LIGHTS AND MARKS S pier lt, Fl WRG 3s 12m 12/9M, 253°-G-270°-W-286°-R-329°, Bell (2) 10s (fishing). Ldg lts, both FR 5/8m, lead 234° into outer hbr. Traffic signals:

B ● (●) at CG stn on S Head = hbr closed by weather.
B ● (●) at S pier head = caution; hbr temp obstructed.

COMMUNICATIONS (Code 01955) HM 602030; MRCC (01224) 592334; Police 101; Ⓗ 602434, 602261.

VHF Ch 14 16 (Mon-Fri 0800-1700).

FACILITIES Poss temporary ⌓ on pontoons in Outer Harbour. **Wick Marina** (Inner Harbour) 70 inc 15 🅥 dredged to 2·0m; £20/craft up to 10m; max 25m LOA; BH, shower block 50m from marina. **Fish Jetty** D, ⚓, 🖳; **Services:** ◣, ✕, 🏧, ◣, C(15/100 ton), Gas. **Town** 🍴, Gas, Gaz(at Heat Centre), 🛒, ✕, 🏧, ✉, Ⓑ, ⇌, ✈.

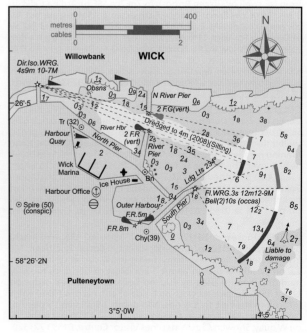

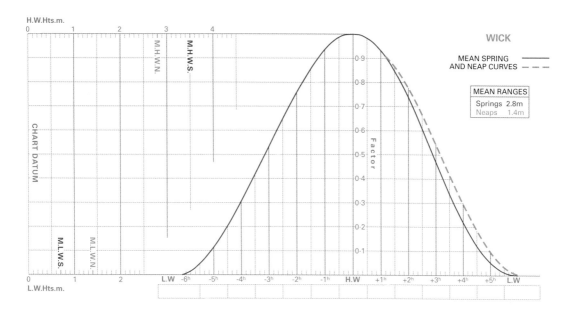

WICK

MEAN SPRING ——————
AND NEAP CURVES — — —

MEAN RANGES	
Springs	2.8m
Neaps	1.4m

PENTLAND FIRTH

(AC 2162, 2581) ▶ *This potentially dangerous chan should only be attempted with moderate winds (less than F4), good vis, no swell and a fair np tide.* In such conditions it presents few problems. A safe passage depends on a clear understanding of tidal streams and correct timing. The Admiralty Tidal Stream Atlas for Orkney and Shetland (NP 209) gives large scale vectors and is essential. Even in ideal conditions the races off Duncansby Hd, Swilkie Pt (N end of Stroma), and Rks of Mey (Merry Men of Mey) must be avoided as they are always dangerous to small craft. Also avoid the Pentland Skerries, Muckle Skerry, Old Head, Lother Rock (S Ronaldsay), and Dunnet Hd on E-going flood. For passages across the Firth see CCC SDs for Orkney. ◀

At E end the Firth is entered between Duncansby Hd and Old Hd (S Ronaldsay), between which lie Muckle Skerry and the Pentland Skerries. Near the centre of Firth are the Islands of Swona (N side) and Stroma (S side). Outer Sound (main chan, 2·5M wide) runs between Swona and Stroma; Inner Sound (1·5M wide) between Stroma and the mainland. Rks of Mey extend about 2ca N of St John's Pt. The W end of the Firth is between Dunnet Hd and Tor Ness (Hoy).

▶Tide flows strongly around and through the Orkney Islands. *The Pentland Firth is a dangerous area for all craft, tidal flows reach 12 knots between Duncansby Head and S Ronaldsay.* W of Dunnet Hd and Hoy is less violent. There is little tide within Scapa Flow. Tidal streams reach 8-9kn at sp in the Outer Sound, and 9-12kn between Pentland Skerries and Duncansby Hd. The resultant dangerous seas, very strong eddies and violent races should be avoided by yachts at all costs.

The E-going stream begins at HW Aberdeen +0500, and the W-going at HW Aberdeen –0105. **Duncansby Race** *extends ENE towards Muckle Skerry on the SE-going stream, but by HW Aberdeen –0440 it extends NW from Duncansby Hd. Note: HW at Muckle Skerry is the same time as HW Dover. A persistent race off* **Swilkie Pt***, at N end of Stroma,* **is very dangerous with a strong W'ly wind over a W-going stream. The most dangerous and extensive race in the Firth is Merry Men of Mey.** *It forms off St John's Pt on W-going stream at HW Aberdeen –0150 and for a while extends right across to Tor Ness with heavy breaking seas even in fine weather.* ◀

<table>
<tr><td>

FLOOD
Pentland Firth & Orkneys

(a) Aberdeen +0500 to Aberdeen –0105
(b) Aberdeen +0310 to Aberdeen –0330
(c) Aberdeen +0400 to Aberdeen –0150

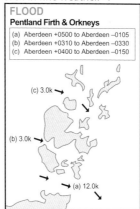

(c) 3.0k

(b) 3.0k

(a) 12.0k

</td><td>

EBB
Pentland Firth & Orkneys

(a) Aberdeen –0105 to Aberdeen +0500
(b) Aberdeen –0330 to Aberdeen +0310
(c) Aberdeen –0150 to Aberdeen +0400

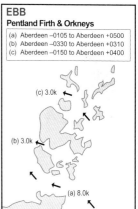

(c) 3.0k

(b) 3.0k

(a) 8.0k

</td></tr>
</table>

Passage Westward: This is the more difficult direction due to prevailing W winds. ▶ *Freswick B, 3·5M S of Duncansby Hd, is a good waiting anch; here an eddy runs N for 9 hrs. Round Duncansby Hd close in at HW Aberdeen –0220, as the ebb starts to run W. Take a mid-course through the Inner Sound to appr the Rks of Mey from close inshore. Gills Bay is a temp anch if early; do not pass Rks of Mey until ebb has run for at least 2 hrs. Pass 100m N of the Rks (awash).◀*

Passage Eastward: ▶ *With a fair wind and tide, no race forms and the passage is easier. Leave Scrabster at local LW+1 so as to be close off Dunnet Hd not before HW Aberdeen +0340 when the E-going flood starts to make. If late, give the Hd a wide berth. Having rounded the Rks of Mey, steer S initially to avoid being set onto the rky S tip of Stroma, marked by unlit SCM bn.◀* Then keep mid-chan through the Inner Sound and maintain this offing to give Duncansby Hd a wide berth.

217

STANDARD TIME (UT)
For Summer Time add ONE hour in **non-shaded areas**

WICK — LAT 58°26′N   LONG 3°05′W
TIMES AND HEIGHTS OF HIGH AND LOW WATERS

Dates in red are **SPRINGS**
Dates in blue are **NEAPS**

YEAR 2015

JANUARY

Time	m	Time	m
1 TH 0158	1.2	**16** F 0106	1.4
0813	3.1	0722	2.9
1425	1.3	1340	1.5
2034	3.2	1949	2.9
2 F 0253	1.2	**17** SA 0210	1.3
0911	3.2	0823	3.1
1519	1.1	1442	1.3
2134	3.2	2053	3.1
3 SA 0337	1.1	**18** SU 0303	1.1
1000	3.4	0919	3.3
1604	1.0	1532	1.1
2223	3.3	2150	3.3
4 SU 0416	1.1	**19** M 0349	1.0
1043	3.5	1008	3.5
1644	0.9	1617	0.8
2306	3.3	2241	3.5
5 M 0452	1.1	**20** TU 0433	0.8
1122	3.5	1055	3.6
1722	0.8	1702	0.6
○ 2346	3.4	● 2329	3.6
6 TU 0527	1.0	**21** W 0516	0.7
1158	3.6	1141	3.8
1758	0.8	1746	0.4
7 W 0022	3.3	**22** TH 0015	3.7
0600	1.0	0559	0.7
1234	3.6	1226	3.9
1833	0.8	1831	0.3
8 TH 0058	3.3	**23** F 0102	3.7
0632	1.1	0643	0.7
1307	3.5	1311	3.9
1907	0.9	1917	0.4
9 F 0132	3.2	**24** SA 0148	3.6
0704	1.1	0727	0.8
1341	3.4	1357	3.8
1941	0.9	2004	0.5
10 SA 0207	3.1	**25** SU 0235	3.4
0737	1.2	0812	0.9
1415	3.3	1444	3.7
2017	1.0	2054	0.7
11 SU 0244	3.0	**26** M 0324	3.2
0811	1.3	0902	1.1
1453	3.2	1536	3.4
2056	1.2	2151	0.9
12 M 0325	2.9	**27** TU 0420	3.1
0851	1.4	1003	1.3
1535	3.1	1636	3.2
2145	1.3	◑ 2257	1.2
13 TU 0413	2.8	**28** W 0522	2.9
0941	1.6	1121	1.4
1626	2.9	1745	3.0
◑ 2248	1.4		
14 W 0511	2.8	**29** TH 0014	1.3
1100	1.7	0631	2.9
1729	2.9	1253	1.4
2358	1.4	1901	2.9
15 TH 0617	2.8	**30** F 0137	1.4
1224	1.6	0746	2.9
1840	2.8	1413	1.3
		2021	3.0
		31 SA 0240	1.3
		0853	3.1
		1510	1.2
		2123	3.0

FEBRUARY

Time	m	Time	m
1 SU 0326	1.3	**16** M 0242	1.2
0944	3.2	0851	3.1
1555	1.0	1514	1.0
2212	3.1	2132	3.2
2 M 0404	1.2	**17** TU 0333	1.0
1027	3.4	0947	3.4
1632	0.9	1602	0.7
2253	3.2	2225	3.4
3 TU 0437	1.1	**18** W 0418	0.8
1106	3.4	1037	3.6
1706	0.8	1646	0.4
○ 2329	3.3	● 2313	3.6
4 W 0509	1.0	**19** TH 0501	0.6
1141	3.5	1123	3.8
1739	0.7	1730	0.2
		2358	3.7
5 TH 0003	3.3	**20** F 0543	0.5
0540	0.9	1209	3.9
1214	3.5	1814	0.2
1811	0.7		
6 F 0035	3.3	**21** SA 0043	3.7
0611	0.9	0625	0.5
1246	3.5	1254	3.9
1842	0.7	1857	0.2
7 SA 0106	3.2	**22** SU 0127	3.6
0641	0.9	0707	0.5
1317	3.4	1339	3.8
1913	0.8	1941	0.4
8 SU 0137	3.2	**23** M 0211	3.4
0711	1.0	0750	0.7
1348	3.4	1424	3.6
1944	0.9	2025	0.7
9 M 0210	3.1	**24** TU 0256	3.3
0742	1.1	0836	0.9
1421	3.2	1513	3.4
2017	1.0	2114	1.0
10 TU 0245	3.0	**25** W 0346	3.2
0816	1.2	0932	1.1
1458	3.1	1610	3.1
2054	1.1	◑ 2215	1.2
11 W 0326	2.9	**26** TH 0445	2.9
0856	1.3	1049	1.3
1543	3.0	1719	2.9
2142	1.4	2334	1.4
12 TH 0417	2.8	**27** F 0556	2.8
0951	1.5	1228	1.4
1639	2.8	1839	2.7
◑ 2256	1.4		
13 F 0521	2.8	**28** SA 0112	1.5
1127	1.5	0714	2.8
1755	2.8	1357	1.3
		2004	2.8
14 SA 0020	1.4		
0635	2.8		
1300	1.5		
1915	2.8		
15 SU 0139	1.3		
0747	2.9		
1417	1.2		
2030	3.0		

MARCH

Time	m	Time	m
1 SU 0223	1.4	**16** M 0112	1.3
0829	2.9	0714	2.9
1454	1.1	1353	1.1
2107	2.9	2009	2.9
2 M 0311	1.3	**17** TU 0221	1.2
0923	3.1	0824	3.1
1537	1.0	1454	0.8
2154	3.0	2113	3.1
3 TU 0347	1.2	**18** W 0314	0.9
1006	3.2	0924	3.3
1612	0.9	1542	0.5
2233	3.1	2206	3.4
4 W 0419	1.1	**19** TH 0359	0.7
1044	3.3	1016	3.6
1644	0.8	1627	0.3
2307	3.2	2253	3.5
5 TH 0449	0.9	**20** F 0441	0.5
1118	3.4	1103	3.8
1715	0.7	1710	0.2
○ 2339	3.2	● 2338	3.6
6 F 0519	0.8	**21** SA 0523	0.4
1150	3.4	1149	3.9
1745	0.6	1752	0.1
7 SA 0009	3.3	**22** SU 0021	3.7
0548	0.8	0605	0.4
1222	3.4	1235	3.9
1814	0.6	1834	0.2
8 SU 0039	3.3	**23** M 0103	3.6
0617	0.8	0647	0.4
1252	3.4	1319	3.7
1844	0.7	1915	0.4
9 M 0109	3.2	**24** TU 0145	3.4
0647	0.8	0729	0.6
1322	3.3	1404	3.5
1913	0.8	1957	0.7
10 TU 0140	3.2	**25** W 0228	3.2
0717	0.9	0814	0.8
1354	3.2	1452	3.3
1944	0.9	2040	1.0
11 W 0213	3.1	**26** TH 0314	3.0
0750	1.0	0908	1.0
1431	3.1	1547	3.0
2019	1.0	2134	1.3
12 TH 0252	3.0	**27** F 0410	2.9
0829	1.1	1021	1.2
1514	3.0	1653	2.7
2102	1.2	◑ 2250	1.5
13 F 0339	2.9	**28** SA 0519	2.7
0918	1.3	1154	1.3
1610	2.8	1811	2.6
◑ 2205	1.4		
14 SA 0440	2.8	**29** SU 0030	1.6
1045	1.4	0635	2.7
1725	2.7	1326	1.2
2345	1.4	1934	2.6
15 SU 0557	2.7	**30** M 0154	1.5
1230	1.3	0752	2.8
1851	2.7	1426	1.1
		2040	2.8
		31 TU 0244	1.3
		0852	2.9
		1508	1.0
		2127	2.9

APRIL

Time	m	Time	m
1 W 0322	1.2	**16** TH 0251	0.9
0937	3.0	0859	3.3
1543	0.8	1520	0.5
2205	3.0	2144	3.3
2 TH 0354	1.0	**17** F 0337	0.7
1016	3.2	0953	3.5
1615	0.7	1605	0.3
2239	3.1	2232	3.5
3 F 0424	0.9	**18** SA 0421	0.5
1051	3.2	1043	3.6
1646	0.7	1648	0.2
2311	3.2	● 2316	3.6
4 SA 0455	0.8	**19** SU 0504	0.4
1123	3.3	1130	3.7
1716	0.6	1730	0.2
○ 2341	3.3	2358	3.7
5 SU 0525	0.7	**20** M 0547	0.3
1155	3.3	1215	3.7
1746	0.6	1811	0.4
6 M 0011	3.3	**21** TU 0040	3.5
0554	0.7	0629	0.4
1227	3.3	1301	3.6
1815	0.6	1851	0.6
7 TU 0042	3.3	**22** W 0121	3.4
0625	0.7	0712	0.5
1259	3.3	1345	3.4
1846	0.7	1931	0.8
8 W 0114	3.2	**23** TH 0202	3.3
0657	0.8	0758	0.7
1334	3.2	1432	3.1
1919	0.8	2012	1.1
9 TH 0148	3.2	**24** F 0247	3.1
0733	0.8	0849	0.9
1412	3.1	1524	2.9
1955	1.0	2059	1.3
10 F 0228	3.1	**25** SA 0338	2.9
0814	1.0	0953	1.1
1458	2.9	1625	2.7
2040	1.1	◑ 2203	1.5
11 SA 0315	2.9	**26** SU 0440	2.8
0906	1.1	1109	1.2
1554	2.8	1734	2.6
2143	1.3	2327	1.6
12 SU 0414	2.8	**27** M 0551	2.7
1031	1.2	1232	1.2
1708	2.7	1846	2.6
◑ 2320	1.4		
13 M 0528	2.8	**28** TU 0059	1.5
1208	1.1	0701	2.7
1831	2.8	1341	1.1
		1955	2.7
14 TU 0046	1.3	**29** W 0203	1.4
0646	2.9	0806	2.8
1328	0.9	1429	1.0
1947	2.9	2048	2.8
15 W 0156	1.1	**30** TH 0247	1.2
0756	3.0	0858	2.9
1430	0.7	1508	0.9
2051	3.1	2130	2.9

Chart Datum: 1·71 metres below Ordnance Datum (Newlyn). HAT is 4·0 metres above Chart Datum.

》》 FREE monthly updates from **《《**
www.reedsalmanac.co.uk

WICK LAT 58°26'N LONG 3°05'W
TIMES AND HEIGHTS OF HIGH AND LOW WATERS

STANDARD TIME (UT)
For Summer Time add ONE hour in **non-shaded areas**

Dates in red are **SPRINGS**
Dates in blue are **NEAPS**

YEAR 2015

MAY

Time	m		Time	m
1 0323	1.1	**16** 0317	0.8
0941	3.0	0932	3.3
F 1542	0.8	SA 1543	0.5
2206	3.0	2210	3.4
2 0357	1.0	**17** 0403	0.6
1018	3.1	1024	3.5
SA 1615	0.7	SU 1627	0.4
2239	3.2	2255	3.5
3 0429	0.8	**18** 0447	0.5
1054	3.2	1113	3.5
SU 1646	0.7	M 1709	0.5
2312	3.2	● 2338	3.5
4 0501	0.7	**19** 0531	0.4
1129	3.2	1159	3.5
M 1718	0.6	TU 1750	0.6
○ 2344	3.3		
5 0533	0.7	**20** 0019	3.5
1204	3.3	0615	0.5
TU 1750	0.7	W 1244	3.4
		1829	0.7
6 0018	3.3	**21** 0100	3.4
0607	0.7	0658	0.5
W 1241	3.2	TH 1328	3.2
1824	0.7	1908	0.9
7 0053	3.3	**22** 0140	3.3
0643	0.7	0742	0.7
TH 1319	3.2	F 1412	3.1
1901	0.8	1947	1.1
8 0130	3.2	**23** 0222	3.2
0723	0.7	0828	0.8
F 1401	3.1	SA 1459	2.9
1942	0.9	2028	1.2
9 0212	3.2	**24** 0308	3.0
0808	0.8	0920	1.0
SA 1449	3.0	SU 1551	2.7
2030	1.1	2119	1.4
10 0300	3.1	**25** 0400	2.9
0905	0.9	1021	1.1
SU 1546	2.9	M 1649	2.6
2133	1.2	◑ 2226	1.5
11 0358	3.0	**26** 0502	2.7
1024	1.0	1127	1.2
M 1656	2.8	TU 1752	2.6
◑ 2258	1.3	2342	1.5
12 0507	2.9	**27** 0606	2.7
1146	0.9	1235	1.2
TU 1811	2.8	W 1855	2.6
13 0017	1.3	**28** 0059	1.5
0621	2.9	0708	2.7
W 1301	0.8	TH 1337	1.1
1921	2.9	1954	2.7
14 0128	1.1	**29** 0201	1.3
0730	3.0	0807	2.8
TH 1404	0.7	F 1425	1.0
2026	3.1	2044	2.8
15 0227	0.9	**30** 0247	1.2
0834	3.2	0859	2.9
F 1457	0.6	SA 1506	0.9
2121	3.2	2127	3.0
		31 0326	1.1
		0943	3.0
		SU 1543	0.8
		2206	3.1

JUNE

Time	m		Time	m
1 0403	0.9	**16** 0436	0.6
1024	3.1	1100	3.3
M 1618	0.8	TU 1652	0.7
2243	3.2	● 2320	3.4
2 0438	0.8	**17** 0520	0.5
1104	3.2	1146	3.3
TU 1653	0.7	W 1732	0.8
○ 2319	3.3		
3 0515	0.7	**18** 0002	3.5
1144	3.3	0602	0.5
W 1729	0.7	TH 1229	3.3
2357	3.4	1810	0.8
4 0553	0.6	**19** 0041	3.4
1225	3.3	0643	0.6
TH 1808	0.7	F 1310	3.2
		1847	0.9
5 0036	3.4	**20** 0120	3.3
0634	0.6	0723	0.7
F 1308	3.3	SA 1350	3.1
1849	0.8	1923	1.0
6 0117	3.4	**21** 0158	3.2
0718	0.6	0802	0.8
SA 1353	3.2	SU 1430	3.0
1933	0.9	1959	1.1
7 0201	3.3	**22** 0238	3.1
0806	0.6	0844	0.9
SU 1441	3.1	M 1513	2.8
2022	1.0	2039	1.3
8 0249	3.2	**23** 0321	3.0
0902	0.7	0933	1.0
M 1536	3.0	TU 1601	2.7
2120	1.1	2128	1.4
9 0344	3.1	**24** 0410	2.9
1010	0.8	1028	1.1
TU 1639	2.9	W 1655	2.7
◑ 2232	1.2	◑ 2234	1.5
10 0448	3.1	**25** 0508	2.8
1122	0.8	1129	1.2
W 1747	2.9	TH 1754	2.6
2346	1.2	2347	1.5
11 0557	3.0	**26** 0610	2.7
1232	0.8	1233	1.2
TH 1854	2.9	F 1853	2.7
12 0058	1.2	**27** 0100	1.4
0705	3.0	0712	2.7
F 1339	0.8	SA 1335	1.2
1959	3.0	1951	2.8
13 0205	1.0	**28** 0205	1.3
0812	3.1	0812	2.8
SA 1437	0.8	SU 1427	1.1
2059	3.1	2044	2.9
14 0301	0.9	**29** 0256	1.2
0916	3.2	0907	2.9
SU 1526	0.7	M 1512	1.0
2150	3.3	2131	3.1
15 0350	0.7	**30** 0339	1.0
1011	3.3	0956	3.0
M 1611	0.7	TU 1553	0.9
2237	3.4	2215	3.2

JULY

Time	m		Time	m
1 0419	0.8	**16** 0509	0.6
1042	3.2	1132	3.2
W 1633	0.8	TH 1715	0.9
2257	3.4	● 2345	3.3
2 0459	0.7	**17** 0547	0.6
1126	3.3	1212	3.2
TH 1713	0.7	F 1750	0.9
○ 2339	3.5		
3 0541	0.5	**18** 0022	3.5
1211	3.4	0623	0.6
F 1755	0.7	SA 1249	3.2
		1824	0.9
4 0021	3.6	**19** 0058	3.4
0624	0.4	0658	0.6
SA 1256	3.4	SU 1324	3.1
1837	0.7	1857	1.0
5 0105	3.6	**20** 0133	3.3
0709	0.4	0733	0.7
SU 1342	3.4	M 1359	3.1
1922	0.8	1930	1.0
6 0150	3.5	**21** 0208	3.2
0757	0.5	0808	0.8
M 1429	3.3	TU 1435	3.0
2009	0.9	2004	1.1
7 0237	3.5	**22** 0244	3.1
0849	0.6	0845	1.0
TU 1521	3.1	W 1514	2.9
2101	1.0	2042	1.3
8 0328	3.3	**23** 0324	3.0
0948	0.7	0929	1.1
W 1617	3.0	TH 1559	2.8
◑ 2203	1.1	2129	1.4
9 0427	3.2	**24** 0412	2.8
1054	0.8	1026	1.2
TH 1719	2.9	F 1652	2.7
2316	1.2	◑ 2239	1.5
10 0533	3.1	**25** 0510	2.7
1204	1.0	1133	1.3
F 1825	2.9	SA 1754	2.7
11 0033	1.2	**26** 0002	1.5
0643	3.0	0619	2.7
SA 1317	1.0	SU 1243	1.3
1933	2.9	1859	2.8
12 0150	1.1	**27** 0120	1.4
0757	3.0	0729	2.7
SU 1422	1.0	M 1349	1.2
2039	3.0	2001	2.9
13 0252	1.0	**28** 0226	1.3
0906	3.1	0834	2.9
M 1515	1.0	TU 1445	1.1
2135	3.2	2058	3.1
14 0344	0.9	**29** 0317	1.0
1002	3.1	0932	3.0
TU 1559	1.0	W 1532	1.0
2223	3.3	2149	3.2
15 0428	0.7	**30** 0401	0.8
1050	3.2	1022	3.2
W 1638	0.9	TH 1615	0.8
2306	3.4	2235	3.4
		31 0444	0.6
		1109	3.4
		F 1657	0.7
		○ 2320	3.6

AUGUST

Time	m		Time	m
1 0526	0.4	**16** 0001	3.5
1155	3.5	0558	0.6
SA 1739	0.6	SU 1224	3.3
		1800	0.9
2 0005	3.7	**17** 0034	3.4
0610	0.3	0630	0.6
SU 1240	3.6	M 1256	3.2
1822	0.6	1831	0.9
3 0049	3.8	**18** 0106	3.4
0654	0.2	0701	0.7
M 1325	3.5	TU 1328	3.2
1905	0.6	1901	0.9
4 0134	3.7	**19** 0138	3.3
0740	0.3	0732	0.8
TU 1411	3.4	W 1400	3.1
1950	0.7	1932	1.0
5 0220	3.6	**20** 0210	3.2
0827	0.5	0805	0.9
W 1459	3.3	TH 1434	3.0
2037	0.9	2006	1.2
6 0310	3.5	**21** 0247	3.1
0920	0.7	0840	1.1
TH 1551	3.1	F 1513	2.9
2134	1.1	2045	1.3
7 0406	3.2	**22** 0329	2.9
1023	1.0	0925	1.2
F 1650	3.0	SA 1600	2.8
◑ 2248	1.2	◑ 2137	1.4
8 0512	3.0	**23** 0423	2.8
1136	1.2	1032	1.4
SA 1756	2.9	SU 1700	2.8
		2308	1.5
9 0014	1.3	**24** 0533	2.7
0625	2.9	1156	1.4
SU 1259	1.3	M 1812	2.8
1909	2.9		
10 0141	1.2	**25** 0040	1.5
0747	2.9	0652	2.7
M 1412	1.3	TU 1315	1.4
2022	3.0	1922	2.9
11 0246	1.1	**26** 0158	1.3
0858	3.0	0807	2.9
TU 1506	1.2	W 1421	1.2
2120	3.2	2027	3.1
12 0336	0.9	**27** 0255	1.0
0952	3.1	0910	3.1
W 1547	1.1	TH 1512	1.1
2207	3.3	2123	3.3
13 0416	0.8	**28** 0342	0.8
1036	3.2	1003	3.3
TH 1623	1.0	F 1556	0.9
2249	3.4	2213	3.5
14 0452	0.7	**29** 0425	0.5
1115	3.2	1050	3.5
F 1656	1.0	SA 1638	0.7
● 2326	3.5	○ 2259	3.7
15 0526	0.6	**30** 0507	0.3
1151	3.3	1136	3.6
SA 1728	0.9	SU 1720	0.5
		2345	3.9
		31 0550	0.2
		1220	3.7
		M 1803	0.5

Chart Datum: 1·71 metres below Ordnance Datum (Newlyn). HAT is 4·0 metres above Chart Datum.

STANDARD TIME (UT)
For Summer Time add ONE hour in **non-shaded areas**

WICK LAT 58°26′N LONG 3°05′W
TIMES AND HEIGHTS OF HIGH AND LOW WATERS

Dates in red are **SPRINGS**
Dates in blue are **NEAPS**

YEAR 2015

SEPTEMBER

Day	Time m	Time m	Time m	Time m
1 TU	0030 3.9	0633 0.2	1304 3.7	1845 0.5
16 W	0038 3.5	0630 0.7	1256 3.3	1834 0.9
2 W	0115 3.9	0717 0.3	1348 3.5	1928 0.6
17 TH	0109 3.4	0659 0.8	1327 3.2	1905 1.0
3 TH	0201 3.7	0801 0.5	1433 3.4	2014 0.8
18 F	0141 3.3	0730 0.9	1400 3.2	1937 1.1
4 F	0249 3.5	0850 0.8	1522 3.2	2109 1.0
19 SA	0217 3.1	0803 1.1	1437 3.1	2014 1.2
5 SA	0345 3.2	0949 1.1	1619 3.0	2224 1.2
20 SU	0259 3.0	0843 1.3	1522 3.0	2102 1.4
6 SU	0452 3.0	1105 1.4	1727 2.9	2357 1.3
21 M	0351 2.9	0940 1.4	1618 2.9	2221 1.5
7 M	0610 2.8	1238 1.5	1843 2.9	
22 TU	0500 2.8	1117 1.5	1730 2.8	
8 TU	0130 1.3	0735 2.8	1359 1.4	2000 3.0
23 W	0008 1.4	0624 2.8	1245 1.5	1847 2.9
9 W	0234 1.1	0845 2.9	1451 1.3	2100 3.1
24 TH	0130 1.2	0742 2.9	1356 1.3	1956 3.1
10 TH	0320 1.0	0936 3.1	1531 1.2	2147 3.3
25 F	0231 1.0	0847 3.1	1450 1.1	2056 3.3
11 F	0357 0.9	1017 3.2	1603 1.1	2227 3.4
26 SA	0319 0.7	0941 3.4	1535 0.9	2148 3.6
12 SA	0429 0.8	1052 3.2	1634 1.0	2302 3.5
27 SU	0403 0.5	1028 3.6	1618 0.7	2237 3.8
13 SU	0500 0.7	1125 3.3	1704 0.9	2335 3.5
28 M	0445 0.3	1113 3.7	1700 0.5	2323 3.9
14 M	0530 0.6	1156 3.3	1735 0.9	
29 TU	0528 0.2	1157 3.8	1742 0.5	
15 TU	0007 3.5	0600 0.7	1227 3.3	1804 0.9
30 W	0009 4.0	0610 0.3	1240 3.7	1824 0.5

OCTOBER

Day	Time m	Time m	Time m	Time m
1 TH	0055 3.9	0652 0.4	1323 3.6	1908 0.6
16 F	0044 3.4	0630 0.9	1259 3.4	1842 1.0
2 F	0141 3.7	0735 0.7	1407 3.5	1954 0.8
17 SA	0118 3.3	0702 1.0	1332 3.3	1916 1.0
3 SA	0230 3.5	0820 1.0	1454 3.3	2049 1.0
18 SU	0155 3.2	0736 1.1	1410 3.2	1955 1.1
4 SU	0325 3.2	0914 1.3	1549 3.1	2202 1.2
19 M	0238 3.1	0817 1.3	1454 3.1	2043 1.3
5 M	0431 2.9	1028 1.6	1656 2.9	2332 1.3
20 TU	0330 2.9	0911 1.5	1549 3.0	2158 1.4
6 TU	0547 2.8	1203 1.7	1811 2.9	
21 W	0438 2.8	1043 1.6	1658 2.9	2339 1.3
7 W	0104 1.3	0710 2.8	1333 1.6	1927 3.0
22 TH	0600 2.9	1214 1.5	1816 3.0	
8 TH	0209 1.2	0820 2.9	1427 1.5	2030 3.1
23 F	0059 1.2	0716 3.0	1327 1.4	1925 3.2
9 F	0254 1.1	0910 3.0	1506 1.3	2119 3.2
24 SA	0203 0.9	0821 3.2	1424 1.2	2028 3.4
10 SA	0329 1.0	0949 3.2	1539 1.2	2159 3.3
25 SU	0254 0.7	0917 3.4	1512 0.9	2124 3.6
11 SU	0400 0.9	1024 3.3	1609 1.1	2234 3.4
26 M	0340 0.5	1005 3.6	1556 0.7	2215 3.8
12 M	0431 0.8	1056 3.3	1640 1.0	2308 3.5
27 TU	0423 0.4	1050 3.7	1640 0.6	2303 3.9
13 TU	0501 0.7	1127 3.4	1710 0.9	2340 3.5
28 W	0505 0.4	1134 3.8	1723 0.5	2350 3.9
14 W	0531 0.7	1157 3.4	1740 0.9	
29 TH	0548 0.5	1217 3.8	1807 0.5	
15 TH	0011 3.5	0600 0.8	1227 3.4	1810 0.9
30 F	0036 3.8	0629 0.6	1300 3.7	1851 0.6
31 SA	0123 3.6	0711 0.9	1343 3.5	1938 0.8

NOVEMBER

Day	Time m	Time m	Time m	Time m
1 SU	0212 3.4	0753 1.2	1428 3.4	2031 1.0
16 M	0140 3.3	0719 1.1	1351 3.4	1945 1.0
2 M	0304 3.2	0841 1.4	1520 3.2	2135 1.2
17 TU	0224 3.2	0802 1.3	1435 3.3	2035 1.1
3 TU	0405 2.9	0943 1.6	1621 3.0	2252 1.3
18 W	0317 3.0	0856 1.4	1528 3.2	2144 1.2
4 W	0514 2.8	1105 1.7	1731 2.9	
19 TH	0420 3.0	1013 1.5	1632 3.1	2310 1.2
5 TH	0015 1.4	0626 2.8	1239 1.7	1841 2.9
20 F	0535 3.0	1139 1.5	1745 3.1	
6 F	0126 1.3	0737 2.9	1348 1.6	1947 3.0
21 SA	0026 1.1	0646 3.0	1253 1.4	1855 3.2
7 SA	0216 1.1	0832 3.0	1433 1.5	2041 3.1
22 SU	0133 1.0	0752 3.2	1357 1.3	2000 3.4
8 SU	0255 1.1	0915 3.1	1510 1.3	2125 3.2
23 M	0229 0.8	0851 3.4	1450 1.1	2101 3.5
9 M	0329 1.0	0952 3.2	1543 1.2	2204 3.3
24 TU	0318 0.7	0943 3.5	1538 0.9	2156 3.7
10 TU	0401 0.9	1026 3.4	1615 1.1	2239 3.4
25 W	0403 0.6	1030 3.7	1624 0.7	2247 3.8
11 W	0432 0.9	1058 3.4	1647 1.0	2314 3.4
26 TH	0446 0.6	1114 3.8	1709 0.6	2335 3.8
12 TH	0503 0.9	1130 3.5	1719 0.9	2348 3.4
27 F	0528 0.7	1157 3.8	1754 0.6	
13 F	0535 0.9	1202 3.5	1752 0.9	
28 SA	0021 3.7	0609 0.8	1240 3.7	1838 0.7
14 SA	0023 3.4	0607 0.9	1236 3.5	1826 0.9
29 SU	0108 3.6	0650 1.0	1322 3.6	1924 0.8
15 SU	0100 3.4	0641 1.0	1311 3.5	1903 1.0
30 M	0153 3.4	0730 1.2	1405 3.5	2011 1.0

DECEMBER

Day	Time m	Time m	Time m	Time m
1 TU	0241 3.2	0811 1.4	1451 3.3	2102 1.1
16 W	0214 3.3	0752 1.2	1422 3.5	2028 0.9
2 W	0332 3.0	0859 1.6	1543 3.1	2202 1.3
17 TH	0303 3.1	0841 1.3	1511 3.4	2127 1.0
3 TH	0430 2.9	1000 1.7	1643 3.0	2308 1.4
18 F	0401 3.1	0944 1.4	1609 3.3	2239 1.1
4 F	0533 2.8	1116 1.8	1747 2.9	
19 SA	0507 3.0	1101 1.5	1716 3.2	2352 1.1
5 SA	0018 1.4	0636 2.8	1238 1.7	1851 2.9
20 SU	0616 3.0	1217 1.4	1827 3.2	
6 SU	0123 1.3	0739 2.9	1347 1.6	1952 3.0
21 M	0103 1.1	0723 3.1	1330 1.3	1936 3.3
7 M	0214 1.3	0832 3.0	1436 1.5	2046 3.1
22 TU	0207 1.0	0827 3.3	1433 1.2	2043 3.4
8 TU	0255 1.2	0916 3.2	1516 1.3	2131 3.2
23 W	0302 0.9	0924 3.4	1526 1.0	2143 3.5
9 W	0332 1.1	0954 3.3	1553 1.2	2212 3.3
24 TH	0349 0.9	1014 3.5	1615 0.8	2236 3.5
10 TH	0406 1.0	1030 3.4	1628 1.1	2250 3.4
25 F	0432 0.9	1059 3.7	1700 0.7	2324 3.6
11 F	0440 1.0	1106 3.5	1702 1.0	2328 3.4
26 SA	0514 0.9	1142 3.7	1744 0.7	
12 SA	0514 1.0	1141 3.6	1737 0.9	
27 SU	0009 3.6	0553 0.9	1224 3.7	1825 0.7
13 SU	0007 3.4	0549 1.0	1218 3.6	1815 0.8
28 M	0052 3.5	0631 1.0	1304 3.6	1906 0.8
14 M	0047 3.4	0627 1.0	1257 3.6	1855 0.8
29 TU	0133 3.3	0707 1.1	1343 3.5	1946 0.9
15 TU	0129 3.4	0708 1.1	1337 3.5	1939 0.9
30 W	0214 3.2	0743 1.2	1423 3.4	2027 1.0
31 TH	0256 3.1	0821 1.4	1505 3.2	2112 1.2

Chart Datum: 1·71 metres below Ordnance Datum (Newlyn). HAT is 4·0 metres above Chart Datum.

》》 **FREE** monthly updates from 《《
www.reedsalmanac.co.uk

5.19 SCRABSTER

Highland **58°36'·61N 03°32'·61W** ✶✶✶✶✿✿✿✿

CHARTS AC 1954, 2162, 1462; Imray C68

TIDES -0240 Dover; ML 3·2; Duration 0615

Standard Port WICK (←)

Times				Height (metres)			
High Water		Low Water		MHWS	MHWN	MLWN	MLWS
0200	0700	0100	0700	3·5	2·8	1·4	0·7
1400	1900	1300	1900				

Differences SCRABSTER

–0255	–0225	–0240	–0230	+1·5	+1·2	+0·8	+0·3

GILLS BAY

–0150	–0150	–0202	–0202	+0·7	+0·7	+0·6	+0·3

STROMA

–0115	–0115	–0110	–0110	–0·4	–0·5	–0·1	–0·2

LOCH ERIBOLL (Portnancon)

–0340	–0255	–0315	–0255	+1·6	+1·3	+0·8	+0·4

KYLE OF DURNESS

–0350	–0350	–0315	–0315	+1·1	+0·7	+0·4	–0·1

SULE SKERRY (59°05'N 04°24'W)

–0320	–0255	–0315	–0250	+0·4	+0·3	+0·2	+0·1

RONA (59°08'N 05°49'W)

–0350	–0350	–0350	–0340	–0·3	–0·4	–0·2	–0·4

SHELTER Very good except for swell in NW and N winds. Yachts usually lie in the Inner (0·9–1·2m) or Centre Basins (0·9–2·7m). Pontoons in inner hbr. ⚓ is not advised.

- A good hbr to await the right conditions for E-bound passage through Pentland Firth (see 5.4).
- Beware floating creel lines in E of hbr.

NAVIGATION WPT 58°36'·58N 03°32'·09W, 278°/0·25M to E pier lt. Can be entered H24 in all weathers. Beware FVs and the Orkney ferries.

LIGHTS AND MARKS No ldg marks/lts but entry is simple once the conspic ice plant tr and/or pier lts have been located. Do not confuse hbr lts with the shore lts of Thurso.

COMMUNICATIONS (Code 01847) MRCC (01224) 592334; Police 101; Dr 893154. HM ☎ 892779, Mobile 07803 290366.

Call HM VHF Ch 12 16 (H24) for berthing directions, before entering hbr. From the W reception is very poor due to masking by Holborn Head.

FACILITIES www.scrabster.co.uk ⚓ £8.00 (£35/week) on quay, pontoon by request ⚓ ⚓, D, ⌂, ⚲, ⌂, ⌂, ⚒, C (15, 30, 99 ton). **Pentland Firth YC** M, ✗, ⌂, Showers (keys held by Duty HM). **Thurso** Gas, Gaz, ☜, ✗, ⌂, ✉, Ⓑ, ⚒, ✈ (Wick). **Ferries**: Stromness; 3/day; 1½ Hrs; Northlink (www.northlinkferries.co.uk). Faroe Islands (Torshavn); weekly (seasonal); 12 Hrs; Smyril (www.smyril.co.uk). Bergen; weekly (seasonal); 16 Hrs; Smyril.

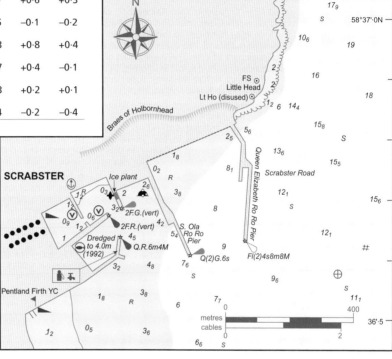

ANCHORAGES BETWEEN SCRABSTER AND CAPE WRATH

KYLE OF TONGUE, Highland, **58°31'·97N 04°22'·67W** (ent). AC 2720, 1954. HW +0050 on Ullapool; HW ht –0·4m; see 5.19. The Kyle runs about 7M inland.

Entry (see 5.4) should not be attempted in strong N winds.

⚓ at Talmine (W of Rabbit Is) protected from all but NE winds; at Skullomie Hr, protected from E'lies; off Mol na Coinnle, a small bay on SE side of Eilean nan Ron, protected from W and N winds; off S of Rabbit Is, protected from W to N winds. No ldg lts/marks. Facilities: Limited ☜ at Talmine (½M from slip) or at Coldbachie (1½M from Skullomie).

LOCH ERIBOLL, Highland, **58°32'·58N 04°37'·48W**. AC 2076. HW –0345 on Dover; ML 2·7m. See 5.19. Enter between Whiten Hd and Klourig Is in W sector of White Hd lt. See 5.3.

In SW winds fierce squalls funnel down the loch.

Yachts can enter drying Rispond Hbr and dry out alongside; no lts/marks and very limited facilities. Good ⚓s at: Rispond Bay on W side of loch, ent good in all but E winds, in approx 5m; off Portnancon in 5·5m; at the head of the loch; Camus an Duin and in bays to N and S of peninsula at Heilam on E side of loch. Beware numerous marine farms in the S half of the loch.

PENTLAND FIRTH TO CAPE WRATH

(AC 1954) Dunnet B, S of Dunnet Hd (lt) gives temp anch in E or S winds, but dangerous seas enter in NW'lies. On W side of Thurso B is Scrabster sheltered from S and W. ▶ *Between Holborn Hd and Strathy Pt the E-going stream begins at HW Ullapool –0150, and the W-going at HW Ullapool +0420, sp rates 1·8kn. Close to Brims Ness off Ushat Hd the sp rate is 3kn, and there is often turbulence.* ◀

SW of Ushat Hd the Dounreay power stn is conspic, near shore. Dangers extend 2½ca seaward off this coast.▶ *Along E side of Strathy Pt (lt) an eddy gives almost continuous N-going stream, but there is usually turbulence off the Pt where this eddy meets the main E or W stream.*◀ Several small bays along this coast give temp anch in offshore winds, but should not be used or approached with wind in a N quarter.

Kyle of Tongue is entered from E through Caol Raineach, S of Eilean nan Ron, or from N between Eilean Iosal and Cnoc Glass. There is no chan into the kyle W of Rabbit Is, to which a drying spit extends 0·5M NNE from the mainland shore. Further S there is a bar across entrance to inner part of kyle. There are anchs on SE side of Eilean nan Ron, SE side of Rabbit Is, off Skullomie, or S of Eilean Creagach off Talmine. Approach to the latter runs close W of Rabbit Islands, but beware rks to N and NW of them.

Loch Eriboll (AC 2076) provides secure anchs, but in strong winds violent squalls blow down from mountains. Eilean Cluimhrig lies on W side of entrance; the E shore is fringed with rks up to 2ca offshore. At White Hd (lt) the loch narrows to 6ca. There are chans W and E of Eilean Choraidh. Best anchs in Camas an Duin (S of Ard Neackie) or in Rispond B close to entrance (but not in E winds, and beware Rispond Rk which dries).

The coast to C Wrath is indented, with dangers extending 3ca off the shore and offlying rks and ks. Once a yacht has left Loch Eriboll she is committed to a long and exposed passage until reaching Loch Inchard. The Kyle of Durness is dangerous if the wind or sea is onshore. ▶ *Give Cape Wrath a wide berth when wind-against-tide which raises a severe sea.*◀ A firing exercise area extends 8M E of C. Wrath, and 4M offshore. When in use, R flags or pairs of R lts (vert) are shown from E and W limits, and yachts should keep clear.

ORKNEY ISLANDS

(AC 2249, 2250) The Islands are mostly indented and rocky, but with sandy beaches especially on NE sides. ▶*Pilotage is easy in good vis, but in other conditions great care is needed since tides run strongly. For details refer to* Clyde Cruising Club's Orkney Sailing Directions *and the* Admiralty Tidal Atlas NP 209*. When cruising in Orkney it is essential to understand and use the tidal streams to the best advantage, avoiding the various tide races and overfalls, particularly near sp.*◀

A good engine is needed since, for example, there are many places where it is dangerous to get becalmed. Swell from the Atlantic or North Sea can contribute to dangerous sea conditions, or penetrate to some of the anchorages. During summer months winds are not normally unduly strong, and can be expected to be Force 7 or more on about two days a month. But in winter the wind reaches this strength for 10-15 days per month, and gales can be very severe in late winter and early spring. Cruising conditions are best near midsummer, when of course the hours of daylight are much extended.

Stronsay Firth and Westray Firth run SE/NW through the group. The many good ⚓s include: Deer Sound (W of Deer Ness); Bays of Firth, Isbister, and off Balfour in Elwick B (all leading fm Wide Firth); Rysa Snd, B of Houton, Hunda Snd (Scapa Flow); Rousay Sound; and Pierowall Road (Westray). Plans for some of these are on AC 2622. A wave test site with turbine platform is between Eday and Muckle Green Holm, and an offshore wave test site marked by cardinal buoys NNW of Hoy Mouth (emec.org.uk). A major oil terminal and associated prohibited area is at Flotta, on the S side of Scapa Flow.

▶ *Tide races or dangerous seas occur at the entrances to most of the firths or sounds when the stream is against strong winds. This applies particularly to Hoy Sound, Eynhallow Sound, Papa Sound (Westray), Lashy Sound, and North Ronaldsay Firth. Also off Mull Head, over Dowie Sand, between Muckle Green Holm and War Ness (where violent turbulence may extend right across the firth), between Faraclett Head and Wart Holm, and off Sacquoy Hd. Off War Ness the SE-going stream begins at HW Aberdeen +0435, and the NW-going at HW Aberdeen –0200, sp rates 7kn.* ◀

5.20 ORKNEY ISLANDS

The Orkney Islands number about 70, of which some 24 are inhabited. They extend 5 to 50M NNE from Duncansby Hd, are mostly low-lying, but Hoy in the SW of the group reaches 475m (1560ft). Coasts are rocky and much indented, but there are many sandy beaches. A passage with least width of about 3M runs NW/SE through the group. The islands are separated from Scotland by the Pentland Firth, a very dangerous stretch of water. The principal island is Mainland (or Pomona) on which stands Kirkwall, the capital. For inter island ferries see www.orkneyferries.co.uk.

Severe gales blow in winter and early spring. The climate is mild but windy, and very few trees grow. There are LBs at Longhope, Stromness and Kirkwall.

CHARTS AC 2162, 2250 and 2249, at medium scale. For larger scale charts, see under individual hbrs; Imray C68

TIDES Wick (5.18) is the Standard Port. Tidal streams are strong, particularly in Pentland Firth and in the islands' firths and sounds.

SHELTER/MARINA CHARGES There are piers (fender board advised) at all main islands www.sailnorthscotland.com. Details of charges at marinas or piers throughout the Orkney Islands, except St Margaret's Hope, are at www.orkneymarinas.co.uk. Some of the many ⚓s are listed:

MAINLAND Scapa Bay: good except in S winds. No yacht berths alongside pier due to heavy hbr traffic. Only ents to Scapa Flow are via Hoy Snd, Hoxa Snd or W of Flotta.
St Marys (Holm/Ham): 58°53'·80N 02°54'·50W; N side of Kirk Sound; ⚓ in B of Ayre or berth E side of Pier, HW±4. 🛎 & 🛢, ✉, 🍴, ✕, Bus to Kirkwall & Burwick Ferry.

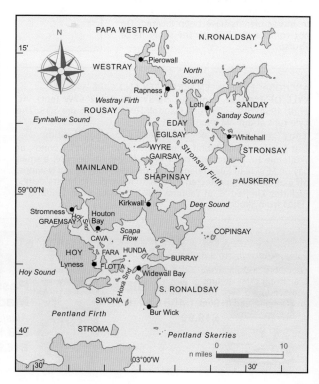

Kirk Sound (E ent): ⚓ N of Lamb Holm; beware fish cages.

Deer Sound: ⚓ in Pool of Mirkady or off pier on NW side of sound; very good shelter, no facilities.

Hunda Sound: good ⚓ in all winds.

SOUTH RONALDSAY/BURRAY **St Margaret's Hope/Water Sound**: ⚓⚓⚓⚓⚓⚓⚓⚓. Ldg Lts, F.G, 174°. ⚓ in centre of bay; or 🛟 £7/day at pier (but limited space and keep clear of ferry berth on S side of pier), beware salmon farm. HM ☎ 01856 831440, mob 07879 688040; Dr 831206. ⚓, 🏠 & 🏠, 🛒, ✕, 🏧, ✉, Bus Kirkwall, Vehicle ferry to Gill's Bay/Caithness.

Widewall Bay: ⚓ sheltered except SW'lies.

FLOTTA **58°50'·20N 03°07'·90W**; berth on Sutherland Pier, SW of oil terminal. HM ☎ 01856 701411. 🏠 & 🏠, 🛒, ✉.

HOY **Long Hope: 58°48'·07N 03°12'·25W**; ⚓ E of Pier, used by ferry, or berth on pier (safest at slack water). 2 ⚓'s < 18 tonnes close to Pier. ☎ 01856 701263; Dr 701209. Facilities: ⚓, 🏠 & 🏠, ✉, 🛒, 🏧.

Lyness: 58°50'·20N 03°11'·40W; berth on Pier; avoid disused piles; ⚓ in Ore Bay. HM ☎ 01856 791387. ⚓, 🏠 & 🏠, 🏧, ✉. Beware fish cages.

Pegal Bay: good ⚓ except in strong W winds.

ROUSAY **Wyre Sound: 59°09'·40N 02°44'·70W**; ⚓ E of Rousay Pier or berth on it. ✉, 🛒, ✕. Piermaster ☎ 01856 821261.

EDAY **Fersness Bay**: good holding, sheltered from S winds. Dr ☎ 01857 622243.

Backaland Bay: 59°09'·40N 02°44'·70W: berth on Pier clear of ferry; Piermaster ☎ 01856 622282; or ⚓ to NW. Beware cross tides. ⚓, P & D, 🛒, ✉.

Calf Sound: ⚓ in Carrick B; good shelter from SW-NW'lies.

PAPA WESTRAY **Bay of Moclett 58°21'·40N 02°26'·30W**: Good ⚓ but open to S. Pier. Piermaster ☎ 01857 644259;

South Wick: ⚓ off the old pier or ESE of pier off Holm of Papa. Backaskaill: 🏠 & 🏠, 🛒, ✉.

SANDAY **Loth Bay: 59°11'·50N 02°41'·80W**; berth on Pier clear of ferry. Piermaster ☎ 01857 600227; Beware strong tides.

Kettletoft Bay: 59°13'·90N 02°35'·80W; ⚓ in bay or berth on Pier, very exposed to SE'lies. HM ☎ (01857) 600227, Dr 600221; 🏠 & 🏠, ⚓, Gas, ✉, Ⓑ, 🛒, hotel.

North Bay: on NW side of island, exposed to NW.

Otterswick: good ⚓ except in N or E winds.

NORTH RONALDSAY **South Bay: 58°21'·40N 02°26'·30W**; ⚓ in middle of bay or berth on Pier. Piermaster ☎ 01857 633239; open to S & W and swell. 🛒, ✉.

Linklet Bay: ⚓ off jetty at N of bay, open to E.

NAVIGATION From the mainland, appr from Scrabster to Stromness and Scapa Flow via Hoy Mouth and Hoy Sd. From the Moray Firth keep well E of the Pentland Skerries if going N to Kirkwall. If bound for Scapa Flow via Hoxa Sd, keep close to Duncansby Hd, passing W of the Pentland Skerries and between Swona and S Ronaldsay. Keep clear of Lother Rk (dries 1·8m) off SW tip of S Ronaldsay. Time this entry for slack water in the Pentland Firth (about HW Aberdeen –1¾ and +4). Beware of tankers off Flotta oil terminal and in S part of Scapa Flow, where are the remains of the German WW1 Battle Fleet; classified as Historic Wrecks (see 0.29) protected, but authorised diving allowed.

Elsewhere in Orkney navigation is easy in clear weather, apart from the strong tidal streams in all the firths and sounds. Beware races and overfalls off Brough of Birsay (Mainland), Noup Head (Westray) and Dennis Head (N Ronaldsay). Keep a good lookout for the many lobster pots (creels).

LIGHTS AND MARKS The main hbrs and sounds are well lit; for details see 5.3. Powerful lts are shown offshore from Cantick Hd, Graemsay Island, Copinsay, Auskerry, Kirkwall, Brough of Birsay, Sanday Island, N Ronaldsay and Noup Hd.

Orkney Hbrs Navigation Service (call: *Orkney Hbr Radio*, Ch 09 11 20 16 (H24)) covers Scapa Flow and apprs, Wide Firth, Shapinsay Sound and Kirkwall Bay.

COMMUNICATIONS Area Code for islands SW of Stronsay and Westray Firths is 01856; islands to the NE are 01857.

MEDICAL SERVICES Doctors are available at Kirkwall, Stromness, Rousay, Hoy, Shapinsay, Eday, S and N Ronaldsay, Stronsay, Sanday and Westray (Pierowall); Papa Westray is looked after by Westray. The only hospital (and dentist) are at Kirkwall. Serious cases are flown to Aberdeen (1 hour).

MARINE FARMS Fish cages/farms approx 30m x 50m may be found anywhere in sheltered waters within anchoring depths. Some are well buoyed, others are marked only by poles. Too many to list but the following will show the scale of the operations:

Beware **salmon cages** (may be marked by Y buoys/lts) at:

Kirkwall Bay	Toy Ness (Scapa Flow)
Rysa Sound	St Margaret's Hope
Bring Deeps	Backaland Bay (Eday)
Pegal Bay (Hoy)	Hunda Sound
Lyrawa Bay	Kirk Sound
Ore Bay (Hoy)	Carness Bay
Widewall Bay (S Ronaldsay)	Bay of Ham
	Bay of London (Eday)

Beware **oysters and longlines** at:

Widewall Bay	Bay of Firth
Swanbister Bay	Damsay Sound
Water Sound	Millburn Bay (Gairsay)
Hunda Sound	Pierowall
Deer Sound	Bay of Skaill (Westray)
Inganess Bay	Longhope

MINOR HARBOURS IN THE ORKNEY ISLANDS

HOUTON BAY, Mainland, **58°54'·85N 03°11'·33W**. AC 35, 2568. HW –0140 on Dover, –0400 on Aberdeen; HW ht +0·3m on Kirkwall; ML 1·8m; Duration 0615. ⚓ in the bay in approx 5·5m at centre, sheltered from all winds. Ent is to the E of Holm of Houton; ent chan dredged 3·5m for 15m each side of ldg line. Keep clear of shipping/ferries plying to Flotta. Ldg lts 316°: front Fl G 3s 8m, rear FG 16m; both R △ on W pole, B bands. Ro Ro terminal in NE corner marked by Iso R 4s with SHM Fl G on edge of ldg line. Bus to Kirkwall; ⚓ close E of piers. Yachtsmen may contact **M.Grainger** ☎ 01856 811397 for help.

SHAPINSAY, Orkney Islands, **59°01'·97N 02°54'·10W**. AC 2249, 2584. HW –0015 on Dover, –0330 on Aberdeen; HW ht –1·0m on Aberdeen. Good shelter in Elwick Bay off Balfour on SW end of island in 2·5-3m. Enter bay passing W of Helliar Holm which has lt Fl WRG 10s on S end. Keep mid-chan. Balfour Pier lt Q WRG 5m 3/2M; vis 270°-G-010°-W-020°-R-090°. Piermaster ☎ 01856 711358; Tides in The String reach 5kn at sp. Facilities: ⚓, 🏠 & 🏠, ✉, shop, 🏧.

AUSKERRY, Orkney Islands, **59°02'·02N 02°34'·65W**. AC 2250. HW –0010 on Dover, -0315 on Aberdeen, HW ht -1m on Aberdeen. Small island at ent to Stronsay Firth with small hbr on SE side. Safe ent and good shelter except in SW winds. Ent has 3·5m; 1·2m alongside pier. Yachts can lie secured between ringbolts at ent and the pier. Auskerry Sound and Stronsay Firth are dangerous with wind over tide. Auskerry lt at S end, Fl 20s 34m 18M, W tr. No facilities.

PIEROWALL, Westray, **59°19'·32N 02°58'·51W**. AC 2250, 2622. HW –0135 on Dover; ML 2·2m; Duration 0620. See 5.23. The bay is a good ⚓ in 2-7m and well protected. Marina pontoons in deep water alongside pier at Gill Pt. From S, beware Skelwick Skerry rks, and from the N the rks extending approx 1ca off Vest Ness. The N ent via Papa Sound needs local knowledge; tide race on the ebb. A dangerous tide race runs off Mull Hd at the N of Papa Westray. Lights: E Pier Hd Fl WRG 3s 7m 11/7M. W Pier Hd 2 FR (vert) 4/6m 3M. VHF Ch 16. HM ☎ (01857) 677216. **Marina** ☎ 07810 465784 www.orkneymarinas.co.uk, £2.00m (see 5.4), ⚓, 🗘. Facilities: 🏠 & 🏠, Gas, 🏧, ✉, Ⓑ, ✕, 🛒. Dr ☎ (01857) 677209.

RAPNESS: 58°14'·90N 02°51'·50W, berth on Pier clear of Ro-Ro. Piermaster ☎ 01857 677212; Open to SSW.

5.21 STROMNESS

Orkney Islands, Mainland **58°57'·78N 03°17'·72W**
❀❀⚓⚓⚓❀❀❀

CHARTS AC 2249, 2568; Imray C68

TIDES –0145 Dover; ML 2·0; Duration 0620

Standard Port WICK (←—)

Times				Height (metres)			
High Water		Low Water		MHWS	MHWN	MLWN	MLWS
0000	0700	0200	0700	3·5	2·8	1·4	0·7
1200	1900	1400	1900				
Differences STROMNESS							
–0225	–0135	–0205	–0205	+0·1	–0·1	0·0	0·0
ST MARY'S (Scapa Flow)							
–0140	–0140	–0140	–0140	–0·2	–0·2	0·0	–0·1
BURRAY NESS (Burray)							
+0005	+0005	+0015	+0015	–0·2	–0·3	–0·1	–0·1
WIDEWALL BAY (S Ronaldsay)							
–0155	–0155	–0150	–0150	+0·1	–0·1	–0·1	–0·3
BUR WICK (S Ronaldsay)							
–0100	–0100	–0150	–0150	–0·1	–0·1	+0·2	+0·1
MUCKLE SKERRY (Pentland Firth)							
–0025	–0025	–0020	–0020	–0·9	–0·8	–0·4	–0·3

SHELTER Very good. Northern Lights Board have sole use of pier near to ldg lts. Marina in N of hbr; or ⚓ where shown.

NAVIGATION WPT 58°56'·93N 03°17'·00W, 317°/0·9M to front ldg lt.

- Entry from the W should not be attempted with strong wind against tide due to heavy overfalls.
- If entering against the ebb, stand on to avoid being swept onto Skerry of Ness.
- Tides in Hoy Sound are >7kn at springs. No tidal stream in hbr.

LIGHTS AND MARKS For Hoy Sound, ldg lts 104° on Graemsay Is: front Iso 3s 17m 15M, W tr; rear Oc WR 8s 35m 20/16M, ldg sector is 097°-R-112°. Skerry of Ness, Fl WG 4s 7m 7/4M; shore-W-090°-G-shore. Hbr ldg lts 317°, both FR 29/39m 11M (H24), W trs, vis 307°-327°. Stromness Marina ent. Fl(2)R 5s.

COMMUNICATIONS (Code 01856) MRCC 01595 692976; Police 850222; Dr 850205; Dentist 850658. HM 07810 465825; Fuel 851286.

VHF Ch 14 16 (0900-1700 LT). (See also 5.22.)

FACILITIES Stromness Marina: ☎ 07810 465825, 10❶ £2.00m (see 5.4), ⬡, ⊥, Showers, WC, ⚒, ⊡, Ⓔ, ⚲, C (mobile, 30 ton), P & D (0800-2100 ☎ 8851286), ⚓. **Town** ⊥, ⬡, ⬡, ✕, ⬡, Gas, ⊠, ⊡, Ⓑ, ⇌ (Ferries to Scrabster, bus to Thurso), ✈ (Kirkwall). Yachtsmen may contact for help/advice: **Orkney Marinas** ☎ 871313.

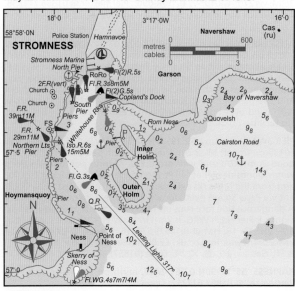

5.22 KIRKWALL

Orkney Islands, Mainland **58°59'·30N 02°57'·70W**
❀❀❀⚓⚓❀❀❀

CHARTS AC 2250, 2249, 2584, 1553; Imray C68

TIDES –0045 Dover; ML 1·8; Duration 0620

Standard Port WICK (←—)

Times				Height (metres)			
High Water		Low Water		MHWS	MHWN	MLWN	MLWS
0000	0700	0200	0700	3·5	2·8	1·4	0·7
1200	1900	1400	1900				
Differences KIRKWALL							
–0042	–0042	–0041	–0041	–0·5	–0·4	–0·1	–0·1
DEER SOUND							
–0040	–0040	–0035	–0035	–0·3	–0·3	–0·1	–0·1
TINGWALL							
–0200	–0125	–0145	–0125	–0·4	–0·4	–0·1	–0·1

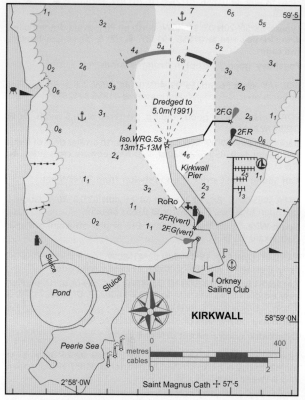

SHELTER Good except in N winds or W gales when there is a surge at the ent. Berth in marina on E of main pier, or SW end of main pier in inner hbr (very full in Jun/Jul). Safe ⚓ between pier and Crow Ness Pt. Hatston RoRo terminal in NW of bay (2 FG (vert)).

NAVIGATION WPT 59°01'·37N 02°57'·10W, 188°/2·2M to pier hd lt. Appr in W sector of pier hd lt, leaving newly extended Hatston Pier (2FG) / commercial terminal to W. Bay is shoal to SW beyond hbr.

LIGHTS AND MARKS See 5.3 and chartlet. Appr with St Magnus Cathedral (conspic) brg about 185°.

COMMUNICATIONS (Code 01856) MRCC (01595) 692976; ⚓ 873802; Police 872241; Dr 888000 (Ⓗ). HM 872292; Port Office 873636; Fuel 873105.

Kirkwall Hbr Radio VHF Ch 14 16 (0800-1700 LT). Orkney Hbrs Navigation Service, call: *VTS Orkney* Ch 09 11 20 16 (0915–1715).

FACILITIES Kirkwall Marina ☎ 879600 (berths 07810 465835), 71 inc ❶ £2.00m (see 5.4). Pier P & D (HO ☎ 873105), ⊥, ⬡, C (mob, 25 ton); **N and E Quays** M; **Orkney SC** ☎ 872331, M, L, C, ⬡ (£15/4days), ⚓. **Town** @ Library & Support Training Orkney (HO) P, D, ⚲, ⬡, ✕, ⬡, ⬡, Gas, ✕, ⬡, Ⓑ, ⊡, ⊠, Ferries to Scrabster, Aberdeen and Shetland, ✈.

5.23 STRONSAY

Orkney Islands, Stronsay 59°08'·57N 02°36'·01W ✿✿⛵⛵✿✿

CHARTS AC 2250, 2622; Imray C68

TIDES As Dover; ML 1·7; Duration 0620

Standard Port WICK (⟵)

Times				Height (metres)			
High Water		Low Water		MHWS	MHWN	MLWN	MLWS
0000	0700	0200	0700	3·5	2·8	1·4	0·7
1200	1900	1400	1900				
Differences WHITEHALL (Stronsay)							
–0030	–0030	–0025	–0030	–0·1	0·0	+0·2	+0·2
LOTH (Sanday)							
–0045	–0045	–0055	–0105	–0·4	–0·3	+0·1	+0·2
EGILSAY (Rousay Sound)							
–0125	–0125	–0125	–0125	–0·1	0·0	+0·2	+0·1
KETTLETOFT PIER (Sanday)							
–0030	–0030	–0025	–0025	0·0	0·0	+0·2	+0·2
RAPNESS (Westray)							
–0205	–0205	–0205	–0200	+0·1	+0·1	+0·2	0·0
PIEROWALL (Westray)							
–0150	–0150	–0145	–0145	+0·2	0·0	0·0	–0·1

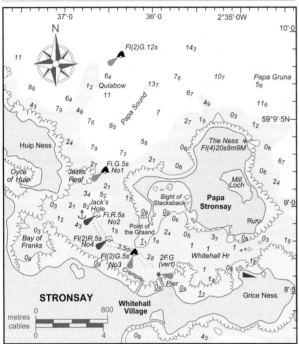

STRONSAY

SHELTER Good from all winds. Good ⚓ between seaward end of piers, or berth on outer end of W pier and contact HM. The extended E pier head is berth for Ro-Ro ferry. There are many other sheltered ⚓s around the bay.

NAVIGATION WPT 59°09'·82N 02°36'·31W, Quiabow SHM lt buoy, 189°/6·5ca to No 1 lt buoy. 800m NE of Huip Ness is Quiabow, a submerged rk. Jack's Reef extends 400m E from Huip Ness, and is marked by No 1 SHM lt buoy. A bank extends 350m SW from Papa Stronsay. Crampie Shoal is in mid-chan, marked by No 3 buoy. The buoyed chan to Whitehall pier is dredged 3·5m. Spit to E of Whitehall pier extends 400m N. The E ent is narrow and shallow and should not be attempted.

LIGHTS AND MARKS See chartlet.

COMMUNICATIONS (Code 01857) MRCC (01595) 692976; Police (01856) 872241; Dr 616321. Piermaster 616317. See Kirkwall for VHF comms.

FACILITIES W Pier M, L, 🍺; Main (E) Pier M, L, ⚓, 🍺 clear of ferry. Village (Whitehall) 🏪 & 🏬, ⛽, 🗑, ⌂, ✉, Ⓑ, 🚂 (Ferry to Scrabster, bus to Thurso), ✈.

SHETLAND ISLANDS

(AC 3281, 3282, 3283) ▶ *These Islands mostly have bold cliffs and are relatively high, separated by narrow sounds through which the tide runs strongly, so that in poor vis great care is needed. Avoid sp tides, swell and wind against tide conditions. The tidal flow around the Shetland Islands rotates as the cycle progresses. When the flood begins, at –0400 HW Dover, the tidal flow is to the E, at HW Dover it is S, at Dover +0300 it is W, and at –0600 Dover it is N.* ◀

Between Mainland and Whalsay passage can be made E or W of W Linga with spring rates of about 2kts with weaker streams to be found to the W in Lunning Sound.

▶ *Slack water at Lunning Sound occurs simultaneously at Lerwick, either 4 hours before or 2 hours after HW Lerwick.* ◀

Passage further Northward can be made through Yell Sound or Colgrave/Bluemell Sounds with shelter at Cullivoe.

▶ *Tides in Yell Sound are slack at the same time as high and low water in Lerwick. The stream normally runs at about 4 kts between the islands at the narrowest part between Yell and the Mainland but may reach 8 kts at springs. Colgrave Sound to the W of Yell experiences somewhat less tidal stream.* ◀

Bluemull Sound between Yell and Unst is a longer narrower passage. Well marked, passage is best attempted in daylight keeping to the middle of the channel clear of the fishing vesssels en-route to Cullivoe.

▶ *The stream runs at up to 6 knts at springs for longer duration and may be carried throughout a transit.* ◀

Although there are many secluded and attractive ⚓s, remember that the weather can change very quickly, with sudden shifts of wind. Also beware salmon fisheries and mussel rafts (unlit) in many Voes, Sounds and hbrs. Lerwick is the busy main port and capital; other hbrs are Scalloway, Walls (Vaila Sound), Uyesound(S Unst), Mid Yell (E Yell), Cullivoe (N Yell), Burravoe (S Yell), Symbister (Whalsay, Out Skerries (Skerries Isle) and Balta Sound. Refer to the CCC's *Shetland Sailing Directions.*

▶ *Coming from the S, beware a most violent and dangerous race (roost) off Sumburgh Hd (at S end of Mainland) on both streams. Other dangerous areas include between Ve Skerries and Papa Stour; the mouth of Yell Sound with strong wind against N-going stream; and off Holm of Skaw (N end of Unst). Tidal streams run mainly NW/SE and are not strong except off headlands and in the major sounds; the Admiralty Tidal Atlas NP 209 gives detail. The sp range is about 2m.* ◀

The 50M passage from Orkney can conveniently be broken by a stop at Fair Isle (North Haven). ▶ *Note that races form off both ends of the Is, especially S (Roost of Keels).* ◀

Recommended Traffic Routes: NW-bound ships pass to the NE (no closer than 10M to Sumburgh Hd) or SW of Fair Isle; SE-bound ships pass no closer than 5M off N Ronaldsay (Orkney). Lerwick to Bergen, Norway, is about 210M.

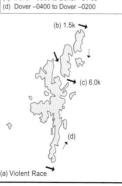

FLOOD
Shetland Islands
(a) Dover –0410 to Dover +0020
(b) Dover –0400 to Dover +0030
(c) Dover –0530 to Dover +01·00
(d) Dover –0400 to Dover –0200

(b) 1.5k
(c) 6.0k
(d)
(a) Violent Race

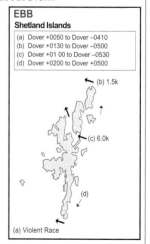

EBB
Shetland Islands
(a) Dover +0050 to Dover –0410
(b) Dover +0130 to Dover –0500
(c) Dover +01·00 to Dover –0530
(d) Dover +0200 to Dover +0500

(b) 1.5k
(c) 6.0k
(d)
(a) Violent Race

5.24 SHETLAND ISLANDS

The Shetland Islands number about 100 islands, holms and rks with fewer than 20 inhabited. Lying 90 to 150M NNE of the Scottish mainland, the biggest island is Mainland with Lerwick (5.25), the capital, on the E side. Scalloway, the only other town and old capital, is on the W side. At the very S is Sumburgh airport, with other airstrips at Baltasound, Scalsta and Tingwall. Two offlying islands of the Shetland group are Fair Isle, 20M SSW of Sumburgh Hd and owned by the NT for Scotland, and Foula, 12M WSW of Mainland. Mariners in the vicinity of inter island ferry ports should check carefully for ferries entering or leaving the following ports and allow them free passage. (Fair Isle North Haven, Grutness, Dury Voe, Vidlin Voe, Symbister Out Skerries, Mossbank, Ulsta, Gutcher, Belmont, NW Fetlar and West Burrafirth.)

There are LBs at Lerwick and Aith. The MRCC is at Lerwick, ☎ (01595) 692976, with an Auxillary Stn at Fair I.

CHARTS AC: medium scale 3281, 3282, 3283; larger scale 3271, 3272, 3292, 3293, 3294, 3295, 3297, 3298.

TIDES Standard Port Lerwick. Tidal streams run mostly N-S or NW-SE; in open waters to the E and W they are mostly weak. Rates >6kn can cause dangerous disturbances at the N and S extremities of the islands and in the two main sounds (Yell Sound and BlueMull/Colgrave Sounds). Keep 3M off Sumburgh Head to clear a dangerous race (Röst) or pass close inshore.

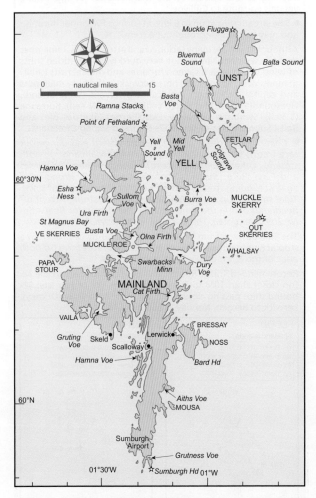

SHELTER Weather conditions are bad in winter; yachts should only visit Apr–Sept. Around mid-summer it is daylight H24. Some small marinas are asterisked* in the column on the right (see www.visitshetland.com); they may have room for visitors. Of the many ⚓s, the following are safe to enter in most conditions:

NAVIGATION A careful lookout must be kept for marine farms, mostly marked by Y buoys and combinations of Y lts. Clyde CC's *Shetland Sailing Directions and Anchorages* are essential for visitors. Local magnetic anomalies may be experienced.

LIGHTS AND MARKS See 5.3. Powerful lighthouses at Fair I, Sumburgh Hd, Kirkabister Ness, Bound Skerry, Muckle Flugga, Pt of Fethaland, Esha Ness and Foula. All inter-island ferry ports have leading sectored lights.

COMMUNICATIONS (Code 01595; 01806 for Sullom Voe) MRCC 692976; Sullom Voe Port Control (01806) 242551, ℻ 242237; ☜ 692239; Forecaster (01806) 242069; Sumburgh Airport (01950) 460654. Port Radio services see 5.25. No Coast Radio Station.

FACILITIES All stores obtainable in Lerwick and Scalloway. Elsewhere yachts should be prepared for extended offshore cruising and obtain water and diesel as and when they can:

MAINLAND (anti-clockwise from Sumburgh Head)

Grutness Voe: 1·5M N of Sumburgh Hd, a convenient passage ⚓, open to NE. Beware 2 rocks awash in mid-ent.

Pool of Virkie*: 59°53'N 01°17W; Close N of Grutness Voe. Ness Boating Club Marina ☎ 01950 477260, ☒ (pontoon 1❶< 1m £10/craft/week), slip, ⌑, ⏚, toilet. Shallow and narrow/entrance.

Cat Firth: excellent shelter, ⚓ in approx 6m. Facilities: ✉ (Skellister), ⏚, 🛒 (both at Lax Firth).

Grunna Voe: off S side of Dury Voe, good shelter and holding, ⚓ in 5-10m; beware prohib ⚓ areas. Facilities: 🗲, ⏚, ✉ (Lax Firth).

South of Yell Sound*: Tides –0025 on Lerwick. W of Lunna Ness, well protected ⚓s with good holding include: Boatsroom Voe, W Lunna Voe (small hotel, ⏚), Colla Firth* and Dales Voe. No facilities.

Vidlin: marina shop, bus service.

Sullom Voe: Tides –0130 on Lerwick. 6·5M long deep water voe, Commercial harbour. Contact Sullom Voe VTS (Ch14) prior to entry. ⚓ S of the narrows. Facilities at Brae: ⏚, 🗲, ✉, ⌑, ⬡, ✗, ⎄.

Hamna Voe: Tides –0200 on Lerwick; very good shelter. Ldg line 153° old house on S shore with prominent rock on pt of W shore 3ca within ent. Almost land-locked; ⚓ in 6m approx, bottom foul with old moorings. Facilities: ❶s, L (at pier), ☎ (1·5M), ✉ (0·5M), cafe, 🆆🅲/showers and 🅾 at nearby campsite.

Ura Firth: NE of St Magnus Bay, ⚓ off Hills Wick on W side or in Hamar Voe (no facilities) on E side, which has excellent shelter/good holding in all weathers. Facilities: **Hills Wick** ⏚, ✉, ☎, ⌑, ⬡, ✗, 🗲, ✗, ⎄.

Busta Voe: N of Swarbacks Minn. 4 ❶ (< 12m LOA) at Delting Marina in 2m (☎ 01806 522479); Brae (½M): 🗲, ✉, ☎, ⌑, ⬡, ✗, ✗.

Olna Firth: NE of Swarbacks Minn, beware rk 1ca off S shore which dries. ⚓ in firth, 4-8m or in Gon Firth or go alongside marina or pier at Voe. Facilities: (Voe) ⏚, 🗲, ☎, ⎄.

Swarbacks Minn*: a large complex of voes and isles SE of St Magnus Bay. Best ⚓ Uyea Sound or Aith Voe, both well sheltered and good holding. No facilities.

Aith Voe*: 60°17·3'N 01°22·3W; Good shelter from all directions ☒ depth LW 1.2m (marina pontoon 2 ❶s) otherwise on pier access H24, D, ⌑, ⏚, slip, ⌑, ✗, 🆆🅲/showers (leisure centre), 🗲, ✗, ⎄, ✉.

Vaila Sound (Walls), 60°13'·65N 01°33'·87W. AC 3295. Tides approx as Scalloway (above); see 5.25. Very good shelter. Appr to E of Vaila island (do not attempt Wester Sound) in the W sector (355°-012°) of Rams Head lt, Fl WRG 8s 16m 9/6M. Gruting Voe lies to the NE. Enter Easter Sound and go N for 1·5M, passing E of Linga islet, to Walls at the head of Vaila Voe. Navigate by echo sounder. Beware fish farms. ⚓ N of Salt Ness in 4-5m in mud. Temporary ☒ on Bayhaa pier (covers). Close E, ☒ £1 Peter Georgeson's pontoon. **Marina:** Sec ☎ (01595) 809273, ⏚. **Walls Regatta Club** welcomes visitors; showers, ⎄, ▬. **Village:** ☎ & ☎, ☒.

Gruting Voe*: HW –0150 on Lerwick, ⚓ in main voe or in Seli, Scutta or Browland* voes. Facilities: 🗲 and ✉ at Bridge of Walls (head of Browland Voe).

Skeld, 60°09'·65N 01°27'W. AC 3283, 3294. Tides approx as Scalloway. Appr from Skelda Voe which is subject to heavy seas and swell in strong S'lies. Beware Braga Rk (dries 2m) and drying rk 1ca S of it. At E of ent also Snap Rk (dries 3.5m) with isolated rks inshore. **Marina** offers good shelter as virtually landlocked, welcomes visitors; 8❶ £10/craft/week; James Scott ☎ (01595) 860287, ⏚, ⌑, 🆆🅲/showers, ☎ & ☎, bus to Lerwick 2/daily.

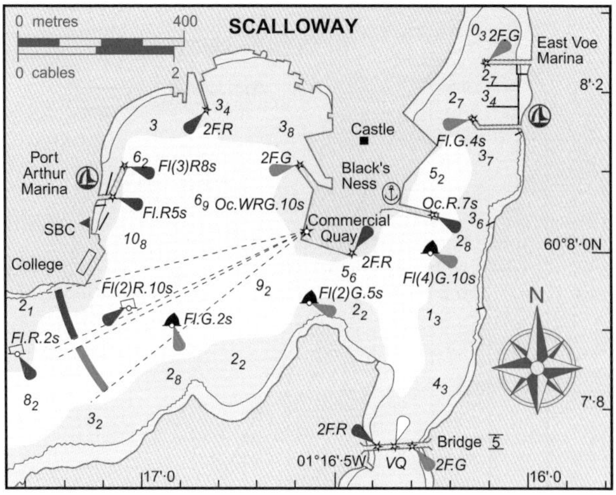

Scalloway, 60°08′·02N 01°16′·59W. AC 3294. HW –0200 on Dover; ML 0·9m; Duration 0620. See 5.25. A busy fishing port; good shelter and ⚓ in all weathers. Care is needed negotiating the islands in strong SW'lies. The N Chan is easier and safer than the S Chan, both are well lit and marked. Castle and warehouse (both conspic) lead 054° through S Chan. Dir Oc WRG 10s on hbr quay leads 064·5° into hbr. Hbr lts as chartlet. Ⓥ pontoon in 3m off SBC is best option; marina close N or new marina in E Voe (though mostly full of local boats). ⚓s in hbr 6–10m or in Hamna Voe (W Burra). Info at www.shetland.gov.uk/ports/scalloway or e-mail scalloway.harbour@shetland.gov.uk (cc to sullomvoevts@shetland.gov.uk). Call *Scalloway Hbr Radio* VHF Ch **12** 16 (Mon-Fri 0600-1800; Sat 0600-1230LT). Piermaster ☎ (01595) 744221. Facilities: **Scalloway Boat Club** (SBC) ☎ 880409 welcomes visitors; ⛴, ⚡. **Town** ⛽, & , , BY, , C, , , , ✉, R, 🛒, , bus to Lerwick.

Hamna Voe*: 60°06·3′N 01°20·3W (West Burra) Entered between Fugla Ness and Alta Ness. Open to the NW; good shelter in small marina. Small village, bus to Lerwick and all other routes.

WHALSAY*: 60°20′·60N 01°01′·60W; Fishing hbr with small marina at Symbister welcomes visitors. , D, (pontoon or pier 20Ⓥs) £7.17/craft/4 days, , , , D, P, WC/showers, 🛒, ✕, , ✉.

FOULA: 60°08′·02N 02°02′·92W. AC 3283. HW -0150 on Dover; ML 1·3m. See 5.25. Highest ground is 416m. S Ness sectored Lt ho, Fl WR(3) 15s, is at the S tip. Beware both Foula Shoal (7·6m) 4·3M E of the island and Hœvdi Grund (1·4m), 2M to the SE of Ham Voe. **Ham Voe:** is a narrow inlet on the E coast with a quay; rks on both sides. Two R ▲ ldg marks, approx 270°, are hard to see. ☆ 2 FG (vert) on pierhead. Berthing or landing is only possible in settled weather with no swell. Take advice from mail boat skipper out of Walls and call Foula, ☎ (01595) 753222. Small ✈. No other facilities.

OUT SKERRIES, 60°25′·3N 00°45′·1W AC 3282. Good shelter at pier. The NE entrance is buoyed and is the easier and has a leading light (Local ferry port). There are two Historic Wrecks (*Kennemerland* and *Wrangels Palais*) on Out Skerries at 60°25′·2N 00°45′·0W and 60°25′·5N 00°43′·3W (see 0.29). Shops, WC/showers at pier. Beware strong tidal conditions off the NE entrance ferries approaching or leaving. Pier (£2/craft/night); , , D (by arrangement), toilet/showers, wi-fi; Village ✉, shop. Good ⚓ at Bruray.

YELL Mid Yell Voe*: 60°36′N 01°03·4W; tides –0040 on Lerwick, enter via S Sd or Hascosay Sd, good ⚓ in wide part of voe 2·5-10m. Berth at marina £5/week or Pier £7.17/4 days/craft. Facilities: ✉, at pier on S side, D, 🛒, , , .

Basta Voe: good ⚓ above shingle bank in 5-15m; good holding in places. Facilities: , 🛒, Hotel, ✉.

Blue Mull Sound/Cullivoe*: 60°42′N 00°59′·7W; Hbr with small craft marina depth 1.2m £5/craft/day, , D. Pier 20Ⓥs £7.17/craft/4 days, , , , D, P, WC/shower. **Town** 🛒, ✕, , ✉. ⚓ off pier and slip.

Burra Voe*: 60°29′·8N 01°02′·4W; Entrance to voe has 2.5m bar. Good ⚓ at head of voe, but buoy ⚓ as precaution against fouling old moorings. at small marina £5/visit or on Pier £12/visit , , WC/showers , 🛒, , ✉.

UNST **Balta Sound: 60°44′·32N 00°48′·12W.** AC 3293. HW –0105 on Dover; ML 1·3; Duration 0640. See 5.24. Balta Sound is a large almost landlocked inlet with good shelter from all winds. Beware fish farms and bad holding on kelp. Safest and main entry is via S Chan between Huney Is and Balta Is; inner chan marked by two PHM lt buoys. N Chan is deep but narrow; keep to Unst shore. ⚓ off Sandisons Wharf (2FG vert) in approx 6m pontoon on W side of pier is derelict and reported unsafe (Oc WRG 10s 5m 2M, 272°-G-282°-W-287°-R-297°). Small boat marina has single shallow Ⓥ berth. VHF Ch 16; 20 (HO or as required). Facilities: BY, , D, , , , hotel. **Baltasound village**, , ✕, 🛒, ✉.

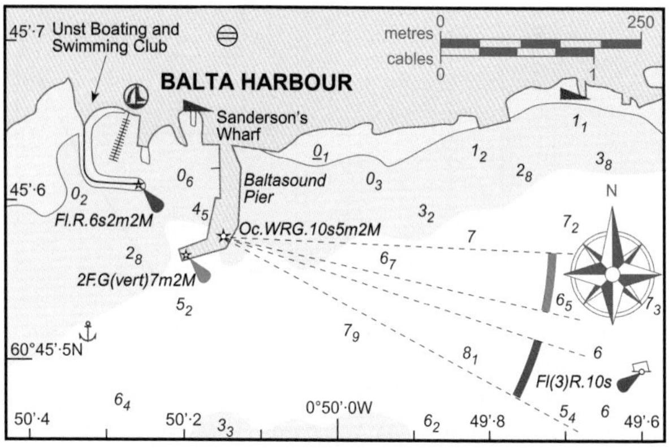

FAIR ISLE: 59°32′·37N 01°36′·21W. AC 3299. HW -0030 on Dover; ML 1·4m; Duration 0620. See 5.25. Good shelter in North Haven, except in NE winds. on pier or ⚓ in approx 2m. Beware strong cross-tides in the apprs; rocks all round Fair Isle, esp in S Haven and S Harbour which are hazardous. Ldg marks 199° into N Haven: front, Stack of N Haven (a dark 'tooth' sticking up from the jumble of blocks which form the bkwtr) in transit with conspic summit of Sheep Craig (rear). Dir lt into N Haven, Oc WRG 8s 10m 6M; vis 204°-G-208°-W-211°-R-221°. Lights: N tip, Skroo Fl(2) 30s 80m **22**M, S tip, Skadan Fl(4) 30s 31m **22**M. **Facilities:** 🛒, ✉ at N Shriva, ✈, bi-weekly mail boat to Grutness. No fuel or water. Bird observatory offers WC/showers/meals. Use large fenders supplied against pier to protect from scend/swell.

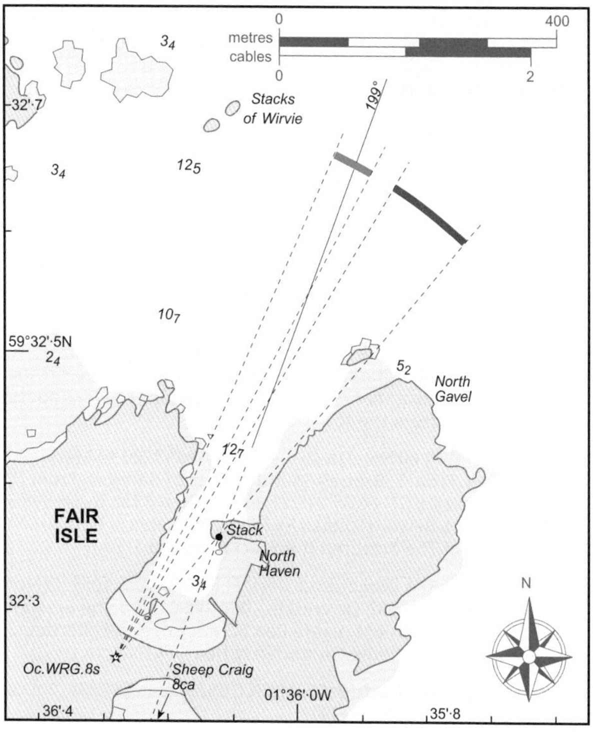

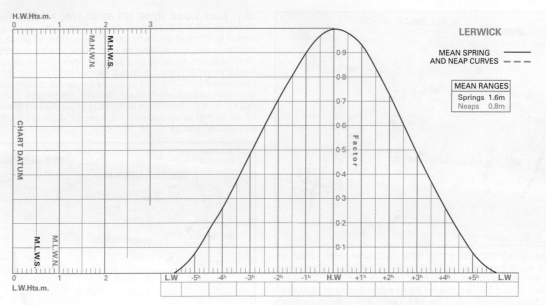

LERWICK

MEAN SPRING AND NEAP CURVES

| MEAN RANGES |
| Springs 1·6m |
| Neaps 0·8m |

5.25 LERWICK

Shetland Is, Mainland **60°09'·26N 01°08'·42W** ✿✿✿◊◊✿✿

CHARTS AC 3283, 3272, 3271

TIDES −0001 Dover; ML 1·4; Duration 0620

Standard Port LERWICK (◄—)

Times				Height (metres)			
High Water		Low Water		MHWS	MHWN	MLWN	MLWS
0000	0600	0100	0800	2·1	1·7	0·9	0·5
1200	1800	1300	2000				
Differences FAIR ISLE							
−0006	−0015	−0031	−0037	+0·1	0·0	+0·1	+0·1
SUMBURGH (Grutness Voe)							
+0006	+0008	+0004	−0002	−0·3	−0·3	−0·2	−0·1
DURY VOE							
−0015	−0015	−0010	−0010	0·0	−0·1	0·0	−0·2
BURRA VOE (YELL SOUND)							
−0025	−0025	−0025	−0025	+0·2	+0·1	0·0	−0·1
BALTA SOUND							
−0040	−0045	−0040	−0045	+0·3	+0·2	+0·1	0·0
BLUEMULL SOUND							
−0135	−0135	−0155	−0155	+0·5	+0·2	0·0	0·0
SULLOM VOE							
−0135	−0125	−0135	−0120	0·0	0·0	−0·2	−0·2
HILLSWICK (URA FIRTH)							
−0220	−0220	−0200	−0200	−0·1	−0·1	−0·1	−0·1
SCALLOWAY							
−0150	−0150	−0150	−0150	−0·5	−0·4	−0·3	0·0
FOULA (23M West of Scalloway)							
−0140	−0140	−0130	−0130	−0·1	−0·1	0·0	0·0

SHELTER Good. HM allocates berths in Small Dock or Albert Dock. FVs occupy most alongside space. ⚓ prohib for about 2ca off the waterfront. Gremista marina in N hbr, is mainly for local boats, and is about 1M from the town.

NAVIGATION WPT 60°05'·97N 01°08'·62W, 010°/3·5M to Maryfield lt, in W sector. From S, Bressay Sound is clear of dangers. From N, WPT 60°11'·60N 01°07'·88W, 215°/1·34M to N ent Dir lt (Oc WRG 6s, 214°-W-216°). Beware Soldian Rk (dries), Nive Baa (0·6m), Green Holm (10m) and The Brethren (two rocks 2m and 1·5m).

LIGHTS AND MARKS Kirkabister Ness, Fl (2) 20s 18m 10M; Cro of Ham, Fl 3s 3M; Maryfield, Oc WRG 6s, 008°-W-013°; all on Bressay. Twageos Pt, L Fl 6s 8m 6M. Loofa Baa SCM lt bn, as on chartlet. 2 SHM lt buoys mark Middle Ground in N Hbr.

COMMUNICATIONS (Code 01595) MRCC 692976; ⚓ 692239; Police 692110; Dr 693201. HM 692991.

Lerwick Harbour VHF Ch **12** 16 (H24) for Vessel Information Service. Other stns: *Sullom Voe Hbr Radio* broadcasts traffic info and local forecasts on request Ch **14** 12 20 16 (H24).

FACILITIES Hbr ⚓, M, P, D, L, ⚓, ⚒, ✗, Gas.
Lerwick Port Authority ☎ 692991, ⓥ pontoons £0.60, ⓓ, M, ⚓, D, P, ♿ ramps/toilet.
Lerwick Boating Club ☎ 692407, L, C, ⌂, ▣; **Services:** ⚒, ⌂, Ⓔ, ✗, ⚓, BY, ⛽, △, Gas, ACA.
Town ⌂, ✗, ⌂, ✉, Ⓑ, @, **Ferries:** Aberdeen via Kirkwall; daily; overnight; North Link (www.northlinkferries.co.uk), ✈. See www.shetlandtimes.co.uk and www.lerwickboating.co.uk.

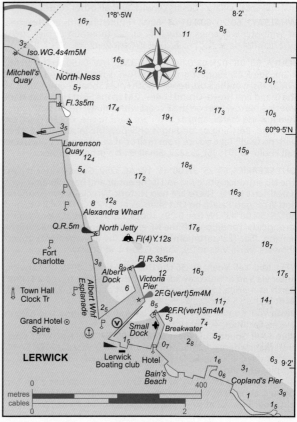

NE Scotland

STANDARD TIME (UT)
For Summer Time add ONE hour in **non-shaded areas**

LERWICK LAT 60°09'N LONG 1°08'W

TIMES AND HEIGHTS OF HIGH AND LOW WATERS

Dates in red are **SPRINGS**
Dates in blue are **NEAPS**

YEAR **2015**

JANUARY

Day	Time	m		Day	Time	m
1 TH	0140 / 0751 / 1408 / 2016	0.8 / 2.0 / 0.9 / 2.0		16 F	0053 / 0702 / 1330 / 1934	1.0 / 1.8 / 1.0 / 1.8
2 F	0234 / 0847 / 1502 / 2114	0.8 / 2.0 / 0.8 / 2.0		17 SA	0151 / 0804 / 1425 / 2034	0.9 / 1.9 / 0.9 / 1.9
3 SA	0321 / 0936 / 1548 / 2204	0.8 / 2.1 / 0.7 / 2.1		18 SU	0243 / 0855 / 1515 / 2127	0.8 / 2.1 / 0.7 / 2.1
4 SU	0402 / 1020 / 1629 / 2248	0.8 / 2.2 / 0.6 / 2.1		19 M	0331 / 0943 / 1602 / 2217	0.7 / 2.2 / 0.6 / 2.2
5 M ○	0441 / 1100 / 1708 / 2327	0.8 / 2.3 / 0.6 / 2.1		20 TU ●	0417 / 1030 / 1647 / 2306	0.6 / 2.3 / 0.4 / 2.2
6 TU	0517 / 1136 / 1745	0.8 / 2.3 / 0.6		21 W	0502 / 1116 / 1731 / 2355	0.5 / 2.4 / 0.3 / 2.3
7 W	0004 / 0552 / 1212 / 1821	2.1 / 0.8 / 2.3 / 0.6		22 TH	0545 / 1202 / 1816	0.5 / 2.4 / 0.2
8 TH	0039 / 0625 / 1246 / 1855	2.1 / 0.8 / 2.2 / 0.6		23 F	0043 / 0629 / 1249 / 1901	2.3 / 0.5 / 2.4 / 0.3
9 F	0113 / 0657 / 1319 / 1930	2.0 / 0.8 / 2.2 / 0.7		24 SA	0131 / 0713 / 1336 / 1947	2.2 / 0.6 / 2.4 / 0.4
10 SA	0147 / 0730 / 1353 / 2006	1.9 / 0.9 / 2.1 / 0.7		25 SU	0218 / 0759 / 1425 / 2036	2.1 / 0.6 / 2.3 / 0.5
11 SU	0223 / 0805 / 1430 / 2046	1.9 / 1.0 / 2.0 / 0.8		26 M	0306 / 0849 / 1516 / 2130	2.0 / 0.8 / 2.1 / 0.7
12 M	0303 / 0846 / 1513 / 2133	1.8 / 1.0 / 1.9 / 0.9		27 TU ☽	0359 / 0948 / 1614 / 2237	1.9 / 0.9 / 2.0 / 0.8
13 TU ☽	0350 / 0938 / 1604 / 2232	1.8 / 1.0 / 1.8 / 1.0		28 W	0500 / 1109 / 1724	1.8 / 1.0 / 1.9
14 W	0444 / 1053 / 1704 / 2345	1.7 / 1.1 / 1.8 / 1.0		29 TH	0004 / 0613 / 1244 / 1847	0.9 / 1.8 / 0.9 / 1.8
15 TH	0548 / 1224 / 1817	1.7 / 1.1 / 1.8		30 F	0121 / 0727 / 1356 / 2003	0.9 / 1.8 / 0.9 / 1.8
				31 SA	0221 / 0830 / 1453 / 2104	0.9 / 1.9 / 0.8 / 1.9

FEBRUARY

Day	Time	m		Day	Time	m
1 SU	0310 / 0922 / 1539 / 2152	0.9 / 2.0 / 0.7 / 1.9		16 M	0223 / 0831 / 1456 / 2110	0.8 / 1.9 / 0.6 / 2.0
2 M	0351 / 1005 / 1618 / 2233	0.8 / 2.1 / 0.6 / 2.0		17 TU	0315 / 0924 / 1545 / 2201	0.7 / 2.1 / 0.5 / 2.1
3 TU ○	0427 / 1044 / 1654 / 2309	0.8 / 2.2 / 0.6 / 2.0		18 W ●	0401 / 1013 / 1630 / 2251	0.6 / 2.3 / 0.4 / 2.2
4 W	0500 / 1119 / 1726 / 2343	0.7 / 2.2 / 0.5 / 2.0		19 TH	0445 / 1100 / 1714 / 2338	0.4 / 2.4 / 0.2 / 2.3
5 TH	0532 / 1152 / 1758	0.7 / 2.2 / 0.5		20 F	0528 / 1146 / 1757	0.4 / 2.4 / 0.1
6 F	0015 / 0602 / 1224 / 1828	2.0 / 0.7 / 2.2 / 0.5		21 SA	0023 / 0610 / 1232 / 1840	2.3 / 0.3 / 2.4 / 0.2
7 SA	0046 / 0631 / 1253 / 1900	2.0 / 0.7 / 2.1 / 0.6		22 SU	0108 / 0653 / 1318 / 1924	2.2 / 0.4 / 2.4 / 0.3
8 SU	0116 / 0702 / 1323 / 1932	2.0 / 0.7 / 2.1 / 0.6		23 M	0152 / 0738 / 1404 / 2009	2.1 / 0.5 / 2.2 / 0.5
9 M	0147 / 0734 / 1357 / 2007	1.9 / 0.8 / 2.0 / 0.7		24 TU	0237 / 0826 / 1454 / 2059	2.0 / 0.6 / 2.1 / 0.7
10 TU	0222 / 0811 / 1435 / 2047	1.9 / 0.9 / 1.9 / 0.8		25 W ☽	0325 / 0921 / 1548 / 2158	1.9 / 0.8 / 1.9 / 0.9
11 W	0305 / 0855 / 1523 / 2135	1.8 / 0.9 / 1.8 / 0.9		26 TH	0421 / 1039 / 1656	1.8 / 0.9 / 1.7
12 TH ☽	0356 / 0952 / 1621 / 2239	1.7 / 1.0 / 1.7 / 1.0		27 F	0534 / 1221 / 1825	1.7 / 0.9 / 1.6
13 F	0457 / 1119 / 1732	1.7 / 1.0 / 1.7		28 SA	0057 / 0659 / 1338 / 1947	1.0 / 1.7 / 0.8 / 1.7
14 SA	0008 / 0610 / 1255 / 1858	1.0 / 1.7 / 1.0 / 1.7				
15 SU	0123 / 0729 / 1401 / 2012	0.9 / 1.8 / 0.8 / 1.8				

MARCH

Day	Time	m		Day	Time	m
1 SU	0204 / 0807 / 1436 / 2047	1.0 / 1.8 / 0.8 / 1.7		16 M	0057 / 0656 / 1337 / 1952	0.9 / 1.7 / 0.7 / 1.8
2 M	0253 / 0900 / 1521 / 2132	0.9 / 1.9 / 0.7 / 1.8		17 TU	0203 / 0807 / 1435 / 2051	0.8 / 1.9 / 0.5 / 1.9
3 TU	0333 / 0943 / 1557 / 2210	0.8 / 2.0 / 0.6 / 1.9		18 W	0255 / 0902 / 1524 / 2142	0.6 / 2.0 / 0.3 / 2.0
4 W	0408 / 1021 / 1630 / 2245	0.7 / 2.1 / 0.5 / 2.0		19 TH	0342 / 0952 / 1610 / 2230	0.5 / 2.2 / 0.2 / 2.2
5 TH ○	0439 / 1056 / 1700 / 2317	0.6 / 2.1 / 0.5 / 2.0		20 F ●	0425 / 1040 / 1653 / 2316	0.3 / 2.3 / 0.1 / 2.2
6 F	0508 / 1128 / 1730 / 2347	0.6 / 2.1 / 0.4 / 2.0		21 SA	0508 / 1127 / 1735	0.3 / 2.4 / 0.1
7 SA	0537 / 1158 / 1759	0.6 / 2.1 / 0.4		22 SU	0000 / 0550 / 1213 / 1817	2.2 / 0.2 / 2.4 / 0.1
8 SU	0016 / 0606 / 1227 / 1829	2.0 / 0.6 / 2.1 / 0.5		23 M	0043 / 0633 / 1258 / 1900	2.2 / 0.3 / 2.3 / 0.3
9 M	0044 / 0636 / 1256 / 1901	2.0 / 0.6 / 2.0 / 0.5		24 TU	0124 / 0717 / 1344 / 1943	2.1 / 0.4 / 2.1 / 0.5
10 TU	0113 / 0709 / 1329 / 1935	1.9 / 0.6 / 2.0 / 0.6		25 W	0207 / 0805 / 1433 / 2030	2.0 / 0.5 / 2.0 / 0.7
11 W	0147 / 0746 / 1406 / 2013	1.9 / 0.7 / 1.9 / 0.7		26 TH	0252 / 0859 / 1525 / 2124	1.9 / 0.6 / 1.8 / 0.9
12 TH	0227 / 0829 / 1453 / 2059	1.8 / 0.8 / 1.8 / 0.8		27 F ☽	0344 / 1012 / 1628 / 2245	1.7 / 0.8 / 1.6 / 1.0
13 F ☽	0315 / 0923 / 1552 / 2157	1.7 / 0.9 / 1.7 / 0.9		28 SA	0450 / 1147 / 1754	1.6 / 0.8 / 1.5
14 SA	0417 / 1038 / 1704 / 2325	1.7 / 0.9 / 1.6 / 1.0		29 SU	0023 / 0620 / 1307 / 1918	1.0 / 1.6 / 0.8 / 1.6
15 SU	0530 / 1222 / 1833	1.7 / 0.8 / 1.6		30 M	0135 / 0734 / 1407 / 2017	1.0 / 1.7 / 0.7 / 1.6
				31 TU	0228 / 0828 / 1452 / 2101	0.9 / 1.8 / 0.6 / 1.7

APRIL

Day	Time	m		Day	Time	m
1 W	0308 / 0913 / 1528 / 2139	0.8 / 1.8 / 0.6 / 1.8		16 TH	0233 / 0839 / 1501 / 2120	0.6 / 2.0 / 0.3 / 2.0
2 TH	0342 / 0951 / 1600 / 2213	0.7 / 1.9 / 0.5 / 1.9		17 F	0320 / 0930 / 1547 / 2207	0.4 / 2.1 / 0.2 / 2.1
3 F	0412 / 1027 / 1630 / 2246	0.6 / 2.0 / 0.4 / 1.9		18 SA ●	0405 / 1019 / 1631 / 2252	0.3 / 2.2 / 0.1 / 2.2
4 SA ○	0442 / 1059 / 1659 / 2316	0.5 / 2.0 / 0.4 / 2.0		19 SU	0448 / 1107 / 1713 / 2335	0.2 / 2.2 / 0.1 / 2.2
5 SU	0511 / 1131 / 1729 / 2345	0.5 / 2.0 / 0.4 / 2.0		20 M	0531 / 1154 / 1755	0.2 / 2.2 / 0.2
6 M	0542 / 1201 / 1801	0.5 / 2.0 / 0.4		21 TU	0017 / 0615 / 1240 / 1836	2.1 / 0.2 / 2.1 / 0.4
7 TU	0014 / 0614 / 1233 / 1833	2.0 / 0.5 / 2.0 / 0.5		22 W	0058 / 0659 / 1326 / 1919	2.1 / 0.3 / 2.0 / 0.5
8 W	0045 / 0649 / 1307 / 1909	2.0 / 0.5 / 1.9 / 0.6		23 TH	0140 / 0747 / 1413 / 2004	2.0 / 0.4 / 1.9 / 0.7
9 TH	0119 / 0728 / 1347 / 1948	1.9 / 0.6 / 1.9 / 0.7		24 F	0224 / 0839 / 1503 / 2055	1.9 / 0.6 / 1.7 / 0.9
10 F	0159 / 0813 / 1435 / 2035	1.9 / 0.6 / 1.8 / 0.8		25 SA ☽	0312 / 0943 / 1558 / 2201	1.7 / 0.7 / 1.6 / 1.0
11 SA	0247 / 0908 / 1536 / 2134	1.8 / 0.7 / 1.7 / 0.9		26 SU	0408 / 1100 / 1709 / 2329	1.6 / 0.7 / 1.5 / 1.0
12 SU ☽	0348 / 1018 / 1648 / 2256	1.7 / 0.7 / 1.6 / 0.9		27 M	0525 / 1216 / 1831	1.6 / 0.7 / 1.5
13 M	0502 / 1153 / 1812	1.6 / 0.7 / 1.6		28 TU	0049 / 0648 / 1321 / 1933	1.0 / 1.6 / 0.7 / 1.6
14 TU	0031 / 0626 / 1310 / 1930	0.9 / 1.7 / 0.6 / 1.7		29 W	0149 / 0747 / 1410 / 2021	0.9 / 1.6 / 0.7 / 1.6
15 W	0139 / 0741 / 1410 / 2029	0.7 / 1.8 / 0.4 / 1.9		30 TH	0234 / 0835 / 1449 / 2101	0.8 / 1.7 / 0.6 / 1.7

Chart Datum: 1·22 metres below Ordnance Datum (Local). HAT is 2·5 metres above Chart Datum.

STANDARD TIME (UT)
For Summer Time add ONE hour in **non-shaded areas**

LERWICK   LAT 60°09'N   LONG 1°08'W
TIMES AND HEIGHTS OF HIGH AND LOW WATERS

Dates in red are **SPRINGS**
Dates in blue are **NEAPS**

YEAR 2015

MAY

Time	m		Time	m
1 0309	0.7	**16**	0259	0.5
0916	1.8		0910	2.0
F 1523	0.5		SA 1525	0.3
2138	1.8		2144	2.0
2 0342	0.6	**17**	0346	0.3
0953	1.9		1001	2.1
SA 1555	0.5		SU 1610	0.3
2211	1.9		2229	2.1
3 0413	0.5	**18**	0431	0.3
1029	1.9		1051	2.1
SU 1628	0.4		M 1652	0.3
2244	2.0		● 2313	2.1
4 0446	0.5	**19**	0515	0.2
1103	2.0		1138	2.1
M 1701	0.4		TU 1735	0.4
○ 2316	2.0		2355	2.1
5 0520	0.4	**20**	0559	0.3
1138	2.0		1224	2.0
TU 1735	0.4		W 1816	0.5
2348	2.0			
6 0555	0.4	**21**	0036	2.1
1214	1.9		0643	0.3
W 1811	0.5		TH 1309	1.9
			1858	0.6
7 0023	2.0	**22**	0117	2.0
0633	0.4		0729	0.4
TH 1253	1.9		F 1353	1.8
1849	0.5		1941	0.7
8 0100	2.0	**23**	0159	1.9
0715	0.4		0817	0.5
F 1337	1.8		SA 1438	1.7
1932	0.6		2026	0.8
9 0142	1.9	**24**	0244	1.8
0803	0.5		0909	0.6
SA 1428	1.8		SU 1525	1.6
2021	0.7		2118	0.9
10 0232	1.8	**25**	0332	1.7
0858	0.5		1008	0.7
SU 1528	1.7		M 1619	1.5
2120	0.8		☽ 2225	1.0
11 0332	1.7	**26**	0427	1.6
1004	0.6		1113	0.7
M 1635	1.6		TU 1725	1.5
☾ 2233	0.8		2341	1.0
12 0442	1.7	**27**	0541	1.6
1125	0.6		1216	0.7
TU 1751	1.6		W 1838	1.5
13 0000	0.8	**28**	0050	0.9
0600	1.7		0656	1.6
W 1242	0.5		TH 1313	0.7
1904	1.7		1934	1.6
14 0111	0.7	**29**	0145	0.8
0714	1.8		0752	1.6
TH 1345	0.4		F 1400	0.7
2004	1.8		2019	1.7
15 0209	0.6	**30**	0229	0.8
0815	1.9		0838	1.7
F 1438	0.4		SA 1442	0.6
2056	1.9		2059	1.8
		31	0308	0.7
			0919	1.8
			SU 1520	0.6
			2137	1.9

JUNE

Time	m		Time	m
1 0345	0.6	**16**	0418	0.4
0959	1.9		1039	2.0
M 1558	0.5		TU 1636	0.5
2213	2.0		● 2256	2.1
2 0422	0.5	**17**	0503	0.3
1038	1.9		1126	2.0
TU 1636	0.5		W 1718	0.5
○ 2250	2.0		2338	2.1
3 0500	0.4	**18**	0546	0.3
1118	2.0		1210	2.0
W 1714	0.5		TH 1758	0.6
2328	2.1			
4 0540	0.4	**19**	0018	2.1
1200	2.0		0627	0.4
TH 1754	0.5		F 1251	1.9
			1837	0.6
5 0007	2.1	**20**	0057	2.0
0621	0.3		0709	0.4
F 1244	1.9		SA 1331	1.9
1836	0.5		1916	0.7
6 0048	2.0	**21**	0136	2.0
0705	0.4		0750	0.5
SA 1332	1.9		SU 1410	1.8
1921	0.6		1955	0.8
7 0133	2.0	**22**	0215	1.9
0754	0.4		0833	0.6
SU 1423	1.8		M 1450	1.7
2010	0.7		2036	0.8
8 0224	1.9	**23**	0257	1.8
0847	0.4		0919	0.7
M 1519	1.8		TU 1533	1.6
2105	0.7		2124	0.9
9 0321	1.9	**24**	0342	1.7
0947	0.5		1012	0.7
TU 1619	1.7		W 1622	1.6
☽ 2208	0.8		☾ 2228	1.0
10 0425	1.8	**25**	0434	1.6
1058	0.5		1113	0.8
W 1725	1.7		TH 1720	1.6
2326	0.8		2344	1.0
11 0535	1.8	**26**	0538	1.6
1213	0.5		1215	0.8
TH 1835	1.7		F 1831	1.6
12 0043	0.7	**27**	0050	0.9
0649	1.8		0656	1.6
F 1320	0.5		SA 1312	0.8
1937	1.8		1932	1.7
13 0147	0.7	**28**	0147	0.9
0755	1.9		0756	1.7
SA 1417	0.5		SU 1402	0.7
2033	1.9		2020	1.8
14 0243	0.6	**29**	0235	0.8
0854	1.9		0845	1.8
SU 1507	0.5		M 1449	0.7
2124	2.0		2104	1.9
15 0332	0.6	**30**	0319	0.6
0948	2.0		0931	1.8
M 1553	0.5		TU 1532	0.6
2211	2.0		2146	2.0

JULY

Time	m		Time	m
1 0401	0.5	**16**	0451	0.4
1016	1.9		1113	2.0
W 1615	0.6		TH 1703	0.6
2228	2.1		● 2322	2.1
2 0443	0.4	**17**	0530	0.4
1101	2.0		1152	2.0
TH 1657	0.5		F 1740	0.6
○ 2311	2.1			
3 0526	0.3	**18**	0000	2.1
1147	2.0		0607	0.4
F 1740	0.5		SA 1229	2.0
2354	2.2		1815	0.6
4 0609	0.3	**19**	0036	2.1
1234	2.1		0644	0.4
SA 1823	0.5		SU 1304	1.9
			1849	0.7
5 0038	2.2	**20**	0111	2.0
0654	0.3		0719	0.5
SU 1322	2.0		M 1339	1.9
1908	0.5		1923	0.7
6 0125	2.1	**21**	0145	2.0
0740	0.3		0755	0.6
M 1411	2.0		TU 1413	1.8
1955	0.6		1957	0.8
7 0214	2.1	**22**	0221	1.9
0830	0.4		0833	0.7
TU 1502	1.9		W 1451	1.7
2045	0.7		2036	0.9
8 0307	2.0	**23**	0301	1.8
0925	0.5		0916	0.7
W 1556	1.8		TH 1533	1.7
☽ 2143	0.7		2124	0.9
9 0406	1.9	**24**	0348	1.7
1028	0.6		1009	0.8
TH 1657	1.7		F 1623	1.6
2254	0.8		☾ 2230	1.0
10 0512	1.8	**25**	0443	1.7
1145	0.7		1118	0.9
F 1805	1.7		SA 1721	1.6
			2359	1.0
11 0018	0.8	**26**	0550	1.6
0627	1.8		1228	0.9
SA 1300	0.7		SU 1832	1.7
1913	1.8			
12 0132	0.7	**27**	0108	0.9
0739	1.8		0711	1.7
SU 1402	0.7		M 1328	0.8
2014	1.9		1940	1.8
13 0232	0.6	**28**	0205	0.8
0844	1.8		0815	1.7
M 1455	0.7		TU 1422	0.8
2109	1.9		2034	1.9
14 0324	0.6	**29**	0256	0.7
0941	1.9		0908	1.9
TU 1542	0.7		W 1511	0.7
2158	2.0		2122	2.0
15 0409	0.5	**30**	0342	0.5
1030	1.9		0957	2.0
W 1624	0.6		TH 1557	0.6
2242	2.1		2208	2.1
		31	0426	0.4
			1044	2.1
			F 1641	0.5
			○ 2254	2.2

AUGUST

Time	m		Time	m
1 0510	0.3	**16**	0543	0.4
1132	2.2		1202	2.0
SA 1724	0.4		SU 1750	0.6
2339	2.3			
2 0553	0.2	**17**	0011	2.2
1219	2.2		0615	0.5
SU 1807	0.4		M 1234	2.0
			1821	0.6
3 0024	2.3	**18**	0042	2.1
0637	0.2		0647	0.5
M 1305	2.1		TU 1305	2.0
1850	0.4		1851	0.7
4 0111	2.3	**19**	0113	2.1
0722	0.2		0719	0.6
TU 1352	2.1		W 1336	1.9
1935	0.5		1923	0.7
5 0158	2.2	**20**	0146	2.0
0809	0.3		0753	0.7
W 1440	2.0		TH 1410	1.9
2023	0.6		1959	0.8
6 0249	2.1	**21**	0223	1.9
0859	0.5		0831	0.8
TH 1530	1.9		F 1449	1.8
2118	0.7		2042	0.9
7 0345	2.0	**22**	0308	1.8
0959	0.7		0917	0.9
F 1627	1.8		SA 1537	1.7
☽ 2227	0.8		☾ 2136	1.0
8 0449	1.8	**23**	0403	1.7
1118	0.8		1016	1.0
SA 1734	1.8		SU 1634	1.7
			2258	1.0
9 0002	0.8	**24**	0508	1.7
0608	1.8		1143	1.0
SU 1243	0.9		M 1741	1.7
1850	1.8			
10 0122	0.8	**25**	0033	1.0
0730	1.7		0630	1.7
M 1351	0.9		TU 1259	0.9
1959	1.8		1900	1.8
11 0225	0.7	**26**	0139	0.9
0837	1.8		0749	1.8
TU 1445	0.8		W 1359	0.9
2056	1.9		2006	1.9
12 0316	0.6	**27**	0234	0.7
0931	1.9		0847	1.9
W 1530	0.8		TH 1451	0.7
2144	2.0		2059	2.0
13 0358	0.5	**28**	0322	0.5
1015	1.9		0937	2.0
TH 1609	0.7		F 1538	0.6
2226	2.1		2148	2.2
14 0435	0.5	**29**	0407	0.3
1054	2.0		1025	2.2
F 1645	0.7		SA 1622	0.5
● 2303	2.2		○ 2234	2.3
15 0510	0.4	**30**	0450	0.2
1129	2.0		1112	2.2
SA 1718	0.6		SU 1705	0.5
2338	2.2		2320	2.4
		31	0533	0.1
			1158	2.3
			M 1747	0.4

Chart Datum: 1·22 metres below Ordnance Datum (Local). HAT is 2·5 metres above Chart Datum.

》 **FREE** monthly updates from 《
www.reedsalmanac.co.uk

STANDARD TIME (UT)
For Summer Time add ONE hour in **non-shaded areas**

LERWICK LAT 60°09'N LONG 1°08'W
TIMES AND HEIGHTS OF HIGH AND LOW WATERS

Dates in red are SPRINGS
Dates in blue are NEAPS

YEAR 2015

SEPTEMBER

Time	m	Time	m
1 0005 2.4 / 0616 0.1 / TU 1243 2.2 / 1830 0.4		**16** 0013 2.2 / 0614 0.5 / W 1231 2.1 / 1823 0.7	
2 0052 2.4 / 0659 0.2 / W 1328 2.2 / 1914 0.4		**17** 0043 2.1 / 0645 0.6 / TH 1300 2.0 / 1855 0.7	
3 0139 2.3 / 0745 0.4 / TH 1413 2.1 / 2002 0.6		**18** 0115 2.0 / 0719 0.7 / F 1332 2.0 / 1931 0.8	
4 0229 2.1 / 0833 0.6 / F 1502 2.0 / 2056 0.7		**19** 0151 2.0 / 0755 0.8 / SA 1410 1.9 / 2013 0.9	
5 0325 2.0 / 0929 0.8 / SA 1556 1.9 / ☽ 2206 0.8		**20** 0236 1.9 / 0839 0.9 / SU 1457 1.8 / 2105 0.9	
6 0429 1.8 / 1050 1.0 / SU 1703 1.8 / 2348 0.9		**21** 0332 1.8 / 0934 1.0 / M 1555 1.8 / ☾ 2216 1.0	
7 0552 1.7 / 1226 1.0 / M 1827 1.8		**22** 0440 1.7 / 1056 1.1 / TU 1704 1.7	
8 0109 0.8 / 0719 1.7 / TU 1336 1.0 / 1940 1.8		**23** 0000 1.0 / 0601 1.7 / W 1232 1.0 / 1824 1.8	
9 0212 0.8 / 0824 1.8 / W 1430 0.9 / 2037 1.9		**24** 0113 0.8 / 0725 1.8 / TH 1337 0.9 / 1939 1.9	
10 0300 0.7 / 0913 1.9 / TH 1513 0.8 / 2123 2.0		**25** 0210 0.7 / 0825 1.9 / F 1430 0.8 / 2036 2.1	
11 0339 0.6 / 0953 1.9 / F 1550 0.8 / 2203 2.1		**26** 0300 0.5 / 0916 2.1 / SA 1517 0.6 / 2125 2.2	
12 0413 0.5 / 1029 2.0 / SA 1623 0.7 / 2239 2.2		**27** 0345 0.3 / 1003 2.2 / SU 1601 0.5 / 2212 2.4	
13 0445 0.5 / 1102 2.1 / SU 1654 0.6 / ● 2312 2.2		**28** 0428 0.2 / 1049 2.3 / M 1644 0.4 / ○ 2259 2.5	
14 0515 0.5 / 1133 2.1 / M 1723 0.6 / 2343 2.2		**29** 0511 0.2 / 1133 2.3 / TU 1727 0.3 / 2345 2.5	
15 0545 0.5 / 1202 2.1 / TU 1753 0.6		**30** 0554 0.2 / 1217 2.3 / W 1810 0.4	

OCTOBER

Time	m	Time	m
1 0032 2.4 / 0636 0.3 / TH 1301 2.3 / 1855 0.4		**16** 0017 2.1 / 0616 0.6 / F 1230 2.1 / 1832 0.7	
2 0120 2.3 / 0721 0.5 / F 1346 2.2 / 1943 0.6		**17** 0051 2.1 / 0650 0.7 / SA 1303 2.1 / 1910 0.7	
3 0211 2.1 / 0808 0.7 / SA 1433 2.0 / 2037 0.7		**18** 0129 2.0 / 0728 0.8 / SU 1341 2.0 / 1953 0.8	
4 0305 2.0 / 0902 0.9 / SU 1526 1.9 / ☽ 2147 0.8		**19** 0214 1.9 / 0812 0.9 / M 1426 1.9 / 2045 0.9	
5 0408 1.8 / 1018 1.1 / M 1630 1.8 / 2323 0.9		**20** 0311 1.8 / 0907 1.0 / TU 1524 1.9 / ☾ 2151 0.9	
6 0528 1.7 / 1157 1.1 / TU 1754 1.8		**21** 0419 1.7 / 1022 1.1 / W 1634 1.8 / 2324 1.1	
7 0044 0.9 / 0655 1.7 / W 1311 1.1 / 1911 1.8		**22** 0538 1.7 / 1201 1.1 / TH 1753 1.8	
8 0146 0.8 / 0758 1.8 / TH 1407 1.0 / 2008 1.9		**23** 0044 0.8 / 0659 1.8 / F 1311 1.0 / 1910 1.9	
9 0234 0.7 / 0844 1.9 / F 1450 0.9 / 2054 2.0		**24** 0144 0.7 / 0801 2.0 / SA 1406 0.8 / 2010 2.1	
10 0312 0.7 / 0923 2.0 / SA 1526 0.8 / 2134 2.1		**25** 0235 0.5 / 0852 2.1 / SU 1455 0.7 / 2102 2.2	
11 0345 0.6 / 0958 2.0 / SU 1558 0.7 / 2210 2.1		**26** 0322 0.4 / 0940 2.3 / M 1540 0.5 / 2151 2.4	
12 0415 0.6 / 1030 2.1 / M 1627 0.7 / 2244 2.2		**27** 0406 0.3 / 1025 2.3 / TU 1624 0.4 / ○ 2239 2.4	
13 0445 0.6 / 1101 2.1 / TU 1657 0.6 / ● 2315 2.2		**28** 0449 0.3 / 1109 2.4 / W 1708 0.4 / 2327 2.4	
14 0514 0.6 / 1131 2.1 / W 1727 0.6 / 2346 2.2		**29** 0532 0.4 / 1153 2.4 / TH 1752 0.4	
15 0545 0.6 / 1200 2.1 / TH 1759 0.7		**30** 0015 2.4 / 0615 0.5 / F 1237 2.3 / 1838 0.4	
		31 0104 2.3 / 0659 0.7 / SA 1321 2.2 / 1926 0.6	

NOVEMBER

Time	m	Time	m
1 0154 2.1 / 0745 0.8 / SU 1407 2.1 / 2019 0.7		**16** 0115 2.0 / 0709 0.8 / M 1321 2.1 / 1940 0.7	
2 0245 2.0 / 0836 1.0 / M 1457 2.0 / 2122 0.8		**17** 0202 2.0 / 0755 0.9 / TU 1407 2.0 / 2031 0.8	
3 0342 1.8 / 0940 1.1 / TU 1555 1.9 / ☽ 2241 0.9		**18** 0259 1.9 / 0849 1.0 / W 1503 2.0 / 2132 0.8	
4 0449 1.7 / 1107 1.2 / W 1707 1.8		**19** 0403 1.7 / 0955 1.1 / TH 1610 1.9 / ☾ 2248 0.8	
5 0000 0.9 / 0610 1.7 / TH 1229 1.2 / 1828 1.8		**20** 0514 1.8 / 1120 1.1 / F 1723 1.9	
6 0106 0.9 / 0716 1.8 / F 1332 1.1 / 1930 1.9		**21** 0010 0.8 / 0629 1.9 / SA 1239 1.0 / 1839 2.0	
7 0158 0.8 / 0806 1.8 / SA 1419 1.0 / 2019 1.9		**22** 0116 0.7 / 0734 2.0 / SU 1341 0.9 / 1945 2.1	
8 0238 0.8 / 0847 1.9 / SU 1457 0.9 / 2101 2.0		**23** 0211 0.6 / 0828 2.1 / M 1433 0.7 / 2041 2.2	
9 0312 0.7 / 0924 2.0 / M 1530 0.8 / 2139 2.1		**24** 0301 0.5 / 0917 2.2 / TU 1522 0.6 / 2133 2.3	
10 0343 0.7 / 0958 2.1 / TU 1601 0.8 / 2215 2.1		**25** 0346 0.5 / 1004 2.3 / W 1608 0.5 / ○ 2224 2.3	
11 0414 0.7 / 1031 2.2 / W 1633 0.7 / ● 2249 2.2		**26** 0430 0.5 / 1049 2.4 / TH 1653 0.4 / 2314 2.4	
12 0446 0.6 / 1102 2.2 / TH 1705 0.7 / 2323 2.2		**27** 0514 0.5 / 1133 2.4 / F 1738 0.4	
13 0519 0.7 / 1134 2.2 / F 1739 0.7 / 2358 2.1		**28** 0002 2.3 / 0556 0.6 / SA 1217 2.3 / 1824 0.5	
14 0554 0.7 / 1206 2.2 / SA 1816 0.7		**29** 0050 2.2 / 0640 0.7 / SU 1301 2.3 / 1910 0.6	
15 0034 2.1 / 0629 0.8 / SU 1242 2.2 / 1855 0.7		**30** 0136 2.1 / 0723 0.9 / M 1344 2.2 / 1959 0.7	

DECEMBER

Time	m	Time	m
1 0223 2.0 / 0809 1.0 / TU 1430 2.1 / 2051 0.8		**16** 0154 2.0 / 0742 0.8 / W 1355 2.2 / 2018 0.7	
2 0311 1.9 / 0900 1.1 / W 1519 2.0 / 2150 0.9		**17** 0246 2.0 / 0832 0.9 / TH 1448 2.1 / 2113 0.7	
3 0403 1.8 / 1003 1.2 / TH 1614 1.9 / ☽ 2256 0.9		**18** 0344 1.9 / 0930 1.0 / F 1548 2.0 / ☽ 2217 0.8	
4 0507 1.7 / 1120 1.2 / F 1723 1.8		**19** 0447 1.9 / 1040 1.0 / SA 1655 2.0 / 2334 0.8	
5 0004 1.0 / 0620 1.7 / SA 1236 1.2 / 1839 1.8		**20** 0557 1.9 / 1203 1.0 / SU 1810 2.0	
6 0105 0.9 / 0720 1.8 / SU 1337 1.1 / 1938 1.9		**21** 0047 0.8 / 0706 1.9 / M 1316 0.9 / 1922 2.0	
7 0154 0.9 / 0808 1.9 / M 1423 1.0 / 2026 1.9		**22** 0150 0.7 / 0806 2.0 / TU 1416 0.8 / 2025 2.1	
8 0234 0.9 / 0849 2.0 / TU 1501 0.9 / 2108 2.0		**23** 0244 0.7 / 0859 2.1 / W 1509 0.7 / 2122 2.2	
9 0311 0.8 / 0927 2.1 / W 1536 0.8 / 2148 2.1		**24** 0332 0.7 / 0949 2.2 / TH 1557 0.6 / 2216 2.2	
10 0347 0.8 / 1003 2.2 / TH 1611 0.8 / 2226 2.1		**25** 0417 0.6 / 1036 2.3 / F 1643 0.5 / ○ 2306 2.2	
11 0422 0.7 / 1038 2.2 / F 1647 0.7 / ● 2304 2.1		**26** 0500 0.7 / 1120 2.3 / SA 1727 0.5 / 2352 2.2	
12 0459 0.7 / 1113 2.3 / SA 1724 0.7 / 2343 2.2		**27** 0541 0.7 / 1202 2.3 / SU 1811 0.5	
13 0536 0.7 / 1150 2.3 / SU 1803 0.6		**28** 0035 2.2 / 0621 0.7 / M 1243 2.3 / 1852 0.6	
14 0023 2.1 / 0615 0.7 / M 1229 2.3 / 1844 0.6		**29** 0116 2.1 / 0701 0.8 / TU 1323 2.2 / 1935 0.6	
15 0107 2.1 / 0657 0.8 / TU 1310 2.2 / 1929 0.6		**30** 0156 2.0 / 0740 0.9 / W 1402 2.1 / 2017 0.7	
		31 0236 1.9 / 0820 1.0 / TH 1443 2.0 / 2101 0.8	

Chart Datum: 1·22 metres below Ordnance Datum (Local). HAT is 2·5 metres above Chart Datum.

>> **FREE** monthly updates from <<
www.reedsalmanac.co.uk

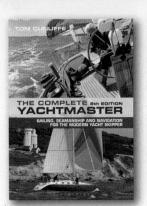

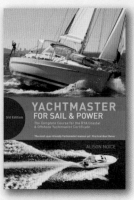
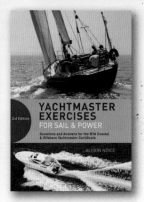
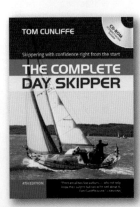

Moclett ... 223
Mònnickendam ... 108
Montrose ... 177, 190
Moray Firth ... 203, 213
Mouth ... 182
Muckle Flugga ... 202
Muckle Skerry ... 224
Muiden ... 108
Muiderzand ... 108

N

Naarden ... 108
Nairn ... 200, 208
Nes (Ameland) ... 92, 102, 105
Ness ... 200
Netherlands ... 14
  Coastguard (IJmuiden) ... 14
  Special notes ... 96
  Weather forecasts ... 14
Newarp ... 142
Newbiggin ... 167
Newburgh ... 189
Newcastle-upon-Tyne ... 163
New Hythe ... 48
Newton Haven ... 168
Nieuwe Waterweg ... 93, 118
Nieuwpoort ... 95, 137
Noodzeekanaal ... 110
Noordwijk-aan-Zee ... 93
Noordzeekanaal ... 93
Norfolk Broads ... 86
North Berwick ... 176, 179
North Fambridge ... 62
North Foreland ... 35
North Rona ... 200
North Ronaldsay ... 201
North Sea, crossing to UK from Netherlands ... 96
North Shields ... 163
North Sunderland (Seahouses) ... 143, 168
Noss Head ... 200
Noup Head ... 201

O

Oil and gas installations ... 144
Olna Firth ... 226
Oostende ... 95, 135
Oosterschelde ... 121
Oostmahoorn ... 102
Ore, River ... 80
Orford Ness ... 34, 68, 81
Orkney Islands ... 200, 222
Orwell, River ... 34, 75
Osea Island ... 66
Oudeschild ... 92, 105
Out Skerries ... 227

P

Paal ... 123
Papa Westray ... 223
Pegal ... 223
Pennan Bay ... 204
Pentland Firth ... 217
Perth ... 189
Peterhead ... 203
Pierowall ... 223, 225
Pittenweem ... 187
Point of Fethaland ... 202
Poplar Dock Marina ... 55
Port Edgar ... 181
Portknockie ... 205
Portmahomack ... 215
Portsoy ... 205

Q

Queenborough ... 46

R

Radio Telephony (R/T) ... 6
Ramsgate ... 36
Ramsholt ... 79
Rapness ... 223
Rattray Head ... 200
Relaxing radio silence ... 7
Richborough ... 38
Richmond Lock ... 52
Roach, River ... 61
Rochester ... 48
Rochford ... 61
Rona ... 221
Roompotsluis ... 121
Rosehearty ... 204
Rotterdam ... 118, 119
Rousay ... 223
Runswick Bay ... 156

S

Sanday ... 223
Sandend Bay ... 205
Sandwich ... 38
Satellite systems, GPS, DGPS, EGNOS ... 6
Scalloway ... 202, 227
Scapa Bay ... 201, 222
Scarborough ... 143, 155
Scheveningen ... 93, 112, 113
Schiermonnikoog ... 101, 102
Schulpengat ... 93
Scrabster ... 221
Seaham ... 143, 162
Seahouses (North Sunderland) ... 168
Sella Ness ... 202
Shapinsay ... 223
Sharfleet Creek ... 48
Sheerness ... 32
Shetland Islands ... 201, 225, 226
Shoeburyness ... 60
Skadan South ... 201
Skegness ... 147
Skeld ... 231
Skroo ... 201
South Dock Marina ... 55
Southend-on-Sea ... 32, 60
South Ferriby ... 153
South Ness ... 202
South Queensferry ... 182
South Ronaldsay ... 223
South Wick ... 223
Southwold ... 34, 81
Special notes
  Belgium ... 129
  Netherlands ... 96
Spurn Head ... 142, 148, 152
St Abb's ... 179
St Abb's Head ... 176
St Andrew's ... 189
Start Point (Orkney) ... 201
Stavoren ... 108
Stellendam ... 93
St Katharine Haven ... 55
St Monans ... 177, 182
Stonehaven ... 177, 191
Stour, River (Essex/Suffolk) ... 34, 74
Stour, River (Kent) ... 36
Strathy Point ... 200
Stroma ... 200, 221
Stromness ... 201, 224
Stronsay ... 225
Sule Skerry ... 200, 221
Sullom Voe ... 202, 226
Sumburgh ... 227
Sumburgh Head ... 201
Sunderland ... 143, 162
Sunk Head ... 66
Sunk Inner Precautionary Area ... 29
Swale, River ... 32, 45
Swarbacks Minn ... 226

T

Tabs Head ... 147
Tarbat Ness ... 200
Tay, River ... 189
Teddington Lock ... 52, 54
Tees, River ... 156
Termunterzijl ... 101
Terneuzen ... 128
Thames Estuary/River ... 32, 35, 37, 52
Thames Tidal Barrier ... 32, 54
Thurso ... 200
Tidal coefficients ... 20
Tidal streams
  Belgium and Netherlands ... 90
  England, E ... 30
  England, NE ... 140
  Scotland, NE ... 198
  Scotland, SE ... 174
  Thames Estuary ... 38
Tide tables
  Aberdeen ... 193
  Harwich ... 76
  Hoek van Holland ... 114
  Immingham ... 149
  Invergordon ... 210
  Leith ... 184
  Lerwick ... 228
  London Bridge ... 57
  Lowestoft ... 83
  Margate ... 40
  River Tees ... 158
  River Tyne ... 164
  Sheerness ... 47
  Vlissingen ... 125
  Walton-on-the-Naze ... 70
  Wick ... 218
  Zeebrugge ... 131, 132
Traffic Separation
  Botney Ground, off ... 88, 96, 97
  Brown Ridge, off ... 88, 97
  Friesland, East ... 97
  Friesland, West ... 96, 97
  German Bight, western approaches ... 97
  Harwich approaches ... 73, 74
  Hinder, West ... 113
  Humber approaches ... 139
  Maas ... 117
  Maas, North ... 88, 117
  Maas, West Inner and Outer ... 117
  Netherlands, North, off ... 88, 97
  Netherlands, South, and Belgium ... 89
  Netherlands, South, off ... 113
  Noord Hinder North ... 88, 113, 117
  Noord Hinder South ... 113
  Terschelling-German Bight ... 97
  Texel, off ... 96, 97
  Vlieland North ... 97
  Vlieland, off ... 96
Tilbury ... 52
Tingwall ... 224
Tollesbury ... 66
Tyne, River ... 143, 163

U

Upnor ... 48
Ura Firth ... 226
Urgency and safety ... 8
Urk ... 108

V

Vaila Sound ... 226
Vessel Traffic Service (VTS)
  Nieuwe Waterweg ... 118
  Noordzeekanaal ... 110
VHF
  Inter-ship channels ... 6
  Port operations channels ... 6
Vlaardingen ... 119
Vlieland ... 104
Vlissingen ... 123
Volendam ... 108

W

Wainfleet ... 147
Waldringfield ... 79
Wallasea ... 62
Walsoorden ... 123
Walton Backwaters ... 33, 69
Wash ... 142, 145
Welland, River ... 147
Wells-next-the-Sea ... 142, 145
West Burra Firth Inner ... 202
Westerschelde ... 113, 122
West Frisian Islands ... 102
Westhoofd light house ... 93
Westkapelle ... 94, 122
West Mersea ... 66
West Schouwen light house ... 94
West Stones ... 145
West Terschelling ... 103, 104
Whalsay ... 201, 227
Whitaker Beacon ... 62
Whitby ... 143, 156
Whitstable ... 32, 44
Wick ... 200, 216
Widewall Bay ... 224
Wielingen Channel ... 94
Winteringham Haven ... 153
Winterton-on-Sea ... 86
Wisbech ... 142, 146
Woolwich ... 52
Workum ... 108
Wouldham ... 48
Wyre Sound (Orkney) ... 223

Y

Yare, River ... 86
Yell Sound ... 201, 202, 227

Z

Zeebrugge ... 130
Zeegat van Terschelling ... 103
Zoutkamp ... 102

A

Aberdeen 192
Aberdour 176, 182
Albert Bridge 52
Aldeburgh 81
Alde, River 80
Allington Lock 48
Althorne 62
Amble 168
Ameland 102
Amsterdam 110
Andijk 108
Anstruther 187
Antwerpen 129
Arbroath 190
Auskerry 201, 223
Avoch 214

B

Backaland Bay 223
Balta Sound 202, 227, 228
Banff 200, 205
Bartlett Creek 48
Basta Voe 226
Bath (Westerschelde) 122
Battlesbridge 62
Beadnell Bay 168
Bee Ness 48
Belgium
    Special notes 129
    Weather forecasts 14
Berghaven 118
Berwick-upon-Tweed 143, 169, 170
Blacktoft 152
Blackwater, River 33, 66
Blakeney 144
Blankenberge 95, 135
Blue Mull 226
Blue Mull Sound 227
Blyth 167
Boddam 204
Boontjes 92
Boston 142, 147
Boulmer 168
Bound Skerry 201
Bradwell 66
Brancaster Staithe 142, 145
Brandaris light tower 92, 104
Brentford Dock Marina 56
Breskens 128
Bressay 201
Bridlington 155
Brightlingsea 33, 67
Broekerhaven 108
Brough Haven 153
Brough of Birsay 201
Buckie 200, 206
Bull Sand Fort 152
Burghead 200, 207
Burnmouth 176, 179
Burntisland 176, 180
Burra Voe 227
Burray Ness 224
Burton Stather 152
Bur Wick 224

C

Caister-on-Sea 86
Caledonian Canal 200, 214
Cantick Head 200
Canvey Island 52, 60
Cape Wrath 200, 222
Cat Firth 226
Chanonry 200
Chatham 48
Chelsea Harbour 55
Clacton-on-Sea 67
Clearances under bridges 15
Clyth Ness 200
Cockenzie 181
Colchester 67
Colne, River 33, 60, 67
Conyer Creek 45
Copinsay 201
Coquet Island 143, 154
Coryton 60
Covesea Skerries 200
Crail 187
Cramond 182
Craster 168
Cromarty 213, 215
Cromer 144

D

Crouch, River 33, 62
Cullen 205
Cullercoats 163

Darnett Ness 48
Deben, River 79
De Block van Kuffeler 108
Deer Sound 224
Delfzijl 92, 101, 102
Den Helder 106, 113
Den Oever 92, 107
Dingwall 213
Doel 123
Doove Balg 92
Dornoch Firth 200, 215
Dunbar 179
Duncansby Head 200, 216
Dundee 189
Dunnet Head 200
Durgerdam 108
Dury Voe 227

E

Edam 108
Eday 223
Eemshaven 101
Egmond-aan-Zee 93
Eierland light house 92
Elie 177, 182
Ellewoutsdijk 95, 122
Enkhuizen 108
Esha Ness 202
Europlatform 119
Eyemouth 176, 178

F

Fair Isle 201, 227
Fambridge 62
Farne Islands 169
Faversham 45
Felixstowe Ferry 79
Felixstowe Pier 79
Fidra 179
Fife Ness 177
Filey Bay 155
Findhorn 200, 208
Findochty 200, 206
Firth of Forth 181
Firths Voe 201
Fisherrow 182
Flamborough Head 143
Flotta 223
Forth and Clyde Canal 183
Forth, River 176
Fortrose 214
Foula 202, 227, 228
Fraserburgh 200, 204

G

Gallions Point Marina 55
Gardenstown 204
Gills Bay 221
Gluss Island 202
GMDSS 8
Goeree light tower 93
Golspie 215
Goole 152
Gorleston 34, 86
Gourdon 191
Grangemouth 176, 182
Granton 176, 182
Gravesend 32, 52
Great Yarmouth 34, 68, 86, 142
Grimsby 153
Grunna Voe 226
Gruting Voe 226
Grutness Voe 226

H

Hammersmith Bridge 52
Hamna Voe 226
Hansweert 122, 123
Haringvliet 93, 113
Harlingen 92, 105
Hartlepool 143, 154, 161
Harwich 33, 34, 68
Havengore 61
Helmsdale 216
Herne Bay 32, 44
Het Vlie 103

Heugh (Hartlepool) 143
Heugh (Holy Island) 143, 169
Hillswick 227
Hindeloopen 108
Hoedekenskerke 122
Holehaven 52
Holliwell Point 62
Holy Island 143, 169
Hoorn 108
Hopeman 200, 207
Houton Bay 223
Hoy 223
Huibert Gat 101
Hull 152
Hullbridge 62
Humber Bridge 143, 148, 152
Hunstanton 145

I

IJmuiden 93, 109
IJsselmeer 107
Immingham 149
Inchcolm 182
Inland waterways
    Belgium 129
    Caledonian Canal 200, 214
    Netherlands 96
Inner Dowsing light tower 147
Inter-ship VHF channels 6
Invergordon 200, 213
Inverness 200, 213
Inverness Firth 200, 214
Ipswich 34
Isle of May 177, 188

J

Johnshaven 191

K

Ketelhaven 108
Kettletoft Pier 201, 223, 225
Kew Bridge 52
King's Lynn 142, 146
Kinnaird Head 200
Kirkaldy 187
Kirkcaldy 177
Kirk Sound 222
Kirkwall 201, 224
Kornwerderzand 107
Kyle of Durness 221
Kyle of Tongue 221

L

Lauwersoog 92, 101, 105
Leigh-on-Sea 32, 60
Leith 176, 181
Lelystad 108
Lemmer 108
Lerwick 227
Lillo 123
Limehouse Basin 55
Linklet Bay 223
Loch Eriboll 221
London Bridge 35, 56
Long Hope 223
Lossiemouth 200, 206
Loth 223, 225
Lowestoft 34, 82
Lybster 200, 215
Lyness 223

M

Maassluis 118, 119
MacDuff 200, 205
Makkum 108
Maldon 66
Margate 32, 44
Marken 108
Markermeer 108
Marsdiep 93
MAYDAY calls 7
McDermott Base 208
Medemblik 108
Medway 32
Medway, River 47
Meikle Ferry 215
Methil 187
Middlesbrough 156, 161
Mid Yell Voe 226
Milton Creek 45
Minsmere 81